Abandoning America

Life-stories from early New England

Abandoning America

Life-stories from early New England

Susan Hardman Moore

THE BOYDELL PRESS

© Susan Hardman Moore 2013

All Rights Reserved. Except as permitted under current legislation no part of this work may be photocopied, stored in a retrieval system, published, performed in public, adapted, broadcast, transmitted, recorded or reproduced in any form or by any means, without the prior permission of the copyright owner

The right of Susan Hardman Moore to be identified as the author of this work has been asserted in accordance with sections 77 and 78 of the Copyright, Designs and Patents Act 1988

First published 2013
The Boydell Press, Woodbridge
Paperback edition 2016

ISBN 978 1 84383 817 3 hardback
ISBN 978 1 78327 141 2 paperback

The Boydell Press is an imprint of Boydell & Brewer Ltd
PO Box 9, Woodbridge, Suffolk IP12 3DF, UK
and of Boydell & Brewer Inc.
668 Mt Hope Avenue, Rochester, NY 14620–2731, USA
website: www.boydellandbrewer.com

A CIP catalogue record for this book is available
from the British Library

The publisher has no responsibility for the continued existence or accuracy of URLs for external or third-party internet websites referred to in this book, and does not guarantee that any content on such websites is, or will remain, accurate or appropriate

For John

Contents

List of illustrations	viii
Acknowledgements	ix
Abbreviations	x
Map: 'The South part of New-England, as it is Planted this yeare, 1634'	xvii
Map: New England, c. 1660	xviii
Timeline	xxi
Introduction	1
Life-stories from early New England	31
Appendix 1 Settlers leaving New England before 1640	334
Appendix 2 Settlers visiting England, 1640–1660	354
Bibliography	379
Index	392

Illustrations

1 'The South part of New-England, as it is Planted this yeare, 1634', William Wood, *New Englands prospect* (London, 1634). This item is reproduced by permission of The Huntingdon Library, San Marino, California.

2 'New England, *c.* 1660'. Originally published in Susan Hardman Moore, *New World settlers and the call of home* (New Haven, CT and London: Yale University Press, 2007). This item is reproduced by permission of Yale University Press.

Acknowledgements

The research for this book started long ago, under the guidance of the late Patrick Collinson. His approach to the history of early modern religion remains an inspiration.

Michael Middeke, Editorial Director of Modern History and Music at Boydell & Brewer, gave generous backing to this project and has seen it into print. I thank him, and others at Boydell & Brewer – especially Megan Milan, and Rohais Haughton, Production Editor – for all their care and professionalism.

Many libraries and archives, on the eastern seaboard of the United States and in Britain, have provided resources and a friendly environment for research. In particular, my thanks are due to Dr Williams's Library in London, and to New College Library and the National Library of Scotland in Edinburgh.

I am grateful to Yale University Press for permission to draw, in the Introduction and in the reproduction of a modern map, on Susan Hardman Moore, *Pilgrims: New World settlers and the call of home* (New Haven, CT and London: Yale University Press). Copyright © 2007 Susan Hardman Moore. I am also grateful to the Huntingdon Library in California for permission to produce a map from William Wood's *New Englands prospect* (1634), and to the Museum Boijmans Van Beuningen, Rotterdam, for allowing the use of Willem van de Velde, 'Vessels in a harbour', for the cover illustration.

On the way to completing this work, my friends Sara Trist, and Iain and Irene Cormack, have tirelessly cheered me on. My memories of visits to New England are warmly coloured by the hospitality and friendship of Harriet Spear and the late Leonard Spear, and of Ruth Drews and Dean Peckham. Last but not least, my family patiently allowed me innumerable hours, desk-bound, to finish the book. It is dedicated to John: he knows why.

Susan Hardman Moore
University of Edinburgh
February 2013

Abbreviations

AAS	American Antiquarian Society, Worcester, Massachusetts.
Al. Cant.	*Alumni Cantabrigienses*, comp. J. Venn and J.A. Venn. Part I: from the earliest times to 1791 (4 vols). Cambridge: Cambridge University Press, 1922–7. Online at http://venn.lib.cam.ac.uk.
Al. Oxon.	*Alumni Oxonienses*, ed. J. Foster (4 vols). Oxford and London: Parker & Co., 1891–2. Online at http://www.british-history.ac.uk/source.aspx?pubid=1270.
ANB	*American National Biography* (24 vols). Oxford and New York: Oxford University Press, 1999. *ANB Online* at http://www.anb.org, 2005– .
Artillery Company	O.A. Roberts, *History of the ... honorable Artillery Company of Massachusetts, 1637–1888* (4 vols). Boston, MA: A. Mudge & Son, 1895–1901. Volume 1, 1637–1738.
Aspinwall	*A volume relating to the early history of Boston, containing the Aspinwall Notarial Records from 1644 to 1651.* Boston, MA: Report of the Record Commissioners, 32, Municipal Printing Office, 1903.
BDBR	*Biographical dictionary of British radicals in the seventeenth century*, eds R.L. Greaves and R. Zaller (3 vols). Brighton: Harvester Press, 1981–4.
BL	British Library, London.
Bodleian	Bodleian Library, University of Oxford.
Boston CR	*The records of the First Church in Boston 1630–1868*, I, ed. Richard D. Pierce. Boston, MA: Colonial Society of Massachusetts, *Publications*, 39, 1961.
BPL	Boston Public Library, Rare Books and Manuscripts Department.
Bush	*The correspondence of John Cotton*, ed. Sargent Bush Jr. Chapel Hill, NC and London: University of North Carolina Press, 2001.
Cambridge TR	City Clerk's Office, City Hall, Cambridge, Massachusetts. Cambridge Town Records, 1632–1703 (transcript).
Canterbury CB	Cathedral Archives and Library, Canterbury, CCA-U37/1, Register, Minute and Account Book of Canterbury Congregational Church, 1645–1715.
CC	*Colonial collegians: biographies of those who attended American colleges before the War for Independence*, ed. Conrad Edick Wright. Boston, MA: Massachusetts Historical Society and New England Historic Genealogical

	Society, 2005. Electronic resource: CD-ROM. Online at http://www.americanancestors.org.
CCEd	*Clergy of the Church of England Database*. http://www.theclergydatabase.org.uk/index.html.
Charlestown CR	'The first record-book of the First Church in Charlestown, Massachusetts', ed. J.F. Hunnewell, *NEHGR* 23: 187–91, 279–84; 24: 9–11; 25: 147–50, 339–44.
Cockermouth CB	Cumbria Record Office and Local Studies Library, Whitehaven. MS YDFCCL 3/1, The Register of Cockermouth Congregational Church, 1651–1771. [References are to the recent printed edition by R.B. Wordsworth, *The Cockermouth congregational church book (1651–c.1765)*. Cumberland and Westmorland Antiquarian and Archaeological Society Record Series, XXI, 2012.]
Conn. Recs.	*The public records of the Colony of Connecticut prior to the union with the New Haven Colony, 1665*, ed. J.H. Trumbull (15 vols to 1776). Hartford, CT: Lockwood & Brainerd Company, 1850–90.
Connecticut VR	*Connecticut vital records to 1870*. Online database, http://www.americanancestors.org, New England Historic Genealogical Society, 2011. From original typescripts, Lucius Barnes Barbour Collection, 1928.
CR	*Calamy revised*, ed. A.G. Matthews. Oxford: Clarendon Press, 1934, reissued 1988.
CSPC	*Calendar of State Papers: colonial series, 1574–1660*, ed. W.N. Salisbury. London: Longman, 1860.
	Calendar of State Papers: colonial series, America and West Indies, 1661–1668, ed. W.N. Salisbury. London: Longman, 1880.
CSPD	*Calendar of State Papers: domestic series, of the Reign of Charles I* (23 vols). London: Longman, 1858–97.
	Calendar of State Papers: domestic series, of the Commonwealth (13 vols). London: Longman, 1875–86.
	Calendar of State Papers: domestic series, of the Reign of Charles II (28 vols). London: Longman, 1860–1939.
DAO	*Dissenting Academies Online* [A project of the Dr Williams's Centre for Dissenting Studies] http://www.english.qmul.ac.uk/drwilliams/portal.html.
Davenport Letters	*Letters of John Davenport, puritan divine*, ed. I.M. Calder. New Haven, CT: Yale University Press, 1937.
Dedham CR	*The record of baptisms, marriages, and deaths, and admissions to the church and dismissals therefrom, transcribed from the church records in the town of Dedham, Massachusetts*, ed. D.G. Hill. Dedham, MA: the Dedham Transcript, 1888.
Dorchester CR	*Records of the First Church at Dorchester … 1636–1734*, ed. C.H. Pope. Boston, MA: G.H. Ellis, 1891.
DRO	Devon Record Office, Exeter.

Dunster MSS	Harvard University Archives, Cambridge, Massachusetts. Papers of Henry Dunster and the Dunster Family (1638–1874, 1914), Boxes 1 and 2.
DWB	*The dictionary of Welsh biography*, eds J.E. Lloyd and R.T. Jenkins. London: Honourable Society of Cymmrodorion, 1959.
DWL	Dr Williams's Library, London.
DWL Baxter Letters	Dr Williams's Library, London, Richard Baxter's Correspondence.
Edwards, *Gangraena*	Thomas Edwards, *Gangraena or a catalogue and discovery of many... errours, heresies, blasphemies and pernicious practices* (3 parts in one volume). London, 1646.
ERO	Essex Record Office, Chelmsford, Essex.
ESRO	East Sussex Record Office, Lewes, Sussex.
Essex Court Files	Philips Library, Peabody Essex Museum, Salem, Massachusetts. Essex Quarterly Court File Papers.
Essex Court Recs.	*The records and files of the Quarterly Courts of Essex County, Massachusetts* (9 vols). Salem, MA: Essex Institute, 1911–75. Online at http://etext.virginia.edu/salem/witchcraft/Essex/.
Essex Deeds	Southern Essex County Registry of Deeds, Salem, Massachusetts. Essex Deeds. Online at http://www.salemdeeds.com/historic.asp.
Essex Probate Recs.	*The probate records of Essex County, Massachusetts* (3 vols). Salem, MA: Essex Institute, 1916–20.
ESTC	*English Short Title Catalogue*. Online at http://estc.bl.uk.
GD	J. Savage, *A genealogical dictionary of New England* (4 vols). Boston, MA: Little, Brown & Co., 1860–2.
GM	Robert C. Anderson, G.F. Sanborn and M.L. Sanborn, eds, *The Great Migration: immigrants to New England, 1634–1635* (7 vols). Boston, MA: Great Migration Study Project, New England Historic Genealogical Society, 1999–2011. Online at http://www.americanancestors.org.
GMB	Robert C. Anderson, ed. *The Great Migration begins: immigrants to New England, 1620–1633* (3 vols). Boston, MA: Great Migration Study Project, New England Historic Genealogical Society, 1995. Online at http://www.americanancestors.org.
Guilford TR	Town Clerk's Office, Guilford, Connecticut. Guilford Town Records A and B.
Harvard Recs.	*Harvard College records*. Part I, Colonial Society of Massachusetts, *Publications*, 15 (Boston 1925). Part III, Colonial Society of Massachusetts, *Publications*, 31 (Boston, MA, 1935). Part IV, Robert W. Lovett, ed. *Documents from the Harvard University archives, 1638–1750*, Colonial Society of Massachusetts, *Publications*, 49 (Boston, MA, 1975).
HSP	Historical Society of Pennsylvania, Philadelphia.

Lechford *NB*	*A note-book kept by Thomas Lechford, Esq., lawyer, in Boston, Massachusetts Bay, June 27, 1638, to July 29, 1641.* Transactions and Collections of the American Antiquarian Society, 7. Cambridge, MA: J. Wilson & Co., 1885. [Citations are to the printed pages, not (as in the index of this edition) to the original folios.]
Lechford *PD*	Thomas Lechford, *Plain dealing: or, newes from New-England.* London, 1642.
LPL, MSS COMM	Lambeth Palace Library, London. Ecclesiastical Records of the Commonwealth, 1643–1660.
Magnalia	Cotton Mather, *Magnalia Christi Americana; or, the ecclesiastical history of New England*, ed. T. Robbins (2 vols). Hartford, CT: Silas Andrus & Son, 1853.
Mass. Archives	Massachusetts State Archives, Boston. The Massachusetts Archives Collection: Records, 1629–1799. 328 volumes. http://www.sec.state.ma.us/arc/arccol/colmac.htm.
Mass. Recs.	*Records of the Governor and Company of the Massachusetts Bay in New England (1626–1686)*, ed. Nathaniel B. Shurtleff (5 vols in 6). Boston, MA: W. White, 1853–4. Reprint, New York: AMS Press, 1968.
MHS	Massachusetts Historical Society, Boston.
MHS, Misc. Bd. MSS	Massachusetts Historical Society, Boston. Ms. N-2196, Miscellaneous Bound Manuscripts Collection, 1629–1908. [Bound into volumes, arranged chronologically.]
MHS, Misc. MSS	Massachusetts Historical Society, Boston. Ms. N-2195, Miscellaneous Manuscripts Collection, 1600-1972. [In boxes, arranged chronologically.]
MHSC	*Massachusetts Historical Society Collections* (Boston, MA, 1792–). [The series number precedes the initials, the volume number follows.]
Middlesex Court Files	Massachusetts Archives, Boston. Middlesex County Court Files, 1649–63.
Middlesex Court Recs.	Massachusetts Archives, Boston. Middlesex County Court Record Book, I, 1649–1663 (transcribed by David Pulsifer). [Originals and transcript at Massachusetts Archives.]
Middlesex Deeds	Middlesex South District Registry of Deeds, Cambridge, Massachusetts. Middlesex Deeds, I, II, III.
Middlesex Probate Recs.	Massachusetts Archives, Boston. Middlesex Probate and Family Court, Cambridge, Massachusetts. Middlesex County Probate Records, First Series, 1648–1876.
Milford CR	Connecticut State Library, Hartford, Connecticut. Milford, First Congregational Church Records, 1639–1837.
Morison	S.E. Morison, *Harvard College in the seventeenth century* (2 vols). Cambridge, MA: Harvard University Press, 1936.
Munk's Roll	William Munk, ed., *The roll of the Royal College of Physicians of London*, I, 1518–1700. London: Longman,

	Green, Longman and Roberts, 1861. Online at http://munksroll.rcplondon.ac.uk/.
NA	National Archives, Kew, London.
NA, PROB	National Archives, London, Wills. Online at http://www.nationalarchives.gov.uk/records/wills-and-probate.htm.
NEHGR	*New England Historical and Genealogical Register.* Boston, MA: New England Historic Genealogical Society, 1847–. Online at http://www.NewEnglandAncestors.org, New England Historic Genealogical Society, 2001–.
New Haven Recs.	*Records of the Colony and Plantation of New Haven* (2 vols), ed. C.J. Hoadly. Hartford, CT, 1857–8.
New Haven TR	*New Haven town records*, ed. Franklin B. Dexter. Vol. 1, 1649–1662. New Haven, CT: New Haven Colony Historical Society, 1917.
Norwich CB	Norfolk Record Office, Norwich, FC 19/1, Norwich Old Congregational Church Book, 1642–1839.
ODNB	*The Oxford Dictionary of National Biography* (61 vols). Oxford: Oxford University Press, 2004. *Oxford DNB Online* at http://www.oxforddnb.com, 2004–.
Pilgrims	Susan Hardman Moore, *Pilgrims: New World settlers and the call of home*. New Haven, CT and London: Yale University Press, 2007.
Roxbury CR	*Roxbury land and church records*. Sixth Report of the Boston Record Commissioners. Boston, MA: Rockwell and Churchill, 1884.
SP	State Papers, National Archives, London.
Salem CR	*Records of the First Church in Salem, Massachusetts, 1629–1736*, ed. R.D. Pierce. Salem, MA: Essex Institute, 1974.
Salem TR	*Town records of Salem, Massachusetts: 1634–1659*, ed. W.P. Upham. Salem, MA: Essex Institute, 1869.
Saltonstall Papers	*The Saltonstall Papers, 1607–1815*, ed. R.E. Moody (2 vols). Massachusetts Historical Society, *Collections*, 80, 81. Boston, MA: Massachusetts Historical Society, 1972–4.
Scituate CR	'Scituate and Barnstable Church Records', *NEHGR*, 9: 279–87; 10: 37–43.
Shepard's confessions	*Thomas Shepard's confessions*, eds George Selement and B.C. Woolley. Boston, MA: Colonial Society of Massachusetts, *Publications*, 58, 1981.
Sibley	J.L. Sibley, *Biographical sketches of graduates of Harvard University . . . 1642–1689* (3 vols). Cambridge, MA: C.W. Sever, 1873–85.
Stepney CB	(i) London Borough of Tower Hamlets, Local History Library and Archive, W/SMH/A/1, Records of Stepney Meeting: Church Book, 1644–1894 and (ii) National Archives, London, RG 4/4414, London, Stepney, Bull Lane (Independent). [The church book was divided in the 19th century: baptisms, marriages and burials (fols

	118–185, 300–2, 302–12) are in the National Archives; the Tower Hamlets MS contains records of admissions, dismissals, and discussion.]
Suffolk Deeds	*Suffolk Deeds*, eds W.B. Trask, F.E. Bradish, C.A. Drew and A.G. Small (14 vols). Boston, MA: Rockwell and Churchill, 1880–1906.
Surman	*Surman Index Online*, http://surman.english.qmul.ac.uk/. Online database of C.H. Surman's biographical card index at Dr Williams's Library, London.
Thurloe	T. Birch, ed., *A collection of state papers of John Thurloe* (7 vols). London, 1742.
Thwing	Annie Haven Thwing. 'Inhabitants and Estates of the Town of Boston, 1630–1800' [electronic resource] and *The Crooked and narrow streets of the town of Boston, 1630–1822* (originally published Boston, MA: Marshall Jones Company, 1920). CD ROM. Boston, MA: Massachusetts Historical Society and New England Historic Genealogical Society, 2001.
Waters	H.F. Waters, *Genealogical gleanings in England and Wales* (2 vols paginated as one). Boston, MA: New England Historic and Genealogical Society, 1901.
WJ	*The Journal of John Winthrop, 1630–1649*, eds Richard S. Dunn, James Savage and Laetitia Yeandle. Cambridge, MA and London: The Belknap Press of Harvard University Press, 1996.
WP	*The Winthrop Papers*, ed. A.B. Forbes and Francis Bremer (6 vols). Boston, MA: Massachusetts Historical Society, 1929–.
WR	*Walker revised*, ed. A.G. Matthews. Oxford: Clarendon Press, 1948, reissued 1988.
Wrentham CB	Suffolk Record Office, Lowestoft Branch, 1337/1/1, Wrentham Congregational Church Book, 1649–1971.
Wyllys MSS	The Wyllys Papers, Connecticut Historical Society, Hartford, Connecticut.
Wyllys Papers	*The Wyllys Papers ... 1590–1796*. Collections of the Connecticut Historical Society, 21. Hartford, CT: Connecticut Historical Society, 1924. [Selected manuscripts.]
Yarmouth CB	Norfolk Record Office, Norwich, FC 31/1, Great Yarmouth, Middlegate Congregational Church Book, 1643–1855.

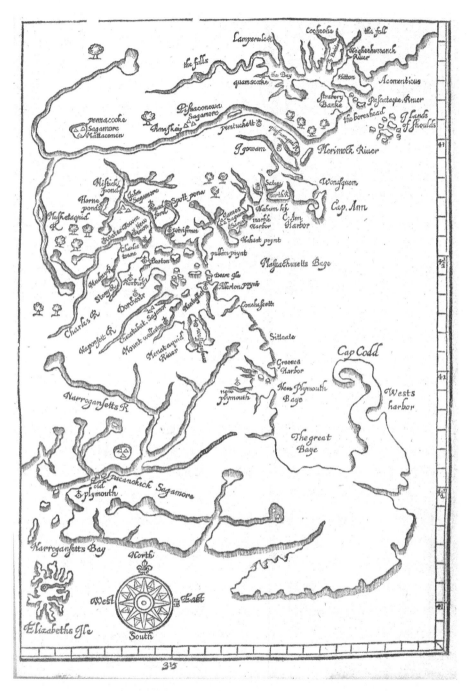

'The South part of New-England, as it is Planted this yeare, 1634': the frontispiece of William Wood's *New Englands prospect* (London, 1634). Wood offered a lively account of the land and its inhabitants, to inform not only 'the future Voyager' but also 'the mind-travelling Reader'. He spent four years in New England but seems to have returned home for good in 1633.

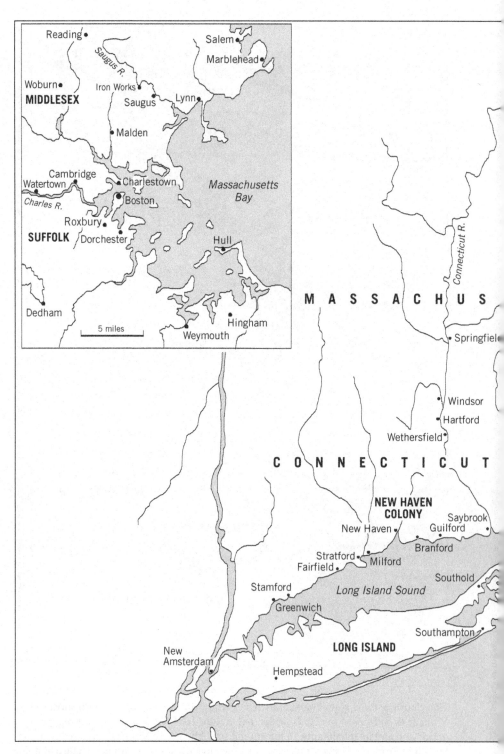

New England, *c.* 1660

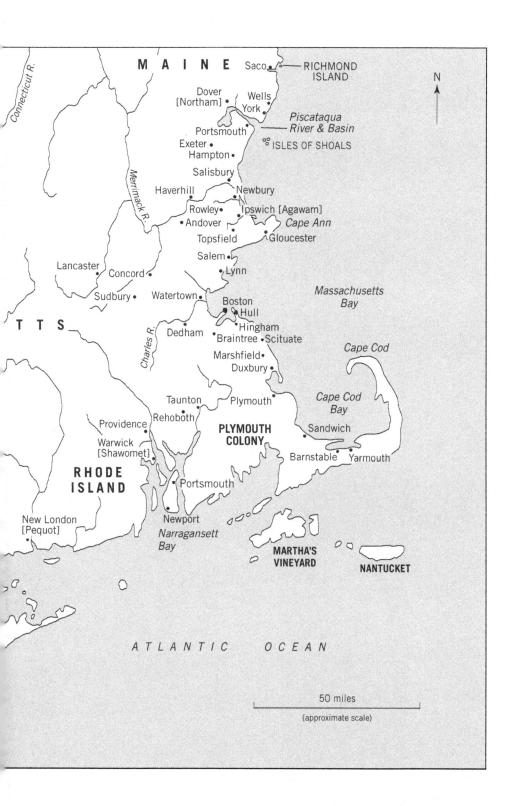

Timeline

New England	**England**
	1620
The *Mayflower* arrived at Plymouth. The Plymouth Colony came into being, self-governing until combined with Massachusetts in 1692.	The English cloth trade suffered a severe depression. A royal patent awarded substantial land rights in North America to a joint stock company, the Council for New England. Across the Channel, the Huguenots declared war on Louis XIII of France.
	1621
Harvest thanksgiving held at Plymouth: the precursor of modern-day Thanksgiving.	James I called his third English parliament, the first since 1614. William Laud became bishop of St David's, Wales. The Scottish parliament ratified the Five Articles of Perth, which enforced kneeling to receive communion.
	1622
A short-lived settlement established at Wessagusset, on the site of modern Weymouth, Massachusetts, 1622–3.	James I dissolved his third parliament. The first English newspaper appeared. The Council for New England granted the province of Maine to Sir Ferdinando Gorges and Captain John Mason.
	1623
A fishing settlement founded at the mouth of the Piscataqua river, on the site of modern Portsmouth, New Hampshire.	The 'Fatal Vesper' at Blackfriars, London: a floor collapsed during Catholic worship, with many deaths; anti-Catholic propaganda took this as a judgment from God. The 'First Folio', the first collected edition of Shakespeare's plays, was published.
	1624
Edward Winslow's *Good newes from New-England*, published in London, reported on the Plymouth Colony. The 'Dorchester Company' (reorganised in 1628 as the New England Company) founded a community at Cape Ann. Thomas Morton settled at 'Ma-re Mount'.	James I called his fourth parliament. The Virginia Company's charter was revoked: Virginia became a crown colony.

New England	England
1625	
The Dutch settled New Amsterdam (modern New York), west of New England. The first English ship reached Barbados.	James I died. Charles I became king. Charles's first parliament assembled in June, but was dissolved in August after MPs voted the king 'tonnage and poundage' (customs revenue) for only one year, not for the whole of his reign as was customary.
1626	
The Plymouth Colony built its first trading house, on the southwestern side of Cape Cod, for trade with native Americans from Narragansett and Cape Cod.	Charles I called a second parliament in February but dissolved it in June. The 'Forced Loan', collected 1626–7, raised about £250,000 for the king. William Laud became bishop of Bath and Wells.
1627	
English settlers colonised Barbados; Nevis was settled in 1628, Antigua and Montserrat in 1632.	The Anglo-French War, 1627–9: the English crown supported French Huguenots in their conflict with the French king.
1628	
A small group, led by John Endecott and supported by the Massachusetts Bay Company, landed at Salem, Massachusetts. They joined a small community established by colonists who had moved south after the failure of the Dorchester Company's settlement at Cape Ann.	Charles I called his third parliament. The Petition of Right (against the Forced Loan and other actions by the king) received royal assent in June, but the king soon prorogued parliament. William Laud became bishop of London and started to enforce conformity. A royal proclamation forbade preaching or printing on the topic of predestination.
1629	
The Massachusetts Bay Company secured a royal charter. The earl of Warwick and others received a charter to promote settlement at Providence Island in the Caribbean.	Parliament re-assembled in January, but was dissolved by the king in March. From this point until 1640, the king exercised Personal Rule, without parliament.
1630	
John Winthrop and the 'Winthrop fleet' of eleven ships left England for New England. Massachusetts Bay Colony established. The towns of Boston, Cambridge, Charlestown, Dorchester, Roxbury, Watertown founded. A harsh winter.	Alexander Leighton severely punished in London for his radical campaign against episcopacy.

TIMELINE   xxiii

New England	England
1631	
Roger Williams arrived in Boston. Settlement of the 'other puritan colony', Providence Island in the Caribbean, began.	Sir Ferdinando Gorges given a land grant by Charles I for what later became Maine.
1632	
Thomas Hooker formed a church at Cambridge, Massachusetts, but moved to settle Hartford, Connecticut, in 1636.	Charles I granted Lord Baltimore a charter for Maryland. Publication of newsbooks suspended, 1632–8, by order of the Court of Star Chamber.
1633	
John Cotton of Boston, Lincolnshire, emigrated and became minister of Boston, Massachusetts. John Davenport, later of New Haven, fled to Holland.	William Laud became archbishop of Canterbury. Charles I's decision to reissue the Book of Sports, originally published in 1618, caused controversy.
1634	
William Wood published *New Englands prospect* in London. The towns of Wethersfield, Connecticut and Ipswich, Massachusetts, founded.	Charles I began to levy Ship Money: this continued until 1640. From 1634–7, Archbishop Laud conducted metropolitical visitations in numerous dioceses, in a drive for religious conformity.
1635	
Saybrook colony established, named in honour of the English lords Saye and Brooke. Roger Williams banished from Massachusetts for his religious opinions. Newbury, Massachusetts, founded.	Sir Ferdinando Gorges secured the dissolution of the Council for New England and was appointed governor-general of New England by Charles I.
1636	
Roger Williams settled Providence, Rhode Island. A 'New College', Harvard, began at Cambridge, Massachusetts. The colony of Connecticut established. Dedham, Massachusetts, founded.	Matthew Wren's visitation articles as bishop of Norwich showed his determination to implement Laudian altar policy. William Prynne published, anonymously, *Newes from Ipswich*. The rate of emigration to New England increased rapidly.
1637	
Pequot War: the Pequots defeated by forces from the colonies of Massachusetts, Connecticut and Saybrook. The Antinomian Controversy broke out in Massachusetts: Anne Hutchinson stood trial.	Charles I issued a proclamation to control the flow of emigration to New England: passenger traffic was monitored. Prynne imprisoned and had his ears cropped for criticising bishops and the Book of Sports.

New England	England
1638	
Anne Hutchinson banished from Massachusetts. New England experienced an earthquake. Rowley, Massachusetts, established. New Haven Colony founded. The New Sweden Company promoted the settlement of Delaware.	The Scottish National Covenant signed at Greyfriars, Edinburgh. The General Assembly of the Church of Scotland voted to abolish episcopacy and establish presbyterianism. The flow of migrants from England to New England peaked.
1639	
The first printing press in America set up at Cambridge, Massachusetts. John Humfrey acted as an agent to recruit New England colonists to move south to Providence Island.	The First Bishops' War, between the Scots and the English: the initial salvo in the wars that engulfed the three kingdoms of England, Scotland and Ireland.
1640	
Immigration to New England all but ended. Settlers start to return to England, until deterred by the outbreak of civil war in 1642. William Hooke preached at a fast for England: his sermon was published in London, 1641, as *New Englands teares, for old Englands feares*.	The Second Bishops' War. Charles I's need for funds to fight the Scots led to the calling of the Short Parliament (April–May) and then the Long Parliament (November 1640–December 1648). The House of Commons impeached Archbishop Laud for high treason in December.
1641	
A small fleet sailed from Massachusetts to take settlers to Providence Island, but discovered it had been captured by the Spanish. The Piscataqua area (modern New Hampshire) came under the control of Massachusetts, 1641–79. Massachusetts sent colonial agents to represent its interests in London.	Laud imprisoned in the Tower. Parliament declared Bishop Matthew Wren unfit to hold office, and abolished the Courts of High Commission and Star Chamber. Control of printing relaxed. The Irish Uprising began – another stage in the escalation of conflict within England, Ireland and Scotland.
1642	
The first class of nine students graduated from Harvard. Seven later went to England.	The First Civil War, August 1642–May 1646. The first battle, at Edgehill, had no clear result.

New England	England
1643	
The New England Confederation established: a military alliance between the colonies of Plymouth, Massachusetts, Connecticut and New Haven. Colonial military men went to England to join the parliamentary army. New England tracts published in London included Hugh Peter and Thomas Weld's *New Englands first fruits*, Richard Mather's *An apologie of the churches in New England for church covenant*, and Roger Williams's *A key into the language of America*.	Negotiations for peace broke down. The Westminster Assembly met, 1643–52, as a committee to advise parliament on religious reform. Tensions mounted: a majority (with the Scots) favoured presbyterianism; a vociferous minority argued for Independency, also known as the 'New England Way' or congregationalism. The Solemn League and Covenant was signed: a military alliance between the English parliament and Scottish Covenanters.
1644	
The colony of Rhode Island and Providence Plantations received a charter from the Long Parliament. In London, Roger Williams's *The bloody tenent of persecution* put the case for religious toleration. Saybrook was incorporated into Connecticut.	The Army of the Covenant marched from Scotland, to support the parliamentary army. Royalists suffered defeat at the battle of Marston Moor.
1645	
Massachusetts received a letter of protest from leading English congregationalists about its intolerant treatment of baptists. John Cotton's *The way of the churches of Christ in New-England* published in London.	The Westminster Assembly produced a *Directory of Worship* to replace the *Book of Common Prayer*. Archbishop Laud executed. Parliament established the New Model Army, which inflicted a decisive defeat on the Royalists at the battle of Naseby.
1646	
The 'Remonstrant Controversy' in Massachusetts saw dissidents prepare to petition the English parliament for greater religious and civil liberties. Ironworks at Saugus, Massachusetts, began production. Peace in England encouraged settlers to go home.	Charles I surrendered to the Covenanter army at Newark. The First Civil War ended. The Westminster Assembly produced the *Westminster Confession of Faith*.
1647	
Massachusetts passed a law to ensure all towns established schools: this followed legislation in 1642 which required that all children should be taught to read and write. Renewed hostilities in England inhibited the flow of return migration.	The Second Civil War, 1647–9, began after negotiations with Charles I faltered and the king signed a secret agreement with the Scots to gain a promise of military support. At this point the Long Parliament and the army were locked in a power struggle.

New England	England

1648

| A synod at Cambridge, Massachusetts, accepted the *Westminster Confession* apart from presbyterian clauses about church government. The synod produced a definitive statement of the New England Way, congregationalism, in the *Cambridge Platform*. | The Scottish parliament demanded the establishment of presbyterianism in England. English presbyterian MPs tried to negotiate with the king, but failed. The Long Parliament was purged by the New Model Army. The 'Rump Parliament' remained until dissolved by Oliver Cromwell in 1653. |

1649

| John Winthrop, the first governor of Massachusetts, died. In London, the colonial agent Edward Winslow published *The glorious progress of the gospel amongst the Indians in New England*, to promote the work of the New England Company. | Charles I executed. The Commonwealth followed, 1649–53. Cromwell led an army to subdue Ireland. The Third Civil War, 1649–51, started after the Scots proclaimed Charles II king and gave him military support. New England Company founded. |

1650

| The early 1650s saw substantial migration from New England to England. Cromwell's regime also encouraged settlers to move to Ireland and deployed colonists in Scotland. Anne Bradstreet, New England poet, published in London *The tenth muse lately sprung up in America*. | Cromwell returned from Ireland. He invaded Scotland and secured an important victory at the battle of Dunbar in September. Edinburgh surrendered to Cromwell in December. |

1651

| Scottish prisoners, captured after the battles of Dunbar and Worcester, were sent over to New England to work at the Saugus ironworks and as labourers. In London, on behalf of the New England Company, Henry Whitfield published *The light appearing more and more towards the perfect day. Or, a farther discovery of the present state of the Indians in New-England, concerning the progresse of the Gospel amongst them.* | Charles II crowned at Scone. He invaded England with support from the Scots. General George Monck took command of English forces in Scotland. Cromwell pursued the king south. Charles was defeated at the battle of Worcester and fled to France. A new Navigation Act allowed only English ships to import freight, a measure aimed against Dutch trade. |

1652

| The Massachusetts authorities issued 'A declaration concerning the advancement of learning', which set minimum salaries in an effort to keep Harvard graduates from leaving New England. Maine came under the jurisdiction of Massachusetts. | The First Anglo-Dutch War, 1652–4, fought at sea, meant rapid expansion for Cromwell's navy: ex-colonists' naval skills were valued. From 1652–9, Scotland was placed under English government, in a forced union backed up by military garrisons. |

New England	England
1653	
New England communities close to the Dutch settlements of New Netherland feared conflict with the Dutch would spread to the New World.	Sea-battles with the Dutch at Portland, the Gabbard, Scheveningen. Cromwell expelled the Rump Parliament and brought in the Nominated (Barebones) Assembly, which lasted only six months. The Army's 'Instrument of Government' paved the way for Cromwell to become Lord Protector.
1654	
Under authority from Cromwell, Robert Sedgwick led a New England force to conquer the French colony of Acadia (these troops had originally been gathered to defend New England against the Dutch).	Cromwell's Protectorate, 1654–8. 'Triers' and 'Ejectors' put in place: Triers, national commissioners, vetted clerical appointments; Ejectors, county commissioners, ousted unsuitable ministers. Cromwell promoted religious toleration along with a broad national church. The English made peace with the Dutch. The First Protectorate Parliament met. Cromwell launched his 'Western Design' to capture Spanish territory in the West Indies.
1655	
Cromwell encouraged New England settlers to move to the West Indies to support the Western Design – which failed to meet its objectives, except for the capture of Jamaica.	Cromwell dissolved the First Protectorate Parliament and introduced direct military government, appointing major-generals to govern regions of England and Wales. Henry Cromwell became major-general of the army in Ireland.
1656	
The Massachusetts authorities whipped and banished the first Quakers to arrive in the colony.	The Second Protectorate Parliament met in September.
1657	
New Haven ironworks start production.	A new constitution, the 'Humble Petition and Advice', ended the rule of major-generals; the crown was offered to Cromwell, who declined it. Henry Cromwell became Lord Deputy of Ireland. England and France signed an alliance against Spain.

New England	England
1658	
Theophilus Eaton, first governor of the New Haven Colony, died. Massachusetts enacted a law to apprehend and banish Quakers.	The Second Protectorate Parliament was dissolved. Oliver Cromwell died in September. Richard Cromwell was proclaimed his successor.
1659	
Massachusetts imposed a five-shilling fine on anyone caught observing Christmas. This formalised existing practice and echoed legislation passed in England in the 1640s.	The Third Protectorate Parliament assembled but was dissolved in May, when the Rump Parliament was reinstated. Richard Cromwell resigned after the Rump refused to recognise the Protectorate.
1660	
Mary Dyer, a Quaker, hanged in Boston. The regicides William Goffe and Edward Whalley fled from England and went into hiding in New Haven. New England expected a fresh wave of migrants from England but in the event few came.	General George Monck marched south from Scotland and arrived in London in February. The Long Parliament was restored. Charles II was proclaimed king since 1649 and made a triumphal return to London in May.
1661	
Massachusetts issued a 'Declaration of Rights': this declared allegiance to Charles II but in effect claimed self-rule (and so contributed to the revocation of the colony's royal charter in 1684).	Charles II forbade Massachusetts to execute Quakers. The Cavalier Parliament met, and ensured the Restoration Settlement reflected Royalist interests.
1662	
Connecticut received a royal charter. The New Haven Colony amalgamated with Connecticut.	The Act of Uniformity required episcopal ordination, use of the prayer book, and religious conformity.

Introduction

> Some have observed that since the year 1640, more persons have removed out of *New England*, than have gone thither . . .
>
> Increase Mather, *A brief relation of the state of New England, from the beginning of that plantation to this present year* (London, 1689)

The stories of those who went over to New England but did not stay are at odds with the onward march of American history. They have largely been overlooked. Yet the newly-built Harvard College saw almost half its graduates sail away to England before 1660. Of the godly preachers who left England in the 'Great Migration' of the 1630s – inspiring members of their congregations to emigrate too – around a third abandoned their flocks after 1640 and returned home. Among the population at large, perhaps as many as a quarter of New England's earliest settlers sailed back across the Atlantic: not only the Harvard graduates and ministers (for whom the hardest evidence survives), but also magistrates, merchants, religious and political dissidents, widows and children, servants, apprentices, military men, surgeons, shoemakers and shopkeepers. Some set a course for home within weeks or months; many more packed their bags after ten or twenty years. Their life-stories undermine the traditional understanding of the Great Migration as a one-way ticket across the Atlantic.[1]

The lives of around six hundred individuals, gathered in this book – mostly obscure lives – witness to a neglected aspect of settling America. The evidence comes from thousands of scattered fragments in the earliest records of New England, and from archives and libraries up and down England.

The criterion for inclusion here of a settler's life-story is that he or she emigrated to New England – usually in the 1630s, exceptionally in the 1620s or 1640s – and returned to England before the Restoration of Charles II in 1660. All the life-stories concern New England settlers, the majority from the larger colonies of Massachusetts, New Haven and Connecticut, with others from the smaller communities of Plymouth, New Hampshire, Maine and Rhode Island.[2]

Some might argue that to focus only on New England, and only on this period, is to set the lens too narrowly; that there is need for a wider angle

---

[1] Susan Hardman Moore, *Pilgrims: New World settlers and the call of home* (New Haven, CT and London: Yale University Press, 2007), 1, 14. I am grateful to Yale University Press for allowing me to draw on *Pilgrims* in this Introduction.

[2] Carla Gardina Pestana, *The English Atlantic in an age of revolution, 1640–1661* (Cambridge, MA and London: Harvard University Press, 2004), 229–34, discusses the relative size of English American colonies in 1640.

on Atlantic migration. However, it would have been impractical in this context to tackle a broader area or a longer timeframe, because of the extremely disparate nature of the evidence. Crucially, no-one kept a roster of the people who sailed *from* New England, away from America. Valuable work has been carried out on migration *to* New England and other American colonies, based on passenger lists that survive in the port books of England.[3] But in the colonial ports of Boston, Plymouth and New Haven, no passenger lists were kept. Goods might be tallied at the quayside, but not people. To trace homeward-bound traffic, then, a different approach has had to be found. The method of this project has been to map out return migration by retrieving personal histories, very often starting from some incidental, passing, reference. A large and evocative collection of individual stories has thus been assembled. The information has a human face: it is the departing settlers' experience that is central, not population statistics. The method affords a panoramic perspective which is quite different from what would emerge from a study of, say, a limited number of characters who happen to stand out in the sources. Yes, the research contributes to a broader understanding of migration in the Atlantic world. But above all it recovers the rich detail of forgotten lives.

There are special reasons for looking at migration back from New England to England between 1640 and 1660. The flow of emigrants in the Great Migration to New England had been catalysed by religious and political tensions during the Personal Rule of Charles I, a period when the king had called no parliament, from 1629 to 1640. In particular, the 'godly' – as puritans liked to call themselves – had feared a return of Catholicism. Much changed when a reinvigorated parliament met in 1640 and provided effective opposition to the king. The chaos of civil war led to regicide in 1649, and to Cromwell's Commonwealth in the 1650s. Many of the religious anxieties that originally stirred up emigration vanished with the changes that came after 1640, and did not reappear until the Restoration of Charles II in 1660. The decision of many settlers to return home, once the situation in England altered, underlines the nature of the Great Migration as a special and specific reaction to the tensions of the 1630s.

This introduction sets the stage for the individual life-stories. It starts by giving a broad sketch of the historical context, introducing the cast of characters, and pointing out certain themes in their histories. Next, it locates this book on a map of recent historical writing, and assesses how common it was for settlers to go home. Then it discusses the particular contribution this material can make for understanding religion in the Atlantic world, and in early modern England. Finally, it surveys the range and type of seventeenth-century

[3] Virginia DeJohn Anderson, *New England's generation: the Great Migration and the formation of society and culture in the seventeenth century* (Cambridge: Cambridge University Press, 1991); Alison Games, *Migration and the origins of the English Atlantic world* (Cambridge, MA and London: Harvard University Press, 2001). Anderson followed the fortunes of almost 700 individuals who left England on seven ships in 1637 (the most complete set of passenger lists). Games based her study on almost 5,000 passengers who left the port of London for America in 1635, to thirteen different destinations (the largest contingent to depart from a single port in a single year).

sources that proved valuable for the investigation, and ends with some information about the structure and approach of the book, to guide its use.

I

Increase Mather – reviewing New England's history from the vantage point of 1689, and determined to boost its reputation with the regime of William and Mary after the 'Glorious Revolution' of 1688 – contended that New England was robust, despite the rumour that for years more people had left its shores than had arrived there.[4] There is an irony about *Increase* Mather mounting a defence against the apparently decreasing attractions of New England. His father Richard Mather, the minister of Dorchester, Massachusetts, had bestowed this unusual first name in 1639, to mark the 'great Increase of every sort' with which 'God favoured the country ... about the time of his nativity'. Yet only two years later, in 1641, Richard Mather received a request to baptise a child with the name *Return*, reflecting a sea-change in the atmosphere in Massachusetts, with 'the unsettled humours of many men's spirits to return for England'.[5]

With hindsight New England's success might seem inevitable, but it had not looked that way at the start. In the early days, prospects were uncertain, and not simply because of the perils any new colony might expect to encounter. Doubts about whether New England was a wise location for settlement were strengthened by the icy winter of 1630–1, when numerous settlers, weakened by scurvy from the voyage over, perished in the cold. John Winthrop, the first governor of Massachusetts, noted how many survivors sailed back to England as soon as they could, 'for feare of deathe or famen & c'.[6] (In the 1630s some of New England's best potential backers turned their interest towards warmer climes – Providence Island, far to the south.[7] This rival venture crumbled when the island fell to the Spanish in 1641, but by that time the overall context had altered for the settlements in New England.)

Between 1630 and 1639, schemes for godly plantations had gathered momentum. The migrants drawn to New England had not been typical Atlantic

---

[4] Increase Mather, *A brief relation of the state of New England, from the beginning of that plantation to this present year, 1689* (London, 1689), 5.
[5] Cotton Mather, *Memoirs of the life of the Rev. Increase Mather D.D.* (London, 1724), 2–3; C.H. Pope, ed., *Records of the First Church at Dorchester . . . 1636–1734* (Boston, MA: G.H. Ellis, 1891), 151, 153. 'Unsettled humours': John Cotton to Richard Saltonstall Jr, [1649], Boston Public Library, MS Am. 1506, pt 3, app. No. 5 [printed in Sargent Bush Jr, ed., *The correspondence of John Cotton* (Chapel Hill, NC and London: University of North Carolina Press, 2001), 420, but with 'Humyrs' transcribed as 'Hurryes']. As an adult, Return Munnings defied his name by staying on in America, whereas Increase Mather defied his name by sailing to England as soon as he could: *Pilgrims*, 54.
[6] John Winthrop, *The Journal of John Winthrop*, ed. Richard S. Dunn, James Savage and Laetitia Yeandle (Cambridge, MA and London: Harvard University Press, 1996), 46; *Pilgrims*, 35–7.
[7] Karen Ordahl Kupperman, *Providence Island, 1630–1641: the other puritan colony* (Cambridge: Cambridge University Press, 1993).

migrants (young, single, unskilled males). New England attracted a spectrum of ages, in a family-centred migration. It recruited more skilled people than other colonies in the New World: gentry, graduates, yeoman farmers, craftsmen, traders. The level of literacy was higher than in England, reflecting the connection between print and Protestantism – Bible-reading habits. For a decade this distinctive stream of voyagers had increased year on year.[8]

But then, in 1640, New England experienced a sudden about-turn in passenger traffic. Settlers started to return to England in noticeable numbers. Soon after this turnaround, a pamphlet called *New Englands first fruits* – published in London in 1643, just after civil war broke out – directly addressed the question of colonial deserters. This anonymous tract was the work of Thomas Weld and Hugh Peter, two New England ministers sent back to England as agents for Massachusetts. It formed part of their strategy to promote the Bay Colony's achievements, to attract investment, and (no small part of the task) to see off reports that New England was not paying its way. In its final pages, the authors answered a series of objections to the viability of settlement in New England: 'Your ground is barren ... You have no money there ... You are like to want clothes hereafter ... Your winters are cold ... Many are growne weaker in their estates since they went over ... Many speak evill of the place.' These led up to an awkward question: 'Why doe many come away from thence?' Weld and Peter presented a sweeping riposte in an attempt to sideline the issue. Surely, they argued, people often move from one country to another, 'yet none likes the Country the lesse because some depart from it'. Some of the traffic back to England could be attributed to voyagers who had only ever intended to visit New England 'on some speciall busines' and then to return home. Certain people had emigrated on 'sudden undigested grounds', without considering costs and difficulties, and 'so have they returned upon as sleight headlesse, unworthy reasons as they went'. Others 'must have elbow-roome, and cannot abide to be so pinioned with the strict Government in the Common-wealth, or Discipline in the Church': New England was not sorry to be rid of these. Of the settlers who had returned home, 'some of the wisest repent them already' and wished to be in New England again. Weld and Peter concluded with a flourish: 'though some few have removed ... yet (we may truly say) thousands ... would not change their place for any other in the World'. Unfortunately, the reality of this optimistic assertion, when put to the test in their own lives, failed to hold water. Both Weld and Peter stayed on in England and never returned to America. Hugh Peter's frequent protestations that he was about to set sail became a joke.[9]

Changes in politics and religion in England tipped the balance. The circumstances that had originally provoked emigration had altered, and fresh opportunities opened up in the old world. Taking the difficulties of life in New

---

[8] *Pilgrims*, 2, 21, 53.
[9] [Anon.], *New Englands first fruits* (London, 1643), 24–6; *Pilgrims*, 58; Thomas Edwards, *Gangraena, or a catalogue and discovery of many ... errours, heresies, blasphemies and pernicious practices* (London, 1646), i. 98–9. Biographies of Hugh Peter and Thomas Weld appear in the main text.

England into account, for many settlers the future looked brighter back home. In the years up to 1660, the stream of migrants leaving New England never stopped. Admittedly, the flow varied depending on news from home: during the 1640s it slowed to a trickle while civil war raged in England, and swelled at times of peace. After the execution of Charles I in 1649 and the establishment of Cromwell's regime, transatlantic relations became more settled and predictable. The strongest ebb-tide of return came in the early 1650s. Cromwell, who had himself so nearly set out for New England in the 1630s, played a significant part in tempting settlers away. By the time he came to power he thought New England had outlived its usefulness, except as a recruiting ground to find well-qualified people who could serve his regime in other places. Cromwell's armed forces and navy drew on the expertise of colonial soldiers and sailors. At the new frontiers of his regime, in Ireland, Scotland and the Caribbean, he looked for support from New England, not merely from individuals but by transplanting whole communities. John Astwood of Milford, Connecticut, felt the pressure at an audience with Cromwell early in 1654. Astwood had come to England to ask for help to defend New England's settlers against the Dutch of New Netherland. But Cromwell more than hinted that colonists should move to the Caribbean: would it not 'be better that new England were removed to some place where they might have cittyes ready builded and land ready'?[10]

After Cromwell's demise and the Restoration of Charles II in 1660, New England hoped for a fresh wave of immigrants, but it never came. The ships that docked in Boston harbour carried relatively few passengers. And most of these were colonists who had returned to England in the 1650s and were now coming over to New England again: usually youngsters with good prospects in New England, like Increase Mather, who came back in 1661.[11] New England's population had certainly risen by the time Mather wrote his *Brief relation of the state of New England* in 1689, but the growth came from births not inward migration. So there was truth in the observation Mather recorded: after 1640, more people abandoned New England than came over to settle there.

II

What kind of people left New England? If they were all markedly different from their neighbours, they might be dissidents or misfits who would reveal little about the general character of their communities.[12] In fact, although

---

[10] For Cromwell's close connections with emigrants and his intention of going to New England, see *ODNB*, John Morrill, 'Cromwell, Oliver (1599–1658)'. Astwood's experience was reported by William Leete in a letter to Samuel Desborough, 10 October 1654: British Library, London, Egerton MS 2519, fol. 10. *Pilgrims*, 12, 25, 66, 75, 80, 83, 84, 109–17.

[11] *Pilgrims*, 143–4.

[12] Some scholars have argued that those who left were mismatched with the general settledness of New England, and that the story of those who stayed is infinitely more important: Anderson, *New England's generation*, 122n.; Roger Thompson, *Mobility and migration: East Anglian*

some had long been unsettled in New England, most differed little in outlook or fortune from their colonial neighbours who stayed on. Usually, their decisions to leave America took shape in the midst of common aspirations and anxieties. For every individual who resolved to go home, others in similar circumstances decided to stay. What clinched the decision was often a subtle mix of factors. So, paradoxically, the histories of those who departed (which might at first sight appear to say little about those who remained) can add to an understanding of life in early New England. The debate about return – which drew in many who stayed on in America but hankered to go home, as well as those who left – uncovers strains and disappointments that are often masked by the apparent stability of New England's early communities.[13]

Few of the people in this book are well-known: only a small number of those who returned from New England stand out for the mark they made in national life – most notably, the preacher Hugh Peter and the politician Sir Henry Vane junior, both exempted from Charles II's pardon and executed at the Restoration. New England's opponents made capital of the fact that some who came back could be pilloried as radical extremists, like Thomas Venner, the Fifth Monarchist convicted in 1657 of plotting to blow up the Tower of London and then of fomenting rebellion in 1660. In one notorious case the career of a migrant took a striking turn: Sir George Downing (from whom Downing Street in London takes its name) was a Harvard graduate who served the Cromwellian regime but switched sides at the Restoration and rose high in the king's service.[14]

Looking beyond the infamous few, dozens of less prominent settlers played a part in significant events of their day: at the frontiers of Cromwellian government in Ireland and Scotland; in the middle ranks of 'the State's servants'; and up and down the land as parish ministers in the national Church. Military men like Stephen Winthrop, George Cooke and Thomas Reade became stalwarts of Cromwell's forces. Merchants and mariners turned naval commissioners in Cromwell's service, like Nehemiah Bourne, Edward Hopkins, Robert Tomson and Francis Willoughby. New England provided government officials: for example, Hezekiah Haynes, deputed to implement Cromwellian government in East Anglia; Samuel Desborough, highly placed in Cromwell's regime in Scotland; Roger Ludlow, who served as master of chancery in Ireland; John Humfrey and Edward Winslow, charged with disposing of Charles I's assets, including the king's priceless art collection. Sixty former colonists entered parish ministry. Most migrants' histories are jigsaws with many missing pieces, but information about clerical careers is more complete because eighteenth-century historians collected material to document the history of Dissent. In the context of migration from New England to England, clerical histories are particularly valuable, since a high proportion of the clergy who went to America in the 1630s – a third – eventually returned to their

---

   founders of New England, 1629–1640 (Amherst, MA: The University of Massachusetts Press, 1994), 223.

[13] *Pilgrims*, 87.

[14] All the settlers mentioned in this paragraph, and this section, have entries in the main text.

native country. Ministers such as John Phillip, Thomas Larkham, Thomas Weld and Giles Firmin pioneered the reform of local religious life informed by their New England experience.[15]

Many 'ordinary' and inconspicuous lives make up the rest of the picture. Some settlers – perhaps the silent majority – returned quietly to where they had come from. John Caffinch, of Tenterden in Kent, waited for his wife and children to sail back from New Haven and rejoin him in the house he had owned before emigration. Ferdinando Adams, a shoemaker of Dedham, Massachusetts, set off to visit England in 1641, then sent word for his family to follow him back. In the 1630s, Adams had clashed with Bishop Matthew Wren in Ipswich, Suffolk, and had been hauled before the courts. But times had changed: the bishop was under investigation. Soon after Adams reached England, parliament locked up Wren in the Tower of London.

For others, returning to England sprang from disgrace and disenchantment. Thomas Fugill, a pillar of New Haven's civil and religious community, returned to his native East Yorkshire after being fined and excommunicated for falsifying documents to give himself more land. Back home, he was said to be in a 'melancholly frame ... his spirit soe imbittered against the whole way and worke of Christ'.[16] Another settler, Mary Oliver, had landed in New England with a reputation as someone who had resisted Laudian religious innovations in England. She was soon marked out in Massachusetts as a troublemaker of a different stripe: making no secret of her dim view of New England's church practices and arrested for (among other things) making speeches at the arrival of newcomers – conjuring up an image of her haranguing immigrants on the quayside as they stepped off the boat. Her husband went back to England before she did. Pressure from the colonial authorities eventually ensured she rejoined him in her native Norwich.[17]

The vessels that sailed out of Boston harbour also carried home people not so much disenchanted with New England, as tempted by better prospects back home. Atlantic traffic was developing fast, with London as the hub for trade. A settler like Thomas Bell of Roxbury built up his business interests to a point where, in the late 1640s, it made sense to relocate from New England to the heart of London's merchant community. Another entrepreneur, Edward Bendall, invested in Boston's docks and invented an ingenious diving bell: like Thomas Bell, he may have returned to England to trade but (in a final twist to a colourful career) seems to have ended his days as a minister. Under Cromwell, new possibilities abounded, of all sorts. Early in 1651, Nathaniel and Samuel Mather, fresh out of Harvard and back in England, made much of the chances their fellow-graduates could expect to enjoy. Nathaniel wrote: 'the naked truth is, here is great encouragement for any to come over ... I think they need not much to question a living here, for it is with the honestest

---

[15] *Pilgrims*, 110–17, 123–42, 201–4.
[16] Thomas Harrison to John Winthrop, 14 February 1647, Allyn B. Forbes et al., eds, *The Winthrop Papers, 1498–1654*, 6 volumes (Boston, MA: Massachusetts Historical Society, 1929–), V, 198.
[17] *Pilgrims*, 43, 44.

on both sides a matter of high account to have been a New-English man'.[18] Samuel Mather reported on the fortunes of a long list of Harvard students in England, remembering how he himself, when in New England, had always been 'very desirous to hear of the students that went ... how they did & how they were disposed of'.[19] Harvard's first class graduated in 1642: seven out of the nine graduates in this first batch eventually found their way back to England.[20] Others left before their studies were over. Nathaniel Rowe, sent to Harvard by his father Owen Rowe (a London silk-maker and one of those who signed Charles I's death warrant in 1649), asked Governor Winthrop to 'make the waie cleare for mee to go to England' – whatever his father might think – and sailed home without a degree.[21] In 1652, the Massachusetts General Court tried to stem the flow of students who 'as soone as they grow up ready for publique use ... leave the Country & seeke for, or accept of, imployment elsewhere'. The Court's remedy, a minimum wage for ministers of £50 a year or £40 for Harvard fellows, was to little avail. It must have seemed small beer in comparison with salaries back home.[22]

Leaving New England could cause friction with friends and relations who stayed on. After Samuel Desborough had left, William Leete (still at Guilford, on the shores of Long Island Sound) reported how he had been forced to insist to his neighbours that Desborough had not tried to tempt him back across the Atlantic: 'I told them over and over that you had wrote nothing to invite or give a call.' Leete saw how the settlers who stayed resented the deserters: they had 'an aptnes to have harsh thoughts on almost all men that go for England'.[23] Family tensions show in the story of George Wyllys, son of Governor George Wyllys of Connecticut. Before George junior left for England, on what was meant to be a temporary visit to take care of family business – and get married if the opportunity arose – Governor Wyllys took the precaution of asking his son to sign a solemn and sacred promise to return to America. (Governor Wyllys's copy of this oath survives at the Connecticut Historical Society.) But despite his written promise, Wyllys junior flatly refused to return to New England, much to his father's fury and dismay – even after his father sent the original paper to him in England, to stir his conscience.[24]

Such frictions happened partly because settlers worried about the viability

---

[18] Nathaniel Mather to John Rogers, 23 March 1650/1, Massachusetts Historical Society, *Collections*, 4th series, 8 (1868), 3.

[19] Samuel Mather to Jonathan Mitchell, Massachusetts Historical Society, Boston, Ms. N-2196, Miscellaneous Bound Manuscripts Collection, 26 March 1651.

[20] Benjamin Woodbridge, George Downing, John Bulkeley, William Hubbard, Henry Saltonstall, Nathaniel Brewster and Tobias Barnard. The graduates from 1642 to 1660 are listed in *Harvard College records I*, Colonial Society of Massachusetts, *Publications*, 15 (1925), 82–4. *Pilgrims*, 70.

[21] Nathaniel Rowe to John Winthrop, c.1642, *WP* IV, 344.

[22] 'A Declaration concerning the Advancement of Learning in New England', Massachusetts General Court, October 1652, Massachusetts Archives, Boston, Massachusetts Archives Collection, vol. 58: 21.

[23] Leete to Desborough, 10 October 1654, British Library, London, Egerton MS 2519, fol. 10v.

[24] Only Governor Wyllys's copy of the paper signed by his son survives (without signature or date): Connecticut Historical Society, Hartford, Wyllys Papers, MS VII, 24A; printed in *The*

of their fragile communities, but also because settlers believed that they had been led over to New England by God. This conviction could encompass, and even draw strength from, mixed motives. Religious aspirations kept company with hopes of profit and efforts to revive flagging careers. Weavers left the beleaguered textile industry of East Anglia. The promise of furs and timber tempted entrepreneurs. West Country fishermen looked for new ways to exploit North Atlantic fishing grounds: the way to the Great Migration was paved by earlier ventures in the 1610s and 1620s to establish fishing settlements – not so much God as cod. A strong streak of providentialism ran through the debate about emigration, and allowed emigrants to gather many kinds of motive into a religious framework. Providence, they believed, had a knack of presenting the same truth in different guises, so a habit of puritan piety (evident in diaries and letters) was to look for multiple reasons that pointed the same way. Economic and religious motives did not compete, but complemented each other. 'Religion and profit jump together', as one colonist put it. On the way over to America, a dozen different reasons to follow the compass west – religious or otherwise – had confirmed the hand of Providence on the tiller. The godly also looked to each other to test out the truth, in a corporate, social process: reaching a common mind was a stamp of heavenly approval.[25]

Now settlers came up with ways to enlist the support of Providence to go home – to persuade not only themselves but also their neighbours who stayed on. To unravel the logic that carried them to New England, settlers had to find a 'just call' to abandon America. In a mirror image of their deliberations about whether to leave England, colonists weighed up whether they were called by Providence to make their way back. Settlers brought an extraordinary range of reasons into play to justify leaving America: better opportunities for employment; property to attend to in England; an inheritance back home; an invitation from friends; a sick relative; a desire to see England once more; poverty; New England's harsh climate. The minister John Davenport, who wanted to leave New Haven to avoid another New England winter – for his health's sake – used the commandment 'Thou shalt not kill' to argue he had a duty to preserve his life. Settlers aired their reasons for leaving in face-to-face conversations and by letters sent between settlements. Ties of covenant meant that these reasons could be formally scrutinised by the church and (where there was a plantation covenant) by the town. To allow someone to go, communities had to find ways to endorse an individual's call to go to England without undermining the purposes of Providence for those who remained in America. Fellow settlers could be ambivalent, or downright hostile, if someone's wish to leave threatened a town's viability. Even a desire to visit England might be greeted with suspicion. Colonists who disregarded the collective disapproval of their neighbours risked the judgment of God. John Winthrop, a harsh critic of settlers who deserted New England 'for outward advantage', wrote that 'all ways were sought for an open door to get out at; but it is to be feared many

Wyllys Papers . . . 1590–1796, Collections of the Connecticut Historical Society, 21 (1924), 6. *Pilgrims*, 88–90, Plate 4.
[25] *Pilgrims*, 3, 27, 28.

crept out at a broken wall'. Winthrop was quick to interpret disasters on Atlantic voyages as a punishment from the Almighty – at the hands of pirates or Turks, or by storms and shipwrecks.[26]

Certain patterns run through the histories of the hundreds of settlers unearthed in this book.[27] For the colonial elite, wealth and connections gave them a greater ability to pull out of New England, and more incentives to do so. People like John Humfrey and George Fenwick – whatever their losses in the colonies – had excellent prospects in England. For young graduates like Nathaniel Norcrosse, the end of New England's rapid growth meant stunted prospects: they could not find professional opportunities, except perhaps in isolated new settlements, which, though they offered youngsters a chance of leadership, had limited appeal.

For ministers, relations with their flock were crucial. Many felt a deep bond of loyalty. This kept several prominent individuals in America, such as John Cotton, who might otherwise have gone home. A minister like John Phillip evaded tying himself to a church in New England and went home as soon as possible: he stayed in America only three years. Some overrode the commitment by persuading their congregations to let them go: Thomas Allen, with a fine invitation from the city of Norwich in prospect, preached to his Charlestown congregation on the theme 'how shal wee come to know when a minister is caled to remoue from one place to another'.[28] Other clerics experienced a restless cycle of deteriorating relations with different local communities – for ministers like Marmaduke Matthews or Joseph Hull, a return to England came at the end of a chain of moves within New England.

For dissenters – whether they were more radical than the orthodoxy prescribed by Massachusetts, or more conservative – England promised greater freedom in religion and politics. People like Nathaniel Biscoe, a wealthy tanner from Watertown, and Ann Eaton, wife of the governor of New Haven Colony, eventually gave up on living as dissenters in small colonial communities. Some, like the ministers Robert Lenthall or Christopher Marshall, moved outside the control of Massachusetts, to Rhode Island or Maine, before they went to England. The correlation between dissent and setting sail for the godly republic back home was a symptom of the rupture between the two Englands over the question of toleration. Even English allies of New England – including the leading congregationalists Thomas Goodwin, John Owen and Philip Nye – found it necessary in 1645 to protest at Massachusetts' treatment of baptists. Sir Henry Vane and others appealed against the colony's condemnation of William Pynchon for heresy in 1651. New England was well out of step with the drumbeat back home. For dissenters of all kinds, England looked a better prospect than a war of attrition with colonial orthodoxy, or life in an outlying settlement.

For merchants and mariners like Nehemiah Bourne, Freegrace Bendall and

---

[26] *Pilgrims*, 10–11, 62–3, 95, 97.
[27] *Pilgrims*, 86–7.
[28] Thomas Allen's sermon on Psalm 143:8, 9 November 1650: American Antiquarian Society, Worcester, Massachusetts, Richard Russell's Sermon Notebook, fol. 139v.

David Yale, operating in the Atlantic world, trade and toleration spurred them to relocate to London.[29] For settlers in plantations that struggled because of poor land (such as Guilford's 'rocky sandy parts', abandoned by settlers like Nathaniel Whitfield and Thomas Jordan) or because of difficulties with trade (such as Rowley and its cloth industry, abandoned by Matthew Boyes, Edward Carleton and others), a return to their roots across the Atlantic seemed a better option than a move into Boston, or elsewhere in New England.[30] For those in financial straits it could be a struggle to find the money to go home. When the impoverished lawyer Thomas Lechford was about to sail back in 1641, his fellow Bostonians believed that Lechford's old friend, the London lawyer and pamphleteer William Prynne, had sent him the money to pay for his passage.[31] John Morse tried – unsuccessfully – to persuade a ship's commander to let him travel back on credit and pay in London. In the end, Morse managed to borrow the £15 he needed to pay upfront for his party of three. For craftsmen like coopers (John Milam, William Cutter, Thomas Venner), or shoemakers (Ferdinando Adams, George Burden, Thomas Edwards, Angel Hollard), their trade made them mobile. Shopkeepers like Walter Blackborne, a haberdasher in Boston who turned fishmonger in London, could also sell up and move on.

Of all the colonists, yeomen and husbandmen – bound to the land – probably had the most to gain by staying on. Although almost every settler worked the land, these farmers had skills which gave them a comparative advantage. Generous land grants meant most were doing well enough, better than in England. More than a few had close ties to New England ministers, but stayed on to farm even after the minister went home. The yeoman Henry Chickering, for example, had in 1638 followed John Phillip to Dedham, Massachusetts, from Wrentham in Suffolk. Chickering remained in Dedham after Phillip returned to Wrentham in 1641, although he may have teetered on the brink of a decision to leave: he delayed his decision to become a church deacon because of his 'affections to Mr Phillip in England'. The yeoman Joseph Peck lived out his days in Hingham and Rehobeth, Massachusetts, after his brother, the minister Robert Peck, returned to his parish at Hingham in Norfolk.[32]

Were settlers from certain parts of England more likely to return than others? The evidence is impossible to quantify, but it is hard to avoid the impression that many of those who went back came from areas where religious

---

[29] *Pilgrims*, 85, 104–9, 145. See also Louise A. Breen, *Transgressing the bounds: subversive enterprises among the puritan elite in Massachusetts, 1630–1692* (Oxford and New York: Oxford University Press, 2001), 97–143.

[30] *Pilgrims*, 84–5.

[31] *A note-book kept by Thomas Lechford ... in Boston*, Transactions and Collections of the American Antiquarian Society, 7 (Cambridge, MA: J. Wilson & Co., 1885), 431. William Prynne (*ODNB*) had once been Lechford's client.

[32] Thompson, *Mobility and migration*, 102, 108, 112, 234; T.H. Breen and Stephen Foster, 'Moving to the New World: the character of early Massachusetts immigration', *William and Mary Quarterly*, 3rd series, 30 (1973), 216. Chickering: D.G. Hill, ed., *The record of baptisms, marriages, and deaths, and admissions to the church and dismissals therefrom, transcribed from the church records in the town of Dedham, Massachusetts* (Dedham, MA, 1888), 35. Joseph and Robert Peck: *New England Historic and Genealogical Register*, 15 (1861), 26, 27; 121 (1967), 115.

tensions had been highest in the 1630s: East Anglia, Yorkshire, Cheshire and Lancashire, Hertfordshire, Kent and London. That is, those who had been most uprooted from England by events in the 1630s were also the most likely to go back. By contrast, West Country settlers played a smaller role in the return movement, perhaps because their migration had been inspired in part by earlier schemes to promote fishing or trade, along the lines pioneered by the Dorchester Company of Adventurers – or possibly because they had relatively worse prospects back in England.[33] Of the six West Country ministers who emigrated from the diocese of Exeter, three had been recruited early in the 1630s under the aegis of the Dorchester Company; the other three, who emigrated later in the decade, claimed harassment by the church authorities. Who came back to England? Only the three who claimed to have been uprooted under pressure.[34]

III

The common thread that unites all the individuals in this book is that that they crossed the Atlantic not once, but twice – a three thousand mile journey at the mercy of the wind and waves.[35] Some crossed more than twice. (A few criss-crossed the ocean what might seem to modern eyes an alarming number of times, for business or family reasons; these visits home quite often precipitated a permanent return.) The voyage to New England usually took between eight and twelve weeks, though one ship took twenty-six, struggling on the open seas for eighteen.[36] The return voyage to England was much quicker because of the prevailing westerly winds on the Atlantic, and because the Gulf Stream could add a hundred and thirty miles a day to the speed of ships.[37] An English correspondent reported that a traveller on his way back from New England had come 'safely from your coasts to ours ... in 3 weeks and 3 days'.[38] Colonists faced longer at sea if they went north from Boston to Newfoundland and took a passage in a West Country fishing vessel. In 1641 John Winthrop Jr took nine weeks to reach England this way, in 'very foul weather, continual storms'.[39] Another indirect route took a southerly course, by way of the West Indies and the Canary Islands or Spain.[40]

---

[33] These impressions tally broadly with D.G. Allen, *In English ways: the movement of societies and the transferal of English local law and custom to Massachusetts Bay in the seventeenth century* (Chapel Hill, NC: University of North Carolina Press, 1981), 13–14.
[34] John Maverick, William Walton and John Warham stayed on, but William Hooke, Joseph Hull and Thomas Larkham returned to England: *Pilgrims*, 187–8.
[35] This section draws on *Pilgrims*, 33–4, 103–4.
[36] David Cressy, *Coming over: migration and communication between England and New England in the seventeenth century* (Cambridge: Cambridge University Press, 1987), 158.
[37] Ian K. Steele, *The English Atlantic 1675–1740* (Oxford: Oxford University Press, 1986), 7.
[38] Henry Jacie [Jessey] to John Winthrop Jr, 12 June 1633, *WP* III, 126.
[39] John Winthrop Jr to Elizabeth Winthrop, 8 October 1641, *WP* IV, 342.
[40] Cressy, *Coming over*, 156.

In both directions, shipping had a seasonal pattern. English fishing boats crossed to Newfoundland early in the year (when easterly winds were strongest), to catch the cod that appeared off the Grand Banks in May – dried it over two or three months, or salted it, often at fishing stations onshore in New England – and sailed back to England in the late summer. Ships carrying manufactured goods to Boston started out from England in the spring, and made the return journey in the autumn, carrying fish, furs and timber.[41] Thus most passengers travelling back from New England to England sailed in the second half of the year.

Vessels often travelled together, for safety. Passengers slept in hammocks and cots, separated by flimsy canvas partitions. A gentleman might get a cabin. Shipboard rations deteriorated as time went on: a predictable diet of oatmeal, buttered peas, cured beef and pork, biscuits, dried bread; enlivened by eggs and milk from animals aboard and fresh fish when passengers or crew could catch it. John Winthrop recorded how small boats ferried people between ships in mid-Atlantic, to bring shipmasters and eminent passengers together for dinner; to fetch a midwife for a woman in labour.[42] In 1632 Thomas Weld (who returned to England nine years later) sent back to Essex an ecstatic account of God's protection on the way over to New England, as an incentive to persuade more of his parishioners to follow him across the Atlantic:

> Yea, mercy, mercy in the Lord, inwardly outwardly, in spite of devils and storms as cheerful as ever, my wife all the voyage on the sea better than at land, and seasick but one day in eleven weeks, at sea my children never better in their lives. They went ill into the ship but well there and came forth well as ever. Myself had not one ounce of seasickness, nor one motion or inclination thereunto, not all the way. 'Stand still and behold the salvation of the Lord.'[43]

Hanserd Knollys (a minister from Lincolnshire who returned to England within three years, and became a prominent baptist) was more realistic about his fourteen-week voyage over to Boston:

> By the way my little child died with convulsion fits, our beer and water stank, our biscuit was green, yellow and blue, moulded and rotten, and our cheese also, so that we suffered much hardship . . . but God was gracious to us, and led us safe through those great deeps.[44]

---

[41] Steele, *The English Atlantic*, 9–10; Gillian T. Cell, *English enterprise in Newfoundland 1577–1660* (Toronto: University of Toronto Press, 1969), 4–6; Mark Kurlansky, *Cod: a biography of the fish that changed the world* (London: Vintage, 1999), 70–2.

[42] John Winthrop, *The journal of John Winthrop*, ed. Richard S. Dunn, James Savage and Laetitia Yeandle (Cambridge, MA and London: Harvard University Press, 1996), 15, 25.

[43] Weld to his former parishioners in Terling, Essex, 1632, in David D. Hall, ed., *Puritans in the New World: a critical anthology* (Princeton, NJ and Oxford: Princeton University Press, 2004), 33. Weld quoted from Exodus 14:13, Moses' words to the fearful Israelites before God parted the Red Sea so that they could cross safely.

[44] [Hanserd Knollys], *The life and death of . . . Mr Hanserd Knollys* (London, 1692), 17.

For some, unpleasant memories of the journey to New England had to be conquered before they could set foot on a ship again. John Davenport teetered on the brink of returning to England in the early 1650s, but loathed the prospect of the Atlantic voyage, and 'my wife is very weak at sea, not well able to bear the smells and troubles in the vessel'. He thought October or November the best time to travel, as 'the Michaelmas storms will be over, and the cold of the winter avoided'.[45] Everyone knew disaster could strike. Many passengers made a will before they set sail. In 1644 the Boston-built *Sea Fort* – named for its size and strength – set out for England in company with a London ship. Both ships ran aground off the coast of Spain and broke up. Nineteen people died. Survivors came ashore 'naked and barefoot as they went frighted out of their cabins'.[46]

Whatever terrors the wind and waves unleashed, godly travellers looked to Providence for protection. Travellers heard shipboard sermons to cheer them on, and ministers led hardened mariners into prayer. Peter Saxton's conduct became a pattern for sailors in crisis: 'say, as that old Puritan Minister did in a storm coming from New-England, when they were all expecting the Vessell to sink, *O, who is now for Heaven, who is bound for Heaven*'.[47] John Winthrop wrote that preservation from danger was 'so frequent, to such ships as have carried those of the Lord's family between the two Englands, as would fill a perfect volume to report them all'.[48] Despite Winthrop's buoyant attitude, watery deaths were an ever-present hazard. As Providence would have it, Mahalaleel Munnings, a New England merchant, made at least five Atlantic crossings but drowned in Boston's mill creek.[49]

IV

The life-stories of people who travelled between New England and England belong in a larger setting: the history of the British Atlantic world, and the history of religion in that world. A new branch of historical study – Atlantic history – has changed the context for research on the communities and cultures around the ocean, in the Americas, Africa and Europe.[50] Even if some scholars are sceptical about how durable the perspective of Atlantic history

---

[45] John Davenport to John Winthrop Jr, 24 July and 11 September 1650, in Isabel M. Calder, ed., *Letters of John Davenport, puritan divine* (New Haven, CT: Yale University Press, 1937), 93.
[46] Winthrop, *Journal*, 598–9. Abraham and Joanna Pratt died; Giles Firmin survived.
[47] John Ryther, *A plat for mariners* (London, 1672), 55.
[48] Winthrop, *Journal*, 403.
[49] For Mahalaleel Munnings, see Appendix 2.
[50] Bernard Bailyn, *Atlantic history: concept and contours* (Cambridge, MA: Harvard University Press, 2005); Jack Greene and Philip D. Morgan, eds, *Atlantic history: a critical appraisal* (New York and Oxford: Oxford University Press, 2009); Nicholas Canny and Philip D. Morgan, eds, *The Oxford handbook of the Atlantic world, 1450–1850* (New York and Oxford: Oxford University Press, 2011); David Armitage and Michael J. Braddick, eds, *The British Atlantic world, 1500–1800* (New York and Basingstoke: Palgrave Macmillan, 2002).

will prove to be, it has challenged historians to place their work on specific areas (such as New England) into the broader Atlantic setting. In seventeenth-century studies this has brought a new dimension to discussions of migration, trade and religion, and to questions of identity and politics.

Interest in Atlantic history has helped to draw attention to the traffic of people out of New England. David Cressy wove it into his book *Coming over: migration and communication between England and New England in the seventeenth century*. Frank Bremer used the histories of colonists who went back advocating the 'New England Way' (congregationalism) to shape his account of clerical networks between old and New England: *Congregational communion: clerical friendship in the Anglo-American puritan community, 1610–1692*. Andrew Delbanco, in *The puritan ordeal*, believed the histories of those who left exposed a general discontent with colonial life. Philip Gura's *A glimpse of Sion's glory: puritan radicalism in New England, 1620–1660*, considered how religious liberty in England attracted radicals back from New England. Stephen Fender explored how the story of those who left New England defined the story for those who stayed on, in *Sea changes: British emigration and American literature*. Louise Breen, in *Transgressing the bounds: subversive enterprises among the puritan elite in Massachusetts, 1630–1692*, pointed to the allure of England for 'cosmopolitan puritans' frustrated with the provincialism of New England. Alison Games's *Migration and the origins of the English Atlantic world* followed 5,000 migrants who left London in 1635 for New England, the Chesapeake and the Caribbean, and noted how events in England after 1640 drew puritans back home, away from the 'wilderness periphery'. Carla Gardina Pestana, in *The English Atlantic in an age of revolution, 1640–1661*, highlighted the role of New England settlers in England's religious debates.[51] My own book, *Pilgrims: New World settlers and the call of home*, has already built on the individual lives presented here, from the perspective of religious history, to interpret the story of these migrants in relation to religious conflict and experimentation in the mid-seventeenth century. Thus, in various ways, historical writing has taken up the transatlantic agenda

---

[51] Cressy, *Coming over*, 191–205; Francis J. Bremer, *Congregational communion: clerical friendship in the Anglo-American puritan community, 1610–1692* (Boston, MA: Northeastern University Press, 1994), 120–1, 145–6, 150–1, 179–90; Andrew Delbanco, *The puritan ordeal* (Cambridge, MA: Harvard University Press, 1989), 184–214; Philip F. Gura, *A glimpse of Sion's glory: puritan radicalism in New England, 1620–1660* (Middletown, CT: Wesleyan University Press, 1984), 136–43, 222–4; Stephen Fender, *Sea changes: British emigration and American literature* (Cambridge: Cambridge University Press, 1992), 141–7 and *passim*; Games, *Migration and the origins of the English Atlantic world*, 193–206, 236–8; Breen, *Transgressing the bounds*, 97–143; Carla Gardina Pestana, *The English Atlantic in an age of revolution, 1640–1661* (Cambridge, MA and London: Harvard University Press 2004), 56–63, 85. See also Francis J. Bremer, *Puritan crisis: New England and the English civil wars 1630–1670* (New York and London: Garland, 1989); Harry S. Stout, 'The morphology of remigration: New England university men and their return to England, 1640–1660', *Journal of American Studies* 10 (1976), 151–72; Norman Pettit, 'God's Englishman in New England: his enduring ties to the motherland', Massachusetts Historical Society, *Proceedings*, 101 (1989), 56–70.

and reckoned with the phenomenon of settlers leaving New England. Efforts have been made to bring these people from the margins into the mainstream.

The difficulty of exploring this aspect of the Atlantic world has been that, until now, the detailed evidence has been widely scattered and largely unknown. For more than half a century, the pioneering work of William L. Sachse has tended to define the field: two articles from the 1940s, 'Harvard men in England 1642–1714' and 'The migration of New Englanders to England, 1640–1660', and his 1956 book, *The colonial American in Britain*.[52] Sachse identified many individuals who left New England for England, but with a generalised approach, and over a long time-span. He laid out a good trail for others to follow, but those he named loom large in documents from the time: religious, social or political misfits, and the educated elite. While these people are important, they are not necessarily representative. Recent scholarship has extended the boundaries of enquiry, but, on the whole, the settlers Sachse identified have been the individuals that historians have most cited.

The research presented here is a new resource, based on a deep trawl of seventeenth-century sources in America and England. The life-stories from early New England gathered in this book extend the body of knowledge far beyond the small cohort of people who have appeared in the literature so far. The lives collected here, largely unknown or neglected, make up a rich storehouse of evidence for future researchers to explore.

V

In 1987 David Cressy made a stab at quantifying the total number of settlers who left, with some bold suggestions based on broad-brush demographic evidence: he confessed this was tricky, because estimates of New England's population vary quite considerably, but suggested it could be as many as one in six.[53]

Intriguingly, the evidence in this book – derived not from demographics but from individual histories – adds up to something not far removed from Cressy's estimate.[54]

Hard evidence can be mustered for the godly preachers who emigrated to New England in the 1630s. Among these, it turns out that a decision to return to England was far from exceptional. One in three of the godly preachers who emigrated in the 1630s went back to England – in fact, twenty-five out of the seventy who lived to hear of the changed circumstances back home in 1640. Only one minister returned to England before 1640 (and that was in the

---

[52] William L. Sachse, 'Harvard men in England 1642–1714', Colonial Society of Massachusetts, Publications, 35 (1942–6), 120–31; 'The migration of New Englanders to England, 1640–1660', *American Historical Review*, 53 (1947–8), 251–78; *The colonial American in Britain* (Madison, WI: University of Wisconsin Press, 1956).

[53] Cressy, *Coming over*, 192: 'as many as one in six migrants to New England may have either permanently or temporarily returned home'.

[54] For what follows, see *Pilgrims*, 55–6.

earliest days of settlement). But twelve left between 1640 and 1643, after the first news of change came from England.⁵⁵

Equally hard evidence is available for Harvard students, but here the ratio is more dramatic. Almost one in two left New England: forty-three of 108 who graduated with a BA in classes up to 1659, and more who went to England without staying to complete a degree.⁵⁶

Among settlers in general, hard evidence is more difficult to find. Nevertheless, around 600 colonists who returned to England in the 1640s and 1650s are identified in this book.⁵⁷ Most of these people went back for good, although some did so only for a while. Of the 600, a disproportionate number (almost 450) are adult men. To arrive at a figure that includes all the women and children (usually a silent presence aboard ship), it seems reasonable to scale up by using the ratio of adult men to the total number of migrants on lists of passengers who sailed to New England in 1637 – the most complete set to survive.⁵⁸ Of 273 voyagers on these lists, eighty-one were men. If this ratio is brought into play, it gives a fairly secure figure of a minimum of 1,500 settlers who returned to England.

But what was the size of the colonial population from which the travellers came? Estimates of the number of immigrants in the 1630s vary from 13,000 to 21,000. Estimates of the colonial population in 1640 vary from 13,500 to 17,600.⁵⁹ Thereafter, New England saw little growth between 1640 and 1660. From a low estimate of immigrants, 13,000, the 1,500 settlers who returned to England after 1640 represent over one in nine; if the immigrants numbered 21,000, the proportion returning would still be one in fourteen.⁶⁰ These ratios are remarkably high, bearing in mind that they come only from what is known about returning settlers who can be identified by name or by household.

Of course, restricting attention to the settlers *who can be identified* almost certainly leads to a serious underestimate of the actual outflow. In August 1641, John Winthrop recorded that forty passengers set sail for England by way of Newfoundland. Of these, only seven can now be identified – that is,

---

⁵⁵ Between 1640 and 1643: Christopher Blackwood, George Burdett, Samuel Eaton, Richard Gibson, Hanserd Knollys, Thomas Larkham, Robert Lenthall, Hugh Peter (as a colonial agent, with Weld), John Phillip, Robert Peck, Peter Saxton, Thomas Weld. Francis Bright returned to England in 1630. Nathaniel Eaton, the first head of Harvard College, left in disgrace in 1639 for Virginia, but later returned to England. *Pilgrims*, Appendix 3, notes which of the first generation clergy returned home before 1660, and when.

⁵⁶ The Harvard students in this book can be identified through the index. A list of early graduates can be found in *Harvard College records I*, Colonial Society of Massachusetts, *Publications*, 15 (1925), 82–3.

⁵⁷ Not all of these returning colonists have a separate entry in the book. Family members, where they can be identified, are typically subsumed under the head of household's entry.

⁵⁸ In terms of migration out to New England, 'the year 1637 stands out for its relatively complete data ... there had not been such careful recording before and there would not be again': Breen and Foster, 'Moving to the New World', 192–3.

⁵⁹ Pestana, *English Atlantic*, 229–32.

⁶⁰ This tallies with Roger Thompson's finding that sixty of the 718 adult male migrants in his cohort of emigrants returned to England (one in twelve): Thompson, *Mobility and migration*, 207. Thompson's book is based on 2,000 emigrants to New England from 'Greater East Anglia'.

roughly one in six.[61] Of other ships' passengers, the fraction who can be identified falls well short of one in six.[62] On this basis, it is plausible to suggest how many went back by multiplying the figure of 600 by at least six. In other words, it is possible that at least 3,600 came back, rather than a minimum of 1,500.

If this is so, and the estimate of 1630s immigrants is set low (at 13,000), it means that perhaps as many as one in four settlers went back. Even with a high immigrant figure (21,000), the proportion of settlers who left is still one in six.[63] These figures are admittedly only tentative, because the hidden number of returning settlers has been arrived at from those who can be identified. However, the ratios gain more traction when set against the hard evidence that one in three of the original clerical emigrants left for England, along with almost one in two early Harvard students.

Clergy and university graduates were, naturally, more likely to leave – they were more likely to have the resources to pay for a passage home; more likely to have good opportunities in England; more likely to feel the pinch of poverty in New England. (It is ironic that the settlers who provided New England's leadership were also the most liable to pluck up stakes and go home.)[64] Even so, for the settlers *en masse*, about whom so comparatively little is known, the evidence of the roughly 600 people identified in this book suggests that the overall rate of return was significant too.

VI

Others will bring their own research questions to the material, but from my own perspective the life-stories help to interpret religion in the Atlantic world, and in early modern England, amid the turbulent events of the mid-seventeenth century.

---

[61] Winthrop, *Journal*, 354. The seven passengers were Ferdinando Adams, Hugh Peter, Thomas Weld, Thomas Lechford and probably Peter Saxton, who all stayed on in England for good, as well as William Hibbins and John Winthrop Jr, who later returned to New England.

[62] See, for example, various ships bound for England with dozens of passengers aboard, of whom only a tiny handful can be identified: Winthrop, *Journal*, 414–15, 598–9, 643–4; *WP* V, 119; Edward Winslow, *New-Englands salamander* (London, 1647), 20. The difficulties of assessing the number and identity of migrants from what survives are illustrated by another fragment from Winthrop's *Journal*. In the summer of 1638, Winthrop reckoned, 'twenty ships, and at least three thousand persons' came to New England; yet of these only seven ships can be identified, and the surviving passenger lists, drawn up in England, name only 260 migrants – or one in twelve: Winthrop, *Journal*, 261.

[63] This matches the estimate David Cressy arrived at from statistics of colonial population: Cressy, *Coming over*, 192. Cressy suggests that the disparity between the number of emigrants to New England (21,000) and New England's population in 1640 (between 13,500 and 17,600) is accounted for by migration to other colonies or back to England – although he acknowledges that the best figures available are not robust, and that from the raw statistics of colonial population there is no way to discriminate between migrants who moved on within the New World and those who went home.

[64] Thompson, *Mobility and migration*, 41–2, 52, notes the attraction of return for the 'better sort' and the clergy. See also Stout, 'Morphology of remigration'.

The role of religion in catalysing the Great Migration to New England has been hotly debated, but there are good arguments for allowing it a central role. Migrants are sometimes portrayed as religious extremists, attracted to America to put distance between themselves and the 'ungodly'. From this point of view, these were Protestants of a sectarian temper, at odds with the broad church of parish religion. Religious policy in the 1630s played at most a marginal role. But from another perspective, emigrants came not from a radical fringe. Rather, they came from a movement central to the newly protestant Church of England, part of a lively campaign to win hearts and minds – a movement far from monolithic, carrying many shades of opinion and practice within a broad commitment to Reformed Protestantism. In the 1630s these zealous Protestants felt threatened by Laudian policies that seemed anti-Calvinist: for example, a prohibition on sermons about predestination, and changes to the communion service that seemed to bring back elements of the Catholic mass. They feared these innovations would snuff out Protestantism. This stirred up interest in a tactical retreat from England, in order to preserve true religion. A great deal of soul-searching went on about whether it was right to desert England at a time of crisis, but migrants found plenty of precedents for taking flight to a place of safety in the cause of truth. The Marian exiles – the Protestants who fled abroad during the reign of the Catholic queen Mary Tudor (1553–8) – came most quickly to mind. The godly had felt under threat many times before, but in the 1630s it seemed the old room for manoeuvre had gone. Places of temporary refuge on the Continent, like English congregations in the Netherlands, came increasingly within reach of the long arm of Laud. New England looked a safe haven.

Undeniably, an assortment of motives, economic and social as well as spiritual, drew them across the Atlantic. Does this reduce religion to merely one of many factors in a decision to sail for America? No: the mindset of godly emigrants shows their determination to weave a providential story for their lives out of an untidy mass of events and aspirations. In the ethos of Reformed Christianity that defined the puritan movement, godly ministers encouraged their people to set everything in the framework of divine Providence. To find inner certainty about a call to leave England, godly migrants weighed up the signs, for and against. Providence would show itself first one way, then another. Everything was grist for the mill: disappointments and dangers in old England, incentives in New.[65]

Perhaps the strongest evidence for the overarching significance of religious factors is that the flow of migrants reflected the development and demise of Laudian initiatives, diocese by diocese. The pressure – or threat of pressure – that the godly believed would uproot preachers and limit the practice of piety pushed them into evasive tactics which, for some, ended in a decision to leave their native country. Although information about most emigrants is fragmentary, and the harder evidence comes from an identifiable cohort of emigrant ministers, without putting religious motives centre stage it would be difficult

---

[65] *Pilgrims*, 4.

to explain why thousands set sail for New England between 1630 and 1639, and only a trickle before or after.⁶⁶

The distinctive religious culture of early New England is also important. Within a few years of the arrival of the Winthrop fleet in 1630, settlers had translated vague principles into what became known by the 1640s as the 'New England Way', or congregationalism. This was a new and controversial model of what a pure church should be: distinct from what settlers had known in England; distinct from the practice of other Reformed churches in Europe; distinct even from the views of the puritan theologian William Ames (1576–1633), which had influenced a whole generation of zealous English Protestants. The unique character of New England's churches came about because the convictions that carried settlers away from England, in the tough environment of the New World, turned pious practices into the foundations for pure churches. Old habits took new forms. Settlers' inventive use of covenants, and the local horizons that circumscribed their churches, all had deep roots in migrants' experiences back home, but led to innovations in the New World. The most striking was this: although everyone still had to attend sermons, in order to join a church settlers had to leap the hurdle of giving a satisfactory spiritual testimony (as judged by the rest of the members). Only then could they could they be admitted to the sacraments; that is, receive communion, or have their children baptised. What started out in England as voluntary strategies among the godly – used to express their identity as zealous Protestants – became essentials in New England, to define the identity of the Church.⁶⁷

If religion played an important part in galvanising people to leave England – and the context of emigration and the religious culture of New England suggest that it did – then the return to England of many settlers who had once felt impelled by Providence to set out for the New World is significant.

The drift back to England in the 1640s and 1650s highlights the role of New England as a refuge in the 1630s, when Laudian policy delivered a push for people to cross the Atlantic. When times changed, why stay on? This was more than a casual question. The minister Nathaniel Ward, about to leave Ipswich, Massachusetts, drew attention in his feisty satire *The simple cobler of Agawam* (1647) to what some settlers, at least, made part of their 'American Creed': 'no man ought to forsake his own country, but upon extraordinary cause, and when that cause ceaseth, he is bound in conscience to return if he can'. Ward's authority for this maxim was a respected puritan of an earlier generation, William Perkins (1558–1602). Perkins argued that:

> as a man is not to depart out of that land where God hath appointed him to dwell, but upon good and sufficient causes: so, when those causes cease, which drew him out, he is not to stay longer from home; but to repair again to the place of his ordinary dwelling.⁶⁸

---

⁶⁶ *Pilgrims*, 4, 23–6.
⁶⁷ *Pilgrims*, 38; Larry Gragg, *Englishmen transplanted: the English colonization of Barbados, 1627–1660* (Oxford: Oxford University Press, 2003), 85–6.
⁶⁸ Nathaniel Ward, *The simple cobler of Aggawam in America* (London, 1647), 23; William

The ministers John Phillip and Robert Peck returned to their parishes in 1641, as soon as news reached New England that Bishop Matthew Wren had been declared unfit for office.[69] In 1644, George Wyllys put it to his father that as he could now enjoy 'the purity of gods ordinances' back home, there was no need for him to be in New England.[70] One of Winthrop's correspondents wrote from England in 1647 that, now colonists could enjoy 'soul comfort' in their native country, there was no need to risk the hardship of life in the American colonies.[71] William Cutter (who once lived in Cambridge, Massachusetts, but had returned to Newcastle upon Tyne) wrote to Henry Dunster of Cambridge in 1654 that, though he often wished to see his family and friends in New England, he would not leave England again: 'truly the sad discouragements in coming by sea is enough to hinder: unless it were as formerly: that we could not enjoy the ordinances of God'.[72] The argument gained momentum as time went on, up to 1660, when the religious context in England changed again.

Those who abandoned America show up an intriguing counterpoint between the traffic of ideas through people and the traffic of ideas in print – between the flow of settlers back across the Atlantic and the flood of colonial tracts from London presses.[73] The settlers who went back to England usually show neither simple dissent from the New England Way, nor a wish to broadcast it as gospel. Admittedly, some ministers came back and put their colonial convictions into practice in a divisive fashion: Thomas Weld caused uproar in Gateshead when he preached to the whole parish but restricted the sacraments to all but a handful of people.[74] Other ministers, although they supported New England's style of primitive purity, were judicious about how far and how fast they transplanted colonial ways onto English soil. The kind of church that could exist in a New World might not be possible – or essential – for old England's parish churches. Justifying this approach, Giles Firmin argued:

> You must put a difference between Churches new erecting, and these in England, which have been churches for so long; when I raise a house from new from the ground, I may then doe as I please, but if I be mending of an old house, I must doe as well as I can, repair by degrees.[75]

Perkins, *A cloud of faithfull witnesses, leading to the heavenly Canaan, or a commentary on the 11. chapter to the Hebrewes* (London, 1607), 199 [on Hebrews 11:9]; *Pilgrims*, 54, 72.

[69] *Pilgrims*, 233 n.47: Wren was judged unfit for office on 5 July 1641, Peck and Phillip sailed home at the end of October.
[70] George Wyllys's arguments, sent in a letter dated 29 May 1644, can be deduced from his father's response: *Wyllys Papers*, 68.
[71] Laurence Wright to John Winthrop, 10 March 1646/7, *WP*, V, 137–8.
[72] William Cutter to Henry Dunster, 19 May 1654, 'Dunster Papers', Massachusetts Historical Society, *Collections*, 4th series, 2 (1854), 196.
[73] Pestana, *English Atlantic*, 235-40, lists and categorises 'London Pamphlets about New England, 1641–1649': she concludes that of 125 tracts (from authors in New England and old), 105 had strongly stated opinions: seventy-one pro-New England, thirty-four against.
[74] *Pilgrims*, 133–5.
[75] Giles Firmin, *Separation examined* (London, 1652), 82.

Firmin's distinction between 'new-build' and 'restoration' meant he looked for implicit signs of a true church in his parish: for the present, that was enough. Firmin perhaps seems atypical: it is often assumed that those who came back from New England were aggressive agitators for change (indeed, the presbyterian polemicist Thomas Edwards painted Firmin in that light). But in the crucial debates of the 1640s, printed books, not New Englanders, articulated the New England Way. Ironically, the most vociferous advocates of replicating the New England Way in England usually turn out not to be people who had been there, but those who had read about it. The ambiguities in settlers' personal histories contrast with the certainties of print.[76]

Many settlers who chafed against orthodoxy in Massachusetts went home. The kinds of dissent that precipitated their departure were many and various, and this is not surprising. Events of the 1630s had radicalised people into emigration, but not necessarily into a particular view of church government or of the theology of grace. Differences intrinsic to the English puritan movement, hidden before emigration, showed themselves in New England, most notably in the Antinomian Controversy of 1636–8 (an anguished theological dispute about whether costly grace is free, as the antinomians argued, or whether free grace is costly, as their opponents alleged). New England lost antinomian sympathisers, like Sir Henry Vane, Thomas Tillam, William Aspinwall and Richard Hutchinson; people who disliked New England's strict criteria for church membership, such as Robert Lenthall, Richard Sadler and Mary Oliver; newly convinced baptists, like Hanserd Knollys and Thomas Patient; emerging Quakers, like Ann Burden and Richard Lippincott; and advocates of godly episcopacy (like Thomas Lechford) or godly presbytery (like Newbury residents Thomas Rashley, John and Benjamin Woodbridge, Henry Sewall, and Stephen and Alice Dummer – an interconnected clan). These dissenters of various shades left New England not only because Massachusetts' drive to create a united 'orthodoxy' shook out diversity, but also because – to look at this from a different angle – a great variety of people, radicalised into emigration by the particular context of the 1630s, found that their ties to the New World worked loose when circumstances in England changed.[77]

VII

To track down the people who returned to England before 1660 has required some ingenuity, and a search of many types of sources on both sides of the Atlantic. Since no passenger lists exist for ships that left New England, the key to identifying a homeward-bound settler is often a document signed on the eve of setting sail. To judge from the records of the Boston notaries Thomas Lechford and William Aspinwall – who could not have been far from the

[76] *Pilgrims*, 125, 135–8.
[77] *Pilgrims*, 56, 87, 123–42.

quayside – there was usually a flurry of activity in advance of going aboard ship, as people bound for England put paperwork in order before they risked the Atlantic again.[78] A will, a deed of sale, a power of attorney granted to a relative or neighbour: such documents provide clues to who left, and when. Evidence also comes from church records, since (in theory, at least) church members were expected to seek either a formal dismissal, or 'letters of recommendation' to carry to England. In practice, people often waited until they wanted to join a new church in England and wrote back to seek release.[79] A wide variety of other early colonial sources – personal letters, diaries and journals, papers from court cases, petitions to the Massachusetts General Court, and so on – can provide fragments of evidence about people ready to depart, or already gone. On the English side, the range of sources that can yield information includes manuscript records from the national church in Cromwell's time and (since New England's single printing press at Cambridge, Massachusetts, was hardly in operation for the period covered here) books printed in London. Regrettably, tracing the less well-known people in English records can be tricky. Unless a paper trail exists to make a link to the colonies, many settlers disappear (lost in a mass of people with similar names) soon after they return to England. Occasionally, however, a source is extremely clear. When Elizabeth Edwards was admitted to the congregational church in Yarmouth, the church book filled out the detail nicely: 'by dismission from the Church of Christ at Salem in New England'.[80]

So, from scraps of evidence in early sources, it is possible to gather the names of colonists who left New England for England. Once an individual has been identified, their history can be traced backwards and forwards in time. In addition to manuscript and printed sources, the work of earlier scholars has provided good leads and relevant information: for example, the work of A.G. Matthews in *Calamy revised* and some nineteenth-century editions of sources, and local and denominational histories.[81]

Over the time my investigation of these life-stories has taken – several decades since the late 1970s when I started my doctorate[82] – the mechanics of research have altered. The work began with an old-fashioned card index at a time when nothing was available online. The research involved a

---

[78] Lechford's records of these 'quayside transactions' run from 1638 until mid-1641 (when he went to England). There is a gap in surviving records of this type until Aspinwall started his work, late in 1644. Aspinwall's record ended in 1651 when the authorities removed him from office. *Pilgrims*, 234 n.48. Biographies of Aspinwall and Lechford can be found in the main text.

[79] *Pilgrims*, 96.

[80] Norfolk Record Office, Norwich, MS FC 31/1, Great Yarmouth, Middlegate Congregational Church Book, 1643–1855, fol. 27; *Pilgrims*, 118.

[81] A.G. Matthews, *Calamy revised* (Oxford: Clarendon Press, 1934; reprint, Oxford: Clarendon Press, 1988): Matthews revised the work of the minister and historian Edmund Calamy (1671–1732, *ODNB*) on nonconformist ministers ejected in 1660–2. For nineteenth-century sources, see bibliography.

[82] The research for both *Abandoning America* and *Pilgrims* originated with my doctoral thesis, 'Return migration from New England to England, 1640–1660' (University of Kent at Canterbury, 1986).

good deal of legwork in libraries and archives on both sides of the Atlantic, checking unwieldy catalogues and ploughing through heaps of paper. Some of the research was undertaken in London, where the British Library and Dr Williams's Library provided seventeenth-century printed books and nineteenth-century editions of early records, and, most of all, manuscripts. More manuscript material was gathered at Lambeth Palace Library and at the National Archives in London, at the Bodleian Library in Oxford, and at county record offices across England (Essex, East Sussex, Suffolk, Norfolk, Devon and Cumbria in particular). On the New England side, the work was mainly with manuscripts in major collections across Massachusetts and Connecticut: in Boston, at the Massachusetts Archives, the Massachusetts Historical Society and Boston Public Library; in Cambridge, at the Harvard University Archives in the Houghton Library, Harvard Yard; in Worcester, at the American Antiquarian Society; in Salem, at the Phillips Library at the Peabody Essex Museum; in Hartford, at the Connecticut State Library and Connecticut Historical Society. The Gratz Sermon Collection at the Historical Society of Pennsylvania in Philadephia also yielded valuable information. For a British scholar used to England's local record offices it was a surprise that so many seventeenth-century records in New England remained, until recently, with the original body that created them. In Middlesex County, Massachusetts, for example, the Cambridge town records can be consulted in the city clerk's office at City Hall. The ancient court files which used to be in the basement of the Middlesex County Courthouse are now at the Massachusetts Archives, as are the probate records which used to at the busy Middlesex County Probate and Family Court. The Middlesex South District Registry of Deeds still keeps the early deeds.

Much has changed in recent years. Many manuscripts can now be found online, as can elderly but important editions of original records. The number of online resources is increasing rapidly. In addition, two significant new resources have come onstream in recent years: *The Great Migration Study Project*, available online and in print, the brainchild of Robert Charles Anderson; and the online *Clergy of the Church of England Database*, initiated by Arthur Burns, Kenneth Fincham and Stephen Taylor. Both projects are ambitious. The former aims to provide biographies of all migrants to New England from 1620 to 1640.[83] The latter intends to document, as far as the surviving diocesan records will permit, all the clergy in the established church, 1540–1835.[84] In the final stages of writing this book, these online databases have been invaluable for adding and cross-checking information. Online resources have the potential to revolutionise this kind of research, to simplify

---

[83] Published, to date: R.C. Anderson, ed., *The Great Migration begins: immigrants to New England 1620–1633*, 3 vols (Boston, MA: New England Historic Genealogical Society, 1995); R.C. Anderson, G.F. Sanborn and M.L. Sanborn, eds, *The Great Migration: immigrants to New England, 1634–1635*, 7 vols (Boston, MA: Great Migration Study Project, New England Historic Genealogical Society, 1999–2011). Accessible online at http://www.AmericanAncestors.org.

[84] *Clergy of the Church of England Database*, http://www.theclergydatabase.org.uk/index.html.

and speed up the investigation. However, for a good while yet it will still be essential to visit libraries and archives to interrogate sources in person. This project has been built on that kind of scholarly detective work.

VIII

The book presents the life-stories in three categories. First and foremost, in the main body of the text, come settlers who left New England for England from 1640, when the the tide of passenger traffic turned and flowed back home, up to the time of the Restoration in 1660. These life-stories – of settlers who abandoned New England for good (or at least until 1660) – occupy the bulk of the book. Here the research has been most exhaustive, to capture as many individuals as possible from the surviving records.

The second group of life-stories (Appendix 1) provides examples of people who returned home earlier, in the 1630s: driven back by sheer hardship, or driven out by the pressure for orthodoxy which accompanied the Antinomian Controversy in Massachusetts. The decision to present examples, rather than an exhaustive account, was partly determined by the difficulty of tracking down these people. Record-keeping in the earliest days of New England was sparser, and plenty of voyagers hardly stayed long enough to leave a trace. Quite often, individuals listed in London as passengers bound for New England simply disappear from view. Did they change their mind and jump ship before it sailed, or die on the way, or take fright when they saw the conditions in America and seize the first chance of a passage home? Presenting these settlers as a separate group also makes sense because the context for return in the 1630s was different: the political and religious climate in England had not yet changed. Those who went home in this decade travelled against the prevailing tide of migrants coming over to New England. A particular feature is the number of settlers who went back home temporarily – almost as soon as they arrived in the New World – to sort out unfinished business, or to get married, or to drum up more migrants to join their community.

The third category of migrants is a miscellany of travellers who at some point in the 1640s or 1650s crossed the Atlantic to visit England, but returned to New England before 1660 (Appendix 2). These Atlantic voyagers – both seasoned mariners and temporary sojourners back home – are important to keep in view. When they returned to New England they brought the most recent news, by word of mouth and in letters and newsbooks, fresh off the boat. This helped to shape the resolve of others to leave.

All the entries follow certain conventions. Each entry traces the biography of a subject or subjects. Years of birth and death are listed at the head only if they have been confidently established. If another individual mentioned within a particular biography has their own entry elsewhere in the book, their name is marked with an asterisk. Also, most names appear in the index. Sometimes, *ODNB* or other initials appear after names within the text: this is a reference to a standard biographical dictionary (see 'Abbreviations' to decipher the code). These references have been provided as a help to identify individuals who are less well-known: they have not been used for individuals who are prominent or who appear repeatedly, such as Oliver Cromwell or John Winthrop. Another important convention to note in the entries is the style of dates: seventeenth-century documents used the old style or Julian calendar which started the new year from 25 March, and this book renders dates between 1 January and 24 March in the style 1650/1. At the end of each entry, publications by the individual (if any) are listed: these seventeenth-century sources are printed in London unless otherwise stated. Finally, a list of sources for the biography is provided: abbreviations are used for core texts, but otherwise full details of the works cited are provided; if any modern biographical dictionaries contain an entry for the individual, these are listed at the end. The bibliography at the close of the book lists all the manuscript sources cited, and a selection of primary printed sources together with a selection of secondary sources (printed and online).

IX

It is important to note that the life-stories in this book differ from those provided by the *Great Migration Study Project*, because the drive behind my project is not genealogy. Although there is plenty of material that will be of interest to family historians – the milestones of 'hatches, matches and dispatches' are present – the dominant themes in the individual histories are journeys: a physical journey of thousands of miles, from England to one or more settlements in New England, and then back home across the Atlantic again; a personal journey over a life-time, shaped by circumstances and connections, motives and mindset.

There is a kind of history that celebrates the 'richness of the ordinary': filling up, 'like a huge pointillist painting, the background to all those well-known central figures ... with depth and colour from thousands of dots of new historical knowledge'.[85] In its own way, this book aims to do just that, putting dots of new evidence about individual people onto the canvas of two Englands in an Atlantic world.

People who dropped out of the onward march of American history are easily written out of the story. They can be overlooked, or ignored as atypical, or deemed unpatriotic. Or, going to the other extreme, they can be elevated as ambassadors for the New England Way, taking light to old England from their 'city on a hill'. A search in colonial records soon digs out prominent settlers or noisy dissenters who left New England. But this does not give the whole picture. The hundreds of personal histories presented here follow idiosyncratic paths, and often concern obscure lives that would not otherwise

---

[85] The novelist Sarah Dunant, in 'Presenting the past', *A Point of View*, BBC Radio 4, 5 October 2012 (http://www.bbc.co.uk/programmes/b01n1vwm, text at http://www.bbc.co.uk/news/magazine-19844685).

come into view. Collectively, the anxieties and aspirations of these people speak eloquently about the experience of being a New Englander – for those who stayed on, as well as for those who left. And their life-stories show how America could be a stage in a journey, not an end in itself.

Life-stories from early New England

A

ADAMS, Ann

Ann Adams, the wife of Ferdinando Adams*, probably arrived in New England with her husband in 1637. She was received into the church at Dedham, Massachusetts, on 2 September 1639, 'with very good satisfaction and testimony of the frute of gods ordinances in the church in hir conversion to god'.

She returned to Suffolk after her husband – 'his wife being sent for by him departed to England 1642' – probably with their children, born and baptised at Dedham: Abigail, Bethia and Nathaniel (born after his father's departure).

Dedham CR, 21, 23, 26, 37; *NEHGR* 1: 99, 4: 274.

ADAMS, Ferdinando

Ferdinando Adams, a shoemaker, was a churchwarden at St Mary-le-Tower in Ipswich, Suffolk, in 1636. Samuel Ward (*ODNB*), town preacher at Ipswich from 1605, had been suspended by the Court of High Commission in November 1635. Adams then refused to unlock the church for the church authorities when they came on a visitation in 1636. He was excommunicated for refusing to put the communion table in place of seats against the east wall of the chancel, and for failing to remove a wall inscription of Mark 11.17 ('My house shall be a house of prayer, but you have made it a den of thieves'). Clement Corbet (*ODNB*), chancellor of the diocese of Norwich, told his bishop, Matthew Wren: 'We heard . . . of the business concerning Adames. There be too many Adames in that towne, both Ecclesiasticks and Laickes.' In a subsequent court case, Adams was represented by William Prynne (*ODNB*) and Thomas Lechford*.[1]

Adams left for New England in 1637 and settled with his wife Ann* at Dedham, Massachusetts. Governor John Winthrop wrote out a bond for Adams on 5 July 1637, which noted that he was 'under question in some of his majesties Courts for matter of Contempt or misdemeanour, for which some engagement may lye upon others there, for his departure, or some displeasure or damage may arise to the magistrates or others heere for receivinge of him'. Adams promised to pay any costs in England or New England arising from this, and to appear in English courts if required. Adams was admitted to the Dedham church on 25 January 1639/40, some months after his wife, 'giving very good testimony of the grace of god in him and of his repentance from his distempers which had become offensive'. He became a freeman of Massachusetts on 13 May 1640.[2]

On 20 July 1641, Adams presented to the Dedham church his reasons for wishing to return to England for a while 'out of the watch of the church'. 'His undertaking and reasons were thought by the whole Church to be according to god', and at his request, after satisfying a brother about some unresolved questions (which are not spelt out in the record), 'he had from the elders a testimony of his unblameable conversation amongst us and departed 3d 6m [August] 1641'. Adams sailed back at the same time as Thomas Lechford (who had acted as his lawyer in England) and the colonial agents Hugh Peter* and Thomas Weld*. After his return he sent for Ann, but then – despite his memorable name – disappears from sight.[3]

[1] NA, SP 16/302, fols 320–2; [William Prynne], *Newes from Ipswich* (Ipswich [i.e. London?] 1636), [sig.A4]; Corbet to Wren, 20 May 1636, Bodleian, Tanner MS 68, fol. 94; *CSPD, 1635–6*, 565; *CSPD, 1636–7*, 420; Roger Thompson, *Mobility and migration: East Anglian founders of New England, 1629–1640* (Amherst, MA: University of Massachusetts Press, 1994), 82, 98, 265; *Pilgrims*, 25.
[2] *WP* III, 439–40; *Dedham CR*, 22; *NEHGR* 3: 188.
[3] *Dedham CR*, 36–7; *Pilgrims*, 56n.11, 57–8, 61, 96.

ALLEN, Ann (d. by 1656)

Ann Allen was the daughter of John Sadler, vicar of Patcham, Sussex, and sister of John Sadler (*ODNB*), Master of Magdalene College, Cambridge, 1650–60. She married, first, John Harvard (*ODNB*), and emigrated to New England with him in 1637. John and Ann Harvard were admitted to the Charlestown church on 6 August 1637. After Harvard died in 1638, Ann married Thomas Allen*. She signed a deed to William Dade with Allen in New England, 17 October 1651, just before Allen left for England.

Ann Allen left Charlestown for Norwich in 1651 with her husband and their children Thomas and Mary, both born in New England. She died by 1656, when Thomas Allen married Joanna Sedgwick*.

CR; Middlesex Deeds II, fol. 112; *NEHGR* 4: 183, 9: 169; Roger Thompson, *From deference to defiance: Charlestown, Massachusetts, 1629–1662* (Boston, MA: New England Historic Genealogical Society, 2012), 21.

ALLEN, Thomas (c.1609–1673)

Thomas Allen was the son of John Allen, a Norwich dyer, and the brother of Robert Allen, later prominent in Norwich city politics. Allen graduated from Caius College, Cambridge, BA in 1628 and MA in 1631. He was ordained priest on 2 March 1633/4 in Norwich, a few days after he had been installed as rector of St Edmund's, 26 February 1633/4. Allen was suspended for disregarding Bishop Matthew Wren's injunctions on 26 March 1636. The authorities accused him of reading prayers and catechising so late on Sunday afternoons that 'strangers' came from other churches to listen and would not stand up or kneel in the service. Allen did not appear at the visitation of May 1636 and was excommunicated on 20 June. He submitted a protestation against the sentence, declaring it illegal. He claimed he had sought absolution from the bishop's chancellor Clement Corbet (*ODNB*). Allen disappeared from Norwich. He was reputed to be at Rotterdam in November 1636. In his absence, others brought a legal action on his behalf against Corbet, churchwardens and others of St Edmund's parish for putting a communion rail and chancel steps in the church. The revenue of the benefice was sequestered, but many parishioners would only pay Allen or his deputies. Allen was named in a petition of Norwich citizens, which protested against the treatment of several ministers. He was back in Norwich in May 1637, although already rumoured to have gone to New England. On 11 June 1637 the secular and ecclesiastical authorities raided the house of his brother Robert to find him. His brother petitioned parliament *c.*1640, to release Allen from a £40 fine imposed by the Court of High Commission, so Allen could have liberty to return from New England. The petition alleged that Allen had been 'compelled to live in forreigne parts'. Among his parishioners at St Edmund's were Thomas* and Mary Oliver*, and also Michael Metcalfe (of Dedham, Massachusetts, who later wrote about his own experiences in Norwich).[1]

Allen emigrated to New England in 1638 and was admitted to the Boston church on 27 February 1638/9, as 'a studyent'. On 9 June 1639, he was dismissed from Boston to the church at Charlestown 'upon theire and his desire'. Between 1639 and 1651 Allen was minister at Charlestown, acting as the 'teaching elder' alongside the pastor, Zechariah Symmes. A letter of Allen's to John Cotton in 1642 about congregational polity survives, and also sermon notes taken down by hearers in 1644 and 1649–51. He married Ann*, the widow of John Harvard, in 1638. The last trace of him in Charlestown is on 17 October 1651, when he signed a deed with Ann. He had been considering return for some time: on 5 November 1650 one of his sermons addressed the theme 'how shal wee come to know when a minister is caled to remoue from one place to another[?]'[2]

Allen returned to England in the autumn of 1651. Formal letters from the city council of Norwich had arrived earlier in the year, inviting Allen to become Sunday preacher to the mayor and aldermen – who now included Allen's brother Robert. Allen reached Norwich before 8 January 1651/2, when he wrote a letter about preaching to the Indians, soon printed in the New England Company's *Strength out of weakness*. On 5 February he received a gratuity of £10 from the Norwich Assembly (city council), and on 20 April his salary was set at £20 a quarter. In 1655 the Norwich congregational church urged Allen to leave his work for the city and be their pastor in succession to Timothy Armitage (d. 1655); after much discussion Allen joined the Norwich church on 31 December 1656, was elected pastor on 12 January 1656/7. He continued to give his Sunday sermons to the aldermen until the summer of 1657, when a 'combination lectureship' (a rota of preachers) replaced him. The city authorities were reluctant to let him go, and commissioned him to preach Wednesday sermons. When he became pastor of the Norwich congregational church, Allen also became rector of St George Tombland, the building in which the church met, described by William Hooke* in 1662 as 'a consecrated place formerly purchased by themselves'. At St George Tombland he was paid £80 a year, far higher than the salary Armitage had received, to match the salary he had received from the city. After the death of his wife Ann, c.1656, Allen married Joanna Sedgwick* (formerly a member of his flock at Charlestown, Massachusetts). After the death of Oliver Cromwell, Allen initiated a meeting in Norwich to discuss religious matters. In 1659 he and John Knowles* joined a board of trustees set up in England by the Massachusetts General Court to solicit and receive gifts for the colony. Funds for his lectures were cut in November 1661, as the influence of the Commonwealth party in city government waned.

At the Restoration, in 1662, Allen was ejected as rector of St George Tombland. In 1669 he was preaching on Sundays and once in the week in St Clement's parish, Norwich; he was licensed (as a congregationalist) in St Andrew's parish on 10 June 1672. He served as pastor of the Norwich congregational church until his death on 21 September 1673. His will was proved on 27 October 1673.[3]

Allen had sold off property in Charlestown before he left New England, but also kept some, and gained more through his marriage to Joanna Sedgwick – including the town brewhouse, on which he was owed £35 rent in 1667. William Dade became Allen's attorney in Charlestown, 20 April 1657. In 1659/60, Allen sold his house to his successor as teacher at the Charlestown church, Thomas Shepard junior, and in 1670 disposed of more land and a stable. Charlestown rents and sales may have eased his fortunes as a nonconformist in the 1660s. After Allen's death, his son Thomas (of Norwich, late of London, 'gentleman') also made William Dade his attorney, and sold property in Charlestown in 1677, 1680 and 1681.[4]

Publications *A chain of Scripture chronology* (1659). Allen contributed a letter to *Strength out of weakness* (1652), and saw through the press two works by John Cotton, *The covenant of grace* (1655) and *An exposition upon the thirteenth chapter of the Revelation* (1655). Ten of his sermons were printed posthumously, with a preface by Martin Finch (CR): *The way of the Spirit in bringing souls to Christ* (1676).

[1] CR; Bodleian, Tanner MS 68, fols 3v, 115–19, 120, 155, 160v–161, 205v, 230, 234, 242; Bodleian, Tanner MS 220, fols 1–3; *NEHGR* 16: 279–84 (Metcalfe); *Pilgrims*, 16–18 and *passim*; Matthew Reynolds, *Godly reformers and their opponents in early modern England: religion in Norwich, c.1560–1643* (Woodbridge: Boydell Press, 2005), 218–23.

[2] *Boston CR*, 22, 29; 3 *MHSC* 3: 93; Allen to Cotton, 21 November 1642, printed in Bush, 368–75; AAS, MSS Octavo Vols S, Thomas Shepard I (1605–49), sermons by Allen and Shepard, fols 1–28v (notes on three sermons by Allen, 1644, in the same volume as a shorthand diary of Francis Willoughby*); AAS, MSS Octavo Vols R, Richard Russell's notes of sermons by Thomas Allen and Zechariah Symmes at Charlestown, 1649–51 (the quotation from his sermon in November 1650 is on fol. 139v); Middlesex Deeds II, fol. 112.

[3] Norfolk Record Office, Norwich, NCR Case 16d/6, 'Norwich City Assembly Book of Proceedings, 1642–68', fols 102, 106v, 120, 123; [New England Company], *Strength out of weakness* (1652), 32–3; Norwich CB, 26 and 30 December 1655, 31 December

1656, 12 January 1656/7; W. Hooke to J. Davenport, 31 March 1662, 4 *MHSC* 8: 195; LPL, MS COMM. III/1, fol. 85; John T. Evans, *Seventeenth-century Norwich: politics, religion, and government, 1620–1690* (Oxford: Clarendon Press, 1979), 196, 234; W.L. Sachse, *The colonial American in Britain* (Madison, WI: University of Wisconsin Press, 1956), 107; *CR*; Norwich Old Congregational Church Book, 21 September 1673.
[4] Middlesex Deeds II, fols 104–5, 111–13; *Charlestown CR*, 282; Roger Thompson, *From deference to defiance: Charlestown, Massachusetts, 1629–1662* (Boston, MA: New England Historic Genealogical Society, 2012), 96, 198, 205.

BDBR, CR, ODNB.

ALLIN, John (1623–*c*.1700)

John Allin, born at Wrentham in Suffolk, emigrated in 1637 with his parents John and Margaret Allin. He settled at Dedham, Massachusetts, where his father (the town's first minister) was instrumental in gathering a church and in calling John Phillip* to office. John Allin attended Harvard and graduated BA in 1643.

Allin returned to England and held a lectureship in London. In March 1649/50, as of Rye in Sussex, he subscribed to the oath of engagement, which affirmed loyalty to the Rump Parliament. Samuel Mather* reported to Jonathan Mitchell from London 1651 'Sir Allin is with his friends ... and some that know him in the citty tell mee hee is of the same disposition, that he was in new england.' Mather failed to spell out what that meant. The MP William Hay (*BDBR*) recommended Allin for appointment as vicar of Rye in January 1652/3: Allin presented certificates from the minister Elidad Blackwell of St Andrew Undershaft, London, Thomas Greenfield (probably a Rye connection – a John Greenfield was mayor of the town in 1651), Thomas Marshall, one of the chief jurates of Rye, and Thomas Osmanton (vicar of Lydd, Kent, by 1656).

At the Restoration, in 1662, Allin was ejected as vicar of Rye. By then a widower, he went to London and left his children with friends in Rye. He wrote regularly between 1663 and 1674 to two close friends in Rye – Philip Frith, an apothecary, and Samuel Jeake (*ODNB*) – who shared his interest in alchemy, astrology and medicine. Allin preached in London during the Plague of 1665, and wrote in vivid detail to Frith and Jeake about what he saw. He also commented on the medical work of George Stirk*. Allin practised medicine himself from 1668.

Allin returned to America in the mid-1670s. He had inherited property in Dedham, Massachusetts, from his father. By February 1673/4 he planned to claim it, sent a letter appointing an attorney in advance, then went over to Dedham with his children. He visited London with his son in May 1680. By September that year he was preaching at Woodbridge, New Jersey, and acted as pastor there until 1686. He died before 1700.

Dedham CR; MHS, Misc. Bd. MSS, 26 March 1651, Samuel Mather to Jonathan Mitchell; LPL, MS COMM. III/3, fols 72–3; Anthony Fletcher, *A county community in peace and war: Sussex 1600–1660* (London: Longman, 1975), 112; ESRO, Frewen MSS 5421–5634, letters from Allin to Frith and Jeake (extracts printed in T.W.W. Smart, 'A notice of Rev. John Allin, vicar of Rye, 1653–1662, an ejected minister', *Sussex Archaeological Collections*, XXXI (1881), 123–56). For Allin's return to New England, and visit to London, see Frewen MSS 5632–4. For Thomas Marshall, see *Thurloe* II, 333.

CC, CR, Sibley.

AMBROSE, Joshua (d. 1710)

Joshua Ambrose was the elder son of Peter Ambrose, of Toxteth, Lancashire, and brother of Nehemiah*. Peter Ambrose, who served on Lancashire's county committee for sequestrating royalist estates, sent both his sons to Harvard in 1650. Joshua Ambrose enrolled three months before Nehemiah and appears as 'Ambros Senior' in the college steward's books. He graduated BA in 1653. He received a diploma attesting this, dated 1 July 1654, and returned to England soon afterwards. He had just inherited property from his father, who wrote his will on 22 December 1653 and died before 10 January 1653/4, when the will was proved.

Joshua Ambrose had his Harvard diploma recorded at Oxford and was admitted with advanced standing on 31 May 1655. He graduated MA from Pembroke College on 6 March 1655/6. He became curate of West Derby, Walton, Lancashire, and conformed at the Restoration. Ambrose was vicar of Childwall, Lancashire, from 15 October 1664 until 1686, and died there in 1710.

Harvard Recs. III, 96n.; Samuel Eaton and Timothy Taylor, *A just apologie for the church at Duckenfield* (1647), 12; Waters, 739; NA, PROB 11/232/331, will of Peter Ambrose, gentleman of Toxteth Park, Lancashire, 10 January 1654.

CC, CR, Sibley.

AMBROSE, Nehemiah (d. 1668)

Nehemiah Ambrose, the younger son of Peter Ambrose, of Toxteth, Lancashire, started his account at Harvard three months after his brother Joshua, on 13 December 1650, as 'Ambros Jeunior'. He graduated BA in 1653 and MA in 1656. He was a fellow at Harvard from 1654; the last payment to him was on 5 September 1657.

Ambrose returned to England in 1657. His father had left him property in Lancashire in 1653 and named him as an executor with his mother: she proved the will in his absence, but reserved rights for Nehemiah when and if he should come back to England. Edmund Calamy stated that Nehemiah Ambrose was ejected from the curacy of Kirkham (or Kirkby), Walton, Lancashire, but no other evidence has been found that he held this living. On 17 July 1660, as of Toxteth, Ambrose married Hannah, daughter of John Beadle (*ODNB*) at

St Olave's, Old Jewry, London. He made his will, as of Toxteth Park, on 2 September 1668; it was proved on 27 October.

> *Harvard Recs.* III, 98n.; Waters, 739; NA, PROB 11/232/331, will of Peter Ambrose, gentleman of Toxteth Park, Lancashire, 10 January 1654.

CC, CR, Sibley.

AMES, John

John Ames was a son of the minister and theologian William Ames (*ODNB*) and Joan Ames, and nephew to John Phillip*. William Ames* was his brother. John's father had hoped to come to New England but died in Rotterdam in 1633. Joan Ames initially returned from the Netherlands to England but emigrated with her children William, John and Ruth in 1637, and settled at Salem in 1638. She died in 1644. John Ames attended Harvard in 1646, but did not graduate. He seems to have left for England soon afterwards. He may have joined his uncle John Phillip and brother William Ames at Wrentham in Suffolk. Some sources reckon he died in 1655, and was buried at Wrentham.

> *CC; CR s.n.* William Ames; Morison, 77; J. Browne, *The congregational church at Wrentham in Suffolk: its history and biographies* (London: Jarrold & Sons, 1854), 14.

AMES, William (c.1624–1689)

William Ames was the eldest son of the minister and theologian William Ames (*ODNB*) and Joan; brother to John Ames* and nephew to John Phillip*.

Ames went to New England in 1637 with his widowed mother and siblings John and Ruth. They settled at Salem in 1638, under the ministry of Hugh Peter*. John Phillip lived briefly at Salem too. Joan Ames died in December 1644, during William Ames's last year at Harvard. He graduated BA in 1645, and became a member of the church at Cambridge, Massachusetts, around that time. His testimony on admission to the church dated the stirrings of his spiritual awakening to hearing Hugh Peter preach at Salem. In December 1645, Thomas Shepard, the minister at Cambridge, asked Hugh Peter (by then in England), to do something for the orphans John and William Ames, describing William as 'a fruit of your ministry'. Ames was admitted a freeman of Massachusetts on 26 May 1647.[1]

Ames soon left New England to join his uncle John Phillip at Wrentham, Suffolk (Phillip's parish since 1609). He was one of the first subscribers to the covenant which gathered a congregational church at Wrentham, 1 February 1649/50. A parliamentary survey of 15 October 1650 recorded Ames as assistant to Phillip. Alongside this role in Wrentham, Ames took office as public preacher in nearby parishes. He became rector of South Cove on 18 June 1653. On 5 September 1656 he was admitted rector of Frostenden, with certificates from Robert Brewster (*BDBR*, patron of Wrentham); Francis Brewster (an MP in 1653 and 1656); Francis Morse; Benjamin Bende; Thomas Dunne; John

Phillip, minister of Wrentham; Samuel Stoneham, minister at Southwold; William Bridge (*ODNB*), minister of Yarmouth congregational church and once a colleague of Ames's father. Francis Brewster, Francis Morse and Benjamin Bende were all members of the congregational church at Wrentham.

At the Restoration, Ames resigned his church livings. He was licensed as a nonconformist preacher at Wrentham in 1672. His will, 27 September 1683, referred to relatives in old and New England, but mentioned no colonial property.[2]

Publication *The saints security, against seducing spirits* (1652).

[1] *Shepard's confessions*, 210–12; Thomas Shepard to Hugh Peter, December 1645, *American Historical Review* 4 (1898), 107
[2] J. Browne, *The congregational church at Wrentham in Suffolk: its history and biographies* (London: Jarrold & Sons, 1854), 16–17; Wrentham CB, fols 7–11, 25–7; LPL, MSS COMM. XIIa/15, fol. 571 and III/5, fol. 107; DWL, MS 38.59, A.G. Matthews's notes of nonconformist ministers' wills, fols 24–5.

BDBR (confuses Ames with his father), *CC*, *CR*, Sibley.

ANGIER, Hannah (1631–1699)

Hannah Angier, the daughter of Elizabeth and William Aspinwall*, was born and baptised in Boston, Massachusetts, and received into full communion by the Boston church on 27 August 1654. She married John Angier* in 1651. A son John was born in 1652, but soon died; another John was born in 1654, and Anna in 1655.

Hannah went to England, probably at the same time as her husband, with their young children. She died at Wigan in Lancashire.

NEHGR 2: 76; *Boston CR*, 55; Thwing; E. Axon, ed., *Oliver Heywood's life of John Angier*, Chetham Society New Series, XCVII (Manchester, 1937), 93–4n.

ANGIER, John (b. 1629, *fl.* 1677)

John Angier was son of the minister John Angier (*ODNB*) of Denton, Lancashire, who had contemplated a move to New England but stayed on at home. The younger John Angier was admitted to Emmanuel College, Cambridge, on 24 July 1647 but his conduct there was unsatisfactory. Ten years later, he had to acknowledge his student misdemeanours during his time at Emmanuel before the Manchester classis would agree to ordain him.

Angier transferred to Harvard, and graduated BA in 1653, MA in 1655. He married Hannah in 1651. Her father William Aspinwall*, before he left for England in 1652, sold Angier a house and land in Boston. When Aspinwall went home, Angier appointed him to collect money in London owed to him by Sampson Shore of Boston.

Angier left for England early in 1656. By June 1656 he was associated with

Ringley chapel at Prestwich, Lancashire, where his father had preached in the early 1630s. In October 1656 he attended the Manchester classis as Ringley's minister. Angier was ordained by the classis on 13 August 1657 and attended regularly until late 1659. On 14 February 1659/60 he was commissioned to preach at its next meeting.

At the Restoration, like his father, Angier stayed on in his living. However, to his father's great dismay, he sought episcopal ordination. Angier was ordained deacon and priest by Samuel Rutter, bishop of Sodor and Man, on 8 August 1661. He stayed at Ringley until 1663 and then became vicar of Deane, Lancashire. His successor was instituted in November 1673. Angier was in Lincolnshire in 1677.

Harvard Recs. III, 64–5n.; Thwing; *Suffolk Deeds* I, 206, 213; E. Axon, ed., *Oliver Heywood's life of John Angier*, Chetham Society New Series, XCVII (Manchester, 1937), 93–4, 129; *CCEd* Person ID 39319.

CC, *ODNB s.n.* John Angier (1605–1677), Sibley.

ASPINWALL, William (d. 1662)

William Aspinwall's precise origins are unknown but he probably came from Cheshire. He married his wife Elizabeth in Manchester, 1628. By 1634 he was caught up in a legal wrangle with Sir William Brereton (*ODNB*), a powerful figure in Cheshire: depositions for this were taken in Boston.

William and Elizabeth Aspinwall emigrated in 1630 and initially settled at Charlestown. William was admitted to the Boston church with the first group of members on 27 August 1630, when the church covenant was signed at Charlestown. He was made a deacon within a month. He became a freeman of Massachusetts on 3 April 1632. He had moved from Charlestown to Boston by 1635. He was elected a deputy in place of Sir Henry Vane Jr* after Vane's departure. Aspinwall was disarmed and banished during the Antinomian Controversy of 1636–8 for drawing up a petition to protest at the banishment of John Wheelwright*. He became secretary of the new settlement of Portsmouth, Rhode Island, but then moved away from this radical environment to New Haven. In 1642 he was reconciled with the Massachusetts authorities, and rejoined the Boston church. He became a member of the Artillery Company in 1643, and that year was also appointed as Boston town clerk, Suffolk court recorder and public notary. He kept a 'Book of Possessions' to record property transactions in Boston. In October 1651, the Massachusetts General Court removed Aspinwall from office in the heat of several legal disputes. Although other complaints against him were not in the end upheld, in one instance he was found to have misled a jury, tampered with evidence, and tried to halt court investigations into his actions. Aspinwall lost his livelihood and his interest turned to England. In 1651–2 he completed a millenarian manuscript, 'Speculum chronologicum', and sold property in preparation for his departure. In a letter to the General Court, 24 July 1652, he requested permission to take his notarial records with him: 'most of the things therein conteined relate to England whither I am going, and hope may be of more use there ... intending the Lord permitting to make my residence in or about London, where any may have easie Recourse for my attest'. However, the magistrates insisted he should leave his record of transactions behind.[1]

William Aspinwall returned to England in 1652. His wife Elizabeth probably returned at the same time. Aspinwall became a champion of the Fifth Monarchist cause, but rejected the violence of Thomas Venner* and urged cooperation with the magistrates to achieve a millenarian utopia. He drew on his New England experience and published an expanded edition of the law code drafted by John Cotton of Boston, with the subtitle 'wherein as in a mirrour may be seen the wisdome and perfection of the government of Christs kingdome'. He responded to the appeal for preachers to support Cromwell's regime in Ireland: in 1659 a 'Mr Aspinwall of New England' was minister at Kilcullen, County Kildare. In April 1662 he wrote to the Massachusetts magistrates from Chester, about property in Boston. He died in Chester later that year: John Angier (*ODNB*) of Denton lamented the death of his 'brother-in-law' 'Mr. Ashmall' (Angier's son had married Aspinwall's daughter Hannah in Boston). Elizabeth Aspinwall of Chester made her will on 25 October 1679 (proved 1 April 1680).[2]

Publications *A brief description of the fifth monarchy or kingdome that shortly is to come into the world* (1653); *An explication and application of the seventh chapter of Daniel* (1654); *A premonition of sundry sad calamities yet to come* (1654); *Thunder from heaven against the back-sliders and apostates of the times* (1655); *The work of the age: or, the sealed prophecies of Daniel opened and applied* (1655); *The legislative power is Christ's peculiar prerogative* (1656); *The abrogation of the Jewish sabbath* (1657); John Cotton, *An abstract of laws and government* (1655) 'now published after his death by William Aspinall'.

[1] *Aspinwall NR*, i–ix; Bush, 52, 276, 303, 333, 401; Bernard Bailyn, *The New England merchants in the seventeenth century* (Cambridge, MA: Harvard University Press, 1955), 51; Thwing; *Mass. Recs.* 1: 207, 2: 45, 4(1): 68; Darrett Rutman, *Winthrop's Boston: portrait of a puritan town, 1630–1649* (New York: Norton, 1965), 73, 167; *Suffolk Deeds*, 1: 206, 235 and 2: 1–4. Aspinwall's manuscript is held by the Boston Athenaeum, MS L2, and printed as *A volume relating to the early history of Boston, containing the Aspinwall Notarial Records from 1644 to 1651* (Boston, MA: Report of the Record Commissioners, 32, 1903).

[2] J.F. Maclear, 'New England and the Fifth Monarchy: the quest for the millennium in early American puritanism', *William and Mary Quarterly*, 32 (1975), 250–4; G.B. Warden, 'Law reform in England and New England, 1620–1660', *William and Mary Quarterly*, 35 (1978), 668–88; St J.D. Seymour, *The puritans in Ireland, 1647–1661* (Oxford: Clarendon Press, 1921), 207; *Oliver Heywood's life of John Angier*, ed. E. Axon, Chetham Society New Series, XCVII (Manchester, 1937), 129; *NEHGR* 49: 193. For Aspinwall in a wider context, see B.S. Capp, *The Fifth Monarchy men* (London: Faber, 1972), 64, 93, 104, 113, 134, 137, 139–41, 145, 164–5, 170, 240–1.

ANB, BDBR, GMB 55–60, *ODNB*.

ASTWOOD, John (d. 1654)

John Astwood was at Little Hadham, Hertfordshire, in 1634, but he may have had connections with Abbotsley in Cambridgeshire. He emigrated in 1635 on the *Hopewell* in a company led by Isaac Desborough* of Eltisley, Cambridgeshire, together with others from Nazeing in Essex linked to the future 'apostle to the Indians', John Eliot. Astwood, recently widowed, may have left his young son Samuel behind in the care of his mother and brothers: no trace of Samuel survives in New England records, but he was in England at the time of his father's death.

Astwood settled at Roxbury, Massachusetts, where John Eliot was minister. He was admitted to the church before 3 March 1635/6, when he became a freeman. In 1639 he moved to Milford in the New Haven Colony, where the minister Peter Prudden had brought other Hertfordshire families. On 20 November 1639, his name was listed among the town's first 'free planters', with Philip Hatley* and Henry Stonehill*. He served as a deputy for Milford in 1643 and 1644. He was later an assistant of the colony and a commissioner of the United Colonies.

In October 1653, the General Court of the New Haven Colony heard Astwood was 'speedily to make a voyage' to England 'about his owne necessary occasions'. This was perhaps to accompany his sister-in-law Sarah Astwood* back across the Atlantic. The court took the opportunity to appoint Astwood as an agent for the colony, to ask Oliver Cromwell for help to remove the Dutch from New Netherland.

Astwood sailed for England late in 1653. He met Cromwell, who offered to help against the Dutch but proposed that New Haven's settlers should move to the West Indies. Astwood died in England of smallpox soon after he made his will on 27 June 1654. He left his estate in New England to his wife. He had estate in England at 'Abutley' (Abbotsley, Cambridgeshire?), where he left his 'loving mother' use of 'two rooms of my house so long as she please' and made bequests to his brothers and his son. William Leete of Guilford, unaware of Astwood's death in England, wrote to Samuel Desborough* in October 1654 about Astwood's audience with Cromwell. News of Astwood's death had reached John Davenport by 10 March 1654/5. Astwood's son Samuel attested his father's will at a probate court in Westminster in August 1654 and secured administration of the estate.

GM 1: 92–5; Alison Games, *Migration and the origins of the English Atlantic world* (Cambridge, MA: Harvard University Press, 1999), 180–1, 202; *The Connecticut Nutmegger*, 8: 354; *The American Genealogist*, 14: 58; I.M. Calder, *The New Haven Colony* (New Haven, CT: Yale University Press, 1934), 198, 212; BL, Egerton MS 2519, fol. 10, William Leete to Samuel Desborough, 10 October 1654; *Davenport Letters*, 101–2; NA, PROB 11/242/617, will of John Astwood of 'Milford in Newhaven, New England', 31 August 1654.

ASTWOOD, Sarah

Sarah Astwood was married to James Astwood, a merchant. She emigrated with her husband in 1638. Initially, they joined James's brother John Astwood* at Roxbury, Massachusetts, but later moved to Boston. James Astwood died in 1653: his will, made on 17 September 1653 (proved on 13 October) authorised his wife as executrix to sell 'what estate I have' in England. His New England estate stretched to cover only six shillings in the £ of his debts.

Sarah left New England late in 1653, soon after her husband's death. She renounced her executorship after the will had been proved, 'because of hir going to England'. She probably returned with her brother-in-law John Astwood, and took her young children, John (b. 1641), Joseph (b. 1644) and Sarah (b. 1646).

GD; Roxbury CR, 84; NEHGR 7: 337, 9: 40, 10: 71.

AUSTIN, _____

In July 1640 John Winthrop recorded in his *Journal*:

One Austin (a man of good estate) came with his family in the year 1638 to Quinipiack [New Haven], and not finding the country as he expected, he grew discontented, saying that he could not subsist here, and thereupon made off with his estate, and with his family and £1000 in his purse, he returned for England in a ship bound for Spain, against the advice of the godly there, who told him he would be taken by the Turks; and it so fell out, for in Spain he embarked himself in a great ship bound for England which carried £200,000 in money, but the ship was taken by the Turks, and Austin and his wife and family were carried to Algiers, and sold there for slaves.

Winthrop's cautionary tale provides all that is known of this colonist.

WJ, 333.

AUSTIN, Francis (d. 1646)

Francis Austin of Guilford borrowed £2 10s from his fellow townsman Thomas Dunck to buy a handsome coat and sword to wear when presenting himself to his father in England. He sailed from New Haven for London in January 1645/6, on a ship captained by George Lamberton*, but never reached his destination. All lives were lost when the ship went down.

Guilford TR, A, fol. 19, 31 December 1646; WJ, 630–1, 643–4; I.M. Calder, *The New Haven Colony* (New Haven, CT: Yale University Press, 1934), 161.

AVIS, Elizabeth

Elizabeth Avis, 'a poor lame maid', who 'much desireth to go for England to her friends', was costing her master four shillings a week to keep. In 1654 the Massachusetts authorities paid for her passage home.

David Cressy, Coming over: migration and communication between England and New England in the seventeenth century (Cambridge: Cambridge University Press, 1987), 197.

B

BACHILER, Stephen (c.1561–1656)

Stephen Bachiler graduated BA from St John's College, Oxford, on 3 February 1585/6. From 1587 he was rector of Wherwell, Hampshire, but lost this living in 1605 during James I's campaign for greater conformity. Bachiler may have been in Holland for a time (by the early 1630s his son was a minister at Gorcum). By 1614 Bachiler was within two miles of Wherwell again, at Newton Stacey: Sir Robert Paine later complained that some of his tenants, misled by Bachiler, a 'notorious' nonconformist, had demolished a chapel there. c.1630 Bachiler became involved with a group of London merchants, the 'Company of Husbandmen' or 'Plough Company', who wanted to develop a patent at Saco, Maine. Richard Dummer* of North Stoneham, Hampshire, who was related to Bachiler by marriage, was also part of this enterprise. Bachiler seems to have been living near Dummer, at South Stoneham, immediately before he left England. The Plough Company sent over two groups of settlers, in the *Plough* (1631) and the *William & Francis* (1632). Bachiler and his wife travelled with the second group. At some point his daughters Deborah and Theodate, and his grandson Stephen Sanborn*, also came to New England.[1]

John Winthrop noted the arrival of 'olde mr. Batchelder ... aged 71' in June 1632. On 3 October Bachiler was forbidden by General Court to exercise public ministry (unless it was to those he had brought with him), but this prohibition was lifted in March 1632/3. In 1635 Bachiler became minister at Lynn, Massachusetts. The congregation dismissed him in 1636 after an internal dispute – an early example of the power of New England laity to fire as well as hire their pastor. He may have gone to Ipswich. In 1637 Robert Stansby wrote from Suffolk in England, regretting rumours that had reached him about Bachiler laying down his ministry. Bachiler tried to start a new settlement at Yarmouth, and then moved to Newbury in 1638. From 1639 he was minister at Hampton, New Hampshire, alongside Timothy Dalton. John Winthrop recorded the controversy that surrounded him there: 'Mr Stephen Batchellor ... who had suffered much at the hands of the bishops in England, being about 80 years of age, and having a lusty comely woman to his wife, did solicit the chastity of his neighbor's wife'. Bachiler initially denied the charge, but then confessed. The church at first 'silently forgave him' but then cast him out. After that he 'went on in a variable course, sometimes seeming very penitent, soon after again ... casting blame upon others ... when he had seemed most penitent, so as the church were ready to receive him in again, he would fall back again, and as it were repent of his repentance'. This went on for two or three years. Bachiler was eventually debarred from acting as pastor there (he took the town to court in 1650 to recover £40 of wages). Bachiler corresponded with the Boston ministers John Cotton and John Wilson*, and with Governor John Winthrop, about his troubles and hopes of a new post at Casco. This came to nothing, and the magistrates also forbade him to form a new church in Exeter. He was at Strawberry Bank (Portsmouth), New Hampshire, from about 1644. At some point Bachiler remarried: on 9 April 1650 he was fined for 'not publishing his marriage according to law'. In October that year his wife Mary was found guilty of adultery with George Rogers and sentenced to 40 lashes after the delivery of her child (born late in 1651 or early 1652). Bachiler tried, unsuccessfully, to divorce her.[2]

Bachiler left for England soon after this. He seems to have been out of the country in October 1651, when the Massachusetts General Court ordered that 'whatsoever goods or lands have been taken away from the inhabitants of Hampton by Edward Calcord[*] or John Samborne, upon pretence of being authorized by Mr Batchelor . . . shall be returned to them from whom it was taken . . . until there appear sufficient power from Mr Batchilor to recover the same'. Bachiler's grandson Stephen Sanborn went to England in 1654. Mary Bachiler petitioned the General Court for divorce on 14 October 1656, because, she alleged, her husband had a new wife in England: he had 'upon some pretended ends of his own . . . transported himself into ould England', leaving her destitute. Bachiler is sometimes said to have died at Hackney, Middlesex, but he was buried in London on 31 October 1656 at All Hallows Staining, Mark Lane.[3]

[1] *CCEd* Person ID 83757; Kenneth Fincham, *Prelate as pastor: the episcopate of James I* (Oxford: Clarendon Press, 1990), 326; 'Stephen Bachiler and the Plough Company of 1630', *Genealogist* 19 (1903), 270–84; *Al. Oxon.*; *WP* III, 67–71, 101–3, 122–4.

[2] *WJ*, 69, 143, 164–5, 252–3, 368–9; James F. Cooper, Jr, *Tenacious of their liberties: the congregationalists in colonial Massachusetts* (Oxford and New York: Oxford University Press, 1999), 25, 41–2; D.G. Allen, *In English ways* (Chapel Hill, NC: University of North Carolina Press, 1981), 267; *WP* III, 390; 3 *MHSC* 3: 94; R.C. Simmons, 'Richard Sadler's account of the Massachusetts churches', *New England Quarterly* 42 (1969), 425; *GM* 6: 165; Bush, 47, 63, 356–62, 375–80; BPL, MS Am. 1506, pt 3, no. 2 (Cotton to Bachiler, 9 March 1641/2, printed Bush, 356–62) and no. 6 (a fragment of a letter from Bachiler to [?], 22 September 1643, see Bush 360n.); *NEHGR* 10: 296n.

[3] *GM* 6: 610; 4 *MHSC* 8: 583; MHS Photostat MSS, 14 October 1656.

GMB 61–9.

BAKER, John (d. 1662)

This name crops up in various contexts, and may not always refer to the same person: a John Baker appears in the Charlestown records in the 1630s; 'John Baker and Charity his wife' were admitted to the Boston church late in 1631 or 1632. In 1641, John Winthrop recorded how 'one John Baker, a member of the church of Boston, removing from thence to Newbury . . . being grown wealthy from nothing . . . fell into drunkenness'. Winthrop went on to recount how Baker moved from Newbury to 'Acomenticus' (York), then came back to Boston and was reconciled with the church, 'yet this man fell into gross distempers soon after'. In September 1646, the Boston church dismissed Baker to the church at York, Maine. By 1653, in Wells, Maine, a John Baker had attracted attention and rebuke for 'upholding private meetings and prophecying to the hindrance and disturbance of public assemblings &c'.

Baker seems to have returned to England in the 1650s and served Cromwell as a halberdier. On 15 December 1662 John Baker, 'one of Oliver's halberdiers', was sent for from Newgate prison, to be examined 'for treasonable designs against the king and government'. An informer reported Baker had been banished from Massachusetts for 'blasphemy and atheism'. William Hooke* wrote to John Davenport of New Haven that 'John Baker, some time a planter in New England, had his part in trepanning men into treason and then informing against them; he lieth now in Newgate'. Edward Godfrey*, keen to disparage the colony, wrote to the authorities on 7 April 1663 to link the New England radicals who caused trouble in England 'Heugh Peter, Vane: Venner: Baker: Potter'. Baker was hanged at Tyburn in August 1663.

> Boston CR, 14, 26, 35, 47; WJ, 350-1; CSPD, 1661-2, 591, 592, 593, 594; William Hooke to John Davenport, 2 March 1662/3, A.G. Matthews, ed., 'A censored letter', Transactions of the Congregational Historical Society, 9 (1924–6), 263–83 (also CSPD, 1663–4, 65); CSPD, 1663–4, 238 (Godfrey, referring to Baker with Hugh Peter*, Sir Henry Vane Jr*, Thomas Venner*, Vincent Potter*).

> GMB 72–8.

BALCH, Freeborn

'ffreeborne Balch of Wappen [Wapping] Late of New England singleman' was admitted to Stepney church, 15 February 1656/7. Balch was granted 'Letters Recommendatory' to an unnamed church on 24 February.

> Stepney CB, fols 4, 192v.

BARNARD, Tobias

Tobias Barnard gained a BA in Harvard's first graduating class of 1642, and later returned to England. Nothing else is known of his history. In 1651, Samuel Mather* gave a comprehensive account of the fortunes of other Harvard graduates in England, but reported that 'Mr Bernard I hear nothing of him, where hee should bee'. Edward Johnson listed Barnard among the first graduates of Harvard in his *Wonder-working Providence* (1653).

> MHS, Misc. Bd. MSS, 26 March 1651, Samuel Mather to Jonathan Mitchell; [Edward Johnson], *Johnson's wonder-working Providence, 1628–1651*, ed. J. Franklin Jameson (New York: Barnes and Noble, 1952), 202.

> CC, Sibley.

BARTHOLOMEW, Richard (d. 1646)

Richard Bartholomew, a merchant, came from East Anglia in 1637. He settled at Salem, and became a church member in 1640, and a freeman of Massachusetts in 1641. He joined the Artillery Company in 1643. His brother Henry was a prominent merchant in Salem, and his brother William also lived there. Bartholomew's business interests took him across the Atlantic. He was in England on 2 May 1645, when he witnessed (with William Hudson Jr*) the appointment of David Yale* as attorney to Joseph Owfield of London and Richard Crossing of Exeter, executors of Thomas Crossing of Exeter, merchant. Bartholomew was back in New England by 6 January 1645/6 and intending another journey to England. He made a will on the eve of setting sail, 'in Case god should not bringe me to London'. He seems to have died on the voyage or in England: his will was proved on 4 August 1646.

> R.P. Gildrie, *Salem, Massachusetts, 1626–1683: a covenant community* (Charlottesville, VA: University Press of Virginia, 1975), 35, 71, 101; *Salem TR*, 64; *Salem CR*, 10; *Suffolk Deeds* I, 162–3; *Essex Court Recs.* I, 102; C.H. Pope, *Pioneers of Massachusetts* (Boston, MA: C.H. Pope, 1900), 36.

BELL, Thomas (d. 1672) and Susanna (d. 1672/3)

Thomas and Susanna Bell married in Bury St Edmunds on 15 August 1631, and emigrated in 1634. According to Susanna's deathbed testimony – written down by her children and published with her funeral sermon – Thomas was keen on New England and Susanna was not, but when her first child died unexpectedly she took this as a sign from Providence that she should go to America.

Thomas and Susanna settled at Roxbury, Massachusetts, and became church members. Thomas was accepted immediately, but the church initially turned Susanna down. Her narrative of this provides the only surviving account from someone who was at first rebuffed but later succeeded. From Roxbury, Thomas Bell developed his business as a transatlantic trader, exporting timber and furs from New England and importing manufactured goods. By 1639 he was one of the sixteen wealthiest inhabitants of Roxbury.

Thomas Bell's trading interests took him across the Atlantic three times in the 1640s. In 1642, soon after news of change in England came – but before civil war broke out – he joined a swarm of colonists travelling back. His return to New England may have been delayed by the outbreak of hostilities, but he was back by the end of 1644. Bell went a second time to England at the end of 1646, as soon as the First Civil War was over. In December that year, Barbara Weld of Roxbury made Thomas Bell her attorney to obtain all property due to her in England following the death of her husband Joseph Weld*. Bell only stayed a short time: he sailed back from London in the spring of 1647 and arrived by the summer. His next voyage to England took place at the end of that year, and this time he took Susanna and their children with him. In trading and property records over the next few years, Thomas Bell 'of Roxbury' turned into Thomas Bell 'of London, Citizen and Merchant'.

Bell traded with New England and Barbados from London. He was said to be 'of London' by 17 July 1648. David Yale* asked for money to be paid to Bell at 'Seething Lane' in 1651. John Eliot, minister at Roxbury, referred to news sent by 'brother Bell' and also to business Bell had transacted for him, on 20 October 1651. Thomas Bell soon became a member of the New England Company (the Corporation for the Propagation of the Gospel in New England, 1649–60), perhaps as early as September 1652, when he procured a bill of lading on the company's behalf for goods to be shipped to New England. At the request of Thomas and Susanna, the Roxbury church sent 'letters of dismission' (release from membership) to London in September 1654. In 1655, Thomas Bell was one of the ex-colonial merchants who provided a certificates for John Wheelwright* (the minister who played a controversial part in the Antinomian Controversy of 1636–8) when Wheelwright applied for a parish living in Lincolnshire. On 23 January 1656/7 Bell appointed John Johnson of Roxbury as his attorney in New England, and sold his share in a watermill. The Bells lived on in Seething Lane, London, through the Plague of 1665 and the Great Fire of 1666 – as Susanna's autobiographical narrative shows. Thomas Bell's will (made on 29 January 1671/2 and proved on 3 May 1672) left his remaining property in Roxbury to the minister John Eliot, in trust, for educating poor children in the town. Susanna's will (made on 10 May 1672 and proved 21 March 1672/3) left £10 to a son of John Collins*, 20 shillings a year for life to John Knowles*, and 'my black cloth gown and petticoat belonging to it' to Anne Eliot, wife of John Eliot of Roxbury. Susanna Bell died on 13 March 1672/3. Thomas Brooks (*CR*) preached her funeral sermon, which was printed as a preface to Susanna's 'experiences', a spiritual narrative of her life, written down by her children at her deathbed.

> Publication Susanna Bell, *The legacy of a dying mother to her mourning children, being the experiences of Mrs Susanna Bell, who died March 13 1672* (1673).
>
> *Pilgrims*, 1–15 and *passim*; *GM* 1: 237–43; *GD* (confuses Thomas with his namesake below); *NEHGR* 3: 94; Aspinwall, 66–7, 181–2, 388, and *passim*; *Suffolk Deeds* I, 45, 138, 215; Bodleian, Rawlinson MS D. 934, fol. 11v, John Eliot to Edward Winslow*, 20 October 1651; W. Kellaway, *The New England Company 1649–1776* (London: Longmans, 1961), 17–18, 69; *Roxbury CR*, 80, 81; LPL, MS COMM. III/4, fol. 406; *Suffolk Deeds* II, 341–3; Waters, 23–4, 1062; NA, PROB 11/339/17, will of Thomas Bell, merchant of London, 3 May 1672; NA, PROB 11/341/330, will of 'Susann Bell', widow of All Hallows Barking, City of London, 21 March 1673.

BELL, Thomas (b. 1642)

Thomas Bell of Boston was the son of Thomas and Ann Bell. His father died in 1655 leaving estate on Long Island. On 2 July 1667, Thomas Bell, a tailor 'sometime of Boston now of London' sold land on Long Island with his sister Deborah.

> *NEHGR* 2: 77, 9: 40, 252 and 10: 219; *Suffolk Deeds* VIII, 157.

BELLAMY, John (d. 1646)

John Bellamy, a London merchant, settled in New Haven in 1644. He left for England in January 1645/6 on George Lamberton's* ship. This vessel was lost at sea, with all on board.

I.M. Calder, *The New Haven Colony* (New Haven, CT: Yale University Press, 1934), 160; *GD*; *WJ*, 630–1, 643–4, 713–4.

BELLINGHAM, Samuel

Samuel Bellingham emigrated with his parents, Richard and Elizabeth Bellingham, in 1634. Richard Bellingham (*ANB*) played a leading role in colonial government and served several times as governor of Massachusetts. The family settled in Boston, but lived in Rowley between 1643 and 1653. In 1642 Bellingham graduated MA from Harvard. He was in Rowley in 1643. He was still there on 23 July 1650 when he signed a deed with his wife Lucy, to sell his farm and rents to Joseph Jewett. In a later court case, witnesses testified that Jewett bought Bellingham's property at Rowley suddenly, just as Bellingham departed for England, at a time when 'many were unsettled and sold their land cheap'.

Samuel and Lucy Bellingham left New England soon after 23 October 1650, when Lucy signed a document which 'released her dower'. In the following years, their history is obscure, but Samuel Bellingham graduated Doctor of Medicine at the University of Leiden and was later in London. In the spring of 1661, Increase Mather* reported that Bellingham, in a state of agitation, left for Holland without him: 'I was under promise to go with Mr Samuel Bellingham into Holland; but Hee beeing frightened with the noyse of a Massacre went for Holland before I could'. Bellingham was later in touch with Nathaniel Mather* (as well as Samuel Sewall, John Hull and other New Englanders). In 1681, Mather wrote 'Mr Bellingham is so drowned in Melancholy if yet living, for I have not heard of him these 8 or 9 years'. 'Dr Samuel Bellingham' used Richard Wharton as his attorney in New England and in 1672 disputed the veracity of a postscript to his father's will, which reported that Richard Bellingham had cast doubt on his son's ability to handle a substantial inheritance: 'he will trust none to take it up for him, and never come to take it, if I leave it to him, besides he will give it away for a song, therefore I dedicate it to God, and the benefit of this country'. Legal wrangling over the Bellingham estate dragged on for more than a century. In 1695 Samuel Bellingham married a widow in London, Elizabeth Savage, and sent her to New England to look after his affairs. Bellingham was in London in 1698 when his wife died off the coast of Ireland on her voyage back from Boston.

NEHGR 19: 107; M.G. Hall, 'The autobiography of Increase Mather', *Proceedings of the American Antiquarian Society*, 71 (1961), 286; *Essex Court Recs.*, II, 397, 399; *GM* 1: 246, 247.

CC, Sibley.

BENDALL, Edward (1607–c.1659)

Edward Bendall was baptised at Kersey in Suffolk in 1607. He emigrated in 1630 with his first wife, Anne. His widowed mother Jane Scarlett, and two Scarlett stepbrothers, followed him over.

Bendall settled at Boston and was admitted a church member during the winter of 1630/1. He became a freeman on 14 May 1634 and joined the Artillery Company in 1638. His son Freegrace was baptised in 1635 and (perhaps not a coincidence) Bendall soon emerged as a supporter of that advocate of free grace, Anne Hutchinson. He was disarmed during the Antinomian Controversy of 1636–8, and fined and imprisoned for failing to 'acknowledge the justice of the Court'. In 1642 Bendall invented a diving bell to raise the wreck of the *Mary Rose* in Boston harbour. He was an entrepreneur and merchant, with firm links to the London trading community. Bendall acted as attorney for several London traders in New England. He formed two companies to finance the construction of wharves on the Boston waterfront, soon known as 'Town Dock' or 'Bendall's Dock'. The dock was later filled in and is now the site of Faneuil Hall.[1]

Bendall visited England in 1646, perhaps in connection with a plan to dive for ordnance off the West Indies: John Winthrop wrote to the earl of Warwick in support of Bendall's petition to do this, c.1646. It was perhaps during this visit that Bendall married his third wife, Jane, widow of Captain John Gower of London (Bendall's wife Anne had died in 1637, and his second wife, Mary, in 1644).[2]

He was back in New England by 14 March 1647/8, when he mortgaged a house. The Massachusetts authorities refused his petition to patent his diving bell, 2 May 1649. Bendall appointed Thomas Gilbert* his attorney when Gilbert set off to visit England early in 1650. On 6 October 1651 Bendall mortgaged property to cover a debt of £160 due to Simon Lynd, a London merchant, due before 6 April 1652. On 30 December 1651 Bendall mortgaged more property and raised £300. In 1653, Lynd gained a court judgment against Bendall for debt, and seized property – a substantial stone house, with garden, yards and warehouse – to the value of £202 19s 5d.[3]

Bendall probably returned to England in 1652, and (as was not uncommon) wrote back later to request dismission from the church. On 12 February 1653/4, he was 'by his owne desire and the consent of the church dismissed to a church in London'. In a strange twist to an already colourful career, he is likely to be the Edward Bendall who was admitted rector of Cotgrave, Nottinghamshire, on 17 April 1654, with certificates from several people with New England connections: Edward Whalley (*ODNB*), Thomas Harrison*, Nicholas Portrage, Leonard Cook of Islington (*CR* 13, 484, 560), and Edward Winslow*. Some or all of Bendall's family also went to England: his wife Jane, and his children Freegrace*, Reforme, Hoptfor*, More Mercy, Ephraim and Restore. If Bendall was indeed rector at Cotgrave, he probably died before November 1659, when John Clark (*CR*) succeeded to the living. Jane Bendall was a widow by 26 January 1660/1, when she made Samuel Scarlett her attorney in New England.[4]

[1] *GMB* 151–6; *Boston CR*, 13, 20; Bernard Bailyn, *The New England merchants in the seventeenth century* (Cambridge, MA: Harvard University Press, 1955), 40, 207n.109; on Bendall's diving bell, *WJ*, 399–400, 401; Darrett Rutman, *Winthrop's Boston: portrait of a puritan town, 1630–1649* (New York: Norton, 1965), 193, 247; Lechford *NB*, 69–74, 295; Aspinwall, 113, 146–7, 211–12, 248–9, 256–7, 263, 289–90, 363–5; *Suffolk Deeds* I, 89, 96, 142; Louise A. Breen, *Transgressing the bounds: subversive enterprises among the puritan elite in Massachusetts, 1630–1692* (Oxford: Oxford University Press, 2001), 262 n.114; for 'Bendall's Dock', Thwing [*Crooked and narrow streets of... Boston*], 126–8.

[2] *WP* V, 58, 79; Aspinwall, 147.

[3] *Mass. Recs.* 2: 273; Aspinwall, 269; *Suffolk Deeds* I, 163–4, 316–17.

[4] *Boston CR*, 55; LPL, MS COMM. III/3, fol. 11; for his children's baptisms, *Boston CR*, 279, 284, 288, 294, 311, 316; *Suffolk Deeds* IV, 88. *Pilgrims*, 82, 106, 120–1, 154.

BENDALL, Freegrace (1635–1676)

Freegrace Bendall, the son of Edward Bendall* and Ann (d. 1637), was baptised at Boston on 5 July 1635. Bendall embarked on a life of Atlantic trade in 1649, at the age of fourteen, before his father returned to England. He followed in his father's footsteps as a merchant and entrepreneur.

Bendall seems to have been based in England in the 1650s and early 1660s. By 1664, he had married Mary, daughter of Alice and Francis Lisle*. He was living in Boston again by 1666, when he and Joseph Lisle were given administration of Alice Lisle's estate. He joined the Artillery Company in 1667 and in 1668 became a member of the Boston church. In 1673 he invested in land to build a gunpowder mill, in partnership with the Boston ministers John Oxenbridge and James Allen, deacon Robert Sanderson, and the merchant and mintmaster John Hull. From 1673 Freegrace Bendall served as recorder for the county of Suffolk. He and his wife drowned in Boston harbour in 1676, leaving eight children.

Boston CR, 279, 63; *GD*; Darrett Rutman, *Winthrop's Boston: portrait of a puritan town, 1630–1649* (New York: Norton, 1965), 254; Thwing; A.K. Teele, *A history of Milton, Massachusetts, 1640–1887* (Boston, MA: Rockwell & Churchill, 1888), 368–9; *GMB* 154, 155.

BENDALL, Hoptfor (1641–*fl.*1708)

Hoptfor Bendall was born in Boston, son of Edward Bendall* and Mary (d. 1644).

He probably returned to England. In London, 1708, he disposed of property left to him in New England by Samuel Scarlett. A namesake died in Antigua in 1728.

Boston CR, 288; *Suffolk Deeds* XXIV, 249; Thwing; *GMB* 154, 155.

BERNARD, Masakiell (b. 1607)

Masakiell [Musachiell] Bernard, son of the minister Richard Bernard (*ODNB*), was baptised in his father's parish of Worksop, Nottinghamshire, on 27 September 1607. By the 1630s, Richard Bernard was minister of Batcombe, Somerset. Masakiell's sister Mary had married Roger Williams* at High Laver in Essex in 1629 and they emigrated in 1631. Richard Bernard (who had strayed into separatism at Worksop but by the 1630s was vehemently against it) was increasingly suspicious that New England's churches were taking a separatist path, and opposed this.

On 20 March 1635, 'Musachiell Bernard of Batcombe, clothier, in the County of Somersett', with 'Mary Bernard his wife' and two children under three, set sail from Weymouth for New England. He was part of a company that went over with the minister Joseph Hull*. Bernard was listed as owning seventeen acres at Weymouth, Massachusetts, c.1643.

Masakiell Bernard seems to have left New England in 1643 or soon after. He was living in London in 1666, when a colonist from Rhode Island referred to leaving a letter with 'Mr Barnard, who, as you know, is Mr William's wife's brother'.

GM 1: 261–3; *Pilgrims*, 46–7, 49, 62. For Richard Bernard's critique of New England, see Bush, 141–9, 257–62; a reply to Bernard in 1639, attributed to Richard Mather, was printed as *An apologie of the churches in New England for church covenant* (1643).

BETSCOMBE, Richard

Richard Betscombe, a haberdasher, was baptised at Symondsbury, Dorset, in 1601. He married Mary Strong at Devizes in Wiltshire in 1630. They emigrated from Bridport in Dorset, with two daughters, in 1635.

Betscombe and his family settled at Hingham. He must have joined the church before 9 March 1636/7, when he was admitted a freeman of Massachusetts. In 1640 he sent a letter of attorney to his brothers in England, to claim legacies for his children from their grandfather Philip Strong of Devizes. The Betscombes had two more children, Anna and Experience, baptised at Hingham in 1639 and 1641. Mary Betscombe died in Hingham on 6 June 1646.

After the death of his wife, Richard Betscombe went back to England. He left in the autumn of 1647, probably with his children (there is no further record of them in New England). He left soon after 6 October 1647, when James Wyton of Hingham, mariner, appointed Betscombe his attorney to collect legacies left to him by Thomas Wyton of Hook Norton in Oxfordshire.

Lechford *NB*, 289; Aspinwall, 88; *GM* 1: 271–2.

BIDGOOD, Mary

Mary Bidgood, wife of Richard Bidgood*, appeared before the Essex Quarterly Court on 24 September 1650 to explain why she refused to go to her husband in England. Her neighbours testified on her behalf that he could not maintain her, nor did he require her to come to him; his letters showed he had left her to herself and to her friends in New England. The court allowed her to remain for the moment, to see 'what the providence of God may lead unto afterward'. She came before the court on 28 September 1652, again to answer for living apart from her husband. As it was almost time for the ship to sail and the seas were dangerous, the court judged it expedient to send her away at the first opportunity after the winter.

Essex Court Recs., I, 149, 266; *GD s.n.* Richard Bidgood.

BIDGOOD, Richard

Richard Bidgood came from Romsey in Hampshire, and arrived in Massachusetts with his wife Mary* in 1638. He was described as a clothworker, late of London. Bidgood settled first at Boston but moved to Ipswich in 1641. He had been in England for some time when his wife appeared in court, in 1650, for not following him home.

C.H. Pope, *Pioneers of Massachusetts* (Boston, MA: C.H. Pope, 1900), 48; C.E. Banks, *Planters of the Commonwealth* (Boston, MA: Houghton Mifflin, 1930), 198; D.G. Allen, *In English ways* (Chapel Hill, NC: University of North Carolina Press, 1981), 269 (as 'Betgood'); Bernard Bailyn, *The New England merchants in the seventeenth century* (Cambridge, MA: Harvard University Press, 1955), 36.

BIRDEN, John

John Birden graduated BA from Harvard in 1647. Nothing is known of him before this, and very little after. In 1651 Samuel Mather* simply reported that 'Sir Birden and Sir Walver [Abraham Walver*] are preachers in their owne County'. Thomas Hutchinson's *History* repeated the information in Mather's letter, and added 'where their friends lived'.

MHS, Misc. Bd. MSS, 26 March 1651, Samuel Mather to Jonathan Mitchell; Thomas Hutchinson, *The history of Massachusetts from ... 1628 until 1750* (Salem, MA: Thomas Cushing, 1795), I, 112.

CC, Sibley.

BISCOE, Nathaniel

Nathaniel Biscoe [Briscoe] probably came from Buckinghamshire. A 'Nathaniell Biscoe' witnessed the will of John Hawes of Little Missenden in 1630. He may have been a relative of the minister John Biscoe (*ODNB*), who came from High Wycombe, or of John Biscoe, a colonel in the parliamentary army and MP for Amersham in 1658–9. Another connection may be Richard Biscoe, a 'rich tanner' of Uxbridge (possibly the son of the minister John

Biscoe): Richard's house was licensed for nonconformist worship in 1672, and he left property in Little Missenden and Chesham.

Biscoe, a wealthy tanner, settled in Watertown, Massachusetts, by the late 1630s. In 1639 his son Nathaniel became a vital witness in the dismissal of Nathaniel Eaton*, the first head of Harvard College. John Winthrop recorded how Eaton was 'a schoolmaster, and had many scholars, the sons of gentlemen and others of best note in the country, and had entertained one Nathaniel Briscoe, a gentleman born, to be his usher'. But Eaton assaulted his assistant with a cudgel 'big enough to have killed a horse'. This started the unravelling of Eaton's career.

Nathaniel Biscoe senior discovered he had baptist sympathies. His conscience would not allow him to join the Watertown church, and so he could not become a freeman of Massachusetts. Until 1647, this meant Biscoe could attend town meetings, but not vote. Without a vote, Biscoe objected to paying taxes – particularly to support Watertown's ministers. From 1643 he made frequent and noisy use of his right to address fellow townsmen: 'it is a very common thing with the said Mr Biscoe to affront the town in public meetings with high words and to much disturbance'. He drew up a handwritten pamphlet objecting to New England's ways in church and state, which circulated hand to hand. As soon as the non-freemen of Watertown got a town vote, Biscoe was elected to a leading role.

Biscoe was still in New England on 27 October 1651, but was probably making preparations to leave (he signed a power of attorney to release him from duties as an executor). Biscoe went to England to find freedom to express his baptist convictions. Little is known of his history thereafter, except that he might have preferred to stay in Watertown: he wrote back to his son-in-law in Boston in 1652, 'If you in Massachusetts had liberty of conscience, I had rather be there.'

The Mayflower Descendent, 10 (1908), 201; Stephen Wright, 'Biscoe, John (1605/6–1679)' minister, *ODNB*; C.H. Firth and G. Davies, *The regimental history of Cromwell's army* (Oxford: Clarendon Press, 1940), 338, 402–3, 404 (for Colonel Biscoe); NA, PROB 11/348/477, will of Richard Biscoe, tanner of Uxbridge, Middlesex, 22 October 1675; *WJ*, 301–4, 423; Roger Thompson, *Divided we stand: Watertown, Massachusetts, 1630–80* (Amherst, MA: University of Massachusetts Press, 1994), 60, 68–71; *Pilgrims*, 77–8.

BISHOP, Townsend

Townsend Bishop arrived in New England in 1634, and settled at Salem. He was a church member before 2 September 1635, when he became a freeman of Massachusetts. He served as a deputy for Salem to the General Court, and as a selectman and magistrate.

On 9 July 1645, at the Essex Quarterly Court, Bishop was presented for 'turning his back on baptism, and detaining his child'. He was ordered to speak with the church elders, 'to be convinced by them'. Although Bishop had previously brought his children to be baptised, there is no record of another baptism after this, so it seems likely his convictions held firm.

Bishop seems to have returned to England soon after his court appearance. On 11 March 1645/6, Robert Moulton and Michael Shafflin, acting for Bishop, sold his 'new messuage or dwelling house' to Ralph Fogg*.

GM 1: 310–12.

BLACKBORNE [BLACKBURN], Walter and Elizabeth

Walter Blackborne, a shopkeeper and haberdasher, may have been related to the naval official Robert Blackborne and Robert's brother James Blackborne, a customs official in Plymouth.

Walter and Elizabeth Blackborne settled at Roxbury and joined the church at some point before 1639, when Walter became a freeman of Massachusetts. He enrolled in the Artillery Company in 1638. In September 1639, 'late of Roxbury', he sold his house and land in the town. He had moved to the larger trading centre of Boston.

Walter Blackborne left New England in the early 1640s, and Elizabeth followed him. On 22 March 1640/1 he made Elizabeth his attorney, and prepared a will before taking ship, in case 'the Lord should take me away'. Thomas Fowle* was one of the witnesses. Blackborne was in London by August that year, when Elizabeth sold their 'late dwelling house and Shopp new built', including 'the hangings of the parler', to Francis Lisle*. Lisle promised to pay Blackborne £10 a year for four years at the home of Richard Hutchinson of Cheapside, with the first payment on 10 December 1641, 'in commodities merchantable in England if money fail'. Elizabeth appointed Joseph Weld* and John Johnson of Roxbury to receive further debts due to her husband. Thomas Fowle was to convey payments to England. She left for England soon afterwards.

'Walter Blackborne of London fishmonger' declared his wish to leave everything to his 'dearly beloved' wife Elizabeth Blackborne, who was also his executor. He asked to be buried in the north aisle of 'Michaels, Crooked Lane', and gave £4 'to the Church with whom I have walked'. His will was proved in December 1657.

G.E. Aylmer, *The state's servants: the civil service of the English Republic, 1649–1660* (London: Routledge and Kegan Paul, 1973), 266–7, 414; B.S. Capp, *Cromwell's navy: the fleet and the English Revolution, 1648–1660* (Oxford: Clarendon Press, 1989), 294–6; Thwing; *Artillery Company*, 54; Lechford *NB*, 393–5, 429, 435; *Suffolk Deeds* I, 20; NA, PROB 11/271/364, will of Walter Blackborne, fishmonger of London, 30 December 1657; *NEHGR* 151: 408–16.

BLACKWOOD, Christopher (*c.*1604–1670)

Christopher Blackwood came from Yorkshire. He matriculated at Pembroke College, Cambridge, in 1621 and graduated BA in 1625. He was ordained priest on 8 June 1628, aged 24. He may have been the person of this name who became vicar of Stockbury, Kent, in 1630 and resigned in 1631. Blackwood was curate of Rye, Sussex, from 1633 until at least 1637.

Blackwood emigrated to New England in 1640. He succeeded John Lothropp (*ODNB*) as minister at Scituate in 1641. He bought land but sold this before returning to England.

Blackwood went to England in 1642. In 1644, when living near Staplehurst, Kent, he heard Francis Cornwell (*BDBR*) argue at Cranbrook for believers' baptism. Blackwood became a Particular Baptist minister. From 1646 to 1652 he was with Cornwell at Marden in Kent, but still had ties with Rye. In 1646 he remonstrated with the mayor and jurates of the town for their treatment of a baptist. In June 1651 Blackwood was in Chester with Colonel Robert Duckenfield (patron of Samuel Eaton*), and in June 1653 he went to Ireland. Blackwood served as a minister in Kilkenny and Wexford, at a salary of £150 a year, in 1653 and 1654. He became overseer of Dublin's Particular Baptist congregation in 1656. At the Restoration he signed the baptist statement against the rising of Thomas Venner*.

Publications *The storming of Antichrist, in his two last and strongest garrisons* (1644); *Apostolicall baptisme* (1645 [1646]); *A treatise concerning the deniall of Christ* (1648); *A treatise concerning repentance* (1653); *A soul-searching catechism* (1654); *Four treatises* (1654); *Some pious treatises* (1654); *An exposition upon the ten first chapters of the gospel of Jesus Christ, according to Matthew* (1659).

Sussex Archaeological Collections, XIII (1860), 60-62; Lechford *PD*, 41; *GD*; Blackwood, *The storming of Antichrist* (1644), 'Preface to the reader' and 17; Anthony Fletcher, *A county community in peace and war: Sussex 1600–1660* (London: Longman, 1975), 65-7, 119-20; St J.D. Seymour, *The puritans in Ireland, 1647–1661* (Oxford: Clarendon Press, 1921), 60, 87, 112; T.C. Barnard, *Cromwellian Ireland: English government and reform in Ireland 1649–1660* (Oxford: Oxford University Press, 1975), 101-2, 103n., 108; Joel Halcomb, 'A social history of congregational religious practice during the Puritan Revolution' (PhD dissertation, University of Cambridge, 2009), 151, 153; Stephen Wright, *The early English Baptists, 1603–1649* (Woodbridge: The Boydell Press, 2006), 130, 139, 166, 167, 245.

BDBR, *CCEd* Person IDs 39824 and 73718, *ODNB*.

BLINMAN, Richard (1607/8–1681)

Richard Blinman was born at Chepstow in Monmouthshire. He graduated BA at New Inn Hall, Oxford, in 1636, and was ordained at Wells on 24 September. On 12 June 1636 he had been admitted curate of Ubley, Somerset, nine miles north of Wells. Blinman witnessed a will at Llanvaches, Monmouthshire, in 1638. Lady Brilliana Harley reported on 29 March 1639 that he had been preaching at Brampton Bryan, Herefordshire: 'He is nowe without a place, being lately put out of one. He teaches the scoule tell Mr Simons be abell.' On 1 September 1639 he was in Holt, Denbighshire, with Oliver Thomas, who allegedly preached a seditious sermon. Later that year he was at Walcot, Shropshire. On 28 February 1640/1, he was said to be 'goon into New England'. He emigrated with a party of Welshmen at the invitation of Edward Winslow*.[1]

Blinman had probably reached New England by 10 October 1640, when Winslow relayed his greetings to John Winthrop. On 28 January 1640/1 Winslow referred to 'Mr Blinmans friends that are come to live with us and the streightnes of place to receive them'. Blinman settled at Marshfield in the Plymouth Colony and gathered a church. Thomas Lechford* recounted, as an example of forceful ministerial action masquerading as 'advice', dissension at 'Greens harbour' between Blinman and one of his flock, which was resolved by John Wilson*, minister of Boston: 'was not master Blindman [forced] to Connecticot?' If Blinman went west at this point it was only briefly: he became minister at Gloucester (and Cape Ann) from 1641 until 1650. On 4 December 1645, Blinman wrote on behalf of the church there to an erring Gloucester colonist who had become a captain in England:

> I wonder that you would never send a word, neither to my self, nor to any friend of yours . . . Your wife is yet alive, and never received word, nor penny from you; And which is most sadde, we are informed by two Letters, that you have been sometimes ready to marry others . . .

Thomas Edwards, the presbyterian propagandist, published this letter as part of his invective against Independents, noting that he had also seen a letter from the captain's wife in New England, pleading with him to remember his family there. In 1650 Blinman moved to New London, Connecticut, taking with him several families that had come with him from England. The Corporation for the Propagation of the Gospel in New England employed him for work among the Indians. In 1657, Blinman sided with John Davenport and strongly opposed the synod in Boston that proposed to implement the Half-Way Covenant (allowing infants to be baptised by virtue of their grandparents' church membership). In reaction, Blinman tried to reform the New London church further, restricting civil voting rights to church members. The town refused to accept this and other conditions. Blinman left and went to New Haven. He prepared a manuscript for publication (which never saw the light of day) about issues raised by the Boston synod of 1657. With audiences in England and New England in mind, Blinman drew heavily on Richard Baxter's *Confirmation and restauration* (1658), which, in his view, 'doth contribute much to the clearing of the truth, & mind of Christ on this point' although some of Baxter's comments 'reflect some prejudice upon Congregat[ional] church[e]s'. Blinman acted as John Davenport's assistant in New Haven, 1658–9, after William Hooke's* departure. In the summer of 1659 he made ready to leave for England: on 25 May the authorities bought books from him for £8, for use in the school; on 27 July he preached in New London, on his way to take ship. On 28 September Davenport passed on English news Blinman had sent from Newfoundland.[2]

No evidence survives to show whether Blinman held a church living in England, 1659–62. After the Restoration, he was indicted at the Monmouth assizes at Chepstow, 5 August 1661, for unlawful assembly at the church of Llanmartin. He was living in Bristol, 1665. In the 1670s he published on infant baptism and corresponded with Increase Mather*. His son Jeremiah was in

New London in 1663 but married Elizabeth, daughter of the congregationalist William Bartlet (*CR*) at Westleigh, Devon, in 1670. Blinman died in 1681 and was buried in Bristol. His will mentioned his wife Mary and his children. Like many nonconformist ministers, he seems to have worked as an apothecary to eke out a living: he made bequests of drugs since he had no money.[3]

Publications *An essay tending to issue the controversie about infant baptism* (1674); *A rejoynder to Mr Henry Danvers* (1675).

[1] *Surman*; R.G. Gruffydd, *'In that gentle country . . .': the beginnings of puritan nonconformity in Wales* (Bridgend: The Evangelical Library of Wales, 1976), 28; *Letters of the Lady Brilliana Harley*, ed. T.T. Lewis (London: Camden Society, 1854), 37, 76, 84.
[2] *WP* IV, 292, 312; *NEHGR* 3: 189; Lechford *PD*, 54; *WJ*, 389; Edwards, *Gangraena*, iii. 94; P.R. Lucas, *Valley of discord: church and society along the Connecticut River, 1636–1725* (Hanover, NH: University Press of New England, 1976), 52–3; AAS, MSS Misc. Boxes B, Richard Blinman, 'An Answeare to divers Reverend Elders of New England . . .', quotations from 'To the Reader'; Dorothy Deming, *The settlement of the Connecticut towns* (New Haven, CT: Yale University Press, 1933), 16; *NEHGR* 23: 237; *Davenport Letters*, 88, 97, 112–13; *NEHGR* 7: 130, 23: 396–8; I.M. Calder, *The New Haven Colony* (New Haven, CT: Yale University Press, 1934), 85, 139, 173; *Davenport Letters*, 144–5.
[3] Letters to Increase Mather, 4 *MHSC* 8: 328–36; *CR*.

CCEd Person ID 55596, *CR*.

BOURNE, Nehemiah (1611–1691)

Nehemiah Bourne was the son of Robert Bourne, a shipwright of Wapping. He married Hannah, the daughter of Katherine Earning*, in 1631. On 10 April 1638 Nehemiah Bourne 'of Whitechapel' secured permission to travel to America on the *Confidence*, owned by William Rainborowe*. Bourne was described as a 'white baker' (baker of white bread, his grandfather John Bourne's trade) but was already a shipwright and shipowner.[1]

Nehemiah Bourne established himself as a leading shipbuilder and Atlantic trader. He and Hannah stayed briefly at Charlestown, but by 1639 had moved to Dorchester, where they became church members.[2]

In September 1639, in advance of a journey to England, Bourne issued and received various letters of attorney. He commissioned Samuel Shepard* of Cambridge to pursue Nathaniel Eaton* for £100, and put Hannah in charge of collecting debts due in New England. His mother-in-law Katherine Earning appointed him to receive money for her in England. Bourne sailed to England with Thomas Hawkins*, probably on a ship they co-owned, the *Sparrow*. He travelled in the same fleet as John Tinker* and arrived at Plymouth on 10 November 1639. Bourne and Hawkins wrote to John Winthrop from Exeter on 14 November, giving news of naval conflict between the Spaniards and Flemish, and of the Bishops' Wars between Scotland and England. The

Sparrow left for New England again on 19 January 1639/40, but Bourne stayed on in England until later that spring. Writing to John Winthrop from London on 4 March 1639/40, he commented on Scottish and Anglo-Spanish affairs, and on the impending parliament: 'times that are approaching threaten heavy and sad things ... I think it behooves al the lords people to double their duty and improve all the interest they have in heaven for this poor land.' He felt he had made bad use of 'pretious libertyes' in the colony: 'I hope this long abstinence will make me sett a higher price upon New England than ever.'[3]

After his return to New England, Nehemiah and Hannah Bourne settled in Boston, but for a time remained members of the Dorchester church. (Nehemiah became a freeman of Massachusetts on the strength of this, 2 June 1641.) Their son Nehemiah, born in Boston on 10 June 1640, was baptised at Dorchester; a daughter, Hannah, born in Boston on 10 November 1641, was baptised there by 'letters of recommendation' from Dorchester. Nehemiah was 'dismissed' from Dorchester to join the Boston church on 18 September 1642, and his wife Hannah on 2 October. Meanwhile, Bourne pursued new business ventures. In 1641 a committee surveyed the land next to his house for a shipyard. Bourne invested with Governor John Winthrop and Thomas Graves of Charlestown, among others. The first Boston-built ship, the *Trial*, was the result.[4]

In the winter of 1643, Bourne left New England for England again and became a major in the regiment of Thomas Rainborowe (*ODNB*), the brother of William Rainborowe. John Winthrop recorded that Bourne served in the parliamentary army with Israel Stoughton*, John Leverett*, William Hudson Jr*, and Francis Lisle*, 'diverse ... of our best millitary men'.[5]

Bourne set sail for New England again in March 1644/5. A letter from Emmanuel Downing* in London to John Winthrop Jr*, 3 March 1644/5, referred to Bourne's 'suddaine and unexpected goeing away'. Downing and Thomas Weld* had wanted to settle accounts with Bourne about money raised to transport poor children to New England (to counter suspicions that one or more of them had pocketed some of it). Bourne reached Boston by 22 June 1645. In October that year, with Downing, Robert Sedgwick*, Thomas Fowle* and others, Bourne petitioned the Massachusetts General Court against the limiting of residence of unaccredited strangers in Massachusetts to three weeks, and against the banishment of anabaptists. The petitioners complained of the offence these measures gave to the godly in England, so that some churches there denied fellowship to members of colonial churches. They asked the court to provide for the indemnity of those who were to go to England. Winthrop noted many of the Court inclined to support the petitioners, but the elders argued the dangers of anabaptism so forcibly that it was decided the laws should neither be altered nor explained.[6]

Bourne crossed the Atlantic regularly, 1645–50, in command of the ship *Merchant*. He carried goods for leading merchants in London and their colonial counterparts. The seasonal cycle of his journeys – from New England to England in the autumn or winter, and from England to New England in the spring or summer – can be traced in records of business transactions and correspondence, and in the pages of John Winthrop's *Journal*. Late in December 1645, as Bourne was about to set sail for England, Ralph Woory of

Charlestown gave him a power of attorney. By September 1646 Bourne was back in New England and almost ready to sail for England again, but finally left on 19 December, a few days after he sold his shop in Boston to George Davies. At this point Hannah Bourne also 'went on shippbord to goe for England'. John Winthrop recorded this because as soon as the Bournes left a sad truth emerged: their maid Mary, daughter of Francis Martin*, had given birth in secret to an illegitimate child, killed her and hidden the body in a chest. In April 1647 Bourne was about to travel from England to New England: Hugh Peter* resolved to go with him if he could, and Thomas Peter* used Bourne to carry a letter. In October, Bourne secured certificates in Boston attesting the safe delivery of his cargo. He returned to England that winter, possibly after Edward Gibbons bought his part share in a ship, 6 January 1647/8. On 12 July 1648 the arrival of goods shipped by Thomas Graves and Bourne was acknowledged in New England: from a letter Bourne wrote to John Winthrop, 12 August 1648, it seems Graves made the delivery; Bourne stopped short in Newfoundland, but declared his intention of being in New England the following summer. By July 1649 he had come to Boston and was preparing to return to London by way of Malaga. On 18 January 1649/50 the Admiralty Committee in London recorded Bourne's excellent conduct in a dispute with Dutch ships on his journey back, and recommended that he should command a frigate. By April 1650 he had taken another shipment to Boston, but returned to England soon after.[7]

In 1648, in the midst of these voyages, Bourne decided to settle permanently in London. Hannah had sailed with him to London in December 1646, leaving their young children behind in the care of 'Mother Earning'. When Katherine Earning decided to follow Nehemiah and Hannah to London, this precipitated Nehemiah's decision to make London his base – or at least that is what he told John Winthrop, 12 August 1648, in a letter that showed him keen to justify his actions:

> I know I am lyable to the apprehensions and Conclusions that all may conceaue and conclude from my absence, and the present removall of my Family, yet do Assure you that gods providence outwent my purposes, the last voyage I was in New England, For when I came from England to yow, I had it not in my heart that my mother Earning would have returned, whose going was the cause that putt me upon a kind of Necessity of sending home my Children being young: and it was beyond my wife her thought or expectation to se Mother or Children at London. therfore ther was no deshigne in us either at first or last going ouer to pluck up my stakes or to disjoynt myself from yow. But what need I trouble your wor[shi]pp with any such Apologie or Defence. I know none have any cause to complaine of my Absence. I haue cause to bewaile my owne barrenes and unprofitablenes amongst yow ... I bless God I shall now reape the fruits of New Inglish Showers and dewes ... Could I with honor or honesty be discharged and acquitt my selfe in my present employment and trust by my freinds (who have willingly adventured with me, and haue received little incouragement yet) I should bend my might towards you if I might be servisable to yow and the Churches.

William Aspinwall's* notarial records described Nehemiah as 'Major Bourne of Boston' on 15 January 1647/8, but as 'Nehemiah Bourne of London merchant' a year later.⁸

Sir Henry Vane Jr* recommended Bourne for naval service. He became captain of the frigate *Speaker* and commander-in-chief off the Scottish coast, 1650–2. In 1652, as captain of the *Andrew*, Bourne played an important part in a battle against the Dutch and was made rear-admiral (a letter written aboard the *Andrew*, 21 May 1652, is his only publication). Bourne served as one of three naval commissioners from 1652 to 1658, with Edward Hopkins* and Francis Willoughby*. He developed the dockyard at Harwich and, after peace with the Dutch came in 1654, worked in London at the Navy Office. Many letters from Bourne survive among the State Papers. He proved to be a staunch supporter of Cromwell's regime, deploying his skills as a shipbuilder, shipmaster and administrator. He kept up his own business interests at the family shipyard in Wapping and imported masts for the navy from New England. On 26 March 1655 he appointed John Leverett and William Bartholomew of Salem as his attorneys in New England.⁹

On 28 April 1662, in Hamburg, Nehemiah Bourne obtained a pass to travel to New England with his family. On 21 July John Davenport reported their arrival. Nehemiah Bourne clearly had mixed feelings about New England, which echoed his protest in 1645 against its restrictions on anabaptists: he had written to John Winthrop Jr in April 1662, of a 'severe and narrow spirit amongst them who have a large and plentiful experience of the grace of God'; Massachusetts' intolerance marred the beauty of its churches, like the 'prickles that are near the rose'.

The Bournes later returned to Europe, possibly to Rotterdam. They had perhaps already gone back in 1669, when the Boston church voted 'that the two teaching Elders doe writ an answer to some passages in major Bournn letters which they are not satisfied in'. A list of Boston church members, 1687, included Nathaniel and Hannah Bourne, 'in London'. Nehemiah made his will, as a merchant of London, on 11 February 1690/1 (proved 15 May 1691). He asked to be buried with his wife at Bunhill Fields, the nonconformist burial ground in London. His will mentioned his children Nathaniel and Anna, and the shipwrights and seamen of Wapping, but not New England.¹⁰

Publication *The copy of a letter from the reare-admiral of the English fleet for the common wealth of England, to an eminent merchant in London. Being a true and plaine narration of the whole proceedings and fight betwixt them and the Dutch fleet near the Downes, upon the 19. day of May, 1652* (1653).

¹ *NEHGR* 8: 139, 51: 109–12.
² *Dorchester CR*, 4.
³ Lechford *NB*, 195, 197–8, 203; *NEHGR* 8: 144; *WP* IV, 152–5, 213–4.
⁴ *NEHGR* 2: 77, 3: 188; *Dorchester CR*, 152; *Boston CR*, 288, 36.
⁵ Thwing; *WJ*, 402n., 495.
⁵ *WJ*, 604–5.
⁶ *WP* V, 14; R.P. Stearns, *The strenuous puritan: Hugh Peter 1598–1660* (Urbana,

IL: University of Illinois Press, 1954), 164; *WP* V, 30; *WJ*, 611n., 762; *Mass. Recs.* 2: 141, 3: 51; Bernard Bailyn, *The New England merchants in the seventeenth century* (Cambridge, MA: Harvard University Press, 1955), 106.

[7] Aspinwall, 17, 151, 227–8, 230, 367, 403–4, 408, 410, 411–12; *WP* V, 119, 146, 150, 243–5; *WJ*, 681; C.H. Firth, 'Sailors of the Civil War, the Commonwealth and the Protectorate', *Mariner's Mirror*, 12 (1926), 255.

[8] *WP* V, 244; Aspinwall, 151, 180.

[9] G.E. Aylmer, *The state's servants: the civil service of the English Republic, 1649–1660* (London: Routledge and Kegan Paul, 1973), 159, 358; Bailyn, *New England merchants*, 132; Firth, 'Sailors of the Civil War', 254–6; A.C. Dewar, 'Naval administration of the Interregnum', *Mariner's Mirror*, 12 (1926), 420–2, 428–9; *Suffolk Deeds* II, 211. The fullest assessments of Bourne's naval career are in B.S. Capp, *Cromwell's navy: the fleet and the English Revolution, 1648–1660* (Oxford: Clarendon Press, 1989), and W.R. Chaplin, 'Nehemiah Bourne', Colonial Society of Massachusetts, *Publications*, 42 (1952–6), 28–155.

[10] *Davenport Letters*, 198; 4 *MHSC* 7: 305–6; *Boston CR*, 64, 84; Waters, 1254–5; NA, PROB 11/407/124, will of Nehemiah Bourne, merchant of London, 15 May 1691.

ODNB.

BOYES, Matthew (b. 1611)

Matthew Boyes was baptised at Leeds, Yorkshire, in 1611. He married Elizabeth, daughter of the minister Elkanah Wales (*CR*) of Pudsey, Yorkshire.

Matthew and Elizabeth Boyes had settled at Roxbury by 1639, and joined the church. Boyes became a freeman of Massachusetts on 22 May. They soon moved to Rowley, where Boyes was prominent in both church and town government. He served as representative to the Massachusetts General Court in 1641, 1643 and 1645.[1]

c. December 1646, the church at Rowley sent Boyes to England as a 'fitt messenger' to William Sykes of Hull, to discuss propositions for trade made by Sykes. Rowley was trying to establish a cloth industry, to supply New England's needs and to generate revenue for the town. Boyes carried a letter from Ezekiel Rogers, minister at Rowley. Rogers commended Boyes highly to one who was already his 'ancient acquaintance', and added that Sykes's approach had been timely, the settlers 'being now in a deepe consultation (upon prayer) what way to take for some way of trading out of Englande, your Letters were brought to us as by a Speciall hand of Providence; which did not a little affect us'. Boyes also visited his father-in-law Elkanah Wales.[2]

Boyes soon returned to New England. He served as a legal commissioner for resolving small cases at Rowley, with Sebastian Brigham* and Edward Carleton*. He represented the town at the Massachusetts General Court again in 1650. In 1655 he advised the executors of Nathaniel Rogers, minister of Ipswich, and after his return to England played a part in a legal dispute over the terms of Rogers's will. He valued horses for the inventory of John Ward's estate, 25 March 1656.[3]

Matthew Boyes left for England at some point in 1656, probably with

Elizabeth and perhaps as many as ten children. On 6 April 1657 a 'M. Middlebrooke' of Yorkshire wrote to Michael Wigglesworth, minister of Malden, Massachusetts. Boyes had delivered letters to Middlebrooke from New England, and now Middlebrooke encouraged Wigglesworth and others to return home: 'if the Lord should incline any of your hearts to make a return back to our European England we should be glad of it'; 'our climate would better agree with your constitution than New England doth'; a minister from Massachusetts could certainly expect to make a comfortable living, 'even in these parts of Yorkshire about Leeds, if you would come'.

On 16 January 1661/2, describing himself as a 'clothworker' of Leeds, Matthew Boyes swore a deposition at York which was sent to New England as evidence in the legal dispute over Nathaniel Rogers's estate (a dispute which included comments by Ezekiel Rogers on the excessive length of his nephew and namesake's hair). Boyes wrote to the New England minister William Hubbard, 21 February 1661/2, in relation to the case. Boyes was occupying lands at Edstone and Welburn, Yorkshire, 5 August 1662. On 29 May 1668 his son Matthew (born in Rowley, 1644, but at this point in London) forwarded letters from Boyes to Richard Bellingham (*ANB*) in New England. In his will, 27 April 1669, Elkanah Wales asked Boyes to send bequests to his nephews in New England, 'in the fittest and safest way that he can'. In 1670 Boyes was mentioned in correspondence, in connection with Yorkshire rents. By 1679 he was said to be 'so ill and weak in his knees, he goes on crutches'. Joseph Boyse (*ODNB*), a son of Matthew and Elizabeth Boyes born in Leeds *c.*1660, became a well-known nonconformist preacher.[4]

[1] D.G. Allen, *In English ways* (Chapel Hill, NC: University of North Carolina Press, 1981), 245; *NEHGR* 61: 385; *Roxbury CR*, 83; *NEHGR* 3: 187; Waters, 230.
[2] BL, Additional MS 4276, fols 72, 72a; Bernard Bailyn, *The New England merchants in the seventeenth century* (Cambridge, MA: Harvard University Press, 1955), 71–4.
[3] *NEHGR* 93: 42; G.B. Blodgette and A.E. Jewett, *Early settlers of Rowley, Massachusetts* (Rowley, MA: [s.n.], 1933), 23; Waters, 230; G.B. Blodgette and M. Mighill, *The early records of the town of Rowley, Massachusetts, I, 1639–1672* (Rowley, MA: [s.n.], 1894), 86; *Essex Probate Recs.* I, 222, 235; *NEHGR* 22: 33.
[4] Waters, 230; *NEHGR* 7: 274, 11: 107, 110–11, 232, 12: 65–7, 41: 181, 156: 312; *GM* 7: 196. Joseph Boyse [Boyce]: *DAO* Person ID 4344.

BRADSTREET, Samuel (*c.*1632–1682)

Samuel Bradstreet, born in Boston, Massachusetts, was the son of Simon Bradstreet (*ODNB*), governor of Massachusetts, and the poet Anne Bradstreet (*ODNB*). The Bradstreets, who came from Horbling, Lincolnshire, initially settled at Boston in 1630 but during Samuel's youth moved to Cambridge (1634), Ipswich (1636), Salem (1646) and Andover (1652). Samuel was their eldest child. His mother wrote 'It pleased God to keep me a long time without a child, which was a great greif to me, and cost me many prayers and tears before I obtained one.' Samuel Bradstreet attended Harvard from June 1650 and graduated BA in 1653 and MA in 1656. He was a tutor in 1656–7, and became a freeman of Massachusetts on 14 May 1656.

Bradstreet spent four years away from New England. His mother wrote a poem, 'Upon my Son Samuel his goeing for England, Novemb. 6, 1657.' He left with Daniel Gookin* and other 'good company'. A ship that sailed at the same time was lost: among its passengers were Bradstreet's fellow Harvard students John Davis*, Jonathan Ince*, Nathaniel Pelham*, and the young minister Thomas Mayhew*.

Almost four years later, Anne Bradstreet marked Samuel's arrival back in Boston with a poem, 'On my Sons Return out of England, July 17, 1661'. While he was away, Bradstreet seems to have studied medicine; he became known as a physician. He represented Andover at the Massachusetts General Court in 1670. Later, he moved to Jamaica, where he died.

GM 1: 213; *Harvard Recs.* III, 86n.; *NEHGR* 3: 194; *The complete works of Anne Bradstreet*, eds Joseph R. McElrath Jr and Allan P. Robb (Boston, MA: Twayne, 1981), 228, 230–1.

CC, Sibley.

BRECY, Mr

Cotton Mather recorded a 'Mr Brecy', minister of Branford, Connecticut, but knew little more: 'I say nothing, because I know nothing of Mr Brecy; but this, he also returned into England.'

Mather's minister is not to be confused with Thomas Brecy, a London linen draper, who may be a brother. Thomas Brecy emigrated in 1634 and at some point married Phoebe Bisby, the daughter of a London merchant, William Bisby. Susanna and John 'Bracey', who appear to be children of Thomas and Phoebe, were baptised at New Haven on 5 September 1647. William Bisby wrote to Mary Wyllys at Hartford, 11 May 1646, that he thought the family were coming home: 'I had noe letter from my sonne & daughter neare you this yeare, one tould mee they were purposed to Come over.' However, by the time William Bisby wrote his will in London on 12 February 1649/50, Thomas Brecy had died. His widow Phoebe had married Samuel Martin by 7 April 1647, and moved to Wethersfield, where she was still living in 1683.

If a 'Mr Brecy' left New Haven it is more likely to be John, the brother of Thomas, although the evidence is unclear and circumstantial. A John 'Bracie' took the oath of fidelity at New Haven in 1644. On 3 August and 5 October 1647, he sold his house and land there. John could well have been the husband of 'Mrs Brecy'* who returned to England late in 1647.

From 1649 to 1651, John 'Bressey' appears in a variety of English records, in connection with family business. In 1655 he was described as 'of London, gentleman', and seems to have been a lawyer.

Magnalia, I, 588; C.E. Banks, *A history of York, Maine* (Boston, MA: Calkins Press, 1931), 268; *Davenport Letters*, 82n.; *NEHGR* 9: 358, 112: 41–2; *GM* 1: 372–5; *Wyllys*

Papers, 88, 96–7 (Mary Wyllys's first marriage had been to William Bisby's brother); Wyllys MSS, Box VII, 52A; NA, PROB 11/220/301, will of William Bisbey, salter of London, 19 February 1652.

BRECY, Mrs

On 13 November 1647, John Davenport sent a letter to Mary, Lady Vere (*ODNB*), by 'Mrs. Brasie, who was formerly your houshold servant, and hath lived in this Plantation, sundry yeares, and is a member of our church, well approved among us.' This letter was probably written shortly before 'Mrs. Brasie' set sail for England.

10 March 1654/5 Davenport reported to John Winthrop Jr* that he had received a letter from 'Mrs. Brassey, a member of this church', telling him she had within a month buried three children of smallpox in England; Susanna Evance* had also heard from her.

Davenport Letters, 82–3, 102.

BREWSTER, Francis (d. 1646)

Francis Brewster, a London merchant, was the father of Nathaniel Brewster*. He settled at New Haven in 1640 with his wife Lucy. Along with seventy other passengers, he set sail from New Haven in January 1645/6 on George Lamberton's* ship, heading for London. The ship went down and all lives were lost.

WJ, 630–1, 643–4; *GD*; I.M. Calder, *The New Haven Colony* (New Haven, CT: Yale University Press, 1934), 60.

BREWSTER, Nathaniel (c.1620–1690)

Nathaniel Brewster, the son of Francis* and Lucy Brewster, graduated BA from Harvard in 1642: one of the nine 'young men of good hope' in the first graduating class. His fellow graduates were Benjamin Woodbridge*, George Downing*, William Hubbard, Henry Saltonstall*, John Bulkeley*, John Wilson Jr, Samuel Bellingham* and Tobias Barnard*. Seven of the nine eventually went to England.[1]

Brewster was in 'Walderswick' (Walberswick), Suffolk, by 6 October 1649, when Thomas Pell of New Haven – who had married Nathaniel's widowed mother Lucy – appointed him as his attorney to collect a bond due to Francis Brewster from a Bristol pewterer. At some point Brewster worked at Neatishead and Irstead, Norfolk (seven miles from the parish Thomas Jenner* took near Coltishall in 1650): the council of state, 8 August 1654, ordered an annual augmentation to be paid to the minister there from the time of Brewster's departure. On 31 October 1650, Brewster was proposed as a colleague to William Bridge (*ODNB*) at the Yarmouth congregational church, but was not elected. Samuel Mather* gave news of him, 26 March 1651: 'Mr Brewster is a minister in Norfolk, and hath a good report.' By then, Brewster had become involved in the formation of a congregational church at Alby, Norfolk, gathered with the advice and approval of Bridge and John Tillinghast (*ODNB*). He initiated formal contact between the saints at Alby and the Yarmouth church, February 1650/1, writing on Alby's behalf for advice. A congregational church was gathered at Alby *c*. October 1651; Brewster was set apart as minister sometime after 28 June 1653. At some point, after the sequestration of Richard Ransome, Brewster also became rector of Alby. He also preached in the neighbouring parish of Thwaite. A letter from William Bridge to Henry Scobell (*ODNB*), clerk to the council of state, 16 August 1655, named Brewster as pastor to an independent church at Alby, with an income of £50. He was listed as an approved minister there, 3 September 1656.[2]

Brewster was close to John Tillinghast, a Fifth Monarchist whose millenarian views made him favour missionary work in 'dark corners' – Ireland and the northern counties. Their friendship, as well as financial inducements from the authorities, may have persuaded Brewster to respond to calls for preachers to go to Ireland. In a letter from Alby, 18 June 1655, Brewster asked the secretary of state John Thurloe for a recommendation. By this means he obtained a letter from Oliver Cromwell to his commander-in-chief in Ireland, Charles Fleetwood, 22 June 1655, recommending Brewster as 'a very able holy man'. Brewster arrived in Dublin in July 1655, travelling from Chester with Henry Cromwell, Lord Lieutenant of Ireland. Brewster became minister of St Audoen's, Dublin, shortly afterwards. Henry Cromwell used him as a safe means of communicating with Thurloe. With ex-colonists Thomas Harrison*, Thomas Patient* and Samuel Mather, Brewster gave weekday lectures at Christ Church cathedral, Dublin. In 1655 Brewster was one of only ten ministers in Ireland with a salary over £200. Brewster was in Alby again, 28 January 1655/6, but probably soon returned to Ireland. On 22 October 1656 he wrote to Thurloe from Dublin having returned from a six-week progress with Henry Cromwell. He was 'somewhat weary of hoping for an accommodation' with the anabaptists, finding 'that they are every where unanimous and fixt in separateing from us, even to the ordinance of hearing the word'. While in Ireland he received a Bachelor of Divinity degree from Trinity College, Dublin. He married Sarah, daughter of Roger Ludlow*. Thomas Harrison reported that Brewster had also drawn his Norfolk and New England compatriot Thomas Jenner to Ireland.[3]

By 1657 Brewster was in England again, and for some reason in financial straits. On 26 July 1658 he wrote to Henry Scobell from Alby asking for an advance. After an application by his church, he secured an augmentation of £45 for his parish living. Brewster resigned before the Restoration and was not reckoned among ejected ministers by Edmund Calamy. His letters in 1661–3 from Alby and London to his 'uncle', the mathematician John Pell (*ODNB*), conformist rector of Fobbing, Essex, show financial and other difficulties. In 21 July 1663 Brewster told Pell he was about to take his family abroad.[4]

Brewster returned to New England, arriving in Boston from London with his family around September 1663. Within a month he became a minister at Boston. In 1665 he moved to Brookhaven, Long Island, where he died in 1690.

¹ *WJ*, 416.
² Aspinwall, 268; Yarmouth CB, 31 October 1650, 4 February 1650/1, 21 January 1651/2, 28 June 1653; MHS, Misc. Bd. MSS, 26 March 1651, Samuel Mather to Jonathan Mitchell; G.F. Nuttall, *Visible saints: the congregational way, 1640–1660* (Oxford: Blackwell, 1957), 150; *WR*, 272; J. Browne, *A history of congregationalism in Norfolk and Suffolk* (London: Jarrold & Sons, 1877), 299; LPL, MS COMM. III/1, fol. 51; see also Joel Halcomb, 'A social history of congregational religious practice during the Puritan Revolution' (PhD dissertation, University of Cambridge, 2009), 41, 65, 182–3.
³ *BDBR*, *s.n.* John Tillinghast; Nuttall, *Visible saints*, 147–8, 152–3; Sibley; Browne, *Congregationalism*, 298; St J.D. Seymour, *The puritans in Ireland, 1647–1661* (Oxford: Clarendon Press, 1921), 34, 111, 141, 208; T.C. Barnard, *Cromwellian Ireland: English government and reform in Ireland 1649–1660* (Oxford: Oxford University Press, 1975), 136n.; BL, Lansdowne MS 821, fol. 200, Thomas Harrison to Henry Cromwell, 14 July 1656; see also Halcomb, 'Social history', 50–1, 153–4, 234.
⁴ Francis Peck, *Desiderata curiosa*, 2 vols (London, 1732–5), II, Lib. XIII:19; W.A. Shaw, *A history of the English Church . . . 1640–1660* (London: Longmans & Green, 1900), II, 591; BL, Additional MS 4278, fols 114, 111, 106, 108, Nathaniel Brewster to John Pell, 12 March 1661/2, 16 and 20 May 1662, 21 July 1663.

BDBR, *CC*, *CR s.n.* John Banister, Sibley.

BRIGHAM, Sebastian

Sebastian Brigham came from Holme-on-Spalding-Moor, Yorkshire, and settled at Rowley, Massachusetts, by 1643. He was captain of the town militia in 1647 and a representative at the Massachusetts General Court in 1649. He served as a legal commissioner, with Matthew Boyes* and Edward Carleton*, for resolving small cases in Rowley. Brigham's last appearance in the town records was in 1650. He sold his estate in Rowley to William Hudson and returned to England *c*.1652 or earlier.

D.G. Allen, *In English ways* (Chapel Hill, NC: University of North Carolina Press, 1981), 245; P.T. O'Malley, 'Rowley, Massachusetts, 1639–1730: dissent, division and delimitation in a colonial town' (Boston College, PhD dissertation, 1975), 189; *NEHGR* 93: 42; G.B. Blodgette and M. Mighill, *The early records of the town of Rowley, Massachusetts, I, 1639–1672* (Rowley, MA: [s.n.], 1894), 69.

BROWN, Hugh

Hugh Brown, a fisherman and mariner, emigrated to Salem in 1629. He and his wife Elizabeth had children there but (because neither parent was a church member) the children were not baptised. Elizabeth appeared in court, 29 March 1641, to answer a charge of physically abusing her husband.

Hugh, and perhaps Elizabeth, returned to England soon after the court appearance. His sons John and Daniel were baptised on 9 February 1641/2, in the parish church at Stepney:

John and Daniell, sonnes of Hugh Browne of Ratcliffe, Mariner & Eliz. ux^r both borne at Salam in New England, the said John beinge ten yeares old . . . and the said Daniell being seaven yeares old . . . were baptized this day . . . being Presented by their said Father.

GMB 246–7; NEHGR 21: 256.

BUCKMASTER, Lawrence

Lawrence Buckmaster, a young mariner, made a will on 27 November 1645, 'Seene that I am now bound for the sea, & soe for England'. He made several small bequests – a great coat, black hat, suit, a 'smale caske of mackrells' – to his sister Elizabeth, brother Zachary, and others. He made provision, should he die at sea, for recovering his wages. His will was presented on 2 July 1646.

NEHGR 3: 178–9.

BULKELEY, John (1619–1689)

John Bulkeley [Bulkley] was the son of Peter Bulkeley (*ODNB*), rector of Odell, Bedfordshire. He emigrated to New England with his father, 1635, settling at Concord. He graduated MA from Harvard in 1642: one of the nine 'young men of good hope' in the first graduating class. His fellow graduates were Benjamin Woodbridge*, George Downing*, William Hubbard, Henry Saltonstall*, John Wilson Jr, Nathaniel Brewster*, Samuel Bellingham* and Tobias Barnard*.

Bulkeley became a freeman of Massachusetts in 1642. In 1643 he served as chaplain to the party sent to arrest Samuel Gorton* and bring him from Rhode Island to Massachusetts. He taught at Harvard for a year, with George Downing, from December 1643. He gave land to Harvard for a fellows' garden, 20 December 1645.

Bulkeley went to England late in 1645, at about the same time as Downing. By 1650 he had succeeded Richard Pulley as minister of Fordham, Essex, a living occupied earlier by John Owen. Bulkeley married Anne Try of Odell, Bedfordshire, on 19 March 1650/1 – Samuel Mather* mentioned this in his letter of 26 March 1651 to Jonathan Mitchell. Henry Dunster received a letter from Richard Saltonstall Jr*, c. 15 May 1651: Saltonstall had seen Bulkeley, and asked Dunster to pass on messages to Bulkeley's father. Ralph Josselin (*ODNB*) noted John Bulkeley's presence at a day of humiliation at Wakes Colne, 23 June 1653. Bulkeley served as an assistant to the Essex commissioners for removing unsuitable parish ministers, 1657. After his father died in 1659, Bulkeley administered his estate in England. The historian John Walker called him 'a certain Independent of New England'. With John Sams*, William Sparrow, Samuel Crossman and John Stalham, Bulkeley commended John Beverley's defence of Independency, *Unio Reformantium* (1659). At the Restoration in 1660, Richard Pulley was restored to Fordham.

Bulkeley moved to Wapping, Middlesex, where he practised medicine and ministered to a congregation. His will, made on 11 October 1689 (proved 28 January 1689/90), included bequests to his brothers in New England. His funeral sermon, by John James (*CR*), was printed as *The different end of the wicked and the righteous* (1689).

WJ, 416; *NEHGR* 3: 181, 189; *Harvard Recs*. III, 32; LPL, MS COMM. XIIa/8, fol. 375; MHS, Misc. Bd. MSS, 26 March 1651, Samuel Mather to Jonathan Mitchell; 'Dunster Papers', 4 *MHSC* 2: 194; John Walker, *An attempt towards recovering an account of the numbers and sufferings of the clergy* (London, 1714), Part II, 330; G.F. Nuttall, *Visible saints: the congregational way, 1640–1660* (Oxford: Blackwell, 1957), 39; A. Macfarlane, ed., *The diary of Ralph Josselin 1616–1683* (Oxford: Oxford University Press, 1976), 306; *NEHGR* 10: 167–9; Waters, 541–2; NA, PROB 11/398/20, will of John Bulkeley, gentleman of Saint Katharine by the Tower, City of London, 28 January 1690. For Pulley, see *WR s.n.* Fordham, Essex.

CC, CR, GM 1: 463, *ODNB s.n.* Peter Bulkeley, Sibley.

BULLOCK, Edward (*c*.1603–*c*.1656)

Edward Bullock, a husbandman, was the son of William Bullock, of Barkham, Berkshire. He emigrated in 1635, aged 32, and settled at Dorchester.

He returned to England in 1649, probably to claim estate left to him by his father. On 25 July 1649, 'having by providence a calling and determination to go for Old England', he drew up a will which made provision for his wife and 'daughter-in-law' (stepdaughter) in New England. The next day he obtained a certificate from Elizabeth Clements of Dorchester, sworn before Governor Thomas Dudley, to show that he was the son of William Bullock late of Barkham. Bullock's will, which was to be void when and if he returned to New England, was proved on 29 January 1656/7.

C.E. Banks, *Planters of the Commonwealth* (Boston, MA: Houghton Mifflin, 1930), 147; *GD*; *NEHGR* 6: 355–6; Aspinwall, 227; *Dorchester CR*, 3; *GM* 1: 476–7.

BURDEN, Ann

Ann Soulby married George Burden* at Newcastle upon Tyne in February 1634/5, and emigrated with him to New England later that year.

She was admitted to the Boston church before her husband, on 6 November 1636. However, on 28 September 1651 the church excommunicated her because she had withdrawn 'from the fellowship of the church at the Lord's table, and ... would give no Reason of it, save only shee was commanded silence from the lord'.

Ann Burden left for England soon afterwards. She was in Bristol with her children by 8 April 1652, when she sent her husband power of attorney to sell their property in New England with complete legal freedom, 'as if I had neuer byn married to him'. She became a Quaker. In 1657 she sailed to Boston to settle her husband's estate, but the authorities immediately sent her back to England because of her Quaker convictions.

> GM 1: 487–91; Boston CR, 21, 53–4; Suffolk Deeds I, 264; NEHGR 8: 277–8; R.M. Jones, The Quakers in the American colonies (London: Macmillan, 1911), 45.

BURDEN, George

George Burden, a shoemaker and tanner from Stepney, Middlesex, married Ann Soulby at Newcastle upon Tyne in February 1634/5. He was perhaps the 'Georg Burden' who had been baptised at Newcastle on 22 April 1610.

George and Ann Burden* emigrated in 1635 from London on the *Abigail*. George was admitted to the Boston church on 8 January 1636/7 and became a freeman of Massachusetts on 17 May 1637. He was disarmed in the midst of the Antinomian Controversy for signing a petition in favour of John Wheelwright*, but soon recanted.

Ann Burden went to England first, probably soon after her excommunication in September 1651. George stayed on and disposed of their property. On 18 December 1651 he sold land in Braintree to Joshua Foote of London. On 19 February 1651/2 he sold a farm at Rumney Marsh, and on 14 September 1652 a dwelling house, slaughter house and cellar. He made a will on 15 October 1652, in anticipation of crossing the Atlantic. He made provision for a permanent or a temporary return to his homeland: 'if my wife and children Stay in England', or 'if wee Returne to New England'. He had property in old and New England. George Burden returned to England and died there before 30 April 1657, when probate was granted in New England.

> GM 1: 487–91; WP IV, 96; Boston CR, 21; NEHGR 3: 95, 8: 277–8; Suffolk Deeds I, 206–7, 265; Alison Games, *Migration and the origins of the English Atlantic world* (Cambridge, MA: Harvard University Press, 1999), 149, 183, 204.

BURDETT, George

George Burdett graduated BA at Trinity College, Dublin, and was admitted to Sidney Sussex College, Cambridge, in 1624. He was ordained in 1626 and became curate of Silkstone, Yorkshire. At the visitation of 1627 he was presented for omitting to use the sign of the cross in baptism; he was absent, and excommunicated. He preached as an itinerant lecturer in East Anglia, where he was cited for nonconformity in 1631. He is probably the 'Georgius Burdett' appointed curate at Saffron Walden, 3 February 1631/2. He was elected town preacher at Yarmouth, 1632, but came into conflict with the vicar and curate because they refused to restrict communion to 'the elect': the case came to the Court of High Commission. Burdett was accused of schism, blasphemy and raising new doctrines, and was suspended on 5 February 1634/5. The Providence Island Company asked him, 24 February 1634/5, to persuade some travellers bound for New England to divert south to Providence. Burdett took on this task but would not promise to go there himself. He left for New

England in 1635. His wife and family, still in Yarmouth, petitioned the corporation successfully for an annuity because of destitution.[1]

Burdett settled at Salem. He joined church before 2 September 1635, when he became a freeman of Massachusetts. He started to send letters from Salem to William Laud, archbishop of Canterbury, in December 1635. Burdett had gone into voluntary exile, he wrote, because of 'impetuous and malicious persecution, importable expense' and to achieve a 'tranquillitie in distance'. He urged a review of his case. On 17 April 1637 Robert Stansby wrote from Suffolk, England, to express concern that 'many of the ministers are much sleighted with you, insomuch as although you want ministers (as some wright) yet some amongst you work with ther hands being not called to any place, as Mr Burdett of Yarmouth'. Burdett was perhaps at Dover by then, but, after quarrels in Dover, went on to York, Maine. There he was elected governor. He was accused in 1638 of baptising all comers, which he denied. Late that year the governor of Massachusetts wrote to Burdett and others on behalf of the Massachusetts General Court, objecting to their acceptance of settlers cast out of the Bay Colony. Burdett replied scornfully. John Winthrop noted that 'this was very ill taken, for that he was one of our body, and sworn to our government, and a member of the church of Salem'. The magistrates decided not to summon Burdett, because this 'would ingratiate him more with the archbishops', but to undermine him instead. Winthrop reported in 1639 that, in a copy of a letter to the archbishop found in his study, Burdett had written:

> That he did delay to go into England, because he would fully inform himself of the state of the people here in regard of allegiance; and that it was not discipline that was now so much aimed at, as sovereignty; and that it was accounted perjury and treason in our general courts to speak of appeals to the king.

Burdett's capacity for disputes seemed unbounded. He clashed with the preacher Hanserd Knollys*. Winthrop wrote early in 1640 that everything was out of out of order, 'for Mr Burdett ruled all, and had let loose the reigns of liberty to his lusts, that he grew very notorious for his pride and adultery'. The new governor, Thomas Gorges*, told Winthrop, 23 February 1640/1: 'his time he spends in drinking, dauncing, singing scurrilous songes, and for his companions he selects the wretchedest people of the country. At the Springe I hear he is for Ingland.'[2]

Burdett left in 1641. Winthrop recorded how, back in England, Burdett 'found the state so changed, as his hopes were frustrated, and he, after taking part with the cavaliers, was committed to prison'. For a time Burdett disappears completely, but later he may have been in Ireland: perhaps assisting Claudius Gilbert at Limerick in 1657, and at St Peter's, Cork, in 1660; possibly Chancellor and Dean of Leighlin diocese, 1666.[3]

---

[1] R.A. Marchant, *The puritans and the church courts in the diocese of York 1560–1642* (London: Longmans, 1960), 236–7; Kenneth W. Shipps, 'Lay patronage of East Anglian puritan clerics in pre-Revolutionary England' (PhD dissertation, Yale University, 1971), 236–8; *CCEd* Person ID 106272.

² *NEHGR* 3: 94, 5: 19; *Letters from New England . . . 1629–1638*, ed. Everett Emerson (Amherst, MA: University of Massachusetts Press, 1976), 181; *WP* III, 390; *WP* IV, 86, 322–3; *WJ*, 269, 274, 284, 290–1, 318, 330; C.E. Banks, *A history of York, Maine* (Boston, MA: Calkins Press, 1931), 103.
³ *WJ*, 331; St J.D. Seymour, *The puritans in Ireland, 1647–1661* (Oxford: Clarendon Press, 1921), 208; N.C.P. Tyack, 'Migration from East Anglia to New England before 1660' (PhD dissertation, University of London, 1951), 85.

GM 1: 491–7.

BURY, William

William Bury, a 'gentleman' of Boston, was planning a journey to London in the autumn of 1646. He signed a promise on 8 October 1646 that he would pay William Hudson Jr* £25 within two months of the arrival of the *Paragon* (or on 1 April 1648 – whichever came sooner), at the White Hart in Holborn, London. On 14 October he cancelled this agreement and seems to have abandoned his plans to go to England that year.

However, it seems Bury set off the following autumn. On 21 August 1647 he promised to pay to Joseph Godfrey of New Haven or his assigns £23 within two months of arriving in England. On 14 October, Bury acknowledged (again) a debt of £25 to Hudson, for 'dyet and clothing': he promised to pay this on 1 March 1647/8, 'at the signe of the Cock at Mr Joshua ffoots shopp'. Joshua Foote, a London merchant of Gracechurch Street, had strong ties with New England trade and travellers. William Bury probably stayed on in England: he disappears from the colonial records.

Aspinwall, 89–90, 96, 106; *Pilgrims*, 105, 106, 107n.29, 108.

BUSBY, John

John Busby was the son of Nicholas Busby, a worsted weaver of Norwich. Nicholas Busby and his family were examined at Ipswich, Suffolk, on 8 April 1637, before sailing from Great Yarmouth for New England. In the 1640s, Nicholas Busby was one of ten Norwich citizens listed when the Long Parliament accused Bishop Matthew Wren of driving into exile the most important tradesmen of the diocese.

The date of John Busby's return to England is not known. The family settled first in Newbury but soon moved to Watertown and later to Boston. In his will, 25 July 1657, Nicholas Busby referred to his son John in England, who was to have 'seaventy pounds more then I sent him the Last Yeare, which was thirtie pounds', physic books, 'my blacke Stuffe Cloake', and a weaving loom if 'he come over to New England'.

C.E. Banks, *Planters of the Commonwealth* (Boston, MA: Houghton Mifflin, 1930), 184; T. Breen and S. Foster, 'Moving to the New World: the character of early Massachusetts immigration', *William and Mary Quarterly*, 3rd series 30 (1973),

195, 198, 213; J. Browne, *A history of congregationalism in Norfolk and Suffolk* (London: Jarrold & Sons, 1877), 89; Thwing; *NEHGR* 8: 278–9; Roger Thompson, *Divided we stand: Watertown, Massachusetts, 1630–80* (Amherst, MA: University of Massachusetts Press, 1994), 18, 43, 95.

BUTLER, Henry (1626–1696)

Henry Butler emigrated with his parents, *c*.1637. They came from Ashford in Kent and settled at Dorchester, Massachusetts. His father Nicholas Butler was listed as a church member before 1639. Henry Butler may have acted as schoolmaster at Dorchester from 1648. He became a freeman of Massachusetts on 7 May 1651. That year he graduated BA from Harvard, and in 1654 took an MA. He married Ann Holman on 9 March 1654/5.

Butler returned to England, probably with Ann, in 1655 or 1656. Edmund Calamy believed Butler spent time in Dorchester, Dorset, before settling in Yeovil, Somerset, but he is as likely to have been in Bridport: to secure admission as vicar of Yeovil, 3 April 1657, Butler presented certificates from John Eaton (*CR*) of Bridport, William Sampson (*CR*) and John Hardy (*CR*), of Bradpole and Symondsbury on the outskirts of Bridport, and from William Benn (*CR*) of Dorchester.

At the Restoration Butler lost his living. His successor as vicar of Yeovil was installed in 1660. In 1663, Butler was preaching near Axminster, Devon, and in 1669 at Yeovil, Kingsbury, Martock and North Cheriton. In 1670 he was nominated but not elected as successor to Richard Mather in Dorchester, Massachusetts; perhaps as a consequence, he sold the property he had inherited there in 1673. Butler was licensed (as a congregationalist) at Yeovil on 25 May 1672, described in the application as 'our pastor'. He was also licensed at Maiden Bradley, Wiltshire (as a congregationalist) and (as a presbyterian) of 'Lavington' – Market Lavington or West Lavington, Wiltshire, neither far from Maiden Bradley. In 1690, Butler was preaching at Hengrave and Witham Friary, Somerset. He was buried at Witham.

C.E. Banks, *Planters of the Commonwealth* (Boston, MA: Houghton Mifflin, 1930), 188; *Dorchester CR*, 4; *Harvard Recs.* III, 55n.; *NEHGR* 3: 192; LPL, MS COMM. III/6, fol. 5; *Surman*; *Transactions of the Congregational Historical Society*, 3 (1907–8), 246; *Dorchester CR*, 62; G.F. Nuttall, *Visible saints: the congregational way, 1640–1660* (Oxford: Blackwell, 1957), 83–4, 94.

CC, *CR*, Sibley.

C

CAFFINCH, John (d. 1658)

John Caffinch came from Tenterden in Kent. He joined the settlement established by Henry Whitfield* and others at Guilford, on the shores of Long Island Sound. He was not a signatory of the town covenant on 1 June 1639. However, he put his name to agreements with local Indians on 29 September 1639 and 17 December 1641, and to a declaration about land use on 2 February 1641/2. By 1643 Caffinch had moved to New Haven, where his brothers Samuel and Thomas had settled. He and his wife Sarah had children baptised at New Haven: Sarah, 9 March 1650/1; Mary 9 July 1654; Elizabeth 8 February 1656/7.

Caffinch travelled back to England ahead of his family. He was there on 14 October 1658, when he made a will describing himself as 'now of Tenterden, Kent, and late of New Haven in New England'. He specified that 'my wife Sarah Caffinch and my three daughters Sarah, Mary and Elizabeth Caffinch which were coming to England about a year since should have and enjoy my house and land in Tenterden which I lived in before I went to New England' (together with other property in Tenterden and New Romsey). He made provision in case his wife and family failed to reach England. He died before 19 January 1658/9, when probate was granted.

> MHS, Misc. Bd. MSS, 1 June and 29 September 1639, 17 December 1641, 2 February 1641/2; B.C. Steiner, *A history of . . . Guilford* (Baltimore, MD: privately printed, 1897), 24–34; NA, PROB 11/286/258, will of John Caffinch or Caffynch of Tenterden, Kent, 19 January 1659.

CARLETON, Edward

Edward Carleton, born at Beeford in Yorkshire, 1610, later lived at Barmston and Hornsea. He married Ellen Newton at St Martin, Micklegate, York, on 3 November 1636.

Edward and Ellen Carleton settled in 1639 at Rowley, Massachusetts, with their young son John. Early that year, Edward was among those who lent money to John Winthrop at the request of James Luxford, Winthrop's dishonest steward, unaware that Winthrop knew nothing the transaction. When Luxford's ill-dealing came to light, *c.* March 1640, Carleton agitated for Winthrop to return the money, £79: 'that which your man borrowed of me in your name was most of my estate'. Winthrop thought Carleton and 'mr Nelson' (probably Thomas Nelson*) were among the 'Christian frends' who demanded their money too 'strictly and hastyly', seeking a bargain.

Carleton wrote three letters to Winthrop, in late August and early September 1640, desperately requesting payment of £23 outstanding because he had to find funds immediately for the 'longe and tedious journey' to England. He described himself as having 'few intimate friends . . . in this land: as for kindered none: a stranger I was to those of our owne plantation soe that my desire is that you would help me'. Winthrop did not pay in time for Carleton to sail back on the *Sparrow* as he had planned, 'but I am to goe (god willinge) with the next ship that goes . . . which wilbee the next weeke'; 'I purpose for holland' (perhaps the 'Parts of Holland', Lincolnshire).

If Carleton went to England in 1640, he soon came back. He became a freeman of Massachusetts on 18 May 1642, and so must already have been a church member. He served as Rowley's deputy at the Massachusetts General Court, 1643–7. In 1646, Carleton objected to the heavy fines imposed on the Remonstrants Robert Child*, Thomas Burton, John Smith, Thomas Fowle*, David Yale*, Samuel Maverick and John Dand.

Carleton left New England in 1650. On 9 August he made Humphrey Reyner and Joseph Jewett of Rowley his attorneys, to act in his absence. On 22 May 1651, the Massachusetts General Court noted he had gone to England and appointed someone in his place to survey the bounds of Haverhill. His wife Ellen seems to have returned after him: in 1661 her eldest son John Carleton referred to a sale of land she had made in conjunction with Jewett, Edward's attorney. She probably travelled back with her children Edward, Mary and Elizabeth, all born in Rowley. John Carleton died in New England before 27 November 1678, when Christopher and Elizabeth Babbage petitioned for receivers to determine what was due to John's widow, Hannah, from Edward Carleton's estate.

D.G. Allen, *In English ways* (Chapel Hill, NC: University of North Carolina Press, 1981), 246; G.B. Blodgette and A.E. Jewett, *Early settlers of Rowley, Massachusetts* (Rowley, MA: [s.n.], 1933), 63; *WP* IV, 208–9, 279–81, 282–3, 283–4; *NEHGR* 3: 189, 93: 21, 23, 32, 41, 43, 94: 3–9; G.L. Kittredge, 'Dr. Robert Child the Remonstrant', Colonial Society of Massachusetts, *Publications*, 21 (1919), 38, 56. On the Remonstrants: Robert Emmet Wall, *Massachusetts Bay: the crucial decade, 1640–1650* (New Haven, CT: Yale University Press, 1972), 157–224.

CARTER, Joseph

Governor John Winthrop's correspondent Francis Kirby of London, who lived 'at the signe of the three pidgeons in Bishops-gate-street', sent Joseph Carter to New England with a letter of introduction to Winthrop, dated 11 April 1639. Kirby described Carter as 'my loue deserving son and faithfull servant, who so soone as he was freed from my service had an earnest desire to come to N: England'. Kirby, a London merchant and skinner, was linked to Winthrop by his first marriage to Susan Downing, sister of Emmanuel Downing* (who had married Winthrop's sister). Joseph Carter was Kirby's stepson by his second marriage, to Elizabeth Carter. So, through Francis Kirby, Carter hoped to count on good connections in Massachusetts.

Joseph Carter arrived in New England in the summer of 1639, and settled at Newbury by 1640. He received a land grant of 40 acres, but did not stay long.

Carter went back to London, took up residence at his stepfather Kirby's house and, like Kirby, worked as skinner. He soon married, probably in London. His daughters Eunice and Mary Carter were baptised at St Helen's Bishopsgate (2 July 1643, 8 September 1644), each as 'daughter of Joseph Carter, skinner, and Eunice his wife'. In March 1643/4, Augustinus Petraeus, a scientist, addressed a letter to his close associate John Winthrop Jr* (who was visiting from New England) 'at Mr Joseph Carter his house at the 3 pigeons in bischopgate strete ouer against the black bull London'. Petraeus sent greetings to Carter: 'Remember mi veri kindle to Mr Joseph Charter and his lovingh wife and daughter'. Francis Kirby died before 1 November 1661, and made bequests to Eunice, Rachel and Sarah Carter, daughters of Joseph Carter deceased.

NEHGR 35: 373; *WP* IV, 114, 198, 368, 369; NA, PROB 11/306/242, will of Francis Kirby, skinner of Saint Olave Southwark, Surrey, 1 November 1661.

CHAPLIN, Clement (1593–1656)

Clement Chaplin was the son of William Chaplin of Semer, near Hadleigh, Suffolk. In 1618 he married Sarah Hindes at Rushbrooke in Suffolk, close to Bury St Edmunds. He was a chandler in Bury St Edmunds. He may have carried a letter in 1630 from Jeremiah Burroughes, lecturer at Bury, to John Cotton at Boston, Lincolnshire: Burroughes sought Cotton's advice about whether to move to Tivetshall, Norfolk, or to stay in Bury – 'the causes that moue staying I suppose Mr Chaplin will fully certifie'.

Chaplin emigrated in 1635, on the *Elizabeth & Ann*, aged 48. He settled at Cambridge, Massachusetts, and must have joined the church before 3 March 1635/6, when he became a freeman. He was an elder in the church. In 1636 Chaplin moved with the first minister of Cambridge, Thomas Hooker, to Hartford, Connecticut. By 1640 Chaplin was at Wethersfield, where in 1641 he became an elder in the church. Chaplin was elected five times as deputy for the town at the Connecticut General Court, and acted as the colony's treasurer. On 10 October 1639, with Roger Ludlow* among others, Chaplin joined a committee to record 'passages of Gods providence which have been remarkable since our first undertaking these plantations'.

Clement Chaplin returned to England before 16 August 1656, when he made his will as 'of Thetford, in the County of Norfolke, clerk'. He left his houses in Hartford and Wethersfield to Sarah Chaplin and her heirs; he appointed as overseers his brother Thomas Chaplin of Bury St Edmunds and his nephew William Clarke of Roxbury, Massachusetts.

GM 2: 46–51; Bush, 154; Waters, 32, 1011; C.E. Banks, *Planters of the Commonwealth* (Boston, MA: Houghton Mifflin, 1930), 155; *NEHGR* 3: 94, 56: 183–4; M.J.A. Jones, *Congregational commonwealth: Connecticut 1636–1662* (Middletown, CT: Wesleyan University Press, 1968), 37.

CHAUNCY, Ichabod (1635–1691)

Ichabod Chauncy was the son of Charles Chauncy (*ODNB*) and Catherine (*née* Eyre). His father had been vicar of Ware in Hertfordshire, but emigrated in 1638 and became minister at Scituate in Plymouth Colony. Chauncy emigrated as a small child with his parents, along with his elder brother Isaac*. The name 'Ichabod' means 'the glory has departed' (1 Samuel 4:21). At the time of Ichabod's birth in 1635 Charles Chauncy was engaged in bruising encounters with the archbishop of Canterbury, William Laud.

Ichabod Chauncy grew up in Scituate. He graduated BA at Harvard in 1651, and MA in 1654, the year his father became president of the college. Accounts at Harvard for Isaac and Ichabod, 'Chaunceys Senior and Junior', ran through to June 1654.

Both Ichabod and Isaac Chauncy left New England soon after June 1654. In December 1656, as of Compton Bassett, Wiltshire, Ichabod stood surety for his brother when Isaac sought the living of 'Woodborow' (Woodborough), Wiltshire. William Eyre (*CR*), rector of Compton Bassett, may have been related to their mother Catherine. In 1659 Chauncy was chaplain at Dunkirk to Colonel Roger Alsop's regiment. He was tutor to Bulstrode Whitlocke's sons in London, but lost the post in August 1661 after he struck one of his charges on the head with a heavy book. Chauncy then moved to Coggeshall, Essex, where he joined the congregation led by John Sams*. He went to Bristol *c.*1666, and joined the Castle Street congregational church in 1670. Chauncy became an extra-licentiate of the College of Physicians in 1666. Richard Blinman* wrote to Increase Mather*, 14 August 1677, that Elnathan Chauncy, a younger brother of Isaac and Ichabod, was about to return to New England, having 'had advantages here from his two brothers for the practice of physick'. Letters from Chauncy to Mather, 1682–3, survive. Chauncy acquired a reputation as a strident religious and political radical, the 'bellweather of all the fanatics' in Bristol. He was prosecuted for nonconformity in 1682 and implicated in the Rye House plot of 1683. He was arrested and imprisoned for nonconformity in 1684, and finally ordered out of the country. He studied medicine at the University of Leiden, preached, and published a tract to defend himself, *Innocence vindicated*. He came back to Bristol in 1686 and died there on 25 July 1691.

Publication *Innocence vindicated: by a brief and impartial narrative of the proceedings of the Court of Sessions in Bristol against Ichabod Chauncy, physitian in that city* (1684).

Pilgrims, 26; Waters, 108; 4 *MHSC* 8: 330; NA, PROB 11/407/466, sentence of Doctor Ichabod Chauncey, Doctor of Medicine of Bristol, Gloucestershire, 10 December 1691; NA, PROB 11/410/455, will of Ichabod Chauncey, Doctor of Physic of Bristol, Gloucestershire, 17 February 1692.

BDBR, CC, CR, Munk's Roll, ODNB, Sibley, *Surman*.

CHAUNCY, Isaac (1632–1712)

Isaac Chauncy was the son of Charles Chauncy (*ODNB*) and Catherine (*née* Eyre). Chauncy emigrated with his parents in 1638, along with his younger brother Ichabod*. Like his brother, Chauncy grew up in Scituate, and also graduated BA at Harvard in 1651, MA in 1654. His last appearance in the college accounts is on 8 June 1654, at the time he and Ichabod took their MA degrees: a charge of £6 was made, 'Commencement Charges for both mr Chances'.

On 16 December 1656, Isaac Chauncy was admitted rector of 'Woodborow' (Woodborough), Wiltshire. He presented certificates of support from two Wiltshire ministers, Daniel Reyner of Buttermere (*CR*) and William Hughes of Marlborough (*CR*), and from Isaac Burgess, twice High Sheriff of the county (*CR s.n.* his brother Daniel Burgess).

In 1660, the sequestered rector came back to Woodborough and Chauncy lost the living. He was active as a pastor in Andover from 1662, presented for absence from the parish church in 1664, and accused of sedition in 1669. He was licensed in 1672 (as a presbyterian) at his house, Easton Town, Knights Enham, Hampshire. In 1669 he followed his brother and became an extra-licenciate of the College of Physicians, and received a full licence from the Royal College of Physicians in 1680 after he moved to London. Although Chauncy was licensed in 1672 as a presbyterian, his practice, and increasingly his publications, showed him to be a strong advocate of congregationalism. He clashed in print with Richard Baxter and Daniel Williams over theology, a sign of growing fissures within the dissenting tradition. Chauncy acted as minister to the congregational church in Mark Lane, London, from 1687 until Isaac Watts took over in 1701. Chauncy helped to create, but also to destroy, the 'Happy Union' of 1691 between presbyterians and congregationalists. He was head of a 'dissenting academy' in London from *c.*1698 until his death.

Publications *The catholick hierarchie* (1681); *A theological dialogue* (1684); *Ecclesia enucleata: the temple opened* (1684); *Ecclesiasticum, or, a plain and familiar Christian conference concerning gospel churches* (1690); *The interest of churches: or, a scripture plea for stedfastness in Gospel order* (1690); *Examen confectionis pacificæ* (1692); *A rejoynder to Mr Daniel Williams* (1693); *Neonomianism unmask'd* (Part I 1692, Parts II & III, 1693); *The doctrine which is according to godliness* (1694?); *A plea for the antient gospel* (1697); *A discourse concerning unction, and washing of feet* (1697); *The divine institution of congregational churches* (1697); *An essay to the interpretation of the angel Gabriel's prophesy, deliver'd by the prophet Daniel* (1699); *Christ's ascension to fill all things* (1699); *Alexipharmacon: or, a fresh antidote against neonomian bane and poyson to the protestant religion* (1700); *A letter to a friend concerning Mr. Bowles's late book of church-government* (1702).

LPL, MS COMM. III/5, fol. 170; Waters, 108; 4 *MHSC* 8: 330; *DAO* Person ID 1617.

BDBR, CC, CR, Munk's Roll, ODNB, Sibley, *Surman.*

CHILD, Robert (1613–1654)

Robert Child – physician, metallurgist, agriculturalist, and a 'Remonstrant' in Massachusetts – was born in Northfleet, Kent. He attended Corpus Christi College, Cambridge, and graduated BA in 1631/2, MA in 1635. He also studied at Leiden, and at Padua, where he graduated MD on 13 August 1638.

Child spent two periods in New England, 1638–41 and 1645–7, and between these two visits he travelled widely in Europe. When he came to New England in 1645 his profile was far higher than during his earlier stay in the colonies. He was known to be well-connected in England. Child advised and assisted John Winthrop Jr* in the development of ironworks at Saugus. More controversially, he was at the centre of a storm over the Remonstrance: this 'humble petition' Child presented to the Massachusetts General Court in May 1646 with Thomas Burton, John Smith, Thomas Fowle*, David Yale*, Samuel Maverick and John Dand. William Vassall* was also implicated. The Remonstrants wanted all colonists to be eligible as freemen, whether or not they were members of a church organised in the (congregational) 'New England Way'. They also wanted greater freedom of admission to church membership, or liberty to form their own churches 'according to the best reformations of England and Scotland' – in Child's view, presbyterianism. The Massachusetts authorities investigated Child and his co-petitioners in November 1646 and fined Child £50, Smith £40, Maverick £10 and the rest £30 each.

The Remonstrant controversy quickly crossed the Atlantic, and reached England before Child himself did. Child's ally Thomas Fowle left on the *Supply*, on 9 November (even before the fines were issued), with a copy of the petition. The Massachusetts authorities commissioned Edward Winslow* to go to England to undermine the Remonstrants' case. Winslow set sail in December. Child intended to leave too, but was discovered to be carrying a draft appeal to parliament and papers that questioned the legality of the colony's charter. He was detained, and in June 1647 the General Court inflicted severe penalties on the Remonstrants, Child in particular: he was fined £200 and kept under house arrest at the home of Richard Leader*, manager of the Saugus ironworks. In the meantime, in London, Winslow put Massachusetts' case into the public eye with *New-Englands salamander* (1647). Robert Child's brother John – Major John Child, a parliamentary officer who would join the royalists in the Kentish insurrection of 1648 – presented Child's side of the argument in *New-Englands Jonas* (1647).

Robert Child left Massachusetts by October 1647 and must have reached London by early 1648. Around May 1648, John Winthrop recorded the arrival of '3 shipps from London in one day', bringing news from England that Child had given up his petition. Winthrop also set down the story of how Child met Francis Willoughby* at the Exchange in London: the two came to blows when Child called New England 'a Company of Rogues & knaves'.

Although Child had a turbulent relationship with the Massachusetts authorities, his friendship with John Winthrop Jr survived and continued by letters. In London, Child became well known as an alchemist and introduced his fellow colonist George Stirk* to Robert Boyle (*ODNB*). He was a correspondent of Samuel Hartlib (*ODNB*) and Elias Ashmole (*ODNB*). Child left London for Ireland in 1651. He settled at 'Lisneygarvey' (Lisburn, County Antrim), where he pursued botanical and entomological interests and sent specimens back to London. He died there in 1654.

> G.L. Kittredge, 'Dr Robert Child the Remonstrant', Colonial Society of Massachusetts, *Publications*, 21 (1919), 1–146; *WJ*, 624–5, 647–70, 706–7; Robert Emmet Wall, *Massachusetts Bay: the crucial decade, 1640–1650* (New Haven, CT: Yale University Press, 1972), 157–224; E.D. Hartley, *Ironworks on the Saugus* (Norman, OK: University of Oklahoma Press, 1957), 77–8; Alison Games, *Migration and the origins of the English Atlantic world* (Cambridge, MA: Harvard University Press, 1999), 151–2, 281n.80; Carla Gardina Pestana, *The English Atlantic in an age of revolution, 1640-1661* (Cambridge, MA: Harvard University Press, 2004), 77–8; *WP* V, 221–3, 324; *WP* VI, 57–9.

ANB, ODNB.

CLEMENTS, John (d. *c*. 1659)

John Clements of Haverhill, Massachusetts, was the son of Robert Clements of Haverhill (d. 1658) and the brother of Robert Clements*.

John Clements went to Ireland and may well be the person of this name who was minister at Castledermot, County Kildare, in 1657. Records in New England show that Clements sent for his family. His brother Robert took them to Ireland, 'aiding and assisting his wife and children which otherwise could not have undertaken the voyage'. The cost – travelling up to Piscataqua to find an England-bound ship, the passage to London and on to Ireland, then Robert's fares back to New England again – amounted to a vast sum of over one hundred pounds. Sea raids from pirates and privateers were a risk for Atlantic travellers. Robert Clements's largest single expense was twenty pounds, all he had with him, taken when the ship was seized by Spaniards. He and his brother's family were 'carried captive to Spain and with very great hardship got to England'. In New England, administration was granted on John Clements's estate on 21 July 1659, he 'being by God's providence cast awaye', drowned. In September 1659 a petition was lodged for Robert to be compensated for the 'dammage and Troubles' he incurred taking the family to Ireland: his expenses were deducted from his brother's estate, 26 March 1660.

> J. Farmer, *A genealogical register of the first settlers of New England* (Lancaster, MA: Carter Andrews & Co., 1829); St J.D. Seymour, *The puritans in Ireland, 1647–1661* (Oxford: Clarendon Press, 1921), 209; *Essex Probate Recs.* II, 272, 290–2; *Essex Court Recs.* II, 202; *Pilgrims*, 101.

COCKRAM, William

William Cockram, a mariner from Southwold in Suffolk, first emigrated in 1635. He settled at Hingham, Massachusetts, but within a short time returned to England to fetch his wife and family. On 15 May 1637, 'William Cocram: of Southould in Suff, mariner' was listed at Great Yarmouth as a passenger on the *Mary Anne*, 'to pass for New England to inhabit'. He travelled with his wife Christian, two children and two servants.

William Cockram became a church member at Hingham before 13 March 1638/9, when he was admitted a freeman of Massachusetts.

Peter Hobart, the minister at Hingham, noted in his journal, 3 October 1642, 'Brother Cockram sayled [for En]gland.' Cockram returned to Southwold. In 1657, still describing himself as a mariner, he made his eldest son, 'William Cockraine' his attorney to collect debts due in New England, and to take possession of his property in Hingham. His son sold some land in New England in September 1657, but was back in Southwold by 2 February 1657/8, and witnessed his father's will. William Cockram senior died by 11 February 1660/1.

D.G. Allen, *In English ways* (Chapel Hill, NC: University of North Carolina Press, 1981), 251; C.E. Banks, *Planters of the Commonwealth* (Boston, MA: Houghton Mifflin, 1930), 183; 'The Hobart Journal', ed. C.E. Egan, *NEHGR*, 121 (1967), 11, 15; *NEHGR* 3: 96, 57: 198; *GM* 2: 122–5.

COGAN, Henry (1607–1649)

Henry Cogan was baptised at Taunton in Somerset, 6 April 1607. He emigrated in 1634 and settled initially at Dorchester, Massachusetts.

He returned to England in 1636. On 14 March 1636/7 he married Abigail Bishop at Bridport, Dorset.

Cogan came back to New England by 1638, when his wife Abigail was admitted a church member, and their daughter Abigail was baptised. In 1639 the family moved from Dorchester to Scituate and then to Barnstable in Plymouth Colony. Cogan took the oath of fidelity on 5 June 1644. The will of George Way of Dorchester, Dorset (30 September 1641), mentioned property at Dorchester, Massachusetts, in Cogan's hands.

At some point in the later 1640s, Cogan went to England again, and died there. He might be the 'Mr Cogan' who was in Rotterdam, 7 August 1648, with whom Samuel Winthrop planned to return to New England. Cogan's death in England, *c.* 16 June 1649, was recorded in October that year by the Plymouth authorities.

Cogan's widow Abigail married John Phinney in Barnstable in 1650 but died in 1653. Her father Thomas Bishop wrote from Bridport in Dorset, to make arrangements for the care of his orphaned grandchildren. His granddaughter Abigail Cogan should go to back to Bridport, 'for I purpose to take her for a daughter': she did for a time – the Dorchester church records marked against her name 'went to England' – but young Abigail was back in New England in 1659 when she married in Barnstable. Her brothers Thomas, John and Henry remained in Barnstable with their stepfather Phinney. In a court case in 1659, brought by neighbours after Thomas Cogan died, the younger two were said to 'suffer wrong'. John Phinney was removed as guardian and custodian of their inheritance.

GM 2: 132–6; *Dorchester CR*, 3, 150; Waters, 311; *WP* V, 243; *GD*; *NEHGR* 2: 64; 4: 284.

COGSWELL, John (1622–1653)

John Cogswell, baptised at Westbury Leigh in Wiltshire on 25 July 1622, was the son of John and Elizabeth Cogswell. His mother was the daughter of William Thompson, minister at Westbury. His father, a London merchant, emigrated on the *Angel Gabriel* in 1635 and settled at Ipswich, Massachusetts. John Cogswell and two of his brothers came over in 1639, with their father's servant Samuel Haines*. The younger John Cogswell married in the mid-1640s but soon became a widower.

Cogswell made a will on 13 December 1652, in anticipation of a voyage to England, a journey driven at least in part by the desire to find a wife. In a letter to his parents from London on 30 March 1653, he spoke of returning to New England at the earliest opportunity. 'I am as yet unmarried, and little hope I have to marry here.' He asked that they care for his property, 'that it be not forfeitted, for I am in a very low and sad condition here and have nothing to pay my debts withall nor to maintain my motherlesse children'. Cogswell had borrowed £84 in England, to be repaid as £100 in New England. He begged his relatives to care for his children. On 19 April 1653, Samuel Thomson of Taunton, Somerset, said that his cousin Cogswell had visited him. Cogswell probably took ship from a West Country port, but died before reaching New England. His will was attested on 30 September 1653.

GM 2: 137–40, 3: 191; *NEHGR* 1: 365, 25: 186n.; Bernard Bailyn, *The New England merchants in the seventeenth century* (Cambridge, MA: Harvard University Press, 1955), 36; *New England Quarterly* 4 (1931), 349; MHS, Misc. MSS, 13 December 1652; *Essex Probate Recs.* II, 158.

COLLINS, John (1632?–1687)

John Collins was the son of Edward and Martha Collins. His parents lived in Essex and London before emigration.

Collins was taken to New England by his parents in 1638 and settled with them at Cambridge, Massachusetts. Both parents were church members, and Edward a deacon. John Collins graduated BA from Harvard in 1649, MA in 1652. He was a fellow and tutor, 1651–3. The Cambridge church admitted him to membership in 1653: Michael Wigglesworth noted down his testimony. In 1658, several years after his return to England, Collins was still a member in full communion.

Collins left New England in 1653. On 13 April 1654 he was elected a fellow of Pembroke College, Cambridge, and in July was incorporated MA there. That same month Collins was appointed by the council of state to preach in Scotland with John Stalham (*CR*): he received £50 for his journey and £200 for the first year's stipend. In October 1655 he took part in a private meeting held by General George Monck and Lord Broghill, president of the Council of

Scotland, with the 'Protesting party', a faction within the Church of Scotland; Collins assisted on the English side as a 'faithfull minister of the Gospel'. On 27 March 1658 Lucy Downing* commended Collins as one of the preachers to the Council and to the English church in Edinburgh. In 1659 Collins acted as a chaplain to General Monck on his journey from Scotland to London. Collins attended the meeting between Monck and Independent deputies in London, 1659, as an observer. He lost his post when Monck dismissed his Independent chaplains. He seems to have stayed in London: Edmund Calamy included him among nonconformist ministers in the city without a benefice in 1662; he may have been the 'Mr Collins' named as lecturer at St Antholin's. He was known as a congregationalist. In 1669 he was preaching at Bell Lane, Spitalfields; in 1672 he received a licence to preach, as a congregationalist, at Duke's Place, Aldgate. He served as pastor to the congregational church at Paved Alley, Lime Street, c.1672–87. Collins kept up his links with New England (where his parents outlived him). He corresponded with John Leverett*. In 1672, he joined John Owen and others to recommend the appointment of Leonard Hoar* as president of Harvard. Collins acted as an unofficial agent for Massachusetts in London. In recognition of this the colony granted him 500 acres in 1683. He died in London and was buried at Bunhill Fields. Nathaniel Mather* succeeded him as pastor at Lime Street.

Publications [Mr 'Collings'], a sermon on Jude 3 in *A compleat collection of farewell-sermons* (1663); 'J.C.', *Strength in Weakness* (1676), a funeral sermon for the wife of Thomas Brooks (*CR*), sometimes ascribed to 'John Collinges' but as Brooks was a fellow London congregationalist it is more likely to be by this John Collins; [anon.], 'How the religious of a nation are the strength of it', sermon XXX in Samuel Annesley, *A continuation of morning-exercise questions and cases of conscience* (1683); prefatory epistle (with James Barron) to Ralph Venning, *Venning's remains, or, Christ's school* (1675); prefatory epistle to Jonathan Mitchell, *Discourse of the glory to which God hath called believers by Jesus Christ* (1677).

Shepard's confessions, 81–4, 130–2, and see Patricia Caldwell, *The puritan conversion narrative: the beginnings of American expression* (Cambridge: Cambridge University Press, 1983), 128–9, 175–6; N.C.P. Tyack, 'Migration from East Anglia to New England before 1660' (PhD dissertation, University of London, 1951), xcvi; *NEHGR* 79: 74, 148–50; *Harvard Recs.* III, 35n.; *The diary of Michael Wigglesworth 1653–1657: the conscience of a puritan*, ed. E.S. Morgan (Gloucester, MA: Peter Smith, 1970), 107–13, and see Caldwell, *Puritan conversion narrative*, 190, 192–5; *CSPD, 1654*, 195; Frances D. Dow, *Cromwellian Scotland 1651–1660* (Edinburgh: John Donald, 1979), 200; R. Scott Spurlock, *Cromwell and Scotland: conquest and religion 1650–1660* (Edinburgh: John Donald, 2007), 119, 146; *Thurloe* IV, 127–9; NA, PROB 11/389/175, will of John Collins, Gentleman of St Giles without Cripplegate, Middlesex, 22 December 1687. Manuscript sermons by Collins: DWL, New College London MS L4/2.

CC, CR, ODNB, Sibley, *Surman*.

COOKE, George (c.1610–1652)

George Cooke, the nephew of Thomas Cooke of Great Yeldham, Essex, was a cousin of Joseph Cooke* and the grandson of Thomas Cooke of Pebmarsh, Essex. Both George and Joseph Cooke emigrated in 1635 on the *Defence*, with a company from Earl's Colne, described as servants of Roger Harlakenden.

George Cooke settled at Cambridge and was admitted to the church before 3 March 1635/6, when he became a freeman of Massachusetts. He was chosen captain of the first train band in Cambridge, 9 March 1636/7. He commanded the Massachusetts Artillery Company in 1643, and led the expedition to capture Samuel Gorton*. He served as a selectman in 1638, 1642 and 1643; as a deputy for Cambridge, 1636 and 1642–5; as speaker for the House of Deputies and a commissioner to the United Colonies, 1645. On 7 October 1645, the Massachusetts General Court appointed Cooke, Richard Saltonstall* and others (including Herbert Pelham*) as agents to negotiate in London with the Warwick Commission over territory lost to Roger Williams* of Rhode Island. Saltonstall and Pelham refused the commission, but Cooke agreed.

Cooke left for England late in 1645, probably with Samuel Shepard*. Both Cooke and Shepard were excused from their duties at the General Court in October 1645, and their farms were in the care of Cambridge townsmen by 8 February 1646/7. By the following autumn Cooke, with his record of military experience in New England, had signed up for the parliamentary army. On 29 October 1646 Adam Winthrop reported 'off ouer new England men only Captain Cooke goes for Irlland . . . he goes leftenant Collonell'. Cooke served in the 'Tower Guard' regiment of foot, under Colonel Simon Needham and then Thomas Rainborowe (*ODNB*). He succeeded Rainborowe as colonel in 1648. John Winthrop heard in October 1648 that Cooke had taken part in the siege of Colchester. Cooke's regiment was chosen to go to Ireland again in 1649. After some hard fighting to gain Wexford, Cooke held the town for two years as military governor. He died during an attack from the Irish in April 1652. In June 1653, the council of state received a petition from Anne, 'widow of Col. George Cook, Governor of Wexford', and in July settled £200 a year on her; she was said to be in Ireland, expecting a child. On 22 April 1656 Hugh Peter* asked Henry Cromwell to expedite the allocation of Irish lands due to Cooke.

At the time of George Cooke's death, he was said to have two children by a former wife. Elizabeth (born in Cambridge, 1644) may have already been in England or Ireland. At the time an inventory of Cooke's estate was drawn up in October 1652, only her sister Mary (born in 1646) was in Cambridge, Massachusetts, under the guardianship of Henry Dunster and Joseph Cooke. Both Cooke's daughters later married well-known nonconformist ministers in London: Mary married the widower Samuel Annesley (*CR*, grandfather of the Wesleys) in January 1680/1; Elizabeth married John Quick (*CR*) by 1690.

C. Yuan, 'The politics of the English army in Ireland during the Interregnum' (PhD dissertation, Brown University, 1981), 69–70, 75; C.H. Firth and G. Davies, *The regimental history of Cromwell's army* (Oxford: Clarendon Press, 1940), 579–82; Roberts, *Artillery Company*, 57–8, 110–11; C.E. Banks, *Planters of the Commonwealth* (Boston, MA:

Houghton Mifflin, 1930), 168; *NEHGR* 3: 94; Cambridge TR, fol. 72; *Mass. Recs*. 2: 138, 3: 48; *WP* V, 120, 266; *WP* VI, 197; Middlesex Court Recs., fols 33, 114, 153; Middlesex Probate Recs., case number 4988 (inventory, 'George Cook, Cooke', 4 October 1652); BL, Lansdowne MS 821, fol. 121. *GM* states that George and Joseph Cooke were brothers, but it is more likely they were cousins. There is evidence that Joseph was one of only two sons of Thomas Cooke of Great Yeldham, with a brother Thomas (not George) who stayed in England: Lechford *NB*, 219–22, 301–2; Waters, 674–5.

BDBR, *GM* 2: 171–7.

COOKE, Joseph

Joseph Cooke was the son of Thomas Cooke of Great Yeldham, Essex, and the cousin of George Cooke*. He emigrated with George in 1635 on the *Defence*, with a company from Earl's Colne, listed as a servant of Roger Harlakenden.

Joseph Cooke settled at Cambridge, Massachusetts. He was a church member by 3 March 1635/6, when he became a freeman. He joined the Artillery Company in 1640 and in 1645 was deputed to take charge in the absence of George Cooke. He frequently held office for Cambridge and for the colony of Massachusetts. In 1643 he married Elizabeth, daughter of Governor John Haynes* of Connecticut (and stepsister of the Harvard graduate John Haynes*). He and Elizabeth were listed in the Cambridge church records, January 1658/9, as 'both in full Communion'.

Joseph and Elizabeth Cooke went to England in or soon after 1659. By 1665 they were living at Stanway, Essex. Joseph had sold a 750-acre farm at Cambridge on 22 December 1658, but kept a house and land which he conveyed to his son Joseph in 1665. The Cookes seem to have taken their daughters – Elizabeth, Mary, Grace and Ruth – to England, but left Joseph to finish his studies at Harvard (where he graduated BA in 1661). Another son, Thomas, was born after their return to England.

Artillery Company, 99; C. Yuan, 'The politics of the English army in Ireland during the Interregnum' (PhD dissertation, Brown University, 1981), 70; C.E. Banks, *Planters of the Commonwealth* (Boston, MA: Houghton Mifflin, 1930), 168; *NEHGR* 3: 94; Cambridge TR to 1658, *passim*; Middlesex Court Recs., fol. 153; *GM* 2: 178–83.

CORBET, John and his father

John Corbet and his father were in England by December 1650. Corbet went to Ireland for a time. The identity of both is unclear, although they were well known to Nathaniel Mather* and John Rogers of Ipswich. They may have been relatives of Thomas Cobbet, minister of Lynn, who signed a letter to Cromwell in December 1650 in response to an invitation for colonists to settle in Ireland.

On 23 December 1650 Nathaniel Mather reported, probably to John Rogers, that John Corbet was in England with his father, and about to go to Milford by land, 'and there to take ship and so for Ireland, thence to returne at spring'; Mather added "Tis incredible what an advantage to preferment it is to have been a New English man. I suppose John Corbet hath spoken largely to the purpose.' John Corbet was in Ireland when Mather wrote to Rogers on 23 March 1650/1: Mather reported that he and many others in England would not have received Rogers's letters so soon, had not he and John Tuttle* opened two large packets addressed to Corbet and distributed the letters inside before the packets were sent on to Ireland.

Letters from Nathaniel Mather, 23 December 1650 and 23 March 1650/1: BPL, MS Am. 1502 v.1, nos. 6, 7 (printed, with some inaccuracies, 4 *MHSC* 8: 2, 4–5). Thomas Cobbet: *Pilgrims*, 111–12; *Original letters and papers of state addressed to Oliver Cromwell*, ed. J. Nickolls (London, 1743), 44–5.

CUTTER, William

William Cutter came from Newcastle upon Tyne, the son of William (d. *c.*1646) and Elizabeth Cutter. His sister Barbary married the Cambridge schoolmaster Elijah Corlet. Cutter emigrated in the 1630s with his parents, sister Barbary and brother Richard.

Cutter had settled in Cambridge by 1638, and may have been there as early as 1633. As part of an investigation of Giles Bitleston, a tanner from Newcastle, the English authorities unearthed a letter dated 1 September 1638, which sent greetings to William Cutter (father or son) in 'New Town' (Cambridge), New England, along with 'Guy Bainbridge', 'Thomas Cheasman' and Edward Winshop'. Cutter may be the William Cutter who became a freeman of Massachusetts on 18 April 1637; if so, he was already a church member. His testimony to the church is not extant, although those of his mother, brother and sister are. Cutter was perhaps the William Cutter appointed on 18 October 1648 by the Massachusetts General Court, with John Milam* and Thomas Venner* amongst others: they were to meet with other coopers to appoint wardens to oversee standards. Cutter was still in New England on 10 February 1649/50, when he witnessed a transaction between James Cutter and Nathaniel Bowman.

Cutter was back in Newcastle by 12 January 1653/4, when he sent a letter to New England to appoint attorneys to act for him there: Edward Goffe, Elijah Corlet and Thomas Swatman of Cambridge, with Robert Hale of Charlestown. A letter of Cutter's from Newcastle to Henry Dunster in Cambridge survives, dated 19 May 1654: Cutter had sent 'seurall diurnalls ... to seuerall freinds which I dyrect to Mr Corlett: and some in particular to yourselff'. He gave details of a day of thanksgiving shortly to be held, and praised the religious life of Newcastle – congregational and presbyterian (he had no time for Quakers or baptists). Cutter believed trade to New England would improve, 'for OE never was so full of shiping as now'. He referred to George Hadden*, John Glover* and George Fenwick*. Cutter asked Dunster to comfort his widowed mother, his 'aunt Wilkenson', and his siblings: 'I often wish I could se them again and you all: butt it is not like ffor besides other hindrances: truly the sad discouragements in comeing by sea is enough to hinder: unles it were as formerly: that we could not injoy the ordinances of God.' On 9 April 1656

Cutter witnessed the will of William Reed*. A William Cutter and his wife were arrested for taking part in an early morning conventicle in Newcastle, August 1669.²

CSPD, 1638–9, 418; *GM* 1: 153 (Guy 'Banbridge'), 2: 63–7 (Thomas Chesholm), 7: 487–8 (Edward Winship); *Shepard's confessions*, 89, 144, 178; *NEHGR* 3: 95; MHS, Misc. MSS, 18 October 1648; Middlesex Deeds I, fols 7–9, II, fols 143–5; 4 *MHSC* 2: 195–6; Waters, 889; 'Depositions from the castle of York', *Publications of the Surtees Society*, XL, (1861), 173–4.

D

DAVIS, John

John Davis set sail from London in 1635 on the *Increase*, and settled at Boston. On 31 January 1635/6, 'John Davisse joyner' became a member of the church, and on 25 May 1636 a freeman of Massachusetts. Davis was among those disarmed in 1637 for supporting Anne Hutchinson. By 1645 he lived next to one of the Boston ministers, John Wilson*, and (in the interests of good neighbourly relations) the deed of sale bound Davis to 'maintain the fence between Mr Wilson and him, and not to annoy him with any stinks or jakes'. Davis sold his house and garden to John* and Katherine Trotman*; he also sold land adjacent to another dwelling house to Edmund Jackson. In October 1646 he sold this 'dwelling house and yard' to Jackson.

John Davis left no trace in colonial records after October 1646. Many settlers left for England that autumn, with Davis probably among them.

GM 2: 301–3; *Suffolk Deeds*, I, 60.

DAVIS, John (d. 1657)

John Davis, the son of William Davis of New Haven, graduated from Harvard with a BA in 1651, and an MA in 1654. In 1652 'Brother Davis his sonne was propounded to supply the scoole masters place' at Hartford, Connecticut. He was in Hartford in 1655, when the town allowed him £10 'for preaching and schooling' to 7 February 1655/6, and another payment was made the following May. Davis kept an account at Harvard until September 1657. After 1651 the only charges were for commencements at his BA and MA, apart from July 1657, when he paid £1 1s 5¾d for 'Commons and Sizinges'.

Davis set out for England on 6 November 1657, but his ship was lost at sea. Among his fellow travellers, all drowned, were Harvard students Jonathan Ince*, Thomas Mayhew* and Nathaniel Pelham*.

NEHGR 5: 306; *Harvard Recs.* III, 56n.

CC, Sibley.

DAY, Wentworth

Wentworth Day was admitted to the Boston church on 5 September 1640 as 'Mr Wentworth Day a singleman'. He soon married, and presented children for baptism in 1641 and 1643. He joined the Artillery Company in 1640. On 26

April 1641 he was granted 100 acres at Muddy River. He moved to Cambridge, Massachusetts. Some sources describe him as a surgeon, still in Cambridge in 1652.

Day has been identified with the Wentworth Day who served under William Rainborowe* as a cornet in Thomas Harrison's regiment, 1647, and was later notorious as a Fifth Monarchist. This Wentworth Day left the parliamentary army in 1649/50 and was arrested with the Fifth Monarchist preacher John Simpson (*ODNB*) in 1655 for reading Vavasor Powell's petition, *A word for God*, to a crowd of 500. He took part in Thomas Venner's* plot, 1657, and spent time in prison in 1658. In 1659 he requested reform of law and church on biblical model. He was jailed, 1660–1, for treasonable words. In 1661 Edward Shrimpton of Bethnal Green (brother of Henry Shrimpton of Boston) left 'Mr Wentworth Day' £5, and 'to the Church of Christ whereof Mr John Sympson is pastor', £10.

Boston CR, 31; Thwing; *Artillery Company*, 100; *GD*; B.S. Capp, *The Fifth Monarchy Men* (London: Faber, 1972), 248, and see also 110, 121, 126, 143, 196; Champlin Burrage, 'The Fifth Monarchy insurrections', *English Historical Review*, 25 (1910), 731, 738; Waters, 319–20.

BDBR.

DENTON, Richard (d. *c.*1662)

Richard Denton was born in Yorkshire. He graduated BA from St Catharine's College, Cambridge, in 1623/4. He was ordained a deacon at Peterborough, 9 March 1622/3, and a priest on 8 June 1623. He was perhaps the person licensed as curate of Turton chapel, 'Bolton le Moors', Lancashire, on 7 March 1628. Denton became curate of Coley chapel, near Halifax in the West Riding of Yorkshire, *c.*1631 (licensed in 1633). His conduct did not attract attention from the church courts but according to the later report of Oliver Heywood, 'he could not do what was required, and feared further persecution, and therefore took the opportunity of going into New England'.

Denton settled at Wethersfield, Connecticut, *c.*1638. In 1641 he led twenty-eight families, dissatisfied with church government at Wethersfield, to found Stamford. This was perhaps at the encouragement of John Davenport: Stamford received land from, and was under the jurisdiction of, the New Haven Colony. However, Denton had presbyterian convictions. He disliked New Haven's practice of restricting the franchise to church members and of refusing to baptise the children of those who were not church members. *c.*1644 Denton secured land from the Dutch authorities of New Netherland and moved to Hempstead, Long Island, where he had more freedom. Although Denton was a presbyterian, his flock included congregationalists who, Dutch visitors reported, absented themselves if children of the parish were to be baptised.

Oliver Heywood commented that Denton had 'little comfort' in New England, being 'not altogether of their principles as to church discipline ... at last he returned into Old England about the year 1659; lived awhile in Essex, and there died'.

> CCEd Person ID 33942; R.A. Marchant, *The puritans and the church courts in the diocese of York 1560–1642* (London: Longmans, 1960), 243–4; J. H. Turner, ed., *The Rev. Oliver Heywood, B.A., 1630–1702: his autobiography, diaries* ... , 4 vols, (Brighouse, Yorkshire: A.B. Bayes, 1882–5), IV, 11–12; Dorothy Deming, *The settlement of the Connecticut towns* (New Haven, CT: Yale University Press, 1933), 23–4; *NEHGR* 24: 36; I.M. Calder, *The New Haven Colony* (New Haven, CT: Yale University Press, 1934), 76, 77, 87.

ODNB.

DESBOROUGH, Samuel (1619–1690)

Samuel Desborough [Disbrowe] was born at Eltisley, Cambridgeshire, the son of James and Elizabeth Desborough. His brother John Disbrowe [Desborough] (*ODNB*) married Oliver Cromwell's sister Jane, and became one of Cromwell's major-generals. His brother Isaac* emigrated in 1635 but returned to England before 1640. Samuel set sail for New England in 1639, with Henry Whitfield's* company: he had perhaps already married Dorothy, Whitfield's daughter.

Desborough settled at Guilford with Whitfield, on the shores of Long Island Sound. He did not sign the plantation covenant aboard ship, but put his signature to a deed with local Indians on 17 December 1641. He was one of the original seven members at the church gathering in 1643.

Samuel and Dorothy Desborough left Guilford in the autumn of 1650, with Henry Whitfield. Samuel was in London by January 1650/1, when he wrote to Cromwell in Scotland. Long connected with Cromwell by his brother John's marriage, Samuel hoped to find employment in the regime:

> My Lord, it having pleased God by his divine providence, through many difficulties and dangers, to bring me once again to see my native country, where I have an inclination to abide ... and was I in any way capable of doing your Lordship any service, I hope I have a heart ready pressed ...

By April 1652 he became a member of the board of commissioners dealing with sequestration, based at Leith near Edinburgh. He worked alongside Richard Saltonstall*. Both Desborough and Saltonstall, with George Fenwick*, were appointed in June 1652 as commissioners for the universities in Scotland and for other affairs relating to the ministry. Desborough served as an MP for Edinburgh in 1654; for Midlothian in 1656; and in 1659 for Edinburgh again. He was a founding member of the Scottish council, 4 May 1655, and also became a judge presiding over the Court of Exchequer. Desborough sought land in Ireland: his brother John petitioned Henry Cromwell on his behalf in 1656. On 16 September 1657 Desborough took up office as Keeper of the

Great Seal of Scotland. From July 1658, as Chancellor, he sat with judges for civil causes as their permanent president.

A letter among Desborough's papers from William Leete of Guilford, 10 October 1654, shows that Desborough had written to Oliver Cromwell on behalf of the settlements along Long Island Sound most affected by the threat of conflict with the Dutch. Leete managed Desborough's New England estate, and his letter mentioned others besides Desborough who had already left New England: John Evance*, Hezekiah Haynes*, Edward Hopkins*, John Hoadley*, Thomas Jones*, Thomas Jordan*, John* and Nathaniel Whitfield*. Leete's letter illustrates the delicate relation between the colonists who stayed, and those who went away: Desborough was 'laid up in the breast of people as one of the Cordiall ffreinds of New England'; yet he was suspected of trying to draw Leete away, his reputation tainted by an 'aptnes to have harsh thoughts on almost all men that goe for England, as if they regard not Christ's poor people here'.

At the Restoration Desborough worked with General George Monck, and in 1660 signed his acceptance of the Declaration of Breda in Monck's presence. Desborough received a full pardon and retired to a house he had bought in 1656 at Elsworth, Cambridgeshire, five miles from his birthplace. His wife Dorothy had died of smallpox in 1654.

B.C. Steiner, *A history of... Guilford* (Baltimore, MD: privately printed, 1897), 24–5, 33, 35–7, 39–40, 41; Desborough to Oliver Cromwell, 18 January 1650/1, *Original letters and papers of state addressed to Oliver Cromwell*, ed. J. Nickolls (London, 1743), 54; Frances D. Dow, *Cromwellian Scotland 1651–1660* (Edinburgh: John Donald, 1979), 57, 58, 150, 165, 175, 184, 185, 214, 217, 222, 224, 235 238; Patrick Little and David L. Smith, *Parliaments and politics during the Cromwellian Protectorate* (Cambridge: Cambridge University Press, 2007), 277–81 and *passim*; John Desborough to Henry Cromwell, April 1656, BL, Lansdowne MS 821, fol. 125; Papers of Samuel Desborough 1651–1660, BL, Egerton MS 2519 (especially fols 10–11, William Leete's letter of 10 October 1654); *Davenport Letters*, 102.

BDBR, ODNB.

DOWNING, Emmanuel (1585–c.1659) and Lucy

Emmanuel Downing was a lawyer of Inner Temple, London. He married Lucy, a sister of John Winthrop, in 1622. He had grown up in Ipswich and attended Trinity Hall, Cambridge. He worked in Dublin for a time but came back to London in 1626. He was an adventurer in the Massachusetts Bay Company from the start, and acted as the Company's attorney in England. He also looked after John Winthrop's business interests after Winthrop left for New England in 1630. Some of Downing's children–James, Mary and Susan–preceded him to New England, c.1633. Emmanuel and Lucy Downing emigrated in 1638, with their son George Downing*, at Winthrop's encouragement.[1]

Downing, an investor and entrepreneur as well as a lawyer, settled in Salem, Massachusetts. He was admitted to the church on 4 November 1638, and as a freeman on 14 March 1638/9. He became recorder of deeds for Salem on 7 October 1640, and kept that office into the 1650s. He was active in town government and often acted as a representative at the Massachusetts General Court. Before Hugh Peter*, Thomas Weld* and William Hibbins* returned to England as agents for Massachusetts in 1641, Downing briefed them on legal matters relating to the colony's charter.[2]

Downing seems to have made three visits to England before he returned home for good in 1654. He was in England on business, c. October 1642 to c. June 1643. On this occasion he acted as an attorney for Adam Winthrop, and aided John Winthrop Jr* (with Hugh Peter and Thomas Weld) to promote investment in the Saugus ironworks. Downing returned to New England but set sail for England again in December 1644. On 25 February 1644/5 he reported his arrival in London. The Massachusetts General Court had directed him to gather evidence against Thomas Morton*. He also handled business for the Saugus ironworks, including the recruitment of Richard Leader* as manager. Downing was associated with a scheme promoted by Hugh Peter and Thomas Weld, to send poor children from England to New England. Downing fell under suspicion (with Nehemiah Bourne*) of pocketing some of the money raised by Peter and Weld. He sailed for New England in May 1645 and was back there by August. With Bourne, Thomas Fowle* and Robert Sedgwick*, Downing led a petition against laws restricting the presence of strangers and prohibiting anabaptists, arguing that these colonial policies were deeply unpopular among the godly in England. His son George Downing left New England for good in 1645. Before long, Downing visited England for a third time: he was there in May 1647, but came back to Boston by June 1648. Downing was keenly aware of temptations to return to England: he had heard John Davenport and Theophilus Eaton might go; he knew Hugh Peter was urging John Winthrop Jr to take up opportunities back home.[3]

Emmanuel Downing's fourth journey to England was his last. He received a letter from Hugh Peter in the winter of 1652/3, asking him to come to England, with his wife Lucy. He suspected 'George would have us retorne, and putts Mr Peters upon the invitation'. On 25 September 1654, Emmanuel Downing declared he intended to travel back to England with Robert Sedgwick* within two months. He sailed that winter. Stephen Winthrop* reported, 11 March 1654/5, that Downing had recently arrived in London. By this time George Downing's star was rising as scoutmaster-general in Scotland. Emmanuel Downing joined him there and quickly became clerk to the new Council of Scotland, established in May 1655 (of which Samuel Desborough* was also a member). Later, Downing welcomed Fitz John Winthrop* to Scotland. His wife Lucy and daughter Martha joined him in Edinburgh by 1658. Emmanuel Downing died in Edinburgh in 1659. Lucy Downing lived on in England until her death in 1679, in straitened circumstances – reliant on her son George, who was notoriously rich and notoriously mean.[4]

---

[1] *WP* II, III, *passim*; *WJ* 47, 88, 136, 293; *GMB* 578–81.

[2] N.C.P. Tyack, 'Migration from East Anglia to New England before 1660' (PhD dissertation, University of London, 1951), xcv; *WP* IV, 70–1; *Salem CR*, 7; *Salem*

TR, 5, 180; R.P. Stearns, 'The Weld-Peter mission to England', Colonial Society of Massachusetts, *Publications*, 32 (1937), 193–4n.
³ *WP* IV, 358, 371–2, 396; E.D. Hartley, *Ironworks on the Saugus* (Norman, OK: University of Oklahoma Press, 1957), 55; Sibley, 29n.; *WP* IV, 500, 501; *WP* V, 5–8, 14; *WJ* 538n; Stearns, 'Weld-Peter mission', 217; R.P. Stearns, *The strenuous puritan: Hugh Peter 1598–1660* (Urbana, IL: University of Illinois Press, 1954), 164; *WP* V, 21–2, 38–9, 154, 230; *WP* VI, 97, 184–5, 248.
⁴ *WP* VI 262, 432; 4 *MHSC* 6: 85; 5 *MHSC* 8: 215; Frances D. Dow, *Cromwellian Scotland 1651–1660* (Edinburgh: John Donald, 1979), 185; *CC s.n.* George Downing.

DOWNING, George (1623–1684)

George Downing, son of Lucy and Emmanuel Downing*, emigrated with his parents in 1638 and settled at Salem, Massachusetts. He entered Harvard in 1640 and graduated BA in 1642. John Winthrop listed him as one of the nine 'young men of good hope' in the first graduating class, with Benjamin Woodbridge*, William Hubbard, Henry Saltonstall*, John Bulkeley*, John Wilson Jr, Nathaniel Brewster*, Samuel Bellingham* and Tobias Barnard*. On 27 December 1643 he was appointed to read to junior pupils at a salary of £4 a year. Downing and his fellow students found their prospects in New England looked dim: seven out of the nine who graduated in 1642 eventually found their way back to England.[1]

Downing returned to England via Barbados in 1645, travelling as a ship's chaplain. His mother Lucy wrote that his determination to leave sprang from 'his little expectation, and fears of supply here'. In 1646 Downing became a chaplain to Colonel John Okey's regiment in the New Model Army. The presbyterian polemicist Thomas Edwards singled him out for attention in *Gangraena*, as a 'young Peters' (Hugh Peter*). Downing went north to Newcastle upon Tyne in 1648 as chaplain to the regiment of Sir Arthur Hesilrige (*ODNB*), whose commander was Oliver Cromwell. Cromwell appointed Downing as scoutmaster-general (intelligence-gatherer) of the English forces in Scotland, 1 November 1649, at a salary of £365 a year. Downing served as an MP in all the parliaments of the Protectorate: for Edinburgh in 1654, for Carlisle in 1656 and 1659. Cromwell commissioned Downing to travel to the continent to lodge complaints from England about the massacre of protestants in Piedmont in April 1655. In 1657 he became Cromwell's envoy to The Hague. In the aftermath of Anglo-Dutch hostilities earlier in the 1650s, Downing played a pivotal role in shaping a protestant consensus against the powers of Catholic Europe. He also learned a great deal about Dutch trading practices and economic strategy, which he later brought to bear in England.

Downing turned Royalist at the Restoration. He made an approach to Charles II while the king was still in exile, declaring that his father had taken him to New England where he had 'sucked in principles that since his reason had made him see were erroneous'. He was knighted in 1660 and in 1662 delivered his former commander, the regicide John Okey (*ODNB*), to the scaffold. Downing secured many high offices, and played a vital role in the fortunes of crown and country through his reform of the Treasury. Downing Street, the home of the British Prime Minister, takes its name from him.

> Jonathan Scott provides a definitive biography in the *ODNB*: 'Downing, Sir George, first baronet (1623–1684)'. For Downing's early career, see *WJ*, 416; *WP* IV, 445; *WP* V, 42–5, 207–8; Edwards, *Gangraena*, iii.81–2; Larry Gragg, *Englishmen transplanted: the English colonization of Barbados, 1627–1660* (Oxford and New York: Oxford University Press, 2003), 26–7, 111, 113; Anne Laurence, *Parliamentary army chaplains, 1642–1651* (Woodbridge, Suffolk: Royal Historical Society, 1990), 122–3; Frances D. Dow, *Cromwellian Scotland 1651–1660* (Edinburgh: John Donald, 1979), 150, 185, 317; Patrick Little and David L. Smith, *Parliaments and politics during the Cromwellian Protectorate* (Cambridge: Cambridge University Press, 2007), 269–70, 276–7, 279, 285 and *passim*. For wider perspectives, see J. Beresford, *The godfather of Downing Street, Sir George Downing, 1623–1684: an essay in biography* (London: R. Cobden-Sanderson, 1925); Henry Roseveare, 'Prejudice and policy: Sir George Downing as parliamentary entrepreneur', in D.C. Coleman and P. Mathias, eds, *Enterprise and history* (Cambridge: Cambridge University Press, 1984), 135–50; *History of Parliament Online*, http://www.historyofparliamentonline.org/volume/1660-1690/member/downing-sir-george-1623-84.

CC, ODNB, Sibley.

DOWNING, Joshua

Joshua Downing, the son of Lucy and Emmanuel Downing*, was at school in Maidstone, Kent, c. July 1636. He was in New England c. January 1640/1, 'very eager for sea Imployment'. In 1648 he had been to Barbados, but was discouraged from travelling again to the West Indies by the plague raging there. He was seeking work with a new shipmaster, January 1648/9.

Joshua Downing, like his father, benefited from George Downing's rise in the Cromwellian establishment. Emmanuel Downing reported, 15 March 1652/3, 'George hath putt Joshua into a Customes place in Scotlund'.

WP III, 278; *WP* IV, 304; *WP* V, 290–1, 296–7; *WP* VI, 262.

DUMMER, Stephen and Alice

Stephen and Alice Dummer came from Bishopstoke, Hampshire. Stephen's brother Richard Dummer* had emigrated in 1632, but visited England in 1637–8 and brought Stephen and Alice back to New England with him. They settled at Newbury, Massachusetts, with Richard Dummer. Stephen became a freeman on 22 May 1639. He still owned property in England, on which he received rents.

The Dummers left New England in the winter of 1646/7. According to their grandson Samuel Sewall, this was because of 'the Climat being not agreeable'. They went back with their daughter Jane Sewall* and her husband Henry*, and their niece Joan Nelson*. Stephen Dummer may have been in Warwickshire for a time, but by 1650 he was back at Bishopstoke, Hampshire. After their return to England, both Stephen Dummer and Henry Sewall used Henry Short of Newbury as their attorney in relation to property and rents in New England.

NEHGR 3: 96; *Suffolk Deeds* I, 79; Aspinwall, 59–63; *NEHGR* 1: 111–12; *GMB* 598–95 (Richard Dummer); *GM* 6: 316–17.

E

EARNING, Katherine

Katherine Earning, a widow, probably emigrated in 1638 with her daughter Hannah and son-in-law Nehemiah Bourne*. Her daughter Ellen stayed in England, married to Anthony Earning, a mariner of Limehouse, London. On 27 September 1639 Katherine Earning made Nehemiah Bourne and Anthony Earning her attorneys to collect money due to her in England. She became a church member at Dorchester on 21 December 1639. Along with Nehemiah and Hannah Bourne, she was dismissed from Dorchester to the Boston church on 27 November 1642. When Nehemiah and Hannah set off in December 1646 on a voyage to London, they left their children in her care in Boston.

Not long after the departure of her daughter and son-in-law, Katherine decided to follow them to England. This unexpected news brought the Bournes' children to England, too. On 12 August 1648, Nehemiah Bourne wrote to John Winthrop:

> I had it not in my heart that my Mother Earning would haue returned, whose going [from Boston] was the cause that putt me vpon a kind of Necessity of sending home my Children being young: and it was beyond my wife her thought or expectation either to se Mother or Children at London.

'Mother Earning' probably returned to Limehouse, where family ties were strong. Anthony and Ellen Earning had a child baptised at Stepney on 6 January 1660/1. Anthony Earning, mariner 'of Lymehouse in the parish of Stepney', made his will on 1 January 1672/3: he mentioned his wife Ellen, his brother 'Major Nehemiah Bourne', and a kinsman 'Mr Anthony Earning' (who may be the 'Lymehouse mariner' admitted to William Greenhill's Stepney church in 1658, with his wife Margaret).

C.H. Firth, 'Sailors of the Civil War, the Commonwealth and the Protectorate', *Mariner's Mirror*, 12 (1926), 256; Lechford *NB*, 195; *Dorchester CR*, 5; *Boston CR*, 37; *WP* V, 244; NA, PROB 11/346/18, will of Anthony Earning, mariner of Stepney, Middlesex, 22 September 1674; Stepney CB, fols 4, 121.

EATON, Ann

Ann Eaton, the daughter of George Lloyd, bishop of Chester, married first Thomas Yale and then in 1627 Theophilus Eaton, brother of Nathaniel* and Samuel Eaton*. By her first marriage, she was mother to Ann (Hopkins*), David* and Thomas Yale*; by her second, to Hannah* and Theophilus Eaton

Jr*. She and Theophilus Eaton lived in the parish of St Stephen's, Coleman Street, London, and emigrated with John Davenport in 1637.

Theolphilus Eaton, with John Davenport, moved from Boston in 1638 and founded New Haven. Eaton served as the first governor of the New Haven Colony in 1643, and continued in that role until his death in 1658. The New Haven church excommunicated Ann Eaton in 1645 for her belief in adult baptism. Her seat in the meetinghouse was kept vacant for years, in the hope that she would return to the fold. She never did. In 1646 the New Haven court – in a dispute about whether a court official took down testimony accurately or not – recorded that a witness had said that 'Mrs Eaton would not lie with her husband since she was admonished but caused her bed to be removed to another room.'

Ann Eaton left for England in September 1658, a few months after her husband's death, with her children Hannah and Theophilus. She died by August 1659, within a short time of making the move to greater religious liberty in England. Yale University takes its name from her grandson, Elihu Yale (*ODNB*).

Lilian Handlin, 'Dissent in a small community', *New England Quarterly*, 58 (1985), 193–220; I.M. Calder, *The New Haven Colony* (New Haven, CT: Yale University Press, 1934), 29, 93, 209; *Davenport Letters*, 120n., 143; *NEHGR* 108: 70; 5 *MHSC* 8: 51; *New Haven Recs.* I, 270.

EATON, Hannah and Theophilus Jr

Hannah and Theophilus Eaton, children of Theophilus and Ann Eaton*, returned to England with their mother in 1658. Hannah married William Jones at St Martin-in-the-Fields, 4 July 1659. Theophilus was later in Dublin. Hannah came back to New England with her husband, arriving on 11 August 1660.

Davenport Letters, 137, 172; *GD*.

EATON, Samuel (1597–1665)

Samuel Eaton, son of Richard Eaton, vicar of Great Budworth, Cheshire, was brother to Nathaniel* and Theophilus Eaton. He graduated BA from Magdalene College, Cambridge, in 1625, and MA in 1628. Eaton was ordained at Peterborough in 1625 and became rector of West Kirby in the Wirral, and preacher at Bromborough. He was cited before the church authorities in 1628 and 1629 for (among other irregularities) allowing people to sit to receive communion. In 1630 he was presented for disparaging the reading of homilies. The church authorities suspended and ejected him in 1632. Samuel Eaton went to Holland in 1634, and met John Davenport. In Holland, as Eaton later put it, he 'joyned with others in a Congregational way', but came back to England when the 'unsutablenesse' of the climate 'occasioned much sicknesse'; then, 'finding no rest', he was 'necessitated to transplant himself into New-England'.[1]

Eaton emigrated with his brother Theophilus Eaton and John Davenport in 1637, from London. They went to Connecticut in 1638, and settled New Haven. In 1639 Samuel Eaton became a freeman, by virtue of his membership of another approved church. He seems to have disagreed with Davenport over the policy of restricting civil office to church members. Eaton received a grant of land at 'Totokett' (Branford) on 5 September 1640, on condition that its government was identical to that of New Haven and came under its jurisdiction. He intended to persuade others to come from England to settle it with him. Meanwhile, the Court of High Commission at York, when 'he was out of the Land, and knew nothing of their sommons, he was fined . . . severall summes of money, which together amounted to fifteene hundred and fifty pound'. The court seized Eaton's assets to recover the fine. News of this, and complaints from his tenant in the Wirral, reached Eaton in several letters; 'he was advised to try if by his returning backe, he could . . . free his estate'. Eaton set sail from New England in the autumn of 1640, intending only a temporary absence. He left behind in New Haven books worth £20, which c.1655 were given by Theophilus Eaton to John Davenport, for a college library.[2]

Eaton was the first minister to return from New England to England after 1640. He arrived just before the Long Parliament convened in November. His original intentions were to recruit settlers for 'Totokett', and, chiefly, to rescue his estate. He later claimed that 'if the High Commission at York could have let him alone, he might probably have ended his days [in America]'. As the political climate changed in England, Eaton was diverted. He quickly became notorious as 'the New England Mr Eaton', 'lately come over . . . as from a New Ierusalem'. His preaching immediately attracted attention in Cheshire – at St John's, Chester, on 3 January 1640/1, then at Knutsford, and at Barrow in August 1641 – for attacking episcopacy and proposing congregationalism. Sir Thomas Aston (*ODNB*) found Eaton's ideas dangerous and raised the alarm in the Cheshire petition in support of episcopacy and in his *A remonstrance against presbitery*.[3]

Before long, Eaton enjoyed the patronage of the parliamentary army officer Colonel Robert Duckenfield (*ODNB*), kinsman of Sir William Brereton (*ODNB*). He preached in a chapel at Duckenfield's home, Dukinfield Hall, Cheshire, and formed a congregational church there late in 1643 or early in 1644. Eaton and Timothy Taylor were soon appointed as pastor and teacher. The presbyterian polemicist Thomas Edwards described Eaton as the 'great apostle' of Independency in the region, and the Dukinfield church as the first Independent church in England. Edwards also told the ominous story of an 'invisible drum' at Dukinfield chapel: Eaton's supporters (including Duckenfield and Birch) dismissed this as merely the sound of a dog scratching its ear and striking the wainscot with its foot. Under Duckenfield's aegis, Eaton also became chaplain to the Chester garrison, c.1646, and seems to have established a congregational church in the town (served by Thomas Harrison* in 1660). He may have played a part in encouraging the parliamentarian Thomas Birch (*ODNB*) to promote congregationalism in his chapel at Birch, Lancashire.[4]

Samuel Eaton and Timothy Taylor defended congregationalism in print against the presbyterian Richard Hollingworth (*ODNB*), 1645–6, as part of a pre-existing debate between Lancashire clergy and New England ministers. Among the arguments they adduced was the fact that their church practice was no novelty. Churches made up of 'the choysest Christians of many Parishes' had already existed in the locality: 'for at least fourteen years since, such a Church was extant in Wirrall in Cheshire (the vocall covenant onely wanting)'. This had also been the case at the church of John Angier (*ODNB*) at Denton in Lancashire and at others besides: 'it was accounted a high happinesse to have liberty to make such a Church; but never was accounted by the godly sinfull before'. Eaton and Taylor claimed they took members only from parishes where there was no hope of reform. If and when change came, they would by mutual consent lay down their covenant and join other churches, 'especially where we were sometimes members'. The continuing attachment of members to their parish churches is suggested by the testimony of Adam Martindale, minister of Gorton, Lancashire, who observed that members of his flock who deserted him to join Eaton's covenanted church still paid for their seats in Gorton parish church.[5]

In 1650 Timothy Taylor became a minister in Ireland with, amongst others, Thomas Jenner* and Samuel Mather*. Eaton visited Ireland briefly in 1655, soon after the death in Dublin of the promising young preacher John Murcot (*ODNB*), who had followed Eaton in ministry at West Kirby in the Wirral. Eaton later collaborated in the publication of Murcot's *Several works* with the ministers Samuel Winter, Robert Chambers, Thomas Manton and Joseph Caryl. Although several in Eaton's circle went to Ireland, he declined invitations to take up ministry there himself.[6]

Eaton had resigned from work in Chester by 1650 (perhaps c.1648) 'because I could not fulfil my Ministry to another people, and yet live among you'. According to Adam Martindale, Eaton's work as chaplain to Chester garrison necessitated many journeys to London, Scotland, and elsewhere. On 12 May 1650 he may have been visiting the congregational church at Stepney, Middlesex: the church records note that 'Mr Eaton being heere was desired to speake' on a matter of discipline. He drew pay as a chaplain to Cromwell's regiment of foot in Scotland from May 1650 to October 1651. In Eaton's absence from Dukinfield, Martindale recorded, preaching was provided by 'gifted persons, whereof the best was many degrees below him'. Divisions ensued, which he found hard to control after Taylor's departure. By late 1651 part of the church, led by Eaton, had moved to Stockport. In the 1650s Eaton refuted the Arian views of his successor at Chester, John Knowles (*ODNB*): copies of his tract against Knowles, *The mystery of God incarnate*, were printed with a special title page to be sold by Hezekiah Usher* in Boston, Massachusetts. Eaton also wrote against the Quakers. In 1654 Eaton was appointed an assistant to the Cheshire commissioners for removing unsuitable parish ministers. He supported the appointment of Henry Newcome (*ODNB*) as a preacher at the collegiate church, Manchester. Eaton signed an agreement with presbyterian ministers in Manchester, 1659. He held no parish living, but accepted state augmentation of his stipend.[7]

After 1660, Eaton attended John Angier's parish church at Denton with some of his former congregation (Angier had in the 1640s commended Eaton and Taylor as 'pious men, good scholars, and excellent preachers'). He died at Bredbury, Cheshire, on 9 January 1664/5, and was buried at Denton. Eaton had asked Oliver Heywood to preach his funeral sermon, and supplied Job 19:25–7 as the text. He had also given Heywood an address to read, a final word to his church: 'Some of you to whom I have preached and with whom I have walked have greatly distressed my heart, with your errors in doctrine and disorderly walking, your scandals and divisions. Some of you have returned me evil for good.'[8]

Publications *A defence of sundry positions, and Scriptures alledged to justifie the Congregationall-way* (1645); *The defence of sundry positions & scriptures for the Congregational-way justified* (1646); *A just apologie for the church of Duckenfeild in Cheshire* (1647); *A friendly debate on a weighty subject: or, a conference by writing betwixt Mr Samuel Eaton and Mr John Knowles concerning the divinity of Iesus Christ* ([1650]); *The mystery of God incarnate* (1650); *The oath of allegiance and the national covenant proved to be non-obliging* (1650); *A vindication . . . to prove the divinity of Jesus Christ* (1651); *The Quakers confuted* (1654). Eaton helped to publish *Several works of John Murcot* (1657), to which he contributed an 'epistle to the Christian reader'.

[1] I.M. Calder, *The New Haven Colony* (New Haven, CT: Yale University Press, 1934), 29, 78–9, 106, 139; G.F. Nuttall, *Visible saints: the congregational way, 1640–1660* (Oxford: Blackwell, 1957), 29–32; A. Gordon, *Historical account of Dukinfield chapel* (Manchester: Cartwright & Rattray 1896), 9–23; R.C. Richardson, *Puritanism in north-west England: a regional study of the diocese of Chester to 1642* (Manchester: Manchester University Press, 1972), 40; Samuel Eaton and Timothy Taylor, *The defence . . . justified* (1646), 41.

[2] *WJ*, 223n., 251; *NEHGR* 3: 153; Dorothy Deming, *The settlement of the Connecticut towns* (New Haven, CT: Yale University Press, 1933), 30; Eaton and Taylor, *The defence . . . justified*, 41–2.

[3] Eaton and Taylor, *The defence . . . justified*, 41; John Taylor, *The Brownists conventicle* (1641), 3 (misprinted 5); Bodleian, MS Tanner 65, fols 214r–214v; Sir Thomas Aston, *A remonstrance against presbitery* (n.p., 1641), 5–6; *CSPD, 1641–3*, 77.

[4] Edwards, *Gangraena*, iii. 67–8, 164–5; Samuel Eaton and Timothy Taylor, *A just apologie for the church at Duckenfield* (1647), 15–18; Joel Halcomb, 'A social history of congregational religious practice during the Puritan Revolution' (PhD dissertation, University of Cambridge, 2009), 35, 43.

[5] Ann Hughes, *Gangraena and the struggle for the English Revolution* (Oxford: Oxford University Press, 2004), 208n., and for more on Eaton, 123, 149–50, 213, 250–1, 267, 310, 325, 370, 403; *Pilgrims*, 48; *A defence of sundry positions* (1645), 2; Eaton and Taylor, *The defence . . . justified*, 20-1; *The life of Adam Martindale*, ed. R. Parkinson, Chetham Society, Old Series, IV (Manchester: Chetham Society, 1845, reprint Manchester: Chetham Society, 2001), 74.

[6] St J.D. Seymour, *The puritans in Ireland, 1647–1661* (Oxford: Clarendon Press, 1921), 57 and *passim*; *The autobiography of Henry Newcome*, ed. R. Parkinson, Chetham Society, Old Series, XXVI–XXVII (Manchester, 1852), 55; *Several works of Mr John Murcot* (1657); T.C. Barnard, *Cromwellian Ireland: English government*

and reform in Ireland 1649–1660 (Oxford: Oxford University Press, 1975), 139–40; Halcomb, 'Social history', 51.

[7] Eaton, *Mystery of God incarnate* (1650), 'Epistle to the Church at Chester', sig. A3; *Life of . . . Martindale*, 74, 110; Halcomb, 'Social history', 127 (citing Stepney CB, fol. 192r); Anne Laurence, *Parliamentary army chaplains, 1642-1651* (Woodbridge, Suffolk: Royal Historical Society, 1990), 123–4; *Autobiography of . . . Newcome*, 35–6; Eaton, *Quakers confuted*, title-page; Eaton, *Mystery of God incarnate* (*ESTC* R174842), Houghton Library, Harvard University; Nuttall, *Visible Saints*, 123, 122; *Autobiography of . . . Newcome*, 373; *Life of . . . Martindale*, 128; W.A. Shaw, *A history of the English Church . . . 1640–1660* (London: Longmans & Green, 1900), II, 585.

[8] *Life of . . . Martindale*, 64; [Oliver Heywood], *The whole works of the Rev. Oliver Heywood*, V (1826), 509–16.

BDBR, CR, ODNB, *Pilgrims*, 138–9, Plate 8, and *passim*.

EDWARDS, Nathaniel

Nathaniel Edwards was appointed with his brother Thomas Edwards* to oversee the New England estate of Nathaniel Smith*. He came to New England alone to present Smith's will, in September 1651. He asked for the legal proceedings to be concluded quickly, 'having urgent reasons to hasten his return to England'. He had probably lived in the colony earlier.

Essex Probate Recs. I, 134–6; *Essex Court Recs.* I, 233.

EDWARDS, Thomas and Elizabeth

Thomas Edwards, a shoemaker, was admitted as an inhabitant of Salem on 12 July 1637. He became a church member on 26 February 1642/3 and a freeman two days later. The town granted him a sixty-acre farm in 1644. His wife Elizabeth is probably the 'Edwards' (listed between two other women with the name Elizabeth) admitted to the Salem church on 2 June 1639 and later marked in the church records as 'removed'. 'Jon' and Joseph, sons of 'Sister Edwards', were baptised on 6 June 1639 and 22 May 1642; Joshua, 'son of Bro. Edwards', on 18 June 1643.

Thomas left for England before Elizabeth, probably around the time of his last appearance in the town records, 28 December 1646. On 9 July 1649, Elizabeth sold land by virtue of a letter of attorney. This transaction was recorded on 14 November, by which time Elizabeth had left or was leaving. On 19 March 1649/50 she was admitted to the congregational church at Yarmouth, Norfolk, 'by dismission from the Church of Christ in Salem in New England'.

Thomas Edwards was nominated, with his brother Nathaniel*, to administer the estate of Nathaniel Smith* in New England: Nathaniel Edwards came over in 1651 to do this, without Thomas.

Salem TR, 51, 135–6, 146; Salem CR, 8, 11, 17, 19; Essex Deeds I, fol. 14; Yarmouth CB, 19 March, 1649/50; *Essex Probate Recs.* I, 134–6; *Essex Court Recs.* I, 233.

EELES, John

John Eeles [Eells, Eyles, Iles] emigrated in 1633 and settled at Dorchester, Massachusetts. He must have been admitted to the church before 14 May 1634, when he became a freeman. Eeles moved to Windsor, Connecticut, and joined the church there. He came back to Dorchester for the baptism of his son Samuel, who was baptised there 'by communion of churches' in May 1640. Eeles sold houses and land in Dorchester in October 1640.

Eeles and his family seem to have left for England in 1641, and went to Devon. On 8 July 1641 Eeles had bought a house and garden on Bowport [Boutport] Street in Barnstaple, Devon, from Thomas Allen of Barnstable in New England. Allen gave Eeles power of attorney to collect debts for him in England, which suggests Eeles was about to sail home. John Eeles's son Samuel returned to live in New England in the 1660s.

GMB 618–20.

EVANCE, John and Susanna

John Evance, a London merchant, married Anna [Susanna] Yong at St Stephen's, Coleman Street, in 1624. John and Susanna Evance settled in New Haven in 1639. The shipmaster Joseph Alsop testified in 1644 that he had found Evance hard to work for: he had 'sailed for John Evance for two years, & it was long ere he could get him to account'.

John Evance left New Haven by 1655 to pursue his career as a London merchant. He was probably already there by 17 October 1653, when Susanna acted for him in New England in his absence. In March 1654/5 John Davenport reported that 'Mrs Evance' had received news from England, and she probably returned to London herself soon after that. Governor Theophilus Eaton mentioned in his will that John Evance was in England. Evance made a will on 13 December 1660 (proved on 2 May 1661) which named his wife Susanna and sons Daniel, John, Thomas and Stephen. Susanna Evance [Evanse] married the naval official and politician Henry Hatsell (*ODNB*) at St Leonard's Eastcheap, London, on 17 June 1661, and retired with him to Saltram House, Plympton St Mary, Devon, until Hatsell's death in 1667.

Davenport Letters, 102, 216n.; MHS, Misc. Bd. MSS, 17 October 1653; I.M. Calder, *The New Haven Colony* (New Haven, CT: Yale University Press, 1934), 74, 162, 209; *GM* 1: 48; *GD*; NA, PROB 11/304/221, will of John Evance, merchant of St Mary Aldermanbury, City of London, 2 May 1661; Stephen K. Roberts, 'Hatsell, Henry (d. 1667)', *ODNB*.

EYTON, Sampson

Sampson Eyton was a student at Harvard, but did not graduate. No formal record of his attendance survives. He was there in 1650.

In 1651 Samuel Mather*, reporting on the activities of former Harvard students in England, wrote that Eyton was a fellow of a college. Eyton graduated MA at Oxford in 1652, and became a fellow of University College. In 1658 he was admitted to Gray's Inn.

MHS, Misc. Bd. MSS, 26 March 1651, Samuel Mather to Jonathan Mitchell; W.L. Sachse, 'Harvard men in England 1642–1714', Colonial Society of Massachusetts, *Publications*, 35 (1942–6), 124; *Al. Oxon.*

F

FAIRFIELD, Daniel

Daniel Fairfield settled at Salem, Massachusetts, in 1639. In 1641 he was alleged to have abused John Humfrey's* daughters Dorcas and Sarah, 'especially upon the Lord's days and lecture days'. Fairfield was convicted in 1642, along with two other men who had abused Humfrey's elder daughter, Dorcas. In March 1643/4 the authorities permitted Fairfield to work in Boston and Roxbury, provided he did not go more than five miles from the meeting house, and wore 'an hempen roape about his necke'. His wife Elizabeth petitioned unsuccessfully, on 6 May 1646, for his release from wearing the rope round his neck. She was eventually successful in May 1652.

On 14 October 1652 Daniel Fairfield gained permission to return to England, 'provided if he come agayne he shall forthwith returne to the same condition agayn as now he is in, and be committed forthwith to prison'.

GD; *WJ*, 370–4; *Mass. Recs.* 3: 67, 161, 273–4, 421; Darrett Rutman, *Winthrop's Boston: portrait of a puritan town, 1630–1649* (New York: Norton, 1965), 242.

FARNWORTH, Joseph (d. by 1677)

Joseph Farnworth [Farneworth, Farnsworth] was the son of Joseph and Elizabeth Farnworth of Dorchester, Massachusetts. His parents were early members of the church there. His father was admitted a freeman on 14 March 1638/9. Joseph became a freeman of Massachusetts on 2 May 1649, and so must have been a church member, but there is no record of this at Dorchester. He entered the Harvard class of 1655.

Farnworth left for England without completing his degree at Harvard. He was admitted as rector of South Hanningfield, Essex, on 4 April 1655, presented by Hugh Peter*. He brought certificates from John Williamson of Wapping, Thomas French and William Penry. In 1659/60, in New England, his father left Joseph a remembrance of 20 shillings in 1659/60, 'to be payd when lawfully demanded'; he had already given him 'a Considerable estate, more than a double portion'.

At the Restoration, in 1660, the sequestered rector was restored to South Hanningfield. Farnworth was licensed (as a presbyterian) at his house in Wapping, Middlesex, in 1672. He died in or near London before 7 August 1677, when William Hooke* included his name in a list of nonconformist ministers who had recently died. Richard Baxter later wrote that Farnworth had seen a human sacrifice made to the devil by 'savages' in America. Baxter added that Farnworth, 'being a Nonconformist, and extream poor, dyed, as all about him said, of meer Poverty, for want of warm Cloaths, Fire, and Food, when the Act of Uniformity had begger'd many into extream necessity'.

Dorchester CR, 3; *NEHGR* 3: 96, 191; *Harvard Recs.* III, 105n.; LPL, MS COMM. III/4, fol. 12; *NEHGR* 9: 140–1; 4 *MHSC* 8: 583; Richard Baxter, *The certainty of the worlds of spirits* (1691), 107.

CR.

FENWICK, George (c.1603–1657)

George Fenwick, the son of George and Dorothy Fenwick of Brinkburn, Northumberland, matriculated at Queens' College, Cambridge in 1619 and was called in 1631 to the bar at Gray's Inn, London. Fenwick took an active role in plans to colonise land along the Connecticut River. With other patentees – William Fiennes, first Viscount Saye and Sele, Sir Arthur Hesilrige, Henry Lawrence, Henry Darley and Sir Richard Saltonstall* – Fenwick signed an agreement on 7 July 1635 which made John Winthrop Jr* their agent.[1]

Fenwick arrived in Boston in May 1636 and in July took part with Hugh Peter* in an expedition to the river towns of Connecticut. In June, John Winthrop had written to warn his son of their impending visit, adding 'The gentlemen seeme to be discouraged in their designe heere'. Fenwick knew, from information Sir Henry Vane Jr* had given him, that he would meet discontented settlers. On this occasion, in 1636, Fenwick was only in New England for about six months. He returned to England late that year.[2]

In 1639, Fenwick travelled over to New England again, with Henry Whitfield's* company. This time he brought his wife Alice (daughter of Sir Edward Apsley and widow of Sir John Boteler), his sister Mary Fenwick* and his daughters Elizabeth* and Dorothy*. He intended to settle at Saybrook (named for his fellow patentees) and to succeed John Winthrop Jr as their agent. If Fenwick had high hopes for the venture, they did not last long. On 6 July 1640, Fenwick complained that 'my disappointments have bene so great that I have bene and am lik to be more straitned for moneyes this yeare then in that litle tyme I have lived I have ever bene'. On 5 December 1644 he sold the Saybrook fort and other land along the Connecticut River to the colony of Connecticut. He promised to sell more land if he could (since by then it was apparent the other patentees would not join him), but failed to live up to the promise. As a consequence, in 1657 Connecticut refused Fenwick's heirs possession of his estate in New England until £500 compensation had been paid.[3]

Fenwick returned to England for good soon after 25 December 1644, although his original intention was perhaps only a short visit. Taking advantage of Fenwick's journey, Herbert Pelham* appointed him as his attorney for family business back home, with Godfrey Bosvile (*BDBR*) and Henry Pelham. Soon after Fenwick left, his wife Alice died and was buried within Saybrook fort.

Back in England, Fenwick was persuaded to stand for parliament, and on 20 October 1645 became MP for Morpeth, a seat associated with Sir Arthur

Hesilrige. On 29 June 1646 Thomas Peter*, minister at Saybrook, wrote that many there 'fear Mr Fenwicke will not come more'. Fenwick had by this time asked his sister Mary to follow him to England with his children. Writing to Winthrop about the Remonstrants' petition (see Robert Child*, Thomas Fowle*), and the complaint of Samuel Gorton* that he and his adherents should be allowed to live at Shawomet without interference, Fenwick thought the best service for New England in England would be 'to keep off what we can, the [parliamentary] Comittees intermedling with your affaires ther'; but he warned Winthrop that limiting the franchise to church members looked strange in England, and suggested moderation, 'for what euer yow doe that may have the least shaddow of severitie is hightened hear'. Fenwick served on the earl of Warwick's commission for English plantations in America, and endorsed the ruling in 1646 that Samuel Gorton and his followers should occupy Shawomet.

In 1647 he accompanied Sir Arthur Hesilrige, by then governor of Newcastle, to the north. This move shaped the rest of Fenwick's career. During the Second Civil War he commanded the Northumberland horse. In 1648, he became governor of Berwick, initially as deputy to Hesilrige. He married Hesilrige's daughter Catherine, and his own daughter Elizabeth married Hesilrige's son Thomas. John Winthrop reported, 3 February 1648/9, that 'Colonell Geo: Fenwick of Saybrook' had been made deputy governor of Tynemouth Castle. He was named a commissioner for the trial of the Charles I, but remained in the north. Fenwick's regiment of foot joined Cromwell's invasion of Scotland, with Thomas Reade* as one of his lieutenant-colonels. Fenwick became governor of Edinburgh Castle and Leith in December 1650, and a commissioner for Scotland, 23 October 1651, with (among others) Sir Henry Vane Jr. He mediated between 'Resolutioner' and 'Protester' factions in the Scottish church, and worked with Samuel Desborough* and Richard Saltonstall* as a visitor to the Scottish universities. He was elected MP for Berwick in 1654 and 1656, but was excluded from the Second Protectorate Parliament of 1656 before it met: like Hesilrige (whose exclusion was more prominent), Fenwick seems to have been a 'commonwealthman' who opposed the Protectorate.

Fenwick died on 15 March 1656/7. In a will made on 2 February 1656/7 (proved on 27 April) he made bequests to his wife Catherine and to his daughters Elizabeth and Dorothy: these included 'suites of Hangings' on subjects such as Caesar and Diana. In a codicil added on 9 March 1656/7, describing himself as of 'Worminghurst' [Warminghurst], Sussex', he left £500 'to the Publique use of that Countrie of New England, if my loveing friend Mr Edward Hopkins thinck it fitt', to be employed exactly as Hopkins* 'shall order and direct'. In fact, Hopkins died a few days before Fenwick, which thwarted the terms of Fenwick's bequest.

George Fenwick is remembered in Berwick parish church – a building started during his tenure as governor of the town – with a monument that reads 'a good man is a publick good'.[4]

[1] Robert C. Black, *The younger John Winthrop* (New York and London: Columbia University Press, 1966), 85–8, 96; *WP* III, 198–9.

² *WP* III, 261–2, 268, 281–3.
³ *WP* III, 319–20; *WP* IV, 261; *Davenport Letters*, 75–6; *WJ*, 299, 630n.; Dorothy Deming, *The settlement of the Connecticut towns* (New Haven, CT: Yale University Press, 1933), 15, 20.
⁴ *WP* V, 86, 89, 142, 312; *WJ*, 638–40, 701–4; C.H. Firth and G. Davies, *The regimental history of Cromwell's army* (Oxford: Clarendon Press, 1940), 387–92; Frances D. Dow, *Cromwellian Scotland 1651–1660* (Edinburgh: John Donald, 1979), 32, 39, 58, 60; Patrick Little and David L. Smith, *Parliaments and politics during the Cromwellian Protectorate* (Cambridge: Cambridge University Press, 2007), 90, 303; Waters, 41; NA, PROB 11/263/436, will of George Fenwick of Warminghurst, Sussex, 27 April 1657.

ANB, BDBR, ODNB.

FENWICK, Mary, Elizabeth and Dorothy

Mary Fenwick was the sister of George Fenwick*; Elizabeth and Dorothy were his daughters. They came to New England with him in 1639 and settled at Saybrook, along with Fenwick's wife Alice, who died there in 1645.

On 29 June 1646 Thomas Peter* reported 'Mrs. Mary and the child[ren] are likely to be gon for England'. In a letter to John Winthrop Jr*, 6 July 1646, Mary acknowledged that her brother had sent 'his commands of my presence with him in the land of our nativity'. They were still in Saybrook on 3 September 1646, but by November had reached Salem, probably on their way to England.

Elizabeth Fenwick married Thomas Hesilrige, son of Sir Arthur Heslirige; her father married Thomas's sister, Catherine Hesilrige, *c.*1648. In a codicil to his will, 9 March 1656/7, George Fenwick revoked all his earlier bequests to his daughter Dorothy and placed her in the care of 'my much honoured friend Dame Elinor Selby of Barwick [Berwick]'.

WP V, 86, 89–90, 101, 119; *BDBR s.n.* George Fenwick; NA, PROB 11/263/436, will of George Fenwick of Warminghurst, Sussex, 27 April 1657.

FIRMIN, Giles (1614–1697)

Giles Firmin was born in Ipswich, Suffolk, and grew up in Sudbury. His father, Giles Firmin, was an apothecary. His mother, Martha, was related to John Winthrop by marriage. Firmin entered Emmanuel College, Cambridge, in 1629. He attributed his conversion to John Rogers, minister at Dedham in Essex.

Firmin initially emigrated to Boston in 1632, and was admitted to the church shortly after its first gathering, by 11 October 1632. His father followed him over, was admitted to the church before 8 September 1633. His father died in 1634.

Giles Firmin had returned to England by 10 October 1633, perhaps to study medicine. During the 1630s, and earlier in his childhood, Firmin encountered antinomian ideas through his relative Henry Firmin of Ipswich.[1]

Firmin came back to New England in June 1637. In November that year, he took notes at the trial of the antinomian Anne Hutchinson in Boston, to whom he was not sympathetic. Before long, Firmin moved to Ipswich, Massachusetts: on 4 January 1638/9 he was granted land if he remained three years. On 25 February 1643/4, the Boston church granted him letters of dismission to Ipswich, 'where he hath long inhabited'. He became a freeman on 22 May 1639, and that same year married Susan, daughter of Nathaniel Ward*. Firmin made his living in part by practising physic, but was frustrated with his fortunes. On 26 December 1639 he wrote to John Winthrop asking permission to gather a new plantation with his brother-in-law John Ward and others. He complained the land he had been given was inconveniently placed and had too many conditions attached. Firmin declared 'I am strongly sett upon to studye Divinitie. My studyes else must bee lost: for Physick is but a mean helpe.' On 12 February 1639/40 he wrote again to Winthrop and admitted he had:

> heard a Conclusion gathered against these Plantations, because the Lord hath so sadly afflicted the founders of them in their estates; that therefore it was not a way of God, to forsake our Countrye ... so long as wee might haue enioyed God in any comfortable measure in the place whence wee came, alledginge that it is scarcely knowne that any church in a way of Separation as wee are did euer yet thriue in grace.

His brother-in-law John Ward already had 'diuers enticements ... to returne to England' but – as Ward's wife was utterly against this – was willing to stay, 'iff he might but haue any employment to stay still'. Although Winthrop dissuaded Firmin from moving at this point, his father-in-law Nathaniel Ward agitated for a new settlement at 'Pentukett' (Haverhill, Massachusetts), where John Ward became minister in 1645.[2]

Firmin set sail for England in 1644, probably on the *Sea Fort*, which left on 23 November. He may have intended to stay in England for a short time, as a physician in the civil war: a fellow passenger, the physician Abraham Pratt*, was sailing home for that reason. Firmin's family remained behind, in New England. The *Sea Fort* was shipwrecked off Spain in December 1644. Firmin's daughter cried out that night, moving the family to pray for his safety. Later, Firmin wrote of 'shipwrack, about one of the clock in the night ... the Ship was breaking on the Rocks; there was a dreadful shout amongst some of the Seamen, "I shall be in Hell before the morning"; but yet could be drunk within three dayes after God spared them'. He also recounted fears of being captured by the Turks, and sights he had seen in Spain.[3]

Firmin wrote to Governor John Winthrop from Colchester, 1 July 1646:

> it is not a cleare day in England ... Providence hath placed me in one of the worst places in the kingdom for opinions: full Crosse to my owne spirits and resolutions, but I saw such a hand of God in it the people pressing so urgently upon mee, that I could not tell how to deny them; else I hope I had been in N. England againe before this time ...

He had perhaps already been there a year: a Colchester correspondent of Thomas Edwards reported in August 1645 that an Independent 'of New-England, one Mr F. a Stranger in this Town' had given a sermon; 'an Apothecary Physitian... who is not in Orders, nor ever Preached, as he confesseth, but on Shipboard as he came over'. Edwards wrote of 'Mr Furman' later as one of the Independent ministers who had started to preach lately, 'as much to bare walls and pewes' as any presbyterian. The opinions Edwards stated the Colchester preacher held tally with important themes in Firmin's publications: a defence of New England and its congregationalism, combined with a desire for peace between presbyterians and Independents. His letter to Winthrop, with its dislike of radicalism, prefigures another concern in his writings: he wished Hugh Peter* would not so countenance 'the Opinionists, which wee did so cast out in N. England'.

Firmin's wife and children came to England late in 1646, with Nathaniel Ward. Firmin became vicar of Shalford, Essex, probably in 1648, and was there when Charles I died. In 1650 he was said to hold the living 'by order of the Committee of Plundered Ministers' (it was not a sequestration, but came to the committee when the Chapter of Bath and Wells was dissolved). Firmin delayed his ordination because he wanted presbyterian ordination by laying on of hands, which the Essex congregationalists refused to countenance. Eventually, Daniel Rogers (*ODNB*), Stephen Marshall (*ODNB*) and Nathaniel Ranew (*CR*), with two other ministers, ordained him. In 1657, Firmin became an assistant to the Essex commissioners for removing unsuitable parish ministers. At Shalford, Firmin implemented as much of the 'New England Way' as he felt he could in a parish context. He was not a dogmatic practitioner of congregationalism. He admired Richard Baxter and promoted the Essex Voluntary Association, modelled on Baxter's example in Worcestershire.

At the Restoration, Firmin left Shalford. His successor as vicar was instituted on 15 March 1662/3. Firmin would not conform, although his children urged him to do so. (Firmin's sons Giles and Nathaniel went to Cambridge: Giles was later ordained in the Church of England; Nathaniel became a physician.) He retired to Ridgewell, Essex, perhaps when the Five Mile Act came into effect in 1665. He supported himself by practising medicine. He preached at conventicles (private meetings) for three Sundays a month and attended the parish church on the fourth. He was licensed as a presbyterian at Ridgewell in 1672. He conducted a lively if intermittent correspondence with Richard Baxter, 1654–71.[2]

Publications *A serious question stated* ([1651]); *Separation examined* (1652); *A sober reply to the sober answer of Reverend Mr Cawdrey* (1653); *Stablishing against shaking* (1656); *Of schism* (1658); *Tythes vindicated* (1659); *Presbyterial ordination vindicated* (1660); *The liturgical considerator considered* (1661); *The real Christian* (1670); *Meditations upon Mr Baxter's review* (1672); *The questions between the conformist and nonconformist, truly stated* (1681); *The plea of the children of believing-parents* (1683); *Scripture-warrant sufficient proof for infant-baptism* (1688); *The answer of Giles Firmin* (1689); *Some remarks upon the anabaptist answer* ([1692]);

Panergia: a brief review of Mr Davis's vindication (1693); *Weighty questions discussed* (1692).

---

[1] *GMB* 673–5; *Boston CR*, 15, 16; David Como, *Blown by the spirit: puritanism and the emergence of an antinomian underground in pre-Civil-War England* (Stanford, CA: Stanford University Press, 2004), 326–30, discusses Firmin's experience of antinomianism in England.
[2] Firmin, *Separation examined*, 102; *WP* IV, 163–4, 191–2; *Boston CR*, 41; *NEHGR* 3: 96; *Mass. Recs.* 1: 290; *WJ*, 432, 541.
[3] *WJ* 598–9; J.W. Dean, *A brief memoir of Giles Firmin* (Boston, MA: David Clapp & Sons, 1866), 9; Edmund Calamy, *The nonconformist's memorial* (1775), I, 518; Firmin, *Real Christian*, 31–2, 79, 181.
[3] *WP* V, 88–9; Edwards, *Gangraena*, i. 68–9, ii. 63 (Firmin responded to Edwards in *Separation examined*, 'Epistle to Reader'); Firmin, *Weighty questions discussed*, 'The Prediction of Mr Daniel Rogers ... concerning King Charles the First'; Susan Hardman Moore, 'Arguing for peace: Giles Firmin on New England and godly unity', in R.N. Swanson, ed., *Unity and Diversity in the Church*, Studies in Church History, 32 (Oxford: Blackwell, 1996), 251–61; *Pilgrims* 135–7, 140–1 and *passim*. Firmin's son Giles may have been vicar of Little Waldingfield, Suffolk, 1679–87 (*CCEd* Person ID 124959) and perhaps the Giles Firmin, clerk of Ovington, Essex, whose will was proved on 8 March 1725 (NA, PROB 11/602/139). Correspondence between Firmin and Baxter, in chronological order: DWL Baxter Letters, 4/284; 3/104, 108, 106, 280; 4/206; 5/152, 154–5; summarised in N.H. Keeble and Geoffrey F. Nuttall, eds, *Calendar of the correspondence of Richard Baxter*, 2 vols (Oxford: Clarendon Press, 1991), letters 192, 300, 306, 311, 660, 850, 852.

CR, ODNB.

FLETCHER, Edward and Mary

Edward Fletcher, a cutler, was admitted an inhabitant of Boston on 24 February 1639/40; he became a church member on 18 July and a freeman of Massachusetts on 12 October. He joined the Artillery Company in 1643. Mary Fletcher became a church member on 8 October 1642. Edward Fletcher sold a house, land and shop in Boston on 9 September 1654. He and Mary probably left for England soon afterwards.

Fletcher's whereabouts for a while are unclear. On 4 May 1657 he was admitted rector of Bagendon, Gloucestershire. He brought certificates from Gloucestershire ministers: William Beale of Stow in the Wold (*CR*), Anthony Palmer of Bourton on the Water (*CR*), James Forbes of Gloucester (*CR*), William Tray of Oddington (*CR*), Thomas Jennings of Brimpsfield (*CR*). Fletcher complained to the council of state on 18 November 1658 that his possession of the 'meeting house' at Bagendon had been obstructed by Samuel Broad, the ejected minister of Rendcombe, and others. Fletcher was known as a congregationalist.

At the Restoration, Fletcher had a turbulent time. Early in 1660, 'the most eminent Cavaliers' in the county were said to have ransacked his house looking for arms, along with the houses of other pastors, church members, and officers who had served the Rump Parliament. Fletcher's harassment by those who wanted him ejected from Bagendon was recorded by Henry Jessey, in *The Lord's loud call to England*. Fletcher made a will on 20 February 1659/60 which provided for a nonconformist future. His wife Mary was to keep Fletcher's tenement in Gloucester, 'neere the Little Cloisters within the precincts of Colledge', in repair for use by James Forbes and his flock, who were to have use of the 'great Hall . . . for the worship of God only', at a rent of 40 shillings a year; after Mary's death, Fletcher's sister was to allow Forbes to use the hall free of charge; after his sister's death, Fletcher wanted Forbes and others to use any profits from the property for 'godly poore and needy people'. Fletcher's successor at Bagendon was installed on 16 August 1661.

It has been suggested Fletcher returned to New England, but the evidence is not clear. Mary Fletcher returned to Boston at some point before 1666. An inventory of 'the goods and estate of Edward Fletcher, lately deceased, in Boston' was presented on 31 December 1666; on 12 February 1666/7 Mary presented Edward's will and was permitted to administer his estate.

Thwing; *Boston CR*, 30; *NEHGR* 3: 188; *Artillery Company*, 130; *Suffolk Deeds* III, 120; *GD*; LPL, MS COMM III/7, fol. 17; Henry Jessey, *The Lord's loud call to England* (1660), 17–24; *NEHGR* 16: 231–3. Edward Fletcher is sometimes confused with William Fletcher, minister at Oyster River: D.G. Allen, *In English ways* (Chapel Hill, NC: University of North Carolina Press, 1981), 14. For Samuel Broad, *WR*, 172.

CR.

FLOYD, Richard

Richard Floyd [Lloyd] may have been in Boston in 1642. He joined the Corporation for the Propagation of the Gospel in New England at its foundation on 27 July 1649. Other members included Herbert Pelham*, Richard Hutchinson (uncle of Richard Hutchinson*), Robert Tomson* and Edward Winslow*. Floyd lived in Cheapside, London. He was a kinsman of John, Lord Bradshaw (*ODNB*), and held an office associated with the council of state.

Thomas Hutchinson, *The history of Massachusetts from . . . 1628 until 1750* (Salem, MA: Thomas Cushing, 1795), I, 154; *GD*; Bodleian, Rawlinson MS D. 934, fols 1v, 3; G.E. Aylmer, *The state's servants: the civil service of the English Republic, 1649–1660* (London: Routledge and Kegan Paul, 1973), 135–6.

FOGG, Ralph (*c.*1600–1674)

Ralph Fogg of London, a skinner, arrived in New England in 1633 with his wife Susanna (a niece of Thomas and Katherine Barnardiston of Suffolk) and his young son John. Fogg initially settled at Plymouth, but moved to Salem in 1634. He became a church member before 3 September 1634, when he was admitted a freeman of Massachusetts. He was Salem's town clerk from 1636 until 1647. In 1647 he was presented at the Essex Quarterly Court for 'speaking falsely and dealing corruptly in his place'.

Fogg was in England from late 1647, after this scandal broke around him, but returned to New England in 1649. After his return he made further court appearances. In February 1649/50, the court ordered Fogg, for lying to the church and slandering the governor, to make a public confession or (if he refused) to stand at the whipping post for 'half an hour after lecture with a paper in his hat' on which his offence would be written in capital letters. On 1 May 1652, the Massachusetts General Court turned down Fogg's petition to open an 'office of addresses', to facilitate communication between employers and servants, buyers and sellers.

Fogg returned to England permanently in 1652. The Salem church records marked his wife Susanna as 'removed'. Fogg had ties in London with the colonial trader John Pocock and with Richard Gibbs, a refiner of Foster Lane. He was described as 'Ralph Fogg, skinner of London' in March 1656, when he bought land from Thomas Venner* and assigned it to John Lowle of Boston. Fogg died at Plymouth, Devon, in 1674. His sons John, Ezekiel and David were in Boston at that point, but Ezekiel had been a 'citizen and skinner of London', and John was later at Barnstaple, Devon.

C.E. Banks, *Planters of the Commonwealth* (Boston, MA: Houghton Mifflin, 1930), 207; C.H. Pope, *Pioneers of Massachusetts* (Boston, MA: C.H. Pope, 1900), 171; Lechford *NB*, 335; *Salem CR*, 5, 6; *NEHGR* 3: 93; Aspinwall, 15, 93, 270–1; *Suffolk Deeds* II, 302, 312; *GD*; Waters 742; *GMB* 682–6.

FORRETT, James

James Forrett acted as an agent for William Alexander, first earl of Stirling (*ODNB*), whose vast ambitions for the settlement of 'New Scotland' (Nova Scotia) had come to nothing in the 1620s. Forrett was at New Haven in 1640, when the earl died. Forrett was left without funds or supplies. On 29 July 1641, to obtain money to return to Scotland, he mortgaged Long Island (on which the earl of Stirling had a patent) for £110. The loan was never repaid.

I.M. Calder, *The New Haven Colony* (New Haven, CT: Yale University Press, 1934), 59.

FOWLE, Thomas and Margaret

Thomas Fowle, a Boston merchant, traded in commodities such as 'dry Cod fish', furs and indigo, with counterparts in the ports of London, Barnstaple and Bristol. He was a business associate of Nehemiah Bourne*, Robert Harding*, Robert Sedgwick* and David Yale*. His brother-in-law and sometime 'factor & agent' in England was Vincent Potter*, the future regicide. Fowle's wife Margaret was admitted to the Boston church on 31 January 1640/1, and four of their children were baptised by virtue of her membership. Thomas Fowle joined the church on 25 March 1643/4. In 1645, with Emmanuel Downing*, Bourne and Sedgwick, he objected to the decision by the Massachusetts

General Court to expel anabaptists and place limits on strangers' residence in the colony. Fowle became a selectman but not a freeman. This was deliberate: in November 1646, the Massachusetts General Court observed that 'he likes better to be eased of that trouble and charge'. The previous May, Fowle had signed the Remonstrants' petition with Robert Child*, Samuel Maverick, David Yale, Thomas Burton, John Dand and John Smith: this called for fewer restrictions on becoming church members and freeman. Fowle was the only Remonstrant known to be a church member, and therefore he is likely to be the petitioner Edward Winslow* identified as rejecting the petition's attack on church government in Massachusetts, 'resting and liking what was done there in that kind'. Winslow, who had been commissioned by the Massachusetts authorities to undermine the credibility of the Remonstrants, found four of the petitioners had 'no considerable interest amongst us', including Fowle, who signed 'at such a time when he was resolved to leave the Country'.

Thomas Fowle set sail for London on the *Supply*, 9 November 1646, with another agitator, William Vassall from Scituate in Plymouth Colony. A few days before the *Supply* left, John Cotton had warned at his Thursday lecture in Boston that any petition the ship's passengers carried against New England would be like the biblical prophet Jonah, whose presence meant shipwreck: better to throw the paper overboard than risk death at sea. According to Edward Winslow, the *Supply* encountered 'the terriblest passage that ever I heard of for extremity of weather'. Remembering Cotton's sermon, godly passengers calmed the storm by casting 'New England's Jonas' overboard: 'they cut it into pieces as they thought it deserved, and gave the said pieces to a seaman who cast them into the sea'. Winslow's opponents debunked this version of events: the weather had not been bad – 'in the winter season all passages from New England are tempestuous' – and what had been thrown overboard was not the original petition, just a copy.

John Winthrop observed that not long afterwards, when Robert Child drew up a petition for the attention of a parliamentary committee and included Fowle's name, Fowle 'protested against it, (for God had brought him very low, both in his estate and in his reputation, since he joined in the first petition)'. In October 1647, the Boston merchants Thomas Clerke, Edward Gibbons, Valentine Hill and David Yale appointed 'Thomas ffowle late of Boston gent', with Robert Harding, as their attorney in London to take legal action over the seizure of the ship *Adventure*. Winslow noted in *New-Englands salamander* that Fowle had sent for his wife and family. Fowle never returned to New England and disappears from view.

Aspinwall, 6, 8, 17, 19, 23, 29, 70–1 (Vincent Potter), 91 (power of attorney, 1647), 98, 170–1, 253; *Boston CR*, 38; *NEHGR* 2: 188; *GD*; *WP* V, 355; Bernard Bailyn, *The New England merchants in the seventeenth century* (Cambridge, MA: Harvard University Press, 1955), 87, 106–7; Edward Winslow, *New-Englands salamander* (1647), 3, 7, 14–20; Major John Child, *New-Englands Jonas cast up at London* (1647), 12–13 (irregular pagination); *WJ*, 545, 611n., 624–5, 655–7, 665–6, 705–6, 766; *GM* 4: 505; G.L. Kittredge, 'Dr. Robert Child the Remonstrant', Colonial Society of Massachusetts, *Publications*, 21 (1919), 17, 21, 23, 29–33, 35–6, 47, 50, 67; Robert Emmet Wall,

Massachusetts Bay: the crucial decade, 1640–1650 (New Haven, CT: Yale University Press, 1972), 157–224; *Pilgrims*, 67–8, 69.

FRANKLIN, William

William Franklin, a blacksmith, emigrated in 1634 from Southampton on the *Mary & John*. He settled at Boston and became a church member on 30 January 1641/2. The church cast him out on 26 December 1645 for 'rigorous and cruel correction to his servants, and for sundry lies in his being dealt with about it'. He was restored to fellowship in August 1646, only to be cast out again in October for extortion and deceit in his dealings with a Dutchman, 'Mr Jacob', over ironworks. This time his excommunication ended in June 1652. Franklin played a part in developing grist mills at Mill Creek with John Milam* and George Burden*.

Franklin may have made one or more journeys to England in the late 1640s or early 1650s – he was given letters of attorney, but might have fulfilled his obligations through substitutes. At some point after 1653 he went to England. He died in London before July 1658. His widow Phebe married a Boston merchant in 1660.

> C.E. Banks, *Planters of the Commonwealth* (Boston, MA: Houghton Mifflin, 1930), 111; D.G. Allen, *In English ways* (Chapel Hill, NC: University of North Carolina Press, 1981), 262; Thwing; Darrett Rutman, *Winthrop's Boston: portrait of a puritan town, 1630–1649* (New York: Norton, 1965), 94, 193–4; Aspinwall, 165; *Suffolk Deeds* I, 96, 105, 272, 297; *NEHGR* 9: 344; *GM* 2: 568–73.

FUGILL, Thomas

Thomas Fugill came from the East Riding of Yorkshire. In 1624, he had land at Kirk Ella near Rowley. In 1631 he served in Sir Richard Darley's household at Buttercrambe, while Thomas Shepard was chaplain. Shepard mentioned Fugill as one of three servants in Darley's household who were 'very careful of me, which somewhat refreshed me'. The household would have been familiar with talk of colonisation: in the 1630s, Henry Darley (*ODNB*), Sir Richard's eldest son, supported the Massachusetts Bay Company, the Providence Island Company and the Saybrook project. In 1637, Fugill's son was buried at Rowley, where Ezekiel Rogers (*ODNB*) was minister.

Fugill left for New England in 1638 with Ezekiel Rogers and other Yorkshire families. That autumn he went to 'Quinipiac' (New Haven) ahead of the main party, and stayed there when the majority decided instead to establish Rowley, Massachusetts. Fugill was one of the 'seven pillars' of the New Haven church at its foundation on 4 June 1639. He was chosen as one of four deputies to assist the magistrates (with Robert Newman*), and became public notary on 25 October 1639. However, soon Fugill's reputation was ruined. In 1645 he was found guilty of falsifying surveys and documents to increase his own landholdings. He was ejected from his post as notary and excommunicated from the church.

Fugill left New Haven and was back in northern England by 14 January 1647/8, when Thomas Harrison* wrote to John Winthrop. Harrison passed on news which had reached him in a letter from Fugill:

The face of the kingdome begins to smile, as stroked and demulced by the hand of peace: only one letter out of the North tells me of another black cloud rising there, 4500 Scots ready to enter the kingdome: But I suspect the melancholly frame of the relators spirit, one Fugill lately cast out of the Church at New-Haven, and I fear his spirit soe imbittered against the whole way and worke of Christ, that he cares not how many may be made like him, in his ruinous estate and condition.

I.M. Calder, *The New Haven Colony* (New Haven, CT: Yale University Press, 1934), 70, 84, 92, 107, 121; Michael McGiffert, ed., *God's plot: puritan spirituality in Thomas Shepard's Cambridge* (Amherst, MA: University of Massachusetts Press, 1994), 54–5; Karen Ordahl Kupperman, *Providence Island, 1630–1641: the other puritan colony* (Cambridge: Cambridge University Press, 1993), 333; *New Haven Recs.* I, 221–5, 260, 262–4; *WP* V, 198.

G

GARNESEY, Elizabeth

Elizabeth and William Garnesey lived at Bampton, Devon, in 1641. They came to York, Maine, in 1652, but William died soon after this. Elizabeth Garnesey went back to Pinhoe, Devon. In 1660 William Rogers was granted administration of her estate in New England.

C.E. Banks, *A history of York, Maine* (Boston, MA: Calkins Press, 1931), 222.

GIBBONS, Margaret

Margaret Gibbons was the wife of the Boston merchant Edward Gibbons, who made great losses in the fur trade in French Acadia. Edward Gibbons died on 9 December 1654. His widow returned to England and died not long afterwards, at Plymouth in Devon. Administration of her estate in New England was granted to her daughter Jerusha, wife of Thomas Rea, on 28 February 1656/7; Susanna Gibbons and Captain Samuel Scarlet later presented an inventory.

Darrett Rutman, *Winthrop's Boston: portrait of a puritan town, 1630–1649* (New York: Norton, 1965), 199; *NEHGR* 8: 275–6, 9: 346; 38: 426.

GIBSON, Richard and Mary

Richard Gibson graduated BA at Emmanuel College, Cambridge, in 1636. He emigrated to New England in 1637 or 1638, as minister to a fishing plantation owned by Robert Trelawney of Plymouth, Devon. He wrote to John Winthrop, 14 January 1638/9, describing himself as 'minister of the Gospell at Richmond Iland and Saco', asking Winthrop to procure testimonies from the shoemaker George Burden* and his wife Ann*. They had been fellow passengers with Gibson's new wife, Mary, daughter of Thomas Lewis of Saco, on the voyage to New England. To Gibson's dismay, it was rumoured that Mary had been so troublesome that 'the block was reaved at the mayne yard to have duckt her, and that she was kept close in the ships Cabin 48 houres'. Gibson also alluded to quarrels at Saco and mentioned the possibility of moving: 'I had not stayed here so long, but that I was sent here by a singular providence, upon engagement of time not yett expired, and for that it reigneth in my hart, that god hath here some worke for mee yett to do.' He soon went to Piscataqua and in 1642 was preaching to the fishermen at the Isles of Shoals, which fell within the jurisdiction of Massachusetts. According to John Winthrop, Gibson was 'wholly addicted to the hierarchy and discipline of England'. In opposition to

Thomas Larkham*, Gibson wrote an open letter which questioned the authority of the colony's government. For this he was committed to the marshall and eventually submitted to the court, 'whereupon, in regard that he was a stranger, and was to depart the country within a few days, he was discharged without any fine or other punishment'.

Gibson returned to England in 1642, with his wife. He may be the Richard Gibson, minister of St Botolph without Aldgate, London, whose wife was Mary.

GD; WP IV, 96–7; WJ, 392; NA, PROB 11/202/192, will of Richard Gibson, clerk of Saint Botolph without Aldgate, London, 23 November 1647.

GILBERT, Thomas

Thomas Gilbert was the son of John and Alice Gilbert of Bridgewater, Somerset. He emigrated with his father in 1635 on the *Hopewell*, from Weymouth in Dorset. The family settled at Dorchester, Massachusetts.

Thomas Gilbert visited England at least twice before he went back for good. He made a visit to England in 1636. This appears on the record as an incidental detail in a case against Thomas for drunkenness: it was agreed his brother John could appear in court in his place, 'for that he was to go to England presently, and not known to have been any [other] way disordered'. On his return from England, Thomas Gilbert followed his brother John to Taunton, in Plymouth Colony. He married Jane Rossiter of Dorchester at Taunton in March 1639/40, and became a freeman of Plymouth Colony in 1643. His half-sister Mary Gilbert married Nathaniel Norcrosse*. Thomas Gilbert sailed for England again, late in December 1649, possibly with Nathaniel and Mary Norcrosse. The timing is suggested by papers Gilbert was given around this time: on 1 November 1649, Edward Bendall* gave Gilbert a bill payable ten days after the arrival of John Allen's ship in London; on 28 December 1649 Bendall made Thomas Gilbert his attorney (with power to substitute) to collect a debt from Edward Skinner of Bristol, mariner. Gilbert was back in New England by 1651, when he served as a deputy to the Plymouth General Court. On 22 May 1651, Mary Longe testified that Thomas Gilbert and 'Capt. Poole' had enquired in England about her husband Joseph Longe*, without success.

Thomas Gilbert seems to have gone to England again in 1653, with his wife Jane, and this time did not return. Their daughter Jane stayed on in New England.

WJ, 751; GD; Aspinwall, 255, 269; MHS, Misc. MSS, 22 May 1651; NEHGR 4: 342n.; GM 3: 59.

GILL, Arthur

Arthur Gill of Dorchester, a 'shipcarpenter', became a freeman of Massachusetts on 2 June 1641. He was already a church member. He and his wife Anne moved to Boston by 27 November 1642, when they were admitted to the Boston church by dismission from Dorchester. Their son Thomas* was baptised there in 1644.

On 11 July 1646, Phillip Hinkson appointed Gill to take possession of an inheritance of a house and lands at 'Coskrum in the parish of Houlberton' (Holbeton), Devon, lately occupied by 'George Wadye'. Gill was commissioned to act without power of substitution: it seems he was about to go to England.

Gill was perhaps in England, or about to go again, on 25 July 1650, when William Aspinwall* certified that Gill and Benjamin Gillom were 'able Ship Carpenters', and that Francis Willoughby* (soon to become a naval commissioner in England) had been a Bay Colony magistrate. On 10 January 1654/5 John Sweete deposed an invoice of goods and debts left with him 'by Arthur Gill at his goeing for England'. Sweete rendered an account of Gill's estate in New England, as administrator, on 19 March 1656/7.

NEHGR 3: 189; *Boston CR*, 37, 297; *Aspinwall*, 23, 306; *NEHGR* 8: 356; 9: 228.

GILL, Thomas

Thomas Gill, the son of Anne and Arthur Gill*, was baptised at Boston on 20 October 1644. An account of his father's assets, presented on 19 March 1656/7, allowed for Thomas's 'dyett for above a yeare, for his passage to England'.

Boston CR, 297; *NEHGR* 9: 228.

GLOVER, John

John Glover was the youngest son of Jose [Joseph] and Elizabeth Glover, and the brother of Roger Glover*. He is likely to have been born at Sutton, Surrey, where his father was rector from 1628 to 1636.

Glover emigrated with his parents in 1638. His father – who shipped the first printing press to New England – died on the way over. Glover's mother and siblings settled at Cambridge, Massachusetts. Elizabeth Glover married Henry Dunster on 22 June 1641, and died on 23 August 1643. John Glover graduated BA at Harvard in 1650.

Glover went to England soon after graduation: the charges to Henry Dunster for his support ended late in October 1650. Nathaniel Mather* reported from London, 23 December 1650, 'Sir Glover is like yea more than like sure I think of a fellowship in Oxford worth about £140 per annum'. Within a few years Glover had established himself as a medical practitioner. Like his older brother Roger, he went to Scotland. He graduated MD from the University of Aberdeen on 15 May 1654. William Cutter* reported to Henry Dunster, 19 May 1654, 'your sone Mr John Glouer cald att our house as he went into Scotland to be ouer the hospitall with Coll Fenwicks Bro.' (Colonel George Fenwick*).

Glover's letters back to New England show he was caught up in acrimonious wrangling about inheritances from his grandmother and his father. On 5 March 1654/5, Glover wrote from London to his brother-in-law John Appleton of Ipswich, Massachusetts: 'I am now come out of Scotland my Grandmother being dead. I am to pay a great deale of moneys before I can enjoy my Estate.' In a codicil to her will, his grandmother Anne Glover had insisted that her 'nephew' John Glover must pay arrears of £50 a year owed to her by his father, 'Josse Glover Clerke', or inherit nothing. At least in part to raise the funds needed to claim his inheritance from his grandmother, Glover waged a fierce dispute with Henry Dunster to recover what he believed was owed to him from Jose Glover's estate. The matter was further complicated by disputes over the validity of the will of his brother, Roger.

By the late 1650s John Glover had left Scotland for good. Lucy Downing*, writing from Edinburgh, referred to 'Dr Glover now being in London', 23 February 1658/9. Glover became an honorary fellow of Royal College of Physicians in December 1664. He died by 1668, perhaps during the Great Plague of 1665.

Harvard Recs. I, 83; Nathaniel Mather to John Rogers(?), BPL, MS Am. 1502 v.1, no. 6 (the transcription in 4 *MHSC* 8: 4–5 is inaccurate); 4 *MHSC* 2: 196; Waters, 774–5, 777; NA, PROB 11/240/774, will of Anne Glover of St Stephen Coleman Street, City of London, 26 June 1654; Dunster MSS, 19 May 1654 (William Cutter to Dunster) and Boxes 1 and 2, *passim*; Morison, 315–7.

CC, *Munk's Roll*, Sibley.

GLOVER, Roger (d. 1650)

Roger Glover, the eldest son of Jose and Elizabeth Glover, and brother of John*, emigrated with his family in 1638. His mother, widowed on the voyage, married Henry Dunster in 1641. After her death in 1643, Dunster assumed responsibility for her children.

Glover was probably already in England by 23 July 1649, when what Dunster later called 'his pretended will' was made. Glover, a member of the first wave of Cromwellian forces in Scotland, was killed in December 1650 in the battle to take Edinburgh castle. Dunster described him as 'lately slain at Eden-borough' in a petition to the General Court on 20 October 1652. Difficulties arose over estate left to John and Roger by their father, which had not been divided before Roger's death. Roger (in a will Dunster declared technically void in 1654, when a copy had reached New England) had left his estate in old and New England to the children of his sisters Elizabeth and Sarah.

Dunster MSS, 20 October 1652 (Dunster's petition to the General Court about the settlement of Glover's estate), 4 November 1654 (Dunster's comments on the wills of Jose and Roger Glover), printed in *Harvard Recs.* IV, 26–8, 52–3.

Sibley.

GODFREY, Edward (1584–1663/4)

Edward Godfrey, who came from Wilmington in Kent, was a merchant who had travelled in the Mediterranean. He emigrated to New England from London in 1630 as an agent of the colonizing entrepreneur Sir Ferdinando Gorges (*ODNB*).

Godfrey settled first at Piscataqua, but moved to York, Maine, in 1633. *c.*1638 Godfrey made a brief visit to England to answer (successfully) in the Court of Star Chamber to charges made against him by George Cleeve of Maine. Godfrey served as a commissioner at York in the 1630s and 1640s, as a deputy governor in 1649 and as governor of Maine in 1650 and 1651. In 1652, he endorsed the decision of the settlers at York to put themselves under the government of Massachusetts. However, Godfrey and others found their property rights alienated under the new regime, and this provoked a crisis.

Godfrey set sail for England late in December 1655. The Massachusetts authorities appointed John Leverett* as an agent in London to counter Godfrey's claims. Godfrey struggled to make his case in London, with little recognition until the Restoration. In 1661, he and Samuel Maverick were invited by the Council for Foreign Plantations to present evidence about New England. On 5 October 1661, Godfrey wrote to John Winthrop Jr* from Ludgate prison in London. He died there on 28 February 1663/4.

GMB 778–83; C.E. Banks, *A history of York, Maine* (Boston, MA: Calkins Press, 1931), 41–52, 78–80, 196–205; W.L. Sachse, 'The migration of New Englanders to England, 1640–1660', *American Historical Review*, 53 (1947–8), 275; *WP* III and IV, *passim*; 4 *MHSC* 7: 380.

GODFREY, Oliver

Oliver Godfrey, Edward Godfrey's son and business partner, arrived in New England in 1642 and settled with his father in York, Maine. Edward Godfrey wrote to John Winthrop, 9 November 1645, that – to resolve a dispute between Maine and Massachusetts over jurisdiction of the Isles of Shoals – he had sent his 'onely son to England for atending to your sonne worship Jo: wyntherop [John Winthrop Jr*] and some others to heere and determine or sartify [certify] of my oppressions'. Oliver Godfrey was granted more land in Maine in 1648, but may never have come back to New England. He lived at Seale, Kent, and was buried there on 23 October 1661.

C.E. Banks, *A history of York, Maine* (Boston, MA: Calkins Press, 1931), 163; *WP* V, 57.

GOODYEAR, Stephen (d. 1658)

Stephen Goodyear, a merchant-taylor from London, settled at New Haven *c.*1638. Goodyear played an active role in religious and civic life. He was a church member, an assistant to the New Haven court, and in 1641 deputy governor of New Haven Colony. He took part in the establishment of the New England colonies' confederation, and was appointed to represent New Haven at its meetings, with Thomas Gregson* or Richard Malbon*. Goodyear acted with Robert Newman* as a trustee of Jane Stollyon's estate until her son Abraham Stollyon* came from England. His wife travelled as a passenger on the New Haven ship bound for England, captained by George Lamberton*, which sank in January 1645/6 with all lives lost. Afterwards, Goodyear married Lamberton's widow. In 1652 he offered his house to the New Haven Colony, for a college. Goodyear joined in several innovative trading ventures: along with Theophilus Eaton, Malbon, Gregson and others, he commissioned the building of the fated New Haven ship on which his wife drowned; he invested in a trading post on the Paugasuc River in 1654, and in the development of ironworks at New Haven in 1655.

Goodyear returned to England late in 1657, in part on business connected with the ironworks. John Davenport, minister of New Haven, hoped Goodyear would be elected governor in his absence, but he was not chosen. The townspeople of New Haven hoped Goodyear might come back in 1658, but he died in England that year.

Bernard Bailyn, *The New England merchants in the seventeenth century* (Cambridge, MA: Harvard University Press, 1955), 36, 71; I.M. Calder, *The New Haven Colony* (New Haven, CT: Yale University Press, 1934), 74, 114, 120, 157–9, 160; Dorothy Deming, *The settlement of the Connecticut towns* (New Haven, CT: Yale University Press, 1933), 42; *GD*; *NEHGR* 9: 359; *WP* V, 275; *WJ*, 644; *Davenport Letters*, 110, 122, 132; *New Haven TR*, 346.

GOOKIN, Daniel (1612–1687)

Daniel Gookin, born near Canterbury in Kent, was the third son of Daniel Gookin. In 1616 the family moved to Ireland, to Carragaline, near Cork. Gookin was a nephew of Sir Vincent Gookin (*ODNB*) of Munster, and a cousin of Vincent Gookin (*ODNB*). He went to Virginia with his father in 1621, and in 1631 acted as his agent. The elder Gookin had not been successful in the tobacco trade, and when he died Daniel inherited land claims and debts, rather than cashable assets. Little is known of Gookin's activities in the 1630s. He married Mary Dolling in London on 11 November 1639.

By 1641 Gookin had emerged as a major landowner in Norfolk County, Virginia. He was the second of seventy-two signatories on a letter to Massachusetts 'earnestly entreating a supply of faithful ministers', 24 May 1642. A letter also went to New Haven. As a result, William Thompson, John Knowles* and Thomas James* were sent to Virginia from New England.

In 1644 Gookin fled to New England after the authorities in Virginia enforced an order against nonconformity. Cotton Mather described him as one of William Thompson's 'constellation of Great Converts ... By Thompson's pains Christ and New-England, a dear Gookins gains'. He arrived in Boston on 20 May 1644, became a church member six days later, and a freeman of

Massachusetts three days after that. His wife Mary joined the Boston church on 7 September 1644. Gookin lived in Roxbury, but he and Mary kept their church membership at Boston until 3 September 1648, when they were dismissed to the church at Cambridge. (Gookin had been tempted to Cambridge by the offer of a five hundred-acre farm.) In the decades that followed, he held significant roles for the town of Cambridge and at the Massachusetts General Court. He also took a keen interest in John Eliot's work with local American Indians, and became superintendent of 'praying Indians' in 1656.

Gookin made several journeys to England. He may have gone back on a trading visit in 1646: on 7 October he promised Thomas Bell* £5 in England, followed by £1 18s 6d to be paid in New England. He was there on 24 July 1650, when England's council of state gave permission for him to transport ammunition to New England. In 1655, Cromwell chose Gookin – in England once again – to further his plans in the Caribbean. By this time Cromwell's 'Western Design' had floundered and failed, except for the capture of Jamaica, but Cromwell remained earnest about transplanting New Englanders south. He asked Gookin to advertise Jamaica to New England's settlers. Gookin took this commission to Boston in 1656 and printed a promotional flyer, but met with little success.

Gookin next travelled to England in the autumn of 1657. He went on family business and this time stayed for several years. On 10 March 1658/9, the council of state appointed Gookin a collector of customs at Dunkirk; he became deputy treasurer in September 1659.

At the Restoration Gookin decided his future was not in England. He reached Boston in July 1660 with the regicides William Goffe (*ODNB*) and Edward Whalley (*ODNB*). Gookin brought letters to John Winthrop Jr* from his son Fitz John*. In Massachusetts, Gookin became licenser of the press and an overseer of Harvard. His appointment as superintendent of the 'praying Indians' was renewed, and he championed their cause during the Anglo-Indian conflict of King Philip's War, 1675–6. In the 1680s he vigorously resisted pressure from England to force Massachusetts into renegotiating its charter, and backed up his politics with meticulous attention to military duties. Gookin wrote books on Native American culture, one of which was published posthumously.

Publication 'Historical collections of the Indians in New England', *MHSC* 1 (1792), 141–227.

NEHGR 1: 345–52; F.W. Gookin, *Daniel Gookin, 1612–1687* (Chicago, IL: privately printed, 1912); *WJ*, 508n.; MHS, Henry Dunster's Notebook, fols 107–14 (Dunster's copies of the letters from Virginia); *To all persons whom these may concern in the several townes, and plantations of the United Colonies in New-England* (Cambridge, MA, 1656), *ESTC* W6490; *Thurloe* IV, 440, 449, 601, 635, V, 6–7, 147–8, 374, 509–10, VI, 362; *Magnalia*, I, 440; *Davenport Letters*, 181; 5 *MHSC* 8: 62–3; *Pilgrims*, 116.

ANB, ODNB.

GORGES, Thomas (1618–1670)

Thomas Gorges, born at Batcombe in Somerset, was a cousin of the colonising entrepreneur Sir Ferdinando Gorges. He started legal studies at Lincoln's Inn, London, in 1638. However, he left London to become Sir Ferdinando's deputy governor in New England, 1640–3, based at Agamenticus. He followed in the footsteps of Robert Gorges* and William Gorges*, who had returned to England in the 1630s. Thomas Gorges proved an effective administrator: he consolidated Sir Ferdinando's land-holdings, drew up a code of laws and developed local courts.

In 1642 Gorges asked permission from Sir Ferdinando to return to England, and went back in 1643. Sir Ferdinando had joined with the royalists, but Thomas sided with the parliamentarians. He completed his studies at Lincoln's Inn and became recorder of Taunton. He served as a lieutenant-colonel of horse in the Somerset militia. He was elected MP for Taunton in 1654, 1656, 1659 and 1660. After the Restoration he retired to Heavitree, Devon, where he died in 1670.

> Robert E. Moody, *A proprietary experiment in early New England history: Thomas Gorges and the Province of Maine* (Boston, MA: Boston University Press, 1963); Robert E. Moody, ed., *The letters of Thomas Gorges: deputy governor of the Province of Maine, 1640–1643* (Portland, ME: Maine Historical Society, 1978); *History of Parliament Online*, http://www.historyofparliamentonline.org/volume/1660-1690/member/gorges-thomas-1618-70.
>
> *ANB s.n.* 'Gorges, Robert', *ODNB s.n.* 'Gorges, Sir Ferdinando'.

GOULD, Jeremiah

Job Gould settled at Weymouth in Massachusetts before 1644, and later moved to Rhode Island.

Gould had gone to England by 19 February 1651/2, when William Coddington* complained that Gould and 'Mr Dyer' (William Dyer*) had 'fitted themselves for England' and Gould had 'maid over his estate to defeate me of my right'. c.1653, Gould wrote to Job Lane* from London to tell him that his uncle had left him nineteen acres. He advised Lane to have a good letter of attorney sent over so Gould could sell the land; a fine of £9 10s had to be paid and Gould was having difficulties raising the money and dealing with Lane's brother James. Gould expected to be in England for another year, 'at my son Simon Gould's at the Raven in Fish Street'. On 6 June 1654 Gould wrote to Job Lane again: a letter from Lane dated 4 October 1653 had reached him a fortnight earlier. Gould mentioned an annuity of £15 annuity left to Lane by his uncle. He had seen James Lane, who showed him a letter Job wrote to him 'before I came from you at Boston'.

> 4 *MHSC* 8: 282–3; *NEHGR* 11: 103–4, 17: 266–7.

GRAVES, Thomas (d. 1653)

Thomas Graves, shipmaster and shipbuilder, settled in Charlestown in 1639 but criss-crossed the Atlantic frequently before and after that. John Winthrop, governor of Massachusetts, took an interest in Graves's activities. Graves built the ship *Trial* at Boston in 1642. Winthrop and Nehemiah Bourne* were among the investors.

Along with Nehemiah Bourne, Graves was recruited to serve in Cromwell's navy. He died as a rear-admiral at the battle of Scheveningen, 31 July 1653, during the First Anglo-Dutch war.

> B.S. Capp, *Cromwell's navy: the fleet and the English Revolution, 1648–1660* (Oxford: Clarendon Press, 1989), 165, 195n., 242; Roger Thompson, *From deference to defiance: Charlestown, Massachusetts, 1629–1662* (Boston, MA: New England Historic Genealogical Society, 2012), 53, 153; *WJ*, 53, 69, 91–2, 147, 149, 402n., 495; *GMB* 806; http://www.british-civil-wars.co.uk/military/first-anglo-dutch-war-scheveningen.htm.

GREGSON, Thomas (1598–1646)

Thomas Gregson, a London merchant, was baptised at Sutton-on-Hill, Derbyshire, in 1598. He and his wife Jane married before 1630. Gregson emigrated to New England in 1637, in the company led by Theophilus Eaton and John Davenport.

Gregson followed Eaton and Davenport to New Haven. His daughter Mary was baptised in New Haven on 26 January 1639/40. Gregson was a church member, and served as a magistrate and assistant in the New Haven Colony, and as its first treasurer. With Theophilus Eaton, he signed articles of confederation with other New England colonies in 1643; he was appointed in 1644 to represent the New Haven Colony at meetings, with Stephen Goodyear* or Richard Malbon*.

Gregson was commissioned to go to England as New Haven's agent to procure a patent for the colony from parliament. In January 1645/6 he sailed from New Haven in the ship captained by George Lamberton*. All seventy passengers were lost at sea. John Davenport's sermon manuscripts, carried aboard by Gregson, went down with the ship. Davenport later told John Cotton that he had insisted Mark Pierce* should return his handwritten sermon notes 'by a safe land-messenger',

> remembring that I lost my autographs of all the sermons I preached out of the epistle of christ to the church at Philadelphia Rev. 3 ... and sundry others about christs shaking heaven and earth to establish his kingdom, in Heb: 12. which I gave Mr Gregson, at his request, to carry with him when he went hence for England.

Gregson's son Thomas was in New Haven in 1656, but had crossed the Atlantic to Bristol by 1672; his daughter Mary seems to have gone back too. His wife Jane and daughter Sarah remained in New Haven.

> I.M. Calder, *The New Haven Colony* (New Haven, CT: Yale University Press, 1934), 75, 114, 120, 160; *Davenport Letters*, 227; *NEHGR* 9: 359, 24: 35, 128: 65–73; *WJ*, 431, 630, 644; Bush, 437; Waters, 563–5; *GM* 7: 355.

H

HADDEN, George

George Hadden graduated BA from Harvard in 1647, and stayed on to take an MA. It has been suggested that he might be the son of Garret Haddon, who arrived in 1630, but this seems unlikely. His origins are unknown.

Hadden returned to England by 19 May 1654, when William Cutter* of Newcastle upon Tyne wrote to Henry Dunster, president of Harvard: 'I am sorry to heare lately that Mr hadden is to mary one of the daughters of a very great mallignant: and that he keeps so much socyety with them: he comes seldom hither.' Perhaps Hadden can be identified with George Hayden (Hawden, Hawdon), vicar of Stannington, Northumberland (ten miles north of Newcastle), from 16 September 1657 until 1662. Hayden was ordained priest by the bishop of Durham on 22 September 1661, and became vicar of Nazeing, Essex, from 8 November 1662.

GMB 833; *Harvard Recs.* I, 83; W.L. Sachse, 'The migration of New Englanders to England, 1640–1660', *American Historical Review*, 53 (1947–8), 262; 4 *MHSC* 2: 96; *CCEd* Person ID 136568 [Heyden].

CC [Hadden], *CR* [Hawdon], Sibley [Hadden], *Surman* [Hawden].

HARDING, Robert

Robert Harding, a merchant and mercer, originated in Boreham, Essex, the son of John and Mary Harding. He emigrated in 1630.

Harding joined the Boston church with the first group of members, after the signing of the covenant at Charlestown on 27 August 1630. He became a freeman on 18 May 1631, a member of the Artillery Company in 1637, and served as a Boston selectman. He and his wife 'Philip' (Philippa) were associated with Anne Hutchinson: Robert Harding was disarmed in 1637 and Philippa was disciplined in 1639 for defending Hutchinson. The Hardings moved to Newport, Rhode Island, in 1640. Like Robert Lenthall*, Harding disapproved of the religious radicalism he met there. A fragment of a letter survives from John Cotton, minister of Boston, written to Harding during this period. Harding was eventually reconciled with the Boston church. He kept property in Boston and moved back by 1646. After Philippa died, Robert Harding married in 1645 Esther Wyllys, daughter of George Wyllys, governor of Connecticut. He continued to pursue his business interests. In July 1646 he bought a captured Spanish ship for £250: this deal ran into controversy when the earl of Warwick's agents argued that the captain, who had captured the ship and sold it on, had sold Warwick's property. Harding traded in tobacco and furs, in partnership with Robert Scott* of Boston.¹

Harding's activities as a trader took him on many Atlantic voyages. In the autumn of 1646, for example, Harding entered into several transactions in advance of a journey to England. On 3 October 1646, Thomas Coleman made Harding his attorney to let or sell a house at Eastham, Worcestershire, and to receive rents and a legacy from the will of John Coleman of Cotherstock (Cotterstock), Northamptonshire. On 16 October Harding signed an agreement with John Milam* to do with the ship *Supply*. On 23 October, Thomas and Jane Mayhew empowered Harding to arrange the lease of lands in Northamptonshire. On 2 November, Thomas Hawkins* appointed Harding to recover money from a London shipmaster. According to Edward Winslow*, Harding was present at John Cotton's Boston lecture on 5 November 1646. He sailed for England on 9 November, on the same ship as Thomas Fowle*, John Leverett*, Thomas Peter*, Richard Sadler* and William Vassall*, arriving in Bristol on 19 December 1646.²

After the mid-1640s, Harding was perhaps more often in England than in Boston. In October 1647, Edward Gibbons, Valentine Hill, Thomas Clark and David Yale* appointed Thomas Fowle, with Robert Harding 'late of Boston', as attorneys to deal with the seizure of a ship and cargo in England. By 1651 Harding was describing himself as 'late of Boston in New England and now of Londo[n] marchant'. According to William Aspinwall's* notarial records, Harding acted as attorney to a number of colonists between 1647 and 1649, for business in England. The dates of the letters of attorney may coincide with his presence in Boston. In his absence, Robert Scott acted as his agent. On 17 October 1654 the Massachusetts General Court released Harding from a bond to the court for continuing 'in this country': a formal recognition that he had left New England. Harding died after this, probably in England but possibly in Ireland, if he is to be identified with the colonist below. (However, a deed recorded in Boston on 1 March 1657/8 refers to the 'Late Capt Robert Harding': this makes identification with Robert Harding of Dublin – still living in 1658 – less likely.)³

---

[1] C.E. Banks, *The Winthrop fleet of 1630* (Boston, MA: Houghton Mifflin, 1930), 74; Aspinwall, 11; *Boston CR*, 13; *NEHGR* 3: 91; *Artillery Company*, 41; Bernard Bailyn, *The New England merchants in the seventeenth century* (Cambridge, MA: Harvard University Press, 1955), 40; *WJ*, 248, 364, 627n.; Bush, 382-3; *GD*; *Wyllys Papers*, xxxv–xxxvi; *WP* V, 111–12; *Suffolk Deeds* I, 319–20; Aspinwall, 20, 22, 145; Darrett Rutman, *Winthrop's Boston: portrait of a puritan town 1630–1649* (New York: Norton, 1965), 72, 74–5, 100, 253.
[2] Aspinwall, 30, 35, 36, 31; Edward Winslow, *New-Englands salamander* (1647), 17–20; *WP* V, 161.
[3] Aspinwall, 91, 98; *Suffolk Deeds* I, 319–20, III, 124; Aspinwall, 94, 100, 111, 147, 150, 218 (mistakenly dated 1649), 249; *GMB* 855–8.

HARDING, Robert

Robert Harding of Dublin addressed a petition to the council of state in 1658, to ask for a fresh lease of land, which gave an account of his history. He had left England for New England in the 1630s, driven there by 'the tyranny of the then power'. In New England he had suffered hardship for twenty years. He also claimed to have lost £5000 at sea to the king's forces and to the French.

Harding's petition stated that he took his family to Ireland in 1653, tempted by the encouragements parliament offered new settlers, which included a lease of lands. (It is unclear whether Harding went straight to Ireland from New England or – if he is to be identified with Robert Harding who was in London, 1651 – after a spell in England.) Harding's petition to the council of state came because his lands in Ireland had now been let to someone else. Harding asked for a new lease of land. The Council granted his petition on 3 June 1658.

CSPC, 1574–1660, 466.

HARLAKENDEN, Elizabeth and Margaret

Elizabeth and Margaret Harlakenden were daughters of Roger and Elizabeth Harlakenden of Earl's Colne, Essex. Their mother later became the wife of Herbert Pelham*. Elizabeth was born in Cambridge, Massachusetts, in 1636; Mary was born there in 1638. These two were stepsisters of Waldegrave*, Nathaniel*, Jemima*, Penelope*, Katherine*, Mary* and Frances Pelham*.

There is no trace of Elizabeth or Margaret in New England records after 1645. They probably left New England late in 1646 with their mother Elizabeth and stepfather Herbert Pelham. Elizabeth Harlakenden, of Bures, married Guthlach Tolliot of St Mary le Bow, at St Augustine's, London, on 2 February 1659/60. Elizabeth Tolliot was mentioned in Herbert Pelham's will, 1 January 1672/3.

Cambridge TR, fol. 487; Aspinwall, 17; NEHGR 33: 294; GM 3: 224; NA, PROB 11/352/517, will of Herbert Pelham of Ferrers Bewers Hamlet, Essex, 30 March 1676.

HARRISON, Thomas (c. 1618–1682)

Thomas Harrison was the son of Robert Harrison, a merchant of Hull, Yorkshire. He graduated BA from Sidney Sussex College, Cambridge, in 1638.

By 1640 Harrison had become chaplain to Sir William Berkeley, governor of Virginia, and also minister to a church at Sewells Point, Lower Norfolk, at £100 a year. In 1644 Berkeley dismissed Harrison for his nonconformist views. The authorities in Virginia indicted him in 1645 for refusing to baptise according to the Book of Common Prayer. By 1646 Harrison had moved to a church at Elizabeth River, Nansemond County. Several letters survive that he wrote from Virginia to John Winthrop. Harrison accepted Winthrop's encouragement to stand firm and stay put, and by January 1647/8 could boast '74 haue joyned here in Fellowship, 19 stand propounded, and many more of great hopes and expectations'. He also commented on English news:

The Parliament proceeds to settle the affaires of the Kingdome: That golden apple The ordinance for toleration, is now fairly fallen into the lap of the Saints; no more compelling men to goe to their parish churches, or to sacrifice the abomination of their soules, or to offer up the sacrifice of fooles etc: and yet all such as preach print or practise any thing contrary to the knowne fundamentalls of religion, the peace of the state, or power of godlinesse, are excluded from tasting the swetenesse of this indulgence ...

Winthrop questioned Harrison's praise for toleration, so Harrison found it necessary to qualify this in his next letter: 'if any partake in this indulgence, besides the orthodoxall party, tis noe matter of exultation to me at all'.

Harrison left Virginia in 1648, banished for refusing to use the Book of Common Prayer. He arrived in Boston by 30 October, promising that his congregation would follow him north. Adam Winthrop told John Winthrop Jr*, then at Pequot (New London), that Harrison was anxious 'to consult about some place to settle him selfe and his church. Some thinke that youer plantation will be the fittst place for him'. That autumn, Harrison married Dorothy Symonds, daughter of Samuel Symonds of Ipswich (and a relative of Downing and Winthrop families). Then it became clear his church members from Virginia would not follow him to New England. Harrison came under pressure to return to them. His parishioners petitioned the council of state in England, in October 1649, for Harrison's restoration – by which time the Book of Common Prayer was illegal in Virginia – and the council of state granted this unless the Virginian authorities could show good cause to the contrary.[1]

Harrison set sail, but for England not Virginia. He left in midwinter, 1649/50, perhaps with his wife and a child born in October 1649. Thomas Jenner* was a fellow passenger. In 1650, back in England, Harrison attested Samuel Eaton's* *Mystery of God incarnate* with the ministers Philip Nye, John Owen, Joseph Caryl, William Greenhill, Sidrach Simpson and George Griffiths. He became rector of St Dunstan in the East, London, and in 1651 succeeded Thomas Goodwin as pastor to a gathered church in the parish. With Edward Winslow* and other prominent English Independents, Harrison signed the *Humble proposal* of 1652 (a scheme which proposed a continuing national church under local and national commissioners, both lay and clerical).[2]

Harrison acted as chaplain to Henry Cromwell, when Cromwell went over to Ireland in 1655 as major-general. Harrison preached at St John's, Dublin, and was appointed Sunday morning preacher at Christ Church cathedral, at £300 a year (the highest salary paid to any minister in Ireland). His congregation attracted the elite military leaders. Samuel Mather* had been appointed lecturer at Christ Church in July, and continued as Harrison's assistant until December 1646 when he moved to work with Samuel Winter at St Nicholas, Dublin, which tended to serve civilian members of the regime. Harrison quickly became a member of a committee for trying candidates for ministry in Ireland. He was in London *c.* June–August 1656, acting as Henry Cromwell's agent in negotiations over matters that divided him from Oliver Cromwell, notably the thorny question of the status of baptists in Ireland. Sections of Harrison's letters back to Dublin are in code. He reported that John Hewson

(*ODNB*), formerly military governor of Dublin and a member of the gathered church at Christ Church under the Fifth Monarchist John Rogers (*ODNB*), 'hath attempted to vilifie me to some of our Church but hath not prevailed'. (Hewson, MP for Dublin in 1654 and Guildford in 1656, and highly esteemed by Oliver Cromwell, had become a baptist.) While in London, Harrison preached to 'my freinds of the Church' at Charterhouse, where the minister was George Griffiths (*CR*); he also wrote a letter of recommendation for the former colonist Thomas Jenner to take to Ireland. Back in Ireland, Harrison and Samuel Mather were among those appointed in 1657 to oversee the trust established by Erasmus Smith (*ODNB*) to create a network of protestant schools. In 1658 Harrison published a tract on devotional difficulties, *Topica sacra*, which he dedicated to Henry Cromwell; it was frequently reprinted. As senior chaplain, Harrison preached a sermon in Dublin to mark the death of Oliver Cromwell, *Threni Hybernici*.[3]

On 28 February 1658/9, Harrison married Katherine Bradshaw at St Oswald's, Chester. In 1660 he became a preacher at Chester cathedral, and minister of a congregational church in Chester established by Samuel Eaton. By 1661 he was vicar of St Oswald's. Harrison may have come to Chester through the agency of the Hardware family of Bromborough Hall, Eastham (where Samuel Eaton had connections before emigration, and where Harrison may himself have preached before going to Ireland). Harrison was ejected from St Oswald's in 1662, and in 1663 imprisoned for preaching at Chester. In 1663 he was accused of taking some of Charles I's books from St James's Palace library when it was in the charge of Hugh Peter*. The authorities claimed that a conventicle of a hundred people had been broken up in his house in 1665, and he soon found himself in prison again. Harrison was reported to be holding conventicles at Bromborough Hall in 1669. He was licensed in Chester (as an Independent) in 1672.[4]

Harrison's admirers in Dublin encouraged him to return. His rhetorical power was legendary. Edmund Calamy recorded for posterity a comment by Lord Thomond: 'he had rather hear Dr Harrison say grace over an egg, than hear the bishops pray and preach'. From the early 1670s until his death, Harrison ministered to a congregation that included both presbyterians and congregationalists. When he died in Dublin in 1687, the presbyterian Daniel Williams preached his funeral sermon.[5]

Publications *Old Jacobs accompt cast up* (1655); *Topica sacra: spiritual logick: some brief hints and helps to faith, meditation, and prayer, comfort and holiness* (1658); *Threni Hybernici: or, Ireland sympathising with England and Scotland, in a sad lamentation for the loss of their Josiah* (1659). He contributed a prefatory epistle to *Philo-Carolus, Philo-Jesus. Lemmata mediationum* (1672).

[1] *WP* V, 116–17, 197–9, 212–13, 273–4, 277.
[2] *WP* VI, 17; BL, Lansdowne MS 821, fol. 200 ('Mr Jenner', not Nathaniel Brewster* as stated in *ODNB*); G.F. Nuttall, *Visible saints: the congregational way, 1640–1660* (Oxford: Blackwell, 1957), 32; T.C. Barnard, *Cromwellian Ireland: English government and reform in Ireland 1649–1660* (Oxford: Oxford University Press, 1975), 117.

³ Barnard, *Cromwellian Ireland*, 136n., 147n., 192; St J.D. Seymour, *The puritans in Ireland, 1647–1661* (Oxford: Clarendon Press, 1921), 111, 213; Harrison to Henry Cromwell, BL, Lansdowne MS 821, fols 222, 218, 200; see also fols 155, 164, 212, 214, 232; for Hewson, see Barnard, *Cromwellian Ireland, passim*.
⁴ J.B. Marsh, *Memorials of the City Temple* (London, 1877), 127–8, cited by Barnard, *Cromwellian Ireland*, 140.
⁵ Barnard, *Cromwellian Ireland*, 88.

BDBR, CR, ODNB.

HARWOOD, John

John Harwood settled in Boston by 1645. He was admitted to the church on 25 December 1647, as 'a taylor', and became a freeman of Massachusetts on 2 May 1649. He married Elizabeth, sister of Hezekiah Usher*, by 1650. Harwood, a merchant, traded from Boston, sometimes with Usher and Thomas Bell* of London. Richard Squire of Southwark, a woollen draper, appointed Harwood as his attorney in New England, 27 February 1653/4.

Harwood went to London soon after 4 November 1657, when he signed a deed with Hezekiah Usher in Boston. He probably travelled back with Usher – who was in England over the winter of 1657 to collect paper and type for printing the Indian Bible – and with Elizabeth Harwood and their two children. When John Winthrop Jr* wrote to a potential emigrant on 19 October 1660, he told him 'Mr John Harwood, who hath lived in NE' could give good advice: 'you will heare of him upon the Exchange, in the New-England walke'.

After the Restoration, Harwood had a reputation as a nonconformist. In 1663 he was noted by the authorities as:

> a merchant at Mile end Green, a factious and dangerous Independent and the common Factor for all the Merchants trading, especially to N. England who uses constantly to cover and disguise the Shipps Goods & persons of those of that opinion, in their voyages & passages, so as the Officers of the Customes &c at Gravesend are by his interest and mony corrupted to slipp the Oaths, which otherwise ought to be tendered to all persons going out &c

Harwood took part in plans to bring the congregationalist John Owen to New England. At a public meeting on 11 December 1663, the Boston church voted 'that whatever charg our brother Mr John Harwood should be at in the transporting of Doctor John Owin heither to us the Congregation would make payment to him againe'. In 1663 Harwood was still a member of the Boston church. He sought release only years later: on 16 March 1672/3, he was dismissed from the Boston church to Stepney congregational church, 'Mr Greenhills church in London Mr Matthew Mead beinge pastor'. Harwood was living at Bethnal Green in February 1665/6, when he acted as an attorney for Job Lane* to recover rents from Yorkshire. He made his will on 13 November 1684, as of Pudding Lane in the City of London, with bequests to relatives in

New England and to the London minister John Collins*. Harwood died before 22 June 1685. Elizabeth Harwood's will mentioned profits from 'goods which my late husband sent beyond seas'.

> Boston CR, 50, 59; NEHGR 3: 192, 11: 108, 23: 410; Suffolk Deeds I, 45, II, 192-3, III, 361a; 5 MHSC 7: 66–7; 'Williamson's Spy Book', 1663, Transactions of the Congregational Historical Society, 5 (1911–12), 251; Waters, 256–7, 625–6; NA, PROB 11/380/221, will of John Harwood, merchant of Pudding Lane, City of London, 22 June 1685; NA, PROB 11/387/60, will of Elizabeth Harwood, widow of Bethnal Green, Middlesex, 11 April 1687.

HATLEY, Philip

Philip Hatley was listed in Milford land records on 20 November 1639 as one of the first 'free planters' of the town, among forty-three settlers. Many had come from Buckinghamshire and Hertfordshire, including Hatley's neighbours John Astwood* and Henry Stonehill*. Some had come over in 1637 with Peter Prudden, who became Milford's minister. Hatley was admitted to Milford church on 9 May 1641.

Hatley had 'removed to London' by 1648. He must have written back to request dismission from the Milford church: the records note that on 19 August 1649 he was dismissed, by vote, 'to the church in London wherof Mr Thomas Goodwin is Pastour'. The records also noted Henry Stonehill's dismissal to the same church. Goodwin initially met with his gathered church in London at St Dunstan in the East but from 1648 at All Hallows, Lombard Street. Hatley and Stonehill followed in the footsteps of Richard Hutchinson*, who had been dismissed in 1645 from Boston to 'to the Church of Christ whereof Mr Thomas Goodwyn is pastor'.

> Milford CR, fol. 2; Connecticut VR, Milford, 81; The Connecticut Nutmegger 8: 354; The American Genealogist 16: 30; ODNB, 'Goodwin, Thomas (1600–1680)'; Boston CR, 44.

HAYNES, John (c.1635–1671)

John Haynes was born at Cambridge, Massachusetts, the son of John Haynes*, governor of Connecticut, and his second wife, Mabel Harlakenden. He was brother to Roger Haynes*, and half-brother to Hezekiah Haynes* and Elizabeth Cooke. The family moved to Connecticut in 1637, where Haynes's father played a leading role as governor. Haynes graduated BA at Harvard in 1656 and became a freeman of Connecticut in February 1656/7.

On 14 November 1657, Haynes was admitted to Pembroke College, Cambridge, with advanced standing awarded because of his education in New England. He was a fellow from 1658 and received an MA in 1660. He took the post of 'Logick Lecturer' in 1660 and was forced to resign on 28 August 1661. From 1658 Haynes also held the living of Hemingstone, Suffolk.

At the Restoration, Haynes conformed and stayed on at Hemingstone. He received episcopal ordination as a deacon on 17 December 1662, as a priest on 17 March 1663, and was formally instituted in the parish on 23 March 1663. In a deed to his brother Joseph in New England, dated 3 February 1665/6, he described himself as of Hemingstone, clerk. In 1668 he was appointed to the living of Stanway, Essex: this was near Coggeshall and Hezekiah Haynes's residence at Copford Hall. In 1669 he wrote to Samuel Wyllys about the extent of his debts, in part because 'I have allready Sunk soe much mony in my removeing'. He died in 1671.

Harvard Recs. I, 84 and III, 146n.; *NEHGR* 24: 127; *Wyllys Papers*, 186–8; *CCEd* Person ID 16657, Record ID 161827, Location ID 20986.

CC, Sibley.

HAYNES, Roger

Roger Haynes, a younger brother of John Haynes*, was born c.1640 in Hartford, Connecticut. He attended Harvard: his accounts, partially torn away, started in 1654. He was in the class of 1658, but did not graduate. Haynes left for England, but nothing more is known of him. He may have died on the voyage home.

Harvard Recs. III, 187n.; *CC*, Sibley.

HEFFORD, Samuel

Samuel Hefford [Heifer, Heyford] appointed Richard Coy his attorney on 20 December 1651, 'some days' before his departure for England. Ezekiel Cheever took possession of Hefford's house in the summer of 1652. Coy contested this in court on Hefford's behalf in 1660, as Hefford was still absent.

Essex Court Recs. II, 232–3.

HIGGINSON, Charles (c.1628–1677)

Charles Higginson was the eighth of nine children born to Francis Higginson (*ODNB*) and Anne. He was in New Haven in 1640, when he was awarded £40 from his mother's estate, and placed with Thomas Fugill* 'as his apprentice for nine years, Fugill to have charge of his education and to pay him his portion'. Fugill, a prominent church member and public notary of New Haven, was convicted of fraud in 1645 and soon went back to England.

It is not clear when Charles Higginson left New England, but like his brother Samuel* he was associated with Stepney, and may also have been a mariner: on 10 January 1677/8 he was said to be 'late of the parish of Stepney in Middlesex deceased at sea'.

GMB 935.

HIGGINSON, Francis (c.1619–1673)

Francis Higginson was one of nine children born to Francis Higginson (*ODNB*) and Anne: John Higginson (*ANB*) was the eldest son (with his twin brother Theophilus); Francis came next; Timothy*, Samuel* and Charles* were younger. Francis Higginson and his siblings emigrated with his parents to Salem in 1629. After his father's death in 1630, the family moved to Charlestown, and then to New Haven in 1638. Francis may have gone with them, but perhaps not: on 20 November 1639, John Winthrop Jr* wrote to Jacobus Golius (1596–1667), professor at Leiden and an eminent orientalist and traveller, recommending Higginson as a student.

On 6 October 1648, Higginson became vicar of Kirkby Stephen, Westmorland. The inhabitants had petitioned Philip, Lord Wharton (*ODNB*) for a minster c.1646. Higginson had come from 'Hela.' (Healaugh), Yorkshire, where Wharton also had land. At some point Higginson married Isabel Branthwait, sister to a servant of Lord Wharton. In 1653 he published two tracts against the Quakers.

At the Restoration, Higginson's successor at Kirkby Stephen, Thomas Stopford (appointed on 5 October 1663), failed to take up the post. Higginson was ordained priest on 20 December 1663, and continued in the parish. In an explanatory letter to Wharton, 7 January 1663/4, Higginson referred to Stopford's sudden surrender of the living, to the bishop's displeasure. Higginson had then 'been again to say but the naked truth exceedingly importuned by many of the Parishioners and other freinds as also by diverse Ministers and some Gentlemen of this County to conform, that if God should so please I might yet be minister there'. He was buried at Kirkby Stephen on 20 May 1673.

Publications *A brief relation of the irreligion of the northern Quakers* (1653); *A brief reply to ... a very scurrilous and lying pamphlet, called, Sauls errand to Damascus, shewing the vanitie of the praises there attributed to the sect of the Quakers* (1653).

GMB 934–5; *WP* IV, 155–6; Bodleian, Rawlinson MSS, Letters, 52: 25, 56, 117, 53: 7, 28.

CCEd Person ID 83504, *CR*, *ODNB* s.n. 'Higginson, Francis (bap.1586/7, d. 1630)'.

HIGGINSON, Samuel (c.1622–c.1664)

Samuel Higginson was another son of Francis and Anne Higginson. Francis Higginson recorded his son's sickness with 'the smallpox and purples together' on the journey over to New England in 1629. After his mother's death in 1640 it was ordered that Samuel should have '£40 and to be with Mr Eaton [Governor Theophilus Eaton of New Haven] as his servant for two years'.

Higginson commanded a vessel in the Protectorate navy and is likely to be the 'Higginson of Lymehouse, mariner' admitted a member of William Greenhill's church at Stepney in 1654. 'Samuel Higgenson of Lymehouse, mariner' had a son James baptised on 13 March 1654/5, and married Sarah Graves (perhaps the daughter of the former colonist and rear-admiral

Thomas Graves*) at Stepney on 5 August 1658. Their children, Abigail and Samuel, were baptised there on 18 October 1659 and 24 April 1663. Higginson, known to be a radical, was despatched on an errand in the Baltic to keep him out of the fleet sent to bring Charles II back to England. He died before 17 January 1664/5, when 'Sara Higgenson widow' was given administration of his estate.

> GMB 934–6; *Davenport Letters*, 207; Stepney CB, fols 3, 121, 300; B.S. Capp, *Cromwell's navy: the fleet and the English Revolution, 1648–1660* (Oxford: Clarendon Press, 1989), 303n., 358, 360.

HIGGINSON, Timothy (1620–1653)

Timothy Higginson, son of Francis Higginson and Anne, was the fourth of nine children, older than Samuel* and Charles*, younger than Francis*. He was still in New Haven in 1640, when he and Francis* (the cost of their education taken into account) received £20 apiece from his mother's estate.

Timothy Higginson, like his brother Samuel, served in the Protectorate navy. On 2 October 1653, his widow Sara was given administration of the estate of 'Timothy Higginson, late master of the *Culpepper* in the state service at sea, deceased'. The *Culpepper*, a thirty-gun hired merchant vessel captained by Thomas Cheyney, took part in naval battles of the First Anglo-Dutch War: the defeat at Dungeness (November 1652) and victories at the Gabbard (June 1653) and Scheveningen (August 1653).

> GMB 933, 935; B.S. Capp, *Cromwell's navy: the fleet and the English Revolution, 1648–1660* (Oxford: Clarendon Press, 1989), 78–82; for *BHV Culpepper* (1652), see R. Winfield, *British warships in the age of sail 1603–1714: design, construction, careers and fates* (Barnsley: Seaforth, 2009).

HOADLEY, John (c.1617–1668)

John Hoadley sailed for New England with Henry Whitfield's* company in 1639. Like the rest of the company, he probably came from Kent, Surrey or Sussex. Hoadley signed the 'plantation covenant' aboard ship and settled at Guilford, east of New Haven, under Whitfield's ministry. He was one of Guilford's original seven church members.

Hoadley left for England on 20 October 1653, without his family. He joined Cromwell's forces in Scotland: he arrived at Leith on 29 June 1654 and became chaplain to the Edinburgh garrison. William Leete, replying on 10 October 1654 to a letter from Samuel Desborough* in Scotland, asked him to show 'love and helpfulnesse to poore brother Hodley ... he was my constant Nocturnal Associate, whom I dearely miss'. By then Hoadley had sent for his wife and children: Leete reported that they were to 'come over according to his order this yeare'.

At the Restoration, Hoadley left Scotland. He settled at Rolvenden, Kent, in August 1662. He died at Rolvenden on 28 June 1668.

B.C. Steiner, *A history of... Guilford* (Baltimore, MD: privately printed, 1897), 24–5, 35, 70; MHS, Misc. Bd. MSS, 1 June 1639; BL, Egerton MS 2519, fol. 11; *CR* ['Hoadly'].

HOAR, Leonard (c.1630–1675)

Leonard Hoar was the son of Charles and Joanna Hoare of Gloucester. His father, a brewer who had been an alderman and sheriff of the city, died in 1638. Charles Hoare left money for his son to attend Oxford, but his widow Joanna took her children to New England. The family settled at Braintree, Massachusetts. Leonard Hoar graduated BA from Harvard in 1650, and MA in 1653.

Hoar returned to England in 1653. He was incorporated MA at Cambridge in 1654 and for a time served as a 'preacher of the gospel in divers places'. On 15 September 1656 he became rector of Wanstead, Essex, in succession to Paul Amyraut: the patron of the living was the regicide Sir Henry Mildmay (*ODNB*), father of William Mildmay*, whose time at Harvard had overlapped with Hoar's. Hoar had perhaps already been active in the Wanstead area: he presented certificates from Jeremiah Benton (*CR*) of Richmond, Thomas Walton (*CR*) of West Ham, James Metford of Barking, and John Yates (*CR*) 'late of West Ham'.

Wanstead was a sequestered living, and Hoar lost it at the Restoration. His successor was installed on 10 December 1660. Hoar was still at Wanstead on 27 March 1661, when he wrote to his nephew Josiah Flint, who was about to start at Harvard. Hoar was known as a congregationalist, and was active in and around London in the 1660s. He joined the church where John Collins* was minister.

In 1672 Hoar returned to New England. He had been invited by Boston Third Church to become their minister, but did not take office. Instead, he brought a letter of recommendation from thirteen congregational ministers in the London area, including John Collins, which suggested that he should become president of Harvard. (In the spring of 1671 John Knowles* had offered to alert his contacts in England to the need to find a new president. The colony's reply was addressed to Knowles, Hoar, Collins, William Hooke*, John Owen, Thomas Goodwin, William Mead, Samuel Lee and eleven other ministers.) Hoar was installed as president on 10 December 1672, but his tenure was deeply unsuccessful. He resigned in March 1675 and was succeeded by Urian Oakes*. He died on 28 November 1675 and was buried at Braintree.

Hoar published only one book in his lifetime, *Index Biblicus*. His funeral sermon of 1657 for Lady Anne Mildmay, wife of his patron at Wanstead, was published posthumously in Boston with a prefatory epistle by his nephew Josiah Flint.

Publications *Index Biblicus: or, the historical books of the Holy Scripture abridged* (1668); *The sting of death and death unstung* (Boston, 1680).

Harvard Recs. III, 42n.; LPL, MS COMM. III/5, fol. 22; Morison, 391–414, 639–44.

ANB, *CC*, *CR*, *ODNB*, Sibley.

HOLLAND, Jeremiah

Jeremiah Holland graduated BA at Harvard in 1645, and left for England soon afterwards. Samuel Mather* reported to Jonathan Mitchell, 26 March 1651:

> Sir Holland hath a great living worth 2 or 300 li [£] a yeare in North Hamptonshire; and is not tainted with these new opinions, though I know not whether his abilityes are much esteemed. Hee was at a place neare London but is remooved since we came over.

MHS, Misc. Bd. MSS, 26 March 1651.

CC, Sibley.

HOLLARD, Angel (1614–1670)

Angel Hollard was baptised at Netherbury, Dorset, on 10 April 1614. He married Katherine Richards at Beaminster, Dorset, on 12 August 1635. 'Angell Hollard', aged twenty-one, and 'Katheryn his wife', aged twenty-two, were listed on 20 March 1634/5 as passengers for New England on the *Marygould*, sailing from Weymouth, Dorset. Angel Hollard was a shoemaker.

Hollard settled in Weymouth, Massachusetts. He must have been admitted to Dorchester church (which at this point served the people of Weymouth) before he became a freeman on 3 March 1635/6. He moved to Boston in 1644. In 1651 Hollard was absent, probably in England, when his wife mortgaged their house. He was in Boston in 1653, when the house was mortgaged again.

Sometime in or soon after 1653, Angel and Katherine Hollard returned to England with their six youngest children. Hollard came back over to visit Boston in 1670, and died there. His widow Katherine and a daughter returned to New England in 1671 to settle his estate. Katherine married John Upham of Malden and stayed on. Upham had travelled over to New England in 1635 on the same ship as the Hollards, and also settled at first at Weymouth.

GM 3: 377–9.

HOOKE, Ebenezer

Ebenezer Hooke, son of William* and Jane Hooke*, was born c.1643 in New England. He probably returned to England in 1654 with his mother. Hooke went back to New England in 1663, to serve John Winthrop Jr* for four years.

5 MHSC 8: 595; CR s.n. William.

HOOKE, Jane

Jane Hooke, the daughter of Richard Whalley of Kirkton and Screveton, Nottinghamshire, and Frances (Cromwell), was sister of the regicide and major-general Edward Whalley (*ODNB*) and a cousin of Oliver Cromwell. She was also a niece of Lady Joan Barrington (*ODNB*), in whose household she lived from 1622 until her marriage to William Hooke* in 1630.

Jane Hooke left New Haven for England in 1654, with her children Ebenezer, Mary, Elizabeth, Walter* and perhaps others. John Hooke* left earlier. William Hooke followed in 1656. After the Restoration Jane Hooke corresponded with John Davenport and Increase Mather* in New England. Her brother Edward Whalley fled to New Haven in secret at the Restoration, with his son-in-law William Goffe (*ODNB*).

Barrington family letters 1628–32, ed. A Searle, Camden Society 4th series, 28 (London, 1983), 19, 153, 171–4; *Davenport Letters*, 257; 4 *MHSC* 8: 260–8.

HOOKE, John (1633/4–1710)

John Hooke, son of William* and Jane Hooke*, was born in Axmouth, Devon. He emigrated with his parents, c.1637. Hooke joined the Harvard class of 1655, but left without a degree.

He returned to England by 1652, when he matriculated at Magdalen College, Oxford. In November 1653, his father wrote from New Haven to Oliver Cromwell, to thank him for 'bounty, since I understood of the favour, which my sonne found in your eies'. Hooke graduated MA in 1654. On 3 November 1658 he was admitted as rector of Kings Worthy, Hampshire: he presented certificates from his father William Hooke, from James Prince (*CR*) of Kingsbury and from Thomas Jacombe (*CR*), rector of St Martin's Ludgate, London. In June 1658, Hooke became an assistant to the Hampshire commissioners for removing unsuitable parish ministers.

At the Restoration, Hooke's successor as rector of Kings Worthy was installed on 29 January 1661/2. Thereafter, Hooke never took a parish living, although he conformed. He subscribed and received episcopal ordination as deacon and priest on 21 August 1662, as of the Savoy Chapel, London. He was admitted as a chaplain there on 30 July 1663, and held office until 1702 when the Savoy Hospital foundation was dissolved. By 1674 he was living at Wokingham, Berkshire: Oliver Heywood (*CR*) spent an evening in prayer with 'Mr Hook' of Berkshire in January 1682/3. After 1702 he lived at Basingstoke, Hampshire, preaching 'to a separate congregation from the Church'. He died in 1710, survived by his wife, Elianor (d. 1714), and three daughters.

Harvard Recs. III, 199n; *Thurloe* I, 564–5.

CC, *CCEd* Person ID 49443, *CR*, *ODNB s.n.* William.

HOOKE, Walter (d. 1670)

Walter Hooke, son of William* and Jane Hooke*, was born at Axmouth in Devon and emigrated with his parents c.1637.

He probably returned to England with his mother in 1654: he was admitted to Pembroke College, Cambridge, late in 1654 or early in 1655. He graduated BA in 1656/7. His whereabouts for a time are unknown, but he worked as a chaplain to East India Company in 1668–9. The Company recalled him because he was not duly ordained, but the summons reached him shortly before his death in 1670 at the port of Masulipatam, India, where English traders had established a settlement in 1611.

Harvard Recs. III, 156n.; *CR s.n.* William.

HOOKE, William (1601–1678)

William Hooke was the second son of William Hooke of Hook, Hampshire. He graduated BA from Trinity College, Oxford, in 1620, and MA in 1623. In May 1627 he became rector of Upper Clatford, Hampshire. In 1630, he married Jane*, a cousin of Oliver Cromwell. Hooke was appointed vicar of Axmouth, Devon, on 26 July 1632. He remained at Axmouth until around October 1637: it was said he had been forced to leave 'because of his seditious sermons and nonconformity to the church in all particulars'. The church authorities declared the living vacant on 23 July 1639.

Hooke took his family to New England sometime after October 1637. He settled first at 'Cohannet' (Taunton), in Plymouth Colony. In *Plain dealing* (1641), Thomas Lechford* reported that, in Taunton, there had been:

> a church gathered of late, and some ten or twenty [are] of the Church, the rest excluded. Master Hooke Pastor, Master Streate Teacher. Master Hooke received ordination from the hands of one Master Bishop a schoolmaster and one Parker a Husbandman, and then Master Hooke joyned in ordaining Master Streate.

On 23 July 1640, Hooke preached a sermon on the first colony-wide fast day for England ordered by the Massachusetts authorities. This sermon was printed in England in 1641, as *New Englands teares, for old Englands feares*. This was among the first tracts from New England published after the start of the Long Parliament, and appeared with the support of an MP. A second fast-sermon by Hooke appeared in 1645 as *New Englands sence, of Old Englands and Irelands sorrowes*. In 1644 Hooke moved to New Haven and served as teacher, alongside John Davenport as pastor. In the early 1650s Davenport was intent on returning to England. He wrote to John Winthrop Jr* on 24 July 1654 that he had peace of mind because Hooke was willing to stay until a replacement for Davenport could be found. But Hooke already had 'strong incouragements from England' to go back, and was sending his family ahead.

William Hooke left for England in October 1656, two years after his wife Jane. Edmund Calamy believed he went back briefly to Axmouth. Hooke wrote to John Winthrop Jr on 13 April 1657, 'I am not as yet settled, the protector having engaged me to him'. On 24 October 1657 he was appointed as an assistant to the Middlesex commissioners for removing unsuitable parish ministers. In 1658 he became Master of the Savoy, where Cromwell accommodated members of his court. Shortly after Hooke took up the post, representatives of congregationalist churches from across England gathered there for the Savoy Conference. Hooke served as a trustee for 'the Inlargement of University Learning in New England' in 1659, with Thomas Allen*, John Knowles*, Herbert Pelham* and Richard Saltonstall*.

At the Restoration of Charles II in 1660, Hooke lost his position at the Savoy. That same year, John Winthrop Jr suggested to a prospective emigrant to New England that Hooke could provide first-hand advice. Hooke may have influenced the regicides Edward Whalley (*ODNB*) and William Goffe (*ODNB*) to flee across the Atlantic. He corresponded with New Englanders, including the hidden regicides. The authorities confiscated a letter Hooke wrote to John Davenport in March 1663, and Hooke went into hiding. John Winthrop Jr met him in secret in London, with John Scott of Long Island, Robert Tomson* and Nathaniel Whitfield*, to discuss colonial business. In 1666, Hooke was living in West Harding Street. In 1672, he was licensed (as a congregationalist) at the house of Richard Loton in Spittleyard, Bishopsgate, with John Langston. Hooke died in 1678 and was buried in London at Bunhill Fields.

Publications *New Englands teares, for old Englands feares* (1641); *New-Englands sence, of Old-England and Irelands sorrowes* (1645); *The priveledge of the saints on earth* (1673); *A discourse concerning the witnesses* (1681). Hooke also published the catechism he and Davenport had used at New Haven, *A catechisme containing the chief heads of Christian religion* (1659), and (with Joseph Caryl) a collection of Davenport's sermons, *The saints anchor hold* (1661).

Lechford *PD*, 40; W. DeLoss Love Jr, *The fast and thanksgiving days of New England* (Boston, MA: Houghton Mifflin, 1895), 147–52; *Davenport Letters*, 90–3, 131–2, 137; 140, 173–4, 216n.; W.L. Sachse, 'The migration of New Englanders to England, 1640–1660', *American Historical Review*, 53 (1947–8), 276–7; 4 *MHSC* 8: 122–5, 143–8, 149–56, 177–9, 194–7, 207–10, 582–5 and *passim*; 5 *MHSC* 8: 63–8; William Hooke to John Davenport, 2 March 1662/3, A.G. Matthews, ed., 'A censored letter', *Transactions of the Congregational Historical Society*, 9 (1924–6), 263–83, also *CSPD*, *1663–4*, 63–5.

BDBR, *CCEd* Person IDs 70274 and 98178, *CR*, *ODNB*.

HOOKE, William (1612–1652)

William Hooke, a merchant from Bristol, emigrated in 1634. His father, the Bristol alderman Humphrey Hooke, invested with Sir Ferdinando Gorges (*ODNB*) in the Agamenticus Patent – also known as Pemaquid, Gorgeana and New Somerset. Hooke was commissioned by his father to advance the family's colonial interests.

Hooke settled at York, Maine. He was appointed governor of Agamenticus, 1638–40, and as a councillor for the province of Maine, 2 September 1639 and

10 March 1639/40. By 1640 he was living at Salisbury, Massachusetts: he had joined the church there before he became a freeman of the Bay Colony on 2 October 1640.

'Mr William Hooke of Accamenticus' went to England in the autumn of 1641, carrying a letter of testimonial to declare 'that he hath borne himselfe in this Countrey in all things we knowe of honestly soberly fairely & therefore with us he hath this esteeme to be a sober discreat & religious man'. Hooke returned to Salisbury in 1642 and stayed until 1650. On 24 July that year, he transferred land into the possession of Mary Jewel, making the promise that 'if I . . . do not return for New England, then I do freely give . . . the said land & meadow unto the said Mary'.

Hooke died in England in 1652. He was buried at St Stephen's, Bristol, the parish in which he had been baptised. He seems to have taken his family home. His father Humphrey Hooke was still living, and, in his will of 25 June 1658, wrote that his grandsons William and Josias (born in New England) were 'a couple of the most stubborn and unruly boys' – he gave their brother Jacob a more generous bequest, 'in hope that he may prove better'. William Hooke Jr was married at St Stephen's, Bristol, in 1660, but later went back to the family estate in New England.

GM 3:403–10; Lechford NB, 408; C.E. Banks, *A history of York, Maine* (Boston, MA: Calkins Press, 1931), 74, 76, 79, 80, 92–4, 133–6.

HOOKER, John (d. 1686)

John Hooker, the eldest son of the minister Thomas Hooker and his wife Susannah, was born at Chelmsford or Little Baddow, Essex. His father, under pressure to conform from his bishop, William Laud, went into hiding in 1630 and left for Rotterdam in 1631.

In 1633, when Thomas Hooker took his family to New England, John Hooker was in the party. With his family, he settled at Cambridge, Massachusetts, in 1633, and moved to Hartford, Connecticut, in 1636.

John Hooker may have been in England as early as 1645. It has been suggested that he took two of his father's manuscripts across the Atlantic to London, for publication – *A briefe exposition of the Lords Prayer* (1645) and *An exposition of the principles of religion* (1645). The name 'John Hooker' appears in the Stationers' Register against the first of these texts: this could be a clerical mistake, or an oversight that saw the author's representative named instead of the author. John Hooker was certainly in England on 7 July 1647, when his father made his feelings known in his will: 'I do not forbid my son John from seeking and taking a wife in England, yet I do forbid him from marrying and tarrying there.' He was still in England in 1655, when his uncle left £200 to 'John Hooker, a student at Oxford'.

At the Restoration, John Hooker conformed. On 5 June 1660 he was ordained deacon and priest by Robert Skinner, bishop of Oxford. He became vicar of Marsworth, Buckinghamshire, on 2 February 1661, a parish in the diocese of Lincoln. Hooker was licensed as a preacher throughout the diocese on 29 July

1662. From 15 July 1669 he was rector of Leckhampstead, Buckinghamshire. He died on 30 March 1686.

Sargent Bush, 'Thomas Hooker and the Westminster Assembly', *William and Mary Quarterly*, 3rd series, 29 (1972), 294–6; G.L. Walker, *Thomas Hooker: preacher, founder, democrat* (New York: Dodd, Mead and Co., 1891), 4–5, 179; *CCEd* Person ID 97401.

HOPKINS, Ann

Ann Hopkins, wife of Edward Hopkins*, was the daughter of Ann Eaton* and sister of David* and Thomas Yale*. She was stepsister to Hannah* and Theophilus Eaton Jr*. John Winthrop observed in his *Journal* on 13 April 1645 that she had:

> fallen into a sad infirmity, the loss of her understanding and reason, by occasion of her giving herself wholly to reading and writing, and had written many books ... If she had attended her household affairs, and such things as belong to women, and not gone out of her way and calling to meddle in such things as are proper for men, whose minds are stronger ... she had kept her wits.

Hopkins wrote to Winthrop in 1648 'Your prayers I nead and begg, that the Lord would ... satisfye me with himselfe in this sad and great tryall which almost overwhelmes my spirit'. He left her in New Haven in the care of her family when he went to England in 1652, and later sent for her; she may have gone back with her brother Thomas Yale in 1656. Cotton Mather noted that she suffered from 'distempered melancholy ... an incurable distraction, with ... ill-shaped ideas in her brain'. In his will, Edward Hopkins left £150 a year to be paid to 'Mr David Yale brother to my deere distressed wife for her comfortable mayntenance ... she being not in a condicon fitt to manage it for herselfe ... I do heartily entreate him to bee tender and carefull over her'. After Edward's death in 1657, David Yale cared for his sister. Despite her melancholy, she outlived him, too, and died in London in 1698.

WJ, 223n., 570; *WP* V, 231; *Davenport Letters*, 104n.; *Magnalia*, I, 145; NA, PROB 11/263/464, will of Edward Hopkins, 30 April 1657; *ODNB s.n.* 'Hopkins, Edward'.

HOPKINS, Edward (c.1600–1657)

Edward Hopkins was a younger son of Edward and Katherine Hopkins of Elton, Herefordshire. His uncle, Sir Henry Lello, was a wealthy overseas trader. In 1629 Edward's elder brother Henry inherited from his uncle an estate at Thickoe, Essex, and the positions of warden of the Fleet prison and keeper of the palace of Westminster. Edward Hopkins inherited shares in the East India Company. Hopkins pursued a career as a London merchant 'of good credit and esteem'. By 1631 he was attending St Stephen's, Coleman Street, where

John Davenport was minister, along with future colonists such as Theophilus Eaton, Richard Malbon* and David Yale*. He married Yale's sister Ann in 1631, and (as Ann's mother Ann Eaton* married Theophilus Eaton in 1627) gained Theophilus Eaton as a stepfather-in-law.

Edward and Ann Hopkins left for New England in 1637 in the company led by Theophilus Eaton and John Davenport. Eaton and Hopkins were perhaps the two most important merchants to emigrate in the 1630s. Hopkins stayed briefly in Massachusetts before he moved further west. He did not settle in New Haven with Eaton and Davenport, but at Hartford, Connecticut, in 1638. He was appointed an assistant in 1639, and served as governor of Connecticut in 1640 and 1644, alternating thereafter with John Haynes*. He seems to have visited England in 1642, when George Wyllys* sent £400 to his father by 'Mr Hopkins of Hartford in New England'.

Hopkins was ambivalent about being away from his native country. Cotton Mather recalled how Hopkins quoted Theophilus Eaton, who 'never had a repenting ... thought about his coming to New England'. Hopkins could not share Eaton's confidence: 'surely in this matter he hath a grace far outshining mine ... I cannot say as he can, I have had hard work with my own heart about it'. Ann Hopkins's melancholy weighed heavily on him. In 1648 he canvassed opinion about returning home to England, for the sake of her health, but was dissuaded.

When Hopkins left for England in 1652, it was probably on colonial business. He left his wife behind in New England, in the care of relatives. But what might have been intended as a short visit turned into a permanent re-location. Hopkins reached the safety of England's shores 'after a Tempestuous and terrible Voyage, wherein they were eminently endangered by Fire, accidentally enkindled on the ship, as well as by water, which tore it so to Pieces, that it was Towed in by another ship'. He was soon recruited as a naval commissioner, and worked alongside Francis Willoughby*, Robert Tomson* and Nehemiah Bourne*. With the navy treasurer Richard Hutchinson*, the naval commissioners played a vital role in day-to-day administration – supplies and pay, staff and shipbuilding – at a time when the navy's size and role expanded dramatically, particularly during the First Anglo-Dutch War. Hopkins served as MP for the naval town of Dartmouth in the second Protectorate parliament. When his brother Henry died in 1655, he inherited the posts of warden of the Fleet prison and keeper of the palace of Westminster.

The settlers of Connecticut hoped Edward Hopkins would return. When Governor John Haynes died in 1654, Hopkins was elected governor in his absence. According to Cotton Mather there were 'Publick Supplications for that Mercy, Lord, If we may win him in Heaven, we shall yet have him on Earth.' But Hopkins would not come back:

> I have had many Thoughts about my Return, and my Affections have been bent very strongly that way; and though I have now, blessed be God, received my Family here, yet that shall be no hindrance to my Return ... But ... I incline to think they will not win it in Heaven; and I know not whether the Terrors of my dreadful Voyage hither might not be ordered by the Divine Providence, to Stake me in this Land ...

Instead, he worked for New England in England. In October 1655 the New Haven court wanted copies of its law-code printed, for distribution to every household, and voted to send the manuscript to London to be published. The following June, Governor Theophilus Eaton reported that 'there is sent over now, in Mr Garret's ship, 500 law books, which Mr Hopkins hath gotten printed': this was *New-Haven's settling in New-England* (infamously parodied in the eighteenth century as the 'Connecticut Blue Laws'). Hopkins also helped Edward Winslow* to represent the interests of colonists to Cromwell: the Massachusetts General Court wrote to thank him on 24 November 1655 for aiding God's 'exiled ones in these parts', and asked him to continue to assist their new agent in London, John Leverett*. In his will, Hopkins left the residue of his considerable New England estate (valued at £1476 15s. 4d) 'to give some encouragement in those fforeigne plantations, for the breeding upp of hopefull youths in a way of learning both at the Grammar Schoole and College for the Publique service of the Country in future times'. He also left £500 more, to be released after the death of his wife, to further 'the aforesaid publique ends, which in the simplicity of my heart are for the upholding and promotinge the Kingdome of the Lord Jesus Christ in those parts of the earth'. (His initial bequest founded the Hopkins School in New Haven, 1660. Harvard received £500 in 1710.) Hopkins named his naval colleagues Robert Tomson and Francis Willoughby as overseers.

In the 1650s, Hopkins probably had a house within the Navy Office buildings on Seething Lane, London – his colleague Francis Willoughby had a house there in 1660, which Samuel Pepys commandeered. Hopkins may well have worshipped at St Olave's, Hart Street, which in Pepys's day had a special gallery set apart for members of the Navy Office. Hopkins died in March 1656/7, in the parish of St Olave's, a stone's throw from St Stephen's Coleman Street, where he had worshipped as a London merchant in the 1630s.

Bernard Bailyn, *The New England merchants in the seventeenth century* (Cambridge, MA: Harvard University Press, 1955), 29, 38, 55; *Wyllys Papers*, 49-50; *WP* V, 231; *Magnalia*, I, 135, 143–8; B.S. Capp, *Cromwell's navy: the fleet and the English Revolution, 1648–1660* (Oxford: Clarendon Press, 1989), 49, 165–6, 295; *New-Haven's settling in New-England. And some lawes for government* (1656), *ESTC* R180938; J. Hammond Trumbull, *The true-blue Laws of Connecticut and New Haven and the false blue-laws* (Hartford, CT: American Publishing Company, 1876), 40; *New Haven Recs.* II, 154, 186; MHS, Misc. MSS, 24 November 1655; Claire Tomalin, *Samuel Pepys: the unequalled self* (London: Penguin Books, 2002), 111, 284; *NEHGR* 38: 315–17; NA, PROB 11/263/464, will of Edward Hopkins, 30 April 1657; Waters, 799.

ANB, ODNB.

HORSFORD, William

William Horsford [Hosford] married his first wife, Florence Heyward, at Beaminster in Dorset, January 1620/1. He emigrated with Florence in 1633. Horsford initially settled at Dorchester, Massachusetts, but moved to Windsor,

Connecticut, in 1635. Florence died there in 1641 and he married Jane Foukes. Horsford had joined the church at Dorchester before 1 April 1634, when he became a freeman of Massachusetts. He moved with members of this church to Windsor: with his former Dorchester companions John Witchfield and John Branter, he was a ruling elder at Windsor and often delivered the weekly lecture (a midweek sermon).

William Horsford went back to England briefly in the mid-1640s, to join the parliamentary army – or so it seems from his fleeting re-appearance in Dorset, in records at old England's Dorchester. Before long he returned to Windsor, Connecticut. The church at Windsor had close connections with Springfield, Massachusetts. After George Moxon* left Springfield in October 1652, Horsford may have been invited to preach in Moxon's place.

Horsford left for England again, c. October 1654. In an annex to his will, made on 6 September 1654 in anticipation of setting sail, he made provision in case 'my wife stays in New England but I hope she will come to me in England'. The next summer, on 23 July 1655, Jane Horsford made her will, 'I going after my husband into old England'. Two years later, the Horsfords disposed of their land in Windsor to their children and to the church. Their children – Hester, Sarah and John – stayed on in New England. William Horsford was admitted rector of Calverleigh, Devon, on 25 November 1657. He presented certificates from the patron of the living, John Doble, and from other Devon ministers: Lewis Stucley of Exeter (*CR*), Fortescue Lowman of Ideford (*WR*, 124, *s.n.* Francis Strode) and James Kingswell of South Molton (*WR*, 111, *s.n.* John Coven).

On 23 August 1660, Horsford was replaced as parish minister at Calverleigh. Nicholas Burch took over: he had been appointed in 1646 but had been kept out of the living. John Walker, in his account of the 'intruders' foisted on parishes between 1640 and 1660, wrote of 'one Horsman, a New-England Divine; of whom 'tis reported, that talking in Defence of Extempore Prayer, he said Tho' we speak Nonsense, God will pick out the Meaning of it'. No record has been found of William Horsford's activity after 1660. Jane Horsford was at Tiverton, Devon, in 1671.

NEHGR 3: 92, 5: 227, 336, 6: 261; Waters, 137n.; *GMB* 994–7; David Underdown, *Fire from heaven: life in an English town in the seventeenth century* (London: Fontana, 1993), 136, 138, 201; LPL, MS COMM. III/6, fol. 149; John Walker, *An attempt towards recovering an account of the numbers and sufferings of the clergy* (London, 1714), Part I, 197; *Pilgrims*, 66n.58, 83, 99.

CR.

HOWE, Daniel

Daniel Howe, a soldier and mariner, emigrated in 1633 and settled at Lynn. He was admitted to the church there by 14 May 1634, when he became a freeman of Massachusetts. Howe served as a deputy for the town at the General Court, and also as lieutenant of the train-band. He took part in the Pequot War of

1637, and joined the Artillery Company in 1638. In 1640 nine families from Lynn, led by Howe, pioneered the settlement of Southampton, and then East Hampton, on Long Island.

Howe left for England in 1654, when the communities on Long Island were under pressure from hostilities with the Dutch. He died, probably in England, sometime after 1656.

GMB 1011–13.

HUBBARD, 'Fra:'

'Fr[a: H]ubbard is in Scotland which way I am intending by the first opportunity and I intend to carry your letter to him with me': so wrote Nathaniel Mather in December 1650, to his 'Fra:' ('frater', brother, fellow graduate) in New England, probably John Rogers of Ipswich, Massachusetts. Later in the letter, Mather sent greetings to:

> Mr Hubbard senior and your brother and sister if yet in America. I hope to see them in England shortly, 'twill be the onely good way, and if Mr Hubbard learne but to bee a little more rhetoricall and get a faculty of better delivery I question not but (providing Independent party continuing to bear sway) hee would after a few weeks of making himself knowne be *inter primos* [among the first] of the whole kingdome. Tis incredible what an advantage to preferment it is to have been a New English man.

The 'Mr Hubbard' that Mather hoped would come over and 'bee a little more rhetorical' was almost certainly the future historian of New England, William Hubbard (*ANB*), who graduated from Harvard in 1642, and in 1658 became minister at Ipswich. Hubbard was the eldest son of William Hubbard of Ipswich, and came over to America with his father in 1635. He had married John Rogers's sister Margaret in 1646 (hence the reference to 'your brother and sister'). It seems Nathaniel Mather hoped he could tempt his fellow Harvard graduate William Hubbard, with his wife and father ('Mr Hubbard senior'), to come back to England.

'Fra: Hubbard', the person Mather planned to follow to Scotland, is likely to be Nathaniel Hubbard, a younger brother of the Harvard graduate. He also came to New England in 1635, aged six, but then all but disappears from the records. He would have been a good age in 1650 to seek opportunities in Cromwell's regime north of the border. Twenty years later, Nathaniel Hubbard was in London, and owned land in Essex. His father, William Hubbard senior, still had land at 'Tendring Hundred' in Essex at the time of his death in 1670, which he left to his son William, who could draw rent on it from across the Atlantic. Hubbard made no bequest to Nathaniel, because 'to my son Nathaniel I have already given a sufficient portion in my land at Dover Court and otherwise'. (Dovercourt is today a suburb of Harwich, Essex.) In 1672, William Whittingham, in London but 'late of Boston', named among his executors 'William Hubbert of Ipswich in New

England' and 'my ... uncle Nathaniell Hubbert of London, Gentleman'; he gave Nathaniel's daughters, Mary and Anne Hubbert, 'ffive pounds to each to buy them Rings'.

> Boston Public Library, MS Am. 1506 v.1, no.6 (Mather's letter can be dated to 1650, not '1651?' as in 4 *MHSC* 8: 4); *GM* 2: 437–43; NA, PROB 11/340/432, will of William Whittingham, gentleman of Boston, Massachusetts, New England, 15 April 1672.

HUBBARD, Benjamin

Benjamin Hubbard, a surveyor, settled in Charlestown in 1633 with his wife Alice; both became church members on 30 August 1633. Hubbard became a freeman of Massachusetts on 3 September 1634. In 1637, he signed the remonstrance drawn up by William Aspinwall* in support of John Wheelwright*. He considered moving to Rhode Island: Roger Williams* reported that he had received a letter from 'some in Charlestowne (in special from one Benjamin Hubbard) intimating his and others desire ... to be my neighbours in some place neere adioyning', perhaps with the dismissed minister of Charlestown, Thomas James*. In the end, Hubbard did not go. He was clerk of writs at Charlestown in 1641.

Hubbard went to England in 1644 with an invention to aid navigation. He wrote to thank John Winthrop from London, 25 March 1644/5, for expediting 'so comfortable a voyage' and for a testimonial which 'hath been a meanes to procure me the more favourable acceptance in the sight of sundry gentlemen. I have not yet made tryall of my Invention concerning Longitude before Artists, but a time is appointed for it.' John Winthrop Jr* had written for Hubbard a letter of introduction to Samuel Foster (*ODNB*), the noted mathematician. Hubbard attended Foster's Cambridge lectures and was to meet Foster, and 'Mr Nye, Mr Goodwin' – the congregationalist ministers Philip Nye and Thomas Goodwin – to discuss what he could do about 'some Covenants or promise to me made'. On 25 March 1645, Hubbard sent to his wife Alice, who was still in New England, a journal of God's providences towards him. (Alice and their children disappear from the colonial records after this and probably followed him home.) In 1656, Hubbard published a treatise on navigation: he dedicated this to the master, wardens and assistants of Trinity House, and described himself as a 'late Student of the mathematicks in CharlesTowne in New England'.

> Publication *Orthodoxal navigation. Or, the admirable and excellent art of arithmeticall great circle-sailing* (1656).

> *Charlestown CR*, 191; *NEHGR* 3: 93; 4: 267; 8: 346; *WP* III, 509; *WP* V, 9, 10; *Orthodoxal navigation*, title-page; *GMB* 1032–5; Roger Thompson, *From deference to defiance: Charlestown, Massachusetts, 1629–1662* (Boston, MA: New England Historic Genealogical Society, 2012), 63, 287, 288, 289.

HUDSON, William

William Hudson, a baker, emigrated in 1630. He was the father of William Hudson*, who went to England temporarily, to serve in the parliamentary army c.1643-5 (see Appendix 2). Father and son are easily confused. Hudson senior settled at Charlestown with his wife Susan. He became a member of the Boston church in the winter of 1630/1 and a freeman of Massachusetts on 18 May 1631. He had moved to Boston by 1635.

The elder Hudson left for England soon after 9 October 1647, when his son William Hudson gave him power of attorney to collect debts there. On 23 November 1647 he was described as 'late of Boston'. He was still absent on 14 July 1648 when William Hibbins*, William Colborne, Jacob Eliot and William Hudson Jr*, his 'feofees in trust', sold land he owned at Braintree. In an undated deed c. December 1653, Hudson sold a house to Thomas Yeow of Boston. Yeow did not pay: on 29 April 1656, Hudson appointed 'my two sons vizt William Hudson of Boston . . . innholder & Francis Hudson of the same, fisherman' to collect the debt. At that point Hudson senior described himself as of 'Chatham in the County of Kent'. He died in England after 17 February 1661/2.

Boston CR, 13; *NEHGR* 3: 91; Aspinwall, 91, 113, 235-6, 320-1; *Suffolk Deeds* I, 93, II, 305-6, IV, 243; *GMB* 1035-7.

HULL, Joseph (1596-1665)

Joseph Hull was baptised at Crewkerne, Somerset. He matriculated at St Mary Hall, Oxford, in 1612, graduated BA in 1614, and was ordained deacon at Silverton, near Exeter, in 1619. He became rector of Northleigh, Devon, on 28 March 1622. He resigned this post on 14 March 1632/3 and was licensed on 14 April 1633 as curate at Broadway, Somerset, within the deanery of Crewkerne. Hull emigrated in March 1634/5, with his wife Agnes, seven children by an earlier wife, and three servants. He travelled with a company of other families, mainly from Broadway and Batcombe in Somerset (including Mary and Masakiell Bernard*). The party sailed on the *Marygould* from Weymouth, Dorset. Hull's elder brother, George, had already gone to New England: he settled at Dorchester, Massachusetts, in 1632.

John Winthrop noted in the summer of 1635 that the Massachusetts General Court had made 'wessauscus . . . a plantation & Mr Hull a minister in England, & 21 familys with him allowed to sett downe there: after called weymouthe'. Hull acted as a minister at Weymouth for several years, although until the Weymouth church formally gathered in January 1638/9 the settlers joined the church at Hingham. Hull served as a deputy for Hingham in 1638-9. Peter Hobart, minister of Hingham, noted his farewell sermon there on 5 May 1639. Hull moved into the Plymouth Colony and joined John Lothropp's church at Barnstable: he was there by 2 November 1639, when baptisms took place at his house (the first since Lothropp's church moved from Scituate to Barnstable the previous month). On 15 April 1640, Hull was invested as the teaching elder at Barnstable. On 1 May 1641 the church excommunicated him 'for his willfull breakeing of communion with us, and joyneing himselfe a member with a companie at Yarmouth to be their Pastour: contrary to the advise and Counsell of our Church'. (Joseph and Agnes Hull had joined a group that had broken away from the Yarmouth church gathered by Marmaduke Matthews* in 1639.) On 7 March 1642/3, the Plymouth authorities ordered the Yarmouth constable to bring Hull before a magistrate if he started to exercise his ministry, because he stood excommunicated. Agnes Hull renewed her covenant with the Barnstable church on 11 March 1642/3, and Joseph rejoined the fellowship on 10 August 1643. However, he seems already to have decided to move north to Maine, for greater freedom: in May 1643 John Winthrop criticised the people of 'Acomenticus' (York) for choosing 'one Hull, an excommunicated person and very contentious, for their minister'. Hull was active in this area – York and 'Strawberry Bank' (Portsmouth) – until 1645. Edward Godfrey* reported to John Winthrop that while he himself would be pleased to come under the Bay Colony's jurisdiction, this was 'not Mr Hulles mind'.

At some point after November 1645, Hull returned to England. In 1648 he was admitted as vicar of Launceston, Cornwall, a parish living that included St Mary Magdalene and St Thomas Chapel. On 13 July 1654, Hull was presented (again) to St Mary Magdalene, Launceston, this time with certificates from the ministers George Hughes (*CR*) of Plymouth, 'Samuel' Saunders of Holsworthy ('Humphrey Saunders' in *CR*), Joseph Squire of 'Lister' ('Lifton', *WR*, 95 *s.n.* Bernard Herniman), and from the layman Robert Bennett (*ODNB*), a parliamentary army officer and religious radical with strong ties to Launceston. On 11 April 1656, Hull became rector of St Buryan, Cornwall, with certificates from George Hughes of Plymouth, Edward Collins of Little Petherick, Robert Rous, Richard Mill, William Thrope, and the former colonist and Cornishman Hugh Peter*. Hull gained notoriety for his vast family: in 1655, John Tingecombe of Truro reported to the secretary of the privy council, Henry Scobell (*ODNB*), 'Tis hoped the man is godly. He has a very greate charge of children neare twenty. Some say more.' Hull had seven children by his first wife and ten by his second.

Joseph and Agnes Hull crossed the Atlantic again after the sequestered rector of St Buryan was restored in 1660. They settled at the Isles of Shoals off the Maine coast. Joseph died in New England on 19 November 1665. An inventory presented by Agnes included £20 owed by 'the Isle' for ministry. All their surviving children – including Reuben, baptised at Launceston in January 1648/9 – lived on in New England.

GMB 1040–3; C.E. Egan, ed., 'The Hobart Journal', *NEHGR*, 121 (1967), 11; *Scituate CR*, 281, 37, 41, 39, 40; *WJ*, 150, 281n., 432, 563; *WP* V, 38, 57; LPL, MSS COMM. III/3 lib. 2, fol. 65 and III/5, fol. 8; *CCEd* Location ID 15810; John Tingecombe to Henry Scobell, 16 August 1655, Francis Peck, *Desiderata curiosa*, 2 vols (London, 1732–5), II, Lib. XIII: 8; C.E. Banks, *A history of York, Maine* (Boston, MA: Calkins Press, 1931), 264.

CCEd Person ID 57456, *CR*, *GM* 3: 452–60.

HUMFREY, John (c.1597–1651/2)

John Humfrey, the son of Michael and Dorothy Humfrey of Dorchester, Dorset, matriculated at Trinity College, Cambridge, in Easter 1613 (a few months before Hugh Peter*). He was a scholar in 1614 but left the university before graduation, and in 1615 was admitted to Lincoln's Inn, London. Humfrey married three times: his first wife, Isabel Williams, died before 1621, when he married Elizabeth Pelham, daughter of Herbert and Elizabeth Pelham; Elizabeth died in 1628; c. 1632, Humfrey married Lady Susan Fiennes, daughter of Thomas Fiennes, earl of Lincoln.

Humfrey showed an early interest in New England. In the 1620s, when he lived at Fordington, on the outskirts of Dorchester, Humfrey became treasurer of the Dorchester Company of Adventurers, which established fishing settlements on the coast of Massachusetts. John White, the leading minister of Dorchester, promoted emigration. After the demise of the Dorchester Company, Humfrey and White pressed on with a 'New England Company' which, with fresh support from London investors, secured a royal charter in 1629 as the Massachusetts Bay Company. In 1629, Humfrey surrendered his post as an attorney in the court of wards, as did John Winthrop, the future governor of Massachusetts. In 1629, briefly, Humfrey acted as deputy governor of the Company (chosen to represent West Country interests). He stood down in 1630 because he was not emigrating with John Winthrop's company. In 1630 Humfrey saw through the press John Cotton's sermon to the Winthrop fleet, *Gods promise to his plantation* (for which he wrote a preface as 'I.H.'), and John White's *The planters plea*. Humfrey's doubts about the wisdom of choosing Massachusetts Bay soon became apparent: he thought it would be better to settle further south, on 'a good river and in a less cold and snowy place'. However, in the early 1630s he worked hard for Massachusetts in London, and kept in close touch with John Winthrop Jr*. On 8 May 1632, in anticipation of his arrival in New England, which was 'daily expected', Humfrey was elected an assistant in Massachusetts. Reports of his imminent departure from England continued to cross the Atlantic. With Sir Richard Saltonstall* and Matthew Cradock (*ODNB*), who were fellow-members of the Massachusetts Bay Company in England, Humfrey appeared in 1632 before a committee of the privy council, to refute charges made in a petition by Sir Christopher Gardiner* and Thomas Morton* (in support of an attack on the Bay Colony's charter by Sir Ferdinando Gorges).[1]

John and Susan Humfrey sailed from Weymouth on 27 April 1634, and arrived in Boston in July. They settled first at Lynn, then moved to Salem. John Winthrop noted 'By Mr Humfryes means muche money was procured', and munitions. Humfrey also brought propositions from 'some persons of great quality & estate, (& of speciall note for pietye) whereby they discovered their intentions to join with us, if they might receive satisfaction therein': these may have been the questions sent by Viscount Saye and Sele, Lord Brooke and 'other persons of quality and condition', to which John Cotton replied in 1636. Humfrey was admitted to the Salem church in January 1636/7. He played a role in civic life as an assistant, and worked with John Winthrop Jr and Sir

Henry Vane Jr* to establish Harvard. Soon, though, Humfrey's financial difficulties started to cloud the picture. Hugh Peter, Humfrey's minister at Salem petitioned the General Court on 10 September 1638 that some money should be given to Humfrey: 'without some helpe his frends feare the Gospell may suffer by his sufferings'; 'less than £700 besides the sale of much estate will not cleere him'. Hugh Peter feared Humfrey's losses would diminish the colony's standing in England. In a covering note to his petition, Hugh Peter wrote that Humfrey was 'now bound for England with his sonne only [John Jr*] with him ... purposing to return in the Spring, having left his family and estate in Godly mens hands'. Governor John Winthrop marked on the letter that the court was 'not satisfied that his estate is so lowe as it should call for any such public helpe'. (Humfrey petitioned again later and, controversially, was given £250.)[2]

Humfrey was back in England from around September 1638 until April 1639. After he came back, John Endecott (*ANB*) reported to John Winthrop that the Salem church had enjoyed a 'comfortable day' after Humfrey's return, because 'Mr Humfryes voluntarily did acknowledge with many teares his cariadges of rashnes and hastiness ... in such a manner as hee drew teares from diuers.' Endecott was among those who were suspicious of Humfrey because of Humfrey's interest in the Caribbean settlement of Providence. Winthrop recorded that Humfrey,

> being brought low in his estate, and having many children, and being well known to the lords of Providence, and offering himself to their service, was accepted to be the next governour. Whereupon he laboured much to draw men to join with him. This was looked at, both by the general court, and also by the elders, as an unwarrantable course; for though it was thought very needful to further plantation of churches in the West Indies, and all were willing to endeavour the same; yet to doe it with disparagement of this country, (for they gave out that they could not subsist here,) caused us to fear, that the Lord was not with them in this way.

Humfrey hoped to persuade many people to move south from New England. He was able to promise free transportation at the Providence Island Company's expense. On 27 July 1640 Winthrop noted how 'The Lord showed his displeasure' against those who, 'though godly ... have spoken ill of this country and discouraged the hearts of his people': Humfrey was one – his barn had burnt down, at a cost of £160. Humfrey's recruits for Providence Island failed to leave in the winter of 1640. Early in 1641, Humfrey quarrelled with John Endecott when the Salem church debated whether their minister Hugh Peter should be released to go to England as an agent for Massachusetts. Endecott and others opposed this: they feared Hugh Peter would be kept in England, 'or diverted to the West Indies, for Mr Humfrey intended to go with him, who was already engaged that way by the lord Say ... it was feared he should fall under strong temptations that way, being once in England'. As a result of the furore, Hugh Peter deferred his departure.

Humfrey's hopes of Providence Island were dashed in the summer of 1641, when a small party sailed there with captain William Pierce*, only to discover it had been captured by the Spanish. Winthrop recorded that the passengers were 'ashamed to return' to New England, but the crew refused to put them ashore elsewhere. They arrived back in Boston on 3 September 1641. Winthrop thought the failure of the venture 'brought some ... to see their error, and acknowledge it in the open congregation, but others were hardened'.[3]

Humfrey left for England within a short time. He set sail on 26 October 1641, on the same ship as John Phillip*. He left his family behind. Soon afterwards, one of his daughters 'ran mad, and two other[s] ... being under ten years of age, were discovered to have been often abused by divers lewd persons, and filthiness in his family'. Winthrop judged that Humfrey 'much neglected his children, leaving them among ... rude servants'. Daniel Fairfield* was found guilty of abuse, 'especially upon the Lord's days and lecture days'; as were Jenkin Davis of Lynn, a schoolmaster with whom they had been put to 'board and school', and John Hudson, a servant. Dorcas also accused two of her young brothers. Winthrop interpreted this as divine punishment for Humfrey's desertion of New England: 'Thus was this family secretly polluted, and brake not out, till Mr Humfrey had left the country ... against the advice of his best friends.' In 1642 Humfrey wrote to ask John Winthrop Jr to help his family: 'I heare they want monie.' On 13 January 1643/4, Thomas Cobbet (minister at Lynn) proposed that Timothy Dalton's request to adopt Dorcas, the 'defiled' child, should be granted. At this point she was the only child of Humfrey's left in Lynn, and no-one else was willing or able to take her in. By this, Dalton repaid an old debt: 'Mr Humprhey had formerly aduentured him self for him in england when in the High Commission Court and was a means of his liberty and therefore he would gladly thus requite that his kindness.'[4]

On his return to England, Humfrey was quick to join the 'Adventurers for Ireland'. The Irish Catholic rebellion of 1641 led many to support an expedition in 1642 led by Alexander, Lord Forbes. Its intention (not achieved) was to suppress the rebels, who claimed to have approval from Charles I. Investors who had put money into New England helped to finance the expedition and several former settlers volunteered their military skills. Humfrey acted as sergeant major of land forces. He tried to tempt John Winthrop Jr (in England on a visit to secure expertise and investment for New England's ironworks) to join him: 'You are a thousand times welcome home, and should be 1000000000000000 times ... if you would go along with me.' Winthrop was not to be diverted, but his brother-in-law William Rainborowe* signed up. Hugh Peter, who had been Humfrey's minister at Salem (and, as Endecott had predicted, was being drawn into events back home), served as a chaplain. In the end, the Forbes expedition achieved little, and Humfrey returned to London in September 1642. Humfrey's activities over the next few years are not easy to trace, but he was with Hugh Peter at Gravesend on 4 September 1646, when he reflected on his time in New England in a rare letter to John Winthrop:

> It is true the want of that lost occasion (the losse of all I had in the world) doth upon rubbings of that irreparable blow, sometimes a little trouble me

... yet I desire to looke at his [God's] hand for good ... Sir I thank you againe and againe (and that in sinceritie) for any fruites of your goodness to me or mine, and for anything contrarie, I blesse his name I labour to forget, and desire him to pardon.⁵

At the trial of Charles I in 1649, John Humfrey carried the sword of state in the ceremonial procession that marked the arrival at Westminster Hall of the lord president of the High Court of Justice, John, Lord Bradshaw (*ODNB*). As events unfolded after the trial, Humfrey's association with Hugh Peter continued. John Humfrey and Edward Winslow* were among those who took charge when Hugh Peter surrendered his care of St James's Palace: they were among the eleven trustees appointed by parliament in July 1649 to list and value Charles I's goods and personal estate, and sell everything – including the king's priceless art collection. Humfrey was in Ireland with Hugh Peter in October 1649.

On or about 16 December 1651, 'Collonel John Humfrey of the City of Westminster' made a verbal will which placed all his estate in the hands of John, his 'dutifull and engenious sonne', to be used for the education and maintenance of his younger children. The will received probate on 4 June 1653.⁶

---

¹ A.P. Newton, *The colonising activities of the English puritans* (New Haven, CT: Yale University Press, 1914), 42; David Underdown, *Fire from heaven: life in an English town in the seventeenth century* (London: Fontana, 1993), 131–4; Francis J. Bremer, *John Winthrop: America's forgotten founding father* (New York and Oxford: Oxford University Press, 2003), 147, 152, 160, 161, 188, 231–2; *WP* II, 327–9, 331–3; *WP* III, 111, 165 and *passim*; *WJ*, 68, 90, 119-20, 121, 537, 730, 744.
² *WJ*, 360; Thomas Hutchinson, *The history of Massachusetts from ... 1628 until 1750*, 2 vols (Salem, MA: Thomas Cushing, 1795), I, 433–6; Bush, 243–9; *Salem CR*, 6; *WP* III, 492–3; *WP* IV, 56–7, 62.
³ *WP* IV, 110, 326–7; *WJ*, 323–4, 333–4, 347, 356–7; Newton, *Colonising activities*, 292–3; Karen Ordahl Kupperman, *Providence Island, 1630–1641: the other puritan colony* (Cambridge: Cambridge University Press, 1993), 146–7, 315, 320–5, 343.
⁴ *WJ*, 370–4, 414–5; *WP* IV, 352–3, 451–2.
⁵ *Pilgrims*, 65; *WP* IV, 352–3; *WP* V, 101–2.
⁶ *CSPD, 1653–54*, 451 (payment of £90 to John Humfrey as sword-bearer to the High Court of Justice); Jerry Brotton, *The sale of the late king's goods: Charles I and his art collection* (London: Macmillan, 2006), 215–6; R.P. Stearns, *The strenuous puritan: Hugh Peter 1598–1660* (Urbana, IL: University of Illinois Press, 1954), 338, 345, 355; T.C. Barnard, *Cromwellian Ireland: English government and reform in Ireland 1649–1660* (Oxford: Oxford University Press, 1975), 96–7; NA, PROB 11/230/390, will of John Humfrey, colonel, of City of Westminster, Middlesex, 4 June 1653.

GM 3: 462–8; F. Rose-Troup, 'John Humfry', *Essex Institute Historical Collections*, 65 (1929), 293–308.

HUMFREY, John Jr (b. 1622)

John Humfrey, son of John Humfrey* and Elizabeth [Pelham], emigrated to New England c.1634. He returned to England with his father in 1638. It is unclear whether he came back to New England with his father in 1639, or stayed on in England.

In the summer of 1649 the younger John Humfrey commanded a troop of dragoons in John Okey's regiment in Ireland. He was there with his father and Hugh Peter* in October 1649. He became a colonel, like his father. From 1651 to 1655, Humfrey's regiment of foot joined Cromwell's military force in Scotland. In 1655 he was given command of a regiment in the Caribbean expedition led by Robert Sedgwick*. They ended up in Jamaica, where ill-health decimated Humfrey's soldiers. Humfrey petitioned in 1656 that the sick should be allowed to go back to England. He left the Caribbean, and perhaps went to a post in Ireland and then to Flanders.

>F. Rose-Troup, 'John Humfry', *Essex Institute Historical Collections*, 65 (1929), 293; R.P. Stearns, *The strenuous puritan: Hugh Peter 1598–1660* (Urbana, IL: University of Illinois Press, 1954), 355; W.L. Sachse, *The colonial American in Britain* (Madison, WI: University of Wisconsin Press, 1956), 138; C.H. Firth and G. Davies, *The regimental history of Cromwell's army* (Oxford: Clarendon Press, 1940), 296, 297, 308–10, 722–4; *GM* 3: 465.

HUMFREY, Joseph

Joseph Humfrey, son of John Humfrey* and Susan [Fiennes], was born in New England and baptised on 5 April 1640 at Salem. He was not in Lynn, 1643/4, when the authorities made provision for his sister Dorcas.

Humfrey was in New England from 1661 to 1663, settling his father's estate, with Edmund Batter. He had gone 'out of the country' by 1663, when Batter became the sole executor. Humfrey made a will, 3 July 1663, 'being bound on a voyage for England & understanding . . . the danger of the seas'. He was killed at Lisbon, Portugal, c.1669.

>*Salem CR*, 17; *WP* IV, 451–2; *Essex Probate Recs.* I, 345–7; *GM* 3: 465.

HUTCHIN, George

George Hutchin, a wheelwright, settled in Cambridge, Massachusetts. He had probably come from north-east England, like some others in the town (for example, William Cutter*). He seems to have returned home in 1647. On 11 October, John Watson of Cambridge appointed Hutchin as his attorney, to ask about legacies from his grandfather, Richard Walters, a smith, late of Whickham, County Durham. Hutchin was to receive and dispose of the legacies to Watson's use, as he thought best. Hutchin then disappears from the records.

>Aspinwall, 90.

HUTCHINSON, Edward (1607–*fl.* 1669)

Edward Hutchinson was a brother of William Hutchinson, the husband of the antinomian Anne Hutchinson, and of the London merchant Richard Hutchinson. He was baptised at Alford, Lincolnshire, in 1607.

Edward emigrated with his wife Sarah in 1633 and settled in Boston. He was admitted to the Boston church in October 1633, and 'Sarah Hutchinson the wife of our brother Edward Hutchinson' joined on 15 December. Edward Hutchinson became a freeman of Massachusetts on 4 March 1633/4. On 2 November 1637, during the Antinomian Controversy, he was disenfranchised, fined £40, and put out of office as a 'sergeant' for signing a seditious libel and speaking contemptuously to the court. He was disarmed on 20 November 1637, and given licence to leave Massachusetts. Hutchinson went to Portsmouth, Rhode Island, and became a freeman of the Rhode Island colony on 7 March 1637/8. He was granted land at Portsmouth on several occasions between May 1638 and February 1639/40.

Edward and Sarah Hutchinson returned to England permanently by 1644. Edward was still living in November 1669, when Richard Hutchinson, 'ironmonger', made his will: he bequeathed £10 in cloth, for mourning clothes, to his brother Edward Hutchinson and his wife.

GMB 1052–4; *NEHGR* 20: 363; NA, PROB 11/332/508, will of Richard Hutchinson, ironmonger of London, 11 April 1670.

HUTCHINSON, Richard (1615–1696)

Richard Hutchinson, son of William and Anne Hutchinson, was baptised at Alford, Lincolnshire, on 8 December 1615. Anne, his mother, became notorious in the Antinomian Controversy that divided Massachusetts in 1636–8. His uncle and namesake was the London merchant Richard Hutchinson, who had many dealings with New England. His aunt Mary Hutchinson married John Wheelwright*, the minister who stood alongside Anne Hutchinson (his sister-in-law) in the Antinomian Controversy. Richard emigrated with his parents in 1634 on the *Griffin* and settled in Boston. He was admitted to the Boston church on 9 November 1634, as the son of 'our brother Willyam Hutchinson'. He became a freeman on 4 March 1634/5. He was disarmed during the Antinomian Controversy.

It is unclear exactly when Hutchinson left New England for England. He had settled in London by 1645, when on 28 December the Boston church, 'according to his Desire by letters', dismissed him 'to the Church of Christ whereof Mr Thomas Goodwyn is pastor', St Dunstan in the East in London.

From 1649, Hutchinson took the post of navy treasurer, first as deputy to Sir Henry Vane Jr* (who had supported Anne Hutchinson in the Antinomian Controversy) and then as Vane's successor in 1650. In this role – with naval commissioners that included Francis Willoughby*, Robert Tomson*, Nehemiah Bourne* and Edward Hopkins* – Hutchinson played an important part in the day-to-day administration of the navy, at a time of huge expansion, especially during Anglo-Dutch hostilities in the 1650s. The former colonist is probably the 'Richard Hutchinson of Mile End' who had two children, Theophilus and Ann, baptised at William Greenhill's church in Stepney, 1648 and 1654. In 1655 Hutchinson (or his uncle) joined Thomas Bell*, David Yale* and John Hill, brother of the Boston merchant Valentine Hill, to endorse John Wheelwright's fitness to hold a church living in Lincolnshire. Several decades later, 'Richard Hutchinson the elder of Mile End' made generous bequests to, amongst others, his children – not Theophilus and Ann (who may not have survived) but Richard, John, Edward, Josiah, Elizabeth and Mary; £200 each to his 'two sisters in New England'; £100 to 'Mr Nathaniel Mather'*; £50 to the widow of John Collins*; £200 for ministers and others, to be divided as Mather and his executors thought fit; £60 for the poor.

Boston CR, 19, 44 (Philip Hatley* and Henry Stonehill* also joined Goodwin's church, by dismission from Milford); *NEHGR* 3: 93; *GD*; *Suffolk Deeds* II, 11–13; *GM* 3: 480–1; G.E. Aylmer, *The state's servants: the civil service of the English Republic, 1649–1660* (London: Routledge and Kegan Paul, 1973), 248–9, 408; B.S. Capp, *Cromwell's navy: the fleet and the English Revolution, 1648–1660* (Oxford: Clarendon Press, 1989), 48, 166, 295, 303; Stepney CB, fols 118, 121; *Pilgrims*, 114, 120; NA, PROB 11/453/72, will of Richard Hutchinson of Stepney, Middlesex, 23 November 1696. Aylmer and Capp both identify the colonist (and not his uncle) as the navy treasurer.

J

JAMES, Abraham

Abraham James attended Harvard, but left no trace in the college records. On 26 March 1651 Samuel Mather* wrote to Jonathan Mitchell about the circumstances of all the students who had already left New England. He worked his way through the list in order of seniority, by Harvard class. James appears with the class of 1642 or 1643: 'Mr Brewster [Nathaniel Brewster*] is minister in Norfolk and hath a good report. And so is Abraham James too.'

MHS, Misc. Bd. MSS, 26 March 1651, Samuel Mather to Jonathan Mitchell.

JAMES, Thomas (1595–c.1683)

Thomas James, the son John James, rector of Skirbeck, Lincolnshire, was baptised at Boston on 5 October 1595. He attended Emmanuel College, Cambridge, and graduated BA in 1615, MA in 1618. He was ordained in 1617 and became a schoolteacher, first at Moulton near Spalding, then from 1619 as head of Boston grammar. James was cited to a church court in 1623 for complaining that anyone who held two church livings 'was like to a woman which nursed two children, feeding th'one and pining th'other'.[1]

He arrived in New England on 5 June 1632. With his wife Elizabeth, James initially joined the Boston church, but was soon dismissed with others to form a new church at Charlestown. On 14 October 1632, the Boston church recorded: 'those of Charles towne, who had formerly been ioyned to Boston congregation, now in regarde of the difficultye of passage in the winter, & haveing opportunitye of a pastor, one Mr Iames, who came ouer at this tyme, were dismissed from the Congregation of Boston'. John Winthrop observed later that:

> Sathan bestirred himselfe to hinder the progresse of the Gospell ... he stirred vp a spirit of Iealousye between Mr Iames, the Pastor of Charlton & many of his people: so as Mr No[w]ell & some other who had been dismissed from Boston, beganne to question their facte of breakinge from Boston, & it grewe to such a scruple of Conscience among them, as the advice of the other ministers was taken in it, who (after two meetings[)] could not agree, about their continuance or return.

By 1636 tensions between James and the Charlestown church were acute:

> Some occasions of difference had fallen out betweene the Church of Charl[t] on & Mr Iames their Pastor: The Teacher Mr Simmes [Zechariah Symmes],

& the most of the Bretheren, had taken Offence at diverse speaches of his (he beinge a verye melanckolike man & full of Causelesse iealousyes &c.) for which they had dealt with him, both privately and publicly, but receiving no satisfaction, they wrote to all the neighbor Churches for their advice & helpe in the Case . . .

The elders of neighbour churches found James at fault, but declared that the proceedings against him had been irregular. They recommended he and Elizabeth should seek dismission from Charlestown; if James refused, he could be cast out. (This case was cited by Richard Mather as the only example of an advisory synod he had known in New England, in a letter of 25 June 1636 to two English critics, William Rathband and 'Mr T'.) The upshot was that James left Charlestown and Thomas Allen* took his place.

Over the next few years James was unsettled in New England, without a tie to a congregation. Roger Williams* received a letter from Benjamin Hubbard* and others of Charlestown, late in 1637, who hoped to move to Rhode Island and thought James intended to join them. James was in Rhode Island in 1638, but his flock did not materialise. c.1639, from Providence, he wrote to ask Winthrop for permission to settle at Seekonk (on the boundary of Massachusetts' jurisdiction), and for an assurance that he would never be 'punished in any kind *causa inaudita* before . . . convicted or have liberty to speake for my selfe in a Judiciall way'. In the event, James moved west to New Haven. On 3 November 1639 he was granted land there, and sold his 'lands, rights and privileges' in Providence, 20 March 1639/40. On 11 June 1640 he became a freeman of New Haven, and so must have already been a church member. He worked as a schoolmaster in the town. In October 1642 James was one of three preachers – the others were John Knowles* and William Thompson – commissioned to go to Virginia to assist the godly there. He returned to New Haven in 1643.[2]

Thomas James may have returned to England as early as 1646. The last trace of his presence in New Haven's records is a sale of land on 2 October 1649. From the late 1640s, his career was entwined with the fortunes of Needham Market in Suffolk. A parliamentary survey recorded, 23 October 1650: 'Needham Market a chapell of ease, Mr Thomas James hyred by the towne att their own charge: and allowed by them his salarye at the yeare £50.' James seems to have been there before 1650. In a petition dated June 1651, the town's inhabitants reported that he had had been with them 'some years together', but had departed two years earlier, leaving them without a preacher. Their petition was addressed to Philip, Lord Wharton (*ODNB*), who had taken James away to become his domestic chaplain. In a letter to Wharton, c.1651, written at Wharton's home in Buckinghamshire, James expressed a 'great desire . . . to remaine at Winchingdon and to spend my poor mite in doing your family seruice. if god may please euen to my dying day', and explained:

> it hath bene my misery my Lord theise 16 or 17 yeares that by a secrett contrived current of injustice. . . I have bene driven up and downe the world and never had that right of nations which Agrippa granted paul. thou art

permitted to plead for thy selfe [Acts 26:1]. if wronged innocency ... may at last under your... protection find a resting place, I shall rejoice and study thankfulnes all my dayes.

The Needham Market petitioners asked Wharton to release James to be their preacher again, knowing 'that your honour hath promised that if some people should call him againe into these parts of Suffolk or Essex where he hath lived formerly ... your Lordship would be willing that he should returne'. The upshot was that James went back to Needham Market. He wrote to Wharton from the town on 25 March 1652, acknowledging receipt of £15.[3]

Thomas James was ejected as town preacher of Needham Market in 1662. Edmund Calamy noted 'He had a pretty numerous society after his being silenc'd', and identified him as a congregationalist. He was licensed (as a presbyterian) at West Creeting in 1672, at the house (and licensed presbyterian meeting-place) of Thomas Waterhouse*. He and Waterhouse both applied to be licensed (as congregationalists) in the house of Margaret Rogers of Needham, 1672, but this was not granted. In his will, dated 5 February 1662/3, James described himself as 'of Needham Market, clerk', and mentioned his son Thomas at East Hampton, Long Island.[4]

[1] Helena Hajzyk, 'The Church in Lincolnshire, c.1595–c.1640' (PhD dissertation, University of Cambridge, 1980), 188, 343, 459.
[2] *Boston CR*, 15; *WJ*, 83–4, 112, 172, 261, 426–7; *Letters from New England ... 1629–1638*, ed. Everett Emerson (Amherst, MA: University of Massachusetts Press, 1976), 204; *WP* III, 509; *WP* IV, 3, 90, 90n.; Lechford *PD*, 43.
[3] LPL, MS COMM. XIIa/15 fol. 599; Bodleian, Rawlinson MSS, Letters, 52: 60, 61, 68.
[4] Waters, 1356–7.

CR, *GMB* 1072–6.

JEFFREYS, Robert

Robert Jeffreys emigrated in 1635 on the *Elizabeth & Ann*, with his wife Mary, three young children and two maidservants.

Jeffreys settled first at Weymouth, but moved to Charlestown – where on 17 April 1636 'Mary Jeffreis' joined the church – and to Boston in 1637. At the time of the Antinomian Controversy, he moved out of Massachusetts: first to Portsmouth in 1638, then to Newport, Rhode Island, in 1639. He acted as a surveyor and surgeon. From 1639 to 1643 Jeffreys served as Newport's treasurer. He was also chosen as captain of the Newport train-band. On 11 November 1646, William Coddington* sent a letter to John Winthrop in Boston, 'per Mr Robt. Jeafferyes'. No further record survives of Jeffreys or his family in New England. Many settlers returned to England at the end of 1646, and Jeffreys seems to have been among them.

In England, Robert Jeffreys is likely to be the person of this name who acted as registrar-accountant in London from around October 1649 until November 1652. Edward Winslow*, who set sail from Boston for England in mid-December 1646 (quite possibly with Jeffreys as a fellow passenger), recommended him to the accounts committee on 19 October 1649. Jeffreys submitted a certificate of proficiency as a merchant and accountant, endorsed by the MPs Luke Robinson (*ODNB*), Charles Fleetwood (*ODNB*), Nathaniel Rich (*ODNB*) and Cornelius Holland (*ODNB*).

> GM 4: 33–6; *WP* III, 517; *WP* V, 118; G.E. Aylmer, *The state's servants: the civil service of the English Republic, 1649–1660* (London: Routledge and Kegan Paul, 1973), 63.

JENNER, Thomas (*c.*1607–1676)

Thomas Jenner was the son of Thomas Jenner, a farmer of Fordham, Essex. He matriculated at Christ's College, Cambridge, in February 1623/4, aged seventeen. He seems to have been a minister before emigration, in East Anglia and perhaps at Heddon, Northumberland. (Thomas Shepard, minister at Cambridge, Massachusetts, took refuge at Heddon before emigration. Edward Hall, who had come from Heddon, mentioned Jenner in his testimony at admission to Shepard's church.)

Both Jenner and his father emigrated in the 1630s and settled at Roxbury. In the records, it is hard to disentangle which Thomas Jenner is which. It is more likely that the younger Jenner emigrated in 1635, was admitted to the Roxbury church late that year, and became a freeman of Massachusetts on 8 December 1636. (His father emigrated later and became a freeman in 1639.) Robert Stansby of Westhorpe, Suffolk, wrote to John Wilson* on 17 April 1637, asking about the truth of reports current in England: some ministers, like George Burdett*, had not yet been called to a place; 'Others laye downe their ministery and become priuate members, as Mr Bachelor [Stephen Bachiler*], Mr Jenner, and Mr Nathan[iel] Ward*.' From 1638 to 1640 Jenner served as preacher at Weymouth, Massachusetts. He was the first minister to ask the magistrates for maintenance because the town did not provide enough. In 1640 a new minister, Samuel Newman, formally gathered a church at Weymouth. Thomas Lechford* reported that Jenner had gone to Maine. He was recommended to Saco by, among others, John Winthrop. Jenner was in Saco by 25 January 1640/1. Richard Vines (*ODNB*), who had been at Saco as an agent for Sir Ferdinando Gorges since 1630, expressed his gratitude to Winthrop with rather mixed feelings. Vines opposed congregationalism as 'Separacion', and remained loyal to the Church of England:

> I like Mr Jenner for his life and conversacion, and alsoe his preaching, if he would lett the Church of England alone. that doth much trouble me, to heare our mother Church questioned for her impurity upon every occasion, as if men (ministers I meane) had no other marke to ayme at, but the Paps that gaue them suck ... why should a Son betray his mothers weaknes ... Noah his Son lyes still under a curse for discovering his fathers shame ...

But Jenner had a salary at Saco of £47, and freedom to minister as he wished. His letters to Winthrop show he regarded his work as a preaching mission.

There were 'scarse any religious' at Saco apart from Vines and his family: 'I have not troubled the people at all with Church discipline, or constitutions of Churches . . . but have bent my whole studdies to shew them their miserable and lost estate with out Christ.' Jenner denied publicly attacking the English church. He had simply preached against popish religion 'and condemned those practices which I saw the people here were superstitiously addicted to'. Jenner supported Vines in his battle with George Cleeve, an agent of Sir Alexander Rigby, over rival claims to territory. But in 1645 the two men quarrelled about the action to be taken against Cleeve. Jenner wanted to leave Saco, reporting that Vines 'is fallen out with me bitterly'. In fact, Vines was the first to go, taking himself to better prospects in Barbados when he sensed that parliament would rule in Rigby's favour. Jenner was by then also:

> on the wing of removall, but whither as yet I know not. The Lord direct me. I can not by any meanes abide here any longer. Amongst many other reasons, one is the falling out betweene me and Mr Robison who unknowne to my selfe had secretly gained the affection of my eldest daughter . . . I approve not of the man . . .

From 1646 to 1649 Jenner lived in Charlestown. On 28 December 1649, he sold a house and land at Weymouth (mainly his own property but some his father's), with consent from 'Mrs Jenner'. It looks as if he completed this transaction as part of his preparations to go to England.[1]

Jenner sailed back to England on the same ship as Thomas Harrison*, in late December or early January 1649/50. In 1650 he became rector of the sequestered living of Horstead with Stanninghall and Coltishall, Norfolk, at an annual stipend of £65. On 21 October 1650, John Eliot responded favourably to an offer from the Corporation for the Propagation of the Gospel in New England to buy the libraries of Jenner and Thomas Weld*. In April 1651, Edward Winslow* wrote that poverty led Jenner to part with his books, and he had already persuaded Winslow to advance him £30 – 'to recover it would be a hard matter'. On 20 October 1651 Eliot reported that Thomas Mayhew had decided to accept the books and 'therefore hath taken them, (all that were here) . . . what books are wanting . . . he will request brother Jenner to make good, and untill he make it good, request of the worshipfull Corporation, that no more money be paid unto him'. Jenner's own catalogue of the two hundred books he sold is among the Corporation's papers.[2]

For the second half of the 1650s, Jenner was in Ireland. On 14 July 1656, Thomas Harrison gave him a letter of recommendation to present to Henry Cromwell, which mentioned their shared voyage back from New England. Harrison's letter told Cromwell that Nathaniel Brewster* had first drawn Jenner 'to looke towards Ireland'. (Brewster had held the living of Alby, close to Coltishall. He had gone to Ireland in 1655 and commanded a high salary.) Jenner became minister of a congregational church at Drogheda, County Louth, one of the vital towns in which able ministers were strategically placed to support the Cromwellian forces. In December 1656 he joined with Samuel Winter and Timothy Taylor (formerly co-minister with Samuel Eaton* in

Cheshire) to ordain Samuel Mather* as Winter's assistant in Dublin. Jenner was at Limerick soon afterwards, and at Carlow in 1658. A successor came to Coltishall in 1658. Jenner acted as chaplain to a brigade going to England in 1659 but continued in Ireland, perhaps still at Carlow.

After the Restoration, Jenner stayed on in Ireland. In 1670 he published an attack on the Quakers which led William Penn to brand him 'an Old Peevish Priest', 'a Presbyter-Independent Priest', just out to make money. Jenner's will, made on 4 June 1672 and recorded at Dublin on 26 May 1676, left bequests to his children and grandchildren, including 'the whole stud of horses and mares which I left behind me in New England'. The residue went to his wife, Ellen. Jenner's son, Captain Thomas Jenner of Charlestown, was a formidable transatlantic mariner.[3]

Publication *Quakerism anatomiz'd and confuted* ([Dublin], 1670).

[1] *Al. Cant.*; *Shepard's confessions*, 33; Roger Thompson, *Cambridge cameos: stories of life in seventeenth-century New England* (Boston, MA: New England Historic Genealogical Society, 2005), 213–14; *Roxbury CR*, 81; *NEHGR* 3: 94, 187; *WP* III, 390, 380n.; *WJ*, 244, 281n, 423n.; David D. Hall, *The faithful shepherd: a history of the New England ministry in the seventeenth century* (Chapel Hill, NC: University of North Carolina Press, 1972) 149; Lechford *PD*, 45; *WP* IV, 307–8, 319–20, 331–2, 436; *WP* V, 14–16, 76; Larry Gragg, *Englishmen transplanted: the English colonization of Barbados, 1627–1660* (Oxford and New York: Oxford University Press, 2003), 22, 70, 110; MHS, Misc. MSS., 28 December 1649.
[2] LPL, MS COMM. XIIb/9/1; BL, Lansdowne MS 821, fol. 200; 3 *MHSC* 4: 144; 4 *MHSC* 7: 355n.; Bodleian, Rawlinson MS D. 934, fols 11v., 32–3.
[3] BL, Lansdowne MS 821, fol. 200; G.F. Nuttall, *Visible saints: the congregational way, 1640–1660* (Oxford: Blackwell, 1957); 31; St J.D. Seymour, *The puritans in Ireland, 1647–1661* (Oxford: Clarendon Press, 1921), 215; T.C. Barnard, *Cromwellian Ireland: English government and reform in Ireland 1649–1660* (Oxford: Oxford University Press, 1975), 136; *WR*, 272; William Penn, *The invalidity of John Faldo's vindication of his book called Quakerism no Christianity* ([London?], 1673), 171–2 and margin; Roger Thompson, *From deference to defiance: Charlestown, Massachusetts, 1629–1662* (Boston, MA: New England Historic Genealogical Society, 2012), 216–27, 382–4.

GM 4: 46–50, *ODNB s.n.* 'Jenner, Thomas (*d.*1673)', printseller and writer.

JENNISON, William

William Jennison was a mariner and merchant, engaged in trade with Virginia and Bermuda. He lived in Bermuda before he came to New England.

Jennison settled at Charlestown in 1630. He must have been a church member by 18 May 1631, when he became a freeman of Massachusetts. He moved to Watertown in 1634, where he joined his brother Robert. William Jennison became a leading member of the small group in Watertown who were elected to office again and again. He served as a selectman and deputy for Watertown, and as captain of the train-band. He took part in a raid on the (undefended) Peqout Indians in 1636. He opposed the sentence of banishment passed on the antinomian Anne Hutchinson in November 1637, but, according to John Winthrop, when he and other 'chief military officers' were called to account, they 'did ingenuously acknowledge, how they had been deceived and misled'. Winthrop also noted that Jennison was questioned in 1644 about whether his loyalty lay with king or parliament: although he was reluctant to take sides against his prince, 'he was now satisfied that the parliament's cause was good, and if he were in England he would assist in defence of it'.

Jennison left for England c.1651 and probably died there after 1657.

GMB 1086–9; Roger Thompson, *Divided we stand: Watertown, Massachusetts, 1630–80* (Amherst, MA: University of Massachusetts Press, 1994), 17, 41, 42–3, 58, 68, 96, 97, 147, 170; *WJ*, 119, 183, 248n., 518–19.

JONES, Thomas (d. c.1654)

Thomas Jones came from south-east England and emigrated with Henry Whitfield's* company. He signed the 'plantation covenant' aboard ship, 1 June 1639.

Jones settled at Guilford with Whitfield, and became a member of the church Whitfield gathered. Jones was elected as the first marshall of the plantation, and re-appointed annually until 17 June 1650, when another was chosen 'to succeed in his room in that office when he removes'. Henry Whitfield had already resolved to go back to England, and had presented his reasons formally to the Guilford church on 20 February 1649/50. At that point Jones signalled his willingness to continue payment to a minister. However, he and others in Guilford (notably Samuel Desborough*) were now also contemplating departure. When Jones was next elected marshall, on 9 June 1651, provision was again made for the time 'when Providence shall remove him'. On 10 June 1652 someone else took his place.

Jones went to England c.1652, and may have joined Samuel Desborough in Scotland. William Leete, writing on 10 October 1654 to Desborough at Leith, asked him to 'remember my respects to Mr Jones'. Jones died soon after this: on 10 March 1654/5 John Davenport reported that 'Mrs Disborough, and Goodman Jones, of Gillford, dyed of the small poxe in England or Scotland'. Jones's children were still in New England. On 12 June 1656, his stepdaughter Mary Carter demanded £40 from his estate, which was paid to her. This left estate in New England valued at only £1 3s 8d for Jones's three other children, Samuel, Nathaniel and Sarah. Nathaniel Jones of Branford died in 1668, leaving £52 6s, of which £45 15s was due to him as portion of his father's will in England. On 4 March 1667/8 William Chittenden registered a sale of Jones's property from the early 1650s, made with permission of Jones's son Samuel. Chittenden had arrived in Guilford in 1639 with Jones and acted as his agent after he left.

MHS, Misc. Bd. MSS., 1 June 1639; B.C. Steiner, *A history of . . . Guilford* (Baltimore, MD: privately printed, 1897), 46; BL, Egerton MS 2519, fol. 11; *Davenport Letters*, 102; *NEHGR* 59: 386–7.

JORDAN, Thomas (d. 1705)

Thomas Jordan, younger brother of John Jordan, probably came from Lenham, Kent. He sailed with his brother to New England in Henry Whitfield's* company in 1639. Thomas Jordan settled at Guilford. He acted as a town officer and in 1651 was among the deputies who attended court at New Haven. On 29 June 1653 Jordan was appointed, with William Leete, to represent Guilford at a meeting of the commissioners of the United Colonies of New England, in Boston, to answer the Massachusetts General Court about the proposed war against the Dutch.

Thomas Jordan left New England with Nathaniel Whitfield* in mid-October 1654. William Leete (who perhaps used them to carry his letter) wrote to Samuel Desborough* on 10 October 1654: 'for matters here I refferre you to conference with your Cousen Jordan and your brother Nathaniel; who fully understand the state of things'. After his return, Jordan seems to have lived at Lenham in Kent, but his history is shadowy.

> B.C. Steiner, *A history of . . Guilford* (Baltimore, MD: privately printed, 1897), 24–5, 31, 45; *WP* VI, 438–9; Leete to Desborough, 10 October 1654, BL, Egerton MS 2519, fol. 10.

JUPE, Benjamin

Benjamin Jupe and Mary Morse*, with Anthony Jupe, were the three children of Grace Jupe, given up after her death into the care of her brother, the Boston merchant Robert Keayne. Benjamin Jupe had been brought up in Robert Keayne's household, with his aunt Anne and cousin Benjamin Keayne*. Mary had married John Morse* in 1652.

In his lengthy will, written during the autumn of 1653, Robert Keayne described Benjamin Jupe as 'lame and dim-sighted and not like to do much if anything at all towards his own maintenance'. Keayne regarded Jupe, with 'many infirmities and his inability otherwise to help himself' as in need of special help: 'I do in special manner commend the care of him to the love and tenderness of my wife and son whom I have found to be very indulgent towards him and to see that he may not be wronged.' Keayne initially left Jupe £40, to be invested to supply an income. This would supplement the 'four pounds a year left to him by his mother in a house at London, also . . . tenements in London left him by his uncle, Mr Nicholas Jupe, which will produce 8 or ten pounds per anno to him for 18 or 20 years'. (Nicholas Jupe had bequeathed to his nephew Benjamin a half-share in two houses in the parish of 'St Buttolphes without Aldgate', also 'the house where the stone cutter did dwell and my own dwelling house and garden', and various sums of money.) However, towards the end of his will, Keayne cancelled all the legacies he had given to Benjamin Jupe and to his sister Mary Morse, 'for some occasion of offence that . . . hath been given to me . . . they have pulled it upon themselves against my desire and have withdrawn themselves from that long care and tender love that I have borne to them'.

Benjamin Jupe set sail for London late in 1654 with his sister Mary and her husband John Morse. John made arrangements for the journey, but ran into trouble raising 'fiveteene Pounds for our three passages' and had to turn to Robert Keayne for a loan.

The apologia of Robert Keayne, ed. Bernard Bailyn (New York: Harper and Row, 1965), 36, 38–9, 40, 72–3, 86–7, 88; NA, PROB 11/218/505, will of Nicholas Jupe, merchant tailor of London, 13 October 1651; Waters, 152–3; *Suffolk Deeds* II, 86–7, 182–5.

K

KEAYNE, Benjamin

Benjamin Keayne was the only son of Robert and Anne Keayne, and cousin of Benjamin Jupe* and Mary Morse*. His father was one of Boston's wealthiest merchants. Keayne arrived with his parents in 1635. He joined the Artillery Company at its formation in 1638, with his father as captain; he was a senior sergeant in 1641. Benjamin Keayne married Sarah*, the daughter of Thomas Dudley (*ANB*). On 9 June 1639 both Benjamin and Sarah were admitted to Boston church. Benjamin Keayne became a freeman of Massachusetts on 9 September 1639. He and Sarah moved to Lynn and were recommended to the church there on 3 May 1640. Benjamin was dismissed from the Boston church to Lynn on 10 July 1642.

Keayne went back to his native country to join the parliamentary army. Robert Keayne wrote that his son had been 'in the wars in England'. Keayne may have been a major in Stephen Winthrop's* regiment, or was perhaps the captain 'Kaine' in Colonel Weldon's regiment of foot, fighting in the West Country in 1645. His wife Sarah followed him back and acquired a reputation as a radical: 'My she Cosin Keane is growne a great preacher', Stephen Winthrop reported, 27 March 1645/6. Brampton Gurdon of Assington, Suffolk, reported to John Winthrop, 6 June 1649:

> Heere goes some speech of a N.E. couple that lately came from thence the husband first, And then the wife followed after with what goods she could get together but we heare all her goods miscarryed, and she escaped only with her life. the man was Canes son . . . the woman is returned to N.E. and resolves there to take another Husband. I hope your lawes will not tollerate such wicked actions.

Gurdon's report was accurate, if slightly behind the times. Sarah Keayne had returned to New England in 1646 and in November the Boston church admonished her for 'Irregular prophesying in mixt Assemblies and for Refusing ordinarilie to heare in the Churches of Christ'. Benjamin Keayne soon renounced his marriage. He sent letters from London in March 1646/7 to the Boston ministers John Cotton and John Wilson*, and to his father-in-law Thomas Dudley: because of Sarah's immorality, she had 'unwived herself'. The Massachusetts General Court granted his divorce, and the Boston church excommunicated Sarah in October 1647 for 'odious, lewd, and scandalous behaviour' with Nicholas Hart, an excommunicate of Taunton.

In 1653, Robert Keayne still hoped to lure Benjamin back to New England. He bequeathed him land not goods, because my desire is that he would resolve to live here in this country and here to settle his abode so long as he can enjoy his peace, and keep a good conscience and live comfortably, which I think he may do as well if not better, then in any other part of the world that I know of, [unless] the times should much alter ... Here he will have a comfortable estate to live upon without any great pains or distractions and if he should have an intent to remove himself into England to accomplish that he will be forced to sell his land it may be for half the value of it.

However, Benjamin Keayne established himself as a merchant in London. Brampton Gurdon described him in 1649 as a 'cloake seller in Birching Lane'. He acted as his father's agent. Keayne had business that took him up into Scotland, and made his will in Glasgow, 16 October 1654. This mentioned a debt of £10 owed by 'Major Ducktt ... Captaine Lt in the late Regiment of Coll[onel] Rich' – Charles Duckett, in Scotland with Colonel Nathaniel Rich (*ODNB*) in 1654. Keayne left most of his estate to his daughter Anna, but left a diamond ring to his 'cousin' Stephen Winthrop, who was also in Scotland in 1654. Keayne died in 1662 and left an estate worth £4,000.

Artillery Company, 67–9; *NEHGR* 3: 187; *Boston CR*, 25, 29, 37, 46, 49; *The apologia of Robert Keayne*, ed. Bernard Bailyn (New York: Harper and Row, 1965), 32, 34, 92 (Robert Keayne's will, 16 December 1653, proved 2 May 1656); C.H. Firth and G. Davies, *The regimental history of Cromwell's army* (Oxford: Clarendon Press, 1940), 150, 452; Bush, 394–5; *WP* V, 70, 143–4, 189n., 351; Bernard Bailyn, *The New England merchants in the seventeenth century* (Cambridge, MA: Harvard University Press, 1955), 87; Aspinwall, 92; *GM* 4: 129; NA, PROB 11/308/160, will of Beniamin Kaine, 17 May 1662.

KNIGHT, William

William Knight attended Emmanuel College, Cambridge, and graduated BA in 1630/1, MA in 1634. His sister Elizabeth married Israel Stoughton* in 1627 and emigrated in 1632. Knight followed the Stoughtons to Massachusetts in 1637. He was perhaps the William Knight of 'New Meadows' (Topsfield), who left by 1648.

Knight may have returned to England with Israel Stoughton in 1643, or possibly later. Stoughton made a will in London, 17 July 1644, which appointed 'my deere brother Mr William Knight' as an overseer.

It has been suggested that the former colonist was the William Knight who became preacher at St Matthew, Ipswich, in 1655. This minister, unusually for a New Englander during the Commonwealth, had been ordained on 8 August 1654 by Ralph Brownrigg, bishop of Exeter. At the Restoration he conformed, and was licensed in Ipswich as curate of St Mary at Elms and rector of St Matthew. He was still rector in 1677; a successor was appointed in 1695.

GMB 1775–6; W.L. Sachse, 'The migration of New Englanders to England, 1640–1660', *American Historical Review*, 53 (1947–8), 278; N.C.P. Tyack, 'Migration from

East Anglia to New England before 1660' (PhD dissertation, University of London, 1951), 88; *NEHGR* 4: 52; 7: 333; LPL, MS COMM. II, fol. 380; *CCEd* Person ID 126006.

KNOLLYS, Hanserd (1598–1691)

Hanserd Knollys, the son of Richard Knollys, was born near Louth in Lincolnshire. He had close connections with Scartho, near Grimsby, where his father was rector from 1613. Knollys was educated at St Catharine's College, Cambridge, and ordained deacon and priest in June 1629. After this he became vicar at Humberston, Lincolnshire. On 22 May 1632 he married Anne Cheyney. Knollys, who had encountered puritanism at Cambridge, objected to requirements such as wearing a surplice and making the sign of the cross at baptism. He also had scruples about 'mixed communion' at the Lord's table. A few years into his ministry he became convinced that he must resign his orders: ordination at the hands of a bishop was not a 'seal from Christ of my ministry'. John Williams, bishop of Lincoln, tried to retain Knollys (and even offered him a better living) but Knollys refused. John Wheelwright*, at this point a preacher at Belleau, exercised a powerful influence on him. In the early 1630s Knollys and Wheelwright enjoyed relative freedom, with Williams's tacit protection, but everything changed when Williams's power fell away. In 1636 the Court of High Commission arrested Knollys – he was taken to the house of the man who served the warrant, but managed to get away.

After much deliberation, Knollys decided to emigrate. He seems to have reached Boston in the summer of 1638. Later, he wrote a vivid account of his Atlantic crossing and early days in New England:

> I tarried so long in London waiting for a passage, that when I went aboard I had but 6 brass farthings left, and no silver or Gold, only my Wife had £5 that I knew not of . . . By the way my little Child dyed with Convulsion fits, our Beer and Water Stank, our Bisket was green, yellow and blew, moulded and rotten, and our Cheese also, so that we suffered much hardship, being 12 weeks in our passage; but God was gracious to us, and led us safe through those great Deeps, and e're we went ashore, came one and enquired for me, and told me a Friend that was gone from Boston to Rode Island had left me his house to sojourn in . . . The Magistrates were told by the Ministers that I was an Antinomian, and desired they would not suffer me to abide in their Patent: But within the time limited by their Law in that Case, two Strangers coming to Boston from Piscattuah, hearing of me by a meer Accident, got me to go with them to that Plantation, and to preach there, where I remained for about four years.

Knollys arrived at a sensitive time, just after the Antinomian Controversy which had seen his old friend John Wheelwright exiled. Knollys did not stay in Massachusetts Bay, but went north to Piscataqua. Knollys's ministry in the settlements at York and Dover had the support of John Underhill, who was under censure from the Boston church for adultery. Initially, Knollys competed in ministry with the maverick George Burdett*. Knollys earned a rebuke from the Massachusetts authorities in 1639 for sending letters to England which, according to John Winthrop, described the civil and ecclesiastical government of the colony as 'worse than the high commission... and that here was nothing but oppression... not so much as a face of religion'. Knollys repented and promised to give public satisfaction: he was granted letters of safe passage into Massachusetts for this purpose. A quarrel between Knollys and Thomas Larkham* at Dover (or Northam), c.1641, over 'baptizing children, receiving members, burial of the dead' led to a riot. Thomas Lechford noted that Knollys had gone 'to seek a new place at Long Island'. Winthrop observed that Knollys was discovered to be 'an unclean person', who had 'solicited the chastity of his two maids' in a hypocritical fashion (as he had urged his church to proceed against Underhill for adultery). Winthrop noted how Underhill, Knollys and other antinomians fell into immorality after 'crying down all evidence from sanctification'.

Knollys and his family left New England in the autumn of 1641. Knollys wrote 'being sent for by my aged Father I returned with my Wife and one Child about three years old, and was great with another child, and came safe to London on the 24th of December 1641'. If the attribution of authorship to Knollys is correct, he published a manifesto against episcopacy, *A petition for the prelates*, almost as soon as he got back. Knollys became a schoolmaster, then an army chaplain under the earl of Manchester. By 1644 he declared himself a baptist. In 1645, in London, he gathered the Particular Baptist church with which he was connected for the rest of his life. He converted Henry Jessey (*ODNB*) to the baptist cause, and attracted the ire of the presbyterian polemicist Thomas Edwards. In the 1650s Knollys associated with Fifth Monarchists: some of his followers signed the manifesto that accompanied Thomas Venner's* rising in 1657; as a result Knollys spent eighteen weeks in Newgate prison and some years in the Netherlands and Germany. Throughout his career, he took on teaching and clerical work to support himself. In the mid-1660s he published several educational texts.

An intriguing development in the late 1640s, which must have helped his finances, was a renewed connection with Scartho. Knollys became rector on 2 December 1647, in succession to his father. Knollys's old scruples about ceremonies and episcopal ordination no longer applied – parliament had set aside the prayer book and abolished bishops – but it is still surprising to find the baptist Knollys holding a parish living up in Lincolnshire, in conjunction with his ministry to a gathered church in London. He must have resigned at the Restoration, but kept the living in the family: his son 'Cheney Knollys' was rector at Scartho from 30 September 1662 until his death in 1671. Knollys outlived his son by two decades: as the funeral sermon for this 'venerable old man' observed, 'The minister, like the candle, wastes while he shines. But at his death he rests from his labours.'

Publications [Hanserd Knollys] *A petition for the prelates* (1641), *ESTC* R179508; *Christ exalted* (1645); *A declaration concerning the publike dispute which should have been in the publike meeting-house... concerning infants-baptisme* (1645); *A moderate answer vnto Dr Bastvvicks book; called Independency not Gods ordinance* (1645);

The shining of a flaming-fire in Zion (1646); *The rudiments of the Hebrew grammar in English* (1648); *An exposition of the first chapter of the Song of Solomon* (1656); *Rhetoricæ adumbratio* (1663); *Radices Hebraicæ* (1664); *Radices simplicium* (1664); *Grammaticæ Graecæ compendium* (1664); *Grammaticæ Latinæ compendium* (1664); *Linguæ Hebraicæ delineatio* (1664); *Grammaticæ Latinæ, Græcæ, & Hebraicæ* (1665); *Apocalyptical mysteries* (1667); *The parable of the kingdom of heaven expounded* (1674); *The baptists answer* (1675); *An exposition of the eleventh chapter of Revelation* (1679); *Mystical Babylon unvailed* (1679); *The vvorld that now is; and the vvorld that is to come* (1681); *The gospel minister's maintenance vindicated* (1689); *An answer to a brief discourse concerning singing in the publick worship of God* (1691); [Hanserd Knollys, William Kiffin], *The life and death of... Mr Hanserd Knollys* (1692).

CCEd Person ID 71006 [Richardus Knowles]; Helena Hajzyk, 'The Church in Lincolnshire, c.1595–c.1640' (PhD dissertation, University of Cambridge, 1980), 306, 460, 466; *Life and death of... Mr Hanserd Knollys*, 17–18; *Pilgrims*, 59–60; Lechford *PD*, 44, 53, 54; *Suffolk Deeds* I, 3; *WJ*, 285, 300, 318, 348–50; Anne Laurence, *Parliamentary army chaplains, 1642–1651* (Woodbridge, Suffolk: Royal Historical Society, 1990), 142-3; Ann Hughes, *Gangraena and the struggle for the English Revolution* (Oxford: Oxford University Press, 2004), 163, 174–5, 178–9 and *passim*; B.S. Capp, *The Fifth Monarchy men* (London: Faber, 1972), 182 and *passim*; CCEd Person ID 63576 [Hanserd Knollys] and Person ID 98576 [Cheyney Knowles]; Thomas Harrison, *A sermon on the decease of Mr Hanserd Knollis*, 29, 39. For detail on Knollys's career as a baptist: B.R. White, *Hanserd Knollys and radical dissent in the 17th century* (London: Friends of Dr Williams's Library, 31st Lecture, 1977); Stephen Wright, *The early English baptists, 1603–1649* (Woodbridge: The Boydell Press, 2006).

BDBR, ODNB.

KNOWLES, John (c.1606–1685)

John Knowles, who came from Lincolnshire, graduated from Magdalene College, Cambridge, BA in 1624, and MA in 1627. He was ordained deacon and priest at Peterborough, 1627. Knowles had been elected a fellow of St Catharine's College in 1625, and had a high reputation as a tutor. Hanserd Knollys* and Richard Jennings* passed through the college in his day, and Nathaniel Norcrosse* just after. On 16 November 1635, Knowles became town lecturer at Colchester, and was almost immediately accused of preaching a seditious sermon. In 1636 he preached at the funeral of John Rogers (*ODNB*) of Dedham, a close friend. At a visitation in 1637, Knowles was said not to wear a surplice, not to pray for the king or bishop, and (over scruples about 'mixed communion') had not administered or received the sacrament in two years. He was told to take communion within a month but 'was so zealous, as that he forsook lecture and town and all, rather than... receive'. Knowles lost his licence and resigned before the end of 1637.[1]

Knowles was admitted to the Boston church on 25 August 1639, oddly described as 'a studyent'. This was probably soon after his arrival in New England. Thomas Lechford* noted that Knowles 'never made any mention in his profession of faith, of any officers of the Church in particular, or their duties, and yet was received'. On 1 March 1639/40, the Boston church dismissed him to Watertown, where the following December he was ordained as fellow pastor to George Phillips. John Winthrop noted the irregularity of this: 'The church of Watertown ordained Mr Knolles, a godly man and a prime scholar, pastor, so they had now two pastors and no teacher, differing from the practice of the other churches, as also they did in their privacy, not giving notice thereof to the neighbouring churches, nor to the magistrates, as the common practice was.' Lechford also reported this, adding 'neither will that Church send any messengers to any other Church-gathering or ordination'. Around 1640, Knowles married Elizabeth, daughter of Thomas Willis* of Lynn, Massachusetts. In 1641, Knowles approached the Boston church to ask about the propriety of 'prayinge with ... such as are excommunicated'. This was on behalf of his congregation at Watertown, which had been stirred up by the boasts of Captain John Underhill, who – though excommunicated – claimed he had been received warmly by the church at Salem. In 1642, the Massachusetts authorities, building on Knowles's experience at St Catharine's in Cambridge, put him on the board of governors for Harvard.[2]

In 1642–3 Knowles spent time in Virginia. Philip Bennet had brought letters from Norfolk County, Virginia, 'earnestly entreating a supply of faithful ministers' from New England. George Phillips of Watertown, William Thompson of Braintree and John Miller of Rowley were nominated, and approved by Massachusetts General Court, but Phillips and Miller refused to go. Instead, Thompson went with John Knowles and Thomas James* of New Haven. They reached Virginia after an eleven-week winter journey and acted as preachers to churches there. The Virginian authorities banished Knowles in 1643 for failing to conform to the rites and practices of the Church of England. When he returned to New England, letters from his congregation in Virginia, and from others there, were read aloud at the Boston lecture:

> whereby it appeared that God had greatly blessed their ministry there, so as the people's hearts were much inflamed with desire after the ordinances, and though the state did silence the ministers, because they would not conform to the order of England, yet the people resorted to them in private houses to hear them as before.

George Phillips died in 1644, and Knowles continued at Watertown alone until 1647. In 1650, Cromwell tried to encourage New Englanders to settle in Ireland. Knowles, with John Tuttle* and others, wrote back to spell out the terms that would make Irish settlement palatable.[3]

Knowles left Massachusetts in 1651 and in 1652 became curate of Twickenham, Middlesex. His wife's brother, Thomas Willis*, who returned from New England earlier, had become vicar of Twickenham in 1646. Knowles's father-in-law, Thomas Willis the schoolmaster, had left New England in 1641 and was running his old school close to Twickenham, at Isleworth. Soon after his return to England, Knowles contacted the mayor of Colchester about £100 still owed to him as lecturer; on 5 February 1653/4, he chased up these arrears of pay again. Knowles became rector of St Werburgh's, Bristol, on 4 November 1653, and also a preacher at Bristol Cathedral. In 1654 he was appointed as an assistant to the Somerset commissioners for removing unsuitable parish ministers. By 1659 he was pastor to a congregational church which met at Castle Green, Bristol: this was perhaps a church Knowles himself had gathered in 1654, under the protection of the castle's governor, the regicide Adrian Scrope (*ODNB*). Knowles's connections with Harvard were renewed when the college appointed him, in 1659, as a trustee to solicit gifts (with Thomas Allen*, William Hooke*, Herbert Pelham* and Richard Saltonstall*).

At the Restoration, in 1660, Knowles lost his post as rector of St Werburgh's. His successor was installed on 23 October 1661. In 1662 he was ejected as a cathedral preacher. He had perhaps already moved to London: he was said in 1661 to be preaching in the parish of All Hallows the Great. Knowles was reported to be holding conventicles at various places in London, 1664–5. In August 1664 he was said to have £1000 in his hands for the benefit of 'godly men'. In 1665, like many other nonconformist ministers in London, Knowles was active during the Great Plague. In September 1671 he witnessed the will of William Greenhill of Stepney, by which he received £5 himself and £100 to distribute to ejected ministers. His interest in Harvard continued. In 1671, he told the Massachusetts authorities of his willingness to present the needs of the college to 'persons of special interest, zeal, largenesse of heart, and singular affection to this weighty commencement of the glory of God'; he would also spread the word that Harvard needed a new president. On 25 March 1672, Knowles was offered the post himself – after a glowing reference from Richard Saltonstall – but declined. Leonard Hoar* accepted. (Letters survive from Knowles about Harvard, 1674–7, to John Leverett*, governor of Massachusetts.) Knowles still owned 500 acres of land at Lynn, Massachusetts, which had been given by the town to his father-in-law Thomas Willis: he sold this in 1672. That year Knowles became minister, with Thomas Kentish (*CR*), of a church that met at St Katharine by the Tower, and later at Eastcheap or Cannon Street (it was not listed among those licensed in 1672). Susanna Bell*, who returned from Roxbury to live in that part of London, left Knowles 20 shillings a year for life. He was preaching at Booby Lane, Wapping, in 1676, and made his will, as of Shadwell, on 10 May 1680. Probate was granted on 6 June 1685.[4]

---

[1] T.W. Davids, *Annals of evangelical nonconformity in Essex* (London: Jackson, Walford & Hodder, 1863), 547; Kenneth W. Shipps, 'Lay patronage of East Anglian puritan clerics in pre-Revolutionary England' (PhD dissertation, Yale University, 1971), 321.

[2] *Boston CR*, 25, 28; Lechford *PD*, 4, 10, 38; *WJ*, 339; James F. Cooper, Jr, *Tenacious of their liberties: the congregationalists in colonial Massachusetts* (Oxford and New York: Oxford University Press, 1999), 28–9; Roger Thompson, *Divided we stand: Watertown 1630–80* (Amherst, MA: University of Massachusetts Press, 1994), 66–7, 73.

[3] *WJ*, 405, 426–7; *NEHGR* 3: 92; *Original letters and papers of state addressed to Oliver Cromwell*, ed. J. Nickolls (London, 1743), 44–5; Pilgrims, 111–12.

[4] Davids, *Annals*, 549 (citing Colchester Castle MSS., 41, fol. 79); G.F. Nuttall, *Visible saints: the congregational way, 1640–1660* (Oxford: Blackwell, 1957), 34–6; W.L. Sachse, 'The migration of New Englanders to England, 1640–1660', *American Historical Review*, 53 (1947–8), 276–7; DWL, MS 38.59, A.G. Matthews's notes of nonconformist ministers' wills, fols 421–2 (William Greenhill); W.L. Sachse, *The colonial American in Britain* (Madison, WI: University of Wisconsin Press, 1956), 107; *Saltonstall Papers* I, 159–61; 3 *MHSC* 1: 62, 65; *NEHGR* 30: 463; NA, PROB 11/341/330, will of 'Susann Bell', widow of All Hallows Barking, City of London, 21 March 1673.

BDBR, CR, ODNB.

L

LAHORNE, Rowland

Rowland Lahorne arrived in New England before 14 January 1635/6, when the Plymouth Colony records noted his marriage to 'Flower' (Flora). He was granted eleven acres of land at Duxbury on 6 February 1636/7, which he sold together with a house on 8 November 1639. By 1643 Lahorne was at Charlestown, Massachusetts, where he took town office as a herdsman in 1646 and as a 'field driver' in 1649. He was still in Charlestown on 13 September 1654, when he and Flora acknowledged the sale of a house and fifteen acres of land at Malden. He described himself as a 'planter'.

Lahorne returned to England sometime after September 1654. On 7 April 1663 'Rouland Langhorne of the City of London, cordwainer' appointed Habbakuk Glover of Boston as his attorney to collect debts.

GM 4: 221–2; Roger Thompson, *From deference to defiance: Charlestown, Massachusetts, 1629–1662* (Boston, MA: New England Historic Genealogical Society, 2012), 66, 72.

LAMBERTON, George (d. 1646)

George Lamberton, a merchant, was an early settler of New Haven. In 1641 he promoted attempts by New Haven merchants to establish trading posts on the Delaware: twenty New Haven families took part in this venture, but most came back in 1643 after resistance from the Dutch. Lamberton aided the establishment of the New England Confederation in 1643, and on its behalf negotiated with the director general of New Sweden about Swedish and Dutch opposition to English settlements on the Delaware.

Lamberton sailed for England from New Haven on the *Fellowship*, in January 1645/6. This ship, built in New Haven, was embarking on its first Atlantic voyage. It went down with the loss of all passengers and a valuable cargo of furs and local produce. Among the other travellers aboard were Francis Austin*, Thomas Gregson*, Nathaniel Turner* and Stephen Goodyear's* wife. Lamberton's widow married Stephen Goodyear*.

WJ, 387n., 471n., 479–80, 630–1, 643–4; Bernard Bailyn, *The New England merchants in the seventeenth century* (Cambridge, MA: Harvard University Press, 1955), 57, 58; I.M. Calder, *The New Haven Colony* (New Haven, CT: Yale University Press, 1934), 64, 77, 78, 114, 160, 162, 163, 185–7.

LARKHAM, George (1630–1700)

George Larkham, born at Northam, Devon, was the second son of the minister Thomas Larkham* and his wife Patience*, and brother to Thomas Larkham*, Patience (Larkham) Miller*, and Jane Larkham*. Thomas Larkham took his family to New England in 1639.

Larkham matriculated at Exeter College, Oxford, on 9 April 1647. He may have returned to England not long before this, with his mother and sisters. His father left New England in November 1642, with his eldest son, Thomas, and later wrote that his family had been scattered like 'dry bones' for several years, 'yet did the Lord bring them altogether againe here in England'. During George Larkham's time at Oxford his father settled as vicar of Tavistock, Devon. After he graduated BA in 1651, George went from Tavistock to Cumberland, and became curate of Cockermouth, and also of Embleton, in 1651. His father soon travelled up from Devon to join him, and together they formed a congregational church on 2 October 1651, with members drawn from Cockermouth and surrounding parishes. George Larkham was ordained pastor on 28 January 1651/2. The model of ministry he pioneered at Cockermouth – public preaching in parish pulpits combined with ministry to a gathered church – proved popular in the north-west. During the 1650s Larkham made more or less annual visits to Tavistock.

In 1660 George Larkham lost his parish living, but initially had greater freedom to preach than his father, who came up to Cumberland for a time to escape pressure in Devon. Later in the 1660s George Larkham moved about to escape attention. His daughter Patience was baptised in 1666 at Christopher Marshall's* congregational church at Topcliffe in the West Riding of Yorkshire. By 1669 George Larkham was preaching at Bridekirk, Cumberland, and in 1672 was licensed there (as a presbyterian). George Larkham inherited Thomas Larkham's manuscript diary, which he used from 1670 to 1676 for farming accounts, letter-drafts, sermon notes and occasional poems.

The diary of Thomas Larkham, 1647–1669, ed. Susan Hardman Moore, Church of England Record Society, 17 (Woodbridge: Boydell and Brewer, 2011), 3, 12, 16–17, 26, 27, 162 and *passim*; Cockermouth CB, *passim*; *Pilgrims*, 131–2; Susan Hardman Moore, '"Pure folkes" and the parish: Thomas Larkham in Cockermouth and Tavistock', *Life and thought in the northern Church c.1100–c.1700*, ed. D. Wood (Woodbridge: Boydell, 1999), 493–4, 495–8; W. Smith, ed., *The registers of Topcliffe and Morley in the West Riding of the County of Yorkshire* (London: Longmans, Green & Co., 1888), 14; Bryan Dale, *Yorkshire puritanism and early nonconformity* (Bradford: [Dale's executors], 1910), 252.

CR, Surman.

LARKHAM, Jane

Jane Larkham, the youngest child of Thomas* and Patience Larkham*, was born at Northam in Devon and went to New England with her family in 1639.

She returned to England some years after her father and elder brother Thomas, probably with her mother. By 1650, she was living with her parents in Tavistock and shared responsibility for housekeeping. She married a Tavistock shopkeeper, Daniel Condy, in December 1652: 'money all spent', her father noted. He had ordered wedding clothes for her from London, at a cost of more than £8. Jane and Daniel Condy joined the congregational church Thomas Larkham gathered in Tavistock. Her father's critics alleged he favoured his daughter and son-in-law at the expense of other church members. Larkham lodged with Daniel and Jane Condy for some years in the 1660s, after he resigned as vicar of Tavistock.

The diary of Thomas Larkham, 1647–1669, ed. Susan Hardman Moore, Church of England Record Society, 17 (Woodbridge: Boydell and Brewer, 2011), 12, 27, 34, 52, 53, 55 and *passim*; 'F.G. D.P. W.G. N.W. W.H. &c', *The Tavistocke Naboth proved Nabal: in an answer unto a scandalous narrative published by Mr Tho: Larkham in the name (but without the consent) of the church of Tavistocke in Devon* (1658), 33–4, 70–1, 74.

LARKHAM, Patience (d. 1677)

Patience Larkham, the daughter of George Wilton, a schoolmaster of Crediton, Devon, married Thomas Larkham* in 1622. By this marriage, Thomas Larkham gained an interest in property at Crediton. The rental income bolstered his fortunes for the rest of his life, and was particularly valuable in the 1660s after he resigned as vicar of Tavistock and became a nonconformist. Patience Larkham went to New England with Thomas in 1639.

She returned home some years after her husband and their eldest son Thomas*. She was probably at Crediton, living in a house Thomas Larkham owned, when their daughter Patience Miller* gave birth there to her son, Tom Miller, in June 1648. It is clear from incidental references in Thomas Larkham's diary that Patience soon joined him in the vicarage at Tavistock, but the absence of personal references is striking. In twenty years he made two comments. In 1658 he wrote 'My poore Rocky Untoward Wife! O my unsuitablenes to her! Lord helpe.' In 1661, on his thirty-ninth wedding anniversary – after he had brought all his children and grandchildren before God – he finally came to his spouse: 'For my unworthy selfe & poore wife, My father thou knowest how it is with me and her, O thy spirit is all I crave for us both, And then all will be well enough.' Apart from these telling moments, he stuck to the facts. Every quarter he noted ten shillings given 'to my Wife' out of the Crediton rents that had come to him by their marriage. He paid 'for surgery Wives foote 00-03-00', for spectacles (4d), and splashed out 11s to buy her a Bible. He bought 'a pair of Pantofles' (slippers) and spent 1s on a 'red jumpe' (underbodice). Occasionally, he allowed her something á la mode: 'sarge & lace for a Gowne for my wife 01-13-10 this was bought at Mr foxwells shop in Exeter . . . for making my wives gowne 00-14-00½ and things about it sacke bows shoes &c All au french'. But compared with Thomas Larkham's generosity to both his daughters, Patience came off poorly: 'paid Dan: Sowton for fitting an old gowne for my wife which was a Gowne of Mine 00-06-0'. Larkham's opponents called him 'a bird that loves not his own nest', 'an abuser of his wife', making capital out of talk that he had a bastard child in New England. They also dropped broad hints: he conducted himself in a way unbefitting a pastor 'towards his relations at home, especially the nearest: more we shall not say'. It is not clear whether Patience Larkham went with her husband on his journeys away from Tavistock in the 1660s. She lived for long periods in the household of Daniel and Jane Condy, and died in November 1677.

> *The diary of Thomas Larkham, 1647–1669*, ed. Susan Hardman Moore, Church of England Record Society, 17 (Woodbridge: Boydell and Brewer, 2011), 13, 62, 63, 65, 103, 139, 178n.1, 190, 273, 245, 362 and *passim*; 'F.G. D.P. W.G. N.W. W.H. &c', *The Tavistocke Naboth proved Nabal: in an answer unto a scandalous narrative published by Mr Tho: Larkham in the name (but without the consent) of the church of Tavistocke in Devon* (1658), '74' [76]; DRO, 482A add 2/PR1, Tavistock Parish Register, 1614–1793, burials, 22 November 1677.

LARKHAM, Thomas (1602–1669)

Thomas Larkham was born in Lyme Regis, Dorset, the son of Thomas Larkham, a linen draper. He graduated BA from Trinity Hall, Cambridge, in 1622, and MA in 1626. At Shobrooke, near Crediton in Devon, in 1622, he married Patience*, the daughter of George Wilton, a schoolmaster of Crediton. Larkham was ordained in London on 23 May 1624, and soon became curate of Sandford chapel, Crediton. He was admitted as vicar of Northam, Devon, on 26 December 1626. Larkham later claimed that he had endured 'suffering (in the time of the prelacy) in almost all the courts in England', including High Commission and Star Chamber, but no evidence exists to substantiate this. Northam stood between the ports of Appledore and Bideford. Larkham would have seen ships setting sail to fish for cod off Newfoundland and to carry passengers across the Atlantic. Late in 1639, Larkham and his family joined the 'Great Migration' to New England. In August 1640, the diocesan authorities deprived him of the living of Northam for neglect by absence.[1]

In New England, Larkham began what he later called 'that exile unto which episcopal tyranny and tenderness of conscience forced me'. He settled at Dover, a small fishing community on the Piscataqua River, seventy miles north of Boston. Here he fell into a spectacular dispute with Hanserd Knollys*. When Larkham arrived, the church favoured Larkham over Knollys because, as John Winthrop put it, Larkham was 'a man not savouring the right way of church discipline, but of good parts and wealthy'. Winthrop reported that Larkham admitted to the church 'all who offered themselves, though men notoriously scandalous and ignorant', as long as they promised to repent. This is surprising, given Larkham's reputation in the 1650s as a stickler for making the church less inclusive. The tension was perhaps as much over Knollys's antinomian preaching (or so Larkham alleged). Knollys excommunicated Larkham, who then 'laid violent hands on Mr Knollys'. A riot broke out. Knollys's party took to the streets with a Bible strapped to a pikestaff, and the reverend Mr Knollys brandishing a pistol. Arbitrators from the Massachusetts Bay Colony waded in. Larkham was vindicated and Knollys left for England. Within a year or so, Larkham also sailed home. John Winthrop, jaundiced by this desertion, set down the local scandal: 'it was time for him to be gone, for not long after a widow which kept in his house, being a very handsome woman ... proved to be with child, and being examined, at first refused to confess the father, but in the end she laid it to Mr Larkham'. Larkham – perhaps conveniently for the pregnant widow, who found in him an absent scapegoat – was no longer in New England, but the tale followed him back across the Atlantic to be retold by his enemies in England.[2]

Larkham's time in America held no charm, looking back. He often gave thanks on the anniversary of the day he set sail for home: 'I call to mind with a humble and thankful hearte that upon the 12th day of November 1642 I left my house in the morninge and came down to the Mouth of the River Paskataquacke in New England to come for England.'[3]

For the years immediately after Larkham's return to England there are only fragments to go on. For the first four years he was at Greenwich and 'elsewhere in Kent'. In June 1645, a 'Mr Larkham of Greenwich' appeared in the papers of the Committee for Plundered Ministers, in a dispute with 'Mr Sprat'. In 1646, the presbyterian propagandist Thomas Edwards – keen to make much of Larkham's scandalous conduct in New England and since – reported to his readers that 'In Kent, not farre from Greenwich, there is a feirce Independent, one Master Larkin.' Not long after, Larkham signed up as chaplain to Sir Hardress Waller's regiment of foot in the New Model Army. He went to Ireland with Waller early in 1647, in an expedition that sailed over and came back by April. Perhaps for the rest of 1647, while Waller was occupied in London and the regiment was not on active service, Larkham gravitated back to old haunts in Kent. It was while he was in Kent that Larkham commandeered a notebook that had previously belonged to George Lane, a minister at East Greenwich, who had died in 1641. Larkham made Lane's notebook his own. From 1651 he used it almost daily until his death in 1669. The 'diary' is neither a journal of spiritual experience, nor a narrative of everyday events – although it contains a good dash of both, in passing. Larkham noted down income and expenditure in a Micawberish spirit, and made this the starting point for prayer and reflection. His entries combined ledger-keeping and soul-keeping.[4]

Before long, Thomas Larkham arrived at Tavistock, where he was to be vicar until 1660. Waller's regiment marched into Devon in January 1648, during the Second Civil War, and came to Tavistock in April. During the First Civil War Tavistock had been occupied in turn by royalists and parliamentarians eager to seize Plymouth. The previous minister, George Hughes (*ODNB*), fled to escape battle in 1643. By the time parliament won the day and Larkham came on the scene, the townspeople were eager to find a new vicar. The earl of Bedford, patron of the living, agreed to appoint the parishioners' choice. Larkham later claimed he was 'chosen by the inhabitants of Tavistock ... under many score hands'. During the 1650s, Larkham steered a controversial course in Tavistock, pursuing reformation in a kind of 'parish congregationalism'. He identified himself as both 'public preacher' to the parish at large and pastor to a gathered church within it. He restricted the sacraments to an ever smaller circle, to which only those who signed a covenant were admitted. This was not what even some of Tavistock's more ardent godly citizens had in mind – particularly as they knew their former minister George Hughes, down the road in Plymouth, adopted a softer line. Local resentment erupted in a no-holds-barred pamphlet war.[5]

Larkham later attributed the start of his troubles in Tavistock to the 'implacable malice' of Francis Glanville, who came from a prominent family in the town and was a justice of the peace. Larkham's ministry in Tavistock took shape amid the bitterness of civil war divisions, vented on a parliamentary army chaplain turned vicar. His campaign for purity in the church proved deeply unpopular. His pulpit utterances were declared by some 'to be such unsufferable Sermons as the like have not been Preached'. By 1650, efforts started to oust him from his post. Resistance to Larkham's ministry was intertwined with a refusal to pay him an extra £50 a year (levied as a fine on a local royalist and allocated to the vicar of Tavistock by parliamentary authority). This financial strategy had the desired effect: in the summer of 1651, Larkham decided to abandon Tavistock and go north to join his son George in Cumberland, 'receiving (as I apprehended it) a Call from God, to be employed in my Function elsewhere, I obeyed it; and departed from the ... Towne of Tavistock with a purpose to return thither no more to dwell among them'. That autumn, Larkham gathered a church by covenant at Cockermouth: 'October 2nd 1651 The Foundation of this particular church was laid in the Towne of Cockermouth ... through the instigation of Mr Thomas Larkham Pastor of the church of Christ at Tavistock in Devon.'[6]

Larkham's association with Tavistock might have ended when he left for Cumberland in 1651, but he was persuaded to return to Devon. More than sixty of the 'most considerable persons for Religion' in Tavistock sent him a letter: 'We humbly desire you ... speedily come among us ... let not the work of God amongst us come to nought'. Nicholas Watts headed the signatories – Watts, who later turned against Larkham and so became the 'Judas' of Larkham's tract *Judas hanging himselfe*. Larkham left Cumberland for Devon but first went to London to petition the Committee for Advance of Money for the missing £50 a year. He also wanted to wrong-foot his Tavistock critics by putting his supposedly 'unsufferable' sermons into print. The result, *The wedding-supper*, was a book designed to impress, with a dedication to parliament and a portrait of Larkham by a rising star, the engraver Thomas Cross.[7]

Larkham returned to Tavistock in May 1652. Controversy immediately erupted and continued for much of the 1650s. Soon after his return, he was locked out of the parish church twice by his opponents. On the second occasion, his supporters took action. A witness testified – before Larkham's implacable opponent, Francis Glanville JP – that he had seen several of Larkham's flock 'in a Riotouse manor use violence to the Church dore ... with a Barr of Iron hamer & other thinges with which they broke open the said Church dore'. Larkham and his associates were hauled before the quarter sessions and assizes in Exeter, accused of riot, but secured an acquittal. The campaign to oust Larkham from Tavistock gained new bite when disenchanted supporters also started to speak out against him. For a time, all seemed sweetness and light within 'the church' – the inner circle who agreed to submit to a discipline 'transacted according to the Word of God' – but peace did not last. Towards the end of 1654, a 'plague of divisions' broke out. Several founding members, including Nicholas Watts, were excommunicated. In the streets of Tavistock, Larkham's enemies rejoiced. Watts joined forces with Francis Glanville and others to bring fresh vigour to the lobbying campaign against Larkham. In the late 1650s they orchestrated complaints to the county Ejectors in Exeter (who disciplined scandalous ministers), to the Triers in London (who approved the fitness of clergy for parish livings), and finally to the council of state. The catalyst for the alienation of Watts and others in the church was Larkham's decision to produce a written covenant. He insisted everyone must sign. The penalty? No signature, no sacraments. Larkham's action was not necessarily unusual: gathered churches could take time to settle themselves with a covenant (months or even years), and a shift from verbal consent to written agreement was sometimes part of this; also, the common practice of 'covenant renewal' might well involve a freshly drafted vow. But whatever Larkham had put on paper was a step too far for some of the Tavistock godly. In the unholy row that broke out, Larkham ghost-wrote *Naboth* to defend himself, to which his opponents (Glanville and Watts chief among them) replied with *The Tavistocke Naboth proved Nabal*. Larkham responded with *Judas*, aimed at his renegade disciple, Watts. His opponents had the last word with *A strange metamorphosis in Tavistock*. Larkham's opponents gained ground as the power of the Protectorate authorities started to ebb away.[8]

At the Restoration, Larkham resigned as vicar of Tavistock, under pressure. In October 1660, he drew a thick black line in his diary under an entry that marked a watershed: 'I left mine imployment of preaching in feare & upon demand of the Patron.' The entries that follow show how his fortunes changed as a result: prisoner, fugitive nonconformist preacher, apothecary. He was in jail for several months early in 1661. He was absent from Tavistock for long stretches of time in 1661–2, 1663–4 and 1666–7. Between July 1664 and January 1666 he ran an apothecary shop in Tavistock, with the help of his grandson Tom Miller. The church Larkham had gathered in the 1650s survived to become a nonconformist congregation in the 1660s.

Larkham died in 1669: the Tavistock parish register records his burial. A final twist of the tale suggests that the wounds of Tavistock strife healed up somewhat after 1660, at least among the godly who had fallen out so spectacularly in the 1650s. In the 1670s, Nicholas Watts – Larkham's ferocious opponent in the battle of books – set up a trust to distribute religious literature to the poor of the town, 'that by bestowing of . . . good books, I may testify true repentance and make some amends for those wretched idle pamphlets wrote in my youthful years for my own Vindication wherein I stuck not to cast Dirt on others for the Clearing of myself'. Not long before this, Watts had helped to make an inventory of Larkham's estate – the final reckoning, diary and all.[9]

Publications *The wedding-supper* (1652); *The parable of the wedding-supper explained* (1656); *A discourse of paying of tithes* (1656); [Larkham] *Naboth, in a narrative and complaint of the church of God at Tavistock* (1657); [Larkham], *Judas hanging himselfe* (1658). *Naboth* and *Judas* are included in *The diary of Thomas Larkham, 1647–1669*, ed. Susan Hardman Moore, Church of England Record Society, 17 (Woodbridge: Boydell and Brewer, 2011), 307–75.

[1] This sketch of Larkham's career draws on the introduction to *The diary of Thomas Larkham, 1647–1669*, ed. Susan Hardman Moore, Church of England Record Society, 17 (Woodbridge: Boydell and Brewer, 2011), 1–29. Larkham, *The wedding-supper* (1652), 'The epistle dedicatory'; DRO, CC7/21.

[2] *Diary of Thomas Larkham*, 6; *Pilgrims*, 61–2; *WJ*, 348–50, 421; for the circulation in England of rumours of a bastard child, see 'F.G. D.P. W.G. N.W. W.H. &c', *The Tavistocke Naboth proved Nabal: in an answer unto a scandalous narrative published by Mr Tho: Larkham in the name (but without the consent) of the church of Tavistocke in Devon* (1658), 15, and John Brackenbury*.

[3] *Diary of Thomas Larkham*, 6–7, 100, 120, 138, 162, 188, 211, 258.

[4] *Diary of Thomas Larkham*, 1, 4–5, 7.

[5] *Diary of Thomas Larkham*, 2–3; Larkham, *Parable of the wedding-supper*, 'To the saints and people of England'.

[6] *Diary of Thomas Larkham*, 14–17; Cockermouth CB, 2, 5.

[7] *Diary of Thomas Larkham*, 17–18.

[8] *Diary of Thomas Larkham*, 18–25; *Tavistock Naboth*; [Anon.], *A strange metamorphosis in Tavistock* [1658].

[9] *Diary of Thomas Larkham*, 25–9; DRO, 482A add 2/PR1, Tavistock Parish Register, 1614–1793, burials, 23 December 1669.

BDBR, CCEd Person ID 71334 ['Thomas Larkeham'], CR, ODNB.

LARKHAM, Thomas

Thomas Larkham was the eldest son of Thomas* and Patience Larkham*, brother of George* and Jane Larkham* and Patience Miller*. He emigrated to New England in 1639 with his father.

In November 1642 he left New England with his father. Thomas Larkham senior often noted the anniversary of setting sail, as in November 1659: 'It is now 17 yeares since I left my famely in New England & came with my Eldest Son towards England. O the mercies I have received! O the afflictions I have under gone! O the providences God hath vouchsafed!' Thomas Larkham junior married Mary, the sister of Richard Covert, a London merchant. Thomas himself died in the East Indies on 14 February 1648/9, leaving his widow and two children, Thomas and Mary. Of the two Marys, nothing further is known. His orphaned son Thomas, brought up in Tavistock by his grandparents Thomas and Patience Larkham (and regarded by his grandfather as a troublesome youth), became an Atlantic trader and London merchant.

The diary of Thomas Larkham, 1647–1669, ed. Susan Hardman Moore, Church of England Record Society, 17 (Woodbridge: Boydell and Brewer, 2011), 12–13, 33, 162, 211, 254, 257 and *passim*.

LATHAM, William

William Latham emigrated on the *Mayflower* in 1620, as a servant to John Carver. He left for England sometime after 1640. William Bradford recorded in 1651, in his account of the Carver family, that the 'servant boy' Latham, 'after more than 20 years' stay in the country, went into England and from thence to the Bahama Islands in the West Indies; and there with some others was starved for want of food'.

> William Bradford, *Of Plymouth Plantation, 1620–1647*, ed. Samuel Eliot Morison (New York: Knopf, 1963), 441, 444; *GMB* 1160.

LECHFORD, Thomas (*fl.*1629–d. in or after 1642)

Thomas Lechford was a lawyer of Clement's Inn, London. He had been an 'auditor' who 'hung upon' the words of the preacher Hugh Peter* at St Sepulchre's. Although he was a solicitor rather than a barrister, Lechford was implicated in a number of legal challenges to Laudian religious policy. In 1636 Thomas Allen's* brother, Robert Allen, engaged 'Mr Letchford' on his brother's behalf to take out writs against parishioners at St Edmund's in Norwich for breaking up ground in the church to install altar steps and rails. Lechford also had on his books Ferdinando Adams*, who locked Bishop Wren's officials out of St Mary-le-Tower in Ipswich, Suffolk. In Adams's case, Lechford worked with the barrister William Prynne (*ODNB*). He also acted as solicitor for Prynne in Prynne's own notorious trial for sedition in 1637. In the wake of Prynne's trial, Lechford fled from England with his wife Elizabeth. He chose Massachusetts over Providence Island to the south, and over the offer of a post from George Rákóczy, prince of Transylvania. Lechford later wrote that he 'suffered . . . a kind of banishment'.

New England failed to greet Lechford as he expected. To pass the time on the Atlantic he had written a tract, 'Of Prophesie', which he presented to deputy governor Thomas Dudley (*ANB*) when he reached Boston: 'the next news I had was, that at first dash he accused me of heresy'. The Boston church – where Dudley was a leading member – refused to admit Lechford. The reasons alleged were that Lechford thought the antichrist had not yet come (and so could not be identified with the pope), and affirmed bishops so long as they were godly. The frictions between Lechford and the Boston church are apparent in a letter Lechford wrote to the elders, and a reply to this from the ministers John Cotton and John Wilson*. As he was not a church member, Lechford could not hold civil office in Massachusetts, and so could not be a public notary. He made a living, good enough to buy the 'best sugar' and expensive Spanish tobacco, by writing legal documents such as wills, deeds, leases, letters of attorney and formal copies. However, after he was accused of trying to influence a jury, his reputation sank and his disenchantment rose. By July 1640 Lechford was seriously considering a return to England. His experience in Massachusetts had convinced him that 'Christians cannot live happily without Bishops . . . nor Englishmen without a King'.

Lechford left New England on 3 August 1641. As he was about to set sail, he heard that fellow settlers 'supposed Mr Prynne had sent me money for my passage'. He travelled back on the same boat back as the colonial agents Thomas Weld* and Hugh Peter, and also his former client Ferdinando Adams. Elizabeth Lechford remained in Boston, at least for a while, with £6 13s 10d of household goods to her name. Back in England, Lechford resumed his work at Clement's Inn by November 1641. In 1642, he published *Plain dealing*, a lawyerly witness against the colony with details of church and civil practice. This, because of Lechford's contacts, had the potential to inflict serious damage. Thomas Weld's counterblast, *New Englands first fruits*, was a poor match. Lechford's death cut short his contribution to the debate, but William Prynne took up the cudgels for the cause in *Independency examined* (1644) and *Full reply* (1644).

Publication *Plain dealing: or, Newes from New-England* (1642). Lechford's notarial records: *A note-book kept by Thomas Lechford, Esq., lawyer, in Boston, Massachusetts Bay, from June 27, 1638, to July 29, 1641*, Transactions and Collections of the American Antiquarian Society, 7 (Cambridge, MA: J. Wilson & Co., 1885).

Bodleian, Tanner MS 68, fols 115r, 234r; NA, SP 16/334/23 and SP 16/335/68, Robert Allen to Thomas Lechford, 20 October 1636 and 17 November 1636; Matthew Reynolds, *Godly reformers and their opponents in early modern England: religion in Norwich, c.1560–1643* (Woodbridge: Boydell Press, 2005), 221; Lechford *PD*, 'To the Reader'; Lechford *NB*, 47–50, 274, 431; *WP* V, 85–6; Bush, 328–31; *WJ*, 354; *Pilgrims*, 60–1. See also Thomas G. Barnes, 'Thomas Lechford and the earliest lawyering in Massachusetts, 1638–1641', in Daniel R. Coquillette, Robert J. Brink and Catherine S. Menard, eds, *Law in colonial Massachusetts*, Colonial Society of Massachusetts, *Publications*, 62 (1984), 3–38; Angela Fernandez, 'Record-keeping and other troublemaking: Thomas Lechford and law reform in colonial Massachusetts', *Law and History Review* (Summer 2005), http://www.historycooperative.org/journals/lhr/23.2/fernandez.html (accessed 4 September 2012).

ANB, ODNB.

LENTHALL, Robert (c.1597–1658)

Robert Lenthall, born at Great Missenden in Buckinghamshire, matriculated in 1611 at Oriel College, Oxford, aged fourteen, and graduated BA from All Souls' College, in 1619. He was ordained deacon and priest in 1621. Lenthall was vicar of Great Missenden from 1627 until the living was declared vacant on 10 May 1638.

Lenthall emigrated in 1638. Late that year, John Winthrop reported that Lenthall, a man 'of good report in England' had been invited to Weymouth, Massachusetts, by some of his former parishioners. Lenthall, Winthrop observed, 'drank in some of Mrs. Hutchinson's opinions, as of justification before faith': John Cotton, the minister of Boston, dissuaded him from these views. However, Lenthall's opinions on the question of church membership proved harder to shift. In Massachusetts, controversially, the door to joining the church was a testimony of true religious experience, judged by church members (who might well reject it as inadequate). Lenthall, however, still stuck close to English practice, 'that only baptism was the door of entrance into the church'. Winthrop noted the result: 'the common sort of people did eagerly embrace his opinions, and some labored to get such a church on foot as all baptized ones might communicate in without any further kind of trial of them'. Thomas Lechford* was one of those said to favour his opinions. On 10 February 1638/9 a 'conference of elders' met with Lenthall to stop the disturbance his views were causing. The discussion covered the question of his English ordination – which, John Cotton declared, not being given by election, did not make him a minister in New England. Lenthall delivered a recantation to the Massachusetts General Court in March 1638/9. Thomas Dudley (*ANB*) reported a suspected outbreak of smallpox in Weymouth as a sign of God's judgment: 'If this be true the plague is begun in the Campe for the sinne of Peor' (a biblical reference to Numbers 25). Lenthall left Massachusetts for Newport, Rhode Island, where he became a freeman in 1640. He was said to be 'out of office and employment and lives very poorly'. He worked as a schoolmaster. Lenthall, although he had clashed with the 'orthodoxy' of Massachusetts, was seriously out of step with the radicalism of some of his Rhode Island neighbours. In 1641 he sided with Robert Harding* and others to oppose radical religious opinions.

Lenthall returned to England by late 1643, when he became rector of Great Hampden, Buckinghamshire. In 1647, in the parish register, Lenthall set down a vivid record of how his wife Susanna, and his children Sarah and Adrian, died in an outbreak of plague. *c.*1649 Lenthall became minister at Barnes, Surrey. His will, made on 10 May 1658 and proved on 3 September, mentioned his wife Margaret and two daughters, 'Marrion' and 'Nan'. He made a bequest to his 'Sister Laughton', probably in New England, 'to be sent over to her'. His daughter Anna (Nan) married Samuel Eeles at Milford, Connecticut, in 1663.

Al. Oxon.; CCEd Person ID 8618, Location ID 7208; *WJ*, 281–2, 364; David D. Hall, *The faithful shepherd: a history of the New England ministry in the seventeenth century* (Chapel Hill, NC: University of North Carolina Press, 1972), 103; *Congregational Quarterly*, N.S., 19 (1877), 136–9; *WP* IV, 86; Lechford *PD*, 22; J.F.D. Shrewsbury, *A history of bubonic plague in the British Isles* (Cambridge: Cambridge University Press, 1970), 424; NA, PROB 11/282/184, will of Robert Lenthall, clerk of Barnes, Surrey, 3 September 1658; *GMB* 619–20.

LEVERETT, John (1616–1679)

John Leverett, son of Thomas and Anne Leverett, came from Boston, Lincolnshire. His father had been an alderman in Boston. He emigrated to New England in 1633, with his parents and siblings Jane and Ann.

Leverett and his family settled at Boston, Massachusetts. His parents joined the church in October 1633. His father, 'an ancient, sincere professor of Mr Cotton's congregation in England', became a ruling elder. John Leverett was admitted to the Boston church on 14 July 1639. He joined the Artillery Company that year, and became a freeman on 13 May 1640. Leverett acted as an emissary to the Narragansett Indians in 1642. His first wife, Hannah, died c.1643.

Leverett went to England to join the parliamentary army, as one of the colony's 'best military men'. This was probably late in 1643, when others took the same path: Nehemiah Bourne*, William Hudson Jr*, Francis Lisle* and Israel Stoughton*. Leverett became captain of a foot company under colonel Thomas Rainborowe (*ODNB*). Hudson served as an ensign in Leverett's company. Bourne and Stoughton also served under Rainborowe. While in England, Leverett had his portrait painted, perhaps by Peter Lely, in a leather buff-coat (which may be the buff-coat of his that survives in the collections of the Massachusetts Historical Society).[1]

Leverett came back from the English civil wars to New England. On 12 August 1645 the Massachusetts General Court appointed him commander of an expedition against the Narragansett Indians. Francis Lisle accompanied this force as surgeon. c.1645, Leverett married his second wife, Sarah, a daughter or sister of Robert Sedgwick*. His family ties with Sedgwick linked Leverett in affection and trade with Robert Houghton of St Olave's, Southwark. Houghton, a major importer of colonial fish, and Sedgwick's brother-in-law, also called Leverett his 'brother'.

For the next decade, Leverett built up his activities as a merchant. He imported haberdashery, cloth, ironmongery and gunpowder from England, and acted for London merchants like Houghton in relation to exports from New England. This took him to England several times, and kept him in touch with the broader range of religious opinion back home, and with support there for religious toleration. Leverett sailed for England on 9 November 1646, on the same ship as the Remonstrant Thomas Fowle*, William Vassall* (who sympathised with Fowle), and other settlers such as Robert Harding* and Richard Sadler*. Edward Winslow, in *New-Englands salamander*, cited Leverett as one of the colonists in England who had been present at John Cotton's Boston lecture on 5 November 1646, and heard Cotton's warnings about Fowle's 'Jonas' of a petition before the ship set sail. Leverett returned to New England before long, but probably went to England again in 1648. On 31 October that year, he was appointed attorney by Martha Winthrop, sister of Thomas and William Rainborowe, to receive a legacy due to her in England from her father's executors. Again, he came back to New England soon – certainly by December 1650, when he defended his corner in a dispute over ownership of the *Unicorn* (a ship in which he had bought a one-third share in 1646). Leverett was elected to serve as a deputy at the Massachusetts General Court on several occasions. In 1651, his sympathy with a more tolerant approach to religion showed: he was among the fourteen deputies who dissented from taking the Westminster Confession of 1646 as the standard of orthodoxy; he also opposed the fine levied on members of the Malden church for their ordination of Marmaduke Matthews*.

John Leverett and Robert Sedgwick were well known to the powers-that-be in Cromwell's navy. In 1653 they were commissioned by Cromwell to command a fleet against the New Amsterdam Dutch. Peace with the Dutch came in 1654, before this force saw any action, but Sedgwick put the force to use against the French in Acadia, destroying three forts and taking the area back under English control as Nova Scotia. Sedgwick went to England again after this, but Leverett stayed in New England. The naval commissioner Nehemiah Bourne appointed Leverett as his attorney in Massachusetts on 26 March 1655.[2]

Leverett went to London once again in December 1655, this time as an agent for Massachusetts. In this role, he replaced Edward Hopkins*. Sarah Leverett followed him back to England in 1657.

At the Restoration of Charles II, Leverett abandoned his work as an agent and returned to New England, arriving in 1661. He became major-general of Massachusetts' forces in 1663, and went on to play a distinguished part in colonial government: as an assistant (1665–71), as deputy-governor of Massachusetts (1671–3), and as governor (1673–9).[3]

[1] *GMB* 1177; *Artillery Company*, 91–3; *Boston CR*, 16, 24; *NEHGR* 3: 188; *WJ*, 99, 408n., 604–5; C.H. Firth and G. Davies, *The regimental history of Cromwell's army* (Oxford: Clarendon Press, 1940), 417–18; *Pilgrims*, plates 6–7.

[2] *Artillery Company*, 107; Aspinwall, 49, 172, 254, 308, 351–4, 363–5, 390, 399, 408, 418; Edward Winslow, *New-Englands salamander* (1647), 17, 20; Bernard Bailyn, *The New England merchants in the seventeenth century* (Cambridge, MA: Harvard University Press, 1955), 79–80, 108; 4 *MHSC* 2: 230–3; *Suffolk Deeds* II, 195, 211.

[3] Mass. Archives, 106: 25; 'The Diary of John Hull', *Archaeologica Americana*, Transactions and Collections of the American Antiquarian Society, 3 (1857), 177; Bailyn, *New England merchants*, 160; Graeme J. Milne, 'New England agents and the English Atlantic, 1641–1666' (PhD dissertation, University of Edinburgh, 1993), 304 and *passim*.

ANB.

LEVERETT, Sarah

Sarah Leverett was the sister or daughter of Robert Sedgwick* and his wife Joanna* (who married Thomas Allen* in England after 1656). She married John Leverett* *c.*1645. On 6 December 1655, before Leverett left New England for London as an agent for Massachusetts, he authorised her to sell a house in Boston in his absence; this was done on 27 May 1656. Sarah Leverett was admitted as a member of the Boston church on 12 October 1656.

She followed her husband to England in 1657. She carried a letter to him from the governor of Massachusetts, John Endecott, dated 29 June. She may have taken their young children with her.

Later, she returned to New England, presumably with her husband in 1661.

NEHGR 1: 220–1, 4: 126; *Boston CR*, 57; *Suffolk Deeds* II, 260–3.

LING, Benjamin

Benjamin Ling settled at Charlestown in 1636, but moved to New Haven in 1637, with Theophilus Eaton and John Davenport. He became a freeman of the New Haven Colony in 1640. Davenport's letters of 1653–5 show Ling often travelled between Massachusetts and New Haven, and carried correspondence between Davenport and John Winthrop Jr* of Saybrook.

Ling sold his land in 1655 and returned to England. Little is known of him until after the Restoration, when he came back to New England. Davenport reported that a letter from Ling, dated 4 March 1661/2, 'Informes that the Act of Uniformity was then finished which (he saith) would cause many to remove'. Writing to Henry Rutherford of New Haven, 27 March 1662, Ling declared his intention of sailing for New England at the end of April. In fact he sailed soon after 13 May, carrying a letter to Davenport from John Winthrop Jr, then in London. Ling died in New England in 1673.

Davenport Letters, 87, 89, 95, 99, 141, 202, 218; 4 *MHSC* 8: 189–92; I.M. Calder, *The New Haven Colony* (New Haven, CT: Yale University Press, 1934), 47.

LIPPINCOTT, Richard and Abigail

Richard Lippincott, a barber, settled at Dorchester, Massachusetts, with his wife Abigail. Both became church members: Abigail was admitted on 16 April 1644, and although the date of Richard's admission is not extant, he would have been a member before his admission as a freeman on 13 May 1644. At some point they moved to Boston. The Dorchester church recommended them to the Boston church on 28 December 1644. Several years later, on 27 April 1651, Richard was admonished at Boston, as 'a member of the Church of Dorchester being Recommended from thence by letters to us': he had withdrawn from communion with the church. The Boston church excommunicated Richard Lippincott on 6 July 1651, for not giving reasons for his conduct and for refusing to hear the arguments of the church.

Richard and Abigail Lippincott left New England and soon emerged as Quakers. They sailed home, probably not long after July 1651. (In December 1652, Richard Wilson sold on a house in Boston he had 'lately' bought from Richard Lippincott, 'barber'.) The Lippincotts were in Plymouth, Devon, when their child 'Restore' was born in 1653. In 1655, the Quakers Thomas Salthouse and Miles Halhead stayed 'at the house of one Lippingcott' in Stonehouse, Plymouth. Richard Lippincott signed a protest at their arrest, delivered to the regional major-general, John Disbrowe. A similar protest was printed in Halhead's account of the event, *The wounds of an enemy in the house of a friend*. On 8 January 1655/6, Richard Lippincott was imprisoned at the quarter sessions in Exeter, by judges including John Disbrowe, for denying the scriptures to be the Word of God. He was released the following month.

At the Restoration, Richard and Abigail Lippincott left England for Rhode Island. By 1669 they had moved to Shrewsbury, New Jersey. They are known for the unusual names of their eight children, which could (perhaps) be combined into a prayer: Remember, John, Restore, Freedom, Increase, Jacob, Preserve, Israel.

> A. D. Selleck, 'Plymouth Friends: a Quaker history', Devonshire Association *Transactions*, 99 (1968), Part I, 289 and Part II, 253; *NEHGR* 3: 187; *Boston CR*, 43, 51, 52; *Suffolk Deeds* I, 274–5; DRO, Q/S 1/9 (Quarter Sessions Order Book, 1652-61), 8 January 1655/6; Miles Halhead, *The wounds of an enemie in the house of a friend* (1656), 62; [Anon.], *The west answering to the north in the fierce and cruel persecution of the manifestation of the Son of God* (1657), 167; David Hackett Fischer, *Albion's seed: four British folkways in America* (Oxford: Oxford University Press, 1989), 506–7.

LISLE, Francis

Francis Lisle arrived in Boston in 1637, with his wife Alice. He was admitted to the Boston church, as 'a barber' (barber-surgeon), on 29 September 1639. Lisle may be the freeman of Massachusetts 'Francis Seyle', admitted on 13 May 1640. He joined the Artillery Company in 1640. On 10 August 1641 Elizabeth Blackborne* (by power of attorney from her husband William*) sold Lisle a dwelling house, shop and land.

Lisle left for England, probably late in 1643 – with Nehemiah Bourne*, William Hudson Jr*, John Leverett* and Israel Stoughton*, some of the colony's 'best military men' – to join the parliamentary army. He became a surgeon in the earl of Manchester's forces.

Francis Lisle had returned to New England by 12 August 1645, when the Massachusetts General Court appointed him as surgeon to John Leverett's expedition against the Narragansett Indians: Lisle was said to have 'lately come out of impliment [employment] of the Earl of Manchester, in England'.

According to John Winthrop, Lisle went to England again, and did not return. He probably left in the winter of 1645. On 29 November that year, Henry and Elizabeth Bridgham appointed him as their attorney to collect money due to Elizabeth from estate of her father, John Harding of Boreham, Essex. (Her brother Robert Harding* acted as a witness.) On 13 December, Lisle assigned the office of attorney to Joseph Rudson of St Mary Axe, London, presumably intending to pass the documents on to Rudson once he arrived in England. Lisle died at some point before 1666. His daughter Mary had married Freegrace Bendall*. In 1666, Lisle's son Joseph, with Freegrace Bendall, administered the estate of Francis Lisle's widow Alice.

> *GD*; *Artillery Company*, 107; *Boston CR*, 26; *NEHGR* 3: 187; *Suffolk Deeds* I, 20, Lechford *NB*, 393–5; *WJ*, 605; Aspinwall, 11, 14.

LONGE, Joseph

On 22 May 1651, Joseph Longe's wife Mary petitioned the Massachusetts General Court for permission to remarry if the opportunity occurred. Her petition was granted. Joseph Longe had gone to England *c.*1647, 'about A legacy his father left him of sixty pounds or thereabouts'. He had:

some infirmity of body before he went, which Contynued strongly upon him after hee Came there as did appeare by A letter under his owne hand, but yet Intended his Journey the next day into the Country trauiling at this time beinge very dangerous.

Thomas Gilbert* had spoken to Longe's brother in England, 'with whom his busines was, who told him he neuer came to him nor did he heare of him at all'. John Stolman had received letters from England which reported that Joseph Longe 'cannot be heard of although they have made much inquiry for him but he thinkes him to be dead'. 'Widow Dapen' of Dorchester had received similar letters from her son, and 'many others haue been desired to Enquire for him ever since he went hence both in England and Ireland but can hear nothinge of him'.

MHS, Misc. MSS, 22 May 1651.

LORD, Robert and Rebecca

Robert Lord was the son of Thomas Lord, a smith from Towcester, Northamptonshire. Thomas and Dorothy Lord emigrated in 1635 on the *Elizabeth & Ann*, with their seven youngest children, among them Robert Lord. Their eldest, Richard Lord, had gone to New England ahead of them in 1633. The family joined Richard Lord at Cambridge, Massachusetts, and together moved to Hartford, Connecticut, in 1636.

By 1651, Robert Lord had married Rebecca Phillips, daughter of William and Susanna Phillips of Charlestown, and was living in Boston. Rebecca's sister, Martha*, had married Richard Thurston*. On 18 August 1652 William Phillips gave Rebecca and Martha a house in Boston – half each, to share – as a gift from the estate of their mother Susanna.

Robert and Rebecca Lord went to England with Richard and Martha Thurston at some point before January 1656/7. Robert Lord and Richard Thurston sent a letter back to New England to their father-in-law William Phillips. They instructed him to sell the house in which they both 'did late Inhabitt and dwell before they with each of theire familyes went for England'. It was sold, 8 January 1656/7, on the strength of the authority the letter conferred, but Phillips promised to obtain within three years a conveyance from both couples, 'Sealed Sufficyently Confirmed and witnessed by two persons or more that comes to New England, who will testify the sealing and delivery thereof'.

'Robert Lord of new Gravell Lane mariner' was admitted a member of the Stepney congregational church on 21 June 1657. Rebecca, daughter of Robert and Rebecca Lord of 'Gravell Lane', was baptised on 20 February 1656/7, and further baptisms followed: Nathaniel (6 October 1657), Sarah (28 August 1659), William (11 August 1661). Richard and Martha Thurston also lived on New Gravel Lane.

Suffolk Deeds I, 325, II, 329–30; *GMB* 1198–201; *GM* 4: 333; Stepney CB, fols 4, 121.

LOWLE, Mary (b. *c.*1633)

Mary Lowle was the daughter of John Lowle, who emigrated from Portbury, near Bristol, and settled at Newbury, Massachusetts, by 1642. John Lowle died before 15 October 1650, when Mary petitioned the Massachusetts General Court that a legacy of £10 due to her at the age of 21 should be released: she wished to go to England to some near friends from whom she had received her education. The court granted her petition.

Essex Probate Recs. I, 72, citing *Mass. Recs.* 3: 213; D.G. Allen, *In English ways* (Chapel Hill, NC: University of North Carolina Press, 1981), 264.

LUDLOW, Roger (1590–*c.*1666)

Roger Ludlow, the eldest son of Thomas and Jane Ludlow of Dinton, Wiltshire, matriculated on 16 June 1610 at Balliol College, Oxford, but did not graduate. He was admitted to the Inner Temple, London, in November 1612, as of Warminster, Wiltshire. The lawyer Thomas Lechford* later referred to him as 'my old acquaintance'; Emmanuel Downing* also knew him well. He was a cousin of the army officer and regicide Edmund Ludlow (*ODNB*).[1]

Ludlow emigrated from Plymouth, Devon, *c.*1630, probably with his brother George (who later moved to Virginia). Roger Ludlow settled at Dorchester. He had been appointed an assistant of the Massachusetts Bay Company before emigration, and continued to 1634. In May 1632 he was angry that the governor of Massachusetts was to be chosen by whole General Court, not just the assistants, and 'protested he would then return back into England'. He became deputy-governor of Massachusetts in 1634. Ludlow was not elected a magistrate in 1635, by Winthrop's record, because he objected that the town deputies had decided their votes before coming to the General Court.

Almost immediately, Ludlow moved to Connecticut. He joined a company of Dorchester settlers who left as a church to found the 'Dorchester plantation', soon re-named Windsor. He was at Windsor by the summer of 1635, and a commissioner for the government of Connecticut. On 7 April 1636, John Winthrop Jr* reported to his father that the Windsor settlers had lost cattle worth £2500 over the winter. In 1637 Ludlow was involved in a military campaign against Pequot Indians with Israel Stoughton* and others. In 1639, as deputy governor of Connecticut, he worked with Governor John Haynes* to frame Connecticut's constitution, the 'Fundamental Orders'. That year Ludlow gained permission to begin a new plantation at Pequonnock (Stratford). This led, controversially, to his absence from duties as a magistrate. In 1641 he was allocated more land near there, and in 1651 he founded Fairfield. Ludlow drew up a code of civil law based on biblical principles in 1650.

Early in 1654, Ludlow began to sell off his land at Fairfield. He and others were discouraged by Massachusetts' failure to lend support to the settlements of western Connecticut, which, at a time of Anglo-Dutch hostilities, were under threat from New Netherland. In April 1654, Ludlow left for Virginia with his family, and visited his brother George.[1]

From Virginia, Ludlow sailed to Ireland, then to England. He went back to Dublin again by September 1654, encouraged to settle there by his cousin Edmund. On 3 November 1654 Ludlow was nominated to a judicial body to adjudicate claims on forfeited lands. He had relevant legal experience from adjudicating land claims in Connecticut. Ludlow became master of chancery.

In 1656 Roger Ludlow administered George Ludlow's will: Roger's children Jonathan, Joseph, Roger, Anne, Mary, Sarah (who married Nathaniel Brewster*) were mentioned. Jonathan and Sarah, and perhaps others, were with him in Dublin. He disputed the terms of the will with his nephew Thomas, son of Gabriel Ludlow, February 1660/1. His wife Mary Ludlow (a sister of John Endecott, *ANB*) was buried at St Michan's, Dublin, on 3 June 1664. The date of Roger Ludlow's death is unknown: perhaps *c.*1666.[2]

[1] *Al. Oxon.*; Lechford *PD*, 43; *Dorchester CR*, iii; *WJ*, 36, 55, 66-7, 97, 116, 123, 127n., 144; *WP* III, 246; for involvement in Pequot War and its aftermath, *WP* III, 435, 437, 441, 454, 457 and IV, 36-7, 43-5; *WJ*, 226, 229; Dorothy Deming, *The settlement of the Connecticut towns* (New Haven, CT: Yale University Press, 1933), 22-4.
[2] T.C. Barnard, *Cromwellian Ireland: English government and reform in Ireland 1649-1660* (Oxford: Oxford University Press, 1975), 288-9; administration of George's will, Waters, 172-3. Also, *passim*, R.V. Coleman, *Roger Ludlow in Chancery* (Westport, CT, 1934) and *Mr Ludlow goes for old England* (Westport, CT, 1935); G.H. Dutcher, 'Introduction', *The Fundamental Orders of Connecticut* (New Haven, CT: Publications of the Tercentenary Commission of the State of Connecticut, XX, 1934); J.H. Perry, *Roger Ludlowe: an historical sketch* (Bridgeport, CT, 1914); J.M. Taylor, *Roger Ludlow: the colonial lawmaker* (New York and London: G.P. Putnam's Sons, 1900).

ANB, *GMB* 1211-3, *ODNB*.

LYON, Richard

Richard Lyon acted as a tutor at Harvard to William Mildmay*. Mildmay had been sent over in 1644 by his father, Sir Henry Mildmay (*ODNB*), to study at the college. Lyon is said to have assisted Henry Dunster, the president of Harvard, with a revision of the Bay Psalm Book. Lyon probably left for England with Mildmay in 1651. He could be the 'Mr Lyon' approached between May 1649 and early 1650, along with others, about becoming minister at Malden (where Marmaduke Matthews* eventually took office).

Sibley I, 164-5; *Harvard Recs.* III, 21; MHS, Misc. MSS, 31 October 1651.

M

MALBON, Richard (d. before 1661)

Richard Malbon [Malbone], a London merchant related to Theophilus Eaton, attended the church of John Davenport, St Stephen's Coleman Street. He emigrated in 1637 with his family (including his son, Samuel Malbon*) in Davenport and Eaton's company. With Eaton, Edward Hopkins* and David Yale*, Malbon was one of the most prominent merchants to go to New England.

Malbon settled at New Haven at the start, in 1638. He was soon a church member and assistant in the New Haven Colony, and captain of the New Haven artillery company. In 1643, his daughter Martha was convicted for stealing from her parents and 'filthy dalliances' with servants. John Winthrop noted: 'There was a piece of justice executed at New Haven, which, being the first in that kind, is not unworthy to be recorded. Mr Malbon, one of the magistrates there, had a daughter . . . which was openly whipped, her father joining in the sentence.' In 1644 the colony appointed Malbon to attend distant meetings of New England confederation, with Stephen Goodyear* or Thomas Gregson*. He also acted, with Gregson, as an arbitrator to resolve local disputes out of court. New Haven's merchants investigated the possibility of a trading settlement in Delaware, but without success. Then the townspeople invested in building a ship, the *Fellowship*, to export goods directly to England. With Eaton, Gregson and Goodyear, Malbon joined the 'Company of Merchants of New Haven' who loaded the *Fellowship* with cargo. The ship set sail in January 1645/6, but sank. Gregson was among those lost, with Goodyear's wife and George Lamberton*. Five months later, it was reported, an apparition of the 'Great Shippe' appeared in New Haven harbour.

Malbon went back to England – probably in the autumn of 1650, when his son Samuel abandoned his studies at Harvard to transfer to Oxford. New Haven suffered a loss of settlers like Malbon in the early 1650s, when prospects at home looked bright and conflict with New Netherland looked likely. In the 1660s, Samuel Maverick wrote that the town, with its 'stately and costly houses', was 'not so glorious as once it was', its merchants 'either dead or come away, the rest gotten to their farms'. A witness later recalled that Malbon had gone to England in 1648, but this may be an error, or a report of a temporary visit: the first mention of his absence in the New Haven town records was in February 1650/1. In a court action in New Haven, January 1653/4, Benjamin Ling* acted as Malbon's attorney, and referred to Philip Leeke as his agent. Malbon, with 'Mr Hutchinson' of London (Richard Hutchinson* or his uncle of the same name) sold his houses and house-lot in New Haven, March 1654/5. Malbon's daughter Mary Perry, and her husband Richard, followed Malbon back from New Haven to England. Nothing is known of Richard Malbon's fortunes in England. He died before May 1661.

New Haven TR, 8, 26, 58–9, 63, 198, 232, 253, 481; *WJ*, 425, 630–1, 643–4, 713–14; *Pilgrims*, 83; Bernard Bailyn, *The New England merchants in the seventeenth century* (Cambridge, MA: Harvard University Press, 1955), 95, citing Maverick, 'A brief description of New England', c.1660; I.M. Calder, *The New Haven Colony* (New Haven, CT: Yale University Press, 1934), 30, 60, 84, 120, 136, 160, 162, 208; *NEHGR* 128: 65–7, 70. Richard and Mary Perry: *New Haven TR*, 8, 58–9, 63–4.

MALBON, Samuel

Samuel Malbon [Malbone], son of the London merchant Richard Malbon*, emigrated with his parents in 1637. Malbon attended Harvard, but did not graduate. He received a certificate of residence, dated 19 October 1650, signed by Henry Dunster as president, and by the Harvard fellows Samuel Mather*, Jonathan Mitchell and Comfort Starr*.

Malbon left for England almost as soon as he had the Harvard certificate in his hand. He was back in London by 23 December 1650, when Nathaniel Mather* wrote that 'Sam. Malbone is goeing I think this day to Oxford'. Malbon graduated BA at New Inn Hall, Oxford, on 29 May 1651. On 21 April 1654, he was presented as vicar of Henham, Essex, by Laurence Wright (*ODNB*), Cromwell's personal physician and an old friend of New England. To support his presentation to the living, Malbon brought certificates from well-known congregationalists in Oxford: John Owen, then dean of Christ Church, and 'Jo.' [Thomas] Goodwin, president of Magdalen College. He also brought certificates from his father's associates: the London merchant Richard Hutchinson and Robert Newman* (Newman had been with Richard Malbon at St Stephen's Coleman Street and in New Haven). Robert King, another of Malbon's guarantors, was perhaps the person named in 1648 as an elder for High Laver, Essex. In 1656 Malbon contemplated a move to Devon: he was probably the 'Mr Sam. Malbon' presented on 25 April 1656 as vicar of Heavitree. This time he brought certificates from John Bond (Master of the Savoy, *CR*); Thomas Goodwin; Thomas Trapham; George Wilson (*CR*) of Elsenham, close to Henham; John Haseler of Chorley, named in 1648 as an elder for Messing; John Payne (*CR*) of Bishop's Stortford; Thomas Leigh; 'Jo. Beane' of Berden, Essex. However, Malbon seems to have dropped the living in Devon in favour of a position in Norfolk. On 23 July 1656 he was admitted rector of Blofield, Norfolk, with certificates from Christopher Muschamp, James Cranford (*ODNB*), and Richard Abbott.

In 1660, at the Restoration, Samuel Malbon left Blofield and the sequestered rector came back. William Hooke* reported to John Davenport in 1662 that Malbon was going to Amsterdam. He stayed there for some years. The title page of his *Death and life* (eight sermons on Romans 1:14) described him as 'preacher of the word of life in Amsterdam'. The Yarmouth congregational church dismissed a member to 'the church in Amsterdam whereof Mr Malbourne was pastor', 20 January 1669/70. At some point Malbon came back to England. He died in Norwich before August 1670, described as of St Giles, Cripplegate, London. Two of his sermons were posthumously published.

Publications *Death and life* (1669); *Christs glorious appearance in judgment* (1673).

I.M. Calder, *The New Haven Colony* (New Haven, CT: Yale University Press, 1934), 136; *Harvard Recs.* III, 44n.; Nathaniel Mather to John Rogers(?), 23 December 1650, BPL, MS Am. 1502 v.1, no. 6 [printed, 4 *MHSC* 8: 5, with the date '1651?']; LPL, MSS COMM. III/3, lib. 1 fol. 75 and III/5, fols 19, 94; W.A. Shaw, *A history of the English Church . . . 1640–1660* (London: Longmans & Green, 1900), II, 380, 389; Hooke to Davenport, 31 March 1662, 4 *MHSC* 8: 196; Yarmouth CB, 20 January 1669/70.

CC, CR, Sibley.

MARSHALL, Christopher (1614–1673)

Christopher Marshall was the son of Christopher Marshall, a mercer of Alford, Lincolnshire. In 1632 he matriculated at Magdelene College, Cambridge, but did not complete a degree.

Marshall emigrated in 1634 and continued his education with John Cotton, minister at Boston, Massachusetts. He was admitted to the Boston church, as 'a singleman', on 28 August 1634. He became a freeman on 6 May 1635. According to Edmund Calamy, Marshall married Sarah Hutchinson, daughter of Edward Hutchinson* and niece of the antinomians Anne Hutchinson and John Wheelwright*. Marshall was associated with Wheelwright, whose party in 1637 opposed the regulation limiting visitors' residence in the Bay Colony to three weeks because – according to John Winthrop – 'it was very probable, that they expected many of their opinion to come out of England from Mr Brierly his church'. (This was Roger Brereley, *ODNB*, of Grindleton, Yorkshire, whose followers became known as 'Grindletonians'.) Winthrop recorded that John Wheelwright, banished from Massachusetts for his antinomianism, 'gathered a company and sat down by the falls of Pascataquack, and called their town Exeter'. Marshall followed him north out of Massachusetts. On 6 January 1638/9, Marshall was dismissed from the Boston church, with Wheelwright and seven others, 'unto the Church of Christ at the Falls of Paschataqua if they be rightly gathered and ordered'.[1]

Marshall returned to England c.1642. He may have served in the parliamentary army. According to the parliamentary survey of 1650, he was vicar of Wakefield and Horbury chapel, and rector of West Ardesley (Woodkirk), in the West Riding of Yorkshire. Woodkirk had a record of nonconformity before 1640 and links with New England: Anthony Nutter, who had acted chaplain to John Savile, first Baron Savile (*ODNB*), had been presented for nonconformity there; Samuel Newman, curate in the parish in 1636, emigrated to New England c.1638; Abraham Pierson, 'clerk, of Ardesley', emigrated to Boston in 1640. Oliver Heywood believed Marshall gathered a congregational church at Woodkirk c.1648. Thomas Jollie (*ODNB*) and his congregation at Altham took advice from Marshall before they gathered their church. Baron Savile's son, Thomas Savile, first earl of Sussex, lived at Howley Hall nearby and gave Marshall a stipend. At Woodkirk, James Nayler was a member of Marshall's church before becoming a Quaker. Marshall was a fierce critic of the Quakers: George Fox later accused him of slander. Marshall was appointed in 1654 as an assistant to the West Riding commissioners for removing unsuitable parish ministers.

Marshall was ejected from West Ardesley in 1662. He attended a meeting of congregationalist ministers and others at Sowerby in July that year, ahead of 'Black Bartholomew's Day', 24 August. He seems to have lived at Topcliffe Hall, which belonged to the Savile family, and held meetings there from 1662 to 1665. After the Five Mile Act of 1665, Marshall stayed at Horbury. He appeared at York assizes, 1 August 1666, for saying in the pulpit that 'those that have taken the protestation and after came to the Common Prayer of the Church are perjured persons before God and Man'. In 1669 he was preaching in the parish of Darfield. By 1672 he was living in his own house at Topcliffe, which used to belong to the Saviles: this house was licensed as a congregational meeting place. Marshall was licensed there and at West Ardesley, but was not permitted to preach in the vacant chapel at Morley.

Marshall had children baptised at Boston, Massachusetts, and at Topcliffe. He seems to have married three times. His first wife (who according to Calamy was Sarah Hutchinson) drowned in an accident at Pascataqua in 1639. In the records of Topcliffe church, confusingly, the burial of 'our dear sister Sarah, the wife of our pastor Mr Christopher Marshall' was noted in February 1657/8. Marshall's third wife was also Sarah – Sarah Neustead, who later married Marshall's successor at Topcliffe, Gamaliel Marsden (*CR*). Marshall died in 1673 and left property in Rothwell and Woodkirk.[2]

[1] *Boston CR*, 18, 23; *NEHGR* 3:93; *WJ*, 219, 274, 283; *GM* 5: 30–5.
[2] LPL, MS COMM. XIIa/18 fols 286–8, 320–1; R.A. Marchant, *The puritans and the church courts in the diocese of York 1560–1642* (London: Longmans, 1960), 5, 42, 108–11, 264, 266, 267; Bryan Dale, *Yorkshire puritanism and early nonconformity*. Bradford: [Dale's executors], 1910), 104–7, 129–30; G.F. Nuttall, *The Holy Spirit in puritan faith and experience* (Oxford: Blackwell, 1946, reprinted Chicago, IL and London: University of Chicago Press, 1992), 179; G.F. Nuttall, *Visible saints: the congregational way, 1640–1660* (Oxford: Blackwell, 1957), 123; W. Smith, ed., *The registers of Topcliffe and Morley in the West Riding of the County of Yorkshire* (London: Longmans, Green & Co., 1888), 1–4, 12, 13, 14, 18, 20n., 29–34. For Sarah (Hutchinson) Marshall: *WP* IV, 118; Smith, ed., *Topcliffe and Morley*, 18; *CR*.

BDBR, CR, Surman.

MARTIN, Francis

Francis Martin, a merchant, came from Plymouth in Devon and settled at Richmond Island in Maine by 1640. John Winthrop noted that Martin's father had been mayor of Plymouth. Within a few years, Francis Martin had gone back to England. He left two daughters behind in New England, with no provision 'for their safe bestowinge in his absence, as the Care & Wisdome of a father should have doone'. The eldest, Mary Martin, became a maidservant to Nehemiah and Hannah Bourne* in Boston: 'findinge herselfe to be with child, & not able to beare the shame of it', she gave birth in secret and killed the child. The sad truth emerged in December 1646, just after the Bournes left for England. The dead child was found in a chest. Mary Martin was tried for murder, and hanged.

WJ, 680–2.

MARTIN, Isaac

Isaac Martin was at Hingham, Massachusetts, by 1639. In 1643 he was granted land at Rehobeth. It has been suggested that he was the brother of Abraham and Robert Martin: Abraham, who had settled in Hingham, c.1635; Robert, who came from Batcombe, Somerset, arrived on the *Marygould* in 1635 and settled first at Weymouth, then at Rehobeth in 1644. However, Isaac Martin's roots may lie in East Anglia – or at least, it looks as if he was heading that way when he left New England.

Martin left for England in December 1646, to judge from two letters of attorney given to him at that time. On 2 December, Humphrey Griggs of Braintree appointed Martin to ask for £5 from William Griggs of Cavendish, Suffolk, clerk. This was a legacy due to Humphrey Griggs by the will of Thomas Griggs of Sudbury, tallow chandler. On the same date Humphrey Griggs signed a bill of release to William Griggs, for £5 received (Martin was to hand over this bill of release on receipt of the money in England). On 12 December, Thomas Bayes of Dedham gave Isaac Martin a letter of attorney, in which Martin was described as 'late of Hingham in N: England'. This authorised Martin to collect a legacy from the executors of Bayes's grandfather, one Wiseman of Barrow Apton, Norfolk, without power of substitution. On the same date Bayes acknowledged receipt of £20 from Martin, in consideration of the power given to receive the legacy: it looks as if Martin gave Bayes a sum equivalent to the bequest Martin was to collect.

GM 5: 56, 60; Aspinwall, 49, 69.

MASCALL, Robert

Robert Mascall [Maskall] was admitted to the Boston church on 20 June 1640, as 'one of our brother Mr Willyam Piercs [Pierce*] family'. He never became a freeman. On 5 July 1646, Mascall 'had letters of Dismission granted him unto the Church of Christ at Dover in England according to his desire thereof'.

Thomas Edwards, the presbyterian propagandist, publicised the activities at Dover of a religious radical and customs official, 'one Master Maskall'. He published a letter about Mascall written on 13 April 1646, and sent to a member of the Westminster Assembly. This reported what Mascall had done in the absence of John Davis (CR), pastor to the newly gathered church at Dover:

Mr Mascal (a man employed by the state to be a perfector of the Customes) undertakes to feed the flock, expounds the Scriptures, and with much vehemency cryes out to the people, expressing himself thus against the present Ministery: [']Your Priests, your damned Priests, your cursed Priests, with their fools Coats. Your Levites, who if they get an Ordinance of Parliament will thunder it out, but they let alone the Ordinances of Christ['], and perswades the people of the evil that Synods and Learned men have done to the Church, and therefore presseth them to the uselesnesse of humane learning, and at other times in private meetings, perswades people, that they will fall into most miserable slavery, if they have a Presbytery, and saith, that he shall stand and laugh at them, when they are under their burthens.

Apparently Mascall came to Edwards's house with a mutual friend to deny these charges, 'holding our godly Ministers to have a lawfull calling, and Synods to be needfull'. Edwards did not identify Mascall as a former colonist, which is surprising.

The Canterbury congregational church book mentioned 'Bro. Mascall' as a messenger from the Dover church in 1647. 'Bro. Mascall' was a member at Canterbury by 28 September 1651, when he was nominated as deacon but not elected. After this, he often acted with the pastor and others on behalf of the church. 'Rob. Mascall' gave certificates in 1656 for John Player (*CR*), on his admission as divinity lecturer at Canterbury Cathedral; and (with Player) for Edward Line (*CR*), for admission to the living of 'Hernhill', Kent. In 1663, the authorities reported 'Capt. Mascall' as a member of the Canterbury church, which met frequently and illegally. Comfort Starr* was a minister at Canterbury, 1687.

Boston CR, 30, 46; Edwards, *Gangraena*, ii. 67, 163–4 and iii, preface; Canterbury CB, fols 6r–19v, *passim*; Joel Halcomb, 'A social history of congregational religious practice during the Puritan Revolution' (PhD dissertation, University of Cambridge, 2009), 136–7; LPL, MS COMM. III/5 fols 37, 177; 'Williamson's Spy Book', *Transactions of the Congregational Historical Society*, 5 (1911–12), 255.

MATHER, Increase (1639–1723)

Increase Mather was born in New England at Dorchester, Massachusetts, the son of Richard and Katherine Mather, and the younger brother of Samuel* and Nathaniel Mather*. Richard Mather named his son 'Increase' to mark the 'great Increase of every sort' with which 'God favoured the country... about the time of his nativity'. Two years later, Mather baptised another Dorchester child with the name 'Return' – a sign of changed times in New England, 'the times of the unsettled humours of many men's spirits to return for England'. Increase and Return grew up in the same small settlement. As an adult, Return Munnings defied his name by staying on in America. Increase Mather defied his name by sailing to England as soon as he could: twelve days after he turned eighteen and preached his first sermon.

Mather entered Harvard in 1651 but after six months went to be tutored by

John Norton of Ipswich, 'my parents ... fearing that the Colledge diet would not well agree with my weake natural constitution of Body'. He moved with Norton to Boston in April 1653, and rejoined the graduating class of 1656. He would have graduated in 1655 but stayed on, at his father's request, for the extra year imposed on students by the Harvard president, Henry Dunster. Mather graduated BA in 1656. During his time at Harvard he attended the church at Cambridge and was influenced by Jonathan Mitchell's ministry.

In 1657, Mather recalled, 'My brother Samuel ... wrote to my Father encouraging him to send me to Dublin ... Now having my selfe a marvellous inclination and bent of spirit that way, I prevailed with my Father to give his consent that I should go for England.' He had an emotional parting from his father, who 'as I took my leave of him, laid his hands over my shoulders, and wept over me abundantly (and so did I pour out tears on him) and solemnly blessed me ... so we parted, not expecting to see one another again in this world'. Increase Mather left New England on 3 July 1657.

After an Atlantic crossing of five weeks, Mather landed at Portsmouth. He rode to London and on 24 August 1657 left for Lancashire, 'where I was very kindly entertayned by my Fathers old friends and Christian acquaintance'. In September 1657 he sailed from Liverpool to Dublin, and met Samuel, who he had not seen for seven years: 'Hee did not know me, but by the letters which I brought and discourse with him, Hee was easily convinced of my being his Brother.' Mather studied at Trinity College, Dublin, and graduated MA in June 1658. He declined a fellowship. He received several invitations to be a minister. The Lord Deputy and Irish council settled Magherafelt on him, and were keen for him to stay: 'The Lord Deputy was so respective as to send me word, that I should not go for England for want of encouragement in Irland whilest hee was in power.' Mather, however, felt the 'moyst Irish Air' was not good for his health. He decided to return to England, 'And thither God brought me again in July 1658'.

In London, Mather met John Howe (*CR*), chaplain to the Protector and vicar of Great Torrington, Devon. (Howe had been ordained at Winwick, Lancashire, and so knew Mather's family, but would also have known William Hooke*.) Letters from Howe to Richard Baxter in June 1658 show Howe was having difficulty finding someone to take his place in his parish. Howe put to Baxter a case of conscience which might result in a happy compromise between his duties in Whitehall and in Devon: he proposed to be in Torrington a quarter of the year, or as much of the year as could be allowed 'procuring another (who shall injoy the profits of the place) to bee constantly resident'. His qualm was whether it was lawful, 'continuing related to a people with whom one can so little reside'. Baxter and others persuaded Howe to stay in London. Howe invited Increase Mather to take his place in Devon: Mather recalled 'This overture I closed with, and spent the following winter in Torrington for the most part, only one moneth I continued with my brother Nathaniel who was then preacher at Barnstaple.'

Over the next year, Mather left Devon for Guernsey, contemplated a move to Kent, and then went to Gloucestershire. In April 1659, he arrived in Guernsey as chaplain to Colonel John Bingham – he had been recommended to Bingham by William Benn (*CR*) of Dorchester, Nathaniel Mather's father-in-law. He preached every Lord's Day, in the morning at Castle Cornet and in the afternoon at Petersport, at a salary of £120 a year. Next, he responded to an invitation from the gathered church at Sandwich in Kent, which had come into being through Nathaniel Mather's influence, to be their pastor. Mather left Guernsey for the mainland, but did not continue negotiations after discouragement from his brother's successor as vicar at Sandwich, Thomas Danson (*ODNB*). Meanwhile, a congregational church in Gloucester, of which James Forbes (*CR*) was pastor, 'procured for me a legal Title to a place in the city . . . called St Maries'. Mather was appointed by the Trustees for the Maintenance of Preaching Ministers on 17 November 1659, and took up the post in December. He lived with Forbes, preaching in the morning at St Mary's-de-Lode and in the afternoon at Gloucester Cathedral.

As the Restoration came, Mather left Gloucester with memories of being 'persecuted out'. According to his travel diary, he left the city on 2 February 1659/60, sailed from Weymouth to Guernsey on 1 April, and stayed in the Channel Islands almost a year. While he was there the king and prelacy 'came again into England'. In March 1661, when he had either to depart or conform to certain ceremonies, he left Guernsey.

Until June 1661, Mather lived partly in Weymouth and partly in Dorchester. He still preached every 'Lord's day' and three or four times during the week. His Dorset friends wanted him to continue. Mather was willing to do this without pay, 'provided I might have the Assurance of a publick opportunity to preach the gospell . . . But this none could promise except I would conform'. Some said they could obtain for him 'a living with £400 per Annum, if I would conform and read the Common prayer, But that I durst not do'. He considered going abroad (with Samuel Bellingham* amongst others), but was prevented by various obstructions. Then, 'having a great desire to see my Father, and hoping that I might for some time find shelter in New England I resolved (with submission to the will of God) to return thither'.

On 29 June 1661, Increase set sail from Weymouth for Newfoundland, which he reached in August. Within ten days he found a vessel bound for New England. He arrived on 1 September 1661, and at the sight of his father emotion swept over him – 'the first, and I think the only time that I ever wept for joy'. Soon he had invitations from twelve churches to become their minister. On 27 October, he was admitted at Dorchester. The following winter he divided his time between the churches of Dorchester and Boston. On 6 March 1661/2, he married Maria Cotton, daughter of John Cotton of Boston (who was also his stepsister, since his father had married Cotton's widow in 1656). Mather decided to continue preaching in Boston, living in Cotton's house: he and his wife were dismissed to Boston North church on 12 April 1663. This Boston church had badly wanted Mather to accept office, but he 'withstood that motion finding a great averseness in my Spirit to comply therewith. I had also a great desire to return to England if liberty for Nonconformity should there be granted'. However, he was ordained in Boston on 27 May 1664 and went on to play a leading part in civic and ecclesiastical life of Massachusetts.

From 1688 to 1692 Mather was in England again, as colonial agent. He was received by James II before his fall from power. After the Revolution, Mather was received by the new king, William, at the introduction of Philip, Lord Wharton (*ODNB*). Mather obtained the removal of Sir Edmund Andros (*ODNB*) as governor of New England, gained a new charter for Massachusetts, and returned to the colony with a new royal governor, Sir William Phips (*ODNB*). Increase Mather's son Samuel, who had interrupted his studies at Harvard to go to England with his father, stayed on and became a presbyterian minister at Witney, Oxfordshire: Mather commented 'He liveth where he is able to furnish himself with a variety of books.'

For the rest of his life, Increase Mather had a keen desire to live in England, but stayed in New England. He kept up his ties across the Atlantic by correspondence.

Publications Mather's numerous publications started with *The mystery of Israel's salvation* (1669). For a full list see T.J. Holmes, *Increase Mather: a bibliography of his works* (Cleveland, OH: printed for W.G. Mather, 1931).

Cotton Mather, *Memoirs of the life of the Rev. Increase Mather, D.D.* (1724), 2–3; Pilgrims, 54, 81–2; 'The autobiography of Increase Mather', ed. M.G. Hall, *Proceedings of the American Antiquarian Society*, 71 (1961), 281; Mather, 'Diary' [notes about travel, 3 January 1659/60–26 December 1660, 2 March 1662/3–23 June 1663, 5 February 1663/4–31 December 1664], AAS, Mather Papers 1613–1819, Box 3 folder 1 [typescript]; Francis J. Bremer, *Congregational communion: clerical friendship in the Anglo-American puritan community, 1610–1692* (Boston, MA: Northeastern University Press, 1994), *passim*; David Cressy, *Coming over: migration and communication between England and New England in the seventeenth century* (Cambridge: Cambridge University Press, 1987), 210–12; R. Middlekauff, *The Mathers: three generations of puritan intellectuals, 1596–1728* (Oxford and New York: Oxford University Press, 1971), 84–5; John Howe to Richard Baxter, 1 June and 3 June 1658, DWL Baxter Letters, 4/79, 81, summarised in N.H. Keeble and Geoffrey F. Nuttall, eds, *Calendar of the correspondence of Richard Baxter*, 2 vols (Oxford: Clarendon Press, 1991), letters 455, 457; K.B. Murdock, *Increase Mather, the foremost American puritan* (Cambridge, MA: Harvard University Press, 1925), 56–70. Some of Mather's correspondence has been printed: *The Mather Papers*, 4 MHSC 8.

ANB, CC, CR, *ODNB*, Sibley.

MATHER, Nathaniel (1630–1697)

Nathaniel Mather was born at Much Woolton, Lancashire, the second son of Richard and Katherine Mather, and brother to Increase* and Samuel*. He was taken to New England by his parents in 1635 and settled at Dorchester, where his father became minister. Mather graduated BA at Harvard in 1647, and MA in 1650.

Mather was in London with his brother Samuel by 23 December 1650, when he wrote euphorically about opportunities for Harvard graduates in England. The recipient was probably John Rogers of Ipswich, formerly a fellow student at Harvard: Mather wrote to Rogers in a similar vein on 23 March 1650/1. Mather's letter gave news of John Tuttle*, Comfort Starr*, 'Sergiant Okes' (see Urian Oakes*), John Glover*, Samuel Malbon*, 'Fra: Hubbard'* and John Corbet*, all in England. Nathaniel wrote that he intended to go to Scotland. Whether he went or not is unclear: his whereabouts are uncertain for a time.

On 4 May 1655, the mayor, jurates and common council of Sandwich in Kent approved Mather as one of their ministers and as public preacher for the town. Mather brought certificates from West Country and London ministers, which suggests that is where he had been since his return from New England. From the West Country, Mather had gathered certificates from William Benn of Dorchester, Dorset – whose daughter Mary he married at some point – and from Benn's neighbour minister John Loder (*CR*) of Fordington. He also had a certificate from his brother Samuel Mather, by then at Gravesend in Essex, and from the London ministers Richard Kentish (*CR*), Samuel Smith (*CR*) of Benet Gracechurch, and Thomas Harrison*. At Sandwich, Mather seems to have gathered a congregational church: Increase Mather referred to a church formed there under his influence. Mather provided a certificate on 9 April 1656, 'with divers other Members of the church' at Sandwich, for the admission of Richard Lane (*CR*) as vicar of Northbourne, Kent. The ministers of Dover and Canterbury congregational churches, John Davis (*CR*) and John Durant (*CR*), also provided Lane with certificates. As Northbourne was less than five miles from Sandwich, Lane (a congregationalist) could have combined public preaching in his parish with ministry alongside Mather to a gathered congregation in Sandwich.

Nathaniel Mather moved on, and spent the next few years in Devon. On 5 March 1655/6 he was admitted as vicar of Harberton. He brought certificates from George Thorne (*CR*) of Melcombe, Daniel Bull (*CR*) of Wyke, and John Loder of Fordington. Mather joined the Devon Association, led by George Hughes (*CR*) of Plymouth. With John Howe (*CR*), Nathaniel was among those who provided certificates to support the appointment of John Flavell (*CR*) as lecturer at St Saviour's and St Clement (Townstal), Dartmouth, in 1656. On 26 November 1656, Mather was presented as vicar of Barnstaple, and took up the post in January 1656/7. Certificates to support him came from the congregationalists Lewis Stucley (*CR*) of Exeter; William Bartlet (*CR*) of Bideford; John Chishul (*CR*) and Theophilus Polwhele (*CR*) of Tiverton. Polewhele was Mather's brother-in-law by his marriage to Mary Benn. Mather also presented certificates from eminent figures in the Cromwellian regime: the Devon minister John Howe, and the Dorset politician William Sydenham (*ODNB*). After Nathaniel Mather came to Barnstaple, reports circulated that he had committed a 'misdemeanor with a woman' in New England. In 1659, the mariner John Brackenbury* appeared in court in Boston, Massachusetts, to admit that he had been party to stirring up this rumour. Brackenbury claimed he had confused Mather with someone else (probably Thomas Larkham*, whose enemies liked to keep rumours of his dark past in the public eye).

Mather lost the living of Barnstaple early in 1660, for speaking out against the reinstated Rump Parliament. The sequestered vicar was restored. Soon afterwards, Mather was recommended for appointment as a naval chaplain, but this opportunity for ministry evaporated as the Restoration became established.

Nathaniel Mather joined other nonconformist ministers to sign a declaration against Thomas Venner* in 1661. He was preaching at the English church at Rotterdam in 1663, and at Sudbury, Suffolk, in 1671. He succeeded his brother Samuel as pastor of the congregational church at New Row, Dublin, in 1672. In 1676 (with Thomas Harrison among others) he signed letters to accompany the Irish donation of £450 to help victims of the colonial Indian Wars. In 1688 he succeeded John Collins* in London as pastor of the congregational church in Paved Alley, Lime Street. In 1689 the colonist Samuel Sewall visited Nathaniel Mather at his home in Fenchurch Street. In 1690 Mather became one of the managers of the Common Fund. He refused to subscribe to the 'Happy Union' of 1691 because he thought it was not missionary in intent or faithful to congregationalism; he tried to undermine it, attacking the 'heresies' of Daniel Williams. Mather was a lecturer at Pinners Hall in 1694, and a founder of the Congregational Fund Board in December 1695. He died in London and was interred in the nonconformist burial ground at Bunhill Fields.

Publication *The righteousness of God through faith* (1694).

BPL, MS Am. 1506 v.1 nos. 6, 7 [printed with the date '1651(?)', 4 *MHSC* 8: 1–5]; LPL, MSS COMM. III/4, fols 58, 563 and III/5, fols 181, 184; 'The autobiography of Increase Mather', ed. M. G. Hall, *Proceedings of the American Antiquarian Society*, 71 (1961), 283; B.S. Capp, *Cromwell's navy: the fleet and the English Revolution, 1648–1660*, 313; C.G. Bolam, J. Goring, H.L. Short and R. Thomas, *The English presbyterians* (London: Allen & Unwin, 1968), 102, 113, 115–19. Some of his correspondence is printed in *The Mather Papers*, 4 *MHSC* 8. He wrote an unpublished tract on 'The Purity of Baptisme', critiquing New England and Increase Mather's publications on the theme: BL, Add. MS 23622. His nephew, Cotton Mather, wrote an extensive biography: *Magnalia*, II, 153–76.

BDBR, CC, CR, ODNB, Sibley.

MATHER, Samuel (1626–1671)

Samuel Mather, born at Much Woolton in Lancashire, was the son of Richard and Katherine Mather, and brother to Increase* and Nathaniel*. He emigrated to New England with his parents in 1635 and settled at Dorchester, Massachusetts.

Mather graduated BA from Harvard in 1643. He continued at the college, and was the first fellow named in the Harvard charter of 30 May 1650. He succeeded John Bulkeley* and George Downing* as a teacher there, and attended the Cambridge church under Thomas Shepard's ministry. He had become a freeman on 10 May 1648. Mather briefly assisted Ezekiel Rogers, minister at Rowley, and several New England congregations invited him to be their minister. But according to Cotton Mather he had 'a strong Desire to pass over into

England, and by the Wisdom of Heaven, there fell out several Temptations in this Wilderness, which occasioned him to be yet more desirous of such a Removal. To England then he went, in the Year 1650.'[1]

On 26 March 1651, Samuel Mather wrote from London to Jonathan Mitchell (a fellow Harvard graduate, now minister at Cambridge), sending greetings to his brothers and sisters of the Cambridge church. He reported that 'Here is great need of good ministers and faithfull men for places of trust ... the students who are come over will bee of great use to the nation and service to God here.' Mather proceeded to recount Harvard students' circumstances in England, working through a list in order of seniority of graduating class: Benjamin Woodbridge* ('the first borne of newengland'); Tobias Barnard*; George Downing; John Bulkeley; Henry Saltonstall*; Nathaniel Brewster*; Abraham James*; John Allin*; William Ames*; Jeremiah Holland*; James Ward*; Sampson Eyton*; John Birden*; Abraham Walver*. He omitted 'those who came over this yeare [who] will write I suppose every one of himselfe'. Mather did not mention his own employment, which presumably was not yet settled.[2]

Over the next few years Mather travelled widely in Britain and Ireland. He soon became chaplain of Magdalen College, Oxford, where the leading congregationalist Thomas Goodwin was president. He contributed a preface in 1652 to Samuel Stone's *A congregational church is a catholike visible church* and in the same year, with William Greenhill, to Thomas Shepard's *Subjection to Christ* (which Jonathan Mitchell had prepared for the press after Shepard's death). Mather resigned his post in Oxford in 1653 to attend the parliamentary commissioners in Scotland, whose ranks included George Fenwick*. He exercised a ministry at Leith, without a regular charge, for about two years. Cotton Mather thought that at some point Mather preached at Exeter cathedral. On 22 November 1654, Thomas Troyte (*CR*) presented certificates from Samuel Mather and a number of West Country ministers to support of his presentation as rector of Owermoigne, Dorset. Mather, still described as 'of Leith', may have known Troyte in Oxford, where he was a fellow of New College. Cotton Mather also recounted how Thomas Andrewes (*ODNB*), lord mayor of London, had taken Mather as his chaplain soon after his return to England: 'and by the Advantage of the Post... he came into an Acquaintance, with the most Eminent Ministers in the Kingdom'. Andrewes provided a certificate for Mather's next move, to Gravesend, in January 1654/5. Mather's other certificates came from Thomas Goodwin, John Owen, Hugh Peter* and Thomas Harrison*. Mather also secured a certificate from Samuel Smith 'of London', perhaps the person who was minister at St Benet Gracechurch from December 1655 (*CR*), and later gave a certificate for the Harvard graduate Urian Oakes*. On 4 May 1655 Samuel Mather, with Harrison and Smith among others, provided certificates for his brother Nathaniel Mather's admission at Sandwich, Kent.[3]

Mather stayed only a few months at Gravesend before he went to Ireland, where in July 1655 he was incorporated MA at Trinity College, Dublin, and became lecturer at Christ Church cathedral. Philip Nye (*ODNB*) had recommended Mather as a preacher to the Council of Ireland, urging that he be settled in Dublin. Mather did not (as some sources say) accompany Henry

Cromwell to Ireland, but he was soon established there. Nathaniel Brewster, Thomas Harrison and Thomas Patient* were also preachers in the city. Mather served as a commissioner for approbation of ministers in County Cork, August 1655. He was ordained as a colleague of Samuel Winter at the gathered church at St Nicholas, Dublin, on 5 December 1656 (Thomas Jenner* took part in the service). In 1657 Samuel invited his brother Increase Mather to the city. In 1659 Samuel Mather was paid over £200 a year, one of the highest paid ministers in Ireland.[4]

After the Restoration, Mather continued to preach in Dublin until called to account for preaching against ceremonies. He refused to give his sermon notes to the authorities and was silenced in October 1660. (The offending sermons were later printed in New England as *A testimony from the Scripture against idolatry & superstition*.) Mather returned to England and served as curate of Burtonwood, near Warrington, Lancashire, 1660–2. For a short time he was in London, but returned to a congregation at Smithfield, Dublin, in 1662. He was imprisoned on 20 September 1664 for preaching at a private conventicle, but soon released. He gathered a congregation, which met at his house in Dublin until a meeting place was built at New Row. He wrote to Gamaliel Marsden (*CR*), 12 November 1669, rebuking him for omitting to pray publicly for the king – whose Restoration Mather said had been brought in 'by a very strong hand of providence' – and for reviling the government. Mather, however, declared full agreement with Marsden's hostility to ceremonies: not only had he himself been silenced for speaking out on this issue, but also he had objected to ceremonies 'as oft as occasion hath presented, which were frequent, while I was upon the types, many of the popish ceremonies having been borrowed originally from the jewish'. This was a reference to Samuel Mather's sermon series, *The figures and types of the Old Testament*, printed posthumously by his brother Nathaniel.[5]

Publications *A testimony from the Scripture against idolatry & superstition* (Cambridge, MA, 1671); *A defence of the Protestant Christian religion against popery* ([Dublin, 1672]); *Irenicum: or An essay for union* (1680); *The figures or types of the Old Testament* ([Dublin, 1683]).

[1] *Magnalia* II, 39–59 [quotation from 43]; *NEHGR* 3: 91; MHS, Misc. MSS, 31 Oct. 1651.
[2] MHS, Misc. Bd. MSS, 26 March 1651, Samuel Mather to Jonathan Mitchell (Mather's letter follows the order of seniority in *Harvard Recs.* I, 82–3).
[3] LPL, MSS COMM. III/3 lib. 3 fol. 45, lib. 2 fol. 139 and III/4 fol. 58; *Magnalia*, II, 43–4.
[4] T.C. Barnard, *Cromwellian Ireland: English government and reform in Ireland 1649–1660* (Oxford: Oxford University Press, 1975), 99n., 117n., 136n.; St J.D. Seymour, *The puritans in Ireland, 1647–1661* (Oxford: Clarendon Press, 1921), 90, 141; G.F. Nuttall, *Visible saints: the congregational way, 1640–1660* (Oxford: Blackwell, 1957), 25–6.
[5] Mather to Marsden, 12 November 1669, Bodleian, Rawlinson MS D. 1347, fols 25–31.

BDBR, CC, CR, ODNB, Sibley.

MATTHEWS, Lemuel (b. 1643/4, d. in or before 1705)

Lemuel Matthews, the third son of Katherine and Marmaduke Matthews*, was born in New England, at Yarmouth, a younger brother to Manasseh* and Mordecai*. Matthews went to England with or after his father, and was in Swansea by 6 December 1658. He matriculated at Lincoln College, Oxford, on 25 May 1661. That year, he was also recorded as a schoolmaster at Carrickfergus in County Antrim. He claimed to have graduated MA and DD, but the awarding universities are not known. Matthews served as chaplain to Jeremy Taylor, bishop of Down, Connor and Dromore. Taylor made him vicar of Glenavy and prebendary of Cairncastle. Matthews became vicar of Aghagallon, Magherameske and Aghalee in 1668. He was appointed archdeacon of Down on 2 November 1674, and became vicar-general of Down and Connor in 1690.

Like his father, Lemuel Matthews was no stranger to controversy. In 1693 he was suspected of ecclesiastical malpractice, suspended by a royal commission, and deprived of his posts. He spent more than a decade appealing against this. Eventually he regained the prebendary at Cairncastle but not his other positions. He died in or before 1725. He published *A pindarique elegie* for his patron, Jeremy Taylor, and, after 1700, a sequence of pamphlets to support his appeal.

Publications *A pindarique elegie* (1667). The most significant pamphlets related to his appeal are listed in *ODNB*.

Marmaduke Matthews, *Messiah magnified* (1659), 'Epistle Dedicatory'; *DWB s.n.* Marmaduke Matthews.

ODNB.

MATTHEWS, Manasseh

Manasseh Matthews, the second son of Katherine and Marmaduke Matthews*, was baptised by John Lothropp (*ODNB*) at Barnstable in Plymouth Colony on 24 January 1640/1. He studied at Harvard alongside his elder brother Mordecai*, as 'Mathewes Jeunior'. Manasseh Matthews did not take a degree, but he incurred regular charges on the account of his father 'Mr Mathewes', from 10 December 1651 until 8 June 1655.

Manasseh Matthews left New England with, or soon after, his father. He entered Jesus College, Oxford, on 9 August 1658, but did not graduate. He became rector of Port Eynon, on the Gower Peninsula, and conformed at the Restoration. In 1670 he became vicar of St John's, Swansea, the living from which his father had been ejected.

Scituate CR, 282; *Harvard Recs.* III, 137–9; *Al. Oxon.*; *CC*, *DWB s.n.* Marmaduke Matthews*, Sibley *s.n.* Mordecai Matthews*.

MATTHEWS, Marmaduke (c.1606–c.1683)

Marmaduke Matthews was the son of Matthew Jones of Nydfywch, Llangyfelach, Glamorgan, and Mary (he erected a brass in memory of his parents in Llangyfelach church). Matthews matriculated at All Souls College, Oxford, on 20 February 1623/4, graduated BA on 25 February 1624/5, and MA on 5 July 1627. On 12 June 1627, 'Marmaducus Mathewes' was instituted as rector of 'Penmaine' [Penmaen], on the Gower Peninsula. In 1636, at Penmaen, Matthews was said by the bishop of St David's to be 'preaching against the keeping of holy days'. When the Court of High Commission initiated proceedings against him, he left for New England with his wife Katherine.[1]

Matthews's arrival in New England, 21 September 1638, was recorded by John Winthrop: 'A ship of Barnstaple arrived with about eighty passengers, near all western people. There came with them a godly minister, one Mr Matthews.' Katherine Matthews joined the Boston church on 3 February 1638/9. Marmaduke and Katherine Matthews soon moved to Yarmouth, in Plymouth Colony. A church gathered there on 3 November 1639, to which Marmaduke became pastor. Their sons – Mordecai*, Manasseh* and Lemuel* – were all born at Yarmouth. Matthews became a freeman of Plymouth Colony in 1641, and in 1643 was listed at Barnstable as able to bear arms.

Matthews became minister at Hull, Massachusetts, c.1647. Within the bounds of orthodoxy set by the Bay Colony, his preaching soon proved controversial. In May 1649, Hull's inhabitants petitioned the Massachusetts General Court for Matthews to continue as their preacher, but the court judged it unwise to grant this. The magistrates, who had a duty to protect churches from heresy, declared Matthews had expressed 'several erroneous expressions, others weak, inconvenient and unsafe'. The governor admonished him in the name of the court.[2]

Matthews was out of office by December 1649, describing himself as in an 'unsettled condicion', little wanting 'to eate the bread of idelnes' in Hull for the winter. He thought he would move to Pequot Plantation (New London), where Thomas Peter* had been minister until he went back to England. Matthews hoped perhaps ten Hull families would follow him there. In letters from Boston, he explained to John Winthrop Jr* and the settlers of Pequot why he felt he must accept their invitation. He had received, in fact, urgent and legitimate calls to leave New England and go back to Wales. He and had been weighing these, but

> When my spirit was ... under sail, and steering with a fresh gale towards Europe, the wise disposer of all the preparations of our hearts (in whose stretched-out hand all our times are) ... constrained me (by the wind which he caused to blow upon my soul and conscience ...) to tack about, and to turn my thoughts to harbour in America a while longer ...

After protracted negotiations, Matthews stayed on in New England, but not at Pequot: Richard Blinman* took that post instead.[3]

Matthews soon found himself at the heart of controversy again, this time at Malden. In 1650 he was called to this new settlement, near Charlestown, where a church had been gathered on 11 May 1649. The Malden church had invited several other candidates before Matthews, but without success. Before his ordination, the churches of Charlestown and Roxbury protested at the choice, in light of Matthews's record for dubious orthodoxy. But the Malden church decided to go ahead without securing the usual approval from neighbouring churches and of the magistrates. In June 1650, the Massachusetts General Court called Matthews, on behalf of the church, to justify this. On 4 March 1650/1 the court ordered the Malden church to reconsider its decision to censure one of its members for his testimony against Matthews's 'erroneous opinions'. Matters came to a head in May 1651, when accusations were exhibited against Matthews at court. The following day, Matthews's supporters in the church 'having seriously Considered the Answers that our Reverend Pastor Mr Marmaduke Mathewes hath given' affirmed them as 'the truth and nothing but the truth'. Matthews defended his views, arguing that his opponents had taken his remarks out of context.

The central theological issues in debate were the nature of justifying faith and Christian righteousness – recalling the Antinomian Controversy of 1636–8 – and the role of the civil magistrate in religion. The case also exposed fault lines within the Malden community, and between the Malden church and the magistrates and neighbour churches of Massachusetts Bay. A commission was appointed to examine Matthews further on the doctrines he had preached at both Hull and Malden. Despite a confession given by Matthews on 15 June, the commissioners were not satisfied and tried to levy a fine imposed by the General Court. Matthews said he could only pay in books. In October 1651 the fine was deferred until he could produce other goods. Thirty-six women of Malden and Charlestown petitioned the General Court, 28 October 1651, in his favour: God 'hath Affter many Prayers, Indeavours & long wayting Brought mr Mathews Among us & putt him into the worke of the Minister'. Matthews then renewed his confession to the General Court, but his fine was not dropped. Instead, the court rebuked the Malden church for its sin in ordaining him. Joseph Hills replied, on behalf of the church, that Matthews's offences had occurred before, not after, his ordination at Malden: the earlier events at Hull were not relevant; Matthews's punishment for that was in the past. Beyond this, Hills pointed out that the church knew of no rule that bound them to ordain only with the consent of magistrates and neighbour churches. On 31 October 1651 the General Court fined the church members who had consented to Matthews's ordination £50, levying this fine on Hills and two others, who were to recover it from the rest. Malden's representatives among the deputies refused to cooperate in the action. Messengers of the churches of Charlestown, Cambridge, Lynn and Roxbury considered the case and reported to the General Court on 26 May 1652. Henry Dunster, president of Harvard, was involved in examining Matthews and kept a copy of their report: they hoped Matthews had repented, 'yet could . . . wish that Mr Mathews did not . . . labour to put too fayre a glosse upon his former expressions which in themselves are very unsavoury and ungrounded upon Scripture'. On 19 October 1652 Matthews's fine was remitted, but in 1653 the

General Court forbade anyone to preach or prophesy without the consent of neighbour churches or the county court. Michael Wigglesworth succeeded Matthews at Malden by 1654.

Edward Johnson's *Wonder-working Providence* (1652) marked the controversy with a poem addressed to Matthews:

> Mathews! thou must build gold and silver on
> That precious stone, Christ cannot trash endure
> Unstable straw and stubble must be gone.
> When Christ by fire doth purge his building pure
> In seemly and in modest terms do thou
> Christs precious truths unto thy folk unfold
> And mix not error with the truth . . .

A majority of Malden's male church members acknowledged to the General Court their offence in ordaining Matthews, May 1655, and asked to be released from the remainder of the fine. Perhaps this came after Wigglesworth urged (as he was to do again in June 1658) deep repentance in Malden for the sin of ordaining Matthews, to turn away God's anger.[4]

Matthews returned home, probably in 1654 – he later said he had been away from Wales for sixteen years – but perhaps not until after 8 June 1655, when his account at Harvard for his sons was closed. Katherine and his sons came with him or followed soon after. By December 1655 he had been installed as vicar of St John's, Swansea. He received an augmentation of his salary there, drawn from the tithes of Llanedern and Llancarfan in Glamorgan, and from Llandingat and Llanfairybryn in Carmarthen. Matthews attributed his return to Wales to 'iterated Invitations and Encouragements' from Philip, Lord Jones (*ODNB*). On 6 December 1658 he dedicated *The Messiah magnified* to Jones, as one 'eminently instrumental to the well-being of me and mine, whilest I yet lived in the midst of wild men, and wild Beasts, amongst the Lords Exiles in America'. Jones, a leading member of the Commission for the Propagation of the Gospel in Wales, hailed from Matthews's birthplace, Llangyfelach. Matthews had sent sermons to him from New England. In Swansea, Matthews had a following of 'independents', said to have 'grown bold' under Jones's patronage. Matthews was a member of the Commission for the Approbation of Public Preachers (the 'Triers') in Wales. He also signed a document in support of Cromwell's government, *The humble representation and address to his Highness from several churches and Christians in South-Wales and Monmouth-shire* (1656). Matthews clashed with Quaker preachers, and was said to be their 'envious persecutor'. On the title pages of two tracts published in 1659, both with prefatory letters 'from my study in Swansey', Matthews was described as 'lately a Teaching-Elder of the Church at Maldon in New-England'. In *The Messiah magnified*, he published material from his ministry abroad, already 'precious to New-English Hearers', now presented for 'Old-England Readers'. *The rending church-member*, written as a letter to dissatisfied members of a gathered church, hints at controversy within a flock scattered in and around Swansea.

Matthews was ejected from the parish living of St John's, Swansea, in 1662. He continued to preach in Swansea with tacit permission from magistrates. He was still associated with Philip, Lord Jones, who had not resisted the Restoration and became high sheriff of Glamorgan in 1671. An article published in 1911 had sight of a privately owned copy of Matthews's *The reconciling remonstrance* (c.1670) which contained Matthews's signature and a loose flyleaf inscribed 'at the house, in the hand and heart of the Author's much obliging Benefactor, Mr Alderman Jones, by the key, let this labour of love be left, very respectfully'. Matthews was licensed in 1672, as an Independent, to preach at his own home in Swansea.[5]

> Publications *The Messiah magnified by the mouthes of babes in America* (1659); *The rending church-member regularly call'd back to Christ and to his church* (1659). Matthews published other tracts, which may no longer be extant, and are not in *ESTC*: *The new congregational church, prov'd to be the old Christian church* (c.1659), advertised on the last page of *Messiah magnified*; *The reconciling remonstrance*, published c.1670 with *A shrill-sounding whisper to a sin-loving soul*.

[1] CCEd Person ID 72251, Record ID 230841; Thomas Richards, *A history of the puritan movement in Wales from the institution of the church at Llanvaches in 1639 to the expiry of the Propagation Act in 1653* (London: National Eisteddfod Association, 1920), 27.

[2] *WJ*, 266, 518n.; Lechford *PD*, 41; *NEHGR* 4: 258, 9: 282; *Mass. Recs.* 2: 235, 3: 218; H.F. Worthley, *An inventory of the records of the Particular (Congregational) Churches of Massachusetts gathered 1620–1805*, Harvard Theological Studies, XXV (Cambridge, MA and London: Harvard University Press, 1970), 339, 713.

[3] *WP* V, 379–80, 380–2 (see also letters of Amos Richardson and Adam Winthrop, *WP* V, 378, 382–3); *WP* VI, 29–31, 53–4.

[4] 2 *MHSC* 8: 325; 3 *MHSC* 1: 29–32; MHS, Misc. MSS, 15, 16, 26 May 1651, 28, 31 October 1651, 10 June 1658; MHS, MS N-1143, 'Henry Dunster Notebook, 1628–54', fol. 143; Morison, 305; [Edward Johnson], *Johnson's wonder-working Providence, 1628–1651*, ed. J. Franklin Jameson (New York: Barnes and Noble, 1952), 250–1; R. Frothingham, *The history of Charlestown, Massachusetts* (Boston, MA: C.C. Little and James Brown, 1845), I, 121–30; David D. Hall, *The faithful shepherd: a history of the New England ministry in the seventeenth century* (Chapel Hill, NC: University of North Carolina Press, 1972), 129n.

[5] LPL, MS COMM. VIa/7, fol. 379; Richards, *A history of the puritan movement in Wales*, 220; Thomas Richards, *Religious developments in Wales 1654–1662* (London: National Eisteddfod Association, 1923), 22, 93, 180; Matthews, *The Messiah magnified*, 'Epistle Dedicatory'; *Transactions of the Congregational Historical Society*, 5 (1911–12), 54–8.

DWB, ODNB.

MATTHEWS, Mordecai

Mordecai Matthews, the eldest son of Katherine and Marmaduke Matthews*, brother to Lemuel* and Manasseh*, was born at Yarmouth. He attended

Harvard: as 'mathewes senior' he was charged on 12 September 1651 for 'Entrance Into the Colledge', and had a continuous account for tuition, commons, and study-rent until 8 June 1655, just after he graduated BA. His accounts were recorded with Manasseh's, under a single account for 'Mr Mathewes'.

Matthews returned to Wales with, or shortly after, his father. The Triers approved him for the living of Llancarfan, Glamorgan, in 1657. (Marmaduke Matthews's augmentation at Swansea had been drawn in part from the tithes of Llancarfan.)

At the Restoration, Mordecai Matthews left Llancarfan. He was admitted to the living of Reynoldston on 16 April 1661, and conformed. The title-page of *The Christians daily exercise* described him as 'Minister of God's Word at Roinolston, in Glamorganshire'.

Publication *The Christians daily exercise* (Boston, MA, 1730).

Harvard Recs. I, 83, and III, 137–9; Thomas Richards, *Religious developments in Wales 1654–1662* (London: National Eisteddfod Association, 1923), 22, 374, 458.

CC, *DWB* s.n. Marmaduke Matthews*, Sibley.

MILAM, John

John Milam [Mileham, Millard, Mylam] probably arrived in Boston in 1635. He was admitted to the church on 3 January 1635/6: 'John Mylam, cooper, and Christian his wife'. Milam became a freeman on 25 May 1636, and joined the Artillery Company in 1641. He was a Mill Creek proprietor with, among others, George Burden* and William Franklin*. He arrived poor, but speculated successfully in town plots and shipping. On 18 October 1648, the General Court ordered Thomas Venner*, John 'Mileham', William Cutter* and others to appoint wardens to oversee coopers' standards. He was still in Boston, 24 July 1652, when he sold land to his brother Humphrey Milam (also a cooper).

Milam left Boston in the autumn of 1652, perhaps for reasons of trade. In mid-October he described himself as 'John Milam late of Boston' in a transaction linked to a merchant in Tenerife. He was probably about to set sail across the Atlantic.

Later in the 1650s, Milam seems to have been in Ireland, where he perhaps became a minister. In August 1654 Charles Fleetwood and the Irish council invited John Davenport to come over, promising help with removal expenses. The Council also wrote to four other divines, promising £100 a year and £50 towards removal expenses. A 'John Millard' alone responded: this could have been John Miller, who succeeded Marmaduke Matthews* as minister at Yarmouth and died at Groton in 1663, but no evidence has been found in New England sources that he went to Ireland. However, on the civil list of 1655, a John Millard was named as minister at Passage, near Waterford. This could have been Milam, who seems to have been in Waterford at this time. In May 1655, the baptist auditor-general, Edward Roberts, wrote to Henry Dunster (once the president of Harvard but recently turned baptist and out of office as a result) from Dublin, inviting him to Ireland. 'For the bringing over yourselfe and family' Roberts offered Dunster £50, 'by Mr John Milam of Waterford once an Inhabitant of New England who is bound with a shipp to some parts of New England, and who will send to you and Contrive your passadg, and advise you as to the state of this Countrey and the Christians amongst us'.

Darrett Rutman, *Winthrop's Boston: portrait of a puritan town, 1630–1649* (New York: Norton, 1965), 199–200; *Boston CR*, 20; MHS, Misc. MSS, 18 October 1648; *Suffolk Deeds* I, 249-51, II, 195; *GM* 5: 212–17; St J.D. Seymour, *The puritans in Ireland, 1647–1661* (Oxford: Clarendon Press, 1921), 103, 217; 4 *MHSC* 2: 196–7.

MILDMAY, William

William's father, Sir Henry Mildmay (*ODNB*), had a keen interest in New England. He sent William to Harvard in 1644 with Richard Lyon* as his tutor. The college kept a single account for both. Mildmay graduated BA in 1647, MA in 1650. He continued there for another year: his payments ended in 1651. No trace survives of Mildmay in New England after 1651. He probably returned to England. Sir Henry Mildmay presented Leonard Hoar* to a living in 1656; Hoar had been William Mildmay's contemporary at Harvard.

WP III, 261, and V, 154 (for Sir Henry Mildmay's associations with New England); *Harvard Recs*. III, 21.

CC, Sibley.

MILLER, Joseph and Patience

Patience Miller, the daughter of Thomas* and Patience Larkham*, was baptised at Sandford, Devon, on 26 February 1625/6. She went to New England with her parents in 1639 from Northam in Devon, where Larkham had been vicar, along with her siblings Thomas*, George* and Jane Larkham*. The family settled at Dover – briefly known as Northam during Larkham's time there – where her father was minister until 1642. Joseph Miller's history is more obscure: he may have emigrated to New England in 1635, aged fifteen, on the *Hopewell*. Someone of this name was in Dover, as a 'travelling merchant', in 1642.

On 21 September 1647, Joseph Miller of Dover sold to a fellow townsman, John Goddard, the 'messuage or tenement in Dover' in which he lived, and all his rights to various land grants (amounting to 140 acres) given by the town of Northam or Dover to 'Mr Thomas Larkham'. Larkham had assigned all but ten acres of his land in the town to Miller. From this it seems Patience Larkham married Joseph Miller at Dover. Thomas Larkham had returned to England in 1642 with his eldest son Thomas, but other members of the family followed him home later in the 1640s.

Joseph and Patience Miller must have left soon after the sale of this property.

Larkham later recorded that Patience had her first child, Tom, in the family house at Crediton, Devon, in 1648. Joseph Miller joined the parliamentary army (in which his father-in-law Larkham served as a chaplain). He died in Ireland on 8 May 1656. At that time Patience was living at 'Rossgarland' [Rosegarland] castle, in County Wexford, where Joseph had probably been stationed. Her father Thomas Larkham went to Ireland in the summer of 1656 to help her to settle her estate. Patience Miller spent long spells in Tavistock in the later 1650s. Eventually, she remarried: unwisely, in the opinion of her father, who took steps in his will to ensure that his bequest to her was protected from her new husband, so that he 'may not have the wasting of it as he hath the rest of her estate'.

GM 3: 85, 5: 119; *The diary of Thomas Larkham, 1647–1669*, ed. Susan Hardman Moore, Church of England Record Society, 17 (Woodbridge: Boydell and Brewer, 2011), 12, 33, 100, 124, 131, 132, 286n.1, and *passim*.

MORSE, John and Mary

John Morse, a salt-maker, married Mary Jupe in 1652. Mary, with her brothers Anthony and Benjamin Jupe*, had come under the care of her uncle, Robert Keayne of Boston, after the death of her mother, Grace Jupe. Robert Keayne's will, drafted during the autumn of 1653, initially left legacies to Benjamin Jupe and Mary Morse. Towards the end of his will, Keayne cancelled these completely: 'for some occasion of offence that ... hath been given to me ... they have pulled it upon themselves against my desire and have withdrawn themselves from that long care and tender love that I have borne to them'. In October 1654, Keayne wrote to John Winthrop Jr* about John Morse, 'who I suppose you know; and is become my kinsman by marryinge my owne sisters Daughter; and soe I have the more int[e]rest [in] him, at least by my cownsell and advice'. Keayne, who had just paid off Morse's obligations so he could seek new work, hoped Winthrop could find work for Morse in salt-making. Nothing came of this.

John and Mary Morse returned to England with Benjamin Jupe late in 1654. Mary and Benjamin had inherited property in London from their uncle, Nicholas Jupe. John Morse made arrangements for the journey, but ran into trouble: 'Major Generall Sedgwick, which hath the Command of all the ships, utterly refused to lett me goe except I would give him security that I would pay him fiveteene Pounds for our three passages Vppon the Arrivall of our shipp in England.' When Robert Sedgwick* refused to accept his bond, Morse had to turn to Robert Keayne for a loan. On 9 November 1654, Morse signed a document promising that the £15 would be repaid to Keayne in London by April 1655, at the Golden Crown, Birchin Lane, out of rents belonging to Benjamin or Mary, in hands of Simeon Smith of Southwark, executor of Nicholas Jupe. On the same day, Morse signed another document, acknowledging a further debt to Robert Keayne of almost £50.

Nothing is known of the fortunes of John and Mary Morse back in England. John Morse could perhaps be the person of this name who provided a certificate for the Harvard graduate Edward Rawson* on his admission as rector at Kingston by Canterbury, Kent, in September 1655. Morse and Rawson sailed back from New England at around the same time. It was not unknown for fellow passengers to be called on for a testimonial – see, for example, the recommendation Thomas Harrison* provided for Thomas Jenner*.

NEHGR 3: 193, 35: 277; *The apologia of Robert Keayne*, ed. Bernard Bailyn (New York: Harper and Row, 1965), 36, 38–9, 40, 72–3, 86–7, 88; Robert Keayne to John Winthrop Jr, 2 October 1654, *WP* VI, 373–5; NA, PROB 11/218/505, will of Nicholas Jupe, merchant tailor of London, 13 October 1651; Waters, 152–3; *Suffolk Deeds* II, 86–7, 182–5; LPL, MS COMM. III/4 fol. 219. (This John Morse should not be confused with a temporary visitor to England, the tailor John Morse*, who was in England for the early months of 1656.)

MOXON, George (*c.*1602–1687)

George Moxon was the seventh son of James Moxon, a husbandman of Wakefield in Yorkshire. He attended Sidney Sussex College, Cambridge, and graduated BA in 1624. Moxon was ordained in 1626. He served as a chaplain to Sir William Brereton (*ODNB*): Brereton joined the Massachusetts Bay Company, but never emigrated; he served as an MP and later acted as commander-in-chief of the parliamentary forces in Cheshire. Moxon became curate of St Helen's chapel at Prescot, Lancashire, on 23 December 1628. He was cited there for nonconformity in 1637.[1]

George and Ann Moxon emigrated *c.*1637 and settled at Dorchester, Massachusetts, where they both became church members. They moved with William Pynchon* to Agawam (Springfield), towards the end of 1637. Moxon was chosen minister. Two of Moxon's children, Union and Samuel, were baptised at Springfield. Pynchon commented on the success of Moxon's ministry to John Winthrop, in a letter of 19 February 1643/4. Notes survive on his sabbath-day sermons in 1649, morning and afternoon, made by John Pynchon, William's son. John Pynchon also recorded when his father, or his brother-in-law Henry Smith*, preached in Moxon's place.[2]

Moxon left Springfield in 1652, after controversy broke over William Pynchon's views on the atonement. Another catalyst may have been the acquittal of Hugh Parsons, who (in events that foreshadowed the Salem witch trials) stood trial for bewitching Moxon's daughters.

Back in England, in 1653, Moxon (or perhaps his son George*) requested a position as a naval chaplain – a far from prestigious appointment, perhaps a stopgap until better prospects came along. On 26 June 1654, Moxon was admitted, jointly with John Machin (*CR*), to the sequestered living of Astbury, Cheshire. He became 'one of the publique preachers there'. Moxon presented certificates from William Brereton, John Yates of Astbury, Walter Cradock (*ODNB*) the Welsh congregationalist, and Charles Worsely. Although Moxon's certificates had come largely from fellow travellers in the New England Way, congregationalism, he worked closely with Machin, a keen presbyterian. Moxon and Machin shared the rectory and preached on alternate Sundays. Their arrangement is a practical example of the cooperation Richard Baxter hoped to promote through the Worcestershire Voluntary Association. Their common efforts centred on public preaching and pastoral care. At some point Moxon gathered a congregational church, but it is not clear how far its existence was formalised before the Restoration. From August 1653, Moxon contributed to a fortnightly lecture (midweek sermon), arranged by Machin at various places in north and south Staffordshire; Henry Newcome (*ODNB*) also took part. In 1654 Moxon became an assistant to the Cheshire commissioners for removing unsuitable parish ministers, with Samuel Eaton* among others.

At the Restoration, the sequestered rector reclaimed Astbury. According to Edmund Calamy, Moxon preached at Rushton Spencer from 1660 until 1662. Later he was at a farmhouse in Woodhouse Green, still close to Rushton, where he evaded the penalties of the Five Mile Act. Moxon settled at Congleton, within Astbury parish, in 1667. He was licensed (as a congregationalist) at his house in Astbury, 30 April 1672. In 1674, at a meeting of messengers from the Associated Churches of Yorkshire, Lancashire and Cheshire, Moxon was said to dissent from the Savoy Confession 'on points concerning the satisfaction of Christ'; he may have shared Pynchon's opinions. In 1676 Samuel Campion reported that Moxon was pastor to a congregational church at Congleton, Cheshire, assisted by William Marsh, a husbandman.[3]

[1] J.S. Morrill, *Cheshire 1630–1660: county government and society during the English Revolution* (London: Oxford University Press, 1974), 19n., and for Brereton, *passim*; CCEd Person ID 35200.

[2] Dorchester CR, 3; *WP* IV, 254; *WP* IV, 443; HSP, Gratz Sermon Collection, 250B, Box 1 (John Pynchon's notes on Moxon's sermons, 1649).

[3] *Pilgrims*, 79, 121; D.D. Hall, ed., *Witch-hunting in seventeenth century New England: a documentary history, 1638–1692* (1991), 29–60; B.S. Capp, *Cromwell's navy: the fleet and the English Revolution, 1648–1660*, 313, 315; LPL, MS COMM. III/3 lib. 2, fol. 20; W. Urwick, ed., *Historical sketches of nonconformity in the County Palatine of Chester* (n.p.: Kent & Co., 1864), xxxiv, 155–7; *Transactions of the Congregational Historical Society*, 3 (1907–8), 6 and 6 (1913–15), 172–3; G.F. Nuttall, *Visible saints: the congregational way, 1640–1660* (Oxford: Blackwell, 1957), 19n.; *The autobiography of Henry Newcome*, ed. R. Parkinson, Chetham Society, Old Series, XXVI–XXVII (Manchester 1852), *passim*; Samuel Campion's account of nonconformists in the Marches of Wales, 1676, Bodleian, Rawlinson MS D. 1481.346; DWL, MS 38.59, A.G. Matthews's notes of nonconformist ministers' wills, fol. 705.

BDBR, CR, ODNB.

MOXON, George Jr (d. 1684)

George Moxon, son of Ann and George Moxon*, is likely to have been in New England. He may be the George Moxon who applied for a naval chaplaincy in 1653.

Moxon became vicar of Haverhill, Suffolk, in January 1656/7. He was rector of Radwinter, Essex, in 1660. The sequestered rector was soon restored at Radwinter. Moxon was brother-in-law to Samuel Shute (*ODNB*). He acted as Shute's chaplain when Shute became Sheriff of London in 1681, and died at Shute's house at Eaton Constantine, Shropshire.

> B.S. Capp, *Cromwell's navy: the fleet and the English Revolution, 1648–1660*, 313, 315; T.W. Davids, *Annals of evangelical nonconformity in Essex* (London: Jackson, Walford & Hodder, 1863), 445–6; H. Smith, *The ecclesiastical history of Essex* (Colchester: Benham, 1932), 186, 190; DWL, MS 38.59, A.G. Matthews's notes of nonconformist ministers' wills, fol. 705.
>
> *BDBR s.n.* George Moxon, *CR*, *ODNB s.n.* George Moxon).

MUNNINGS, Edmund (*c*.1595–1666 or 1667)

Edmund Munnings came from Dengie Hundred, Essex. He served on the manorial court at Tillingham, a parish where the antinomian John Traske (*ODNB*) had been active in the 1620s. Munnings emigrated in 1635 on the *Abigail*, with his wife Mary and three children under ten: Mary, Ann and Mahalaleel Munnings*. Edmund and Mary left their daughter Rebecca (aged about four) at Tillingham with her grandfather, Edward Herris. Herris made a will on 18 June 1635, the day after the Munnings set foot aboard ship in London: he left a bequest to be paid when Rebecca turned eighteen, or earlier if she was called to New England. At some point Rebecca followed her parents across the Atlantic.

Edmund and Mary Munnings settled at Dorchester, Massachusetts. Mary was admitted to the church on 16 April 1641. Edmund became neither a church member nor a freeman. His children Hopestill*, Return and Takeheed* were baptised at Dorchester by virtue of Mary's membership. In 1641 he made his mark on a list of Dorchester inhabitants, but although he remained a proprietor until 1658 there is little trace of Edmund or Mary after Takeheed's baptism on 22 January 1642/3. Several of their children were married in New England: Hannah (Ann?) at Dorchester around 1648; Rebecca in Boston around 1651; Mahalaleel by 1655; Return married Sarah Hobart, daughter of the minister Peter Hobart of Hingham.

The Dorchester town records noted in December 1651 'Goodman Moninges desireth to have the land about his house recorded'. Edmund Munnings probably left New England soon after this, if he had not gone already. He returned to Dengie Hundred. In 1658, Joseph Hills of Malden complained he had given Munnings £11 to send over a bullock from England but it had never arrived. On 2 October 1666, as an 'unprofitable servant of God' living at 'Denge', Essex, Edmund Munnings set his mark on his will before Takeheed and other witnesses. Hopestill, his father's executor, gained probate on 18 July 1667. Munnings left bequests to his wife 'Markiet', to his daughters Mary and Rebecca, and to his sons Return, Hopestill and Takeheed. His bequests to Return and Mary were to be paid 'within one year after demand be made', as they were both still in New England. Munnings's son Mahalaleel, a New

England merchant, had already died: he crossed the Atlantic at least five times but drowned in the Boston mill creek.

Alison Games, *Migration and the origins of the English Atlantic world* (Cambridge, MA: Harvard University Press, 1999), 142–3, 203, 278n.44; David Como, *Blown by the spirit: puritanism and the emergence of an antinomian underground in pre-Civil-War England* (Stanford, CA: Stanford University Press, 2004), 61; *Dorchester CR*, 5, 153, 155; *NEHGR* 5: 244, 391, 7: 273; Waters, 10; *GM* 5: 190–5.

MUNNINGS, Hopestill and Takeheed

Hopestill Munnings was the son of Mary and Edmund Munnings* and brother of Mahalaleel Munnings*. Hopestill was born at Dorchester, Massachusetts, on 15 April 1637 and baptised there on 25 April 1641. In the Dorchester church records beside his name is a note: 'went to England'. Hopestill married Sarah Smith at Tillingham, Essex, on 13 October 1659. He was named as executor of his father's will in 1666.

Takeheed Munnings, his brother, was born at Dorchester on 20 October 1642 and baptised on 22 January 1642/3. Named in his father's will, 1666, he was probably the 'Takeheed Munnings' of St Lawrence, Essex (close to Tillingham and Dengie), who made his own will in March 1684/5.

Dorchester CR, 153, 155; *GM* 5: 190–5.

N

NELSON, Joan

Joan Nelson was the daughter of Thomas Dummer of 'Badgeth' [Badgeworth], Gloucestershire, and niece of Richard* and Stephen Dummer*. She married Thomas Nelson* at Rowley, Massachusetts, on 15 February 1641/2: her daughter Mercy was born in February 1643/4, and her son Samuel c.1646.

Joan Nelson followed Thomas Nelson to England. He returned to England in 1646 and died there in 1648. At some point Joan came back to England with her young children Mercy and Samuel. In 1654 they were living at Stoneham, Hampshire. Her uncle Richard Dummer, one of Thomas Nelson's executors, acted for Joan in New England. She was reliant on Dummer for funds for the children's education and maintenance, as Thomas Nelson's estate in England was insufficient. Philip and Thomas, Nelson's sons by an earlier marriage, remained in New England. Mercy Nelson later married John Storke of 'Rumsey' [Romsey], Hampshire. In 1667 Dummer complained Mercy had been of age two years and had not taken steps to secure what was due to her from her father's estate: he set aside cattle for her use.

Essex Court Recs. II, 8ff.; *Essex Probate Recs.* I, 113–14, 116; G.B. Blodgette and A.E. Jewett, *Early settlers of Rowley, Massachusetts* (Rowley, MA: [s.n.], 1933), 243; Mass. Archives, 15B: 159.

NELSON, Thomas

Thomas Nelson was at Cottingham in the East Riding of Yorkshire, in 1626. Later, he was five miles east at Rowley. He emigrated c.1637, perhaps slightly ahead of the party led over to Massachusetts by the minister of Rowley, Ezekiel Rogers. He seems to have been a widower, who travelled over with his sons Philip and Thomas. He was a wealthy immigrant. He stayed briefly in Boston but soon moved to found Rowley, Massachusetts, with Ezekiel Rogers. Nelson was chief town officer in 1638; he joined the church Rogers gathered in 1639, and became a freeman of Massachusetts on 23 May 1639. Nelson built gristmills and a sawmill, c.1642. He married Joan*, niece of Richard* and Stephen Dummer* (who were also wealthy settlers at Rowley) on 15 February 1641/2. Richard Saltonstall* and Ezekiel Rogers acted as witnesses.

On 24 December 1645 Nelson made a will, 'beeing by providence Called now to make a voyage into old England'. He provided for his wife Joan, and children Philip, Thomas and Mercy. He made Richard Bellingham and Richard Dummer his executors; Ezekiel Rogers and John Norton, the ministers of Ipswich, were his overseers. Nelson also gave Richard Dummer power of attorney during his absence in England. Nelson was still in England on 6 August 1648, although preparing to return to Massachusetts. He added a new clause to his will, being 'at present sick in body but enjoying understanding and memory'. He confirmed his earlier will 'left in Newengland with my wiues uncle Mr Richard Dummer', but made new provision for his son Samuel, born since he came away from New England. The witnesses to this addition included the minister Henry Jessey (*ODNB*). Nelson died soon afterwards. His inventory was taken at Rowley on 23 February 1648/9 by Edward Carleton*, Sebastian Brigham*, Thomas Barker and Joseph Jewett. His estate amounted to £1685 14s 9d. On 2 May 1649 the Massachusetts General Court ordered Richard Dummer to give an account to Richard Saltonstall and Samuel Symonds. This was so Dummer could be discharged as Nelson's attorney, and with Richard Bellingham take up his work as executor, to 'enter upon the estate of Mr Nelson and dispose of the same in behalf of Mrs Nelson, widow, and her children, and the children of Mr Nelson by a former wife'.

The winding-up of Nelson's estate led to protracted disputes. In 1656, his elder children, Philip and Thomas, challenged Richard Dummer's actions. Dummer had petitioned the Massachusetts General Court on 14 May 1656 for permission to sell land, in order to be able to pay legacies to Thomas Nelson's children, including Mercy and Samuel, who were by then in England. The court agreed, but Philip (who had recently graduated from Harvard) objected, supported by Ezekiel Rogers. He and Thomas wanted to take up husbandry, the only career they were qualified for: 'if the land be sold away, wee shall be driven out of the countrey and be put to seek farms among strangers we know not where, and we are young and shiftles'. Dummer protested: Philip and Thomas were not fit only for husbandry, and were not yet suitable custodians of their siblings' property; he elaborated his expenses for maintaining the children in England, due to the limits of Nelson's estate there, and refuted the charge that he was selling off the most valuable part of Nelson's assets. The business dragged on. Richard Dummer was still acting as an executor in 1667, when he set aside cattle for Thomas and Joan Nelson's daughter, Mercy.

D.G. Allen, *In English ways* (Chapel Hill, NC: University of North Carolina Press, 1981), 247; C.H. Pope, *Pioneers of Massachusetts* (Boston, MA: C.H. Pope, 1900), 326; *NEHGR* 3:187; *Essex Probate Recs.* I, 111–16; Mass. Archives, 15B: 155–9.

NEWMAN, Robert

Robert Newman came from London, where he was associated with John Davenport's parish at St Stephen's, Coleman Street. His brother Francis Newman also emigrated.

He arrived in Boston, March 1633/4, and moved to New Haven with Davenport's company in 1638. He played an important role in the religious and civil life of New Haven. He was one of the original 'seven pillars' of the New Haven church at its gathering, and was made a deacon. From 1644 to 1650 he was a ruling elder. He became one of the first four deputies for the town, elected on 25 October 1639 with Thomas Fugill*. Newman was consulted about the formation of New England confederation in 1643. With Stephen Goodyear*, he took care of Jane Stollyon's estate until Abraham Stollyon* returned from England.

Late in 1649 or early in 1650, Newman went to London. In 1654 he was described as a citizen and vintner there. Mark Pierce* made his will in London and referred to £40 with Newman and other money with Elizabeth Higginson*. Pierce left Newman a bequest. When Samuel Malbon* sought certificates to support his admission to a church living, Newman provided one: he had known Samuel's father, Richard Malbon*, at St Stephen's Coleman Street and in New Haven. John Winthrop Jr*, advising an unnamed enquirer about emigration in 1660, suggested that it would be helpful to talk with former colonists in London, such as Newman, 'elder of the church of Newhaven when Mr Hooke was teacher', William Hooke* or John Harwood*. In 1660, John Davenport wrote urgently to Robert Newman about the death of his brother Francis, governor of the New Haven Colony from 1658, who had died on 18 November.

Robert Newman made his will on 25 October 1681, as a 'Citizen and Vintner of London', living in the parish of St Magnus the Martyr near London Bridge. He bequeathed £5 apiece 'unto Doctor John Owen Pastor of the Church of Christ whereof I am a member & to Mr Isaac Loeffes Teacher of the same Church'. At this point Owen led a church that met at Leadenhall Street, with Loeffs (CR) as his assistant. Newman also left £4 to 'Mr John Hooke', presumably the nonconformist minister John Hooke*, who had grown up in New Haven. Newman appointed his wife Susanna as executrix.

I.M. Calder, *The New Haven Colony* (New Haven, CT: Yale University Press, 1934), 30, 84, 85–6, 107, 114, 208; *NEHGR* 9:267, 24:34; *GD*; *WP* IV, 161; *WP* V, 275; Waters, 99, 1080; *Davenport Letters*, 183–4; 4 *MHSC* 8:184; NA, PROB 11/372/240, will of Robert Newman, vintner of London, 8 February 1683.

NORCROSSE, Jeremiah and Adrean

Jeremiah and Adrean Norcrosse were of London, c.1618, when their eldest son Nathaniel* was born. They emigrated in the late 1630s, probably soon after Nathaniel's graduation from the university of Cambridge in 1637, with not only Nathaniel but also their children Richard and Sarah.

Jeremiah and Adrean Norcrosse settled in Watertown in 1638. In 1651 Jeremiah served on a jury in Cambridge, Massachusetts, and in 1654 was cited in various Watertown cases. On 25 October 1654, as Watertown's constable, he came to the Massachusetts General Court to give evidence in the trial of Edward Sanders for the abuse of a nine-year-old girl. At this point Norcrosse had recently drawn up a will, 15 September 1654, in anticipation of an Atlantic journey. He probably left later that autumn, with Adrean, intending to return to England for good.

On 30 September 1656, Jeremiah Norcrosse made a second will at Walsingham in Norfolk. He was 'sick of an ague'. He and Adrean were living with his son Nathaniel and his family: he thanked them for 'their loveinge dutye and care of us' and committed his wife to their care. Jeremiah specified that the will he had made in New England should 'stand to a tittle as it is'. He made one or two extra bequests, including a 'scarlet embroidered cushion' for each of his grandchildren in Watertown. He died soon after this. Adrean Norcrosse, as a widow of Walsingham, made her own will on 20 December 1656. She left a black gown to her daughter-in-law in America, and 'my coloured mowhaire gowne with the mowhaire Girtell thereunto belonging' to her grandchild Mary Norcrosse in Walsingham. Everything else went to Nathaniel Norcrosse, who acted as executor for both his parents: their wills were proved in London on the same day, 5 April 1658.

Meantime, in New England on 6 October 1657, the witnesses to Jeremiah Norcrosse's original will – deacon Simon Stone and Norcrosse's brother Charles Chadducke – declared the will 'to be his act, at such time as he went for England'. Norcrosse had made bequests to Adrean, his sons Nathaniel and Richard (Watertown's schoolmaster from 1651), and his daughter Sarah (wife of Francis Macy). He left two ewe sheep to 'members of Jesus Christ in Watertowne', and 20 shillings each to local ministers John Sherman of Watertown, Zechariah Symmes of Charlestown, John Norton and John Wilson* of Boston, John Eliot of Roxbury and Richard Mather of Dorchester.

NA, PROB 11/274/592, will of Jeremiah Norcrosse or Norcross of Walsingham, Norfolk, 5 April 1658; NA, PROB 11/274/591, will of Adrean Norcross, widow of Walsingham, Norfolk, 5 April 1658; Middlesex Court Recs., fols 15, 140; Middlesex Court Files, F.9.G.4, 9/4, 1654-1-4; Middlesex Probate Recs., case number 16026 ('Jeremiah Norcros, Norcross', 1657); Waters, 1041n.; Roger Thompson, *Divided we stand: Watertown, Massachusetts, 1630–80* (Amherst, MA: University of Massachusetts Press, 1994), 61, 78, 114, 115, 121, 187, 236.

NORCROSSE, Nathaniel (*c.*1618–1662) and Mary

Nathaniel Norcrosse, the son of Jeremiah and Adrean Norcrosse*, graduated BA in 1637 from St Catharine's College, Cambridge. He arrived in Massachusetts with his parents in 1638 and settled at Watertown.

Norcrosse started out at Watertown, but was restive, looking for suitable work for a new graduate, and a place to settle. He joined the Salem church on 23 May 1641: later, against his name was marked 'dismist'. He became a freeman of Massachusetts on 10 May 1643. He was one of a company drawn from Watertown that hoped to start a new settlement at Nashaway (Lancaster), in 1645. According to John Winthrop, they wanted to form a church, but the magistrates advised them to build their houses first. Norcrosse left when 'in two years they had not three houses built'. He moved to Exeter. In 1646, sixteen settlers there agreed to share the cost of purchasing John Wheelwright's* house for Norcrosse. In July 1647, writing from Exeter, Norcrosse put cases of conscience to John Cotton, mainly about difficulties in his church: the authority of gifted brethren to preach in the absence of the minister; the proper grounds on which an individual could withdraw from fellowship. He added a more personal question: 'whither churche worke desired may bee deferred in case of marriage, if probability of matchinge bee not likely in such A place that one lives in'. Cotton replied that to this point he was 'loth to speake, as hauing spoken of it to you before. I think noe Place in the countrey, but may finde way for marryage'. By December 1648, Norcrosse was in York, Maine, still hoping to get settled in a better place. Lucy Downing* wrote to John Winthrop Jr* about him: 'if we will goe thither, a hows with 3 chimnyes hee promiseth, if 2 of them blowe not down this winter, wich may be feard, being but the parsons howes. I am willinge to make you smille, but I wish him well and the worke of the lord to prosper in his hands'. Norcrosse eventually found his match – if not with a church, with a wife – Mary, sister of Thomas Gilbert*.[1]

Nathaniel and Mary Norcrosse returned to England late in 1649, perhaps also with Thomas Gilbert. For a short time Nathaniel was a naval chaplain, a stopgap post on the way to a better position ashore. Perhaps through naval connections, he became vicar of St Mary's, Dover, in 1653. Two years later, on 21 December 1655, he became vicar of Little Walsingham, Norfolk. By this time he was well-connected: he brought certificates from the congregationalist ministers William Greenhill (*ODNB*) of Stepney, Middlesex; Thomas Brooks (*CR*) of St Margaret's, Fish Street, London; Matthew Barker (*CR*) of St Leonard's, Eastcheap, London; Thomas Allen*; Timothy Armitage, pastor at Norwich; William Bridge (*ODNB*), pastor at Yarmouth; and also from Samuel Packley and 'J. Tofts'. Norcrosse was also admitted rector of Egmere, Norfolk, on 4 June 1656, with certificates from William Stiward, Richard Worts (*CR*) of Guestwick (an associate of Nathaniel Brewster*), John Hooker (*CR*) of Wood Dalling with Guestwick, and Edwards Bulwer. Adding to his portfolio, Norcrosse became rector of Waterden on 11 August 1658, with certificates from Matthew Sheppard, Nicholas Juxon, Matthew Barker and Thomas Brooks. Walsingham, Waterden and Egmere were within four miles of each other, so it is likely he served all the parishes concurrently. Another 'public preacher', Edmund Turner, was appointed to Waterden on 16 March 1658/9, perhaps to work alongside Norcrosse. Norcrosse may have provided public preaching in all three parishes, and ministered to a gathered church drawn from them all: no firm evidence of this survives, but it was a pattern followed in other places (for example, by John Phillips and William Ames* at parishes in and around Wrentham, Suffolk). Edmund Calamy described Norcrosse as a congregationalist.

At the Restoration, Norcrosse was said to have been ejected from Walsingham, but in fact died 'upon or about the 10th of August 1662', just before 'Black Bartholomew's Day'. He had been in London, 'late of St Dunstan's in the East'. He left all his estate, in old and New England, to his wife Mary.[2]

---

[1] *Salem CR*, 11; *NEHGR* 3:190; *WJ*, 504; *GM* 6:349, 485; his letter to John Cotton, together with Cotton's draft reply, survives in BPL, MS Am. 1506, pt 3, no. 8 (now printed in Bush, 396–9); *WP* V, 291.

[2] B.S. Capp, *Cromwell's navy: the fleet and the English Revolution, 1648–1660*, 313, 315; LPL, MSS COMM. III/4 fol. 433, III/5 fol. 45, III/7 fol. 84; *CCEd* Record ID 141795; Waters, 1041.

CR.

O

OAKES, Urian (1631/32–1681)

Urian Oakes, the son of Edward and Jane Oakes, came from Dedham in Essex. He arrived in New England by 1642, with his parents. Oakes settled at Cambridge, where his father played a prominent role in town and church life. Urian Oakes graduated BA at Harvard in 1649, MA in 1652, and became a fellow of the college.

By 1650, Oakes was seriously considering a return to England. His fellow graduates Nathaniel* and Samuel Mather* were keen to see him follow them back across the Atlantic. His father seems to have been in London with Nathaniel Mather in March 1650/1, when Mather wrote to John Rogers in New England. Mather talked up the opportunities for graduates: he offered 'great incouragement for any to come over, especially such as designe themselves for the ministry . . . it is with the honestest on both sides a matter of high account to have been a New England man'. Mather declared 'Sergiant Oakes is so fully of this mind I thinke hee halfe repents that his son is not here, and he is resolved not to be any hindrance to his comming the next year.' Samuel Mather sent a letter to Urian Oakes at the same time, which has not survived, but a letter of his to Jonathan Mitchell shows how he had Oakes, in particular, in mind:

> I could wish that yourselfe and others who are in power in new England would do so much favour to England as . . . to part with such from amongst you whom you may well spare, and whose hearts were inclined to come to us. Sir oakes his thoughts have beene formerly this way, and I have then spared to say any thing to persuade him, because then was no season for mee to speake my mind; and I was unwilling to bee a meanes of depriving you of one whom I knew you tooke so much Content in. But I desire that now you would not bee his hindrance, partly for that if hee should stay there the season of your lives is now over, or soone will bee for studying together, and hee will soone bee called aside to employment in one place or other . . . and partly because there are many advantages here for his improvement in the hireings above what there are there; In my letter to him I have spoken but sparingly because I would not [raise] expectations, for feare of unexpected disappointments, when hee comes; but of his Incouragement and preferment here I do noe more question, then if the thing were already done.

Oakes left New England around the time of the last entry on his record in the Harvard college accounts, 1 February 1652/3.

In England, according to Cotton Mather, Oakes first became 'chaplain to one of the most noted persons ... in the nation'. Who this was is unclear. Oakes was admitted to the sequestered living of Titchfield, Hampshire, on 9 July 1656. He presented certificates from Samuel Rolls (*ODNB*) of Isleworth, Middlesex; James Thompson of Hampton; John Rocket (*CR*) of Market Bosworth, Leicestershire; and London ministers Samuel Smith (*CR*) of St Benet Gracechurch and Charles Offspring of St Antholin's. On 1 June 1658, he was appointed as an assistant to the Hampshire commissioners for removing unsuitable parish ministers.

At the Restoration, the sequestered vicar of Titchfield was restored, 18 February 1660/1. After this Oakes turned to teaching: for a time he was a schoolmaster at Southwick, near Portsmouth, and co-minister with Richard Symmonds (*CR*) to a congregational meeting there. Oakes's wife died in 1669 (he is sometimes said to have married Ruth, sister of William Ames*, but she married Edmund Angier of Cambridge, and their son married Oakes's daughter).

In 1671, Oakes returned to New England. The church at Cambridge, Massachusetts, invited him to become their pastor after the death of Jonathan Mitchell. In 1675, he succeeded Leonard Hoar* as interim president of Harvard and was fully installed as president in 1680.

Publications *MDCL. An almanack for the year of our Lord 1650* (Cambridge, MA, 1650); *New-England pleaded with* (Cambridge, MA, 1673); *The unconquerable, all-conquering, & more-then-conquering souldier: or, The successful warre which a believer wageth with the enemies of his soul* (Cambridge, MA, 1674); *An elegie upon the death of the Reverend Mr. Thomas Shepard* (Cambridge, MA, 1677); *A seasonable discourse* (Cambridge, MA, 1682); *The sovereign efficacy of divine providence* (Boston, MA, 1682).

Harvard Recs. I, 83; BPL, MS Am. 1502 v.1 no. 7 (printed, 4 *MHSC* 8:3); MHS Misc. Bd. MSS, 26 March 1651; *Magnalia*, II 114–18 (quotation from 115); Tai Liu, *Puritan London: A study of religion and society in the City parishes* (Newark, DE: University of Delaware Press, 1986), 87; LPL, MS COMM. III/5; Roger Thompson, *Cambridge cameos: stories of life in seventeenth-century New England* (Boston, MA: New England Historic Genealogical Society, 2005), 13, 14, 38, 169, 222, 323 and *passim*. For Ruth (Ames) Angier, *NEHGR* 34:409; J. Farmer, *A genealogical register of the first settlers of New England* (Lancaster, MA: Carter Andrews & Co., 1829), *s.n.* Edmund Angier; J. Browne, *A history of congregationalism in Norfolk and Suffolk* (London: Jarrold & Sons, 1877), 70.

ANB, BDBR, CC, CR, ODNB, Sibley.

OLIVER, Mary (b. *c*.1603)

Mary Oliver, the wife of Thomas Oliver*, came from the parish of St Edmund's, Norwich, where Thomas Allen* was rector. She and her husband were both cited before the ecclesiastical authorities in 1633. John Winthrop wrote that she 'had suffered somewhat ... for refusing to bow at the name of Jesus, though otherwise she was conformable to all their orders'.

Mary Oliver took her family to New England in 1637, and settled at Salem. There is no record that she joined the church. In fact, John Winthrop recorded how New England's tight limits on access to sacraments outraged her. In 1638, she stood up in the Salem meetinghouse, when the church members were about to celebrate communion, to argue that she had a right to take part. She took offence 'that she might not be admitted to the Lord's Supper without giving public satisfaction to the church of her faith, etc., and covenanting or professing to walk with them according to the rule of the gospel'. One of the magistrates threatened to get her ejected by a constable. She ended up in court for 'disturbing the peace in the church', and spent several days in prison before admitting she had been wrong to make a public nuisance of herself. However, she stuck to her conviction that 'all that dwell in the same town, and ... profess their faith in Christ Jesus, ought to be received to the sacraments there'. John Winthrop thought Mary Oliver was 'for ability of speech, and appearance of zeal and devotion' far more likely to do damage than the antinomian Anne Hutchinson, 'but she was poor and had little acquaintance'. Mary Oliver continued to campaign against New England's innovations. In 1639 the authorities put her in prison again, for making speeches at the arrival of newcomers – conjuring up an image of her haranguing immigrants on the quayside as they stepped off the boat. Two years later she was admonished for 'contemning the ordinances of God'. In 1646 Winthrop added a passage to his earlier record of her misdemeanours, to report that she had been whipped, and had 'a cleft stick put on her tongue for half an hour', for speeches against the magistrates and elders. She was alleged to have said 'all the ministers in the country are blood thirsty men'. In 1647, she was punished – with an hour in the stocks – for working on the sabbath at service time and saying 'You in New England are theeves and Robbers'. In November 1648, she was said to be 'living from her husband', and ordered to go home. On 26 December 1648 she sued John Robinson successfully for taking her in a violent manner and putting her in the stocks. The court noted a few months later that Mary Oliver was still not living with Thomas. On 11 July 1649, 'having been ordered to go to her husband in England in the next ship ... [she was] further told to go by the next opportunity on penalty of £20'. Mary Oliver came before the court again in December 1649, for stealing goats, and then compounded her offence by saying the governor was 'unjust, corrupt and a wretch and had made her pay for stealing two goats when there was no proof in the world of it'. For this, the court ordered that she should be whipped on the next Salem lecture day ('if the weather was moderate and not more than 20 stripes'). She requested relief from this sentence, which was granted on condition she left town. At the end of February 1649/50, a fine was remitted so long as she used the money 'in transporting herself and children out of this jurisdiction within 3 weeks'.

Thomas Oliver, back in Boston in 1654, testified that Mary had joined him in Norwich in the summer of 1651. There is no evidence that she ever returned to New England.

T. Breen and S. Foster, 'Moving to the New World: the character of early Massachusetts immigration', *William and Mary Quarterly*, 3rd series 30 (1973), 202; *WJ*, 275–6; *Essex Court Recs.* I, 12, 99, 138, 152, 154, 173, 180, 182–3, 185, 186; Essex Court Files, 1646-8, 1-46-1, 1-90-1, 1-97-3; *Mass. Recs.* 2:258, 283; MHS, Misc. MSS, 6 May 1654; *Pilgrims*, 43.

OLIVER, Thomas (b. c.1601)

Thomas Oliver, a 'calender' (calenderer, smoother of cloth), came from of St Edmund's parish, Norwich, where Thomas Allen* was rector. He and his wife Mary* were cited before the ecclesiastical authorities in 1633. He emigrated to New England in 1637, on the *Mary Anne* from Yarmouth, aged 36, with Mary, their children Thomas and John, and two servants. They settled at Salem. Thomas was in court for various small offences – not making a fence, sleeping on the watch – between 1640 and the spring of 1648.

Thomas Oliver was already back in England, presumably in Norwich, when Mary was first ordered to go to him on 15 November 1648. He was there in the summer of 1651 when she arrived, and until at least 6 September 1652, when he received a letter of attorney that authorised him, as of Norwich, to receive money from a Roxbury man.

He seems to have been in Boston on 6 May 1654, when he made a deposition on behalf of one Underwood, a biscuit baker of Salem. He had met Underwood's wife in Norwich and urged her to join her husband in New England:

> in the time of my late being in England I had conference with her severall times in the Cittie of norwich between my selfe and her ... once or twice at my owne house ther, together with my owne wife (sense her coming over in somer 51) and both of us ... used divers arguments to perswade her to come to her husband... But wee could prevaile nothing ... notwithstanding we both perceived a comfortable way of subsistence her husband was in [in] Regard of his biskett Bakeing & allso we[ll] accomodated Both with house and other conveniences and heareby both her owne lively hood and also hir Children's might be much betered; also a way much pleasing to god ... but she [said] in a very passionate maner that her husband wanted her for nothing but to make a drudge of her because he wanted one to helpe him in his calling. And further that he sent for her and sent for her, but did not send her mony to pay her passage: with many divers other objections ... the which ... all ... seemed to proceed from no beter ground then from an headstronge & willfull minde ... [she being able] to Transport her selfe if wifelike duty and loyall affections weare not wanting.

On this occasion, Oliver seems to have remained in Boston only a short time. The next reference to a 'Thomas Oliver' in the Essex county court records is on 26 June 1660. If this is the same man, he was clerk of the foot company of Salem on 11 September 1663, and appeared in court several times over the following years. He married a widow, Bridget Wasselbee, on 26 July 1666. In

1669 he and his wife were charged for fighting one another: a neighbour 'saw Goodwife Olyver's face at one time bloody and at other times black and blue'.

T. Breen and S. Foster, 'Moving to the New World: the character of early Massachusetts immigration', *William and Mary Quarterly*, 3rd series 30 (1973), 202; MHS, Misc. MSS, 6 May 1654; *Essex Court Recs.* I, 21, 137, 152, II, 217, III, 116, 154, 268, 339, 385, IV, 90.

OTTLEY, Adam

Adam Ottley of Lynn acted as attorney for John Humfrey* after Humfrey left for England. Like Humfrey, Ottley was in financial difficulties. Fellow colonists sued him for debt, and on one occasion he was summoned to court for forging a signature. Samuel Whiting and Thomas Cobbett, the ministers at Lynn, intervened unsuccessfully to prevent Ottley's differences with the merchant Joseph Armitage from coming to trial: they wrote to John Winthrop about 'the Great Action at Boston', 10 July 1643. John Endecott reported Ottley's claim that the testimonies against him were false. Ottley admitted he was deep in debt, and acknowledged, c.1643, his 'more then youthfull (I might say grosse) folly' in risking the respect of his friends and his livelihood. On 13 March 1643/4, Thomas Cobbet, consulting Winthrop about the adoption of John Humfrey's abused daughter Dorcas, considered Ottley but ruled him out: 'Mr Ottley is poore, and he cannot helpe her'. Early in 1644, Ottley pressed claims to some goods left by Hugh Peter* in New England (which he claimed had been bought by Humfrey). Endecott asked Winthrop, 22 April, 'to staie the suite till Mr Peter come ouer, who we hope will be heere this spring . . . For Mr Otely is upon going away, and is turning euery stone to get something, For hee is poore and is like to be poorer'.

Ottley seems to have gone to England c.1645.

Essex Court Recs. I, 32, 43, 55, 64, 70, 78; *WP* IV, 365, 411, 452, 456; F. Rose-Troup, 'John Humfry', *Essex Institute Historical Collections*, 65 (1929), 293. (According to the editor of *WP*, Ottley married Ann Humfrey, John Humfrey's daughter, but the evidence is not clear. At some point Ann Humfrey married William Palmes of Tipperary, Ireland, and then in the 1660s the baptist John Miles (*ODNB*), with whom she came back to New England by 1666: *Essex Court Recs.* VIII, 137–8.)

P

PAGE, Margaret

Margaret Page of Salem, Massachusetts, was sent to Boston jail on 5 February 1643/4, as a 'lazy idle and loytering person', to be 'sett to work for her liuinge'. On 15 December 1645, the town offered 'Brother Browning' fifty shillings to keep her in work for a year; if he agreed, she would not go to prison again. Later, c.1646, 'Goodwife Oliver' (Mary Oliver*?) was ordered to give Page house-room.

On 30 September 1647 the town of Salem resolved, 'for the transporting of Margaret Page into England . . . to pay by Rate £5'. She was to leave as soon as possible, either on Francis Willoughby's* ship or 'the next after that goes'.

Salem TR, 124, 140, 142, 147.

PALGRAVE, Anne

Anne Palgrave arrived in New England in 1630 with her husband Richard Palgrave, a physician. They settled at Charlestown and joined the Boston church early in 1631.

Anne travelled back to England as a widow. Richard Palgrave had died in the summer of 1651. Anne gained probate on her husband's will in October that year and went to England soon afterwards. Her daughter Elizabeth (who probably came to New England as a small child) had already married John Edwards of Stepney, Middlesex. At some point between 1651 and 1657, Anne's daughter Lydia married Edmund Heylett of Deptford, Kent. Anne Palgrave was in Stepney by 17 March 1656/7, when she appointed John Pierce [Pearse*] and Edmund Heylett of Stepney as her attorneys for business in New England. She returned to Boston by 1665 and died in Roxbury, 1669.

GMB 1373–6; Roger Thompson, *From deference to defiance: Charlestown, Massachusetts, 1629–1662* (Boston, MA: New England Historic Genealogical Society, 2012), 17, 27.

PARISH, Thomas (1614–1665?)

Thomas Parish [Parrish] was baptised at Nayland, Suffolk. His father, Thomas Parish, was a clothier. At the episcopal visitation of 1629, seven inhabitants of Nayland had been presented for refusing to kneel at communion. At least two of the seven found their way to New England: John Warren in 1630, Gregory Stone in 1635.

Thomas Parish emigrated to New England in 1635 on the *Increase*, described in the custom house record as a clothier. In Massachusetts, he was variously described as a clothier, planter and surgeon. He became a proprietor at Watertown in 1636, but moved to Cambridge c.1637, where he joined the church. He was admitted a freeman of Massachusetts on 18 April 1637.

Parish seems to have visited England between the autumn of 1638 and the spring of 1639. Around October 1638, probably just before he set sail, he entered into a complex agreement with John Hood of Cambridge. Hood, a weaver, had come from Halstead in Essex. He had inherited property in Halstead from his father-in-law and now wished to dispose of most of it. Thomas Parish agreed to sell 'to some person or persons in England for as much money as hee by his best skill and endevours can get . . . and returne the said money unto the said John Hood his executors administratours or assignes'. Parish was to be protected against any costs of effecting a sale; he was also to be given 20 shillings for 'labours and charges in and about the premises' if the property sold, and 10 shillings if it did not. Parish was back in New England in time to be chosen as a selectman in 1639. He joined the Artillery Company in 1641. He married Mary Danforth, sister of deputy governor Thomas Danforth. Their son Thomas Parish* was born in 1641.

Parish returned to England for good by the late 1640s, with his wife Mary and two young daughters. He left his son Thomas in Cambridge under the watchful eye of his uncle Thomas Danforth. Parish was already back in Suffolk by early autumn 1649, when John Sawin of Watertown, a shoemaker, had two letters of attorney drawn up – presumably to send on consecutive ships for safety – commissioning 'Thom Parish of Nailon in the County of Suffolk, chirurgeon' to recover a legacy. On 24 December 1652, Thomas Parish's father, 'Thomas Parrish the elder of Nayland . . . clothier' left him property. Parish secured probate of his father's will in September 1653. He wrote back to Cambridge, Massachusetts, to appoint his brother-in-law Danforth as his attorney in New England. Danforth sold Parish's 'late mansion place' in Cambridge, 'lately burnt downe', on 25 March 1654/5, and 100 acres of land on 1 March 1656/7 (these transactions were both recorded on 5 April 1659).

Thomas Parish made his will on 17 August 1660, with bequests to his wife and children, and to his 'loving ffreind' Alexander Eaton of Wapping, apothecary. He left his 'chirurgions chest with all the medicines instruments Bookes implements and other appurtenances' to his son 'Thomas the younger'. His wife and son, with Eaton, were named executors. Parish died before 26 September 1661.

GM 5: 357–60, 6: 551; for Mary Parish's testimony on admission to the Cambridge church, see *Shepard's confessions*, 136–8; Lechford *NB*, 10–15; Cambridge TR, fols 52, 54, 80; Aspinwall, 231, 249; Middlesex Deeds II, fols 298–302; NA, PROB 11/232/217, will of Thomas Parrish, clothier of Nayland, Suffolk, 29 September 1653; NA, PROB 11/305/433, will of 'Thomas Parish, chirurgeon' of Nayland, Suffolk, 26 September 1661. Parish has been mistakenly identified with Thomas Parris, a London haberdasher trading with New England (father of Samuel Parris, of Salem witch-trial fame): see *Artillery Company*, 117; Bernard Bailyn, *The New England merchants in the seventeenth century* (Cambridge, MA: Harvard University Press, 1955), 87, 88, 111.

PARISH, Thomas (1641–c.1707)

Thomas Parish [Parrish] was born on 21 July 1641 at Cambridge, Massachusetts, the son of Thomas* and Mary Parish. He remained in New England after his parents returned to England in the late 1640s, under the care of Thomas Danforth. In due course he enrolled at Harvard. His accounts from 7 September 1655 to 7 March 1655/6 are marked 'payd by his unkell Thomas Danforth', who was attorney for Parish's father. On 9 June 1656, young Thomas Parish was convicted 'of some foolish and inordinate carriages towards the Towne and Church of Cambridge at a publique meeting'. He was admonished by the Middlesex county court, and told to make a public acknowledgement of his fault at the next public meeting. Parish was in trouble again in January 1658/9, when he took part in 'a great disorder in Cambridge in the night and fighting betweene the schollars and some of the towne'. This time the court ordered that Parish and two other student ringleaders should be publicly censured in the college hall by the Harvard president, Charles Chauncy. Parish graduated BA from Harvard in 1659, and left New England soon afterwards.

A badly torn letter to Thomas Danforth in 1659 (perhaps from his son Joshua Danforth in London), referred to the correspondent having 'taken order' for the passage home of 'young Mr Tho: Parrish'. Parish was expected in London. He was to reside with Alexander Eaton of Wapping, apothecary, until order came from his father. Thomas Parish was incorporated BA at Cambridge on 13 April 1660. In August that year, his father named him as an executor of his will (alongside his mother Mary Parish and Alexander Eaton) and bequeathed him his 'chirurgions chest'. Nothing more is known of Parish's later career. He died c.1707.

NEHGR 4: 182; Middlesex Court Recs. I, 91, 102; Middlesex Court Files, File 7, # 3 (affidavit from Charles Chauncy, 14 March 1658); *Harvard Recs.* III, 213n.; MHS, Misc. Bd. MSS, 1659; *GM* 5: 359; Roger Thompson, *Cambridge cameos: stories of life in seventeenth-century New England* (Boston, MA: New England Historic Genealogical Society, 2005), 82-4; NA, PROB 11/305/433, will of 'Thomas Parish, chirurgeon' of Nayland, Suffolk, 26 September 1661.

CC, Sibley.

PARKER, Nicholas

Nicholas Parker arrived in New England in 1633 and joined the church at Roxbury. He became a freeman of Massachusetts on 4 March 1633/4. In 1636 he moved to Boston, where on 25 February 1642/3 he and his wife Anne were admitted to the church 'upon letters of dismission from the church at

Roxbury'. A 'Mr Parker' was disarmed in November 1637 after a petition in support of Anne Hutchinson, but this was probably Richard Parker, a Boston merchant. Nicholas Parker testified that he 'had no hand in it'.

Parker disappears from New England records after 1651. He made his will at Plymouth, Devon, on 4 April 1659. He left land to his son Nicholas, the mariner 'Captain Nicholas Parker', who left it in turn to siblings scattered between London, Boston and Barbados.

GMB 1394–6; *WP* III, 514; NA, PROB 11/330/37, will of Nicholas Parker, 13 May 1669.

PARRAT, Francis

Francis Parrat [Parrit, Parrot] came from Sutterton, Lincolnshire, and was an early settler at Rowley. He became a freeman of Massachusetts on 13 May 1640, served as a deputy for Rowley at the General Court later that year, and as town clerk in 1641. He acted several times as a juryman, and laid out lands with Matthew Boyes* in June 1652. He and his wife, with William Bartholomew of Ipswich, testified against John Broadstreet, who was brought to court for 'familiarity with the devil' and for using a book of magic. In 1655 Parrat was a deacon of Rowley church.

Parrat made a will on 18 November 1655, 'intending to take a Journey to England'. The will was proved 30 September 1656. He died at sea or in England. His widow Elizabeth remarried in 1657.

D.G. Allen, *In English ways* (Chapel Hill, NC: University of North Carolina Press, 1981), 248; *NEHGR* 3: 187; C.H. Pope, *Pioneers of Massachusetts* (Boston, MA: C.H. Pope, 1900), 346; G.B. Blodgette and A.E. Jewett, *Early settlers of Rowley, Massachusetts* (Rowley, MA: [s.n.], 1933), 266; G.B. Blodgette and M. Mighill, *The early records of the town of Rowley, Massachusetts, I, 1639–1672* (Rowley, MA: [s.n.], 1894), 97; *Essex Court Recs.*, I, 37, 161, 250, 265, 387, II, 5, 57; *Essex Probate Recs.* I, 244–5.

PARSONS, William (d. 1701/2)

William Parsons emigrated to New England in 1635. The custom-house records described him as a tailor. When he was admitted to the Boston church on 20 April 1644, he was said to be a joiner. Parsons became a freeman of Massachusetts in May 1645, and joined the Artillery Company in 1646.

He went to England in the 1650s. With his wife Ruth, he sold land in Boston on 21 July 1654, and perhaps returned home with her. He was in London in 1661: Samuel Sewall recalled that Parsons 'was in the fifth-monarchy fray in London: but slipt away in the Crowd'. Parsons later returned to New England and died at Boston in 1702.

GD; *Boston CR*, 41; *NEHGR* 3: 191; C.H. Pope, *Pioneers of Massachusetts* (Boston, MA: C.H. Pope, 1900), 347; 5 *MHSC* 6: 52; B.S. Capp, *The Fifth Monarchy Men* (London: Faber, 1972), 223.

PATIENT, Thomas (d. 1666)

Thomas Patient [Patience] emigrated in the late 1630s. Looking back, he explained that he had become 'convinced of the unwarrantableness of the Government of the Lordly Prelates, and the Liturgy in the Church of England, and the mixed Communions in the Parish Assemblies'. He had decided to follow others and leave England: 'At this time many godly Christians going to New England, and being come up in my judgement to the way of New England in faith and order, [I] went over thither.'

Patient settled first at Salem, Massachusetts, then at Lynn. Although he later became well-known in England as a baptist, by his own account he arrived in New England with no baptist convictions. But as he listened to numerous New England preachers defend infant baptism, he began to doubt whether this practice was right. In his only published work, *The doctrine of baptism* (1654), Patient depicted his change of mind as a private journey, 'all of which time I was not acquainted with any that opposed Christening children'. He was tempted not to air his views publicly, fearing

> that then I should be generally dispised, and slighted of all the godlie in that Countrie, and not only frustrated of Communion and Fellowship with them, but must expect to suffer imprisonment, confiscation of goods and banishment at least, which would be my ruin, not knowing where to go, but in the woods amongst Indians and wild beasts . . .

However, Patient's claim that he travelled a lonely road to becoming a baptist is rather belied by the Essex county court papers, where Patient's name appears alongside four or five other people in Lynn who were suspected of holding baptist views. The authorities pursued Patient after he and his wife Sarah had a child: a warrant was issued for his arrest in 1641, 'upon vehement suspicion, not only of holding, but also of fomenting the error that baptism of infants is no ordinance of God, and hindering his child from baptism'. Patient declared the warrant 'was no trouble to me, being filled with unspeakable joy, as I walked up and down in the woods in that wilderness'. Before his case came to court on 14 December 1642, Patient had fled: in the court files, against his name was marked 'gone'.

Thomas Patient returned to England, no doubt with his wife Sarah and his unbaptised child. Over the next two years his history is obscure, but his ties with leading advocates of adult baptism soon became clear. In 1644, he signed a Calvinistic Baptist confession with William Kiffin (*ODNB*), as a representative of one of the congregations whose views it set out. He baptised the sectary Laurence Clarkson (*ODNB*) in London, 'in the water that runneth about the Tower'. In 1646 the presbyterian propagandist Thomas Edwards referred to Patient as one 'that would not be suffered in New-England'. In 1647 it was reported that Patient had been ordained in Bell Alley, Coleman Street. On 2 April 1649 he joined other London baptists in a petition to parliament disassociating themselves from the Levellers. He was in Ireland by 15 April 1650, where he showed himself a keen advocate of a strict policy of limiting church membership to those willing to receive 'believer's baptism'; he converted the military governors of Kilkenny and Waterford to his views. Patient's church at Waterford was the strongest baptist community in Ireland. On 14 January 1651/2, he and his flock wrote to rebuke Dublin baptists who remained in communion with the Independent congregation of the Fifth Monarchist John Rogers (*ODNB*). In December 1652, Patient became a preacher at Christ Church cathedral in Dublin (with Nathaniel Brewster*, Thomas Harrison* and Samuel Mather*). He and Harrison served on a commission that examined ministers who applied to come to Ireland. Alongside Christopher Blackwood*, Patient was the most important baptist in Ireland, working through the army, and encouraged by Charles Fleetwood and the Irish council (though later discouraged by Henry Cromwell). His salary, £11 4s a month, was drawn on military funds; he was not, like most other ministers, on the civil list.

After 1660, Patient was in Bristol for a time. He was imprisoned there in 1663-4 for illegal preaching. On 28 June 1666 he was ordained in London as an associate of the baptist preacher William Kiffin – who was also a city merchant of substantial wealth and influence. Hanserd Knollys* took part in the service. Thomas Patient died on 29 July 1666, a casualty of the Great Plague.

Publication *The doctrine of baptism* (1654).

Patient, *The doctrine of baptism*, 'Epistle to the Christian reader'; Essex Court Files, 1641, 1-8-1, 1-10-1 A and B; *Essex Court Recs*. I, 51-2; B.R. White, 'Thomas Patient in England and Ireland', *Irish Baptist Historical Journal*, 2 (1969–70), 36–48; Edwards, *Gangraena*, i. 95 [second pagination]; T.C. Barnard, *Cromwellian Ireland: English government and reform in Ireland 1649–1660* (Oxford: Oxford University Press, 1975), 101–2, 146–7; St J.D. Seymour, *The puritans in Ireland, 1647–1661* (Oxford: Clarendon Press, 1921), 218; Stephen Wright, *The early English baptists, 1603–1649* (Woodbridge: The Boydell Press, 2006), 103, 133, 136, 187, 217.

BDBR, ODNB.

PEARSE, John

'John Pearse of Wappen Mariner late of New England' was admitted to the Stepney church, Middlesex, on 8 February 1656/7. Soon afterwards, Anne Palgrave* appointed him as an attorney for business in New England.

Stepney CB, fol. 4; *GMB* 1374.

PECK, Robert (1580–c.1656)

Robert Peck, born at Beccles, Suffolk, graduated MA from Magdalene College, Cambridge, in 1603. He became rector of Hingham, Norfolk, in 1605. He was convicted of nonconformity in 1615 and 1617. Samuel Harsnett, bishop of Norwich, censured Peck for catechising and singing psalms at his home on

Sunday afternoons. As a result, Norwich citizens included Peck's case in a petition to the House of Commons against Harsnett. The bishop got Peck bound over at the quarter sessions in 1622 for holding conventicles, and in the consistory court it was alleged that Peck 'had infected the parish with strange opinions: as that people are not to kneel as they enter the church; that it is superstition to bow at the name of Jesus; and that the church is no more sacred than any other building'. Some of Peck's neighbours were said to believe that there was 'no Difference between an Alehouse and the Church, till the Preacher be in the Pulpit'. In 1630, Peck was one of four ministers among twelve 'trustees for the Religion in Norwich and Norfolk', who, in a similar fashion to the London Feoffees for Impropriations, worked to establish positions for zealous protestant preachers. Soon after, Peck joined the team of twelve ministers serving the Norwich 'combination lecture' at St George Tombland, the parish of William Bridge (*ODNB*); other preachers included Jeremiah Burroughes (*ODNB*) and William Greenhill (*ODNB*).

In the campaign for conformity led by Bishop Matthew Wren, Peck was excommunicated on 9 October 1636 and deprived of his living on 9 April 1638. According to petitions from his parishioners and his son Samuel – included among papers presented in 1640 to the House of Commons against Wren – Robert Peck had been excommunicated by Wren's chancellor, Clement Corbet (*ODNB*), for not appearing in person at a visitation. Peck had requested absolution but Corbet refused this, according to Samuel Peck's account, unless his father agreed to 'always preach in his surplesse, constantly use Common prayer, read second service att the high Altar, which they had caused to be built in the Chancell (with diverse other Articles commonly called Bishop Wrens pocket injuncions)'. Robert Peck would not assent, claiming the requirements had no legal force in the Church of England. On 4 November 1636, Corbet reported to Wren that Robert's son Thomas Peck (*CR*) had recently officiated at Hingham, and 'did nothing in order': Corbet called him to appear 'but he is returned into Essex from whence he came and it is rumorde the ould fox his father is kenelld ther'. (Thomas Peck had married Abigail, daughter of the well-known preacher John Rogers of Dedham, Essex.) The authorities sequestered tithes from Hingham, worth £160 according to the parishioners, £180 according to Samuel Peck. However, so 'addicted' to Robert Peck were his people that they paid their dues to him, or to his wife or deputies in his absence, defying Corbet. In light of Peck's obstinate refusal to repent, Corbet requested in June 1637 that the case should be taken to the Court of High Commission. On 9 March 1637/8, Corbet urged Wren to proceed against Peck, who had been called back to residence six months earlier but had not appeared. Corbet reported that Peck was soon to go to New England 'and carryeth [with him] many Housholdes in that and other townes adjacent, as I heare'. In the end, the authorities deprived Peck for nonresidency, 'notwithstanding', wrote his parishioners, 'he did always abide in the said Towne where he had soe long lived'. Before Peck set off for New England, he made complex arrangements for family members left behind. He granted the profits of his living to his son Samuel, for maintenance. Samuel petitioned parliament for payment in 1640: this petition described Robert Peck, under threat of proceedings in the Court of High Commission, as 'inforced togeather with his wife and family in his old dayes to forsake his deare contry'. He and his wife were 'made Exiles in their old age'.[1]

Robert Peck sailed for New England on the *Diligent* of Ipswich, which carried 135 East Anglian passengers. He arrived in New England on 10 August 1638, with his wife Ann, two servants, and two of his children, Joseph and Ann. His brother Joseph Peck emigrated with his family at the same time. On 28 November 1638, Robert Peck was ordained teacher at Hingham, Massachusetts, where Peter Hobart, who had grown up in Hingham, Norfolk, was pastor. Peck was granted land in 1638 and became a freeman on 13 March 1638/9. Thomas Lechford* noted that Peck and Hobart 'refuse to baptize old Ottis grandchildren, an ancient member of their own Church'. The Hingham church seems to have included almost the whole community, but this case arose because in 1641 John Otis presented his granddaughter for baptism. Her father, Thomas Burton, had not joined a church, regarding it as a separatist act. Hobart and Peck initially refused baptism, adhering to the practice of baptising only the children of members, not their grandchildren. Later, after Peck's departure, Hobart baptised the child. In 1646 Hobart sided with Thomas Burton and Robert Child* when they petitioned against, among other matters, restricted baptism.[2]

Peck set sail for England on 27 October 1641, with his wife Ann and son Joseph. His daughter Ann stayed in New England, as did his brother Joseph. Robert Peck sailed in the same fleet as John Phillip*. According to Cotton Mather, he went home at 'the Invitation of his Friends at Hingham in England'. His former parishioners had in fact petitioned the House of Commons in 1640, 'humbly crauing redresse that Mr Peck our old minister may be by law and justice of this Court returned to his old possession or att least some godly man may be placed amongst us'.

Peck resumed his ministry at Hingham. The altar rails and mound at the east end of the chancel, erected on the orders of Bishop Wren's chancellor, Clement Corbet, were removed. On 5 July 1647, Captain John Mason (*ANB*), who had married Peck's daughter Ann, sold Peck's house and land in Hingham, Massachusetts. Peck died in 1656, or perhaps somewhat later. His will, made on 24 July 1651, was proved on 10 April 1658. Peck mentioned his wife Martha and asked to be buried at Hingham next to his former wife, Ann; also his sons Thomas, Samuel, Robert (deceased) and Joseph, and his daughter Ann, wife of John Mason of Connecticut. Peck's funeral sermon was preached by Nathaniel Jocelyn (*CR*), pastor of Hardingham, Norfolk, near Hingham.[3]

---

[1] Matthew Reynolds, *Godly reformers and their opponents in early modern England: religion in Norwich, c.1560–1643* (Woodbridge: Boydell Press, 2005), 135–6, 160–9, 171, 173, 226–7; Bodleian, Tanner MS 68, fols 171, 232, 234, 236, 242, 312, 329; Bodleian, Tanner MS 220, fols 54–6, 145.

[2] *WJ* 268; 'The Hobart Journal', ed. C.E. Egan, *NEHGR*, 121 (1967), 11; D.G. Allen, *In English ways* (Chapel Hill, NC: University of North Carolina Press, 1981), 256; Aspinwall, 174; J.J. Waters, 'Hingham, Massachusetts, 1631–1661: an East Anglian

oligarchy in the New World', *Journal of Social History*, I (1968), 359; Lechford *PD*, 37; *NEHGR* 2: 251; 3: 96; on the Otis case and Hingham church membership, Waters, 'Hingham', 362–7.

³ 'Hobart Journal', 14; 'Daniel Cushing's record of Norfolk emigrants', *NEHGR*, 15 (1861), 26, 27; *Magnalia* I, 587; Bodleian, Tanner MS 220, fols 55-6; *Suffolk Deeds* I, 82; Allen, *In English ways*, 258; *NEHGR* 39: 65–6; J. Browne, *A history of congregationalism in Norfolk and Suffolk* (London: Jarrold & Sons, 1877), 104.

PELHAM, Elizabeth (c.1617–c.1659)

Elizabeth was the daughter of Godfrey Bosvile of Yorkshire (*BDBR*). She married Roger Harlakenden of Earls Colne, Essex, and emigrated with him in 1635, aged eighteen.

The Harlakendens settled in Cambridge, Massachusetts, where their daughters Elizabeth* and Margaret Harlakenden* were born. After Roger Harlakenden's death in 1638, Elizabeth married Herbert Pelham*: their children, born in New England, were Mary* and Frances Pelham*, and Herbert (who did not survive long). Pelham's children by his first marriage were Waldegrave*, Nathaniel*, Jemima*, Penelope* and Katherine Pelham*.

Elizabeth Pelham probably returned to England early in 1647, with Herbert Pelham, and various children and stepchildren. She died before 25 August 1659 when her husband was granted letters of administration on her estate.

GM 3: 221, 224; Cambridge TR, fols 487, 488, 493.

PELHAM, Herbert (1600–1673/4)

Herbert Pelham, son of Herbert and Penelope Pelham, was born in Sussex or perhaps Lincolnshire. His father was a half-brother of John Humfrey's* wife, Elizabeth. His uncle, Thomas Pelham, was a member of the Virginia Company. In 1626, as of Boston, Lincolnshire, Herbert married Jemima, daughter of Thomas Waldegrave of Bures, Essex, granddaughter of Robert Gurdon of Assington, Suffolk. She died in England. By Jemima, Herbert Pelham received the manor of Ferrers at Bures, Essex. Through her he was related to the Winthrops. In 1629 Pelham became a member of the Massachusetts Bay Company. He and his brother-in-law Thomas Waldegrave contributed £50 each to the common stock. c. November 1630 John Rogers (*ODNB*), minister of Dedham, sent money to John Winthrop Jr*, or in his absence to 'Mr Pelham of Bures', to buy food for certain poor settlers: one John Page, late of Dedham, had written back that 'unless God stir up some friends to send him some provision, he is likely to starve'. On 23 February 1635/6, Herbert Pelham wrote to Winthrop, thanking him for his 'Care and paynes' with a brother (probably John Pelham, who had recently gone to New England). Pelham was also in touch with Emmanuel Downing* and Sir Richard Saltonstall*. On 19 April 1637, he sent more news of their common acquaintances to 'cosen' Winthrop.[1]

Pelham arrived New England in late 1639 or early 1640, with his children Waldegrave*, Nathaniel*, Jemima*, Katherine* and Penelope*. A number of his siblings had come to New England: John, William*, Penelope (who married Richard Bellingham, governor of Massachusetts), and Elizabeth. The family settled at Cambridge. Herbert soon married Elizabeth*, widow of Roger Harlakenden. He joined the Artillery Company in 1639; in 1643 and 1644 he was town surveyor. He became the first treasurer of Harvard, 27 December 1643. Pelham promoted a new plantation at Sudbury, Massachusetts, and was given land there in 1644. He was admitted a freeman in May 1645, and in the same year was elected as a representative for Cambridge and as an assistant at the Massachusetts General Court; in 1645 and May 1646 he was chosen a commissioner for the United Colonies. On 25 December 1644, letters of attorney were noted from Pelham to Godfrey Bosvile (*BDBR*), George Fenwick*, and his brother Henry Pelham: these were to obtain what was due to him from Thomas Waldegrave's estate, and to his wife from Roger Harlakenden's executors, as maintenance for Elizabeth* and Margaret Harlakenden. Pelham may have visited England himself in 1644, but if so, he was back in New England by August 1645, when George Downing* sent him greetings. By the 1640s, Pelham was without doubt among the wealthiest settlers of Cambridge, if not the wealthiest: with four houses and land-holdings of 934 acres, he topped the list.[2]

William Pynchon* wrote to John Winthrop, 27 October 1646, 'Mr Haines [Governor John Haynes* of Connecticut] is going for England and so I heere is Mr Pelham and many others: which the land can ill spaire without a shaking ague: the pillars of the land seeme to tremble'. Pelham's intention of travelling to England was taken up by the Massachusetts General Court, which proposed that Pelham and Richard Saltonstall* should act as agents in London for Massachusetts, to represent the colony before the Warwick Commission in a dispute with Samuel Gorton*. However, on 17 November 1646, Pelham and Saltonstall petitioned the General Court, refusing to act as agents 'for divers reasons of weight'. The court agreed to appoint Edward Winslow* instead, and the names of Pelham and Saltonstall were removed from a letter to the earl of Warwick.[3]

Pelham and Saltonstall may have been unwilling to act as agents, but both soon left for England. Winslow named Pelham, in a tract published in May 1647, as one of the colonists now in England who had been present at John Cotton's lecture in Boston on 5 November 1646. Pelham left with his wife Elizabeth and, in all likelihood, all his children and stepchildren but one: Nathaniel Pelham, who stayed on and studied at Harvard. On 11 July 1647, Hannah, daughter of 'Mr Pellam of New England', was baptised at the Stepney church where William Greenhill was minister.

Pelham was expected to come back to New England almost immediately, because he was elected an assistant of the Bay Colony in his absence in 1647, 1648 and 1649. This never happened, but on 5 May 1647, in a letter to John Winthrop, Pelham paid at least lip-service to the idea of returning to America:

> I know not as yett when my occasions will give liberty to have thoughts of returning as I unwillingly departed from you, for I know noe place where I more desier to be then amongst your selves, but we have not the disposeing of our time, nor appoynting the Bounds of our habitation.

He reported on local and national events, referring Winthrop for detail to 'printed News' sent to Thomas Dudley. In light of alarming tales of religious radicalism, Pelham believed Massachusetts had the right policy on toleration: 'I hope you will every day more and more see lesse Cause to repent that the doore hath not beene sett soe wide open as some would have had it'. On 19 April 1648, he wrote about a riot that had happened in London ten days earlier: 'you see what need we stand in of all the Prayers of the Churches with you'.

By 1648, Pelham resettled in his home at Bures, Essex, which had come to him through his first wife, Jemina. He was in touch with her grandfather and Winthrop's old friend, Brampton Gurdon of Assington; also with Richard Saltonstall, whose wife Muriel* was Gurdon's daughter. Pelham knew the Essex minister Ralph Josselin (*ODNB*): Josselin noted in his diary in 1651 that he lent £50 to Pelham and his son. Pelham served as a JP in Essex throughout the 1650s, and as an MP for the county in 1654. With the colonial agent Edward Winslow and the former colonist Richard Floyd*, Pelham became an original member of the Corporation for the Propagation of the Gospel in New England, appointed on 27 July 1649. In 1651, Pelham's daughter Penelope married Winslow's son Josiah*: wedding portraits of both survive, together with Penelope's wedding shoe and a portrait of Edward Winslow.[4]

Pelham kept land in New England, and was active in exercising his rights, even though not resident. On 19 October 1648, Henry Dunster of Cambridge presented a petition on Pelham's behalf to the General Court, 'at the motion of the said Herbert by his letters dated Ferrers Aprill 4th 48'. Pelham was described as 'late of Cambridge in Massachusetts now for the present in England resident'. He asked for a land grant of 800 acres in return for the £100 he and Thomas Waldegrave had contributed to the common stock about seventeen years before. Pelham declared he would, 'whither present or absent ... remaine ever mindfull to be yours in what office of love he ... shall be able to pleasure this Colonie'. His petition was granted. On 1 April 1651, Pelham brought a case against Samuel Eldred in Cambridge, Massachusetts, for detaining rent and not keeping the terms of his lease. Pelham and his brother William still had land in Sudbury, Massachusetts, where their wish to cast votes by proxy provoked controversy about non-residents' rights.[5]

Pelham's will, as of Ferrers, in Bures Hamlet, Essex, 1 January 1672/3, was proved on 30 March 1676. He gave land in Lincolnshire to his son Waldegrave, and property in County Cork, Ireland, to his son Henry (born after his return to England). His land in Massachusetts went to his son Edward; his property there, to his son Edward and daughter Penelope Winslow, who had returned to New England after her marriage. Edward, probably born after his parents' return to England, was at Harvard when the will was made. Pelham also left him rents at Smeeth Hall, Swineshead, Lincolnshire, on condition that, if he resided in New England, the governor and four magistrates or assistants would testify 'that he is now grown serious, sober, and solid, and follows his study, and avoids all idle and profuse company, and that they verily conceive there is a real change in him for the better, and not only to attain his ends thereby'.[6]

¹ *NEHGR* 33 285–95; F. Rose-Troup, *The Massachusetts Bay Company and its predecessors* (New York: Grafton Press, 1930), 150–1, 157; *WJ*, 367; *WP* II, 316; *WP* III, 228, 393-4.
² *GD*; Cambridge TR, fols 39, 60, 61, 63 (for other references to property before and after his return to England, fols 70, 79, 80, 81, 83, 93, 135, 137); *Artillery Company*, 94; *WJ*, 490, 574, 621, 763; *NEHGR* 3: 190; Aspinwall, 17; *WP* V, 44; Roger Thompson, *Cambridge cameos: stories of life in seventeenth-century New England* (Boston, MA: New England Historic Genealogical Society, 2005), 18, 20, 38.
³ *WP* V, 115, 120–1.
⁴ Edward Winslow, *New-Englands salamander* (1647), 12; Stepney CB, fol. 118; *WP* V, 156–7, 216–19, 237; ERO, Chelmsford, Assize and Quarter Session Records, 1650s, *passim*; A. Macfarlane, ed., *The diary of Ralph Josselin 1616–1683* (Oxford: Oxford University Press, 1976), 259; Bodleian, Rawlinson MS D. 934, fol. 1v; *Pilgrims*, 99–100, 108n.36, 117, plates 9–11 (portraits and shoe, from the collections of the Pilgrim Hall Museum, Plymouth, Massachusetts).
⁵ Mass. Archives, 45:12 (Dunster's petition, 19 October 1648); *Mass. Recs.* 3: 138; S.C. Powell, *Puritan village: the formation of a New England town* (Middletown, CT: Wesleyan University Press, 1963), 90, 125, 169.
⁶ NA, PROB 11/352/517, will of Herbert Pelham of Ferrers Bewers Hamlet, Essex, 30 March 1676. For Edward Pelham, see *CC*, Sibley.

ODNB.

PELHAM, Jemima, Frances, Katherine, Mary, Penelope, Nathaniel and Waldegrave

Jemima, Katherine, Penelope, Nathaniel and Waldegrave Pelham were the children of Herbert Pelham* and his first wife, Jemima. Waldegrave, the eldest, was baptised at Bures, Essex, on 26 September 1627. Nathaniel was baptised there on 5 February 1631/2. Herbert Pelham emigrated with his five children in late 1639 or early 1640, as a widower. (In New England they acquired Mary and Frances Pelham as half-sisters and Elizabeth* and Mary Harlakenden* as stepsisters.)

All but Nathaniel Pelham seem to have returned to England with their parents late in 1646. Waldegrave Pelham was admitted to the Inner Temple early in 1647: he later married Abigail, daughter of Thomas Glascock of Hedingham Sible, Essex; he administered his father's estate, and died at Bures in 1699. Penelope Pelham married Josiah Winslow* in London in 1651: she returned to New England with Josiah in 1655 and died at Marshfield, Massachusetts, in 1703. Jemima married Samuel Kem (*ODNB*), rector of Albury near Oxford, 10 February 1653/4: she died on 20 August 1657 and was buried at Bures; her daughter, Katherine Clarke, was mentioned in Herbert Pelham's will of 1 January 1672/3. Of Katherine nothing is known.

Mary and Frances Pelham, the daughters of Herbert* and Elizabeth Pelham*, were born in Cambridge, Massachusetts, c.1640 and c.1643. It seems likely that they were taken to England by their parents late in 1646. Mary died unmarried in Essex before 1672, when her father made his will. Elizabeth married

Jeremiah Stonnard and lived in Essex; she died before 1672, but Stonnard was mentioned in Herbert Pelham's will.

Nathaniel Pelham stayed in New England longer than his siblings. He graduated with a BA from Harvard in 1651. He sailed for England in November 1657, but the ship went down, and all the passengers were lost at sea. John Davis*, Jonathan Ince* and Thomas Mayhew* were among his fellow travellers. Herbert Pelham's will, 1 January 1672/3, referred to rent left to Josiah Winslow* 'in satisfaction of a debt which he says my son Nathaniel Pelham owes him'.

> *NEHGR* 33: 285–95; *Pilgrims*, plates 10–11 (Penelope Pelham's portrait and wedding shoe, from the collections of Pilgrim Hall Museum, Plymouth, Massachusetts); NA, PROB 11/352/517, will of Herbert Pelham of Ferrers Bewers Hamlet, Essex, 30 March 1676. On Nathaniel Pelham, see also *Harvard Recs*. I, 83; *CC*; Sibley.

PELHAM, William

William Pelham, a younger brother to Herbert Pelham*, had studied at Emmanuel College, Cambridge. He was the 'Mr Pelham' who intended to cross the Atlantic in the Winthrop fleet of 1630. However, he and John Winthrop's son Henry missed their passage by going ashore to collect cattle and not returning to the ship in time.

Pelham arrived in Massachusetts by July 1630 and requested admission as a freeman on 19 October. He seems to have settled at Watertown, but disappears from view. He may have been away in England. He was at Sudbury, Massachusetts, by 1645. He served the town as captain of the militia, as a selectman, and as a deputy at the Massachusetts General Court in 1647. In 1646, Pelham objected to the Bay Colony's treatment of the Remonstrants Robert Child*, Thomas Fowle*, Samuel Maverick, Thomas Burton, John Smith, David Yale* and John Dand.

William Pelham returned to England in or soon after 1647. In 1652 Edward Johnson wrote that he was 'in England at present'. Pelham kept land in Sudbury: he and his Herbert Pelham tried to vote there by proxy, raising the issue of non-residents' rights. He died in England in 1667.

> *Al. Cant.*; *GMB* 1417–19; *WJ*, 8–9, 730; *NEHGR* 8: 56, 33: 285–95; G.L. Kittredge, 'Dr. Robert Child the Remonstrant', Colonial Society of Massachusetts, *Publications*, 21 (1919), 55–6; S.C. Powell, *Puritan village: the formation of a New England town* (Middletown, CT: Wesleyan University Press, 1963), 84, 88, 90, 111, 115, 125, 169; [Edward Johnson], *Johnson's wonder-working Providence, 1628–1651*, ed. J. Franklin Jameson (New York: Barnes and Noble, 1952), 230. On the Remonstrants: *WJ* 624–5, 647–50, 655–70; Robert Emmet Wall, *Massachusetts Bay: the crucial decade, 1640–1650* (New Haven, CT: Yale University Press, 1972), 209.

PEMERTON, John (d. *c.*1653)

John Pemerton [Pemberton], a weaver, was in Boston by late 1632 or early 1633, when he joined the church. On 11 June 1633 he was whipped for fornication with Elizabeth Marson, who soon became his wife. Pemerton became a freeman of Massachusetts on 1 April 1634. He moved to Newbury by 1639. He was admonished by the Boston church at a public fast on 26 November 1639, 'for his unbrotherly Contention with our brother John Baker[*] and for his unsavory Revyling Speeches given to him, to the Offence of the Church at Newberry to whom thay had beene Recommended'. On 19 July 1640, Pemerton was reconciled to the Boston church after 'poenitentiall acknowledgement' of his fault. On 4 October 1640, he was 'Recommendatorily Dismissed' to Newbury. In 1641 he and the wife of John Robinson of Newbury were presented at court for 'obscene and filthy speeches and carriages'. Pemerton's wife Elizabeth died at Newbury on 22 February 1644/5. He served as constable for the town in 1647.

At some point between 1647 and 1653, Pemerton returned to England. He set his mark to his will, as a weaver of Lawford, Essex, on 9 September 1653. He left all his 'Worldly goods ... in New England, in the custody of Hercules Woodman, livinge in Newbery in the county of Essex or his assignes', to his daughter-in-law Deborah Gofe. If she was no longer living, his property in New England should go to his brother, James Pemerton of Newbury, and to 'sister Robinson' – perhaps his partner in 'filthy speeches'? Pemerton's estate in England was left to his brothers William, Richard and Thomas. Pemerton's executor was his 'loveing Kinsman and faithfull friend' John Beeston of Dedham, Essex. The will was proved on 25 March 1654.

Boston CR, 16, 26, 30, 32; *NEHGR* 3: 93, 39: 61–73; *Essex Court Recs*. I, 39; Waters, 89–90; NA, PROB 11/236/534, will of John Pemerton, weaver of Lawford, Essex, 25 March 1654; *GMB* 1421–2.

PESTER, William

William Pester was granted land at Salem in 1637. He was a wealthy settler, but not a church member. On 13 August 1639, Emmanuel Downing* wrote to John Winthrop about the proposed marriage of one of his daughters to Pester, 'but Mr Hathorne tells me from the Elders of the Bay that it wilbe a scandall to marry my daughter to such a man that hath noe religion'. Downing's daughter feared that, as her father was poorer than once he was, 'if she should refuse Mr Pester, shee may stay long ere shee meet with a better, unles I had had more monie for hir than now I can spare'. Pester was presented in court for defamation, drunkenness and many other misdemeanours.

Pester went to England c.1642. On 31 May 1652, the Massachusetts General Court granted the petition of Dorothy Pester, 'whose husband went into England some ten years since, and was never to this day heard of'. Dorothy was permitted to remarry 'when God ... shall afford her an oppertunitie'.

GD; *WP* IV, 502; *Essex Court Recs*. I, *passim*; *Mass. Recs*. 3: 277.

PETER, Deliverance

Deliverance Peter came to Boston as a widow, 'Mrs Sheffield', with William Hibbins* and his family in 1638. She married Hugh Peter*, minister at Salem, by the summer of 1639 – after some embarrassment because it was thought Peter was contracted to marry Ruth Ames, sister of William Ames*. On 2 January 1639/40 Deliverance Peter was dismissed from the Boston church to Salem at her own request.

Deliverance Peter followed her husband to England, perhaps with Judith, wife of Thomas Weld*. She gained a reputation for insanity: in *Gangraena*, Thomas Edwards's list of misfortunes to be visited on Independents included the threat that 'our wives [would become] starke mad, as Mr Peters wife'. She was there by 25 September 1643, when Thomas Weld reported on plans to return to New England: he and Peter dared not risk 'our owne and our wives healths and lives in a winter voyage'. On 23 June 1645, Hugh Peter wrote to John Winthrop Jr* that he would come to New England soon, 'and have sent my wife before, for divers reasons'. But on 4 September 1646 Deliverance was still in England. Her husband reported, 'I am coming over if I must. My wife comes of necessity to N. Eng: having run her selfe out of breath here: you know all, the lord teach me what to doe.' Hugh Peter added a postscript: 'Bee sure you never let my wife come away from there without my leave and then you love me.'

John Winthrop reported Deliverance Peter's return to New England on 26 October 1646, noting she 'is now as she used to be'. *c.* 10 April 1647, Hugh Peter repeated his intention of returning to Massachusetts soon, and went on:

> If I come not say I am dead, and then let my wife returne, and child [Elizabeth*] if shee will though there I wish them to stay: I am selling my land to inable to come. let what I haue there be wisely sold by peecemeale, to stop my wifes complaynt of want.

On 5 May 1647 he wrote to ask Winthrop 'Why my wife should dispose of any thing of my goods without your order, or the deacons?' and added 'if shee will come hither I hynder not but thought shee might bee better there'.

Sometime after this (the precise date is not known) Deliverance Peter's madness was interpreted as devil-possession. She was excommunicated by the Salem church and sent back to England. She was there by 17 July 1649, when Hugh Peter wrote 'Oh that I ever left New E. or had never had this wife so sent to me!' Roger Williams* reported to John Winthrop Jr, 12 July 1654, having seen Hugh Peter in England, that he 'Cries out against N. English Rigidities and Persecutions ... their unchristian dealing with him in the excommunicating his distracted wife'. Hugh Peter devoted £80 of his £200 salary to her: she 'lives from him, not wholly, but much distracted ... He tould me, that his Afliction from his wife stird him up to Action abroad, and when Successe tempted him to pride, the Bitternes in his bozome Comforts was a Cooler and a Bridle to him'.

Deliverance Peter stayed on in England after Hugh Peter's execution in 1660. In 1677, she was living in London, dependent on charity from the Independent church run by George Cokayn (*ODNB*) at his house on Red Cross Street, outside Cripplegate.

> R.P. Stearns, *The strenuous puritan: Hugh Peter 1598–1660* (Urbana, IL: University of Illinois Press, 1954), 134–7, 168; R.P. Stearns, 'The Weld-Peter mission to England', Colonial Society of Massachusetts, *Publications*, 32 (1937), 220; *Boston CR*, 26; *Salem CR*, 9; Edwards, *Gangraena*, i. 70; *WP* IV, 113; *WP* V, 30, 102, 114, 147, 158, 357; *WP* VI, 402; *ODNB, s.n.* 'Peter [Peters], Hugh (*bap.* 1598, *d.* 1660).

PETER, Elizabeth

Elizabeth Peter, baptised at Salem on 8 March 1640, was the daughter of Hugh* and Deliverance Peter*. She remained in New England when her parents went to England: Thomas Shepard wrote to Peter, 27 December 1645, 'Your child is very well with us what ever reports may come to you to the contrary, and her education is not neglected.' *c.* 10 April 1647, Hugh Peter mentioned the possibility of her departure for England in a letter to John Winthrop: 'If I come not [to New England] say I am dead, and then let my wife returne [to England], and child if shee will though there I wish them to stay.'

Elizabeth probably went to England in the early 1650s, when her mother returned there for the second time. She was in England by 3 March 1654, when her father wrote to John Winthrop Jr* about the actions of his attorneys in selling off his house at Salem, 'whereas by my letters I gave it to you and all I had there, in trust for my daughter if shee come over [to New England]'.

In the autumn of 1660, when Hugh Peter was imprisoned in the Tower of London, Elizabeth visited him daily. He wrote a manuscript for her, with advice and autobiographical reflections: *A dying father's last legacy to an onely child: or, Mr Hugh Peter's advice to his daughter; written by his own hand during his late imprisonment in the Tower of London* (1660). He advised Elizabeth to 'serve in some Godly Family ... But if you would go home to New-England (which you have much reason to do) go with good Company, and trust God there: the Church are a Tender Company'. After her father's death, Elizabeth stayed on in England and married Richard Barker.

> *Salem CR*, 17; Thomas Shepard to Hugh Peter, 1645, *American Historical Review*, 4 (1898), 105; *WP* V, 147; 4 *MHSC* 6: 116; Hugh Peter, *A dying father's last legacy to an onely child* (1660), 116–17; *ODNB, s.n.* 'Peter [Peters], Hugh (*bap.* 1598, *d.* 1660).

PETER, Hugh (1598–1660)

Hugh Peter [Peters] was born in Fowey, Cornwall, the son of a merchant, Thomas Peter (or Dickewoode) and his wife Martha. Thomas Peter* was his elder brother. Hugh Peter attended Trinity College, Cambridge. He graduated BA in 1618 and MA in 1622. He was ordained deacon in 1621 and priest in 1623, then became curate at Rayleigh, Essex. Around this time, Peter married his first wife, Elizabeth Reade, sister of George Cooke* and widow of Edmund

Reade of Wickford, Essex. John Winthrop Jr* married her daughter, another Elizabeth Reade. In 1626 Hugh Peter moved to London and became lecturer at St Sepulchre's in Holborn. He was involved in the work of the London feoffees for impropriations. In 1627, after his preaching licence was suspended, he fled to the Netherlands. Peter moved to and fro between the Low Countries and England, preaching illegally at Rayleigh and St Sepulchre's. He was in prison for some months. In Holland, he briefly took a university post at Friesland where William Ames (*ODNB*, father of William Ames*) was professor of theology; he also worked as a military chaplain. From 1629 to 1635 he served the English reformed church at Rotterdam, which from 1633 he shaped in congregationalist fashion. William Ames joined him at Rotterdam in 1633, but died soon after; John Davenport arrived in 1635. After Archbishop William Laud took direct control of the English churches in the Netherlands in 1633, resistance became more difficult. Hugh Peter looked to New England.[1]

Hugh Peter's arrival in New England in 1635 was noted by John Winthrop: 'Heere arrived 2: great shippes', and among the passengers 'Mr Peter pastor of the Englishe Church in Rotterdam'. Hugh Peter succeeded Roger Williams* as pastor at Salem, Massachusetts, and played a prominent part in church and civil life. Although he had some doubts in advance, he married, as his second wife, Deliverance*.

Five years later, Peter's return to England was under discussion. In 1640, English contacts urged Massachusetts to send agents to London, to solicit financial aid from parliament. This tactic was rejected: it might end in the imposition of laws on the colony, to its disadvantage. Instead, the Massachusetts authorities decided on a less direct approach: they could despatch agents to help with religious reform, who could also explain why Massachusetts had not met its financial commitments. Hugh Peter, William Hibbins* and Thomas Weld* were proposed for the task. The congregations at Salem and Roxbury were asked to release Peter and Weld from their ministry for a time. John Endecott (*ANB*) led opposition from within Salem church: he argued that the agents' mission would confirm the view that New England could never be self-sufficient, and so dishonour God, and discourage immigration and investment. Endecott questioned the wisdom of going 'from a place of safetie provided of God, to a place of danger under the hand of God to seeke reliefe for us', and whether it was proper for Peter and Weld to leave their churches to attend to secular business. Endecott also distrusted the proposed agents, as persons 'well-affected to the West Indies'. John Winthrop believed this last reason was the real cause for Endecott's opposition: Salem feared losing its pastor for good. Hugh Peter intended to leave with John Humfrey* (who was already committed to Lord Saye's venture in the West Indies), and would no doubt 'fall under strong temptations that way, being once in England'. As the matter was still unresolved when the planned time came for the agents to set sail, they deferred their departure. On 2 June 1641, the Massachusetts General Court asked the churches again to release Weld and Peter: this time, they agreed.[2]

On 3 August 1641, Hugh Peter left New England for England with William Hibbins and Thomas Weld. The forty passengers on their ship also included John Winthrop Jr and Thomas Lechford*.

In London, Peter and his fellow agents lobbied to reduce taxes and shipping regulations imposed by Commission for Foreign Plantations, with some success. In March 1641/2, a committee of the House of Lords recommended the removal of all restraints on ships, persons, and goods going to New England. In March 1642/3, parliament freed Massachusetts from customs duties on imports and exports. Alongside their lobbying activities, the agents raised funds. Peter, Hibbins and Weld collected over £2000 in money and supplies for Massachusetts. This included £500 in linens, woollens, other commodities sent in 1642 by Robert Houghton of Southwark, with the cooperation of Robert Sedgwick*, his brother-in-law and trading associate. It also included £500 in goods sent by William Willoughby, father of Francis Willoughby*, in the spring of 1643. During the winter of 1642-3 Hugh Peter and Thomas Weld helped John Winthrop Jr to raise funds for the Saugus ironworks. Also, they published *New Englands first fruits* (1643), which included a description of Harvard's first commencement, to encourage gifts for education and investment. Lady Ann Moulson (*ODNB*) gave £200 for New England and a scholarship of £100 for Harvard. Lady Mary Armine (*ODNB*) gave £20 a year in perpetuity to support preaching to the Indians, but the agents struggled to gain much more for this cause. Weld and Peter began to collect funds for the transportation of poor children from England and Ireland to New England: this project turned out to be fraught with difficulty, not least because some of £875 raised was pocketed by Nehemiah Bourne* and Emmanuel Downing*, and £200 was misappropriated by colonial authorities. In the summer of 1643, twenty children arrived in the colony, and more came later (the precise number is not known). To influence religious reform in England, as the Westminster Assembly prepared to start work in June 1643, Peter and Weld published *Church-government and church-covenant discussed*: this put into print several manuscripts which had been sent back from Massachusetts in the late 1630s, in response to critical enquiries from different parts of England about the nature of the 'New England Way'.[3]

William Hibbins returned to New England early in 1643, but not Weld and Peter. Their voyage was delayed. On 25 September 1643, Thomas Weld wrote to the Massachusetts General Court, on behalf of himself and Hugh Peter, to say that – as time had passed and winter was coming on – they dared not risk 'our owne and our wives healths and lives in a winter voyage'. Moreover, Weld went on:

> the present condition of this kingdome, that is now upon the Verticall point, together with the incredible importunities of very many godly Persons, great and smale (who hapily conceive we by our presence doe more good here, then we ourselves dare imagine that we doe) have made us, after many various thoughts, much agitation, and consultation with god and men, unwillingly willing to venter ourselves upon Gods Providence here, and be content to tarry one six moneths longer from your and our churches most desired presence with whom our hearts are, without the least wavering, fixed. Things cannot long stand at this passe here, as now, but will speedily be better or worse. If better, we shall not repent us to have bene messingers

of the good newes therof unto you. If worse, we are like to bring thousands with us to you.

Weld asked for this letter to be sent out to the churches at Roxbury and Salem, to which he and Peter were still bound as ministers.[4]

Hugh Peter became ever more deeply involved in English affairs. He became famous – infamous – as an army preacher and Independent. In 1642 he joined Lord Forbes's expeditionary force to Ireland, with fellow-colonists John Humfrey and William Rainborowe*. In the summer of 1643 he was active as a propagandist for parliament in Kent, Sussex, Surrey and Hampshire. In the winter of 1643–4, because of his personal knowledge of the Netherlands, he was sent there to raise support for parliament's cause. For this he was rewarded with £100 and 'a Study of Books, to that Value' (part of Archbishop Laud's library). In April 1645, the House of Commons voted him lands worth £200 a year. Nathaniel Ward* accused him of of deserting New England for financial gain. Hugh Peter supported Prides's Purge and the execution of Charles I. He was not a regicide but his name became synonymous with the policies of the Cromwellian regime. In 1651, he published *Good work for a good magistrate*, which set out a model for social reform. He was also concerned for ministry in Ireland and 'dark corners' of England: in 1649, he had been with Oliver Cromwell in Ireland; in 1652, with Cromwell, John Hewson, Charles Fleetwood, John Owen, Thomas Goodwin, Jenkin Lloyd and others, he discussed strategies for supplying Ireland with ministers and a stock of godly people – including inviting settlers back from New England. In 1654 Peter became one of the 'Triers' appointed to vet applicants for parish ministry and (as part of the process the Triers introduced for approving preachers) provided a certificate to vouch for his fellow Cornishman, the ex-colonist Joseph Hull*. As a patron, he presented the Harvard student Joseph Farnworth* to the rectory of South Hanningfield, Essex.[5]

Peter's relations with New England, as time passed, were mixed and on the whole uneasy. In 1649, the work of the Corporation for the Propagation of the Gospel in New England suffered because of Weld and Peter's supposed mismanagement of funds raised in England for the colonies. Weld and Peter managed to clear their names, but suspicion shifted to Massachusetts' misuse of the money. Hugh Peter found that Lady Armine's gift of £20 a year to support preaching to the Indians had not been delivered regularly to John Eliot, 'apostle to the Indians'. It had been diverted to other purposes – including work on the governor's house. In 1654 Peter denounced the Corporation, telling Edward Winslow* 'he heard the worke was but a plaine cheate, and that there was no such thing as gospell conversion amongst the Indians'. He was also dissatisfied in his personal financial dealings with Massachusetts: he complained about his attorney, Charles Gott, deacon of Salem, and in a letter of 3 March 1654 referred to 'the many unkindnesses I had from New England ... They owe me much mony'. Hugh Peter drew his brother, Thomas*, back to England. In 1652 he had urged John Winthrop Jr to come home, but by March 1654 Peter was prepared to support Cromwell's strategy of moving settlers to the West Indies. He advised Winthrop and his friends to 'looke to the

West Indyes, if they remove, for many are here to seeke when they come over'. A major cause of Peter's disenchantment with New England was intensely personal: the excommunication of his 'distracted' wife Deliverance* for devil possession, and the abrupt decision of the Massachusetts authorities to ship her to England.[6]

A particular cause of Peter's strained relations with New England was his strong advocacy of religious toleration. His support for peaceful co-existence with radicals, and his attempts to persuade Massachusetts to change its policy, met with disapproval in New England. Thomas Shepard wrote to him, 17 December 1645:

> you have had experience of the gangreene in New England ... let me be bolde (my deare brother) to perswade you to be watchfull over your selfe, least your heart herein out of love to some men growes cold to God's truth ... is it not high time for all God's ministers to awaken and purge God's floure of such chaff ... I know the honesty of the heart of brother Peters cannot beare with it, but he will take to him the zeale of his God and do worthily herein ...

The former colonist Giles Firmin* wished Peter 'did not too much countenance the Opinionists, which wee did so cast out in N. England. I know hee abhorrs them in his heart, but hee hath many hang upon him, being a man of such use'. Peter responded to his critics by urging change in the colony, pointing out that it was isolating itself from influential currents in English opinion. He cautioned New England to 'bee tender towards those that hold Christ for the head, and would live quietly under your government'. If New England could show more tolerance it would win support in England: 'What will you doe with men dissenting? Devise a way for them to live ... and you will have many frends here.'

Despite awkwardness on various fronts, Massachusetts still called on Peter for help. Thomas Shepard, while taking Peter to task for his conduct in England, tried to secure for Harvard the books Peter had received from Archbishop Laud's library:

> we have very good wits among us and they grow up mightily, but we want books ... we want schoolmen especially ... we were thinking to desire the Archbishop's Library, and that the Parliament would recompence your labours for publike good with somewhat more usefull for your self.

In response to this request, which seems to have come to him from more than one correspondent, Peter assured John Winthrop 'my bookes you may tell the elders I shall bring with mee'. A few years later, worried that conflict with the Dutch would spread to the New World, the Massachusetts General Court asked Peter to deploy his influence in London and intercede with Cromwell for help: the colony needed to 'make use of all our lost friends amongst whome [we] canot but rank yourselfe amongst the chiefe'.[7]

For a long time, Peter kept promising to return to Massachusetts. In the early 1640s, the Salem church and the secular authorities expected him to arrive at any moment. In 1645, when Peter's pledge of returning quickly was well worn out, both ordered him back. The General Court appointed others, including Richard Saltonstall* and George Cooke, to take over the role of negotiating with the Warwick Commission in land disputes with Rhode Island. On 23 June 1645 Peter had asked John Winthrop Jr to 'assure all that I am coming to you'. On 4 September 1646, in a short note that criticised New England for intolerance, he declared 'I am coming over if I must.' In November 1646, his tone shifted: he tried to persuade Governor Winthrop to travel home to England, to 'assiste in the Parliamentes cause'. The following spring, Peter's tone altered again. In a letter to Winthrop, he made extravagant declarations of affection: 'truly nothing but death can part us ... Oh that I were to dye in your bosome. Nothing in the world more affects mee then my being here ... I am resolved to come ... The lord helpe us to wash off all scandalls, we have contracted by our staying here'. A short while later he had to come up with an excuse for his failure to set sail. He had been delayed by poor health and the time it had taken to sell off the land given to him by parliament as pay. But he firmly intended to take next ship: 'I am sure my spirit these 2 or 3 yeares hath bin restles about my stay here, and nothing under heaven but the especiall hand of the lord could stay mee.' Several more letters at this time echoed these sentiments, and he still struck this note in 1654: 'I profes nothing but want of health (I thinke) could detayne me from New England: such is my love to the place.' In *Gangraena*, Thomas Edwards mocked Hugh Peter for wavering on the brink of return:

> one Mr Peters the Soliciter Generall for the Sectaries ... how often in Pulpits he hath taken his leave of Old England, and every Spring for some years told them of his present going to New-England ... And Mr Peters is so bold, daring, and active for the Sectaries, that against all their own Church-Principles (their most sacred, that of the power of the Church) Mr Peters is kept here and must not go to New-England ... [he] had expresse Letters from the Church of which he is Minister, without all excuse or longer delay to come away to New-England as this last Summer; Himself meeting a Minister of my special acquaintance, told him, I am now going for New-England shortly: To whom, my Friend said, I, you have been long a going, I will not believe it. Mr Peters Replied, I, but now I go, certainly I must, the Church hath commanded ... and drew out the Letters. But upon occasion of the Churches writing thus ... there are meetings of several Independent Ministers ... to consult and resolve this case of conscience about Mr Peters going, considering the peremptory call of the Church; the result ... was, that Mr Peters being so useful a man, should not go, but stay in England; and the objection of the command of the Church being urged, it was Answered, and so Resolved, That if the Church were twenty Churches that sent for him, he should not go.

Shortly before his death, Peter expressed deep regret at having stayed in England:

It hath lain to my heart above anything almost, that I left that People I was engaged to in New-England, it cuts deeply, I look upon it as a Root-evil: and though I was never Parson nor Vicar, never took Ecclesiastical promotion, never preached upon any agreement for money in my life, though not without offers and great ones; yet I had a Flock, I say, I had a Flock, to whom I was ordained, who were worthy of my Life and Labours ... but here I was overpowered to stay.

Although Hugh Peter was not a regicide, he and Sir Henry Vane Jr* were added by parliament to those excluded from pardon at the Restoration. He was executed at Tower Hill on 16 October 1660.[8]

Publications *Milk for babes* (1630); *Digitus Dei. Or good newes from Holland* (1631); *A true relation of the passages of Gods providence in a voyage for Ireland* ([1642]); *The full and last relation, of all things concerning Basing-House* (1645); *Mr Peters report from Bristol* (1645); *Mr Peters report from the army* (1645); *Gods doings, and mans duty* (1646); *Master Peters messuage from Sir Thomas Fairfax* ([1646]); *Mr Peters last report of the English vvars* (1646); *Severall propositions... concerning the Presbyterian ministers of this kingdome* (1646); *A word for the Armie. And two words to the kingdome* (1647); *A letter from Ireland* (1649); *Æternitati sacrum* ([1651]); *Good work for a good magistrate. Or, A short cut to great quiet* (1651); *A dying fathers last legacy to an onely child* (1660); *A sermon by Hugh Peters: preached before his death* (1660). Various scurrilous and scathing pamphlets were printed around the time of his death, such as: *Hugh Peters figaries: Or, his merry tales and jests* (1660); *Don Pedro de Quixot, or in English the right reverend Hugh Peters* (1660).

[1] And throughout, R.P. Stearns, *The strenuous puritan: Hugh Peter 1598–1660* (Urbana, IL: University of Illinois Press, 1954).
[2] *WJ*, 156, 345–50, 354, 355 and *passim*; *WP* IV, 112–3; R.P. Stearns, 'The Weld-Peter mission to England', Colonial Society of Massachusetts, *Publications*, 32 (1937), 185–246; Endecott to Winthrop, c. Feb. 1640/1, *WP* IV, 314–15.
[3] *WJ*, 402–4, 429n., 608, 743, 744; Stearns, 'Weld-Peter'; E.D. Hartley, *Ironworks on the Saugus* (Norman, OK: University of Oklahoma Press, 1957), 54–5; *Pilgrims*, 45–9; Graeme J. Milne, 'New England agents and the English Atlantic, 1641–1666' (PhD dissertation, University of Edinburgh, 1993), 305 and *passim*.
[4] Stearns, 'Weld-Peter', 220–1.
[5] Stearns, 'Weld-Peter'; J.E. Christopher Hill, 'Puritans and the "Dark Corners of the Land"', in his *Change and continuity in seventeenth century England* (London: Weidenfeld and Nicolson, 1974), 25, 42–5; T.C. Barnard, *Cromwellian Ireland: English government and reform in Ireland 1649–1660* (Oxford: Oxford University Press, 1975), 96.
[6] Stearns, 'Weld-Peter'; 4 *MHSC* 6: 114–17.
[7] Thomas Shepard to Hugh Peter, 1645, *American Historical Review*, 4 (1898), 105–7; Carla Gardina Pestana, *The English Atlantic in an age of revolution, 1640–1661* (Cambridge, MA: Harvard University Press, 2004), 60, 69–71; *WP* V, 89, 146–7, 157–9; Mass. Archives, 106: 24 (draft of a letter from the General Court to Peter, 1654).
[8] *WJ*, 654–5; Mass. Archives, 106: 4a; *Mass. Recs*. 2: 137, 3: 48; Stearns, 'Weld-Peter',

235; *WP* V, 30–1, 102, 146–7, 157–9 and *passim*; 4 *MHSC* 6: 117; Edwards, *Gangraena*, i. 98–9; Hugh Peter, *A dying father's last legacy to an onely child* (1660), 108–9.

BDBR, CCEd Person ID 42519, *GM* 5: 442–5, ODNB.

PETER, Thomas (1597–1654)

Thomas Peter [Peters], elder brother of Hugh Peter*, was born at Fowey in Cornwall. He attended Brasenose College, Oxford, and graduated BA in 1614, MA in 1625. He was vicar of Mylor, Cornwall, in 1628. On 25 September 1632 he married Anne Rowe. Thomas Peter sailed for New England in 1643, to escape civil war: Edward Winslow* described him as 'a Minister that was driven out of Cornewall by Sir Ralph Hopton in these late Warres, and fled to New England for shelter'.

Peter settled at Saybrook, not long before George Fenwick* returned to England late in 1644. On 29 June 1645, Peter wrote to John Winthrop in the aftermath of conflict between the Narragansett and Pequot Indians, and revealed the fragility of morale among his companions:

> many heer fear Mr Fenwick will not come more and I fear then that this plantation wille flaw . . . we shalbe about 50 soules at the arrivall of Goodman Skidmore, whereof 30 wilbe infants so that we may call it an infant plantation, sine tropo. Mrs Mary [Fenwick*] and the child[ren] are likely to be gon for England if I can guesse, and much talk is in every mouth for the like voyage . . .

Peter's communication with his family, left behind in England, was very poor: 'Sir I thank your inquiry for my letters. Oh keep still on, till some arrive per hands that may testifie my wifes life and childrens welfare.' c.1646 he wrote to John Winthrop of having sent eighteen letters to his brother Hugh, 'and so to my wife, yet never could receive one syllable from either'. In May 1646 Thomas Peter was appointed pastor of Pequot Plantation (New London), but became ill and teetered on the brink of returning home. William Morton feared this: 'If Mr Peters goe for Old england it will much dash our beginnings our plantation beinge in the infancie manye being discouraged.' In September 1646, Hugh Peter wrote from England to John Winthrop Jr* and asked him to 'send my brother to his wife and family'. John Jones of Fairfield agreed to take Thomas Peter's place as preacher at New London that winter.

Thomas Peter was in Boston on 5 November 1646, ready to set sail. He heard John Cotton preach at the Thursday lecture, against Thomas Fowle* and the other Remonstrants who were about to sail for England. Cotton instructed their fellow passengers to throw the Remonstrants' petition into the sea, as a 'Jonas' that would bring disaster. Thomas Peter apparently took this to heart:

> being called back by his people . . . upon Mr Cotton's exhortation, having shipped his goods and bedding to have gone in the Ship with them, amongst other arguments this was the maine, that he feared to go in their company

that had such designes, and therefore took passage to goe rather by way of Spaine.

Peter sailed away from New England on 19 December 1646, taking a ship from Nantasket instead of Boston.

On 27 April 1647, from London, Thomas Peter sent a letter to John Winthrop by means of Nehemiah Bourne*, with the latest national news, and tidings of Hugh Peter and Stephen Winthrop*. He had persuaded some friends to give £10 a year for a schoolmaster at Roxbury, to teach the Indians. He told Winthrop that correspondence could be sent to him via the London merchant William Pennoyer (*BDBR*).

Thomas Peter probably went back to Mylor later in 1647. The content of a letter he sent in June 1648 to John Winthrop Jr, from Falmouth, suggests he had been back in the West Country for a while. In his opinion, 'there is no good to be done for Pequit by the Londoners, who for the major part are base and rotten'. He asked Winthrop to retrieve £10 or £12 owed to him by the planters and send it over in 'beaver' (beaver pelts) to his sister, Bridget Peter, at Limehouse near London. In 1652, as 'Pastor of the Church at Mylor in Cornwall', Peter published an assize sermon he had recently preached at Launceston, Cornwall, *A remedie against ruine*. He addressed the 'Epistle Dedicatory', to Richard Lobb, high sheriff of Cornwall (father of the minister Stephen Lobb, *ODNB*). Thomas Peter had become Lobb's chaplain, and expressed thanks to his patron: 'At my return from New-England to London you sought me diligently and found me out, And ever since have refreshed me with an annuall as personall countenance to my Lecture at Penrin, and contribution to my Labours at Mylor.' In the sermon, Peter vindicated himself against a charge of perjury from Sampson Bond (*CR*). Richard Lobb had written from Falmouth to Edward Winslow, 22 December 1651, warning Winslow about Bond, 'a notorious Insynuatinge Hypocrite' who might have made off with money belonging to the New England Company. Peter's sermon spoke of the need for justice: he opposed the prevalent 'hideous blasphemies, hellish heresies, uncouth Errors'. He died at Mylor in 1654.

Publication *A remedie against ruine* (1652).

R.P. Stearns, *The strenuous puritan: Hugh Peter 1598–1660* (Urbana, IL: University of Illinois Press, 1954), 366, 436; Edward Winslow, *New-Englands salamander* (1647), 18; *NEHGR* 2: 63–4; *WP* V, 20 86, 93, 104, 113, 129–30, 150, 233–4; Thomas Peter, *A remedie against ruine* (1652), t.p., 'Epistle dedicatory', 15–16, 22; Lobb to Winslow, 22 December 1651, Bodleian, Rawlinson MS D. 934, fol. 22.

BDBR, ODNB.

PHILLIP, John (*c.*1582–1660)

John Phillip [Phillips] was admitted to Emmanuel College, Cambridge, on 27 June 1600. He graduated BA early in 1604, and MA in 1607. He was ordained deacon at Peterborough on 16 July 1607, and priest at Norwich on 24 September 1609, aged twenty-four. He served as rector of Wrentham, Suffolk, from 24 July 1609. On 6 January 1611/12 he married Elizabeth Ames, sister of the minister and theologian William Ames (*ODNB*). Hugh Peter* sent a letter to him from Rotterdam on 23 June 1633, which was intercepted by Clement Corbet (*ODNB*). Corbet was chancellor to Matthew Wren, bishop of Norwich. The letter concerned the distribution of Ames's prohibited book, *A fresh suit against human ceremonies in God's worship*. Three years later, Phillip was excommunicated for not appearing at Wren's visitation – the controversial visitation of 1636. Phillip was reported to be:

> a man very factious, and contemptuous of order and government; one that seldom or never read the confession, or Absolution; and in that churching of a woman, uses to receive an handkerchief at hir hand and sayeth welcome abroad neighbour and that's all.

On 27 November 1636 Corbet told Wren that Phillip was rumoured to be in Holland.[1]

John and Elizabeth Phillip left for New England in 1638, with others from Wrentham. Their time in New England was unsettled. John Phillip had many invitations but avoided a binding commitment. He had been encouraged to come over to New England by the Dedham church, whose minister, John Allin (the father of John Allin*), had been married at Wrentham in 1622. In 1637–8, the Dedham godly were gathering a church with difficulty, but 'did expect and much indeavoured the guidance and helpe of Mr Jo. Phillips who came over that summer with some godly company and had bene invited to this plantation by letters formerly'. However, Phillip, 'delaying his resolution', prevented the church from completing its formation. He settled first at Salem, under Hugh Peter's ministry. Salem granted him land, on condition that he remained there. With some of his Wrentham flock, he founded Salem Farms or Wenham. Phillip had also been invited to Cambridge, and seems to have moved from Salem to Cambridge early in 1639, perhaps to act as an interim president of Harvard after the disgrace of Nathaniel Eaton*. John and Elizabeth Phillip lived in one of Herbert Pelham's* houses while building their own. Two Cambridge church members – John Fessenden and Richard Cutter – mentioned a 'Mr Phillip' in their confessions: this was probably John Phillip (not George Phillips as the editors suggest). When the Dedham church called him once again in March 1640, Phillip accepted, 'the lord ordering things so by a speciall providence that he no wher setled but was freed from all ingagements'. He and Elizabeth became church members at Dedham on 31 May 1640. However, Phillip still seems to have avoided being installed as a minister. Thomas Lechford*, who left Boston in August 1641, described John Phillip as 'out of office'.[2]

John Phillip left New England about three months after parliament declared Wren unfit to hold office as a bishop; in other words, as soon as the news reached New England. He and Elizabeth set sail on 26 October 1641, probably in company with Robert Peck* (also returning to his old parish) and the disenchanted John Humfrey*. John Winthrop recalled how the ship had a 'fair and speedy voyage' almost all the way home, but three ministers and a schoolmaster kept up a torrent of complaints against New England. Close to England's shores, the ship ran into such a tempest that it could carry no sail. The passengers fell to prayer, and attributed the storm to the hand of God as a punishment for speaking evil of New England and its people. One man – John Phillip – had spoken up for New England. For his sake, God spared the ship, 'when they expected every moment to have been dashed upon the rocks'. The Dedham church had (on the whole) given its blessing to Phillip:

> our Reverend brother mr John Philips with his wife propounding divers reasons of thier intended departure and returne to England for the satisfaction of the Church therin and further advise about the same the Church though divers were unsatisfied in his reasons yet yeilded consent to his departure . . .

Phillip sold three acres of land and part of a house to the Dedham church in 1641, but kept his house in Cambridge.³

Back in England, Phillip returned to his old parish of Wrentham, probably immediately. Robert Asty (*CR*) had served the parish in his absence. c.1646, Phillip was joined by his nephew William Ames*, a Harvard graduate.

In 1643 Phillip became a member of the Westminster Assembly, one of two ministers appointed for Suffolk. He was the only person present who had first-hand experience of New England: although John Cotton, John Davenport and Thomas Hooker had been invited to return to England to join the Assembly, they had declined. Phillip did not play a major part. In fact, he rarely spoke – like the majority at the Assembly, he was a silent member. His few speeches recorded in the Assembly Minutes made no mention of New England. His name appeared in the records most frequently in the autumn of 1643. Phillip was probably there to put up his hand on 25 September 1643, to affirm the Solemn League and Covenant with the Scots to bring 'a Reformation of three Kingdoms'. He made brief interventions to temper the Assembly's crackdown on antinomian opinion, which tallied with a paper he signed in 1640 in Massachusetts, with Thomas Weld* among others, on 'propositions concerning evidence of God's love'. He spoke up for 'the divine institution of a doctor [teaching elder] in every congregation, as well as a pastor', a reflection of the Reformed ministry he had seen in New England. Phillip made short contributions to other debates in November and December 1643, but then seems to have been absent. In August 1645 he was added to a committee to consider on what grounds people could be suspended from communion. Phillip did not sign a pro-presbyterian petition from Suffolk and Essex ministers to the House of Lords in 1646, but after parliament voted to make England presbyterian he was nominated to a local division of the Suffolk classis (presbytery). The Scottish presbyterian, Robert Baillie, identified Phillip as an Independent.⁴

In the 1640s Phillip was held in high regard by congregationalists in East Anglia. The Wrentham church was treated as a congregational church well before it had formally 'gathered' by covenant. Norwich members of the Yarmouth congregational church, who were thinking of gathering their own church, wrote to Phillip for advice. The Yarmouth church gave one of its members, Brother Purgall, a letter of recommendation to Wrentham. Entries in Wrentham's parish register suggest that Phillip limited baptism to the children of godly families after he came back from New England. From 1641 the register listed most children by date of birth, not baptism (unusual in the 1640s although it became a legal requirement in the 1650s). 'Baptised' was sometimes added later. Once parliament cleared the path for wider toleration, so that forming a congregational church had legal sanction, Phillip gathered a congregational church in his parish at Wrentham. On 1 February 1649/50, he read out a rationale and a confession of faith 'at the first meeting and gathering into Church fellowship'. This described the church-gathering as 're-forming' the church into its primitive purity. His wife Elizabeth was present, and was admitted as a member of the church at the next meeting. This gathered church kept its own records of church life – admissions, baptisms and so on. Phillip continued to act as parish minister, providing public preaching, alongside his ministry to the gathered church. A parochial survey, 15 October 1650, gave Robert Brewster as the patron of Wrentham, and valued the living at £60 a year. Phillip was said to be 'an Antient and Reverend preaching Minister ... [who] supplyes the Cure every Lordes daye with the assistance of Mr William Amys sonne to the late Reverend Doctor Amys'. Phillip acted as pastor, William Ames* as teacher.[5]

Phillip kept his property in Cambridge, Massachusetts, but it went to rack and ruin. On 8 February 1649/50, the president of Harvard, Henry Dunster, wrote to Phillip to ask what he intended to do with his house. It 'now lyeth in so uncertaine a condition that none knowes whose it is, nor who should repaire it though in severall places it becomes ruinous'. There was a move afoot to seize the house and sell it off to pay Phillip's debts.[6]

John Phillip died in 1660, not long after the Restoration came. He was buried at Wrentham on 5 September. He was not ejected from the living at Wrentham, which he had held for more than fifty years. His will, made on 21 March 1658/9, was proved on 6 November 1660 by his wife Elizabeth as executrix. It mentioned lands in Wrentham, and made bequests to relatives, local people, and to the poor of the town and church of Wrentham. It made no reference to New England.[7]

---

[1] *GD*; J. Browne, *A history of congregationalism in Norfolk and Suffolk* (London: Jarrold & Sons, 1877), 422–3; Bodleian, Tanner MS 68, fols 99, 178; Roger Thompson, *Mobility and migration: East Anglian founders of New England, 1629–1640* (Amherst, MA: University of Massachusetts Press, 1994), 261.

[2] Colonial Society of Massachusetts, *Publications*, 18 (1913–14), 208–15; R.P. Stearns, *The strenuous puritan: Hugh Peter 1598–1660* (Urbana, IL: University of Illinois Press, 1954), 131; *WP* IV, 109; *Dedham CR*, 7, 8, 23; *Shepard's confessions*, 177, 180; Lechford *PD*, 38.

[3] *WJ*, 414–5; *Dedham CR*, 37; MHS, Misc. Bd. MSS, 1641; *Pilgrims*, 97.

[4] Bush, 362–5; Sargent Bush, Jr, 'Thomas Hooker and the Westminster Assembly', *William and Mary Quarterly*, 3rd series, 29 (1972), 291–300; Alexander Henderson and Philip Nye, *The covenant: with a narrative of the proceedings and solemn manner*

of taking it by the honourable House of Commons, and reverent Assembly of Divines (1643), 10, 14; Chad Van Dixhoorn, ed. *The Minutes and Papers of the Westminster Assembly 1643-1652*, 5 vols (Oxford: Oxford University Press, 2012), 2: 159-60, 289, 294, 303, 332, 359, 415, 661 (Phillip's contributions to debates) and 2: 30, 261, 491, 3: 5, 647, 652, 4: 124-25, 140-41 (Phillip in lists of committee or Assembly members); *Pilgrims*, 129. 'Propositions concerning evidence of God's love', 7 September 1640, *WP* IV, 286–7: Michael P.Winship, *Making heretics: militant protestantism and free grace in Massachusetts, 1636–1641* (Princeton, NJ and Oxford: Princeton University Press, 2002), 223–4, suggests the propositions are close to the theology of Richard Sibbes (*ODNB*); Phillip's fellow signatories in Massachusetts were Thomas Weld* and John Eliot of Roxbury, John Allin of Dedham, Thomas Shepard of Cambridge, Richard Mather and Jonathan Burr of Dorchester and John Wilson* of Boston.

[5] Norwich CB, 23 April, 29 May, 10 June 1644; Yarmouth CB, 19 March 1645/6; Suffolk Record Office, Lowestoft Branch, 168/D1/1, Wrentham Parish Records; Wrentham CB; NA, RG 4/3098, Suffolk, Wrentham (Independent), Births and Baptisms, 1650–1785 (a record of baptisms in the gathered church, at one time part of Wrentham CB); LPL, MS COMM. XIIa/15/570–1; *Pilgrims*, 123–4, 128–30; J. Browne, *The congregational church at Wrentham in Suffolk: its history and biographies* (London: Jarrold & Sons, 1854), 1–18; W.A. Shaw, *A history of the English Church . . . 1640–1660* (London: Longmans & Green, 1900), II, 425; Browne, *Congregationalism*, 163, 607–8.

[6] MHS, MHS, MS N-1143, 'Henry Dunster Notebook, 1628–54', fol. 117; Cambridge TR, fols 105, 109.

[7] DWL, MS 38.59, A.G. Matthews's notes of nonconformist ministers' wills, fols 768–9; *CCEd* Person ID 126730.

CR.

PIERCE, Mark (1597–1656)

In 1639 Mark Pierce [Peirce] appeared among those who subscribed to the founding agreement of New Haven. He may also have had land at Cambridge, Massachusetts. He was appointed public surveyor for New Haven in 1642. In 1643 he was fined with Theophilus Higginson for being late at militia training. He took the oath of fidelity, 1 July 1644, and was assigned a seat in the New Haven meetinghouse as a church member, 10 March 1646/7. He offered to teach the children of the town, 1645.

By the spring of 1650, Pierce was in Boston, trying to decide whether to go back to England, or stay on. He had just sold his house in New Haven, and its contents. On 6 May 1650, John Davenport, minister at New Haven, wrote to John Cotton, minister at Boston:

> I understand that Brother Pierce hath delivered unto you a Copie of some sermons preached by me, in our weekly lecture . . . The Forenamed brother diligently wrote, as his manner was, but finding that his head and pen could not carry away some materiall expressions, he earnestly desired me to lett him have my notes, to perfect his owne by them, which I promised him in the winter was twelve moneths. Having other hindrances, he called not for

them . . . but being in the Bay, & unresolved about his stay there, or passage for England, or return hither, he wrote for these notes . . . which accordingly I sent to him . . .

Davenport added that he had asked Pierce to send the notes back to New Haven 'by a safe land-messenger': in 1646, he had lost precious manuscript sermons in a shipwreck. He had entrusted them to Thomas Gregson* on the voyage that claimed Gregson's life.

Pierce went back to England in 1652 or 1653. He made a will in London on 10 February 1654/5, against the time when 'it shall please God to put an ende to my fraile life and pilgramage in this world'. He mentioned £40 in hands of his good friend Robert Newman*, 'citizen and vintner of London'. Pierce chose Newman as an executor. He also remembered £10 in hands of Elizabeth Higginson, 'which I lent to her deceased husband Theophilus Higginson, in N.E. and ought to have been paid presently at our arrival in England as by a bill of his hand appeareth'. He left 'unto Master Davenport pastor to the Church in newhaven in new England fortie shillings'. Other bequests were to family and friends in England.

When he made his will, Pierce was on his way to Ireland, and had perhaps already been in Ireland. He referred to goods already there, at the house of 'Mr Ludlow' (Roger Ludlow*) in Dublin, and in the hands of Samuel Caffinch (perhaps formerly of New Haven, brother of John Caffinch*). Pierce attached to his will a lengthy schedule of goods he was about to carry with him to Ireland – cloth, scarves, hoods, buttons, ribbons and thread, hats and hatbands, pearl necklaces, dozens of spectacles, casks of tobacco, a hogshead of ginger. The will was proved on 3 June 1656.

New Haven TR, 60; Bush, 436, 440; NA, PROB 11/256/355, will of 'Mark Peirce' of London, 3 June 1656.

PRATT, Abraham (*c.*1580–1644) and Joanna (d. 1644)

Abraham Pratt emigrated from the parish of St Brides, Southwark, in 1630. He had been appointed surgeon to the ship *Lions Whelp*, and to the Massachusetts Bay Company. He and his wife Joanna [Jane] settled in Massachusetts, at Roxbury and Cambridge for a time, then at Charlestown.

Pratt set off for England with his wife in 1644. He hoped to find work as a surgeon during the civil war. They sailed in the *Sea Fort* of Boston, built by Thomas Hawkins*, on 23 November. In December, the *Sea Fort* was wrecked off the coast of Spain. Abraham and Joanna were among nineteen passengers who drowned. Other passengers aboard included 'Mr Kerman'* and Giles Firmin*, a young 'apothecary physician'. Winthrop recorded the episode and commented on Pratt:

This man was aboue 60: yeares olde, an experienced Surgeon, who had liued in New England many yeares, & was of the first church in Cambridge in Mr Hooke[r]s tyme, & had good practice & wanted nothing. But he had been long discontented, because his employment was not so profitable to himselfe as he desired, & it is like he feared least he should fall into want in his olde age, & therefore he would needes goe backe into England (for Surgeons were then in great request there by occasion of the warres) but God took him awaye, childlesse.

NEHGR 143: 35; *Roxbury CR*, 76–7; Roger Thompson, *From deference to defiance: Charlestown, Massachusetts, 1629–1662* (Boston, MA: New England Historic Genealogical Society, 2012), 18n., 22, 27; *GMB* 1504–7; *WJ*, 598–9; *Pilgrims*, 66.

PRICHARD, Hugh

Hugh Prichard emigrated in Richard Blinman's* company in 1640, one of a party from Wales. He was at Gloucester, Massachusetts, in 1642 but soon settled at Roxbury. He joined the Roxbury church, recommended by the church at Cape Ann (Gloucester), where Blinman preached. He became a freeman of Massachusetts on 18 May 1642, and served as a deputy for Roxbury in 1643, 1644 and 1649. He was captain of the town's train-band in 1644. In May 1647, after the death in October 1646 of Joseph Weld*, captain of the Roxbury train-band,

> the yonge men of the Towne agreed togither: to choose one Geo: denyson a yonge soldier come lately out of the warres in England, which the Ancient & cheife men of the Towne understandinge, they came togither at: the tyme apponted, & chose one mr Pricharde, a godly man & one of the cheife in the town, passinge by their Leiutenant . . . wherevpon muche discontent & murmuringe arose in the Towne: the yonge men were ouer strongly bent to have their will, althoughe their Election was voyd in Lawe (Geo: Denyson not beinge then a freeman) & the Aunceint men over voted them aboue 20: & the Leiutenant was discontented because he was neglected, &c: The cause was comminge to the Court, & all partyes being heard, mr Prichard was allowed, & the young men were pacified, & the Leiutenant . . .

Prichard went to Wales in 1650. On 25 June 1651, 'Capt. Hugh Prichard late of Roxbury' sold land to John Ruggles. In 1657, his attorneys sold 50 acres to John Pierpont, describing Prichard as of Broughton, Denbighshire. A 'Hugh Prichard' signed a letter to John Thurloe about a Cavalier plot, 8 March 1654/5, with Morgan Llwyd and others of Wrexham. In 1655 the name appeared on a petition from several churches in Wales against wickedness in high places; other signatories included Morgan Llwyd (*ODNB*), Vavasor Powell (*ODNB*) and Richard Saltonstall*, although Thurloe noted that many of the signatures were in the same hand.

Artillery Company, 133; *GM* 6: 110; *NEHGR* 3: 189; *WJ*, 687–8, 718; *Thurloe* III, 207, IV, 380–4, 505. For Morgan Llwyd's congregational church at Wrexham, and Vavasor Powell, see G.F. Nuttall, *Visible saints: the congregational way, 1640–1660* (Oxford: Blackwell, 1957), 35–6.

PYNCHON, William (1590–1662)

William Pynchon was born on 26 December 1590 at Springfield in Essex, the son of John and Frances Pynchon. He was one of the original patentees of the Massachusetts Bay Company charter in 1629.

Pynchon arrived in New England in 1630, with the Winthrop fleet. He settled at Roxbury, Massachusetts, where he was first on the list of church members. He was elected as an assistant of the Bay Company, 1630–6, 1642–50. Pynchon used his influence as a magistrate, and capital raised from his sale of English lands, to become the colony's leading fur trader. His wife, Anne, died during their first winter in Roxbury, and in 1632 he married Frances Samford of Dorchester.

In pursuit of profit from the fur-trade, Pynchon established a settlement in 1635 at Agawam (Springfield), further north than other communities. At first Springfield was associated with Connecticut, but in 1641 the town placed itself under the jurisdiction of Massachusetts, with Pynchon in control. His letters in the 1640s commented on English affairs. He blessed God for the covenant between England and Scotland: 'It is the high way of god for deliuerance. I hope it is now the day of Antichrists great overrthrow at Armageddon.' He lamented divisions between the Scots and parliament, and 'the lawlessenesse of liberty of conscience . . . that vile tenet'. In the autumn of 1646, he expressed concern about the number of people leaving New England for England: 'which the land can ill spaire without a shaking ague: the pillars of the land seeme to tremble'. Pynchon noted parliament's refusal to adopt wholesale either the claims of the Scottish presbyterians or of the English independents. He endorsed this:

> the Parliament say that neather of them is the only way of Christ . . . truly where zeale of gods glory and godly wisdome are joyned together: a world of good hath bin don by godly ministers even in England that have held no certain fourme of discipline.

On 19 October 1648 he told John Winthrop he thought that England was 'in the saddest posture that ever they were for danger of ruine'.[1]

In 1650 Pynchon visited England, and, describing himself as a 'New English Gentleman', published *The meritorious price of our redemption*. This tract argued against the imputation of sins only to Christ on the Cross (penal substitution); redemption was achieved, Pynchon argued, by the imputation of the 'mediatoriall obedience' of Christ, shown throughout his life, 'whereof his Mediatoriall sacrifice of Atonement was the Master-piece'. He seems to have held this view for many years, but his decision to publish a book in 1650 had been influenced by Richard Baxter's *Aphorismes of justification* (1649), and the storm it had aroused. Later, he wrote to tell Baxter that he had heard his views

> so much preached against by Mr Wareham [John Warham of Windsor, Connecticut] . . . as if you held justification by works: and for denying faith

to be the instrument of Justification . . . I herd him tosse your name many tymes out in a sermon, at which I was much grieved and spak my mind to friends that beleeved as I did that he did mistake the sense . . .

Pynchon returned from England to face uproar in New England. The Massachusetts General Court ordered his book to be burnt, and Pynchon was summoned to appear in May 1651. He refused to attend, but wrote to say his position had been misunderstood. Letters were sent from England to support him, by Sir Henry Vane Jr[*] and others, much to the embarrassment of the Massachusetts authorities. Pynchon still declined to come to court, despite renewed orders in September 1651 and May 1652. The authorities were concerned that, as Pynchon had styled himself a 'New English Gentleman', many in England might think New England concurred 'in the allowance of such Exorbitant Aberrations'. John Norton, minister at Boston, was commissioned to write a riposte to Pynchon's book. Three elders were appointed to speak with Pynchon.[2]

Pynchon left New England for good in September 1652, with his wife Frances. George Moxon[*], minister of Springfield, who sympathised with Pynchon, also left. Ann and Henry Smith[*], Pynchon's daughter and son-in-law, soon followed. His son John Pynchon, and his daughters Mary Holyoke and Margaret Davis, remained in New England.

As soon as Pynchon reached England, he put another book through the London press: *The Jewes synagogue*, which argued that churches should take their form from Hebrew synagogues, not the New Testament. The book-collector George Thomason (*ODNB*) marked on his copy that he received it on 31 December 1652. On the title page, Pynchon was still described as 'of Springfield in N. England'. Pynchon settled at Wraysbury in Buckinghamshire. He wrote to Richard Baxter c.1654–5, and sent Baxter his book *The time when the first sabbath was ordained* (or its second edition, *Holy time*). In 1655 Pynchon wrote to Baxter again, and this time enclosed his reply to John Norton, *A farther discussion of that great point in divinity the sufferings of Christ*. This described Pynchon as 'Late of New England'. Nicholas Chewney attacked Pynchon's views in his *Anti-Socinianism* (1656).[3]

Pynchon's will, made on 4 October 1662, was proved on 8 December 1662. He made bequests to people in old and New England. Henry Smith and John Wickens were appointed as overseers in England. Wickens also oversaw Pynchon's interests in Virginia. John Pynchon, who played an important role in the government and economy of Springfield, took over his father's interests in New England. His wife Frances Pynchon died at Wraysbury.[4]

Publications *The meritorious price of our redemption* (1650); *The Jewes synagogue* (1652); *The time when the first Sabbath was ordained* (1654); *A farther discussion of that great point in divinity the sufferings of Christ* (1655); *The covenant of nature made with Adam described* (1662).

[1] And throughout, S. E. Morison, 'William Pynchon, the founder of Springfield', MHS *Proceedings* 64 (1930–2), 67–107 and Bernard Bailyn, *The New England merchants*

in the seventeenth century (Cambridge, MA: Harvard University Press, 1955), 29, 31, 53–5; *Roxbury CR*, 73; *WP* III, 267; *WP* IV, 36–7, 54, 84, 98–9, 443–4; *WP* V, 90–2, 114–15, 134–7, 271.

[2] Pynchon to Baxter, 27 April 1655, DWL Baxter Letters 3/186, summarised in N.H. Keeble and Geoffrey F. Nuttall, eds, *Calendar of the correspondence of Richard Baxter*, 2 vols (Oxford: Clarendon Press, 1991), letter 244; John Norton, *A discussion of that great point in divinity, the sufferings of Christ, and the questions about his righteousness . . . and the imputation thereof* (London, 1653), 'Epistle Dedicatory', 13–15, and the appended letter from John Cotton, Richard Mather, Zechariah Symmes, John Wilson* and William Thompson to English ministers who had written in support of Pynchon (Bush, 454–8, reprints the letter).

[3] Pynchon to Baxter, c.1654–5 and 27 April 1655, DWL Baxter Letters, 4/173, 3/186, summarised in Keeble and Nuttall, *Correspondence of . . . Baxter*, letters 206, 244.

[4] NA, PROB 11/309/558, will of William Pynchon, gentleman of Wraysbury, Buckinghamshire, 8 December 1662. For detailed studies of Pynchon's life and thought, see: Philip F. Gura, 'The contagion of corrupt opinions in puritan Massachusetts: the case of William Pynchon', *William and Mary Quarterly*, 3rd series, 39 (1982), 469–91; Philip F. Gura, *A glimpse of Sion's glory: puritan radicalism in New England, 1620–1660* (Middletown, CT, 1984), 304–22; Ruth A. McIntyre, *William Pynchon: merchant and colonizer, 1590–1662* (Springfield, MA: Connecticut Valley Historical Museum, 1961); Joseph H. Smith, ed., *Colonial justice in western Massachusetts (1639–1702): the Pynchon court record* (Cambridge, MA: Harvard University Press, 1961); Michael P. Winship, 'Contesting control of orthodoxy among the godly: William Pynchon reexamined', *William and Mary Quarterly*, 3rd series, 54 (1997), 795–822; Michael P. Winship, 'William Pynchon's *The Jewes synagogue*', *New England Quarterly*, 71 (1998), 290–7.

ANB, GMB 1536–8, *ODNB*.

R

RAINBOROWE, William (*c.*1617–1673)

William Rainborowe [Rainsborowe, Rainsborough] was the younger brother of the parliamentarian army officer and Leveller Thomas Rainborowe (*ODNB*), and son of William Rainborow (*ODNB*), a Levant merchant and naval officer. He grew up in Wapping, Middlesex, close to the Thames, to the east of the City of London. Like his brother Thomas, William was a mariner with ambitions for overseas trade.

Rainborowe emigrated in the late 1630s and in 1639 settled at Charlestown and joined the Massachusetts Artillery Company. He bought the original meetinghouse grounds in Charlestown, and had a house at Watertown, December 1640. On 8 March 1643/4, after he had already left New England, he petitioned the Massachusetts General Court for payment of £6 for gunpowder; he was paid an extra £20 because the payment was so long overdue. Rainborowe's sisters Martha and Judith had also settled in New England. (Martha, widow of Thomas Coytmore, married governor John Winthrop in 1647: after Winthrop's death in 1649 she re-married, but was widowed again, and committed suicide in 1660. Judith married Stephen Winthrop* in 1643.)

Rainborowe returned to England by 1642. In April that year, he had come into a substantial inheritance from his father: houses in Wapping, and a thousand pounds in cash. In June, he married Margery Jenney of Suffolk. Over the summer, he joined Lord Forbes's expedition to Ireland, in a troop commanded by his brother, Thomas, which had Hugh Peter* as chaplain. John Humfrey* also joined this venture. Rainborowe may have returned to New England briefly, but came back to England to serve in the civil wars as a captain in Thomas Sheffield's regiment of horse. Rainborowe became a senior captain under Thomas Harrison (*ODNB*), and then a major. With his brother Thomas, he became an outspoken Leveller and took part in the Putney debates. His radicalism may have been the reason for his dismissal as a major by Cromwell in 1649. In the aftermath of the passage of the 'Act for the Punishment of Atheistical, Blasphemous and Execrable Opinions' on 9 August 1650, Rainborowe was cited in the House of Commons on 27 September for his support for a book by the Ranter, Laurence Clarkson (*ODNB*), *The single eye*. He was discharged from office as a JP of Middlesex and barred from holding such office in England and Wales. His home, first at Fulham and then at Ilford, was a meeting place for Ranters. On 19 July 1659, Rainborowe petitioned the House of Commons on behalf of sheriffs, JPs and gentry of Northamptonshire, and was made a militia commissioner for the county the same day. On 9 August 1659, the restored Rump Parliament made him the colonel of a regiment of horse there.

After the Restoration, on 17 December 1660, a warrant was issued for Rainborowe's arrest, for treason. He was confined to his home at Mile End Green, Stepney. His wife Margery petitioned for his examination, and on 7 February 1661/2 a bond of £500 was posted for his release. At some point Rainborowe went back to New England. He was living in Boston in 1673.

Artillery Company, 95; R.P. Stearns, *The strenuous puritan: Hugh Peter 1598–1660* (Urbana, IL: University of Illinois Press, 1954), 191; NA, PROB 11/189/79, will of William Rainborow or Rainborowe of Saint Leonard Shoreditch, City of London, 8 April 1642; C.H. Firth and G. Davies, *The regimental history of Cromwell's army* (Oxford: Clarendon Press, 1940), 175, 178, 179–80, 184, 198, 576–7; Mark Kishlansky, *The rise of the New Model Army* (Cambridge: Cambridge University Press, 1979), 43, 201; Ian Gentles, *The New Model Army in England, Ireland and Scotland, 1645–53* (Oxford: Blackwell, 1992), 210, 214, 219; B.S. Capp, *Cromwell's navy: the fleet and the English Revolution, 1648–1660*, 167; Mass. Archives, 67: 67; Roger Thompson, *From deference to defiance: Charlestown, Massachusetts, 1629–1662* (Boston, MA: New England Historic Genealogical Society, 2012), 15, 16, 27, 205, 411–16.

RASHLEY, Thomas (*fl.* 1629–1660)

Thomas Rashley entered Trinity College, Cambridge, in 1629, as an exhibitioner from Charterhouse school. He was a scholar in 1631, graduated BA in 1633, MA in 1636, and perhaps became a fellow of Trinity in 1633.

Rashley emigrated by 1640. The Boston church admitted him on 8 March 1640, as 'a studyent'. Soon afterwards he started work as a chaplain to fishermen. Thomas Lechford* reported:

> at Cape Anne, where fishing is set forward and some stages builded, there one master Rashley is Chaplain ... it is farre off from any Church: Rashley is admitted of Boston Church, but the place lyeth next Salem, and not very far further from Ipswich.

By 1644 Rashley had been preaching at Exeter, and may still have been there in 1646. Stephen Bachiler* wrote to John Winthrop about the proposed gathering of a church at Exeter: Bachiler had agreed to allow £40 to purchase the minister John Wheelwright's* house, out of wages which the people had 'proposed to have allowed (and I think payd) to Mr Rashly, yerely'. On 29 May 1644 the Massachusetts General Court ordered that because of 'divisions and contentions' at Exeter, attempts to gather a church there should be deferred. Rashley's wife was with him in New England (he probably met and married her there) and a son, Jonathan, was baptised at Boston on 18 May 1645.[1]

Rashley returned to England by 1648. In that year, as rector of Barford St Martin, Wiltshire, he joined other ministers in the county to sign the presbyterian *Testimony*. (Rashley may have followed Benjamin Woodbridge* at Barford St Martin, and in turn was succeeded there by John Woodbridge*.) In 1650, he became chaplain of St Cross, Winchester. The diarist Samuel Sewall, son of Henry* and Jane Sewall* and grandson of Stephen* and Alice

Dummer*, was baptised at Bishopstoke on 4 May 1652, by 'Mr Rashly (sometime a member of Boston Old Church)'. By 1652 Rashley had become a preacher at Salisbury cathedral. Adoniram Byfield of Marlborough listed 'Mr Rashley', in a letter to Henry Scobell, clerk to the council of state, as one of the 'publique preachers' in Wiltshire who were also pastors of churches. On 24 July 1657, a letter from the Trustees for Ministers stated that Rashley had agreed to preach at Devizes for a year, because few families attended Salisbury cathedral, and Devizes could not otherwise afford a minister.

Rashley left his cathedral living in 1660 and lived at Avebury in Wiltshire. His two sons, Jonathan and Nathaniel, were ministers. Jonathan Rashley, a nonconformist, was at Lydiard, Wiltshire, c.1670–99. Nathaniel conformed, and may be the 'Nathanael Rashleigh' who held livings in the diocese of Ely in the 1690s.[2]

[1] *Boston CR*, 28; Lechford *PD*, 45; *WP* IV, 458.
[2] *WR*, 182, 381; *NEHGR* 1: 112; LPL, MS COMM. V/5, fol. 504; Adoniram Byfield to Henry Scobell, 14 August 1655, Francis Peck, *Desiderata curiosa*, 2 vols (London, 1732–5), II, Lib. XIII:7; Alexander Gordon, ed. *Freedom after ejection* (Manchester: Manchester University Press, 1917), 337; *CCEd* Person ID 18844.

CR.

RAWSON, Edward (d. 1668)

Edward Rawson was the son of Margaret and Edward Rawson, of Gillingham, Dorset. His mother was sister to John Wilson*, and a grandniece of Edmund Grindal, the Elizabethan archbishop of Canterbury.

Rawson came to New England in 1637 with his parents. His father was secretary of the Massachusetts Bay Colony, 1650–86. Initially, the family settled at Newbury but later moved to Boston. Rawson attended Harvard. His name first appeared in the steward's book in 1649, and he gained a BA in 1653. His college accounts suggest he was at Harvard until c. Sept. 1654, but he did not graduate MA.

Rawson's career in England is not easy to trace. An Edward Rawson was vicar of Ab Kettleby, Leicestershire, in 1655 (not far from where John* and Thomas Weld* had earlier held livings). Another person of this name was presented as vicar of Kingston by Canterbury, in Kent, 17 September 1655: he brought certificates from 'B. Needhe' (perhaps Benjamin Needler, minister of St Margaret Moses, Friday Street, London); 'E. Taylor'; John Morse (possibly John Morse* of Boston, who came back to England at the same time as Rawson); William Webb (perhaps the minister of St Martin's, Ironmonger Lane, London). These certificates seem a plausible collection for a Harvard graduate, recently back from America, to accumulate. But no record survives of this man's ejection or continuance at the Restoration, so the trail in Kingston goes cold.

The eighteenth-century historian John Walker identified the Harvard graduate with a different Edward Rawson, the rector of Horsmonden, Kent, presented to the living on 19 March 1655/6. Walker described this man as 'a

New-England Man, and a violent Presbyterian ... He was resolved to have continued in the Living if he could'. Walker might have confused the Rawson of Horsmonden with the Rawson of Kingston. The rector of Horsmonden presented certificates from people in and around Bridlington, Yorkshire, which seems less likely: Roger Atey of Burton Agnes, where a 'James Attey' had been rector in 1649 (*WR* 389); Richard Raikes of Beeford (*WR* 396); 'Jer. Garthwaite' of 'Carnaby', perhaps rector of South Kelsey, Lincolnshire, 1656 (*WR* 248); Thomas Bradley of 'Thornton' (probably Thornton Dale, Yorkshire, or Thornton, Lincolnshire); Thomas Crosier of Bridlington; William Shrubland; Arthur Noell; Robert Johnson, rector of Bainton-on-the-Wold, Lincolnshire (*WR* 393). At the Restoration, 'Eadward Rawson' at Horsmonden conformed. He had petitioned the authorities in 1661 to retain his living, stating that he had suffered for orthodoxy and loyalty.

Whether the Harvard graduate Edward Rawson was at Kingston or Horsmonden in the late 1650s, he was probably in Buckinghamshire in the 1660s. An Edward Rawson was admitted as vicar of Wooburn on 4 February 1661/2, and as rector of Hedsor on 13 May 1664. In a letter of 8 October 1667, Rawson thanked Philip, Lord Wharton (*ODNB*), for his kindness. Wharton had a chapel at Wooburn (*WR* 232). He also acted as a patron to other New Englanders, Francis Higginson* and Thomas James*. Edward Rawson was buried at Wooburn in 1668.

S.E. Morison, *The founding of Harvard College* (Cambridge, MA: Harvard University Press, 1935), 408; D.G. Allen, *In English ways* (Chapel Hill, NC: University of North Carolina Press, 1981), 265; LPL, MSS COMM. III/9 fol. 596, III/4 fol. 219; John Walker, *An attempt towards recovering an account of the numbers and sufferings of the clergy* (London, 1714), Part I, 220; Bodleian, Rawlinson MSS, Letters 53:83; *CCEd* Person IDs 1888 and 101399.

CC, CR, Sibley.

READE, Thomas (d. 1662)

Thomas Reade was the son of Edmund and Elizabeth Reade of Wickford, Essex. The widowed Elizabeth married Hugh Peter*, so Reade became Hugh Peter's stepson. Reade's sisters Elizabeth, Martha and Margaret came to New England: Elizabeth married John Winthrop Jr*; Martha married Samuel Symonds of Ipswich; Margaret married John Lake of Boston. His brothers Samuel and William did not emigrate. John Endecott referred to Thomas Reade as in England, 8 December 1634, but Reade wrote to John Winthrop Jr from Rotterdam on 7 March 1634/5.

Thomas Reade was in New England by 5 March 1635/6, when his brother Samuel reported that he had received letters from him. *c.* February 1640/1 Hugh Peter mentioned that he was trying to find a husband for a cousin now in New England: 'I am somtymes thinking of Thom: Reade though I have my fears.' 'Thomas Reade' appeared on the membership list of Salem church before 1636. Against his name someone later marked 'removed'.

Reade returned to England and joined the parliamentary army. He served as a major in Morgan Lloyd's regiment in 1645. By the start of the Second Civil War he had become a lieutenant colonel, and was under the command of George Fenwick* from 1649. In 1651 he became colonel of a foot regiment. Reade took part in Cromwell's Scottish campaign. After the capture of Stirling he was appointed governor of Stirling castle. Fitz John Winthrop* was commissioned in his uncle Reade's regiment, 1659.

In his will, made on 25 July 1662, Reade referred to his farm at Salem, Massachusetts, called Wickford after his birthplace in Essex.

WP III, 176, 194, 253; WP IV, 316; Salem CR, 5; C.H. Firth and G. Davies, *The regimental history of Cromwell's army* (Oxford: Clarendon Press, 1940), 384–5, 387–8, 389, 563–8; Frances D. Dow, *Cromwellian Scotland 1651–1660* (Edinburgh: John Donald, 1979), 64, 150, 226, 257, 258; NA, PROB 11/309/443, will of Thomas Reade, gentleman of Wickford, Essex, 6 November 1662; David Cressy, *Coming over: migration and communication between England and New England in the seventeenth century* (Cambridge: Cambridge University Press, 1987), 277–84; GMB 1565–7.

REED, William (c.1587–1656)

William Reed [Read] arrived with Thomas Shepard on the *Defence*, in 1635, aged forty-eight. He probably came from Newcastle upon Tyne. He travelled over with his wife Mabel, aged thirty, and three children: George (six), Ralph (five) and 'Justice' (eighteen months).

In New England, the family settled at Dorchester. William Reed became a church member by the time his daughter Abigail was baptised on 30 December 1638. He became a freeman of Massachusetts on 14 March 1638/9. The family moved to Scituate by 1642, but William was still a church member at Dorchester and had his son Israel baptised there. They were at Roxbury by 1647, when that church admitted 'Goodwife Reade'. On 7 July 1648 William Reed bought a house and land in Woburn.

At some point between 1648 and 1656, William and Mabel Reed returned to England with their four youngest children (Israel, Sarah, Rebecca and another). Their older children – George, Ralph and Abigail, by now all married – stayed on in New England. Reed made his will on 9 April 1656 in Newcastle upon Tyne, with William Cutter* and Thomas Gibson as witnesses. He left £60 to Mabel, together with household stuff, and £30 each to 'my four youngest children'. He noted that William Brenton of New England still owed him £60: if it could be got, £5 apiece should go to the four youngest children; £20 should be divided among 'my three children that are married in NE', with the residue to Mabel. She was granted administration, 31 October 1656.

Mabel Reed returned to Woburn, Massachusetts, with Israel, Sarah and Rebecca. She was in New England by 19 June 1660. At that time, Israel, who was lame, was placed under the guardianship of his brother George Reed, to be 'put forth to an apprentice to such a trade as he is most meet for'. She registered her husband's will with the Middlesex county authorities for probate on 17 February 1661/2. Israel, Sarah and Rebecca all married at Woburn. Mabel married Henry Summers of Woburn. In her eighties, as a widow, she moved out of her stepson Summers' home and took him to court for neglect and abuse. She died at Woburn in 1690.

Dorchester CR, 3, 150, 155; *NEHGR* 3: 196; Waters, 889–90; NA, PROB 11/258/403, will of 'William Read', 31 October 1656; Middlesex Probate Recs., case number 18636; *GM* 6: 30–5.

ROWE, Nathaniel

Nathaniel Rowe was the son of Owen Rowe (*ODNB*), a London merchant of St Stephen's, Coleman Street, who became a regicide. Owen Rowe supported the Massachusetts Bay Company and had property in Boston and New Haven.

Rowe was sent to New England by his father in 1637, in the company of John Davenport and Theophilus Eaton. Nathaniel Eaton* taught him in the earliest days of Harvard. After Eaton's disgrace he was one of the students put out to board. He went to the schoolmaster Thomas Willis* of Lynn:

> Theire I liueing privately gott the best part of my lattine-tongue, but yet not by his instructiones, butt . . . onelie by seeing his manner of teachinge, and gatheringe things of my selfe, and alsoe by bribeinge (or giveinge gifts to) his sonnes for patternes; of which Mr Willis never knew, as yett.

Later, Nathaniel studied with Henry Dunster at Harvard.

Around 1642, Rowe wrote to John Winthrop to ask for permission to go to England. He argued that his father had sent him over 'verie hastilie', though 'it is a sore greife to mee, that I should charge my prudent and most deare father with the evill of rash doeinge of things: but yet beinge compelled in this time of straightness, I must say itt'. He declared his willingness to do anything for his father, but asked Winthrop to 'make the waie cleare for mee to goe to England', where he had been promised 'opportunities' in London by an uncle.

After Rowe's departure, Nathaniel Sparhawke of Cambridge, Massachusetts, sent a letter of attorney to the merchant Thomas Adams (*ODNB*), later lord mayor of London. Sparhawke wanted to recover £16 2s 10d from Owen Rowe, 'for clothes, dyet, bookes and other necessaries unto his sonne'.

WP IV, 344; Aspinwall, 5.

S

SADLER, Richard (*c.*1620–1675)

Richard Sadler was born in Worcester. He matriculated in 1637 at Emmanuel College, Cambridge, but never took a degree. He emigrated to New England in 1638, and settled at Lynn. It may be that he came over with his parents, and that his father, also Richard, was a proprietor at Lynn in 1638, and Reading in 1644. Sadler became a freeman of Massachusetts on 14 March 1639/40 and served the town of Lynn as clerk of writs in 1640 or 1641.

Sadler was on his way to England on 5 November 1646, when he attended John Cotton's lecture at Boston. This was at the height of the Remonstrant controversy provoked by Robert Child*, Thomas Fowle* and others. At the lecture, Cotton warned that the petition the Remonstrants were sending to England, which was critical of Massachusetts, could be a 'Jonas', and sink the ship. Cotton recommended anyone who found it to throw it overboard. Sadler set sail from Boston on 9 November, on the *Supply*, with Thomas Fowle, William Vassall* and Robert Harding*. When a storm blew up, the passengers remembered Cotton's instruction to throw the petition into the sea. 'A godly and discreet woman' took a copy of the petition – not the original – to Sadler and others, 'who although they knew it was not the right Petition . . . yet . . . they judged it also to bee very bad . . . they cut it into peeces as they thought it deserved, and gave the said peeces to a seaman who cast them into the Sea'. The storm abated.

Sadler next appears in Shropshire, where he lived out the rest of his days. It has been said he became curate of Whixall, in the parish of Prees, on 1 September 1646 (*CR*), but (as he had not yet come back from New England) the date must be later. He was ordained at Whixall on 16 May 1648. Sadler joined other ministers in the county to sign the *Testimony* in 1648, showing support for the presbyterian style of church government. Sadler became lecturer (preacher) at Ludlow by April 1652, and in 1654 was appointed an assistant to the Shropshire commissioners for removing unsuitable parish ministers.

He lost his post at Ludlow at the Restoration, and moved back to Whixall. In 1669, he was preaching at Whitchurch and Prees; the churchwardens of Prees presented him for not receiving the sacrament in 1669 and 1670. Sadler was licensed (as a presbyterian) in Prees, 1672. He made his will, as of Whixall, 3 November 1674; it was proved on 21 April 1675.

A manuscript of Sadler's, neatly drawn up – almost ready for printing – survives in the National Library of Wales. It describes the 'way and custome of the separate Congregationall Churches' in New England, and is marked in a different hand 'by Mr Ric. Sadler Lecturer at Ludlow, drawn up by him between 1640 and 1650'. It presents a hostile account of New England's theory and practice: 'the matter of their church'; gathering 'separate congregationall churches'; ordination; admitting members; the administration of church ordinances (perhaps an unfinished section, since it only deals with preaching). Sadler probably drew up the manuscript, spiced with personal recollections, after his return to England. He objected in particular to restrictions on church membership and to the extent of lay participation in church government.

NEHGR 3: 96; Edward Winslow, *New-Englands salamander* (1647), 17, 18, 20. For an edition of Sadler's manuscript, see R.C. Simmons, 'Richard Sadler's account of the Massachusetts churches', *New England Quarterly*, 42 (1969), 411–25. The original is in the National Library of Wales, Aberystwyth, MS 6710B.

CR.

SALTONSTALL, Henry

Henry Saltonstall, son of Sir Richard Saltonstall* and his wife Grace, was born at Wragby, Yorkshire. Most of his family went to New England in 1630, but he emigrated later. He probably arrived in October 1638, on William Pierce's* ship, with Emmanuel*, Lucy* and George Downing*, and his brother Robert Saltonstall.

Henry Saltonstall joined his brother Samuel at Watertown: he had a farm of 300 acres by 1642. He joined the Massachusetts Artillery Company in 1639, and studied at Harvard. He was awarded a BA in the first graduating class, 1642: one of nine 'young men of good hope', the others being Benjamin Woodbridge*, George Downing*, William Hubbard, John Bulkeley*, John Wilson Jr, Nathaniel Brewster*, Samuel Bellingham* and Tobias Barnard*.

On 22 April 1644, his sister Rosamund reported to Samuel Saltonstall that her brother Henry was with his father, Sir Richard Saltonstall, in Holland. He matriculated in the philosophical faculty at the University of Leiden, 1644, and studied in the medical faculty, 1646. He took an MD at Padua in 1649. In 1650, Henry Saltonstall became a fellow of New College, Oxford, where William Stoughton* was also a fellow. He was incorporated MD at Oxford on 24 June 1652. As Samuel Mather* reported to Jonathan Mitchell, 26 March 1651, 'Sir Saltonstall is doctor of Physicke and Fellow of New College.'

Saltonstall put his skills to use as an army surgeon. He went with English forces to Flanders, 1657–8, in the war against Spain, and took part in the Anglo-French campaign to occupy Mardyke. Administration was later granted on the estate of 'Henry Saltonstall of New College, Oxford', who was said to have died 'overseas'.

Saltonstall Papers, 8, 22n., 43, 136–7, 150; *WP* IV, 64–5; *Harvard Recs.* I, 82; *WJ*, 416; MHS, Misc. Bd. MSS, 26 March 1651, Samuel Mather to Jonathan Mitchell.

CC, Sibley.

SALTONSTALL, Muriel (c.1613–1688)

Muriel, daughter of Brampton Gurdon of Assington in Suffolk, married Richard Saltonstall* in England on 4 July 1633. She went to New England with him in 1635. Her health was an issue by 10 May 1643, when Saltonstall had permission to leave the Massachusetts General Court because of her illness.

She returned to England, accompanied by Richard, late in 1645. While she stayed on there, he returned immediately to New England. A 'case of conscience' resulted from their separation, which led Richard Saltonstall to consult with John Cotton and others about whether he should abandon his commitment to New England and join her back home.

There is no evidence that Muriel Saltonstall was ever in New England again. Henry Newcome saw the Saltonstalls at Hulme in Lancashire on 19 June 1667, and reported that she was very weak. She died in 1688. Newcome preached her funeral sermon at Didsbury. Muriel Saltonstall's dislike of New England apparently extended to a desire that her portrait should not be sent to Massachusetts after her death.

Saltonstall Papers, 27, 35, 41, 48; Bush, 419–21; *The Autobiography of Henry Newcome*, ed. R. Parkinson, Chetham Society, Old Series, XXVI–XXVII (Manchester 1852), 166, 267.

SALTONSTALL, Richard (1610–1694)

Richard Saltonstall, son of Sir Richard*, grew up at Wragby in Yorkshire and matriculated at Emmanuel College, Cambridge, on 14 August 1627. Saltonstall went to New England with his father in 1630. He stayed on after Sir Richard left in April 1631, and became a freeman of Massachusetts on 18 May.

On 23 November 1631, Saltonstall set sail for England in the *Lyon*, with the shipmaster William Pierce*. In 1633, in England, he married Muriel*. On 13 April 1635, Richard and 'Merriall' Saltonstall, and their daughter 'Merriall' (aged 9 months), were licensed to sail for New England in the *Susan & Ellen*.

Richard Saltonstall joined John Winthrop Jr* at Ipswich, and played an important part in Massachusetts government. He attacked the power of magistrates, and wrote against the idea of a standing council. He was elected an assistant continuously, 1637–49; with Richard Bellingham, he joined the deputies in their opposition to Governor John Winthrop. Matters came to a head over aid given by Massachusetts (at Winthrop's direction) to Charles de La Tour of St John's, Acadia, who was in dispute with d'Aulnay of Port Royal over French claims in the area. A majority of Massachusetts magistrates supported Winthrop, but Ipswich dissidents directed a protest to the governor, assistants and elders on 14 July 1643. The signatories were the laymen Richard Saltonstall, Simon Bradstreet and Samuel Symonds, and the ministers Nathaniel Ward*, Ezekiel Rogers, Nathaniel Rogers and John Norton. Winthrop saw a conspiracy of Essex county men. Saltonstall, Bellingham and Bradstreet also dissented from proceedings against the Remonstrant Robert Child* and his associates. This Essex county group was led by Saltonstall and

Bellingham, who were protected by their social standing from charges which might otherwise have brought them into disrepute or exile. During the depression of early 1640s, Saltonstall may have been under pressure to go to England or to join the Providence venture promoted by Lord Saye and Sele and John Humfrey*. He later revealed that 'In the times of the unsetled Humyrs of many mens spirits to Returne for England', he had tied himself to New England with a solemn vow 'not to leave the countrey, whilest the Ordinances of God continued here in Purity'.[1]

Towards the end of 1645, Saltonstall prepared to take his wife Muriel to England, for her health's sake. On 17 October, he provided for 'such occasions as during my absence in England may arise'. The following day, he submitted a petition concerning some accounts, which began 'having thoughts (if God will) of going for England by the next passage ...'. That month, the General Court appointed Saltonstall, George Cooke*, and others to negotiate with the earl of Warwick's commission in London, and with parliament, about grants of Narragansett land to Roger Williams*. Herbert Pelham* was also named. Saltonstall and Pelham side-stepped this commission to be agents. On this visit to England, Saltonstall returned to New England almost immediately. He came back by 27 July 1646, when he took his assistant's oath late.[2]

Sometime between 1646 and 1649, Saltonstall put a 'case of conscience' to John Cotton. It concerned leaving New England for England. In the early 1640s, Saltonstall had made a vow 'not to leave the countrey, whilest the Ordinances of God continued here in Purity'. This now put him in a difficult position: as his wife had to stay in England for her health's sake, could he break his vow and go to her? Cotton's draft reply survives (without a signature or date). Cotton advised Saltonstall that his vow had been rash. Although he would be a loss to his community and the colony, he should join his wife in England and return to Massachusetts later, if he could.[3]

Armed with this advice, Saltonstall prepared to leave New England for England. In September 1649, 'Being by Gods providence upon a voyage for England', he had appointed the pastor and deacons of Ipswich church to act as attorneys for his estate in New England. In mid-October, the Massachusetts General Court noted his 'intended voyage'. He took back five of his six children: Abigail, Elizabeth, Gurdon, Richard and Muriel – all born in New England except Muriel, who had emigrated as a babe-in-arms. Another son, Nathaniel, remained in New England.

Saltonstall reached England late in 1649. With his father, Sir Richard Saltonstall, he became a member of the High Court of Justice established in March 1650 to try enemies of the Commonwealth. The next step was Scotland. In a letter to Henry Dunster, received in New England c. 15 May 1651, Saltonstall wrote that he was about to go north at the invitation of 'my Lord Generall', to 'some occasions there of a civill nature'; he also reported he had seen John Bulkeley*. In Scotland, he worked with Samuel Desborough* and George Fenwick*. He became a trustee for sequestered estates. By 19 September 1655, he was also a commissioner for customs and excise. Soon after this, he resigned from his posts in Scotland because of ill-health, and went to England. Lord Broghill, president of the Scottish council, wrote to

John Thurloe, secretary of the English council of state, on Saltonstall's behalf. Early in 1656 he was promoted to be customs commissioner for England. Saltonstall may have signed a petition from several churches in Wales against 'wickedness' in high places, 1655, although Thurloe noted that many of the signatures were in the same hand (Hugh Pritchard* was another signatory).

Saltonstall kept up his interest in New England. In 1654 and 1655 he had sent £220 of goods, then £100 more, for Harvard. In 1659, he was the principal agent of the trustees appointed by Massachusetts General Court to raise funds for the college (along with Thomas Allen*, William Hooke*, John Knowles* and Herbert Pelham). He still had considerable amounts of property there.

At the Restoration, Saltonstall chafed under the new regime. William Hooke* reported to John Davenport in March 1663 that Saltonstall had 'lately come out of the Common Gaol at Shrewsbury, to which he was sent ... for refusing to take the oath of Allegiance till he was informed about it touching something that he scrupled which was denied him'.

Soon after this, Saltonstall returned to New England. He was elected as an assistant after his return, but may not have wanted to be involved in government at a time of dispute with the crown (over the extent of Massachusetts' jurisdiction and the enforcement of Navigation Laws). Saltonstall subscribed £50 to support the fugitive regicides William Goffe and Edward Whalley. He was one of the few in New England who knew where Goffe and Whalley were hiding.

Saltonstall crossed the Atlantic several times more. In 1672, he went back to England and was there until 1680: he stirred up support for John Knowles as president of Harvard, and acted to gather funds for the college, but in general scant record survives of his activities. From 1680 to 1687 he was in New England again. In December 1687, he sailed back to England for the last time. The colonist Samuel Sewall visited Saltonstall at his son-in-law Horsey's home, at Newington near London, in June 1689. Saltonstall died in 1694 at the home of another son-in-law, Sir Edward Moseley of Hulme, Lancashire.[4]

---

[1] *Saltonstall Papers*, 25–41 (biographical sketch), 132–6, 138–9; *WP* III, 94-5, 112, 115, 131, 132–3; *WJ*, 390–1, 418–20, 443n., 452, 468n., 579n., 591; *Mass. Recs.* 2: 5; BPL, MS Am. 1506, pt 3, app. no. 5 (printed in Bush, 419–21, but on 420 the original manuscript's 'unsetled Humyrs' is rendered 'Hurryes').

[2] Mass. Archives, 15B: 60; *Mass. Recs.* 2: 144–5, 3: 48; *Saltonstall Papers*, 141–2.

[3] BPL, MS Am. 1506, pt 3, app. no. 5 (Bush, 419–21); *Pilgrims*, 88–9.

[4] Saltonstall to the pastor and deacons of the Ipswich church, September 1649, MHS, Ms. N-2232, Saltonstall Family Papers (copy from Ipswich Deeds, Lib. II, fol. 6); *Mass. Recs.* 2: 283, 3: 171, 180; Frances D. Dow, *Cromwellian Scotland 1651–1660* (Edinburgh: John Donald, 1979), 57, 123, 169, 312; G.E. Aylmer, *The state's servants: the civil service of the English Republic 1649–1660* (London: Routledge and Kegan Paul, 1973), 72–3; 'Dunster Papers', 4 *MHSC* 2: 194; *Saltonstall Papers*, 159–61; *Thurloe* IV, 380–4, 597–8, 659; William Hooke to John Davenport, 2 March 1662/3, A.G Matthews, ed., 'A censored letter', *Transactions of the Congregational Historical Society*, 9 (1924–6), 263–83, also *CSPD*, *1663–4*, 64.

SAMS, John (d. 1672)

John Sams [Sammes] may have been related to Edward Sams of London, grocer, who in his will in 1635 referred to 'my cousin Stone preacher in New England' (Samuel Stone, *ODNB*). He seems to have had family property at Langford, Essex. He probably emigrated in 1640, from Totham Hill, near Maldon in Essex. Sams settled at Roxbury, where the ministers were Thomas Weld* and John Eliot: both had come from Essex. He stayed only a short time in New England, and left little trace. He bought land from Thomas and Joseph Weld, and from John Johnson. He is said to have been educated in New England: perhaps, like Christopher Marshall* who studied with the Boston minister John Cotton, Sams studied with Weld or Eliot.[1]

Sams left New England before September 1642. He owed £50 18s to governor Thomas Dudley, who was at that point living in Roxbury. The Massachusetts General Court ordered that Sams's land should be taken to repay the debt. The valuers estimated that, in total, Sams's land was worth £42 17s 8½d, so Dudley took the lot.[2]

The next trace of Sams is in August 1645, when he was already established as a minister in the sequestered living of West Farleigh, Kent. On 19 March 1645/6, he married Ann Milway of Maidstone. He became vicar of Kelvedon, Essex, on 9 October 1647. Sams followed the 'New England Way', congregationalism, but set this in a parish context. He stepped into the shoes of John Owen at Coggeshall in Essex, as public preacher and as pastor to the church Owen had gathered there. Sams was vicar of Coggeshall from 18 March 1651/2. Ralph Josselin (*ODNB*), minister nearby at Earls Colne, often mentioned Sams in his diary and noted how Sams was set apart as a 'teaching elder'. In 1654, Sams became an assistant to the Essex commissioners for removing unsuitable parish ministers, along with other ministers such as John Bulkeley*, Giles Firmin*, John Stalham and William Sparrow; the commissioners, all laymen, included Dionysius Wakering of Kelvedon, Robert Crane of Coggeshall, Sir Thomas Honeywood and Richard Harlakenden. Ichabod Chauncy* was a member of the Coggeshall church sometime between 1656 and 1659.

At Coggeshall, Sams clashed with the Quakers. Ralph Josselin witnessed some of the disturbances and described the 'fits at Coxall' as being 'like the pow wowing among the Indies'. On 12 July 1655, the Quaker James Parnel disrupted a public fast at Coggeshall, when Sams and other ministers were present. Parnel shouted out that the minister was a false prophet and deceiver. Dionysius Wakering arrested him: Parnel was committed by Wakering, Herbert Pelham*, Thomas Cook, and Richard Harlakenden for trial at Chelmsford assizes. For Parnel, the Coggeshall episode started him on the road to death in gaol at Colchester castle, a martyr for the Quaker cause.

John Sams lost the living of Coggeshall in 1660. After the Restoration, he attended the parish church at first, then gathered a church. He was presented by the Coggeshall churchwardens on 18 May 1664, for absence from parish worship. On 16 November 1665, he was presented for 'exercising at conventicles' and teaching school without a licence. He was preaching at Coggeshall in 1669. The authorities described a 'conventicle' there, 'hard to be suppressed', ministered to by Sams and Thomas Lowry (*CR*). Sams was licensed (as a congregationalist) at house of John Croe, Coggeshall, in 1672. He died in December 1672, and was buried at Coggeshall. Thomas Lowry preached his funeral sermon.³

[1] Waters, 516–17; *The diary of Ralph Josselin 1616–1683*, ed. A. Macfarlane (Oxford: Oxford University Press, 1976), 66n. The Essex Record Office holds documents about the Sams [Sammes] family.
[2] *Suffolk Deeds* I, 37.
[3] *Diary of Ralph Josselin*, 274, 349, 350n., 366 and *passim*; G.F. Nuttall, *Visible saints: the congregational way, 1640–1660* (Oxford: Blackwell, 1957), 38; Bryan Dale, *Annals of Coggeshall* (London: J. Russell Smith, 1863), 171–3; *ODNB*, 'Parnel , James (*bap.* 1636, *d.* 1656)'.

CR.

SANBORN, Stephen

Stephen Sanborn [Samborne], a grandson of Stephen Bachiler*, was living with his grandfather at Hampton in 1643. He returned to England in 1654, with or following his grandfather. He may have been living in London, 1685.

GD; *NEHGR* 6: 207, 8: 50, 10: 272–5; *GMB* 63, 69.

SAXTON, Peter (d. 1651)

Peter Saxton was born at Bramley, near Rotherham in Yorkshire. He may have been related to the map-maker Christopher Saxton (*ODNB*). He attended Leeds grammar school, and was admitted as a sizar at Trinity College, Cambridge, *c.*1595; he graduated BA in 1596, MA in 1603. In 1601 he became rector of Newton-on-Ouse. On 17 January 1602/3, after being called before the Court of High Commission in York on a number of occasions, Saxton was told 'to rede divine service as is set down by the book and to weare the surples as is appointed'. He subscribed, and was licensed as a preacher throughout the diocese of York, on 13 December 1604 and again on 18 April 1611. In 1614 he became rector of Edlington, in the West Riding of Yorkshire. There, at the visitation of 1632, he was reprimanded for nonconformity. In 1636, he was charged for (among other offences) not wearing surplice. On 14 July 1637, the authorities recorded him as absent, and suspended him. He was said to have called the surplice a 'whore's smock'. On 30 April 1640, Saxton's resignation as rector of Edlington was recorded, and the living was declared vacant.¹

Saxton probably sailed to New England in 1640. He replaced John Lothropp as preacher at Scituate, but did not create a gathered church (Lothropp had taken his gathered church to Barnstable in October 1639, and a new church at Scituate was not formed until 2 February 1642, after Saxton's departure). According to Cotton Mather, Saxton failed to put down roots because of 'the unsettled Condition of the Colony, and some unhappy Contention in the Plantation where he lived'. He moved from Scituate to Boston, and did not remain in New England long – although his daughter Silence married Captain Samuel Pool, and stayed on.[2]

Saxton took ship for England in the summer of 1641. Thomas Lechford, who left on 3 August, wrote that he 'was comming away when we did'. Recollections of Saxton's conduct on the way home later surfaced in a book by John Ryther, as a pattern for mariners' prayers in a crisis: 'say, as that old Puritan Minister did in a storm coming from New-England, when they were all expecting the Vessell to sink, *O, who is now for Heaven, who is bound for Heaven*'. Safely back in England, Saxton chose his native Yorkshire over opportunities offered to him in Kent. In April 1646, he was sent 'by the triumph of his party' to be vicar of Leeds. His presence there was noted in a parliamentary survey, 6 June 1650. Saxton continued in Leeds until his death. He had a reputation for lively preaching and as a Hebrew scholar.[3]

[1] R.A. Marchant, *The puritans and the church courts in the diocese of York 1560–1642* (London: Longmans, 1960), 275–6; *CCEd* Person ID 129148.

[2] *Magnalia*, I, 587.

[3] Lechford *PD*, 41; John Ryther, *A plat for mariners* (1672); Benjamin Brook, *The lives of the Puritans* (London: James Black, 1813) III, 139–40; LPL, COMM. MS XIIa/18/350–62.

SEDGWICK, Joanna

Joanna, the wife of Robert Sedgwick, was the sister of Robert Houghton, a brewer of St Olave's, Southwark. Houghton had extensive trading interests in New England. Joanna emigrated to New England with Robert in 1636 and settled at Charlestown. Both were admitted to the church on 27 February 1637.

Joanna followed Robert to England in the 1650s. In November 1655 Robert commended her to Cromwell's care. She was granted administration of his estate, 30 September 1656. In 1657 she was living at Stepney, Middlesex. She married Thomas Allen*, formerly her pastor at the Charlestown church in Massachusetts, and moved to Norwich.

Bernard Bailyn, *The New England merchants in the seventeenth century* (Cambridge, MA: Harvard University Press, 1955), 79–80; *GM* 6: 226; *Charlestown CR*, 279; Colonial Society of Massachusetts, *Publications*, 3 (1901), 174; *NEHGR* 42: 67; Waters, 259; Roger Thompson, *From deference to defiance: Charlestown, Massachusetts, 1629–1662* (Boston, MA: New England Historic Genealogical Society, 2012), 205.

SEDGWICK, Robert (1613–1656)

Robert Sedgwick – colonist, merchant, naval commander – was born at Woburn, Bedfordshire. He was the son of William and Elizabeth Sedgwick, and brother of the radical minister and army chaplain William Sedgwick

(*ODNB*). Before emigration, he was a London merchant. He married Joanna Houghton, of Southwark.

Robert and Joanna Sedgwick emigrated by 1636 and settled at Charlestown. Both were admitted to the church on 27 February 1636/7. Sedgwick became a freeman of Massachusetts on 9 March 1636/7. He was elected a deputy the following month (and often thereafter). He became a founder member of the Massachusetts Artillery Company, 1637: Edward Johnson wrote of him as 'nursed up in London's Artillery Garden'. He served as a captain in 1640, commander of the castle in 1641, and head of the Middlesex regiment in 1643.

Sedgwick was a natural ally of entrepreneurs and Atlantic merchants in Massachusetts. He and others petitioned to be incorporated as a company of free adventurers to explore the Delaware: an expedition went, but with poor results. He traded in partnership with his brother-in-law, Robert Houghton of Southwark. Sedgwick supported the development of the Saugus ironworks. In 1645, he joined with Emmanuel Downing*, Nehemiah Bourne* and Thomas Fowle* to protest against a law limiting the residence of unaccredited strangers to three weeks, and against the banishment of anabaptists.

Sedgwick went to England in 1653. He had been called back by Cromwell, together with his son-in-law John Leverett*, and commissioned to command a fleet against New Netherland. In the event, peace with the Dutch came in 1654, before Sedgwick's force saw any action, but he put it to use against the French in Acadia, destroying three forts and taking the area back under English control as Nova Scotia. He returned to England towards the end of 1654. (Emmanuel Downing told John Winthrop Jr*, 25 September 1654, that he planned to sail with 'Generall Sedgwick' within two months, if not before. John Morse* also sailed back with Sedgwick's fleet.) On 6 June 1655, Sedgwick was paid £1793 7s 8d for his 'publique service in New England and elsewhere against the French'. Next, Sedgwick was sent on a new mission to transport 800 men as reinforcements for Sir William Penn (*ODNB*) and Robert Venables (*ODNB*) in Cromwell's ill-fated Caribbean venture, the 'Western Design'. Edward Winslow*, veteran of the *Mayflower*, took part as a civil commissioner. Sedgwick was named commander-in-chief of the Jamaican forces. In November 1655, he wrote to ask Cromwell if he could return from Jamaica to London – he was disillusioned, his men were sick – but this request was not granted. Sedgwick died suddenly in Jamaica on 24 May 1656.

H.D. Sedgwick, 'Robert Sedgwick', Colonial Society of Massachusetts, *Publications*, 3 (1901), 156–74; *Artillery Company*, 21–3; E.D. Hartley, *Ironworks on the Saugus* (Norman, OK: University of Oklahoma Press, 1957), 104; Bernard Bailyn, *The New England merchants in the seventeenth century* (Cambridge, MA: Harvard University Press, 1955), 37, 51–2, 79–80, 82; B.S. Capp, *Cromwell's navy: the fleet and the English Revolution, 1648–1660*, 87-90, 91, 92; *Thurloe* I, 721–2, II, 259, 418–20, 425–6, 583–4, IV, 4–5, 12, 389–90, 454–8, 600, 604–6, 634–5, V, 12–13; Waters, 260; Roger Thompson, *From deference to defiance: Charlestown, Massachusetts, 1629–1662* (Boston, MA: New England Historic Genealogical Society, 2012), 269–74; Louise A. Breen, *Transgressing the bounds: subversive enterprises among the puritan elite in*

Massachusetts, 1630–1692 (Oxford: Oxford University Press, 2001), 116–18, 124–5, 126–7, 141–2 and *passim*.

ODNB.

SEDGWICK, Samuel

Samuel Sedgwick, a son of Robert and Joanna Sedgwick, was baptised at Charlestown on 31 March 1639. He was in London by 17 June 1657, when he witnessed the will of Jonathan Wade*. On 20 May 1667, he sold a house and land in Charlestown to Francis Willoughby*, describing himself as a 'Citizen and clothworker of London'.

Charlestown CR, 150; GD.

SEELY, Robert (1602–1668)

Robert Seely, baptised at Huntingdon, lived in the parish of St Stephen's, Coleman Street, London. He married Mary Mason there in 1626 and they had a child, Nathaniel, baptised in 1627. Seely was a cordwainer (shoemaker).

He emigrated with Mary and Nathaniel, and settled first at Watertown, Massachusetts. Seely requested admission as a freeman on 19 October 1630 and was admitted, 18 May 1631. He took part in an expedition led by John Oldham to explore the Connecticut River, and this led him to become, in 1636, one of the founders of Wethersfield, Connecticut. He played a significant role as a lieutenant in the Pequot War of May 1637. By 1639 he decided to settle with John Davenport's company at New Haven, which had close links to St Stephen's, Coleman Street. He became a free burgess of New Haven in 1639, and led the colony's defence against Indians.

On 26 October 1646, 'Lieut. Robert Seely had liberty to go for England although a public officer.' He sold his house in November 1646. However, he was still in New Haven in February 1646/7, so he may have deferred the journey, or decided not to go. From early 1648 his name appears again in the colony's records, so if he went back it was a short visit.

In May 1649, Seely asked to be relieved of his role as lieutenant, to free him for other opportunities: 'there is a way open for him, and he desires to attend providence in it, if he cannot see a way of comfortable subsistence here'. In November that year, it was suggested the town should help Seely to buy a house, 'for he is now resolved to stay here & to follow his trade of shoemaking, and shall not remove unless the town be satisfied that God by his providence calls him away'. In 1650 Seely helped to plan for New Haven settlers to move south to the Delaware. In 1654, he led the force raised in New Haven for service under Robert Sedgwick* and John Leverett* against New Netherland.

In 1659 he went to England. He was there on 22 November 1659 when his son Nathaniel sold off land for him at New Haven harbour.

Seely returned to New England at the Restoration, soon after 12 October 1661, seeking refuge from the changes in England. He was at Saybrook and

Stratford in 1662, and captain of the militia at Huntingdon on Long Island in 1663. He died by October 1668.

> I.M. Calder, *The New Haven Colony* (New Haven, CT: Yale University Press, 1934), 16, 67, 106, 179, 180, 183, 191–2, 209; *WP* III, 453; *Davenport Letters*, 194n.; *New Haven Recs*. I, 275, 457, 500; *GMB* 1647–50; *GM* 7: 353.

SEWALL, Henry Jr (1615–1700) and Jane

Henry Sewall, baptised at Manchester, was the eldest son of Henry Sewall, a draper who originated in Coventry, Warwickshire. Sewall emigrated from London in 1634 on the *Elizabeth Dorcas*, probably at the prompting of his father. Henry Sewall senior had already sent livestock to New England and sold off some of his land in Coventry. He followed his son to New England in 1635.

Sewall settled at Ipswich, but moved to Newbury in 1635. His father settled at Rowley. 'Henry Seawall, Junior' became a freeman of Massachusetts on 17 May 1637. Sewall soon complained his farm at Newbury was too small. The town's authorities responded that it was 'sufficient and competent both in respect of the quality and quantity of the ground and farther that they see not for the present any ground or reason either to add any more land to his farm or else to alter any part or parcel thereof'. On 25 March 1646 he married Jane, daughter of Stephen* and Alice Dummer* of Newbury.

In the winter of 1646/7, Sewall returned to England with his wife Jane and her parents. At first they went to Warwick, then to Hampshire. Both Henry Sewall and Stephen Dummer appointed Henry Short of Newbury, Massachusetts, to look after their affairs back in New England. Henry Sewall's son Samuel, the diarist, was born on 28 March 1652 at Bishopstoke, Hampshire, his grandfather Dummer's native town. Samuel Sewall later recounted how he was 'baptised by Mr Rashly (sometime member of Boston Old Church) in Stoke Church, May 4th 1652'. Thomas Rashley* preached a sermon before the baptism and afterwards 'an entertainment was made for him and many more'. Henry and Jane Sewall were living at North Baddesley, Hampshire, in October 1654 when their son John was born: he was baptised by Henry Coxe (*CR*), minister of Bishopstoke.

At some point in the 1650s Henry Sewall became the minister at North Baddesley. This is clear from a letter of recommendation by Richard Cromwell, the Lord Protector, written when Sewall went to New England to take possession of his father's estate at Rowley (Henry Sewall senior had died intestate). Cromwell wrote to the governor and magistrates of Massachusetts, 23 March 1658/9, describing Sewall as 'personally knowne to us to be laborious and industrious in the work of the ministry, and very exemplary for his holy life and good conversation'. Cromwell requested speedy attention to Sewall's case, 'that soe he may the sooner returne to his ministeriall charge at North Baddesley'.

While Sewall was in New England, the Restoration of Charles II came. He sent word for his family to leave England and come back to Massachusetts.

Samuel Sewall remembered 'being at Bishopstoke and Baddesley, April 23, 1661, the day of the Coronation of K. Charles the 2d, the Thunder and Lightening of it'. Soon afterwards, Jane Sewall boarded a ship at Gravesend with five small children. She arrived in New England in July 1661, after two months at sea.

Henry and Jane Sewall lived out the rest of their lives at Newbury, Massachusetts, but Sewall still kept his English property. In his will, made 17 August 1678, he left Samuel Sewall a tenement at Lee near Romsey, Hampshire, and land in Coventry; to his youngest son, Stephen, he left a house, lands, barns and orchards in Bishopstoke, Hampshire. Samuel Sewall later visited Samuel Blower (*CR*) chaplain to the household of Samuel Dunch at Baddesley, Hampshire, and John Goldwire (*CR*), an ejected minister also living in Baddesley.

> *GM* 6: 246, 317; *NEHGR* 1: 111–112, 3: 95; D.G. Allen, *In English ways* (Chapel Hill, NC: University of North Carolina Press, 1981), 114; *Essex Court Recs.* I, 54, 66, 418; *Essex Probate Recs.* I, 232–3; Thomas Hutchinson, *The history of Massachusetts from ... 1628 until 1750* (Salem, MA: Thomas Cushing, 1795), I, 455; MHS, Misc. Bd. MSS, 17 August 1678; *ANB*, s.n. 'Sewall, Samuel'.

SHEPARD, Samuel (*c.*1613–*c.*1673)

Samuel Shepard was the son of William Shepard of Towcester, Northamptonshire and Banbury, Oxfordshire, and a younger half-brother to the minister Thomas Shepard. Samuel and Thomas Shepard emigrated in 1635 from London on the *Defence.*

Shepard settled at Cambridge, Massachusetts, and in February 1635/6 became one of the first members of the church gathered by his brother. He became a freeman on 3 March 1635/6. He was a deputy for Cambridge to the General Court on several occasions, and joined the Artillery Company in 1640. He became involved in the scandal of Nathaniel Eaton's* dismissal as head of Harvard (he investigated Eaton's accounts) and from 1639 until 1641 looked after the finances for building the college.

Shepard visited England in 1641 and 1645, and on each occasion was absent for up to two years. In 1641, he left at the same time as Hugh Peter*, who sailed on 3 August. This emerges from Henry Dunster's account of the construction work at Harvard. Dunster recounted how this was to be supervised by Hugh Peter, Samuel Shepard and Joseph Cooke*, 'who prudently declined the trouble and left it to the two first'. Peter and Shepard, however, then 'went for England, leaving the work in the Carpenters and Masons hands without Guide or further direction', with the result that Dunster had to step in and supervise from October 1641. Shepard had returned to New England by 23 December 1643, when he sent a letter to Sir Thomas Barrington (*ODNB*) in England, 'I have not beene wanting in my best endeavours this yeare to make you returnes of the Debts which you was pleased to Comitt me to receive for you.' He pointed out the difficulty of converting pay into commodities fit to send, and also 'the extreme danger and hazard in transporting anything from hence to England'. Barrington's reply, 5 June 1644, made reference to 'the poore orphanes business which we committed to your Charge' (the scandal which tainted Hugh Peter, Thomas Weld and others over the misappropriation of money raised for transporting children to New England).

In 1645, Shepard went to England again, this time with George Cooke*: both were excused duties at General Court in October, and their farms were put into the care of fellow-townsmen. On 16 May 1646 Shepard appeared in a case at the High Court of Admiralty, London, and said he had 'lived in New England, for the most part, these 10 years'. He was back in New England by October 1647, when he presented a letter of attorney (dated 10 May 1647) from Sir Gilbert Gerard and Sir William Masham, executors of Robert Barrington, and recorded £520 paid to Barrington's estate by the Boston merchant Robert Keayne. (It seems that Shepard failed to paid over all the money due to the Barrington estate: to comply with a court verdict of 27 September 1652, his agent Thomas Marshall was ordered to levy £591 9s 1d to satisfy Gerard and Masham. Shepard's farm – 500 acres and a dwelling house – was appraised in February 1653/4, to pay what was still due.)

Shepard had already left New England for the last time by February 1649/50, when Henry Dunster (in a letter to John Phillip*) referred to 'S. S.' being 'in England not with us'. On 28 March 1650, Shepard wrote from London to deacon Edward Collins in Cambridge, appointing Collins his attorney in New England: 'I am within a few days to be in Ireland, if God will; but the next letters will, I hope, settle me.' His wife Hannah joined him, leaving their daughter Jane, aged four, in Collins's care. Shepard's activities in Ireland have left little trace, yet he seems to have been there for most of the 1650s. The Cambridge church records noted, in January 1658/9, 'Mr Samuell Shepard & his wife now living in Ireland do yet stand in memberly relation to us. And here with us is their daughter Jane Shepard now under the care of Mr Edw[ard] Collins.'

Samuel Shepard's history after 1660 is obscure. He died in England or Ireland before 18 September 1673, when administration of his estate in New England was granted to Edward Collins.

GM 6: 269–73; NEHGR 3: 94; *Shepard's Confessions*, 172; *Artillery Company*, 110; Cambridge TR, fols 40, 72, 80; Dunster MSS, Dunster's memorandum of December 1653 (about the construction of the first college building); BL, Egerton MS 2648 fols 10, 74b; MHS, MS N-1143, 'Henry Dunster Notebook, 1628–54', fol. 117; Middlesex Deeds II, fol. 104. *GD* reports that Shepard was a major in Ireland, but this may be a 'William Sheappard': Robert Dunlop, *Ireland under the Commonwealth* (Manchester: Manchester University Press, 1913), 397.

SMITH, Henry (c.1610–1682) and Ann

Henry Smith came from Dorchester, Dorset, and was the son of Frances (Samford), who later married William Pynchon*. Smith emigrated with his mother on the *Mary & John*, in the Winthrop fleet, and was at Dorchester in 1630. He requested freemanship on 19 October 1630 and was admitted on 18 May 1631. Ann Smith was William Pynchon's daughter. She arrived with Pynchon in 1630, settled at Roxbury, and married Henry Smith c.1635. In 1636 Henry and Ann moved with Pynchon to settle Springfield. Henry Smith served as a representative in 1651.

Henry Smith left New England with William Pynchon and George Moxon*, September 1652. Ann Smith travelled back later: Pynchon wrote to Richard Baxter, 27 April 1655, that he had been in London (probably earlier that year) to 'meete a daughter of mine and her children that was then newly arrived from NE'.

Henry and Ann Smith seem to have settled at Wraysbury, Buckinghamshire, with Pynchon. Henry's will, made 1 August 1681, and proved 24 October 1682, left most of his property to his wife 'Anna', but made bequests to his children Martha, Mary (in New England, the wife of Richard Lord of Hartford), Rebecca, Elizabeth and Elisha. Rebecca Lee of Wraysbury, his daughter, attested the will.

GMB 1691–2; NEHGR 3: 90, 91; WP III, 214; WP IV, 98; DWL Baxter Letters 3/186; Waters, 723, 859; NA, PROB 11/371/163, will of Henry Smith or Smyth of Wraysbury, Buckinghamshire, 24 October 1682.

SMITH, James Jr

James Smith, a mariner, was the son of James Smith, a smith and husbandman. Smith senior and his family settled at Salem, Massachusetts, by 1635. The family were in Gloucester, 1642, and at Marblehead in 1645.

Both father and son appeared frequently in the Essex court records in the early 1640s for minor misdemeanours and petty theft. James Smith senior held some town offices in the 1650s, but in 1659 was suspected of being a Quaker and admonished for absence from 'public ordinances on the Lord's day'. The younger Smith was often in court between 1640 and 1642: on 12 July 1642, he was sentenced 'to be moderately whipped for pilfering and stealing on the Lord's day'.

James Smith Jr probably returned to England around 1642. There is no clear record to place him in New England between 1642 and 1666. James Smith senior's will, made in 1656, referred to 'mine only son James Smith living at Bristol in England'; the will of Smith's mother Mary will shows James was still there in 1663.

James Smith, 'of the city of Bristol, mariner', returned to New England in 1666 to live in the property he had inherited at Marblehead. Family disputes with his brothers-in-law ensured more court appearances thereafter for 'Captain James Smith'.

GM 6: 361–73.

SMITH, Nathaniel

Nathaniel Smith, of Malden, Massachusetts, made a will on 1 January 1648/9 which included the clause 'if it please god to restore any thing of the plundered estate my will is . . .'. Smith seems to have drawn up this will in anticipation of a voyage to England to reclaim property lost during the civil war.

He made a fresh will in England, 19 February 1650/1, and died soon afterwards. This will also mentioned plundered estate – clearly his campaign to retrieve it had not yet succeeded – and also his 'kinsman' Thomas Edwards* and 'cosen' Nathaniel Edwards*, and other relatives in New England. On 30 September 1651, Nathaniel and Thomas Edwards (at that point both also in England) were appointed administrators of Smith's estate in New England. Nathaniel proved the will in England and brought it to New England, where he submitted it to the Essex county probate court.

MHS, Misc. MSS, 1 January 1649; NA, PROB 11/216/17, will of Nathaniel Smith, 20 March 1651; *Essex Probate Recs.* I, 133–4.

SMITH, Richard

Richard Smith came from Shropham in Norfolk, six miles southwest of Hingham. He was a proprietor at Ipswich, Massachusetts, by 1641. His daughter married Edward Gilman junior, whose family had come from Hingham, Norfolk, to Hingham, Massachusetts. In preparation for leaving New England, Smith sold off land in Ipswich to his son-in-law Gilman in October 1647.

Smith went back home to Shropham in the autumn of 1647. Edward Gilman, father of Gilman junior, took the opportunity to give a power of attorney to his 'brother' Richard Smith (and to Nehemiah Bourne*) for the recovery of money due from captain Thomas Hawkins* 'late of New England'.

D.G. Allen, *In English ways* (Chapel Hill, NC: University of North Carolina Press, 1981), 77, 252, 275; C.H. Pope, *Pioneers of Massachusetts* (Boston, MA: C.H. Pope, 1900), 423; Aspinwall, 86.

SMITH, Robert

Robert Smith, a wine cooper of London, arrived New England c.1637, with his wife and a sister, Mary Smith. His sister Ann had already come over in 1636.

Smith and his wife returned to England, but his sisters stayed on. In 1648, Peter Gardner* of Roxbury, Massachusetts, visited London. He found Smith keeping the Golden Lion Tavern in Fetter Lane. Gardner gave Smith news of his sister Mary. In 1650 Gardner visited Smith's tavern again, bringing messages and tokens from New England. Robert Smith suggested his sister Mary should send over a son from New England for him to adopt as his heir.

David Cressy, *Coming over: migration and communication between England and New England in the seventeenth century* (Cambridge: Cambridge University Press, 1987), 267–8.

SMITH, Zephaniah

Zephaniah Smith was a tanner of Windsor, Connecticut. He seems to have left New England around December 1648, when he promised to pay Thomas Bell* £40 in London before 5 May 1649.

A former New England colonist of this name was minister at Roscrea in Tipperary, Ireland, by mid-1656. He was to have been sent to 'Queen's County' (now County Laois) in August 1656, but did not go. He was in the Barony of Corkaree in West Meath, 1659.

> Aspinwall, 160, 183–4; St J.D. Seymour, *The puritans in Ireland, 1647–1661* (Oxford: Clarendon Press, 1921), 221; *Pilgrims*, 83, 107n.29, 111n.61, 179, 203. The colonist is not the ejected minister Zephaniah Smith (*CR*).

STARR, Comfort (1624–1711)

Comfort Starr was born in Ashford, Kent, son of Comfort and Elizabeth Starr. His father was a surgeon. His parents emigrated in 1635 from Sandwich, Kent, on the *Hercules*. Their party included Comfort, his siblings Thomas and Mary, and a 'Truth-shall-prevail Starre' – listed as a servant but perhaps the sister of Comfort Starr senior.

Starr's family settled first at Cambridge, but moved to Duxbury in 1638 and Boston by 1646. Starr attended Harvard and graduated BA in 1647. He was paid £11 10s for being a 'fellow [for] part of 2 yeeres', before he took his MA, one of five fellows named in the college charter dated 10 May 1650.

Starr left for England in 1650, probably in the autumn, around the same time as Nathaniel* and Samuel Mather*. Samuel Mather failed to mention him in his letter to Jonathan Mitchell, 26 March 1651, but wrote that 'those who came over this yeare will write I suppose every one of himselfe, and therefore I shall spare my paines concerning them'. Nathaniel Mather reported to John Rogers, 23 March 1650/1, that neither he nor his brother Samuel nor Starr had received letters from fellow students.

By 1651, Starr was a preacher at Dalston and Sebergham, Cumberland. In 1654 he was appointed an assistant to the Commission for the Propagation of the Gospel in the Four Northern Counties, which recruited and approved preachers for the north. On 11 January 1655/6, the Trustees for the Approval of Public Preachers took steps, in response to a petition from the people of Carlisle, to settle Timothy Tullie (*CR*) and Comfort Starr in the city: Tullie was to preach at St Mary's, Starr at St Cuthbert's. On 22 April 1656 the Trustees for Maintenance of Ministers (whose members included Edward Hopkins*) ordered an augmentation of £80 for both Tullie and Starr. Starr was admitted to the living at St Cuthbert's on 23 April 1656: he had certificates from Thomas Craistor and Cuthbert Studholme, members of Carlisle corporation; Roger Baldwin (*CR*) of Penrith, who had been vicar of St Cuthbert's in 1648; George Larkham* of Cockermouth; James Cave (*CR*), preacher of Crosthwaite. All but Cave were ministerial assistants to, or lay commissioners of, the Commission for the Propagation of the Gospel in the Four Northern Counties. In 1657 and

1658, the salaries of both Tullie and Starr were augmented again. By 1659 they both had £100 a year. Tullie and Starr preached the election sermon for the mayor of Carlisle by turn, and divided their preaching duties. Starr attended the Savoy Conference in London, in 1658. No evidence survives to show that he joined the Cumberland Association. 'Mrs. Grace Starr', his wife, joined George Larkham's congregational church at Cockermouth, thirty-sixth on the list of women members (she was later dismissed from membership, presumably when the Starrs moved south after the Restoration). The baptism at Carlisle, 28 May 1657, of 'Comfort the son of Comfort Starr', was recorded in the Cockermouth church book.

Comfort Starr lost his post in Carlisle in 1660, and went back to his native Kent. His father, who had died in New England in January 1659/60, had left him a house and land at Ashford. (His father's will shows that Comfort's sister Hannah was also in England: the will specified that if Hannah came back to New England she could have a 'silver guilt double salt Celler', but otherwise her father left her any money due in England and £50 from the rents of the property at 'Eshtisford' [Ashford], which Comfort was to inherit.) Comfort was at Sandhurst in August 1663, and preaching at Cranbrook in 1669. In 1672 he was licensed (as a congregationalist) at his house in Sandwich, where Nathaniel Mather had worked in 1650s. In Starr's application for a licence he was described as 'teacher'. He petitioned four times to have use of the old chapel that belonged to hospital of St Bartholomew's, Sandwich, 'without the walls' of the town. His wife Grace died before March 1674/5, when he married Jane Chauntler of Maidstone. On 12 August 1687, Starr was elected pastor of the congregational church at Dancing House Yard, Canterbury (see Robert Mascall*). In 1690 he was said to be living with his son, an apothecary, on Little Tower Hill in London. Thereafter, Starr served in Dover as assistant to Nathaniel Wilmot (*CR*); he was minister at Goudhurst, Kent, in July 1691, and at Lewes, Sussex, *c.*1696–*c.*1708. He died at Lewes. His will, 21 June 1709, was proved on 20 December 1711. It mentioned property at Ashford and Shadoxhurst, Kent, but made no reference to New England. His widow, Jane, died on 11 April 1712.

> *Harvard Recs.* I, 83; MHS, Misc. Bd. MSS, 26 March 1651, Samuel Mather to Jonathan Mitchell; Mather to Rogers, 23 March 1650/1, BPL, MS Am. 1506 v. 1, 7 (printed 4 *MHSC* 8: 2–3); Benjamin Nightingale, *The ejected of Cumberland and Westmorland* (Manchester: Manchester University Press, 1911), I, 158–73; LPL, MS COMM. III/ 5 fol. 16; W.A. Shaw, *A history of the English Church . . . 1640–1660* (London: Longmans & Green, 1900), II, 585; Cockermouth CB, 133, 152, 155; Canterbury CB, fol. 6r; *NEHGR* 8: 128 (the will of Comfort Starr senior); Waters, 651-2; NA, PROB 11/524/542, will of Comfort Starr, clerk of Lewes, Sussex, 20 December 1711.
>
> *CC, CR, GM* 6: 487–94, Sibley.

STIRK, George (d. 1665)

George Stirk [Starkey] was the son of George Stirk, a minister in the Somers Islands (Bermuda). He went to Massachusetts in 1639, after his father's death, to continue his education. Patrick Copeland, the governor of Bermuda, commended him to John Winthrop as 'a small Poesie of one of our Preachers, whom the Lord hath taken to himselfe. if there be any good Schole or Scholemaister with you, I could wish with all my heart that hee might have his education with you, [rather] then in old England'. In due course Stirk studied at Harvard, where he graduated BA in 1646, and later MA. Copeland wrote again to John Winthrop in September 1647: 'I doubt not but you will afford your grave counsel to George Stirke, whom both his father and my selfe dedicated unto God. I heare he practices Physick. I ever intended Divinity should be his main study.' But Stirk followed the trail blazed by John Winthrop Jr*, showing interest not only in medicine, but also in science and alchemy. A letter Stirk wrote to the younger Winthrop, August 1648, shows he had been drawing on Winthop's expertise and private library for some time: he asked for the key to unlock book cabinets, wanted to see 'chemical books', requested supplies of antimony and mercury, and reported 'I have built a furnace, very exquisitely.' Stirk seems still to have been in New England in July 1650, when William Aspinwall* noted his testimony about a lame and sick mariner. But he left soon after this, possibly with his grandfather Stephen Painter, who arrived in Boston in August 1650, on his way from Bermuda to London.

Stirk soon became connected with leading intellectuals in London. In 1651, Robert Child* introduced him to the natural philosopher Robert Boyle (*ODNB*), no doubt as a result of John Winthrop Jr's recommendations. Stirk and Boyle conducted some experiments before Boyle went to Ireland in 1652. Stirk wrote medical and scientific tracts, some of which were published only after his death.

At the Restoration Stirk made little secret of his royalist convictions. He lived in London. He signed a prefatory epistle to *Pyrotechny* (1658) 'from my chamber at the White Swan in Foster-lane'; later, he had a house at 'St Thomas Apostles, next door to Black-Lyon-Court'. He died in the city during the Great Plague of 1665. John Allin* reported on Stirk's experiments with plague victims, in which he and his associates

> would give money for the most infected body they could heare of . . . upon the opening whereof a stench ascended from the body, and infected them every one . . . they are all dead since, the most of them distractedly madd, whereof G. Starkey is one.

Publications [as George Starkey] *The marrow of alchemy* (1655); *Nature's explication* (1657); *Pyrotechny* (1658); *George Starkey's pill vindicated* ([1660?]); *Royal and innocent blood crying to heaven for vengeance* (1660); *The dignity of kingship* (1660); *Monarchy triumphing* (1661); *Via ad vitam* (1661); *A smart scourge for a silly sawcy fool* (1664); *A brief censure and examination of several medicines* (1664); *An epistolary discourse to the . . . author of Galens-pale* (1665); *Liquor alkahest* (1675); *The admirable efficacy of . . . true oyl* (1683) [in Eireneaus Philalethes, *Collectanea chymica* (1684), 139–154].

WP IV, 158; *WP* V, 184, 241–2; Aspinwall, 304; G.L. Kittredge, 'Doctor Robert Child the Remonstrant', Colonial Society of Massachusetts, *Publications*, 21 (1919), 100–1; Stirk, *Nature's explication* (dedicated to Robert Tichborne, lord mayor of London), 'Epistle to Reader'; Stirk, *Pyrotechny*, dedicatory epistle to Robert Boyle; Stirk, *Royal and other innocent blood*, sig.A2v; *Collectanea chymica*, 148; John Allin to Philip Frith of Rye, 14 September 1665, ESRO, Frewen MS 5466.

CC, Sibley.

STOLLYON, Abraham

Abraham Stollyon [Stolion, Stolyon] came from London to New Haven, *c.*1640, with his mother Jane. His siblings Thomas and Elizabeth stayed in England.

He went back to England *c.*1645, at Jane's behest, on family business. While he was away, Jane Stollyon died. On her deathbed she had produced her will and appointed Stephen Goodyear* and Robert Newman* as trustees of her estate until Abraham got back. The terms of her will, at first, seemed simple enough: she left all her estate in England to Thomas, and all her estate in New England to Abraham. The trouble was, she left only £4 to her daughter Elizabeth Combes, and that was to be paid out only after her son Abraham died.

Abraham Stollyon went to England again in the winter of 1646, and proved his mother's will, 4 May 1647. He bought up his brother's share of the estate in England, and stayed on. In 1648, 'Mr Combes', Abraham's brother-in-law, arrived in New England to lay claim to more of Jane Stollyon's estate on Elizabeth Combes's behalf. Abraham Stollyon sent word from England that Combes had been fully paid, and appointed two more trustees in New England to sell off his mother's property. Theophilus Eaton laid out the whole history in a letter to John Winthrop, 30 October 1648, to alert Winthrop that the matter had been fully considered in New Haven. 'Mr Combes' did not have a case.

WP V, 274–6; Waters, 999; NA, PROB 11/200/597, will of Jane Stolion, widow of London, 4 May 1647.

STONE, John (*c.*1634–1660)

John Stone was born at Cambridge, Massachusetts, the eldest son of the minister Samuel Stone (*ODNB*). He moved with his family to Hartford, Connecticut, in 1636. He graduated BA from Harvard in 1653. Charges on his account continued until 8 December 1654.

On 10 March 1653/4, Stone was admitted to Pembroke College, Cambridge. He became a fellow on 6 July 1654. On 6 April 1655 he was incorporated BA at Cambridge, and graduated MA in 1657. His history after that is uncertain. There is no clear evidence to identify him with John Stone (*CR*), vicar of Hellingly in Sussex from 1657, who was ejected in 1662. A 'John Stone' with a Cambridge MA was ordained priest in the diocese of Chichester, 9 June 1663.

Harvard Recs. III, 79n.; *GMB* 1771, *s.n.* Samuel Stone; *CR*; *CCEd* Person ID 70475.

CC, Sibley.

STONEHILL, Henry

Henry Stonehill came from Aston Clinton, Buckinghamshire. He was listed in the Milford land records, 20 November 1639, as one of the first 'free planters' of the town. Some of the settlers had come over in 1637 with Peter Prudden, who became Milford's minister. Among Stonehill's Milford neighbours were John Astwood* and Philip Hatley*. 'Hennery Stonehill' was admitted to Milford church on 13 June 1641.

Stonehill had 'removed to London' by 1648, as Philip Hatley had done. Stonehill, like Hatley, wrote back to New England to request dismission from the church: the Milford records note that Stonehill was dismissed 'to the church in London wherof Mr Thomas Goodwin is Pastour (in Colman Street)'. The record-keeper confused Thomas Goodwin with John Goodwin of St Stephen's Coleman Street. Thomas Goodwin's gathered church met initially in London at St Dunstan in the East but from 1648 at All Hallows, Lombard Street; another colonist who joined Goodwin's church was Richard Hutchinson*, dismissed in 1645 from Boston.

NEHGR 26: 296–7, 38: 166, 170; Milford *CR*, fol. 2; *Connecticut VR*, Milford, 153; *The Connecticut Nutmegger* 8: 354; *The American Genealogist* 14: 58, 16: 30; *ODNB*, 'Goodwin, Thomas (1600–1680)'; *Boston CR*, 44.

STORER, Richard

Richard Storer spent some years as an apprentice to a London goldsmith. He travelled to New England in 1635 with his mother Elizabeth and stepfather Robert Hull. Storer's stepbrother John Hull (*ANB*) became eminent in Boston as a silversmith and mintmaster. Storer was granted land in Braintree, November 1639, but after that there is no clear trace of him in New England.

Storer wrote from Bristol on 19 April 1643 to John Winthrop Jr*, then in London. Winthrop was known for his medical skills. Storer reported that his wife had developed 'a stronge Consumtion'. He now feared for her life and sought any advice Winthrop could give, and any financial help. Storer had been forced to sell his 'flocke bed and other thinges' to make ends meet. He had found work in the service of 'Corronall Finnes': Colonel Nathaniel Fiennes (*ODNB*), in charge of parliamentary forces in Bristol at that point. Storer was employed in 'a messengers place ... to runne of messeges for him and the Counsell of warr'. Given the state of his wife's health, Storer thought a return to New England impossible, for the present.

GMB 460–2; *WP* IV, 374–5.

STOUGHTON, Israel (1602/3–1644)

Israel Stoughton, baptised at Great Coggeshall in Essex, on 18 February 1602/3, was the youngest son of Thomas and Elizabeth Stoughton. His father, a minister, was deprived in 1606 and moved to Great Totham, Essex. Israel married Elizabeth Knight at Rotherhithe in 1627. His brother, John Stoughton (*ODNB*), was a West Country minister with links to New England emigrants. Another brother, Thomas, sailed for New England in 1630 and settled in Dorchester, Massachusetts.

Israel and Elizabeth Stoughton emigrated in 1632 and also settled at Dorchester. Israel was admitted a freeman of Massachusetts on 5 November 1633. In 1636, he and his wife headed the list of members at the gathering of a new Dorchester church; they are likely to have been part of the earlier Dorchester church, whose members moved together to settle Windsor, Connecticut. Israel Stoughton was a leader in the church, and may be the captain Thomas Lechford wrote of: 'I have heard a Captaine delivered one to Satan, in the Church at Dorchester, in the absence of their Minister.' Stoughton became the first captain of the Dorchester train-band, 1636, and joined the Artillery Company in 1637. When it was decided to send town representatives to the General Court in 1634, Stoughton was elected as the first representative for Dorchester. He led the campaign for constitutional checks on the arbitrary power of the governor and assistants. In 1635 John Winthrop accused him of being an 'underminer of the state', and Stoughton's tract against the governor's power of veto was ordered to be burnt. Stoughton was barred from office for three years, but in the crisis of the Antinomian Controversy his orthodoxy made him valuable. He served as an assistant, 1637–44. He played a leading military role in the defeat of the Pequot Indians, May 1637, and in 1641 became sergeant-major-general of Massachusetts.

Stoughton's military skills led him to England. He joined the parliamentary army in 1643. He had crossed the Atlantic *c.*1642 on business – 'mr Israell Stoughton one of the magistrates havinge been in England about merchandice ... returned with good advantage' – but then went back, '& entered into the Parliamentes service'. Stoughton served as lieutenant colonel to Thomas Rainborowe (*ODNB*). John Winthrop recorded that Stoughton left in company with 'diverse other of our best millitary men': Nehemiah Bourne* (who became a major in Stoughton's regiment), John Leverett* (captain of a foot company), William Hudson* (an ensign in Leverett's company) and Francis Lisle* (a surgeon).

Stoughton made a will in London, 17 July 1644, 'being now likely to run some part of the hazard of warre'. He fell sick, and died at Lincoln towards the end of 1644. An inventory of his goods was taken in New England on 2 April 1650. He left half his small library to his son William Stoughton*, 'for his incouragement to apply himself to studies, especially to the holy Scriptures; unto which they are mostly helpful'. He also left 200 acres of land to the newly founded Harvard College.

NEHGR 3: 92, 4: 51–2, 162; 7: 333; *Dorchester CR*, 4; Lechford *PD*, 12 (3 *MHSC* 3: 72, refers to a copy with a manuscript note in the margin that identifies Stoughton with the captain); *Mass. Recs.* 1: 137; *WJ*, 604–5 (see also 142, 145–6, 215, 218, 225–7, 229, 373n., 390n., 574, 762); *Wyllys Papers*, 53; C.H. Firth and G. Davies, *The regimental history of Cromwell's army* (Oxford: Clarendon Press, 1940), 417–18; *GMB* 1773–7.

ODNB.

STOUGHTON, William (1631–1701)

William Stoughton, son of Elizabeth and Israel Stoughton*, was born at Dorchester, Massachusetts, on 30 September 1631. He graduated BA from Harvard in 1650, and on 2 August 1651 received a diploma signed by Henry Dunster as president and by Jonathan Mitchell, Urian Oakes* and John Collins* as fellows.

Stoughton carried his Harvard diploma to England. He was incorporated BA at Oxford on 28 April 1652 and elected a fellow of New College on 14 September. He graduated MA on 30 June 1653. He had leave of absence from New College, 29 September 1653, 'quod privitia aliqua negotia praesentiam suam in Scotia requirunt'. He was back in Oxford by 1656 and bursar of New College in 1657. He lost this post in 1660, and also the curacy of Rumboldswyke, Sussex, to which he had been presented on 6 December 1659.

Stoughton returned to New England in 1662, and became a freeman of Massachusetts on 3 May 1665. He was invited three times to become a minister at Dorchester, but refused. After Jonathan Mitchell's death in 1668 he also refused an invitation from the church at Cambridge. In 1671 John Hull wrote that Stoughton was 'an able preacher and very pious, but not yet persuadable to take any office charge in any church'. He devoted himself to landowning and to politics. He was in England again, as a colonial agent, 1677–9, and also refused invitations to ministry there. He served as an assistant, 1671–86; as a selectman for Dorchester, 1671–4; as a federal commissioner, 1673–7 and 1680–6; and as a member of Andros Council, 1686, which made unpopular concessions to the crown. In 1691 he became lieutenant governor of Massachusetts, and in 1692 was chief justice at the Salem witch trials. He died at Dorchester.

Publications *New-Englands true interest* (Cambridge, MA, 1670); *A narrative of the proceedings of Sir Edmond Androsse* ([n.p., 1691); official publications as lieutenant governor of Massachusetts.

NEHGR 4: 51–2; *Harvard Recs.* III, 37n.; LPL, MS COMM. VIa/10, fol. 137; *Dorchester CR*, 54, 59.

ANB, CC, CR, ODNB, Sibley.

STOWE, John (1619–1643)

John Stowe was the son of John and Elizabeth Stow of Biddenden, Kent, and the nephew of Smalehope Bigg, a clothier at Cranbrook. His parents emigrated in 1634, with six children – Thomas, Elizabeth, John, Nathaniel, Samuel and Thankful – and settled at Roxbury.

Stowe went back to Kent and set up as a clothier at Cranbrook, where his uncle, Smalehope Bigg, had died in 1638. John Stowe's will, made on 28 September 1643 and proved on 2 December, included bequests to his father and siblings in New England. His uncle, Peter Masters of Cranbrook, acted as executor.

GM 6: 563; NEHGR 93: 297–8.

STOWERS, John

John Stowers probably came from Parham, Suffolk, the community to which he returned in the 1650s.

Stowers arrived in Watertown in 1634 or 1635. He became a freeman of Massachusetts on 25 May 1636, and so (as only church members could become freemen) must have already been admitted to the church. In 1643 Stowers supported Nathaniel Biscoe*, a wealthy tanner, in a battle with their minister, George Phillips. Biscoe opposed infant baptism. Stowers read out passages from a handwritten pamphlet by Biscoe, which allegedly made offensive remarks against the 'officers and church of Watertown'. The authorities fined Stowers forty shillings for causing a disturbance. George Phillips, however, judged Biscoe's work to be relatively harmless, 'fuller of teeth to bite and reproach the ministers ... than arguments to convince the readers'. He petitioned the Massachusetts General Court in Stowers's defence:

> The man hath been a member with us a long time & though he be not free from human frailties yet I am persuaded he is free from all Anabaptistical opinion neither have I ever observed in him any carriage towards God's ordinances but such as well becometh his place.

Stowers left for England in the autumn of 1650, to judge from the evidence on record, and made his way to Parham in Suffolk. In October 1650, he sold off land and housing in Watertown. That month also, his neighbour Thomas Hammond agreed to send Stowers £40 by 28 December 1652, 'at the dwelling house of John Stowers (the father of the said Stowers) situate in Parham in the county of Suffolk in old England'. Stowers's daughter Elizabeth, baptised at Watertown in 1637, was married at Parham on 20 March 1654/5. John Stowers's father died at Parham in January 1657/8: his will, proved on 11 May 1658, mentioned 'John Stowers my eldest son' and made other bequests to children and grandchildren.

Some years after the Restoration, John Stowers returned to New England. In

1685, as 'John Stowers of Newport in Rhod Island . . . formerly of Watertowne', he sold off 130 acres in Watertown.

> GM 6: 565–70; Roger Thompson, *Divided we stand: Watertown, Massachusetts, 1630–80* (Amherst, MA: University of Massachusetts Press, 1994), 69–70, 79; NA, PROB 11/278/418, will of John Stowers, yeoman of Parham, Suffolk, 11 May 1658.

SWINFIELD, Raphael

Raphael Swinfield had travelled to New England. In 1653 he spoke about this in Dublin, in his testimony to the church gathered by the Fifth Monarchist John Rogers (*ODNB*), at 'a publick place called Michaels':

> I went into New-England, and had much comfort from them, and their Ministers, and was much affected with their way; but by reason I could not (before) bring my Wife and Family over thither with me, I came home again hither to my Wife and Family whom I found (I thank God) all well and living; and ever since I have been here, but walking alone, and very disconsolate for want of such a society as this; and I shall now much rejoyce, if I may be one with you in this onenesse of love and spirit, which (I perceive) you are in.

> John Rogers, *Ohel or Bethshemesh: a tabernacle for the sun* (1653), 397.

SWINNOCK, Joseph (d. 1662)

Joseph Swinnock studied at Harvard with the class of 1651, but there is no record of his graduation. The index to the steward's book refers to pages (now missing) headed 'Swineoke'.

Swinnock became chaplain of New College, Oxford, on 19 January 1648/9, and graduated MA in 20 June 1653. He was said to have spent '7 years in academical study here [at Oxford], and at Cambridge, N.E.'. William Stoughton* was also at New College. Nathaniel* and Samuel Mather* did not mention Swinnock in their letters about other Harvard students in 1651. He was admitted rector of St Martin Orgar, in London, 19 March 1656/7, with certificates from Elidad Blackwell of St Andrew Undershaft, John Meriton of St Nicholas Acons, Thomas Irons, William Wickens and William Blackmore. Ninian Butcher, of St Mary Aldermanbury in London, left legacies in 1658 to his cousins Joseph, Caleb and Samuel Swinoke.

At the Restoration, Swinnock conformed. William Hooke* mentioned this in a letter – intercepted by the authorities – to John Davenport of New Haven:

> one Swinock (sometimes a New England scholar ... and known to Mr Corbet) living lately in Thames street, or thereabout, yielding to put on the surplice, but with reluctancy, read the service with a disturbed spirit, and was so smitten in it, that he took his bed, and died (I take it) within two or three days following.

Hooke cited Swinnock's fate as the first of several examples of how 'the hand of God hath gone out against several who have submitted to this devised worship'. Swinnock's successor was installed at St Martin Orgar in October 1662.

Harvard Recs. III, 55n.; LPL, MS COMM. III/5, fol. 233; W.A. Shaw, *A history of the English Church ... 1640–1660* (London: Longmans & Green, 1900), II, 590; Waters, 22, 75–6; *NEHGR* 38: 416; William Hooke to John Davenport, 2 March 1662/3, A.G Matthews, ed., 'A censored letter', *Transactions of the Congregational Historical Society*, 9 (1924–6), 266, also *CSPD, 1663–4*, 63.

CC.

T

TARE, Jane and Richard

Jane Tare was described in a deed of 1656 as formerly the wife of John Parker of Boston, now the wife of Richard Tare. She had two sons by her marriage to Parker, Noah and Thomas. On 7 October 1656, Jane Tare, with her son Thomas Parker, sold off land given to her by the town of Boston to Clement Corbin, for 'tenn pounds to them in hand paid'.

The land was sold to raise money for a passage to England. The going rate for the journey to England was £5 for an adult (as in the case of John Morse*, who struggled to raise £15 for a party of three). The deed of sale stated that 'the said monies together with other parcells from others receaved was to helpe transport the said Jane and Thomas with his Brother Noah into England'. Richard Tare was said to be 'late of Boston': he must have already been in England.

Suffolk Deeds II, 303.

THOMPSON, Edmund and Martha

Edmund and Martha Thompson came from Framlingham, Suffolk. They arrived in New England in 1637 or 1638, with William Fiske (perhaps Martha's father) of Laxfield, Suffolk. Edmund was a seaman – perhaps the 'Mr Thomson' plying between Barbados and New England via Bermuda in August 1646. They settled at Salem, Massachusetts.

In December 1647 they left New England for Great Yarmouth in Norfolk. On 11 January 1648/9, Francis Chickering of Dedham, Massachusetts, made Francis Morse of Wrentham, Suffolk and John Morse of Beccles, Suffolk, attorneys to collect £5 from Edmund Thompson 'late of Salem in New England'. Francis Morse was one of the first lay people to sign the covenant of the Wrentham church, gathered by John Phillip* and William Ames*.

N.C.P. Tyack, 'Migration from East Anglia to New England before 1660' (PhD dissertation, University of London, 1951), 85; *WP* IV, 96, 236n., 464; Aspinwall, 186–7; Wrentham CB, fol. 25.

THORNTON, Thomas (*c.*1608–1699/1700)

Thomas Thornton came from London. On 23 April 1633 he married Ann Tinker at St Margaret Moses, London.

Thomas and Ann Thornton emigrated in 1633. They settled at Dorchester initially, but moved to Windsor in 1636 and to Stratford in 1650. Thomas was a representative for Stratford in 1651. He served on the town's war committee in May 1653, at a time when hostilities with the Dutch at New Netherland threatened communities like Stratford.

Thomas Thornton left New England by 1654, probably with his family. He escaped the threat of conflict with the Dutch, and seems to have been attracted by Cromwell's campaign to recruit settlers for Ireland. A former colonist called Thomas Thornton was on the civil list in Ireland, as a minister at Six-Mile-Bridge (probably in County Clare). The same man was a preacher in County Limerick, at Galbally before December 1656 and at Caherconlish c.1657.

A Thomas Thornton came to Boston in 1663, with his wife and family. He served as minister at Yarmouth for thirty years. The evidence suggests this was the Thomas Thornton who had been in Stratford.

D.G. Allen, *In English ways* (Chapel Hill, NC: University of North Carolina Press, 1981), 179; *GD*; *NEHGR* 5: 365, 33: 274; St J.D. Seymour, *The puritans in Ireland, 1647–1661* (Oxford: Clarendon Press, 1921), 222; *GMB* 1814–17.

THURSTON, Richard and Martha

Martha Thurston was the daughter of William Phillips. Her husband, Richard Thurston, was described in October 1650 as a Boston mariner of the ship *John Adventurer*. Martha's sister Rebecca* had married Robert Lord*. The Thurstons and the Lords shared a house in Boston. Richard Thurston, Robert Lord and William Phillips, with Charles Thurston, all 'of New-England in the parts beyond the seas Marriners' signed a bond in 1654 for £100 to Thomas Fowke, a London grocer: this debt remained unpaid in 1655.

Richard and Martha Thurston moved to England at some point in the early 1650s, with Robert and Rebecca Lord. On 8 January 1656/7, William Phillips, by a power of attorney from his two sons-in-law, sold the Boston house Rebecca and Martha had inherited from their mother, in which 'the said Captaine Richard Thurston and Robert Lord did late Inhabitt and dwell before they with each of theire familyes went for England'. Phillips was to get, within three years, 'a good sufficyent Ample Legall and firme deede or conveyance of the aforesaid house'. The document, to be signed in England by Richard Thurston and Robert Lord, should be 'sealed sufficiently Confirmed and wittnessed by two persons or more that comes to New England, who will testify the sealing and delivery thereof'.

The records of the congregational church at Stepney, Middlesex, show that the Thurstons and the Lords both lived on 'New Gravel Lane', perhaps again in the same house. Both couples had children baptised at the Stepney church, where William Greenhill was minister.

Aspinwall, 323, 332; *Suffolk Deeds* II, 329–30; *WP* VI, 392; Stepney CB, fol. 121.

TOMLINS, Edward

Edward Tomlins, a carpenter, was the son of Edward Tomlins of Todenham, Gloucestershire. He emigrated in 1630, and his younger brother Timothy followed him to New England in 1632. Both settled at Lynn.

'Mr Edw: Tomlyns' became a freeman of Massachusetts on 18 May 1631. Tomlins was a deputy for Lynn at the General Court in 1634, 1635, 1639, 1643 and 1644. In 1634 the Court charged him with checking the condition of 'ordinances, powder and shot', and gave him power 'to press men & carts for ordinary wages, to help towards the making of such carriages and wheels as are wanting for the ordinances'. In 1637, the year he joined the Massachusetts Artillery Company, 'Sargent Tomlines' was appointed 'cannoneer'. In 1642 he was put on a committee to oversee the making of saltpetre (used in the manufacture of gunpowder) at Lynn. He served as clerk of writs for Lynn in 1643.

Tomlins's radical religious convictions are suggested by two short entries in colonial records. On 1 June 1641, the General Court recorded that 'Mr Edward Tomlins, retracting his opinions against singing in the churches, was discharged'. On 28 September 1641, John Winthrop drew attention to the illegal occupation of land on Long Island (part of the patent of the earl of Stirling), by 'Edward Tomlins and Timothy Tomlins, together with one Hanserd Knowles, clerk, & others'. Hanserd Knollys* sailed for England in December 1641 and became a prominent baptist. The last record of Edward Tomlins in New England is on 9 December 1644.

A 'Capt. Ed. Tomlins' was resident in London on 1 February 1648/9, when Joseph Redknap of Lynn sold him land at Hampton Court in Middlesex. He was still living, 23 July 1661, when his brother Samuel left him a bequest.

GMB 1825–30; *GM* 7: 23, *s.n.* Edward Thomlins.

TOPPING, Richard and Alice

Richard Topping, a draper, arrived in Boston in 1633, with his family. He and his first wife, Judith, joined the Boston church in November that year. Topping became a freeman of Massachusetts on 4 March 1633/4. Judith Topping died in 1635. Topping remarried: his second wife, Alice, was admitted to the Boston church on 17 April 1647.

On 29 August 1654, Richard and Alice Topping sold their 'dwelling house ... in Boston ... with all the houses, outhouses, shops, buildings, orchards & backside thereunto adjoining'. This is the last record of them in New England: they left for England soon afterwards, with their youngest children Joseph and Benjamin (baptised in Boston, 1648 and 1650).

Richard Topping of Soulbury, Buckinghamshire, made a will on 20 August 1657. He named four older children still in New England; also, in England, his eldest son Richard and youngest children Joseph, Benjamin and Lydia. The will was proved on 9 April 1658.

GMB 1830–2; NA, PROB 11/274/291, will of Richard Topping of Soulbury, Buckinghamshire, 9 April 1658.

TRACY, Stephen

Stephen Tracy was probably the 'Stephen Trace' baptised at Great Yarmouth, Norfolk, in 1596. Before emigration he was at Leiden, Holland, employed as a 'say worker', or cloth-worker. He married Tryphosa Lee in Leiden, 1621.

He sailed to New England in 1623, in the *Anne*. Tryphosa and their daughter Anne followed in 1625. Tracy settled at Plymouth initially, but by the early 1630s had moved within the Plymouth Colony to Duxbury.

On 20 March 1654/5, Stephen Tracy made a will in London, describing himself as 'att present of great yarmouth in old England'. The will was in the form of a power of attorney to John Winslow of Plymouth. Tracy referred to land and houses at 'Duxburrow', and divided his property between his five children in New England.

GMB 1832–4; *The Mayflower Descendant*, 10 (1908), 143–4.

TRAVERS, Henry

Henry Travers's origins are unknown. He sailed from Southampton on the *Mary & John*, 24 March 1633/4, with the minister Thomas Parker (*ODNB*) and his company. With others in that group, he probably settled initially at Ipswich and then moved with Parker to Newbury.

On 26 July 1648, Henry Travers made a will, 'having occasion to go to sea and know not whether I shall live to Com againe'. He left his house and most of his property to his son, who was at that time not yet three.

In 1655, his wife 'Bridgett Travers of Newbury' told the Ipswich court that Travers 'went away to England from me seven years agone, and left me two children'. She had not heard from him for five years. She petitioned to be allowed to 'enjoy my house and land' until her son was of age, and after that to receive 'the thirds during my natural life'. Life had been hard: 'I and my children was very mean in apparel . . . I had not so much as an house to dwell in and left me also five pounds in debt.' The court would not grant probate at this point. Several years later, on 15 July 1659, an inventory of Travers's estate was taken. The value amounted to £92 17s 6d, of which £80 was tied up in the house and land. On 27 September 1659, the Ipswich court granted administration to Bridget, who had by that time remarried.

GM 7: 88–93; D.G. Allen, *In English ways* (Chapel Hill, NC: University of North Carolina Press, 1981), 266; Bridget Travers's petition, *Essex Probate Recs.* I, 292–4 (assigned a date of 1661 by the editors, but redated to 1655 by *GM*).

TROTMAN, John and Katherine

John and Katherine Trotman [Totman] perhaps initially settled at Roxbury, where 'Totman the wife of John Totman' became a member of the church. Later, they were in Boston.

John Trotman wrote to Katherine from London, 16 February 1644/5, giving authority for her to sell 'my house and ground and the appurtenances belonging thereunto'. He expected her to hurry back to England, travelling light: 'I pray wife make sale of all your goods, bedding, pewter, brasse, Iron potts, all your weareing clothes, safeing the bed you lye on, and the clothes that you bring on your backe.' William Aspinwall*, in his capacity as public notary, entered this authority in the records of Suffolk county deeds. On the same day, he noted Katherine Trotman's sale of a house to the baker Thomas Hawkins, and details of John Trotman's earlier purchase of this house from John Davis*. Katherine Trotman presumably left for England soon after this.

Roxbury CR, 85; *Suffolk Deeds* I, 60–1.

TROWBRIDGE, Thomas

Thomas Trowbridge [Trobridge], a mercer of Taunton, Somerset, settled in Dorchester *c.*1636 and perhaps joined the Artillery Company in 1637 ('Strawbridge'). He moved to New Haven, and soon ran into financial difficulties. By April 1644 he had gone away, abandoning not only his debts but also his children: the New Haven court impounded his estate and put his children into care.

Trowbridge may have returned to Taunton and perhaps served as an army captain under Robert Blake (*ODNB*), parliamentary governor of Taunton. In 1647, Robert Keayne of Boston appointed attorneys in London to receive debts from (among others) Thomas Trowbridge, late of New Haven. In 1660, a 'Thomas Trewbridge' owed money to the estate of Mahalaleel Munnings*.

Dorchester CR, 4, 150; *Artillery Company*, 51; *New Haven Recs.* 1: 59, 61, 92, 124, 133, 219; Somerset Record Office, Taunton Quarter Session Records, petitions of Richard Hillard, Emmanuell Butler (Q\SPET/1/115, Q\SPET/1/125); Aspinwall, 92, 96; *NEHGR* 10: 177; F.B. Bacon, *The Trowbridge Genealogy* (New Haven, CT: privately printed, 1908), 37, 43, 44-8.

TURNER, Nathaniel (d. 1646)

Nathaniel Turner arrived in New England in 1630 and settled at Lynn, Massachusetts, where he served as a magistrate, a deputy to the General Court, and as captain of the militia. Turner moved to New Haven in 1638, where he became a church member and (as at Lynn) played an important role in civil and military affairs.

Turner sailed for London in January 1645/6, from New Haven, on the *Fellowship*. This ship, then on its maiden voyage, had been built by a consortium of merchants in the town to export goods directly to England. In a disaster that haunted the people of New Haven, the *Fellowship* was lost at sea, with all aboard. As yet unaware of this, on 23 February 1645/6 the town chose a new captain to lead the New Haven militia 'instead of Captain Turner, not knowing when he will return'.

I.M. Calder, *The New Haven Colony* (New Haven, CT: Yale University Press, 1934), 160; *WJ*, 630-1, 643-4, 713-14; *GMB* 1847-50.

TUTTLE, Hannah

Hannah Tuttle was the daughter of John* and Joanna Tuttle*, who settled at Ipswich, Massachusetts, in 1635. She was probably born at Ipswich, not long after their arrival.

By April 1657 Hannah was in Carrickfergus, Ireland. Her mother reported: 'Hanna is to be married shortly to a good husband, one that loves her well and a handsome man.' By 20 March 1657/8 Joanna was living with Hannah and her husband, who had taken over John Tuttle's job as a receiver of revenue.

Essex Court Recs. II, 142, 173.

TUTTLE, Joanna

Joanna [Joan], as the widow of Thomas Lawrence, married John Tuttle* in 1628. They lived at St Albans, Hertfordshire. She was listed as a passenger to New England in 1635 on the *Planter*, aged forty-two, with John, her elderly mother Joan Antrobus, and four children from her marriage to Tuttle – Abigail, Simon, Sara and John, aged from six down to one. Also aboard the *Planter* were children from her marriage to Thomas Lawrence: John, Mary, Thomas and William Lawrence, and Jane Giddings with her husband George.

John and Joanna Tuttle settled in Ipswich in 1635, but moved to Boston by 1650. Some of their children put down roots in Ipswich and Boston; Simon and John Tuttle travelled to Barbados; John and Thomas Lawrence moved west – John Lawrence was in New Amsterdam by 1657.

After John Tuttle went to Ireland, Joanna Tuttle left New England and followed him over with her youngest daughter Hannah*. She was there by 1655. Among the papers of the Essex Quarterly Court, three letters survive which Joanna sent back to New England from Ireland. The first, sent to her daughter Jane (wife of George Giddings of Ipswich, who acted as John Tuttle's attorney in New England), was dated 3 October 1656. She reported all were in good health, and

> The letter I receaved from you I lay by me as a cordiall which I often Refresh my selfe with. If you know how much it Rejoyced me to hear from you, you would nott omitte. I pray let me hear how your breach is made up in Respect of the ministrey which I long to hear, if you have Mr Cobete [Thomas] I pray present my love to him and tell him I live under a very honest man [Timothy Taylor], wher I inJoy the ordinances of god In new england way. We want nothing but more good company. The lord increase the number.

On 6 April 1657 she wrote to George Giddings to tell him of John Tuttle's death, and to warn against letting her sons Simon and John – who were then in Barbados – meddle with her estate in New England. She might herself return from Ireland: 'It may be I may se new ingland againe I pray louke to my house that it be nott Reuined.' On 20 March 1657/8 she wrote again to Giddings about her estate in New England:

> If I should com to new Ingland I feare I should goe a beging if Reportes be true my estate de Cays apase for want of lookeing to. I heare the house goes to Ruine, the land spends itselfe, the cattell dye, the horses eate them selves outt in keeping; so I am like to have a small a count butt I hop it will nott prove as I heare. If it should he that knows all things will a veneg the widows cause.

At this point she was living with Hannah and her husband: Hannah 'remembers her love to you all'. Joanna was also able to send greetings from an old acquaintance, someone she had known before she went to New England in the 1630s: 'Mrs haries the potecaris wife that lived in Saint Albanes: she dwellse next house to me.' Joanna was still living in 29 January 1660/1, when she wrote to make her son Simon Tuttle her attorney in New England. On 15 May 1661 he petitioned the General Court for her against a debt, 'that the widdow and fatherlesse may have releese'.

Essex Court Recs. I, 142–3, 172–4, 335, 365; Essex Court Files, 4-139-1, 5-31-1; *Essex Probate Recs.* I, 278; Mass. Archives, 15B: 248. *GM* 7: 125–35; see also *GM* 1: 67–9 (Antrobus), 3: 52–6 (Giddings), 4: 254–68 (Lawrence).

TUTTLE, John (*c.*1596–1656)

John Tuttle was the son of Simon and Isobel Tuttle of Ringstead, Northamptonshire. He married Joanna* in 1628 and lived at St Albans, Hertfordshire. Tuttle was listed in 1635 as a passenger for New England, with Joanna, his mother-in-law Joan Antrobus, and his children and stepchildren. His brothers Richard and William Tuttle were also aboard. They all sailed on the *Planter*, from London.

Tuttle became a proprietor at Ipswich in 1635. He was admitted to the church before 13 March 1638/9, when he became a freeman of Massachusetts. He served as a deputy for Ipswich at the General Court in 1643. By 1650 he had moved to Boston. He engaged in trade with Barbados.

His decision to leave New England was catalysed by a trading venture that went sour. In the summer of 1649, Tuttle travelled to Barbados, and then on to England (the timing and route are suggested by letters of attorney he was given to take with him). Back in England, Tuttle signed a contract with two Southampton merchants on 16 February 1649/50: this was the deal that went awry. William Stanley and Peter le Gay agreed to supply Tuttle with £1200 by 15 March 1650, to be invested in goods to be shipped to New England. They expected a return by November 1650. However, by 5 June 1650 they were already dissatisfied. Tuttle had gone back to New England, so they appointed attorneys to pursue him. Tuttle, in Boston, was called to appear before William Aspinwall*, the public notary, to answer the accusations relayed by the attorneys. He admitted 'he had not provided the full complement of goods according to agreement' and so stood liable to pay damages. On 28 December 1650, he showed Aspinwall the value of his bills of lading for fish, beef and goods, on ships in Boston harbour, ready to set sail for England.

By this time Tuttle already had it in mind to go to Ireland. He was tempted by the encouragements Oliver Cromwell had sent over to Massachusetts to steer settlers in that direction. On 31 December 1650, just before he set off to England, Tuttle signed a letter to Cromwell with John Knowles*, Thomas Corbet, Samuel Whiting and George Dennison, setting out conditions for moving to Ireland. Tuttle must have carried the letter back across the Atlantic himself.

Tuttle was in Southampton on 1 March 1650/1, when he signed a document to sort out his financial and legal predicament – partly by mortgaging his house and land at Ipswich. (This was recorded in Boston, 30 December 1651, endorsed by the attorney for Stanley and le Gay, acknowledging 'full satisfaction' from Tuttle and releasing him from the mortgage.) He was in London with Nathaniel Mather* by 23 March 1650/1, when Mather wrote to John Rogers of Ipswich that he would not have received Rogers's letter had he and Tuttle not opened a large packet addressed to John Corbet*, who was already in Ireland.

Tuttle's sights were still set on Ireland. By the time Joanna leased out their house and land in Ipswich on 18 March 1653/4 he was said to be 'now living in Ireland'. He had become a receiver of revenue at Carrickfergus. Joanna was with him by 1655. Both were members of the congregational church run by Timothy Taylor (a former colleague of Samuel Eaton*). Tuttle carried letters between Taylor and Thomas Harrison* of Dublin in 1655, at a time when disputes with baptists were rife.

Tuttle died at Carrickfergus on 30 December 1656. George Giddings (his son-in-law) and Joseph Jewett, who had acted as his attorneys in Massachusetts in his absence, were given oversight of his estate. On 27 September 1659, 'there being no will or administration and the heir appearing', it was ordered that if Simon Tuttle gave security to repay rent received and kept the house in repair, he could take possession of his father's estate for the moment, the 'widow's thirds' being reserved for her life. Simon was allowed as an attorney for his mother 1661, when he produced a letter from Joanna as executrix; probate on Tuttle's estate been granted in Ireland.

GM 7:125–45; Aspinwall, 113, 225, 344, 345–6, 382–4, 423–4; *Original letters and papers of state addressed to Oliver Cromwell*, ed. J. Nickolls (London, 1743), 44–5; *Suffolk Deeds* I, 265–71; Mather to Rogers, Boston Public Library MS Am. 1506, v.1, 7 (printed 4 *MHSC* 8: 2); *Thurloe* III, 29; *Essex Court Recs.* II, 142–3, 150, 172–4, 178, 335, 365; *Essex Probate Recs.* I, 277–8; T.C. Barnard, *Cromwellian Ireland: English government and reform in Ireland 1649–1660* (Oxford: Oxford University Press, 1975), 136; *Pilgrims*, 84, 111–12.

V

VASSALL, William (1592–c.1655)

William Vassall, a merchant, was the son of John Vassall (*ODNB*) of Stepney, and the brother of Samuel Vassall (*ODNB*). He married Anna King at Cold Norton, Essex, in 1613. He and Samuel became assistants under the first Massachusetts Bay Company charter on 23 March 1628/9. Two of his children were baptised, in 1626 and 1628, at Little Baddow in Essex, but shortly before he emigrated he was said to be 'late of Pritellwell [Prittlewell] in the countie of Essex'.

Vassall and his family crossed the Atlantic to New England twice in the 1630s. They joined the Winthrop fleet in 1630, and arrived in late June or July, but went home within weeks. When the *Lyon* set sail for England, it carried 'Mr Vassall, one of the Assistants, and his family'. William and Anna Vassall came back to New England in 1635, on the *Blessing*, with five children – Judith, Francis, John, Margaret and Mary. 'Mris Anna Vassaile the wife of Mr William Vassaile' joined Roxbury church in 1635, but in 1636 the family moved to Scituate, in Plymouth Colony, where William joined the church on 28 November. In both the Massachusetts Bay Company and Plymouth Colony, Vassall held office as a magistrate.

Vassall argued for greater liberty of conscience and more latitude in admitting church members. When he did not gain satisfaction he resolved to petition the English parliament. He supported the aims of the Remonstrants in 1646 – Robert Child*, Thomas Fowle*, Samuel Maverick, Thomas Burton, John Smith, David Yale* and John Dand. John Winthrop described Vassall as 'a man of a busy & factious spirit, & allwayes opposite to the Civill Governmentes of this Country, & the way of our Churches'.

Vassall sailed for England in December 1646, in company with the Remonstrant Thomas Fowle. The Remonstrants' petition – or at least a copy of it – was thrown overboard by fellow passengers. This course of action, suggested by the minister John Cotton in a sermon a few days before the ship left, delighted Edward Winslow*. Winslow had been commissioned by Massachusetts to act as an agent in London, in part to limit damage from the Remonstrant affair. Vassall influenced the pamphlet put out by John Child to support his brother Robert, *New Englands Jonas cast up* (1647), but Winslow out-manouevered both Vassall and Child with his riposte, *New-Englands salamander* (1647).

Vassall went to Barbados in 1648 and became a factor for New England merchants. He made his will there on 31 July 1655. Most of his family were with him, but his wife is not mentioned and probably predeceased him. He had estate in Barbados and New England. His daughter Margaret married Joshua Hobart* in Barbados, 25 April 1656.

GMB 1871–5; *ODNB*, s.n. 'Vassall, John (d. 1625)'; *WP* II, 295–6; Thomas Dudley to the countess of Lincoln, March 1630/1, *Letters from New England . . . 1629–1638*, ed. Everett Emerson (Amherst, MA: University of Massachusetts Press, 1976), 72; *Roxbury CR*, 80; *NEHGR* 9: 280; Alison Games, *Migration and the origins of the English Atlantic world* (Cambridge, MA: Harvard University Press, 1999), 150–1; *WJ*, 578n., 624, 647, 705–6, 730, 765, 766; *Pilgrims*, 67–8; Edward Winslow, *New-Englands salamander* (1647), *passim*; Bernard Bailyn, *The New England merchants in the seventeenth century* (Cambridge, MA: Harvard University Press, 1955), 36, 39, 88, 107; Waters, 1319; Graeme J. Milne, 'New England agents and the English Atlantic, 1641–1666', (PhD dissertation, University of Edinburgh, 1993), 305–6 and *passim*; Robert Emmet Wall, *Massachusetts Bay: the crucial decade, 1640–1650* (New Haven, CT: Yale University Press, 1972), 102–4, 157–224 and *passim*.

VENNER, Thomas (1608/9–1661)

Thomas Venner probably came from Littleham, Devon, but was in London by 1633 when he became a member of the Coopers' Company. He testified before the High Court of the Admiralty in 1637, with the separatists Praisegod Barbon [Barebone] (*ODNB*) and Stephen More, about wine bound for Virginia. He was said to be of the parish of All Hallows Barking, close to the Tower of London, when he set sail for New England in 1637.

Venner was admitted to the church at Salem on 25 February 1637/8, and became a freeman of Massachusetts shortly afterwards. He was keen to recruit settlers from New England for Providence Island, as was John Humfrey*, but the venture failed in 1641. Venner and his wife Alice had a son, Thomas, baptised at Salem in 1641. They moved to Boston by February 1644/5, when their daughter Hannah was baptised there by 'communion of churches' (that is, by virtue of Venner's church membership at Salem). Their son Samuel was baptised on the same basis in February 1649/50. Venner joined the Artillery Company in 1645, and had a 'mansion' in Boston, on the waterfront. On 18 October 1648, the Massachusetts General Court appointed Venner to meet with other coopers (including John Milam* and William Cutter*), to appoint wardens to oversee standards. On 26 December 1648, Venner became a Warden of the Company of Coopers.

Venner left for England sometime after October 1651. His wife Alice, and children Thomas and Hannah, probably travelled back with him, or soon after him. They were certainly in London later.

In England, Venner emerged as a radical Fifth Monarchist, prepared to advance the cause of the kingdom of God by force. By 1655, he was back in his old haunts, with a job at the Tower of London as a master cooper. However, he was dismissed and arrested for plotting to blow up the Tower and to assassinate Cromwell. He was already leading a Fifth Monarchist congregation at Swan Alley, Coleman Street. Not long after this, Venner disposed of property in New England – cutting ties with Massachusetts, and raising funds. He sold part of the land on which he had built his house in Boston to Ralph Fogg* of London, a skinner (the deed was witnessed by Nathaniel Williams and the Atlantic sea-captain James Garrett); Fogg assigned it to John Lowle, a cooper.

On 9 April 1656, Thomas and Alice Venner sold their Boston house to Lowle (this deed was witnessed by Jonathan Wade*, with Henry Powning and John Woodmancey, who were all from New England and visiting London).

Venner's plotting gathered momentum. He planned an uprising in April 1657, through a network of armed supporters organised into secretive cells. One of his co-conspirators was the former colonist Wentworth Day*. Another was his son-in-law, William Medley (who had married Venner's daughter Hannah). Medley was the scribe of the 'Vennerite' manifesto, *A standard set up* (1657). When the plotters gathered to launch their revolt, troops swiftly stepped in. For his part in this, Venner was imprisoned in the Tower until 1659. In the early days of the Restoration, he unleashed another assault, 'Venner's rising'. On 6 January 1660/1, he rallied his followers. The rebels had some success in the City of London, where they briefly controlled St Paul's before being pushed back. The authorities tried Venner for treason at the Old Bailey. On 19 January 1660/1 he was hung, drawn and quartered outside his meeting-house in Coleman Street. Efforts were made to show he had orchestrated a national plot. As a result of Venner's rising, the activities of nonconfomists came under harsher scrutiny, and even moderate presbyterians like Adam Martindale felt under threat.

After Venner's death, his son-in-law William Medley continued the cause: 'Mr Medley in Seething Lane, that married Venner's daughter . . . is as right as his father for rebellion', wrote William Pestell to Sir Edward Nicholas, 28 November 1661. In 1674, the authorities raided Alice Venner's house over Medley's activities. Thomas Venner's son, Thomas, also took a radical path: he served as an officer in an English regiment, but joined the ranks of the Monmouth rebels in 1685, appointed a lieutenant-colonel by the duke; in the aftermath, he was said to believe that Christ's earthly kingdom would come in 1688.

B.S. Capp, *The Fifth Monarchy Men* (London: Faber, 1972), 135, 272; C.E. Banks, 'Thomas Venner: the Boston wine-cooper and Fifth-Monarchy Man', *NEHGR* 47: 37–44; *Artillery Company*, 154; MHS, Misc. MSS, 18 October, 26 December 1648, 22 October 1651; Champlin Burrage, 'The Fifth Monarchy insurrections', *English Historical Review*, 25 (1910), 722–47; J. F. Maclear, 'New England and the Fifth Monarchy: the quest for the millennium in early American puritanism', *William and Mary Quarterly*, 3rd series, 32 (1975), 223–60; *Suffolk Deeds* II, 302, 315a–316; *CSPD, 1660–1*, 470–1;*The life of Adam Martindale*, ed. R. Parkinson, Chetham Society, Old Series, IV (Manchester: Chetham Society, 1845, reprint Manchester: Chetham Society, 2001), 143; Richard L. Greaves, *Deliver us from evil: the radical underground in Britain, 1660–1663* (Oxford: Oxford University Press, 1986), 50–7 and *passim*.

BDBR, ODNB.

VERMACE, Mark

Mark Vermace [Vermais, Vermase, Fermayes, 'ffermais', 'ffirmace'] is likely to have been a son of Alice Vermace, who emigrated from Great Yarmouth,

Norfolk, in 1638. Alice set sail with six children, in company with Margaret and Robert Buffam, her sister and brother-in law. They followed other relatives: William and Joanna Towne, who left Yarmouth in 1635, and Edmund Towne, who left in 1637. All settled at Salem: an extended family network of twenty settlers, if household servants are included. Mark Vermace was not separately identified in the emigration record, but was admitted an inhabitant of Salem on 29 October 1638. He became a church member ('Fermayes') on 22 September 1639, and a freeman on 13 May 1640 ('ffermais').

Vermace returned to England before January 1651/2, when he was admitted to the congregational church at Great Yarmouth 'by dismission from the Church in New England'. In the Salem church records, the word 'removed' is entered against his name. He may well have been in Yarmouth several years earlier: there are references in the church book from early 1648 to baptisms of children of Mark and Ruth 'Vermase' (or 'ffirmace'). Congregational practice would have allowed this, even before Mark Vermace became a member at Yarmouth, by 'communion of churches' from Salem. The gathered church at Yarmouth met in the chancel of St Nicholas, where their pastor William Bridge (*ODNB*) had been town preacher since 1642. Their use of this ancient parish church continued until the Restoration. On 18 November 1661, they were locked out.

> Roger Thompson, *Divided we stand: Watertown, Massachusetts, 1630–80* (Amherst, MA: University of Massachusetts Press, 1994), 148, 190; *Salem TR*, 72, 74; *Salem CR*, 8; *NEHGR* 3: 187; Yarmouth CB, 20 January 1647/8, 30 March 1649, 20 January 1651/2, 17 August 1658.

W

WADE, Joan

Joan Wade was the wife of Robert Wade, who arrived at Dorchester in 1635. (He may have been related to Richard Wade, who arrived that year from Symondsbury, Dorset, and also settled in Dorchester.) Robert Wade soon moved to Hartford, where he was admitted a freeman in 1640. By 1657 Robert was in Saybrook.

Joan Wade abandoned her husband and went back to England. In 1657, Robert petitioned for divorce. The divorce was granted on the grounds of

> his wives unworthy, sinfull, yea unnaturall carriage towards him ... notwithstanding his constant and commendable care and indeavours to gaine fellowship with her in the bond of marriage, and that either where she is in England, or for her to live with him here in New England; all which being slighted and rejected by her ... for neare fifteene yeares ...

Conn. Recs. I, 301; *GM* 7: 182–3, 'Richard Wade'.

WALVER, Abraham

Abraham Walver graduated BA at Harvard in 1647, but did not stay to take an MA. He had already gone to England by 26 March 1651, when Samuel Mather* reported to Jonathan Mitchell that 'Sir Birden [John Birden*] and Sir Walver are preachers in their owne county'. To this the historian Thomas Hutchinson later added 'where their friends were'. The Harvard graduate of 1647 could well be the person of this name in Ireland: the minister at 'Maglass' (Mayglass), County Wexford, on the Irish civil list of 1654, who moved to County Galway before June 1658.

Harvard Recs. I, 83, III, 125n.; MHS, Misc. Bd. MSS, 26 March 1651, Samuel Mather to Jonathan Mitchell; Thomas Hutchinson, *The history of Massachusetts from ... 1628 until 1750* (Salem, MA: Thomas Cushing, 1795), I, 112; St J.D. Seymour, *The puritans in Ireland, 1647–1661* (Oxford: Clarendon Press, 1921), 222. Another 'Walver', probably a relation, appears in the Harvard college steward's records from 1651–5.

CC, Sibley.

WARD, James

James Ward was the son of Nathaniel Ward*. He emigrated with his father in 1634. Ward settled at Ipswich, Massachusetts, and James was sent to Harvard. In the spring of 1644, James Ward and John Weld* (son of Thomas Weld*) broke into the houses of Joshua Hewes and Joseph Weld*, and stole money and gunpowder. John Winthrop recorded:

> Two of our ministers' sons, being students in the college, robbed two dwelling houses in the night . . . Being found out, they were ordered by the governours of the college to be whipped, which was performed by the president himself – yet they were about 20 yeares of age . . .

A document survives which says Ward was 'whipp'd publiquely in the Colledge at Cambridge . . . and expelled out of the said Colledge', but Ward graduated BA in 1645. On 3 December 1646 his father obtained a certificate attesting the degree, to take to England.

James Ward was incorporated BA at Oxford, 10 October 1648, the first Harvard student to take up that opportunity. In 1648 he graduated MA and became a fellow of Magdalen College. In 1649, he graduated Bachelor of Physic.

WJ, 510; Mass. Archives, 38B: 39; *Harvard Recs*. I, 83.

Al. Oxon., *CC*, Sibley.

WARD, Nathaniel (1578–1652)

Nathaniel Ward, the son of John Ward, minister of Haverhill, Suffolk, was the brother of the preachers John Ward and Samuel Ward (*ODNB*), and stepbrother of Ezekiel Rogers (*ODNB*). He was admitted sizar at Emmanuel College, Cambridge, in 1596. He graduated BA in 1600, MA in 1603. Ward studied law and travelled on the continent. In 1618 he was ordained, and from 1620 to 1624 served as chaplain to English merchants at Elbing, Prussia. He became curate of St James's Piccadilly, in London, 1626–8. In 1628 Sir Nathaniel Rich, as patron, presented him as rector of Stondon Massey, Essex. The Massachusetts Bay Company invited Ward in 1629 to leave for New England, but he declined. He joined other ministers, notably Thomas Hooker, to resist the campaign for conformity promoted by William Laud as bishop of London. On 13 December 1631, eight months after Hooker fled to Holland, Ward wrote to John Cotton about the pressure he was still under from Laud's officials. Laud himself interviewed Ward on several occasions. Ward was suspended, then excommunicated and deprived on 10 December 1632. The rectory of Stondon Massey was declared vacant in August 1633.[1]

Ward travelled to New England in 1634, and settled at Ipswich, Massachusetts. From an early stage, he worried about the progress and policy of the Bay Colony, both in terms of the poor calibre of colonists and (in his view) the over-large grants of land. He opposed John Winthrop Jr's* move from Ipswich to Connecticut, and wrote to him about this in December 1635:

> I feare your tye or obligation to this state and in speciall to this towne is more then you did well consider when you ingaged your self another way ... I am in a dreame att least not awake if it be a way of God for so many to desert this place turning their backs upon us and to seeke the good of their cattell more then of commonwealth ... God doth justly rebuke our state by the losse of so many men vessells and victuals ... for their facility in giving way to ... departure.

Ward drew up a petition from Ipswich inhabitants to the Massachusetts General Court, to resist Winthrop's removal: 'It was for his sake that many of us came to this place and without him we should not have come.' Later, Ward was involved in the decision to establish Haverhill, with his son-in-law Giles Firmin* and son John Ward.

After a short time in New England, Ward withdrew from active ministry, ostensibly for the sake of his health. He served as teacher of the Ipswich church from 1634 to 1636, but after that was 'out of office' (Robert Stansby of Westhorpe, Suffolk, expressed some surprise and alarm that this should be so, in a letter to John Winthrop).

However, this did not stop Ward from playing a vigorous role in Massachusetts' affairs. He provided evidence against the antinomian Anne Hutchinson. He supported the deputies (representatives of the freemen) in their struggle to provide checks and balances to the power of the magistrates: he preached a controversial election sermon on the issue in 1641, chosen as preacher for this occasion by the freemen, though 'now no minister by the received determination of our churches'. As part of the campaign, Ward drew up a lawcode, the *Body of liberties*, to limit the scope for magisterial discretion in interpreting the law. In 1644 the deputies made an unsuccessful attempt to change to the way government was run between sessions of the General Court: instead of the magistrates holding power alone, there should be committee of seven magistrates, three deputies and Ward. This was in part a reaction to the decision in 1643 by John Winthrop and other magistrates to provide military assistance to Charles de la Tour, French lieutenant general at Acadia, against his rival Charles d'Aulnay. The fiercest protest against this 'arbitrary' and unpopular decision had come from magistrates and ministers in Essex County: Richard Saltonstall*, Simon Bradstreet, Ezekiel Rogers, Nathaniel Rogers, John Norton and Nathaniel Ward.[2]

Ward's son-in-law Giles Firmin left for England in 1644, leaving his family in Ward's care. Soon, Ward began to write his satire *The simple cobler of Aggawam in America*. He completed this by the autumn of 1646, and – although he was already planning to cross the Atlantic – sent the manuscript ahead, to his brother John, a member of the Westminster Assembly. It was printed in January 1646/7 under a pseudonym, 'Theodore de la Guard'. The simple cobbler urged the king to bring reform, opposed religious toleration, and criticised the Westminster Assembly for its lack of progress: 'If publique

Assemblies of Divines cannot agree upon a right way, private Conventicles of illiterates will soone finde a wrong.' Ward's cobbler was frustrated with the religious divisions that had opened up: 'He that sayes the Presbyterian and Independent way, if rightly carryed doe not meet in one, he doth not handle his Compasses so considerately as he should.' The cobbler gave his own opinion:

> for Church worke, I am neither Presbyterian, nor plebsbyterian, but an Interpendent: My task is to sit and study how shapeable the Independent way will be to the body of England, then my head akes on one side; and how suitable the Presbyterian way, as we heare it propounded, will be to the minde of Christ, then my head akes on the other side: but when I consider how the Parliament will commoderate a way out of both, then my head leaves aking.

At the end of 1646, Ward took final steps to prepare for a return to England: he sold land in Haverhill on 25 November; he obtained a certificate from Harvard for his son James Ward* on 3 December; a week later, he transferred to Harvard 600 acres he had been given by the General Court, in lieu of £20 owed for his son's education.[3]

Soon afterwards he set sail. He wrote later of a 'hard winter voyage over the vast raging seas'. Ward may well have carried back with him the manuscript of John Eliot's *The day breaking if not the sun rising of the gospell with the Indians.* This appeared in print in April 1647 with a prefatory letter from Ward. He was back home by March 1647, because Edward Winslow's *Hypocrisie unmasked*, which went to press then, included details of a conversation with Ward in London.

Ward never set out to make himself popular, and his robust conservatism was out of step with the times. On 30 June 1647, in a sermon to the House of Commons, he criticised the army. He was not formally thanked and invited to print the sermon, as was customary (it was printed, but Ward said this was done privately, at the prompting of friends). Stephen Winthop* reported, 29 July 1647, that Ward 'hath mad himselfe odious and rediculous heere by books and sermons'. A controversy with Hugh Peter* ensued. Peter replied to Ward's *A religious retreat sounded to a religious army* (published in August 1647), in which Ward argued caution and respect for parliament, to avoid further civil war. Peter's riposte, *A word for the armie and 2 words to the kingdom* was answered anonymously (probably by Ward) with *A word to Mr Peters and two words for the parliament and kingdom*. This tract accused Peter of deserting his New England flock for gain: 'I am sensible (so are you too) that Church-cures in New England are not so gainfull as State-cures in old'; Peter's return 'hath brought you in more gains in Old England in one yeer, then you could have gotten in New-England in seven'. Using the kind of extravagant language that had characterised *Simple cobler*, the author declared that Ward had not changed his opinions since coming back from America: he was 'not given to pyrrohonian fluctuation as many of you who are possest with a spirit of giddinesse'.

At some point between January and May 1648, Ward was admitted to the sequestered rectory of Shenfield, Essex, near his former parish at Stondon Massey. He signed the *Essex testimony* in 1648, to accept the Solemn League and Covenant, and in 1649 *The Essex watchman's word*, against toleration. George Thomason attributed to Ward a 'petition', *To the high and honorable Parliament of England*, which protested that presbyterianism and action against heresy and blasphemy had not been pursued as promised. The parliamentary survey of 1650 noted that Ward was an 'able preaching minister'. He died before November 1652, when his successor took over at Shenfield.[4]

Publications *The honest welch-cobler* (1647); *A religious retreat sounded to a religious army* (1647); *A sermon preached before the honourable House of Commons . . . on Wednesday, June 30. 1647* (1647); *The simple cobler of Aggawam in America* (1647); *A word to Mr Peters, and two words for the parliament and kingdom* (1647); *An ansvver to a declaration of the commissioners of the Generall Assembly, to the whole kirk and kingdome of Scotland* ([1648]); *Mercurius anti-mechanicus. Or The simple coblers boy* (1648); *To the high and honorable parliament of England now assembled at Westminster* (1648); *A religious demurrer* ([1649]); *Discolliminium. Or, A most obedient reply* (1650). Ward wrote a postscript to Samuel Ward's *Jethro's justice of peace* (1618); one of his verses introduced the first edition of Anne Bradstreet's poems, *The tenth muse lately sprung up in America* (1650).

[1] Ward's postscript to Samuel Ward, *Jethro's justice of the peace* (1618); Giles Firmin, *Presbyterial ordination vindicated* (1660), 38; Giles Firmin, *The real Christian* (1670), 51, 60, 229; Bush, 162-4; WP III, 60; Tom Webster, *Godly clergy in early Stuart England: the Caroline puritan movement, c.1620-1643* (Cambridge: Cambridge University Press, 1997), 195, 197-9 and *passim*; CCEd Person ID 63166.
[2] WP III, 215-17, 390, 432; WP IV, 221-2, 299-300; David D. Hall, ed., *The antinomian controversy, 1636-1638* (Durham, NC: Duke University Press, 1990), 325, 335; on conflict between the magistrates and deputies, *WJ*, 359-60, 511-12, and Stephen Foster, *Their solitary way* (New Haven, CT: Yale University Press, 1971), 67-98; on La Tour and d'Aulnay, WP IV, 397-401, 402-10 and *WJ*, 440-50; on the lawcode, *WJ*, 314-15, 380, and G.B. Warden, 'Law reform in England and New England, 1620-1660', *William and Mary Quarterly*, 3rd series, 35 (1978), 668-88.
[3] Nathaniel Ward, *The Simple cobler of Aggawam in America* (1647), 39, 35-6; J.W. Dean, *A memoir of the Rev. Nathaniel Ward* (Albany, NY: J. Munsell, 1868), 76-7, 88, 167; *Suffolk Deeds* I, 81; Sibley, s.n. James Ward; *Mass. Recs.* 4(2): 113.
[4] Ward, *A sermon preached before the honorable House of Commons* (1647); J.F. Wilson, *Pulpit in parliament* (Princeton, NJ: Princeton University Press, 1969), 131-2; WP IV, 175; [Ward], *A word to Mr Peters*, 3, 29; LPL, MS COMM. XIIa/8/108-9. See also Jean Béranger, *Nathaniel Ward* (Bordeaux: Études et Recherches Anglaises et Anglo-Américaines, Université de Bordeaux, 1969); Simon P. Newman, 'Nathaniel Ward, 1580-1652: an Elizabethan puritan in a Jacobean world', *Essex Institute Historical Collections*, 127 (1991), 313-26; *Pilgrims*, 54-5, 68-9, 72, 73, 119, 127-8 and *passim*.

ANB, GM 7: 229-35, ODNB.

WATERHOUSE, Thomas (d. 1680)

Thomas Waterhouse was the son of a London barber-surgeon, Edward Waterhouse. He attended Charterhouse school, and then Emmanuel College, Cambridge, graduating BA in 1635. He became an assistant to Mathias Candler (*CR*), vicar of Coddenham, Suffolk. He married Ann Mayhew of Coddenham.

He emigrated by 1639 and became schoolmaster at Dorchester, Massachusetts. He and Ann were admitted to the church on 4 February 1639/40; their daughter Anna was baptised there, 5 April 1640. Thomas became a freeman on 13 May 1640.

When Ann Waterhouse inherited lands at Coddenham from her father, the family returned to England. Thomas Waterhouse was elected a master at Colchester grammar school in June 1643. He remained in Colchester until the end of 1647, on the eve of the siege of the town. He was preaching in the locality, as articles presented on 10 June 1644 against Thomas Bond, vicar of Debenham, Suffolk, show:

> The said Mr Bond since this parliament did most maliciously on purpose read the letany and other service ... to offend weak consciences ... when Mr Waterhouse, a godly Devine (lately come from New England) being to preach in his parish on a lecture day ... [Bond] being demanded why he did read the same then, he knowing it would much offend him he answered he did it for the nonce or words to that effect.

Waterhouse was at Brandeston, Suffolk, in November 1648, when the minister Nicholas Stanton of Ipswich drew up his will. On 2 July 1652 Waterhouse became vicar of Ash Bocking. On 15 January 1657/8 he was admitted to the sequestered rectory of Little Hallingbury, Essex, presented by his old school, Charterhouse: he brought certificates from various Suffolk clergy and the congregationalist John Owen.

In 1660, at the Restoration, the sequestered rector was restored to Little Hallingbury. According to Edmund Calamy, Waterhouse then took up work as a schoolmaster in Ipswich, but was ejected in 1662. His application to be licensed in 1672 at Needham Market (as a congregationalist, along with Thomas James*) was not granted, but his home at West Creeting, Suffolk, was licensed as a presbyterian meeting place, with Thomas James as preacher. Two letters survive from Waterhouse to Increase Mather* in the 1670s, sent over to New England. In a letter of 24 February 1678/9, Waterhouse mentioned his only surviving son, David (a London merchant, buried at West Creeting in 1714), who was at that time in Boston. Waterhouse endorsed Mather's support for the Half-Way Covenant and reported on his discussions with 'divers Nonconformist Ministers of whom some had been in N.E., and found them of my mind'. Thomas died on 20 August 1680 and was buried at West Creeting. The date of his wife's death is unknown.

Dorchester CR, 5, 152; *NEHGR* 3: 187; T.W. Davids, *Annals of evangelical nonconformity in Essex* (London: Jackson, Walford & Hodder, 1863), 573; J. Browne, *A history of congregationalism in Norfolk and Suffolk* (London: Jarrold & Sons, 1877), 368; Clive Holmes, ed., 'The Suffolk Committees for Scandalous Ministers 1644–46', *Suffolk Record Society*, XIII (1970), 82–3; Waters, 1120; LPL, MS COMM. III/6, fol. 177; 4 *MHSC* 8: 588–90, see also 590–2.

CR.

WELD, Edmund (1631–c.1668)

Edmund Weld, son of Thomas Weld*, emigrated as a babe-in-arms with his parents in 1632. He graduated BA from Harvard in 1650, and is not mentioned in the college records after that year. He probably went to England soon. His parents and brother John* had been back in England for some time.

Weld was in Ireland by 1654, on the civil list. He was at Bandon in County Cork, September 1655, and at St Finbarr's, Cork, in May 1656. He was excluded from taking part in a weekly lecture at Cork in 1656: Justice John Cooke reported to Henry Cromwell that the presbyterians who had established the lecture kept out anyone they regarded as not immediately or derivatively ordained by a bishop. Hugh Peter* thanked Cromwell on 24 August 1656 for his 'care of young Mr Weld and men of his constitution'.

Harvard Recs. I, 83; St J.D. Seymour, *The puritans in Ireland, 1647–1661* (Oxford: Clarendon Press, 1921), 54, 104, 162, 223; John Cooke to Henry Cromwell, *Thurloe* V, 353; Hugh Peter to Henry Cromwell, BL Lansdowne MS 823, fol. 364.

CC, Sibley.

WELD, John (1625–*fl.*1669)

John, son of Thomas Weld*, was baptised in his father's parish of Terling, Essex, in 1625. He emigrated with his parents in 1632 and attended Harvard for a time. In the spring of 1644, he and a fellow-student, James Ward* (son of Nathaniel Ward*) broke into the houses of Joshua Hewes and Joseph Weld* at night, and stole money and gunpowder. Both were whipped by the president of the college.

Weld left Harvard without taking a degree. His father had gone to England as a colonial agent in 1641, and stayed on. John Weld followed his father home. In 1645, he became rector of Pickwell, Leicestershire. His father held a living nearby, at Wanlip. Both father and son later went to the northeast of England. John Weld was rector of Boldon, near Sunderland, in 1651. On 17 October 1655 he became rector of Ryton, County Durham: he presented certificates from the Leicestershire ministers Samuel Blackerby of Church Langton (*CR*) and his assistant Walter Hornby Jr (*CR*); William Cooke of Tilton-on-the-Hill (*CR*); Thomas Lowry of Market Harborough (*CR*); and from Edward Chambers. Blackerby and Lowry were assistants to the Leicestershire commissioners for the removal of unsuitable parish ministers. Weld's successor at Ryton was installed on 10 December 1660.

John Weld conformed on 7 March 1665/6. He was ordained at Durham on 19 September 1669 and served as curate of St Andrews, Newcastle upon Tyne.

WJ, 510; LPL, MS COMM. III/4, fol. 240; *WR*, 140, 142.

CC, CR.

WELD, Thomas (1595–1661)

Thomas Weld was the son of Edmund Weld, a linen draper of Sudbury, Suffolk, and brother to Joseph Weld*. He matriculated at Trinity College, Cambridge, in 1611, and graduated BA in 1613/14, MA in 1618. He was ordained deacon at Peterborough, 1 March 1617/18, and priest the following day. For a short time Weld was vicar of Haverhill, Suffolk. He soon became vicar of Terling, Essex, presented by Robert Mildmay: his entries in the register start in February 1624/5. Weld was suspended on 16 December 1630, during a visitation by William Laud, bishop of London, for refusing to subscribe to required articles. He was then excommunicated, and deprived for non-appearance at the church court, 1 September 1631. John Humfrey* wrote to John Winthrop on 18 December 1630: 'Divers godly lecturers and ministers dayly are put by. Mr Weld of Essex is now upon the stage and expects his doome.' Weld went to Amsterdam, along with other exiled preachers who would soon find their way to New England: Thomas Hooker, Hugh Peter* and John Davenport.[1]

Weld set sail for Massachusetts from London on 9 March 1631/2, and arrived on 5 June. He sent back to Essex an ecstatic account of God's protection on the way over, as an incentive to persuade more of his parishioners to follow him:

> Yea mercy mercy in the Lord inwardly outwardly, in spite of devils and storms as cheerful as ever, my wife all the voyage on the sea better than at land, and seasick but one day in eleven weeks, at sea my children never better in their lives. They went ill into the ship but well there and came forth well as ever. Myself had not one ounce of seasickness, nor one motion or inclination thereunto not all the way. 'Stand still and behold the salvation of the Lord' [Exodus 14:13].

Weld praised New England – 'here the greater part are the better part' – and reported that four congregations had approached him to be their minister. On 5 July 1632, Weld became pastor at Roxbury, alongside John Eliot as teacher. In the Antinomian Controversy of 1636–8, he proved a zealous critic of Anne Hutchinson. He became an overseer of Harvard in 1638 – where his son John* was soon in disgrace for theft. Weld was one of the anonymous translators who worked on a new metrical version of the psalms, the first book published in the English American colonies: *The whole book of Psalmes, faithfully translated into English metre* (Cambridge, MA, 1640).[2]

Weld set sail for England on 3 August 1641, as a colonial agent. Although he intended to return to New England, he never came back. The Massachusetts General Court chose him, along with Hugh Peter and William Hibbins*, to promote the colony's cause in London. (For details of their joint activities, see Hugh Peter.) Back in England, Weld paid a visit to his old adversary, William Laud, in the Tower of London: according to Laud, Weld demanded to know, 'in a boisterous manner', whether Laud had repented or not.

In October 1645, the Massachusetts authorities sent Weld and Peter a firm order to return to New England: 'The house of deputies think it meete that as Mr Peeters and Mr Weld being sente over as persons fitt to negotiate for the Country, having bine long absent desire they may understand the Courts minde, that they desire their presence heere and speedy returne.' Neither came back. Weld later prepared a statement to be printed in their defence. This manuscript, never published, included a declaration of their absolute sincerity in saying they would return to Massachusetts, 'that none might think we did equivocate, or had mentall reservations, when we so expressed ourselves'. Weld pinned the blame on Providence, which 'appeared clearly to our consciences to stop us in our way ... in our ... preparation for the voyage putting such crosbarrs in our way that indeed we could not with good conscience break throw them'.[3]

Weld had already made a mark in print as a promoter and defender of New England. In 1643, with Hugh Peter, he published *New Englands first fruits*. Weld and Peter also saw through the press *Church-government and church-covenant discussed* (1643), which put into print several manuscript defences of the 'New England Way'. This provoked a reaction from the presbyterian William Rathband, to which Weld responded with *An answer to W.R.* In 1645 he followed this with *A brief narration of the practices of the churches in New-England*. On another front, in the fight against radicalism, Weld published various (largely anonymous) manuscripts, assembled and edited by John Winthrop to show New England's stern response to antinomianism: *A short story of the rise, reign and ruine of the antinomians*. Thomas Hooker thought Weld had been goaded into some of these publications by the devious planning of the Scots Samuel Rutherford and Robert Baillie, who proceeded in a 'Jesuit-like' manner. He told Thomas Shepard in 1646,

> these men had a secret hand to provoke Mr Weld to set forth his short story touching occasions here in Mr Vane his reign ... I say I cannot but think ther was by some cunning contrivements and underhand working some trayne layd to provoke the setting forth of these; that he [Baillie] might have testimony upon record in writing for what he doth express in an oppobious manner ... and so attayne his end, and yet save him self from being a privy slanderer. This I suspect is ther working but Gods ways in this are wonderfull.

Many allegations against Weld and Peter – for their conduct as agents and in fomenting religious anarchy by promoting the New England Way – came from the hostile pen of the presbyterian Thomas Edwards. Weld's reputation was clouded by questions about his financial dealings as an agent: the

Massachusetts General Court did not audit and approve his accounts until 1651.[4]

As time passed, Weld put down roots and his commitment to return to New England vanished. Initially, he served as assistant minister at St Giles Cripplegate, London, 1643–4: at this point Thomas Edwards described him as dithering between 'Giles Cripplegate and New England'. Weld may have been in his old parish of Terling for a time. He was rector of Wanlip, Leicestershire, in 1646. Then, on 1 February 1649/50, Weld was installed as rector of Gateshead. Here he stayed until the Restoration in 1660.

In Gateshead, Weld gathered a congregational church and worked as parish preacher. His policy of restricting sacraments to the tiny membership of the gathered church proved controversial. It led to an unsuccessful effort from his parishioners to oust him in 1658. He cooperated with local ministers of presbyterian and congregationalist convictions, but fiercely attacked Quakers and baptists. In 1653 Weld was involved in the case of Thomas Ramsay (*ODNB*), the 'false Jew of Hexham': the baptists in Hexham, led by Thomas Tillam*, claimed 'Joseph ben Israel' as a convert, but he turned out to be an English-born Catholic agent. Weld supported Cromwell's abortive plans for a new college at Durham, to stand alongside Oxford and Cambridge. In 1651, he sold his library to the New England Company for £34: a list of these books survives in the company's records.

At the Restoration, or shortly before, Weld withdrew to London. His successor at Gateshead was presented as rector early in 1660 and read the Thirty-nine Articles to the congregation on 26 August. There is little trace of Weld in London. He signed the congregational ministers' condemnation of Thomas Venner's* rebellion and died about two months later.[5]

Publications *A briefe recitall of the unreasonable proceedings of Dr. Laud* (1641); *An answer to W.R. his narration of the opinions and practises of the churches lately erected in New-England* (1644); *A brief narration of the practices of the churches in New-England* (1645); *The perfect Pharise[e]* (1653); *A further discovery of that generation of men called Qvakers* (1654); *Mr Tillam's account examined* (1657). Weld also had a hand in [Anon.], *A vindication of Mr Weld* (1658). Weld played a key role in *The whole Booke of Psalmes faithfully translated into English metre* ([Cambridge, MA] 1640), and in seeing through the press *Church-government and church-covenant discussed* (1643), *New Englands first fruits* (1643), and *A short story of the rise, reign, and ruin of the antinomians* (1644).

[1] Tom Webster, *Godly clergy in early Stuart England: the Caroline puritan movement, c.1620–1643* (Cambridge: Cambridge University Press, 1997), 189–90, 195–6 and *passim*; *WP* II, 335–6; *CCEd* Person ID 59547.

[2] *GMB* 1961–3; *WJ*, 69, 71; David D. Hall, *Puritans in the New World: a critical anthology* (Princeton, NJ and Oxford: Princeton University Press, 2004), 33; David D. Hall, ed., *The Antinomian Controversy, 1636–1638* (Durham, NC: Duke University Press, 1990); Michael P. Winship, *Making heretics: militant protestantism and free grace in Massachusetts, 1636–1641* (Princeton, NJ and Oxford: Princeton University Press, 2002), 51, 53–4, 55, 195–6 and *passim*; David D. Hall, *Ways of writing: the practice*

and politics of text-making in seventeenth-century New England (Philadelphia, PA: University of Pennsylvania Press, 2008), 12, 82, 89, 95, 112.

[3] *WJ*, 353–4; R.P. Stearns, 'The Weld-Peter mission to England', Colonial Society of Massachusetts, *Publications*, 32 (1937), 185–246; Graeme J. Milne, 'New England agents and the English Atlantic, 1641–1666' (PhD dissertation, University of Edinburgh 1993), 306 and *passim*; R.P. Stearns, *The strenuous puritan: Hugh Peter 1598–1660* (Urbana, IL: University of Illinois Press, 1954); the deputies' call, cited in Roger Howell, 'Thomas Weld of Gateshead: the return of a New England puritan', *Archaelogia Aeliana*, 4th series, 48 (1970), 303–32, quotation from 318–19; Weld's 'Innocency cleared' (April 1647), Bodleian, Rawlinson MS D. 934, fol. 29.

[4] Hall, *Ways of writing*, 62–66; *Pilgrims*, 46–9; Hooker to Shepard, 17 September 1646, Mass. Archives, 240: 100; Edwards, *Gangraena*, i. 40-2, ii. 289–90; Stearns, 'Weld-Peter mission'.

[5] Edwards, *Gangraena*, ii. 84; Bodleian, Rawlinson MS D. 934 (Papers relating to the New England Company), fols 5, 19–21, 26–31, 34–5; *Pilgrims*, 130–1, 133–5 and *passim*.

ANB, BDBR, CR, ODNB.

WESTGATE, John

John Westgate was admitted to the Boston church on 12 September 1640, as 'a singleman'. He lived in the household of John Cotton, minister at Boston. Westgate joined the Artillery Company in 1641.

Westgate moved back to England by the mid-1640s, to Pulham Market in Norfolk. He was keen to observe the formalities of the 'New England Way', which required church members to be dismissed from one congregation before they joined another. He had written back to Boston for a 'letter of dismission', but this letter failed to arrive. This set off a consultation among the congregational churches in the area. On 26 February 1645/6, the congregational church at Yarmouth recorded a missive from the Norwich congregation, conveying questions from 'Pullam' church, among which was the query: 'Whether a member of a Church in New England should joyne here by confession of faith, or without any dismission in case that his dismission miscarry, or is not sent him.' There is no answer noted in the Yarmouth record, and no records survive from the gathered church at Pulham Market to show how the discussion progressed. However, Westgate's dismission was eventually agreed by the church in Boston. On 26 September 1647, 'Our brother John Westgate at the Desire of the Church of Pulham Mary in Norfolk in England and his owne was dismissed unto them with the consent of the Church by their silence.'

Westgate's interest in New England continued over several decades. On 5 April 1653, he wrote to John Lake from Harleston, Norfolk, to ask if reports of John Cotton's death were true. In 1677, he wrote to Increase Mather* after the Indian Wars:

The sad condition of N.E. (where sometimes I lived several years) have been much upon our hearts, we have had many solemne days of humiliation, and

25 January last we had a solemne day of thanksgiving for the great deliverances we heard the Lord had given you. This was very general among all the congregationall churches in City and countrey round about, we sending one to another and agreeing of the day before hand, which was also kept by many of the Baptist congregations . . .

Westgate wrote of a need for a reformation in Boston, 'you being set up as a Beacon upon the top of a mountain': 'your Fathers with much hazard, difficult and danger went to that wildernesse (even when it was a neer wildernesse) to set up the pure worship of God, and to enjoy the liberty of their conscience'. He criticised Massachusetts' harsh treatment of Quakers and baptists.

In 1672, the preacher Samuel Petto (*CR*) was licensed to conduct worship at John Westgate's house in 'Redenhall cum Harleston' (Redenhall with Harleston). Petto corresponded with Increase Mather in Boston, and conveyed letters from Mather to Westgate. In a postscript to a letter written *c.* January 1681/2, Petto sent Mather news of Westgate's demise: 'Mr Wesgate is dead. He died very suddenly.'

Boston CR, 31, 49; *Artillery Company*, 118; Yarmouth CB, 26 February 1645/6; 4 *MHSC* 8: 342, 350, 577–81.

WHEAT, Joshua

Joshua Wheat left London for New England in April 1635 as a passenger on the *Elizabeth*, and settled at Concord, Massachusetts. His brother Moses was also at Concord by 1640.

In 1640 or 1641, Joshua Wheat returned to his father in England. Before he left, Joshua made an agreement with his brother Moses: while Joshua was in England, Moses should use Joshua's six acres of land in Concord as if it were his own, and if Joshua never came back to New England, Moses could keep the land. In return, Moses granted his brother Joshua whatever legacy might come to him from his father in England. The Concord town records set down how Moses Wheat recalled this agreement forty-nine years later, in February 1689/90. No-one had ever come to demand the six acres, 'though my brother Joshua lived most of the time'.

GM 7: 323–4.

WHEELWRIGHT, John (1592?–1679)

John Wheelwright came from Lincolnshire. He was probably the son of Robert and Catherine Wheelwright of Saleby. He attended Sidney Sussex College, Cambridge, and graduated BA in 1614, MA in 1618. He was ordained in 1619 and served as vicar of Bilsby, Lincolnshire, from 1623. He was convicted of simony in 1632, because he had sold the living back to the patron. He stayed in Lincolnshire until early in 1636.

Wheelwright arrived in New England on 26 May 1636, and settled at

Boston with his wife and five children. Some years earlier, he had married Mary Hutchinson, sister to Anne Hutchinson. Wheelwright arrived just as the storm of the Antinomian Controversy was about to break: the events of 1636–8 centred on Anne Hutchinson's robust and controversial interpretation of John Cotton's teaching. Wheelwright sided with her. Those who favoured Hutchinson tried to install Wheelwright as teacher in the Boston church, alongside Cotton and John Wilson*. Wilson and John Winthrop fiercely opposed this. Wheelwright became minister at Mount Wollaston, and preached a fast-day sermon at Boston, 19 January 1636/7, which advocated the antinomian cause. He was tried and banished. Wheelwright went north, and founded the town and church of Exeter (now in New Hampshire); after Massachusetts annexed that area in 1643, he moved to Wells, Maine. In 1644 Massachusetts lifted the sentence of banishment, but at the same time Wheelwright's orthodoxy was thrown into serious doubt in England through *A short story of the rise, reign and ruin of the antinomians* (1644) brought to press by Thomas Weld*. Wheelwright sent a riposte to England to be printed, to defend himself: *Mercurius Americanus, Mr Welds his antitype* (1645).

Wheelwright left for England in the summer of 1655. By this time, he had managed to gain a half-hearted endorsement of his orthodoxy from the Massachusetts General Court. Back in England, he enjoyed the patronage of Sir Henry Vane Jr*, who had been an ally in the Antinomian Controversy. In 1650, Vane had acquired the manors (and rectories) of Belleau, Aby and Swaby in Lincolnshire. On 7 December 1655, John Wheelwright was admitted as minister to Belleau, Aby and Swaby. In support of this, he presented certificates from merchants with strong connections in New England: Thomas Bell*, David Yale*, Richard Hutchinson* (or Hutchinson's uncle and namesake), and John Hill of London (brother of Valentine Hill of Boston) – a reminder of the support Wheelwright had enjoyed from Boston merchants in the heat of the Antinomian Controversy.

Wheelwright ended his days in New England. In 1662, the year Sir Henry Vane was executed, he left England for America. He became a minister at Salisbury, Massachusetts, and died there in 1679.

Publications *Mercurius Americanus, Mr Welds his antitype* (1645); *A brief, and plain apology written by John Wheelwright* (1658).

David D. Hall, ed., *The Antinomian Controversy, 1636–1638* (Durham, NC: Duke University Press, 1990); Bush, 300–19 and *passim*; David Como, *Blown by the spirit: puritanism and the emergence of an antinomian underground in pre-Civil-War England* (Stanford, CA: Stanford University Press, 2004), 441–4; LPL, MS COMM. III/4, fol. 406; *Pilgrims*, 119, 120; V. Rowe, *Sir Henry Vane the younger* (London: The Athlone Press, 1970), 172, 242.

ANB, ODNB.

WHITE, Nathaniel

Nathaniel White was the son of Nathaniel White, a minister who worked in the Somers Islands and later in the Bahamas. White graduated from Harvard with a BA in 1646 and MA in 1649. In 1650, when supplies were short in the Bahamas, six or eight churches in New England gathered supplies and funds. A note by Increase Mather* on a manuscript account of this venture names 'Mr White's son Nat:' as one of the 'messengers' who took the shipload of goods south. The party returned with a cargo of wood, sold for £124, to Harvard's benefit. White's accounts at Harvard ended in November 1653. He may have gone to England in the 1650s. His father's will shows he was there in 1668.

Harvard Recs. III, 29n. *CC*, Sibley. (He was not the ejected minister of Lavington, Wiltshire, as Sibley suggests: see *CR*, 'White, Nathaniel'.)

WHITFIELD, Henry (1597–1657)

Henry Whitfield was the son of Thomas Whitfield, an attorney of Mortlake in Surrey. Whitfield matriculated at New College, Oxford, on 16 June 1610, but the only record of a degree is an MA noted in diocesan records, 1631. Cotton Mather thought Whitfield originally intended to qualify as a lawyer, but there is no record of him at the Inns of Court either. Whitfield was ordained in 1618 and became rector of Ockley, Surrey, a post he held until 1638. In 1618, he married Dorothy Sheafe, daughter of Dr Edmund Sheafe of Cranbrook, Kent. Whitfield played a pivotal role in discussions about emigration to New England: the ministers John Cotton, Thomas Hooker, Philip Nye and John Davenport met at his home, *c.* December 1633, in what is sometimes called 'the Ockley conference'. Whitfield had already come to the attention of Archbishop Laud and the Court of High Commission, for not reading Book of Sports and for not performing certain ceremonies. Although Whitfield did not emigrate as early as Cotton and Hooker, by late 1638 or early 1639 he accepted the need for, in Cotton Mather's words, a 'moderate secession'. When he was cited again to appear in the archbishop's court, he relinquished his post and left for New England.[1]

In 1639, Whitfield led a company of family and friends across the Atlantic: among his party were Samuel Desborough*, John Hoadley*, Thomas Jordan* and John Caffinch*; also, Dorothy Whitfield's brother Jacob Sheafe, and her sister Joanna Chittenden with her husband William. Their ship was the first to sail directly across the Atlantic to New Haven. George Fenwick* helped to prepare the way and travelled over with them. Whitfield's plan was to settle within the limits of the Saybrook patent (held by puritan nobles like Lord Saye and Sele and Lord Brooke), between Saybrook and the New Haven Colony but independent of both. On the way over, Whitfield's company made a shipboard covenant, which included the promise 'not to desert or leave each other or the plantation, but with the consent of the rest, or the greater part of the company'. After their arrival they started negotiations with native Americans for more land: their settlement originally kept an Indian name, Menumkatuck, but was renamed Guilford. Fenwick granted the Guilford settlers more land to enlarge their plantation, but, in a letter to William Leete on 22 October 1645, he set one condition:

> that is, when you are all suited to your present content, you will bind yourselves more strictly for continuing together; for however in former times ... some here gained by removes ... yet in these latter times it doth not only weaken and discourage the plantation desired, but also wastes and consumes the estates of those that remove. Rolling stones gather no moss in these times, and our conditions now are not to expect great things. Small things, nay moderate things, should content us, a warm fireside and a peaceable habitation with the chief of God's mercies, the gospel of peace, is no ordinary thing, though other things were mean.

Guilford was independent of other colonies for twenty years. Six planters bought land in name of all, but in June 1643 surrendered this into the hands of the church. The church had seven founder members: Whitfield, Desborough, Whitfield's son-in-law John Higginson, John Mepham and John Hoadley. Whitfield served as pastor and Higginson as teacher; there were no elders or deacons as such. The church had no covenant, but examined prospective members about their religious experience and asked them to accept a simple confession of faith. Only church members could be freemen, but most in the town belonged to the church. It was a close-knit community: when some settlers requested permission to move, c.1645, others opposed this, 'feareing if ... many should ... desert the burden might be too heavy for the rest'.[2]

After a decade in New England, Henry Whitfield decided to return home: 'At a general Court held the 20th of February 1649[/50]. Mr Whitfield's reasons, tendered to the church here for his removall were read in publique.' The document that was read out does not survive. The historian William Hubbard, writing later, attributed Whitfield's decision to a mixture of factors, in New England and old:

> the sharpness of the air, he having a weake body ... the toughness of those imployments wherin his livelhood was sought, he having been tenderly and delicately brought up ... [his] estate very much wasted ... and many other things concurring, especially the strong inducements held out for his return from England by those who sought his help and counsel in the mother country ...

In the summer of 1650, Whitfield made preparations to leave. On 20 August, he sold the land Fenwick had given him to the people of Guilford for £20. He was paid in wheat at four shillings a bushel. He had other assets he could not sell – even at a low price – because his neighbours thought they might follow him to England. The London merchant Robert Tomson* eventually bought these up after Whitfield's death. Whitfield had built a substantial stone house, which still stands. Whitfield set out from Guilford for Boston at the end of August 1650, in a small vessel. According to Cotton Mather, 'at the time of parting, the whole town accompanied him unto the water-side, with a springtide of tears, because "they should see his face no more"'.[3]

Contrary winds forced the ship to put into Martha's Vineyard, where Whitfield spent ten days with Thomas Mayhew observing his work with the Indians. Mayhew gave Whitfield a written narrative about his work, dated 7 September 1650, to carry to England. Whitfield and Mayhew rode together to Boston. On the way, they visited John Eliot at Roxbury. Whitfield heard Eliot preach to Indians, and helped him to catechise Indian children. Whitfield himself preached to the Indians through an interpreter. Eliot, like Mayhew, gave Whitfield documentary evidence to carry to England with him, in the form of a letter addressed to Edward Winslow*, dated 21 October 1650.

Whitfield sailed to England that autumn. Immediately after he arrived, he published in London – as 'late pastor to the church of Guilford', 'late come from thence' – *The light appearing more and more towards the perfect day. Or, a farther discovery of the recent state of the Indians in New England, concerning the progresse of the Gospel amongst them. Manifested by letters from such as preacht to them there.* John Eliot was not pleased with the result: Whitfield had failed to add his own testimony about what he had seen. Eliot wrote to Edward Winslow*, 20 October 1651, 'you mention . . . Mr Whitfi[e]ld silence, in not saying what he saw among our Indians[.] I cannot but observe it, and have so much of man in me as to think, that his saying he was with them, and giving no reason of his silence, is to say lesse then nothing.' Whitfield joined William Gouge and other prominent ministers in lending support to a fresh set of testimonials printed by the New England Company, *Strength out of weakness* (1652).

Whitfield became a preacher at Winchester, and gathered a congregational church that met in the cathedral. It is not clear when he took up this post, but he was well-established by 14 August 1655, when he wrote to Henry Scobell, clerk to the council of state, about the churches in Hampshire: 'We are not so happy in this Countie, as to reckon many Churches gathered, especially in the purest Way. Here be divers godly men that are Presbyterians, that have gathered some churches in a hopeful Way.' Winchester was the administrative centre for Major-General William Goffe (*ODNB*). Henry Whitfield declared his will on 17 September 1657, in the presence of his children Nathaniel* and Mary Whitfield. He left all his estate to his wife Dorothy. She was granted probate on 29 January 1657/8. On 23 October 1657, Theophilus Gale (*CR*) had become Whitfield's successor as pastor to the congregational church in Winchester, and preacher at the cathedral.

Dorothy Whitfield visited New England in 1659, perhaps to settle her husband's estate at Guilford. Her son-in-law (and Whitfield's former assistant), the minister John Higginson (*ANB*), brother of Francis Higginson*, almost returned to England in 1659. He and his family may have intended to accompany Dorothy back home. They were all aboard ship and on their way to England when the ship had to put into Salem, Massachusetts, because of bad weather. The church at Salem persuaded Higginson to be their minister and stay on in New England.[4]

Publications *The light appearing more and more towards the perfect day* (1651).

[1] Tom Webster, *Godly clergy in early Stuart England: the Caroline puritan movement, c.1620–1643* (Cambridge: Cambridge University Press, 1997), 58, 157–8, 160, 164, 165–6, 167, 257, 267; *Magnalia*, I, 592–4; *Al. Oxon.*; *CCEd* Person ID 108525; Waters, 1348.
[2] *WP* IV, 261; *Davenport Letters*, 75–6; MHS, Misc. Bd. MSS, 1 June 1639 (shipboard covenant); MHS, Misc. Bd. MSS, 23 August and 29 September 1639, 20 September 1641, 2 February 1642; B.C. Steiner, *A history of. . .Guilford* (Baltimore, MD: privately printed, 1897), 22–3; MHS, Misc. Bd. MSS, '1645?'.
[3] Hubbard, *c.* 1680, cited by Steiner, *Guilford*, 62–3; MHS, Misc. Bd. MSS, 20 August 1650; 4 *MHSC* 7: 399 *Magnolia*, I, 593.
[4] Henry Whitfield, *The light appearing* (1651); Bodleian, Rawlinson MS D. 934, fol. 11; [New England Company], *Strength out of weakness* (1652), 'To the Christian Reader'; Whitfield to Scobell, 14 August 1655, Francis Peck, *Desiderata curiosa*, 2 vols (London, 1732–5), II, Lib. XIII:6; LPL, MS COMM. II/728; Waters, 1351; NA, PROB 11/272/141, will of 'Henry Whitfeild', clerk of Winchester, Hampshire, 29 January 1658; Steiner, *Guilford*, 64. In general: I.M. Calder, *The New Haven Colony* (New Haven, CT: Yale University Press, 1934), 55, 56, 70–3, 87, 175; *Pilgrims*, 41, 83, 84, 95, 130; Steiner, *Guilford*, 12–40, 60–5.

ODNB.

WHITFIELD, Nathaniel

Nathaniel Whitfield, son of Henry and Dorothy Whitfield*, emigrated with his parents in 1639, along with other siblings – Dorothy, who married Samuel Desborough*, John and Mary. After his parents left in 1650, Nathaniel moved to New Haven. In 1654, he and his brother-in-law John Higginson were still trying to sell off Henry Whitfield's property in Guilford.

Nathaniel left New England in mid-October 1654, with Thomas Jordan*. Back in England, he took employment as a clerk to the naval commissioners, whose ranks included Nehemiah Bourne*, Edward Hopkins* and Francis Willoughby*. In April 1656, Major-General William Goffe (*ODNB*) wrote from his headquarters at Winchester, where Henry Whitfield was a minister, recommending Nathaniel for a 'custom waiter's place', as an improvement on his current position.

Nathaniel Whitfield and his sister Mary witnessed their father's will in 1657. Nathaniel went on to become a prosperous merchant. He met with John Winthrop Jr* in London, early in 1663, to negotiate in the controversy between the New Haven Colony and Connecticut. He acted as an agent for Guilford in London.

Waters, 1351; W.L. Sachse, 'The migration of New Englanders to England, 1640–1660', *American Historical Review*, 53 (1947–8), 259n.; B.C. Steiner, *A history of. . . Guilford* (Baltimore, MD: privately printed, 1897), 64; John Higginson to John Winthrop Jr, 20 September 1654, *WP* VI, 438–9; G.E. Aylmer, *The state's servants: the civil service of the English Republic, 1649–1660* (London: Routledge and Kegan Paul, 1973), 126; *Davenport Letters*, 216n., 217; William Hooke to John Davenport, 2 March 1662/3,

A.G. Matthews, ed., 'A censored letter', *Transactions of the Congregational Historical Society*, 9 (1924–6), 263–83.

WHITING, John (d. 1690)

John Whiting was the son of Samuel Whiting, minister of Lynn, Massachusetts, and formerly rector at Skirbeck, Lincolnshire, 1625–36. Samuel Whiting emigrated to New England in 1636. Whiting – 'whittinge Jewner' – appears in the Harvard college accounts from October 1653 until June 1656. He graduated BA in 1657 (and is not to be confused with the older graduate John Whiting, who stayed in New England and married Sybil, sister of John Collins*).

Whiting seems to have returned to England soon after his graduation. He is likely to be the John Whiting who conformed at the Restoration, and worked in parishes within ten miles of his father's old parish at Skirbeck in Lincolnshire. John Whiting was ordained deacon on 11 July 1661 and priest on 22 August 1662. He became rector of Butterwick in Lincolnshire on 11 July 1661. His BA was noted in the records, but not the awarding university. On 13 August 1662, Whiting subscribed, and was licensed as a preacher throughout the diocese of Lincoln. (This time an MA was recorded, which does not tally with Sibley's record that Whiting had his Harvard degree incorporated at Cambridge in 1669, and received an MA that year from Queens' College.) From December 1667 until his death in March 1690 John Whiting served as rector of Leverton (North and South Moiety), two miles from his former parish at Butterwick.

Harvard Recs. III, 180n.; G. F. Nuttall, 'Peterborough ordinations', *Journal of Ecclesiastical History*, 30 (1979), 240; CCEd Person ID 104970, Location IDs 8028, 9077, 9078.

CC, Sibley.

WILKES, Thomas

Thomas Wilkes lived at Salem, Massachusetts, and was probably a haberdasher: an inventory of his estate included haberdashery in Salem and cloth in Boston. Wilkes returned to England with his wife and his younger brother Robert. He died there. On 24 June 1662, Edmund Batter was granted administration of Wilkes's estate in New England. Batter presented an inventory of £100 6s 11d. He was told to send £40 to Wilkes's widow in England and to keep the remainder until the court made a further order. In 1666, £30 was sent to Robert Wilkes, who had come of age.

Essex Probate Recs. I, 381–3.

WILKES, William and Joan

William and Joan Wilkes settled at Boston in 1633 and joined the church. When they moved to New Haven in 1639, the Boston church recommended

'Jane' Wilkes to the church there. William left for England sometime in the early 1640s. On 12 January 1645/6, Joan made a will, 'being called to go to my husband but not knowing whether he be living or not'. She set sail for England from New Haven, on the *Fellowship*, with George Lamberton* and others. The ship was lost at sea with all aboard. William Wilkes had died by 1648, presumably in England.

GMB 1989–91.

WILLIS, Thomas (1582/3–1666)

Thomas Willis came from Fenny Compton, Warwickshire. He studied at St John's College, Oxford, and graduated BA in 1606, MA in 1609. He was a schoolmaster, and ran his own establishment at Isleworth, Middlesex.

Willis emigrated to New England and settled at Lynn by 1638, when he received the largest land grant in the town's land distribution. On 11 March 1638/9 he signed a petition with, among others, Richard Sadler*. On 14 March 1638/9 he became a freeman of Massachusetts, and so was already a church member. Willis served as a magistrate at the Essex county court for several sessions. Nathaniel Rowe* had been sent to learn Latin from 'Mr Willis of Linne the schoole-master'. His sons, including Thomas*, were in Lynn with him. John Knowles* married Thomas Willis's daughter, Elizabeth, c.1640.

Willis left for England in 1641 or 1642. He was perhaps the schoolmaster hostile to New England who sailed back with John Phillip* in October 1641. He returned to his school at Isleworth and became known as a grammarian. He died at Isleworth in 1666.

Publications *Vestibulum linguae Latinae* (1651), a Latin dictionary for children; *Proteus vinctus* (1655), a dictionary of Latin idioms.

Al. Oxon.; GMB 2011; WP IV, 104, 343–4; Waters, 1250; WJ, 414–15; *Pilgrims*, 70n.84, 183, 192.

ODNB.

WILLIS, Thomas (c.1618–1673)

Thomas Willis, son of Thomas Willis* the schoolmaster, emigrated with his father by 1638 and settled at Lynn. In 1660 it was said he had attended no university but had been 'bred in New England'. There is no firm record of him at St John's College, Oxford, where it is sometimes claimed he studied (perhaps confusing him with his father). Nor is there any trace of him at Harvard, which during the years Willis was in New England, had only just begun. In fact, after the disgrace of the first head of Harvard, Nathaniel Eaton*, scholars like Nathaniel Rowe* were sent to board with Thomas Willis senior at Lynn. So Willis is likely to have been taught by his father.

Willis perhaps sailed home with his father, or may have followed later. In

October 1646, he was admitted vicar of the sequestered living of Twickenham, Middlesex, close to his father's school at Isleworth. His brother-in-law John Knowles* joined him as curate, 1652–3. In 1654, Willis became an assistant to the Middlesex commissioners for removing unsuitable parish ministers.

On 23 August 1660, some of his parishioners at Twickenham presented a petition to the House of Lords asking for his removal, with a stream of complaints: he had attended no university but had been 'bred in New England'; he had not been lawfully ordained; he had caused discord between neighbours; he was an enemy of the king – and much more. On 7 December 1660, JPs in Middlesex convicted him of preaching maliciously against the king. His successor was installed in 1661. In 1669, Willis was said to be preaching in a warehouse near Radcliffe Cross; on 30 August 1673, the churchwardens of Stepney presented him for preaching there. On 7 August 1677, William Hooke* included Willis in a list of London nonconformist ministers who had recently died.

4 *MHSC* 8: 583–4; *Pilgrims*, 70n.84, 144n.13, 168, 183, 192, 200, 203. Willis is often confused with another Thomas Willis, who served as a chaplain in the parliamentary army and as rector of Billingsgate, and conformed at the Restoration. C.S. Knighton, in the *ODNB*, disentangles the threads.

CR, *ODNB*.

WILLOUGHBY, Francis (d. 1671)

Francis Willoughby was the son of William and Elizabeth Willoughby of Wapping. (William died in 1651. Elizabeth is likely to be the 'Mrs Willowbie of Wapping' who became a member of William Greenhill's church at Stepney in 1647, and as 'Elizabeth Willowbie of Wapping' married John Wood there in 1653.)

Francis Willoughby trained as a shipwright in Wapping. He emigrated from Portsmouth in 1638, with his wife Mary and son Jonathan, aged two. They settled at Charlestown, Massachusetts, where he joined the church on 8 December 1639. Willoughby joined the Artillery Company in 1639 and became a freeman on 13 May 1640. He lived in an area of Charlestown named Wapping, and engaged in shipbuilding.

He visited England more than once in 1640s. After Israel Stoughton* died at Lincoln in 1644, it was Willoughby – who had been in England – who brought Stoughton's will back to New England. He was in England again early in 1648. In London, he met the Remonstrant Dr Robert Child* at the Exchange, a gathering place for merchants with colonial interests, and home to the 'New England Walk'. Willoughby and Child fell out and came to blows. John Winthrop recorded the episode in his journal:

> falling in talke about N: E: the doctor rayled against the people, sayinge they were a Company of Rogues & knaves: mr willoughby Answered that he who spake so &c: was a knave, whervpon the docter gave him a boxe on

the eare: mr willoughby was readye to have closed with him &c: but beinge vpon the exchange, he was stayed, but presently arrested him: & when the doctor sawe the danger he was in, he imployed some frendes to make his peace: who ordered him to give 5:^{li} to the poore of N: E: (for mr willoughby would have nothinge of him) & to give mr willoughby open satisfaction in the full exchange, & to give it vnder his hande, never to speake euill of N: E: men after, not to occasion any trouble to the Contry or to any of the people all which he gladly performed.

Winthrop described Francis Willoughby's father as a 'colonel' in the City of London. William Willoughby had been appointed as one of sixteen regulators of the navy in January 1648/9, and served as a resident naval commissioner in Portsmouth from 16 February 1648/9 until his death in July 1651.

Willoughby's return to England, at the end of 1651, followed his father's death. He had considered this step for some time. In July 1650, more than a year before he left New England for good, Willoughby procured a certificate from the notary William Aspinwall*, to show he had served as a Massachusetts magistrate. Willoughby's spiritual diary survives, in shorthand, with 'daily observations' from 20 November 1650. The entries show a struggle between his aspirations as a merchant and his desire to undertake public service. He referred to a 'call to England the latter end of the year if God spare my life'. He made his last note in the diary on 28 December 1651, just before he set sail for England on the *Adventure*, a ship he had built.

Back in England, Willoughby took his father's post as naval commissioner at Portsmouth in September 1652. He briefly served as the town's MP in 1659. He was an associate of Nehemiah Bourne*, Edward Hopkins* and Robert Tomson*. With Tomson, he had responsibility for conveying £500 from Hopkins's estate to New England, to found a school. In July 1660, 'Major Willoughby' lived in a Navy Board house in Seething Lane, close to the Tower of London. Samuel Pepys turned up with a pair of bedsheets and asked to stay the night: Pepys had his eye on Willoughby's house, and within two days claimed it for himself. Willoughby, part of the old republican regime not the new royalist administration, moved out within two weeks.

Willoughby returned to New England by May 1662, with his new (third) wife, Margaret. In 1665 he became deputy governor of Massachusetts, and died one of New England's wealthiest citizens.

Willoughby's second wife, Sarah, and their five children – Jonathan, Sarah, Nehemiah, Jeremiah and William – probably sailed with him to England in 1651, or soon followed him back. Jonathan (born in 1636) was at Harvard, 1651–4, but married in London in 1661. He worked briefly as a minister in Connecticut, 1664, but when he died at Tangiers in 1680 was described as lately of St Katherine Coleman, London. Francis Willoughby, in his will in 1671, called Jonathan 'an unnaturall and most disobedient childe'. Sarah, Nehemiah and William all went back to New England in the 1660s: Sarah moved to Connecticut, Nehemiah became a merchant in Salem, William died of smallpox in 1677. Nothing is known of Jeremiah.

Charlestown CR, 280; *Artillery Company*, 98; *NEHGR* 3: 187; Bernard Bailyn, *The New England merchants in the seventeenth century* (Cambridge, MA: Harvard University Press, 1955), 34, 160; *WP* V, 11, 14; *NEHGR* 7: 333; *WJ*, 706; Aspinwall, 306; A.C. Dewar, 'Naval administration of the Interregnum', *Mariner's Mirror*, 12 (1926), 425, 428–9; *Davenport Letters*, 273; G.E. Aylmer, *The state's servants: the civil service of the English Republic, 1649–1660* (London: Routledge and Kegan Paul, 1973), 204, 399; B.S. Capp, *Cromwell's navy: the fleet and the English Revolution, 1648–1660* (Oxford: Clarendon Press, 1989), 49, 144, 166n., 280–1, 290–1, 295, 301, 371; *Pilgrims*, 13, 107, 108n.44, 109, 114–15, 143, 144, 162, 183, Plate 13; Roger Thompson, *From deference to defiance: Charlestown, Massachusetts, 1629–1662* (Boston, MA: New England Historic Genealogical Society, 2012), 274–9 and *passim*; Willoughby's manuscript diary, AAS, Shepard Family Papers, MSS Box 1, folder II; see Francis Sypher, 'The "Dayly Observations" of an impassioned puritan: a 17th-century shorthand diary attributed to Deputy Governor Francis Willoughby of Massachusetts', *Proceedings of the American Antiquarian Society*, 91 (1981), 91–107, and Thompson, *From deference to defiance*, 278–9; Claire Tomalin, *Samuel Pepys: the unequalled self* (London: Penguin Books, 2002), 111. On Willoughby's family: Stepney CB, fols 1v, 300; Capp, *Cromwell's navy*, 49; *CC*; *GD*; *NEHGR* 4: 270, 8: 347; 25: 340; Waters, 970, 971–2, 974–6, 977; Thompson, *From deference to defiance*, 418–22.

WINSLOW, Edward (c. 1594–1655)

Edward Winslow, born at Droitwich, Worcestershire, was the eldest son of Edmund and Magdalen Winslow. His father was a wealthy yeoman farmer and saltmaker. In 1613, Edmund apprenticed himself for seven years to a London stationer and learnt the printing trade. In 1617, he travelled to Leiden with English separatists, to set up a radical printing press. After three years, under serious pressure from the English authorities, the Dutch shut the press down.

Winslow arrived in New England on the *Mayflower* in 1620, with his wife Elizabeth. His brother Gilbert* sailed over with them, and his other brothers – John, Kenelm and Josiah – soon followed. Winslow was elected assistant governor of Plymouth Colony, and took that role almost continuously (except in 1633, 1636 and 1644, when he served as governor instead of William Bradford). Elizabeth died on 24 March 1620/1, and Winslow married Susanna White, a widow, on 12 May.

Winslow travelled back to England several times before 1640. In 1623–4, he was there as an agent for the Plymouth Colony, and published *Good newes from New-England*. In 1624–5 he went back again. In 1635 he acted as an agent for both Plymouth and Massachusetts, to get assistance against the incursions of French and Dutch and to answer complaints against Massachusetts by Thomas Morton*. During this visit, Winslow, a layman, was accused of teaching in church and of conducting marriages. The authorities imprisoned him.

In 1646, Winslow returned to England again, this time as an agent for Massachusetts. William Bradford and others in the Plymouth Colony disapproved of his absence. Winslow's principal task was to protect the Bay Colony against the territorial challenges and religious radicalism of Samuel Gorton*. When the Remonstrant controversy blew up, Winslow undertook to minimise the damage from the petition against Massachusetts that Thomas Fowle* carried to England. Winslow set sail in mid-December 1646, with about a hundred other passengers. He was at the Boston lecture on 5 November 1646, with Thomas Peter*, Herbert Pelham*, John Leverett*, Robert Harding* and Richard Sadler*. Soon after arriving in London, Winslow delivered to the press *Hypocrisie unmasked*, a tract against Gorton. He took on William Vassall* and the Remonstrants in print shortly after that, in *New-Englands salamander*. Winslow attended meetings of the Warwick Commission in London and, by stressing the autonomy that Massachusetts' charter bestowed, resisted interference.

Winslow's role as an agent for Massachusetts led to his engagement in a range of activities that promoted New England's interests. He became a member of the New England Company, or 'Corporation for Propagating the Gospel in New England', 27 July 1649. Winslow promoted this cause with *The glorious progress of the gospel among the Indians of New England.* The corporation's president, William Steele, wrote that although Winslow was unwilling to be kept longer from his family across the Atlantic, his presence in London was essential. The papers of the New England Company include letters to and from Winslow. In September 1651, Cromwell's council of state ordered that one hundred narratives of the battle of Worcester should be sent to Winslow, for transmission to New England. In July 1652, Winslow secured a supply of ammunition and swords for New England, to arm colonists against the Dutch. That same year he signed *The humble proposal for the furtherance and propagation of the gospel in this nation*, an Independent scheme for church government under the Commonwealth. Other signatories included the ministers Thomas Harrison*, John Owen, Philip Nye, William Bridge, Sidrach Simpson, William Greenhill and John Dury. (Roger Williams* of Rhode Island protested at the national ministry and 'new conformity' this would bring.) In 1653 Winslow published his last tract, *A platform of church discipline in New England*, an accurate printing of the 'Cambridge Platform' of 1648. This was a response to the scandal caused in England by Massachusetts' treatment of the baptists Obadiah Holmes, John Clarke and John Crandall.

Winslow also took on other responsibilities in the early days of Cromwell's regime. He was a trustee for the sale of the king's goods, including Charles I's art collection. He was one of seven commissioners for compounding, 1650, and later joined the 'Committee for Sequestration and Advancement of Money and for Compounding with Delinquents' (at salary of £300 a year). After he petitioned against the forced dissolution of parliament in 1653, he fell out of favour for a time. Unusually, he came back into office after the beginning of the Protectorate.

At the end of 1654, Winslow sailed with the force Cromwell despatched to the West Indies. He had been appointed as one of the civilian commissioners to govern Jamaica, at a salary of £1000 a year. He died at sea. His will, made on 18 December 1654 before he set sail for Jamaica, was proved in London on 16 October 1655 by his son Josiah Winslow*.

Susanna Winslow remained in New England throughout Edward Winslow's years in England. In 1651, on the occasion of Josiah's marriage to Penelope

Pelham*, Winslow had his portrait painted, holding a letter – on which the only words legible are 'From yr loving wife Susanna'.

Publications *Hypocrisie unmasked: by a true relation of the proceedings of the governor and company of the Massachusetts against Samuel Gorton, a notorious disturber of the peace* (1647); *New-Englands salamander* (1647); *The glorious progress of the gospel among the Indians of New England* (1649); *A platform of church discipline in New England* (1653).

GMB 2023–6; *Mass. Recs.*, 3: 79 (Winslow's commission as an agent, 4 November 1646); Edward Winslow, *New-Englands salamander* (1647), *passim*; Bodleian, Rawlinson MS D. 934, Papers relating to proceedings of the Corporation for the Propagation of the Gospel in New England, 1649–1656, *passim*; W.L. Sachse, *The colonial American in Britain* (Madison, WI: University of Wisconsin Press, 1956), 141; G.E. Aylmer, *The state's servants: the civil service of the English Republic, 1649–1660* (London: Routledge and Kegan Paul, 1973), 218–19; Jerry Brotton, *The sale of the late king's goods: Charles I and his art collection* (London: Macmillan, 2006), 216; Waters, 179; *Pilgrims*, 12n.42, 68, 69, 100, 103, 108n.36, 111n.63, 116, 120, 183, Plate 9. See also W.T. Whitley, 'Edward Winslow, 1595–1655', *Transactions of the Congregational Historical Society*, 9 (1924–6), 132–43, 208–19; W. Sterry Cooper, *Edward Winslow* (Halesowen: Reliance Printing Works, 1953); Graeme J. Milne, 'New England agents and the English Atlantic, 1641–1666 (PhD dissertation, University of Edinburgh, 1993), 307 and *passim*.

ANB, ODNB.

WINSLOW, Josiah (1629–1680)

Josiah Winslow, son of Edward Winslow* and Susanna, was born in New England. He attended Harvard in the 1640s but did not graduate.

In 1651, Josiah travelled to England to marry Penelope Pelham*, the daughter of Herbert Pelham*. (Edward Winslow and Herbert Pelham had known each other in New England, and were associates in London in the work of the New England Company.) Just before Josiah left New England, the minister John Eliot gave him a letter to deliver to his father. In a jocular spirit, Eliot warned Josiah against drunkenness, 'lest by occasion of many taking their leave, he should be too often at the wine'.

Portraits of Josiah and Penelope were painted in London, to mark their wedding. Josiah proved his father's will in England, 16 October 1655. Josiah and Penelope Winslow later returned to New England. Josiah became a successful merchant and prominent magistrate, and a governor of Massachusetts.

Morison, 76; John Eliot to Edward Winslow, 20 October 1651, Bodleian, Rawlinson MS D. 934, fol. 11; *Transactions of the Congregational Historical Society*, 9 (1924–6), 219; Bernard Bailyn, *The New England merchants in the seventeenth century* (Cambridge, MA: Harvard University Press, 1955), 70, 153; *Pilgrims*, 103, 175, 184, Plate 10.

ANB, CC.

WINTHROP, Fitz John (1639?–1707)

Fitz John Winthrop, eldest son of John Winthrop Jr*, was probably born in Boston in 1639. He grew up in New London. Although it is sometimes said that he attended Harvard without taking a degree, there is no trace of him in the college records.

He was in or near Scotland by 2 February 1657/8, when Emmanuel Downing* wrote to him from Edinburgh: 'I am glad Providence hath brought you safe into these parts, and shall rejoice to have your companie here . . . my advise is when the seasons will permitt, that you come downe hither. I know your unkle Reade wilbe glad to see you.' Thomas Reade*, Fitz John's uncle, was commander of a regiment and governor at Stirling castle. Fitz John became a lieutenant in Reade's regiment in 1658. General George Monck made him a captain on 21 December 1659. Winthrop and his regiment accompanied Monck south from Scotland into England in 1660.

Winthrop was expected back in New England in 1660, but his return was delayed by smallpox. Edmund Tooly, a servant of John Davenport who was back in London, saw Fitz John Winthrop with Thomas Reade at the Exchange. His father, John Winthrop Jr, wrote to him on 28 September 1660, recommending that he should not come back to New England if he could find better employment in England. In the event, Fitz John stayed on in London until his father came over as a colonial agent in 1661–3. He returned to New England in 1663 with his father, and his brother Waitstill Winthrop, and settled once more in New London. His puritan convictions evaporated towards the end of his time in England, but from the 1670s until his death he played an important role in colonial government and diplomacy.

4 *MHSC* 6: 84, 86, 87; C.H. Firth and G. Davies, *The regimental history of Cromwell's army* (Oxford: Clarendon Press, 1940), 566–9; Frances D. Dow, *Cromwellian Scotland 1651–1660* (Edinburgh: John Donald, 1979), 257–8; *Davenport Letters*, 153, 173, 216; 5 *MHSC* 8: 68–71, 72; *GD*.

ANB, *ODNB*.

WINTHROP, Stephen (1619–1658)

Stephen Winthrop, son of John and Margaret Winthrop, was born at Groton, Suffolk. He emigrated with his father in 1630, and became a member of the Boston church in 1634. He was appointed recorder for Massachusetts in 1639 and joined the Artillery Company in 1641. c.1644 he married Judith Rainborowe, sister of William* and Thomas Rainborowe (*ODNB*). Winthrop became a merchant, an Atlantic trader, selling goods from Massachusetts to the Canaries, shipping produce on to London, and from there bringing goods to Massachusetts again.

Winthrop's trading activity took him to London more than once. On 1 March 1644/5, when he was there with Emmanuel Downing*, he wrote of the damage caused by Massachusetts' treatment of baptists: 'heere is great

Complaint against us for our severitye against Anabaptists it doth discourag any people from coming to us for feare they should be banished if they discent from us in opinion'. He returned to New England a short time later, but *c.* March 1645/6 was on his way to England again, via Tenerife, when he sent news to John Winthrop. He arrived safely in London, but he and Joseph Weld* were immediately arrested and sued in a court case brought by Alderman William Berkeley over the seizure of cargo in New England.

The delay caused by the legal wrangling diverted Winthrop into the New Model Army. On 4 September 1646, Hugh Peter* reported that Stephen Winthrop would be 'captayn of a Troope of horse with us'. By 26 October, his father John Winthrop reported that he 'means to stay in Engl. with his brother Rainsborough [Thomas] who is governor of Worster and he is Capt. of a Troope of horse'. Laurence Wright wrote to John Winthrop, 10 March 1646/7, that the way of George Downing and of 'your sonns' in England were 'full of weakenes idlenes vayn hopes of fancye: religion makes no man such a one'; Hugh Peter, however, said Stephen 'does all here by good counsayle'.

Stephen Winthrop had hoped to return to New England with Hugh Peter in May 1647, but his intentions were thwarted. He could not pay his creditors and they would not allow him to leave the country. He seized the chance of further employment in the army as an opportunity Providence had opened up: 'the kingdome is now upon a great turn'. As he was staying longer in England, he sent for his wife and children – leaving one child behind in New England, as a guarantee that he would return. He did not want any of his New England estate sold, except to pay debts. On 1 March 1647/8, he reported Judith Winthrop's safe arrival in England with 'hir Litle ones'.

Winthrop's career prospered. His father reported early in 1649 that Stephen had sent a 'very punctuall relation' of the battles against the Scots. Although some of Winthrop's troops were involved in the Leveller rising of May 1649, he was not implicated in or blamed for their conduct. He was sympathetic to the religious outlook of Cromwell's regime, and became an increasingly vocal advocate of religious toleration. In January 1654, he went to Scotland as colonel of a regiment, but returned to England in May because of ill health. In September 1656 he became MP for Banff and Aberdeen in the Second Protectorate Parliament and (despite continuing illness) served until its dissolution in February 1657/8.

Winthrop had long wanted to return to New England, but died in the summer of 1658. He was buried at his birthplace, Groton in Suffolk.

WP V, 13 (see also 20, 22, 44), 62–4, 69–70, 97–8, 102, 114, 138, 147, 158, 161, 174–5, 203, 266, 280, 320–1; 5 *MHSC* 8: 211–18; Frances D. Dow, *Cromwellian Scotland 1651–1660* (Edinburgh: John Donald, 1979), 185; C.H. Firth and G. Davies, *The regimental history of Cromwell's army* (Oxford: Clarendon Press, 1940), 179, 184, 185, 191–2, 235, 418; Francis J. Bremer, *First founders: American puritans and puritanism in an Atlantic world* (Durham, NH: University of New Hampshire Press, 2012), 113–29. On the Berkeley affair: Roger Thompson, *From deference to defiance: Charlestown, Massachusetts, 1629–1662* (Boston, MA: New England Historic Genealogical Society, 2012), 162–6.

BDBR.

WITHEREDGE, Edward

On 28 August 1651, Edward Witheredge, 'of Boston church in New England', had a daughter, 'Willmot', baptised at Stepney. By 1656, when Edward and Rachel Witheredge had their son Edward baptised, Witheredge was said to be 'of Lymehouse, mariner'.

Stepney CB, fols 120, 121.

WOODBRIDGE, Benjamin (1622–1684)

Benjamin Woodbridge was the son of John Woodbridge, rector of Stanton Fitzwarren, Wiltshire, and Sarah, sister of Thomas Parker (*ODNB*). John Woodbridge* was his elder brother. Woodbridge matriculated at Magdalen Hall, Oxford, on 9 November 1638, but because of strict requirements for religious conformity, he left Oxford without taking a degree.

Woodbridge emigrated to New England in 1639 with his brother John, who had first gone over in 1634. He may have studied with John Cotton for a time, in Boston. He was awarded a BA at Harvard in 1642, at the head of the first graduating class, the 'first-born' of the college. He, or perhaps his brother John, worked as a schoolmaster in Boston, 1644: the constable was told to pay 'Mr Woodbridge' £8 for the previous year.

Woodbridge returned to England. He may have been at Barford St Martin, Wiltshire, after its sequestration in 1646. At some point he was in Salisbury: he later mentioned that he 'had formerly been a Preacher in that City for some time together'. Woodbridge was admitted rector of Newbury, 25 February 1647/8, following William Twisse (*ODNB*). Samuel Mather* reported this to Jonathan Mitchell:

> Mr Woodbridge the first borne of newengland is Dr Twisse his successor at newbury; inclines to the presbyterians scripture but is orthodox and sound and not malignantly disaffected. I have not seene Him as yet, but I have heard of him by sundry newbery men who gave him an high Testimony.

Woodbridge graduated MA from Magdalen Hall, Oxford, on 16 November 1648. In 1654, he became an assistant to the Berkshire commissioners for removing unsuitable parish ministers.

Woodbridge stepped into the fray to oppose radical religion – lay preaching, Quaker beliefs, antinomianism. In 1648 he published, under the pseudonym 'Filodexter Transilvanius', *Church members set in joynt*, a rebuttal of 'private' (lay) preaching: this was in response to *Preaching without ordination* (1647), by the baptist Edmund Chillenden (*ODNB*). He wrote a preface to his uncle Thomas Parker's letter rebuking the prophet Elizabeth Avery (*ODNB*), who was Parker's sister and Woodbridge's aunt: *The copy of a letter written by Mr Thomas Parker, pastor of the church of Newbury in New-England, to his sister, Mrs Elizabeth Avery* (1650). In 1652, Woodbridge and William Eyre (*CR*) started a substantial exchange in print, on justification. Eyre had been preaching what Woodbridge called 'that Antinomian Error, that Justification is before Faith'. Woodbridge sent a manuscript to Christians in Salisbury, for private use. They printed it without his consent as *Justification by faith* (1652). As part of wider controversy on the matter, Richard Baxter defended Woodbridge in *The right method for a settled peace of conscience and spiritual comfort* (1653). Eyre published *Vindiciae justificationis gratuitae* (1654), against which Baxter published his *Admonition* (1654), and Woodbridge *The method of grace* (1656). Baxter described Woodbridge as 'a very judicious man'. Eyre retorted that he was 'but a spark out of Mr Baxters forge'.

At the Restoration, Benjamin Woodbridge became a chaplain-in-ordinary to Charles II, and one of the puritan commissioners at the Savoy Conference of 1661. Bishop Henchman of Salisbury reported, 17 October 1661, that Woodbridge was 'so farr pliant his Curat shall read Common Prayer'. Woodbridge was ejected as rector of Newbury in 1662. He was offered a canonry at Windsor, which he refused. In 1665, to gain greater freedom for preaching, he accepted ordination from the bishop of Salisbury. However, he regretted this and resumed his nonconformist ministry at Newbury. In 1669 he was preaching at Newbury, Wantage and Childrey in Berkshire, and at Burghclere in Hampshire. In 1672 he was licensed (as a presbyterian) to preach in the market place at Newbury. In 1678 he was preaching every Sunday at Highclere, Hampshire. He died at Newbury in 1684 and was buried in the parish church.

Publications *Church-members set in joynt* (1648); *Justification by faith* (1652); *The method of grace in the justification of sinners* (1656).

Bush, 69; *Boston TR* II, 82; *WJ*, 416n; MHS, Misc. Bd. MSS, 26 March 1651, Samuel Mather to Jonathan Mitchell; Thomas Parker, *The copy of a letter* (1650), 'Epistle to the Reader' (where Woodbridge reported that he also knew of letters to Avery from the New England ministers John Cotton, John Wilson and James Noyes); Woodbridge, *The method of grace* (1656) 'Epistle to reader'; William Eyre, *Vindiciae* (1654) 'To the Christian reader'; letters from Woodbridge to Richard Baxter, 6 January 1658/9 and from Baxter to Woodbridge, 30 July 1667, DWL Baxter Letters 5/160, 150; N.H. Keeble and Geoffrey F. Nuttall, eds, *Calendar of the correspondence of Richard Baxter*, 2 vols (Oxford: Clarendon Press, 1991), letters 539, 738.

CC, CR, ODNB, Sibley.

WOODBRIDGE, John (1613–1695)

John Woodbridge was the son of John Woodbridge, rector of Stanton Fitzwarren, Wiltshire, and Sarah, sister of Thomas Parker (*ODNB*). He was the elder brother of Benjamin Woodbridge*. He entered Magdalen Hall, Oxford, but left because of demands for conformity and continued his studies privately. Woodbridge emigrated in 1634 from Southampton, on the *Mary & John*, with his uncles Thomas Parker and James Noyes.

Woodbridge settled at Newbury, Massachusetts, where Parker and Noyes were ministers, He returned to England briefly in 1637, to settle his father's estate, but came back to Newbury in 1639 with his brother Benjamin. By 1640, Woodbridge married Mercy, daughter of Thomas Dudley (*ANB*). He held civil appointments at first, as Newbury town clerk, and as a deputy to the General Court. He joined the Artillery Company in 1644. His father-in-law Dudley suggested to him, 28 November 1642, that he ought to pursue his studies and turn from husbandry to ministry or teaching. He (or perhaps Benjamin) served as a Boston schoolmaster in 1644, and was paid £8 for the year. On 24 October 1645, Woodbridge became pastor at Andover, Massachusetts, a community he had helped to found.

Woodbridge returned to England in 1647, and this time stayed until after the Restoration. His wife and children travelled back with him, or followed soon after. He served as chaplain to a parliamentary commissioners negotiating with Charles I on the Isle of Wight in the autumn of 1648. By 1650 he had became rector of Barford St Martin, Wiltshire, succeeding Thomas Rashley* and possibly also his brother Benjamin. He and Benjamin supported each other in the public controversy with William Eyre over justification. Adoniram Byfield listed John Woodbridge in 1655 as one of the public preachers who also held office as a pastor of a church. On 29 September 1657 he became an assistant to the Wiltshire commissioners for removing unsuitable parish ministers.

The ejected rector was restored to Barford St Martin in 1660, after a lawsuit. According to Edmund Calamy, John Woodbridge served as schoolmaster at Newbury until 1662 (when his brother Benjamin was ejected as rector).

Woodbridge sailed back to New England in 1663, probably with Mercy and their twelve children. He kept a journal of goods taken aboard ship, of the journey itself (from 26 May until 27 July), and of what he brought ashore. James Noyes had died in 1656, and Woodbridge assisted his uncle Thomas Parker in ministry at Newbury. He was dismissed in 1665/6 after a faction in the church turned against him: they objected to the fact that he had been brought into office in presbyterian style, without the consent of the congregation. Letters survive from his son John to Richard Baxter, 1669–71. Out of office as a preacher, Woodbridge took up the role of a civil magistrate. He died at Newbury in 1694.

NEHGR 6: 279; *Artillery Company*, 147–8; *WJ*, 541, 614, 764.; *Boston TR* II, 82; *NEHGR* 32: 292; *WP* IV, 327–8; *WR*, 381; William Eyre, *Vindiciae justificationis gratiae* (1654), 84; Benjamin Woodbridge, *The method of grace* (1656), 'Epistle to reader'; Adoniram Byfield to Henry Scobell, 14 August 1655, Francis Peck, *Desiderata curiosa*, 2 vols (London, 1732–5), II, Lib.XIII:7; Woodbridge's Journal, 1663, *Wyllys Papers*, 139–44; DWL Baxter Letters 2/235, 237, 233. *CR*, *GM* 7: 500–10; *ODNB* s.n. 'Woodbridge, Benjamin'. For Woodbridge and the Newbury dispute in the 1660s, see Stephen Foster, *The long argument: English puritanism and the shaping of New England culture, 1570–1700* (Chapel Hill, NC and London: University of North Carolina Press), 209–10.

Y

YALE, David (d.1690)

David Yale was the son of Ann Eaton* and stepson of Theophilus Eaton. He was brother to Thomas Yale* and Ann Hopkins*, brother-in-law to Edward Hopkins*, and stepbrother to Hannah Eaton* and Theophilus Eaton Jr*. Yale was a London merchant, of St Stephen's, Coleman Street. He and his wife Ursula had a family estate, Plas Grono, near Wrexham in Denbighshire.

Yale emigrated with Theophilus Eaton in 1637, along with other merchants from St Stephen's, Coleman Street. He owned land in New Haven, where Eaton was governor, but was soon to be found in Boston. He is not known to have been a church member or a freeman. In 1646 Yale joined the 'Remonstrants' – Robert Child*, Thomas Fowle*, Samuel Maverick, Thomas Burton, John Dand and John Smith – who prepared a petition which aimed to place Massachusetts under closer parliamentary supervision from England.

Yale returned to England in 1651. He appointed Thomas Clarke and Thomas Lake of Boston as his attorneys in New England on 8 July 1651, and probably set sail soon after that. Ursula Yale, and their children born in New England – David, Elihu and Theophilus – followed in 1652. Yale divided his time between London and the family estate in Denbighshire. On 7 December 1655, Yale provided a certificate for John Wheelwright* on his admission to the living of Belleau, Aby and Swaby in Lincolnshire, together with other merchants who had strong ties with New England. David Yale cared for his distracted sister, Ann Hopkins, after Edward Hopkins's death in 1657. Hopkins had left Yale £150 a year for Ann's maintenance, 'she being not in a condicon fitt to manage it for herselfe', and entreated his brother-in-law Yale 'to bee tender and carefull over her'.

David Yale's son Elihu, left New England as an infant and never went back again. He was a highly successful merchant in India, trading in precious stones and much else. His gifts endowed Yale University.

WJ, 570, 625, 665–6; Bernard Bailyn, *The New England merchants in the seventeenth century* (Cambridge, MA: Harvard University Press, 1955), 29; *Artillery Company*, 111–12; Suffolk Deeds I, 192; W.L. Sachse, 'The migration of New Englanders to England, 1640–1660', *American Historical Review*, 53 (1947–8), 255; Robert Emmet Wall, *Massachusetts Bay: the crucial decade, 1640–1650* (New Haven, CT: Yale University Press, 1972), 164; LPL, MS COMM. III/4, fol. 406; *Pilgrims*, 12, 67, 71n.92, 85, 92n.17, 106, 115, 120, 184; NA, PROB 11/263/464, will of Edward Hopkins, 30 April 1657; *ANB* and *ODNB s.n.* 'Yale, Elihu (1649–1721)'.

YALE, Thomas

Thomas Yale was the son of Ann Eaton*. His siblings were David Yale* and Ann Hopkins*. Like his brother, he was a London merchant, and emigrated with his stepfather Theophilus Eaton to New Haven in 1637.

Yale left for England in 1656, having sold off land at New Haven. It is likely that Ann Hopkins, the 'deere distressed wife' of Edward Hopkins, travelled home with him to join her husband.

Thomas Yale returned to New Haven in 1659 to administer his mother Ann Eaton's estate, and also brought over Edward Hopkins's will. At the Restoration, he stayed on in New England.

Davenport Letters, 104n., 141n., 143, 162, 172; *Pilgrims*, 92n.17, 115, 144n.7, 165, 184.

Appendix 1: Settlers leaving New England before 1640

This section contains brief accounts of settlers who returned to England before 1640. It is not an exhaustive account, for reasons explained in the Introduction, but provides examples of people who left for England soon after they arrived in New England. Some left for good – disappointed, disenchanted or deported – like Thomas Sharpe, Thomas Tillam or Abigail Gifford. Some had only ever intended a short stay in New England, like Robert Cushman, who crossed the Atlantic (more or less) to preach a sermon at Plymouth. Some went back to visit England in the 1630s to sort out their affairs: not infrequently affairs of the heart, as the stories of George Alcock and Richard Brackett illustrate.

ALCOCK, George (*c.*1605–1640)

George Alcock emigrated in 1630 with his wife (Anne?), a sister of the minister Thomas Hooker, and settled at Roxbury, Massachusetts. He joined the church and was chosen deacon. His wife died in the winter of 1630/1. Alcock made two return journeys to England before 1640, first to fetch his son John and then to marry and bring over a new wife, Elizabeth. The Roxbury church records noted: 'He maide two voyages to England upon just calling thereunto; wherein he had much experiens of Gods preservation and blessing'. He died in December 1640.

GMB 15–18; *Roxbury CR*, 76.

BRACKETT, Richard

Richard Brackett, of Sudbury, Suffolk, emigrated in 1632. He was admitted to the Boston church in November that year. He travelled back across the Atlantic in 1633. In London, on 6 January 1633/4, at St Katharine by the Tower, he married Alice Blower. They set sail for New England in 1634. Their first child, Hannah, was baptised at Boston on 4 January 1634/5. Alice was admitted to the Boston church on 8 November 1635. Richard Brackett acted as Boston jailkeeper, 1637–40. In 1641 the family moved to Braintree. Both Richard and Alice Brackett died at Braintree in 1690.

GMB 203–6.

BROWN, John and Samuel

John and Samuel Brown appeared in the records of the Massachusetts Bay Company from March 1628/9 as patentees. Samuel Brown came from Roxwell, Essex. According to William Hubbard's history, the two were brothers. John Brown, a lawyer 'experienced in the laws of our kingdom', was made an assistant. Both were placed on the council to advise John Endicott as governor of the plantation at Salem. The Browns sailed for New England on 25 April 1629, and arrived on 29 June. The authorities censured John for letters to 'private friends' in England, which reported scandalous innovations in religion. They objected to the Salem church, gathered in July 1629. They returned to London by 19 September 1629.

GMB 254–5.

BRUISE, 'Goodman'

Bruise had been in New England in 1632. He delivered a letter to Henry Jessey (ODNB) in Suffolk from John Winthrop Jr* in Massachusetts. Jessey commented, in his reply to Winthrop, that 'g[oodman] Bruise of Boxford' came 'safely from your coasts to ours ... in 3 weeks and 3 dayes'. The Winthrop family had close ties with Boxford, Suffolk, close to their home at Groton, but nothing more is known of this traveller. The journey back from New England was always faster, because of the Gulf Stream and the prevailing westerly winds, but twenty-four days seems remarkably quick. The journey over to New England usually took eight to twelve weeks, sometimes more.

WP III, 126; *Pilgrims*, 33–4, 103–4; Francis J. Bremer, *John Winthrop: America's forgotten founding father* (New York and Oxford: Oxford University Press, 2003), 42, 61–2, 77, 118, 131.

CRANE, Robert

Robert Crane seems to have settled briefly in Ipswich, Massachusetts, but was back in England by 1639, when he wrote with John Spencer* and others to claim money owed to him by the Massachusetts Bay Company. His identity is not clear. He could be Robert Crane of Coggeshall, Essex, a grocer who was later a member of the gathered church formed by John Sams*, and who collected money in 1653 for the propagation of the gospel in New England. Or perhaps the transient Ipswich settler was this man's son, the fishmonger Robert Crane of St Giles Cripplegate in London, an adventurer in the Massachusetts Bay Colony, who died in 1646.

WP IV, 91–2; D.G. Allen, *In English ways* (Chapel Hill, NC: University of North Carolina Press, 1981), 277; *Suffolk Deeds* I, 335–7; A. Macfarlane, ed., *The diary of Ralph Josselin 1616–1683* (Oxford: Oxford University Press, 1976), 29; Waters, 1140;

F. Rose-Troup, *The Massachusetts Bay Company and its predecessors* (New York: Grafton Press, 1930), 107, 140.

CUSHMAN, Robert (1577/8–1625)

Robert Cushman, originally a grocer from Canterbury, Kent, was in Plymouth, briefly, in 1621. For several years he had acted as chief agent to secure finance and supplies for the Leiden separatists who became Plymouth's settlers. He set sail for New England on the *Speedwell* in 1620, alongside the *Mayflower*, but stayed on in England when the *Speedwell* had to turn back. Cushman travelled to New England in the autumn of 1621, and reached Plymouth on 11 November. On 12 December Cushman preached a sermon to convince the settlers to accept terms offered by London merchants. This was later printed. Cushman reached London again by February 1621/2, to continue negotiations for trade and supplies. He carried back from New England an account of Plymouth, by William Bradford and Edward Winslow*, published as *A relation, or journall of the beginning or proceedings of the English plantation settled at Plymouth* (1622). Cushman died in England in 1625.

Publication *A sermon preached at Plymouth* (1622).

GMB 502–4; Nathaniel Philbrick, *Mayflower: a voyage to war* (London: HarperPress, 2009), 125–6, 187.

DAVIS, Barnabas (d. 1685)

Barnabas Davis, a tallow chandler, came from Tetbury and Tewkesbury, Gloucestershire. In 1635 he was hired by the London merchant William Woodcock (at £10 a year with expenses) to manage Woodcock's interests in Connecticut. Woodcock, along with the earl of Warwick, Sir Richard Saltonstall, Lord Saye and Sele and Lord Brooke, was intent on exploiting the commercial potential of the 'Warwick Patent', 400 acres of land along the Connecticut River valley. Davis was to stock Woodcock's land with sheep and cattle.

'Barnabie Davis' set sail in the *Blessing* at Easter, 1635. He travelled with a shipload of carpenters and servants led by Francis Stiles, who were to build a house and fence land for Woodcock. But Stiles reneged on most of what he was commissioned to do, and Davis pursued him on Woodcock's behalf. After William Woodcock's death in 1639 Davis continued to work for John Woodcock, William's brother.

Between 1635 and 1639, Davis made five transatlantic voyages, following Stiles to and fro, and responding to the commands of his employers. He received little or no payment for his work and expenses, and the case came to court in 1641. Thomas Lechford* of Boston acted as a notary for Davis, and left a paper trail in his notebook of Davis's business dealings and disappointments.

When Davis landed at Boston in June 1639, he came with his wife Patience and four children. They settled in Charlestown where Barnabas became a church member and pursued his work as a tallow chandler. He died there in 1685.

GM 2: 286–92 (Davis), 6: 519 (Stiles); Roger Thompson, *From deference to defiance: Charlestown, Massachusetts, 1629–1662* (Boston, MA: New England Historic Genealogical Society, 2012), 33–5; Lechford *NB*, 367–72, 381–3, 396–401, 407; Karen Ordahl Kupperman, *Providence Island: the other puritan colony* (Cambridge: Cambridge University Press, 1993), 325–32.

DESBOROUGH, Isaac (1615–1658)

Isaac Desborough, son of Isaac and Mary Desborough of Eltisley, Cambridgeshire, emigrated in 1635 on the *Hopewell*. He was the elder brother of John Disbrowe (*ODNB*) and Samuel Desborough*. Desborough settled at Lynn, Massachusetts. There is no record of his landholding, but in the Essex Quarterly Court, 1638–9, 'Isaac Disberoe' was involved in a defamation case against Hugh Burt. The court found in Desborough's favour. Burt sued Desborough in September 1639, but when the case came to the Court of Assistants in March 1639/40, Desborough failed to appear. He had probably already gone to England.

Isaac Desborough was soon back in Cambridgeshire. He married, and had a number of children baptised in the parish of Eltisley in the 1640s and 1650s. He died there in 1658.

GM 2: 338–44.

EATON, Nathaniel (c.1609–1674)

Nathaniel Eaton was the son of Richard Eaton, vicar of Great Budworth, Cheshire. He was brother to Theophilus Eaton, first governor of New Haven, and to the minister Samuel Eaton*. He is said to have attended Trinity College, Cambridge, without taking a degree, but could perhaps be the 'Nathaneel Eaton' who in 1633 graduated MA, was ordained deacon in the Salisbury diocese, and became curate at Dinton, Wiltshire. Eaton studied with William Ames (*ODNB*) at Franeker, c.1633–4. He returned to England and is said to have worked briefly as a schoolmaster. Given his Cheshire connections, he could have been the 'Eaton' who served in 1635 as a curate at Siddington chapel in Prestbury, twenty miles from Great Budworth.

Eaton emigrated to New England in 1637, with his wife and brothers, and settled at Cambridge. He joined the church: his testimony on admission survives in Thomas Shepard's records. He became a freeman of Massachusetts on 9 June 1638. That same year he was appointed head of the new college, Harvard, where he planned and planted 'Harvard Yard'. A year later, in 1639, the Massachusetts General Court hauled Eaton in for mistreating students: he gave them 'nothing but porridge and pudding, and that very homely'; worse, he had a reputation for cruelty to servants and scholars, inflicting 'twenty or thirty stripes at a time, and would not leave till they had confessed what he required'. The General Court dismissed him in September 1639 and revoked his licence to teach. He was also ordered to answer to the Cambridge church, but fled to New Hampshire and then to Virginia, where he served as an assistant rector. After he left Massachusetts it emerged that he had plundered Harvard's coffers and run up debts of more than £1000. He sent for his wife and younger children to come to Virginia in 1641: they perished on the journey, and Eaton remarried – a wife he apparently deserted when he left Virginia.

Eaton went from Virginia to the University of Padua, where he graduated PhD and MD in 1647. He lived 'privately' in England during the Interregnum. In 1657 and 1661 he published books as 'Nathanael Eaton, Doctor of Philosophy and Medicine'. In 1661 he became vicar of Bishops Castle, Shropshire. He is likely to be the Nathaniel Eaton, MD, who was ordained priest by the bishop of Exeter on 15 March 1662/3, and became rector of Bideford, Devon, in 1668. He was arrested for debt in 1665, and again in 1674. He died in prison in Southwark.

Publications *Mēno-Ezeologia; or a treatise of moneths and years* (1657); *De fastis Anglicis, sive calendarium sacrum. The holy calendar: being a treble series of epigrams upon all the feasts observed by the Church of England* (1661).

Shepard's confessions, 53–7; *NEHGR* 3: 96; *WJ*, 301–5, 343, 744; *WP* IV, 142, 173–4, 204, 249, 251, 253–4; Lechford *NB*, 196, 197–8; *Magnalia* II, 10; *Pilgrims*, 24, 26n.53, 55n.6, 70n.84, 159, 177, 191, 204; *CCEd* Person IDs 94099, 33274 and 96470.

ANB, ODNB.

GARDINER, Sir Christopher

Sir Christopher Gardiner (a knight of the Golden Melice, a title conferred by the Pope) arrived in New England in April 1630, as an agent for Sir Ferdinando Gorges (*ODNB*). Gardiner had been told to pursue Gorges's claim to the territory of Massachusetts. He settled on the south shore of the Bay.

In February 1630/1, John Winthrop received letters which alleged that Gardiner had abandoned two wives in England. The Massachusetts authorities attempted to detain Gardiner, who fled into Plymouth Colony. There he fell into the hands of Indians, who handed him over to the Plymouth authorities. William Bradford recorded how they discovered 'a little notebook that by accident slipped out of his pocket ... in which was a memorial what day he was reconciled to the Pope & church of Rome'. Gardiner, sent back to Massachusetts, spent the summer under house arrest and then fled with Thomas Purchase. He spent the winter with Purchase (and ran up debts that the courts were still trying to recover from Purchase years later).

Gardiner returned to England by August 1632. With Thomas Morton* and Philip Ratcliffe*, he continued to support Gorges's efforts to challenge the Bay Colony's patent. Thomas Morton opened his *New English Canaan* with a poem in praise of Gardiner.

WJ, 51, 53, 88, 90, 92, 94, 332-3, 535; Thomas Morton, *New English Canaan* (1637), 8; *WP* III, 110n., 112, 120; William Bradford, *Of Plymouth Plantation, 1620–1647*, ed. Samuel E. Morison (New York: Knopf, 1963), 247–9, 421–2; *GMB* 729–30.

ANB.

GIFFORD, Abigail

In December 1635, John Winthrop recorded:

> One Abigaell Gifford widy beinge kept at the charge of the parishe of wilsden in midelsex neere London, was sent by mr Babbs shippe into this Contrye, & beinge fonde to be sometimes distracted; & a very burdensome woman The Governor & Assistantes returned her backe by warrant to the same parishe in the ship Rebecka.

Thomas Babb's ship, the *Griffin*, arrived in September 1635. By December the widow Gifford had been shipped back on the *Rebecca* to Willesden, Middlesex.

WJ, 139.

GILLETT, Jonathan

Jonathan Gillett was the son of William Gillett, rector of Chaffcombe, Somerset. He and his brother Nathan were in New England by 1633. Both went to Dorchester, Massachusetts. Jonathan Gillett returned to England and married Mary Dolbiar at Colyton, Devon, on 29 March 1634. Jonathan and his new wife immediately returned to Dorchester: in the family bible, their son recorded 'my father Gille[tt] came into new-ingland the second time in June in the year 1634'. Jonathan Gillett became a freeman of Massachusetts on 6 May 1635. He and Mary moved to Windsor in 1638, following Jonathan's brother Nathan. Jonathan died at Windsor in 1677, Mary in 1685/6.

GMB 766–70; *CCEd* Person ID 57041, 'Gillett, Willimus'.

GOAD, Thomas

Thomas Goad arrived in 1635, apprenticed to serve John Winthrop Jr* for four years. He stayed in New England only a few months.

Alison Games, *Migration and the origins of the English Atlantic world* (Cambridge, MA: Harvard University Press, 1999), 202; *GM* 3: 76–8.

GORGES, Robert (1595–1624?)

Robert Gorges was the son of the colonising entrepreneur Sir Ferdinando Gorges. Sir Ferdinando sent his son to Massachusetts Bay in 1623, with authority from the Council for New England to settle a new plantation. Robert Gorges was to be governor-general. The settlement, on the site of modern Weymouth, Massachusetts, failed to prosper. Robert Gorges returned to England in 1624. William Bradford observed that Gorges thought New England not fit for someone of his quality, and went home having 'scarcely saluted the country'.

William Bradford, *Of Plymouth Plantation, 1620–1647*, ed. Samuel E. Morison (New York: Knopf, 1963), 133–6; *GMB* 794–5.

ANB.

GORGES, William (1606–1659)

William Gorges was the son of Sir Edward Gorges of Wraxall, Somerset, and the nephew of Sir Ferdinando Gorges. He emigrated in 1635, to act as governor for another colonial venture his uncle wanted to develop, on territory granted to him to the north of Massachusetts. In August 1636 Sir Ferdinando referred to his nephew as 'Captain William Gorges, Governor of New Somersetshire'. By 27 February 1636/7 William Gorges was back in England. He was recalled by Sir Ferdinando after a dispute with his fellow colonist George Cleeve.

GM 3: 120–1; *ANB, s.n.* 'Gorges, Robert'.

HAINES, Samuel

Samuel Haines came from Westbury Leigh in Wiltshire. He emigrated in 1635 on the *Angel Gabriel*, as a servant to John Cogswell (senior) of Ipswich. Haines returned to England late in 1637 or 1638. On 1 April 1638, he married Eleanor Neate at Dilton, Wiltshire. In 1639 he came back to New England with his wife. He also brought back 'between fourscore and an hundred pounds worth of goods' for Cogswell, and Cogswell's sons William, John* and Edward. Haines moved to Dover in 1640, and to Portsmouth in 1650. He died in 1684.

GM 3: 187–93.

HARRISON, John Jr

John Harrison had been in New England since at least 1637, perhaps earlier. He was well-known to John Winthrop Jr* and in 1638 seems to have been living in Governor John Winthrop's household in Boston. In the early summer of 1639 Harrison left for England on a 'suddenly-undertaken voyage'. He was in debt. On 1 August 1639, John Coggan, a Boston merchant, appointed an attorney in London to sue Harrison for payment. Harrison sent English news to John Winthrop Jr on his passage back, 11 August 1639, and from the Inner Temple in London on 18 February 1639/40 and 15 April 1640. Harrison reported that on his arrival in London his father was displeased with him: he had not yet obtained leave to visit him. Harrison continued his legal studies at Inner Temple and was called to the Bar on 20 May 1647.

WP III, 517; *WP* IV, 87, 93, 138, 193–6, 226–7; Lechford *NB*, 145–6, 147.

HATHERLY, Timothy

Timothy Hatherly, a feltmaker and merchant, came from Winkleigh in Devon. He travelled from St Olave, Southwark, to the Plymouth Colony in 1623 but returned to England later that year. Hatherley transacted business for the Plymouth Colony in London and made annual trips over to New England in 1631, 1632 and 1633. Finally, in 1634, he settled at Scituate. He died there in 1666.

GMB 876–81.

HAYNES, Hezekiah (d. 1693)

Hezekiah Haynes was the second son of John and Mary Haynes of Copford Hall, Essex. His father John Haynes* became governor of Massachusetts in 1635 and served repeatedly as governor of Connecticut from 1639. Hezekiah's sister Elizabeth married Joseph Cooke*; he was half-brother to John* and Roger Haynes*.

Hezekiah Haynes emigrated with his parents in 1633. The family settled initially at Cambridge, Massachusetts. Like George Wyllys*, son of Governor George Wyllys of Connecticut, Hezekiah was despatched to England on family business and stayed on.

He left New England in 1637, around the time his father moved to Hartford, Connecticut. Haynes joined the parliamentary army when the First Civil War broke out. He became a captain in Colonel James Holborne's foot regiment, and by 1645 was a major in the regiment of Charles Fleetwood (*ODNB*). He led Fleetwood's regiment at the battle of Dunbar in 1650.

In the 1650s Haynes turned from military service to administration. He became an Essex JP and a lay ejector of clergy, and served as MP for Essex in the Second Protectorate Parliament, 1656. In 1655 Fleetwood deputed him to act as major-general of Norfolk, Suffolk, Essex, Cambridgeshire and the Isle of Ely. Haynes took a lead in urging the suppression of Quakers, baptists and Fifth Monarchists. Haynes was disenchanted by the failure of Cromwell's Protectorate to deliver what it promised. After Cromwell's death, he joined Fleetwood in calling for the restoration of the Rump Parliament. A few months later, his support for Fleetwood's abortive suppression of the Rump cost him his commission, and he was ordered by parliament to leave London. He retired to the family seat at Copford Hall, which he had inherited from his brother in 1657. Haynes was arrested for treasonable conspiracy in 1660, and imprisoned in the Tower of London for eighteen months. He was released in 1662 after providing a bond of £5000 to guarantee good conduct. In 1672 Copford Hall was licensed as a presbyterian place of worship, with John Argor

(*CR*) as its preacher. Haynes lived at Copford until 1684, when his son took over and Haynes moved to Coggeshall.

Haynes kept up his connections with New England. He visited in the 1640s: the diarist and minister Ralph Josselin (*ODNB*), a good friend of Haynes, recorded on 8 February 1647/8, 'Mr Haines tooke his leave of us to goe for New England.' Josselin also noted, on 11 January 1651/2, 'wee had this day a comfortable presence of god in word and breaking bread, the Major Haynes joyned with us in breaking bread being a member of a church in New-England'. In 1653 Hezekiah Haynes was one of the friends of New England asked to support colonists' request to Cromwell for aid against the Dutch. After his father's death in 1654, relations grew more strained. On 17 June 1675 Haynes wrote to John Winthrop Jr*, then governor of Connecticut, about his right to land at 'Mattabesett' (Middletown) 'by the free donation of the Sachem... which was expressed... in a formall way when I was presentt in New-England'. He had been advised of the Indian's death by his father, and expected to be assigned a 'considerable lott' when the area was settled, but had heard nothing. Samuel Wyllys replied, offering Haynes land – if he came over to New England – but not in Middletown. In a letter of 29 May 1677 Haynes responded, with some bitterness, that the colony had obviously forgotten how much his father had invested in New England, and had also overlooked his own work in raising £600 from his regiment 'for the purchase of Lands for propagating the Gospel among the Indians'. He complained that his experience verified what was 'proverbially [said] of NE': 'that they are free in promising but slow in performing & that men cannot have equall Justice liueing out of the Country'.

> GMB 893–7; W.A. Shaw, *A history of the English Church ... 1640–1660* (London: Longmans & Green, 1900), II, 388; T.W. Davids, *Annals of evangelical nonconformity in Essex* (London: Jackson, Walford & Hodder, 1863), 293, 318; *The diary of Ralph Josselin 1616–1683*, ed. A. Macfarlane (Oxford: Oxford University Press, 1976), 111, 268 (see also 38, 110, 196, 239, 277, 302); Wyllys MSS, I, 19B and 20 (printed *NEHGR* 24: 124–5, 128–9); Patrick Little and David L. Smith, *Parliaments and politics during the Cromwellian Protectorate* (Cambridge: Cambridge University Press, 2007), 61–4, 88; Christopher Durston, *Cromwell's major-generals: godly government during the English Revolution* (Manchester and New York: Manchester University Press, 2001), 31, 49–50.

BDBR, ODNB.

JENNINGS, Richard (1616–1709)

Richard Jennings, of Ipswich, Suffolk, graduated BA from St Catharine's College, Cambridge, 1636. His tutor had been John Knowles*. Jennings sailed to New England with the minister Nathaniel Rogers and his family, 1 June 1636, and lived with Rogers at Ipswich, Massachusetts. Jennings returned to England in 1638, and took an MA in 1639. He was ordained in 1645 and became rector of Grundisburgh, Suffolk, 12 March 1645/6. He was admitted rector of

Combs, Suffolk, 15 January 1647/8. His successor at Combs was installed on 13 April 1663, the date of Jennings's deprivation for non-subscription.

CCEd Person ID 125805, Record ID 73805; *CR*.

LEY, Lord James (1618/19–1665)

Lord James Ley, who later became the third earl of Marlborough, arrived in New England on the *Hector*, 26 June 1637: 'being about nineteen years of age', he 'came only to see the country'. Governor John Winthrop reported that Ley was of 'very sober carriage and showed much wisdom and moderation in his lowly and familiar carriage, especially in the ship'. He 'took up his lodging at the common inn'. Although Winthrop offered him lodging, Ley refused, 'saying, that he came not to be troublesome to any'.

Ley left with Sir Henry Vane Jr* in August 1637, and returned to England. After his father died in 1638, Ley took on his title and his debts. During the civil wars, he was appointed admiral of a royalist squadron. He lived quietly during the Interregnum, but after the Restoration took on the role of a commissioner for trade, and travelled widely. He died in the sea-battle of Lowestoft, during the Second Anglo-Dutch War.

WJ 223–4, 225, 228–9.

ODNB.

MINTER, Desire

Desire Minter sailed to New England on the *Mayflower* in 1620, in the household of John Carver. William Bradford recorded 'Desire Minter returned to her friend and proved not very well and died in England'.

William Bradford, *Of Plymouth Plantation, 1620–1647*, ed. Samuel E. Morison (New York: Knopf, 1963), 441, 443–4; *GMB* 1269.

MORTON, Thomas (*c.*1580–1647)

Thomas Morton was a lawyer of Clifford's Inn, London. Little else is known of his background, except that in his lifetime he travelled near the equator as well as three times to New England.

Morton first emigrated to New England in 1624, with a Captain Wollastan. After Wollastan left for Virginia, Morton took charge of the tiny settlement of Passonagessit (located at what would become Quincy, Massachusetts). On 1 May 1627, to the fury of the settlers at Plymouth – the devout *Mayflower* pilgrims – Morton set up a maypole at 'Ma-re Mount', as his settlement was now called. After further controversy (Morton was accused of selling guns to the Indians), the Plymouth authorities banished Morton to the Isles of Shoals and then to England. Thus in 1628 Morton was ejected from New England. A party of newly-arrived settlers from Salem, Massachusetts, led by John Endicott (*ANB*), cut the maypole down. Unabashed, Morton returned to New England for a second time in 1629, to pursue what promised to be a rich trade in furs. He was soon at Ma-re Mount again, and vigorously resisted attempts by the Massachusetts authorities to control either his trading activities or his religious beliefs. As a result, the Massachusetts General Court resolved in 1630 to ship Morton to England as a prisoner. Back in England once more, Morton worked as a lawyer for Sir Ferdinando Gorges in his attempts to overturn the charter of the Massachusetts Bay Colony. Morton wrote *New English Canaan* in 1633–4, expressing his delight in the landscape and native people of New England, and his distaste for the ways of English puritan settlers. Morton returned to New England for a third time in 1643, and travelled to land he owned in Plymouth, Rhode Island and Maine. In 1644 the Massachusetts authorities accused him of plotting against the colony and held him in jail for a year. He died at York, Maine.

Publication *New English Canaan* (1637).

William Bradford, *Of Plymouth Plantation, 1620–1647*, ed. Samuel E. Morison (New York: Knopf, 1963), 204–10, 216–17, 273–4; *WP* II, 267, 269n.; *WJ*, 39, 332–3, 492, 535–9; *GMB* 1299–300.

ANB, *ODNB*.

NEALE, Walter

Walter Neale arrived in New England in 1630, with his sights set on the fur trade. He represented the Laconia company, one of the many colonial ventures supported by Sir Ferdinando Gorges. Neale's task was to explore the upper reaches of the Piscataqua River, in the hopes of finding an inland lake and waterways to revolutionise the transport of furs. Neale established small trading posts on the coast, but his inland expedition was a failure. He was recalled to England in 1633. He commanded the City of London's artillery for a time, and was appointed lieutenant governor of Portsmouth, Hampshire, in 1639.

GMB 1324–6; *ODNB*.

PAULIN, Sebastian

Sebastian Paulin was taken to New England by his uncle, Nicholas Simpkin, and apprenticed to Robert Keayne of Boston for ten years. He was appointed a drum major on the fort at Castle Island. Paulin wrote to his mother in England, asking to go home. She replied in February 1637, enclosing a letter written by a friend to persuade John Winthrop to release her son. It was decided that Simpkin had no power to bind Sebastian into an apprenticeship, so he could go. Sebastian's mother instructed him, if allowed to leave, to 'agree with the master of the ship for your passage at the best rate and cheapest you can, and if it pleaseth God to send you safe hether I will see it duly discharged'.

WP III, 352; *WJ* 749; *GM* 6: 334–6.

PENTON, Edward

Edward Penton of Norwich, a 'Sanctified brother [who] hath bin already at New England', was arrested by the city magistrate John Anguish in 1637 for distributing copies of prohibited books such as Henry Burton's *A divine tragedie lately acted* (1636) and William Prynne's *Newes from Ipswich* (1636). Under examination, Penton disclosed his suppliers and the authorities pursued the matter in the Court of Star Chamber.

Matthew Reynolds, *Godly reformers and their opponents in early modern England: religion in Norwich, c.1560–1643* (Woodbridge: Boydell Press, 2005), 200, citing NA, SP16/346/58 and SP16/349/52.

POTTER, Vincent (1614?–1661)

Vincent Potter is likely to have come to New England from Warwickshire. He was a member of the Massachusetts Bay Company from the start. 'Vyncent Potter', aged twenty-one, signed up as a passenger on the *Elizabeth & Ann*, May 1635. He settled in Boston and was employed on 13 October 1636, 'to serve at the fort [on Castle Island] for one year for £10 wages'. There is no record of church membership. He may have served in the Pequot War, 1637. He took the oath of fidelity at Sandwich, in Plymouth Colony, in 1639. His brother-in-law Thomas Fowle* was also in New England.

Potter set sail for England in October 1639, on the same ship as John Josselyn (*ODNB*). In anticipation of leaving New England, Potter had assigned several of his apprentices or indentured servants to new masters over the previous months. The ship reached Devon on 24 November. From his conduct aboard ship, Josselyn judged Potter a 'sectary'.

Potter pursued a radical path after his return to England. Initially, he traded with New England, but after civil war broke out he joined the parliamentary army as a captain of horse. He became a parliamentary commissioner, liaising between parliament and the New Model Army, and played a prominent and crucial role in settling arrears of army pay. Potter was among those who signed the death warrant for Charles I in 1649. In June that year, by now a colonel, he went to Ireland and masterminded provisions for Cromwell's campaign. In August 1650, he travelled from England to Scotland, to oversee the distribution of supplies to regiments. In 1651–2 he acted as a commissioner for improving the land in Scotland that was under English control. In 1652 he returned to Ireland.

In October 1660, Potter was tried and condemned as a regicide. He was to have been hung, drawn and quartered, but early in 1661 he died a natural death, in prison in the Tower of London.

GM 5: 505–6; Lechford *NB*, 93, 101, 188; *WP* IV, 355; Aspinwall, 70–1.

BDBR, ODNB.

RATCLIFFE, Philip

Philip Ratcliffe was a servant of the London merchant Matthew Cradock (*ODNB*), a prominent English investor in New England. In June 1631 the Massachusetts authorities ordered 'that Phillip Ratcliffe shall be whipped, haue his ears cutt of, fyned £40 and banished out of the lymitts of this Jurisdiccion, for vttering mallitious and scandalous speeches against the gouernment & the church of Salem &c'. Edward Howes wrote to John Winthrop Jr* from London, 3 April 1632, that reports of the severity of colonial government were causing concern, especially 'about cuttinge off the Lunatick mans eares'. Ratcliffe returned to England by 1632. He became an ally of prominent opponents of Massachusetts – Thomas Morton*, Sir Christopher Gardiner*, Sir Ferdinando Gorges – who petitioned the privy council to get the Bay Company's charter revoked.

Mass. Recs. 1: 88; *WJ*, 52, 75, 88, 90, 538; *WP* III, 76; *GMB* 1550.

REVELL, John

John Revell, a London fishmonger, agreed in 1629 to buy a one-sixteenth share in the *Eagle*. This vessel, renamed the *Arbella*, became the flagship of the Winthrop fleet in 1630. Revell's name appeared in the Massachusetts Bay Company records regularly in 1629, and he took on various responsibilities. Revell sailed to New England in 1630, in the Winthrop fleet, on the *Jewel*. On 27 May, in mid-Atlantic, Revell and the master of the *Jewel* rowed to the *Arbella* and stayed for dinner, '& about 2: howers after dinner they went aboard their owne shippes our Captaine giving mr Revell 3: shott, because he was one of the owners of our shippe'. Revell arrived in New England in mid-June, but soon left. Thomas Dudley noted that when the *Lyon* left New England, commissioned to fetch supplies from Bristol, Revell left too: 'With this ship returned Mr Revil, one of the five undertakers here for the joint stock of the company, and Mr. Vassall [William Vassall*], one of the assistants, and his family, and also Mr. Bright [Francis Bright], a minister, sent hither the year before.' Revell stayed less than a month in New England and took the first opportunity to go home.

GMB 1571–2; *WJ*, 24, 35, 730; *WP* II, 305; Bernard Bailyn, *The New England merchants in the seventeenth century* (Cambridge, MA: Harvard University Press, 1955), 203; F. Rose-Troup, *The Massachusetts Bay Company and its predecessors* (New York: Grafton Press, 1930), 152–3; Thomas Dudley to the countess of Lincoln, March 1630/1, *Letters from New England ... 1629–1638*, ed. Everett Emerson (Amherst, MA: University of Massachusetts Press, 1976), 72.

SALTONSTALL, Sir Richard (1586–1658)

Sir Richard Saltonstall, a London lawyer, was first elected an assistant of the Massachusetts Bay Company in England on 23 March 1628/9. He was the father of Richard Saltonstall*. In 1629, he sent servants and cattle ahead of him to New England. Saltonstall sailed to New England in 1630, as a widower, with five of his six children. He settled at Watertown. He attended all the meetings of the Massachusetts Bay Company in New England between 22 August 1630 and 22 March 1630/1.

He left New England on the *Lyon*, 1 April 1631, and arrived in London on 29 April. He was elected an assistant in Massachusetts in 1633, in his absence, but never returned. Saltonstall continued to take an interest in New England. He defended Massachusetts against the charges of Philip Ratcliffe*, Thomas Morton* and Sir Christopher Gardiner*. He diverted his attention to fresh colonising ventures by Lord Saye and Sele and Lord Brooke, outside the boundaries of Massachusetts, but made heavy losses. In 1639 he handed over his New England interests to his son Robert, who had returned there c.1638. Saltonstall spent time in the Netherlands, 1643–4, where Henry Saltonstall* joined him. From 1649 he controlled the sales of crown property, and this profitable post helped him to boost his fortunes. In 1650 he and his son Richard became members of the High Court of Justice, commissioned by the Rump Parliament to try the crimes of the Commonwealth's enemies. From 1658 he lived near Wrexham, and associated with the congregationalist Vavasor Powell (*ODNB*). He criticised Massachusetts for its intolerance: he wrote to John Wilson* and John Cotton c.1652, advocating freedom for Quakers.

Saltonstall Papers, 3–24, 42–7; Bush, 496–504 (Saltonstall's letter to Cotton and Wilson, c.1652, and their reply); *WJ*, 48–9; *GMB* 1618–21; *Pilgrims*, 36, 84, 88, Plate 3.

BDBR, ODNB.

SHARPE, Thomas

Thomas Sharpe, a leatherseller, was chosen an assistant of the Massachusetts Bay Company in England, 1629. He crossed the Atlantic in the Winthrop fleet in 1630, with his wife Tabitha, son Thomas and a daughter. He joined the Boston church at its gathering on 27 August 1630. His daughter's death on 3 January 1630/1 – 'a godly virgin, making a comfortable end after a long sickness' – was reported by Thomas Dudley in a letter to the countess of Lincoln. After this, on 17 March, Sharpe's house was razed by fire. He left for England two weeks later, on the *Lyon*, with Sir Richard Saltonstall*. In the Boston church records, his name was annotated 'gone since'.

In 1636, as of Sandon, Essex, Thomas Sharpe was presented with his wife Tabitha and son Thomas as 'a common depraver of the government ecclesiasticall, and of the rites and ceremonies of this church, since his cominge from new England'. Sharpe became Warden of the Company of Leathersellers, London, in 1641.

F. Rose-Troup, *The Massachusetts Bay Company and its predecessors* (New York: Grafton Press, 1930), 154; *Boston CR*, 13; *WJ*, 47, 48–9, 730; Thomas Dudley to the countess of Lincoln, March 1630/1, *Letters from New England . . . 1629–1638*, ed. Everett Emerson (Amherst, MA: University of Massachusetts Press, 1976), 73, 76, 81; ERO, D/AEA 41, Archdeaconry of Essex Act Book, 1636–38, fol. 102v.; *GMB* 1655–6.

SPENCER, John (d. 1648)

John Spencer probably came from London, though possibly from Wiltshire or Hampshire. He emigrated in 1634 from Southampton on the *Mary & John*.

Spencer settled first at Ipswich. He had joined the church by 3 September 1634, when he became a freeman of Massachusetts. He moved to Newbury at its foundation in 1635. He served as a representative for both Ipswich and Newbury at the General Court. In May 1637, he was turned out of office as captain of Newbury's train-band, for sympathy with John Wheelwright*. In November 1637, along with Richard Dummer*, he was one of the Newbury men disarmed.

Spencer left New England at the height of the Antinomian Controversy. He made a will on 1 August 1637, which Richard Dummer swore in 1649 had been delivered to him 'before Mr. Spencere's going to England'. The content of the will tends to confirm his antinomian leanings: his nephew and heir was under the tutelage of John Cotton in Boston, and all his executors and overseers – including Richard Dummer – had been linked with the antinomian cause.

He was later said to be 'of London' (but he may not be the 'Spenser' who wrote from England, *c*.1639, to demand repayment of his investment in the Massachusetts Bay Company). Spencer was buried on 23 June 1648 at Kingston-on-Thames, Surrey.

D.G. Allen, *In English ways* (Chapel Hill, NC: University of North Carolina Press, 1981), 266; F. Rose-Troup, *The Massachusetts Bay Company and its predecessors* (New York: Grafton Press, 1930), 154; *GD*; *Essex Probate Recs*. I, 107–8; *WP* IV, 91–2 (*GM* argues this 'Spenser' is a different person); Waters, 553n.; *GM* 6: 428–36.

TILLAM, Thomas (*fl*.1637–1668)

Thomas Tillam emigrated to New England in 1638. No evidence of his stay has survived, apart from his poem, 'Uppon the first sight of New England June 29 1638':

> Hail holy-land wherin our holy Lord
> Hath planted his most true and holy Word . . .
> Methinks I hear the Lamb of God thus speak:
> 'Come my dear little flock, who for my sake

> Have left your Country, dearest friends and goods
> And hazarded your lives o'the raginge floods.
> Posses this Country: free from all annoy
> Here I'll bee with you, heare you shall Injoye
> My Sabbaths, sacraments, my ministry
> And ordinances in their puritye ...

Tillam stepped ashore in New England in the aftermath of the Antinomian Controversy. Suspicions of radical opinions ran high and – to judge from Tillam's later career – the drive for orthodoxy in Massachusetts would not have been congenial to him. He left no trace of his time there, and must have gone home soon. By the 1640s, he was a member of a baptist congregation in London, led by another antinominan ex-colonist, Hanserd Knollys*.

By Tillam's own testimony, he was born a Catholic. He became a well-known religious radical in revolutionary England, a Seventh Day Baptist and Fifth Monarchist. He joined Morgan Llywd's church at Wrexham (see Hugh Pritchard*) and clashed with Thomas Weld* in Newcastle. In the 1660s, Tillam was a refugee in Germany, and leader of a tiny community that believed that Christians, like Jews, should celebrate the Sabbath on Saturday, not Sunday.

Harrison T. Meserole, ed. *Seventeenth century American poetry* (New York: Doubleday & Co., 1968), 397–8; J.F. Maclear, 'New England and the Fifth Monarchy: the quest for the millennium in early American puritanism', *William and Mary Quarterly*, 3rd series, 32 (1975), 230, 249; E.A. Payne, 'Thomas Tillam', *Baptist Quarterly*, 17 (1957–8), 61–6.

BDBR, ODNB.

TINKER, John (d. 1664)

John Tinker was living in Governor John Winthrop's household in Boston by 1636, when clothes for him were itemised in a bill for tailoring. Tinker went to England on Winthrop's business, November 1639–c. May 1640. By 1643 he had settled at Windsor, Connecticut, and was later in Boston, Lancaster and Groton. Tinker was in England again in August 1653, when Stephen Winthrop* wrote that 'John Tinker promised to call on me but failed me'. By 1659 he was in New London, a distiller and refiner.

WP III, 220; *WP* IV, 152–3, 205–6, 223–5, 249–52, 326 and *passim*; *WP* VI, 318; 5 *MHSC* 8: 214; Bernard Bailyn, *The New England merchants in the seventeenth century* (Cambridge, MA: Harvard University Press, 1955), 55.

TOMSON, Robert (d. 1694)

Robert Tomson, a prosperous London merchant, was in Boston, briefly, in 1639. He bought property and was granted 500 acres. In 1649, Tomson became one of the original members of the Corporation for the Propagation of the Gospel in New England, with Herbert Pelham*, Richard Floyd* and Edward Winslow* among others. In the 1650s, he was a naval commissioner with Francis Willoughby*, Nehemiah Bourne* and Edward Hopkins*. He was responsible, with Willoughby, for administering some of the terms of Hopkins's will. Tomson met with John Winthrop Jr*, Nathaniel Whitfield* and others in London, early in 1663, to settle a dispute between the New Haven Colony and Connecticut. Tomson bought up Henry Whitfield's* holdings at Guilford after his death.

Davenport Letters, 217n.; Waters, 65–7, 74; William Hooke to John Davenport, 2 March 1662/3, A.G. Matthews, ed., 'A censored letter', *Transactions of the Congregational Historical Society*, 9 (1924–6), 263–83; *ODNB s.n.* 'Thomson, George (*bap.* 1607, *d.* 1691)'.

VANE, Sir Henry Jr (1613–1662)

Sir Henry Vane was born at Debden, Essex, the eldest child of Sir Henry Vane the elder and his wife Frances. Vane was educated at Westminster School, and at Magdalen College, Oxford, where he matriculated but did not take a degree. He travelled for a while on the Continent, taking in Paris, Geneva and Leiden. He also served as an aide to the English ambassador in Vienna. At some point he experienced a religious conversion. By the early 1630s his convictions had hardened into serious resistance to the policies of Archbishop Laud. In 1635 he decided to emigrate to New England.

Vane arrived in Boston in October 1635, and started to intervene actively in Massachusetts' affairs. He joined the church in November and became a freeman on March 1635/6. In a stellar rise for a 'young gentleman' who had only arrived the previous summer, Vane was elected governor in May 1636. When the Antinomian Controversy broke, Vane sided with Anne Hutchinson and John Wheelwright*, as did many members of the Boston church. But Boston's leading layman, John Winthrop, with ministers from other settlements, expressed their opposition. In May 1637, Winthrop regained power as governor, and the writing was on the wall for the Antinomian party. Vane left for England in August 1637, before the full extent of the fallout became clear.

Vane had an immensely influential career in parliament and public life during the 1640s and 1650s. His activity in London was interspersed with short periods of retirement to the country when the political climate was uncongenial. (For more detail see the sources listed below.) He took up the cause of religious toleration, and roundly criticised Massachusetts on this score. In 1655 he provided a parish living for his old antinomian ally, the minister John Wheelwright, at Belleau, Lincolnshire. Vane had bought an estate at Bellau in 1650 and spent a good deal of time there.

After the Restoration of Charles II in 1660, Vane was called to answer for the 'crimes' he had committed in the time of the republic. Although he was not a regicide, he came to represent a hated regime. After two years in prison, the political tide of the Cavalier Parliament led to a trial for treason, and a sentence of execution.

Publications See *ODNB*.

Vane's part in the Antinomian Controversy is discussed in Theodore Dwight Bozeman, *The precisianist strain: disciplinary religion and antinomian backlash in puritanism to 1638* (Chapel Hill, NC: University of North Carolina Press, 2004); Janice Knight, *Orthodoxies in Massachusetts* (Cambridge, MA: Harvard University Press, 1994); Michael P. Winship, *Making heretics: militant protestantism and free grace in Massachusetts, 1636–1641* (Princeton, NJ and Oxford: Princeton University Press, 2002). See also, for his political career, M.A. Judson, *The political thought of Sir Henry Vane the younger* (1969); V. Rowe, *Sir Henry Vane the younger* (London: The Athlone Press, 1970); J.H. Adamson and H.F. Holland, *Sir Harry Vane* (1973); Patrick Little and David L. Smith, *Parliaments and politics during the Cromwellian Protectorate* (Cambridge: Cambridge University Press, 2007), 65, 77, 120–1, 260–4, 291.

ANB, BDBR, GM 7: 161–71, *ODNB*.

WILSON, John (*c.*1591–1667)

John Wilson, minister of Sudbury, Suffolk, arrived in Boston in 1630. He was chosen as a minister of the Boston church, alongside John Cotton. Wilson made two return journeys to England in the 1630s, in 1631 and 1634. On the first occasion, he went to fetch his wife, Elizabeth. She was known to be reluctant to come to New England: in May 1631, Margaret Winthrop reported that 'Mr Wilson is now in london. . . he can not yet perswad his wife to goe, for all he hath taken this paynes to come and fetch hir'. Wilson returned with her in May 1632 on the *Whale*. On the second occasion, Wilson returned to recruit settlers, especially ministers, in East Anglia. He reached New England again in October 1635 and lived out the rest of his life in Boston.

WP III, 33, 34, 36, 61, 175 [quotation from 33]; *WJ*, 69, 156; David Cressy, *Coming over: migration and communication between England and New England in the seventeenth century* (Cambridge: Cambridge University Press, 1987), 50, 95; *GMB* 2012–15; Tom Webster, *Godly clergy in early Stuart England: the Caroline puritan movement, c. 1620–1643* (Cambridge: Cambridge University Press, 1997), 278, 281–2.

ANB.

WINSLOW, Gilbert

Gilbert Winslow of Droitwich, Worcestershire, brother of Edward Winslow*, travelled to New England on the *Mayflower* with Edward in 1620. He settled at Plymouth. William Bradford reported that 'after divers years here, [he] returned into England and died there'. Gilbert Winslow is absent from the Plymouth records from 1627 onwards, and died before 1650.

GMB 2026–7; William Bradford, *Of Plymouth Plantation, 1620–1647*, ed. Samuel E. Morison (New York: Knopf, 1963), 443, 447.

WOOD, William

William Wood stayed in New England four years, and probably arrived in 1629. He became a freeman of Massachusetts on 18 May 1631. He left for England in August 1633. On his return to London, he published a famous account of the colony, *New Englands prospect*. In September 1634, the Massachusetts General Court ordered that 'lettres of thankefulnes' should be signed and sent to 'Mr Wood' and others. Little else is known about Wood. It is unlikely that he came back to New England (in other words, he was not the William Wood who arrived on the *Hopewell* in 1635). He may have lived at Saugus, near Lynn, since his descriptions of that area are particularly vivid and detailed.

Publication *New Englands prospect* (1634).

GMB 2052–4; *GM* 7: 499; Alden T. Vaughan, ed., *New England's prospect* (Amherst, MA: University of Massachusetts Press, 1977), 1–6.

ODNB.

WYLLYS, George (d. 1670)

George Wyllys, the son of Governor George Wyllys of Connecticut, was born at Fenny Compton in Warwickshire. He came to New England with his father in 1638 and settled in Hartford, Connecticut.

In 1639, Wyllys travelled back to his birthplace, to sell land for his father and to find a wife. Governor Wyllys drew up an oath for his son to sign before he sailed away: a solemn promise to come back from England and settle in Connecticut. Governor Wyllys proved unable to hold his son to this. In 1644, after his expectations of seeing his son return had been dashed several times, he wrote a long letter to argue with George junior about the reasons for his failure to honour the oath. He dismissed his son's complaints about lack of funds, and even the dangers of travel in wartime – 'never any ship ever miscarried coming into New England (so merciful and good hath God been in his Providence for the good of his people coming hither and abiding here)'. It was harder to answer his son's argument that he need not cross the Atlantic to New England again because England now had 'many churches gathered ... and the purity of God's ordinances may there be enjoyed'. However, Governor Wyllys composed a vigorous defence of New England's church-fellowship as purer still: in England, 'such as are gathered dwell not together and so cannot watch over one another as they should'; 'with us none are admitted to partake of the seals of the covenant, but such as in the judgment of charity have truth of grace'. In any case, if (as his son had reported) many of 'God's servants' at Fenny Compton had died, it was not likely that George could enjoy church fellowship there – and if his son needed to move within England to find church fellowship, he might as well come back to New England. God would compensate for any financial loss with spiritual gain, 'as he usually doth'. Wyllys sent his son the oath he had signed, 'that you may seriously consider of it'. He

APPENDIX 1: SETTLERS LEAVING NEW ENGLAND BEFORE 1640

invoked the Almighty: 'I see not yet how I can quit you from your engagement as you desire . . . the nature of the engagement being such (as I conceive) that God is become a third party in it.'

Governor Wyllys wrote his will soon after this exchange with his son. He left George Wyllys Jr substantial property at Wethersfield, Connecticut, but only if 'he do come over into New England and settle himself and his family here according as I have wrote him by letter'. After his father's death, George Wyllys fiercely disputed the terms of his inheritance, but never came back to New England. He lived as a landowner and lawyer, and married Susanna Clark, c.1655. He was buried at Fenny Compton on 28 December 1670.

Wyllys MSS, VII, 24a (Wyllys's oath) and 44-45 (will of Governor George Wyllys, 14 December 1644); *Wyllys Papers*, xxiv, xxxv, 6 (Wyllys's oath), 66–78, 82–7; *Pilgrims*, 88, 89–90, 102, 170, 184, Plate 4.

Appendix 2: Settlers visiting England, 1640–1660

Many settlers had reasons to visit England: mariners and merchants, plying their trade; settlers who wanted to drum up investment for a project in New England – to develop ironworks, or a cloth industry; colonial agents, appointed to press a case with parliamentary committees in London and to manage the bad press colonial disputes might receive in England; individuals who needed to claim a bequest, or check on property, or find a wife. This traffic to and fro across the Atlantic is an important backdrop to settlers' decisions to return to England for good, since travellers brought news in person, and carried letters with encouragements and invitations to come home. The following brief biographies are examples to fill out the picture.

BRACKENBURY, John

John Brackenbury was a mariner, of Charlestown and Boston. He made a deposition to the Massachusetts General Court, 14 April 1659, about his part in stirring up rumours about Nathaniel Mather* at Barnstaple in Devon. Mather had been appointed vicar of Barnstaple in March 1656/7, and when Brackenbury was back in Barnstaple, it was reported Mather had been 'culpable in New England of misdemeanour with a women afore he went from hence'. Brackenbury denied being the author of this report, but testified that:

> being there asked whether this thing were so . . . I suddenly and inconsiderately affirmed . . . that the thing was true. But not long after calling to mind my great mistake herein (for my thoughts at that time were upon another man who was so culpable indeed) . . . I thereupon went to the governor or chief magistrate in Barnstaple aforesaid, and before him acknowledged my great mistake.

Brackenbury seems to have confused Mather with Thomas Larkham*, minister at Tavistock, Devon, whose critics were keen to exploit rumours of misconduct in New England.

MHS, Misc. MSS, 14 May 1659; C.E. Banks, *Planters of the Commonwealth* (Boston, MA: Houghton Mifflin, 1930), 59.

BRIDGES, Robert (d. 1656)

Robert Bridges was at Lynn by 1640. He became a freeman of Massachusetts on 2 June 1641, and joined the Artillery Company. He went to England, 1642, with a specimen of iron ore from Lynn. As as a result, a company formed to set up the Saugus ironworks. Bridges returned to New England in 1643. He took part in Massachusetts government as a representative in 1644, and as an assistant, 1647–56.

> W.L. Sachse, *The colonial American in Britain* (Madison, WI: University of Wisconsin Press, 1956), 121; E.D. Hartley, *Ironworks on the Saugus* (Norman, OK: University of Oklahoma Press, 1957), 216; *GD*.

BROWNE, Abraham

Abraham Browne, a mariner, was born in Plymouth, Devon, the son of a shipmaster and merchant. In later life he wrote an autobiography, recounting his travels and religious experience: 'A book of remembrance of God's Providences towards me, A. B. ... written for my own meditation in New England.' He had lived in France as a child, with a Catholic family. Browne first came to New England in 1650 and settled at Boston. In 1655, after a visit to his old home in the West Country, he set off back to New England by way of Madeira and Barbados. His ship was captured by a 'Sallee Rover' – a Moorish pirate ship – off the coast of Africa. Browne spent months in a dark dungeon before he was ransomed and released. He reached England in December 1655 and New England on 22 May 1656. Browne was son-in-law to Hezekiah Usher* of Boston.

> MHS, MS SBd-151, Abraham Browne: volume of reminiscences, 1653–1668; *Pilgrims*, 101; *NEHGR* 2: 45, 9: 229; *GD*. Extracts from Browne's manuscript have been published: Stephen T. Riley, 'Abraham Browne's captivity by the Barbary pirates, 1655', P.C.F. Smith, ed., *Seafaring in Colonial Massachusetts*, Colonial Society of Massachusetts, *Publications*, 52 (1980), 31–42. On attacks by Muslim privateers on Christian ships, see Linda Colley, *Captives: Britain, empire and the world, 1600–1850* (London: Pimlico, 2003), 43–134.

CALCARD, Edward (c.1604–1681)

Edward Calcard [Colcord, Calcord, Calkard] witnessed a deed to John Wheelwright* at Exeter in 1638. On 22 January 1639/40, writing from Dover, Maine, John Underhill reported information from 'Mr Calkard' and others about letters against Massachusetts sent into England by Hanserd Knollys* (this was during Knollys's dispute with Thomas Larkham* at Dover). Later, Calcard was in Hampton. On 14 October 1651, the Massachusetts General Court ordered that 'whatsoever goods or lands have been taken away from the inhabitants of Hampton by Edward Calcord or John Samborne, upon pretence of being authorized by Mr. Batchelor [Stephen Bachiler*] ... shall be returned to them from whom it was taken ... until there appear sufficient power from Mr Batchilor to recover the same'.

Calcard visited England – more specifically, Devon – on at least two occasions. In a deposition made in New England in 1647, he said he had been at 'Tingworth' (probably Teignmouth), Devon, in 1646. He referred to a Dartmouth merchant, Thomas Jago, and to an 'Ambroze Lane'. In April 1656, Thomas Larkham – by then of Tavistock in Devon – noted that he gave £1 'To Calcard of N England in distresse'. Larkham's generosity in this case (he only received £9 15s a quarter for his own salary) may be due to the fact that Calcard had taken his side at Dover years before, in opposition to Hanserd Knollys.

Lechford NB, 223; WP IV, 179; Aspinwall, 18, 124, 289; GM 6: 610; NEHGR 23: 167; *The diary of Thomas Larkham, 1647–1669*, ed. Susan Hardman Moore, Church of England Record Society, 17 (Woodbridge: Boydell and Brewer, 2011), 127, 131.

CHICKERING, Henry

Henry Chickering came from Wrentham, Suffolk, where he had been a ship money defaulter. He brought his family to New England in 1638, in company with the minister of Wrentham, John Phillip*. He settled at Dedham. He became a church member on 29 February 1640 and a freeman of Massachusetts on 2 June 1641. The choice of deacons at Dedham was delayed, partly by 'apprehensions' in the church, and 'sometimes by reason of brother Chickerings delays of acceptance in regard of his relation and affections to Mr. Philips in England'. John Philip left Dedham to return to Wrentham in 1641. Chickering was eventually ordained deacon on 23 June 1650. He may have visited Wrentham c.1649: Henry Dunster, in a letter to Phillip dated 8 February 1649/50, referred to carriers of letters and wrote that he had received a letter from Phillip 'by Mr. Chickering' (although this might simply mean that Chickering had received a parcel of letters from Phillip, to pass on).

J. Browne, *A history of congregationalism in Norfolk and Suffolk* (London: Jarrold & Sons, 1877), 423; Roger Thompson, *Mobility and migration: East Anglian founders of New England, 1629–1640* (Amherst, MA: University of Massachusetts Press, 1994), 261n.20; NEHGR 3: 188; Dedham CR, 24, 35; MHS, MS N-1143, 'Henry Dunster Notebook, 1628–54', fol. 117.

CLEMENTS, Robert

Robert Clements of Haverhill, Massachusetts, the brother of John Clements*, took John's wife Sarah and her children to Ireland at John's request. On the way, the ship was seized by Spaniards. He and his brother's family were 'carried captive to Spain and with very great hardship got to England'. Robert Clements returned to New England and later claimed costs of £105 10 shillings for the voyage from his brother's estate.

Essex Probate Recs. I, 291–2; Pilgrims, 101, 111n.61, 157.

CODDINGTON, William

William Coddington of Boston, Lincolnshire, emigrated to New England in 1630 with his wife Mary and settled at Boston, Massachusetts. He was an assistant of the Massachusetts Bay Company, and joined the Boston church. During the first hard winter in America, his wife died. Coddington returned to England in March 1631 to find a wife – he married Mary Moseley at Terling, Essex, in September 1631 – and stayed on in England for two years. During this time he wrote to John Cotton, who was still in Boston, Lincolnshire. Coddington came back to New England with his new wife on the *Mary & Jane*, arriving in May 1633.

Coddington supported Anne Hutchinson and John Wheelwright* in the Antinomian Controversy. He was banished from Massachusetts on 12 March 1637/8 and went to Aquidneck (Rhode Island). Letters from Coddington to John Cotton, in the years after this, show that the religious differences between Coddington and the Boston church remained unresolved.

Land disputes within Rhode Island, and between Rhode Island and Massachusetts, meant that agents from Rhode Island – John Clarke, Samuel Gorton*, John Greene, Randall Holden, Roger Williams* – played a large part in negotiations back in London in the 1640s and 1650s, out of all proportion to the tiny size of their settlements. Coddington, a self-appointed agent, went to England early in 1649 to secure a commission to govern Aquidneck Island. Also, his wife Mary had died in 1647. He returned to New England by August 1651, commission in hand and a new wife at his side. In later life he became a Quaker. He died at Newport, Rhode Island, in 1678.

GMB 395–401; Bush, 150–1, 172–3, 345–8, 350–1. Graeme J. Milne, 'New England agents and the English Atlantic, 1641–1666' (PhD dissertation, University of Edinburgh, 1993), 61–7, 302–6 and *passim*.

ANB, *ODNB*.

DAVISON, Nicholas (*c.*1611–1664)

Nicholas Davison, a London merchant, had roots in Norfolk. He emigrated from Stepney with his wife Joanna and settled at Charlestown in 1639. Like Francis Willoughby*, he engaged in transatlantic commerce, exporting fish and timber (from trade up the coast with Maine) and importing a variety of goods. Davison acted as a colonial agent for Matthew Cradock (*ODNB*) of London. He seems to have visited England several times. He was there *c.*1645, when Thomas Edwards reported his refusal to join the London Independents. Davison was alleged to have told the Independents, 'You little know ... whose work you further in opposing the Presbyterians ... the Independents in Old-England are nothing like them of New-England no more than black to white: you Independents here do that which we abhorre there.' He was in England again *c.*1655, and returned to New England on the *Speedwell*, leaving 30 May 1656. In 1658 he moved to live chiefly at

Pemaquid, Maine. Davison profited well from business, leaving estate worth £1896 in 1664.

> Edwards, *Gangraena*, iii. 98–9; *Suffolk Deeds* I, 13 and II, 68; *NEHGR* 1: 132; Roger Thompson, *From deference to defiance: Charlestown, Massachusetts, 1629–1662* (Boston, MA: New England Historic Genealogical Society, 2012), 16, 23, 24, 27, 50, 59, 60, 145, 150, 421, 462n.

DELL, George

George Dell, a shipmaster, settled at Salem in 1639 but moved to the larger trading centre of Boston by 1645. He was active in commerce with the West Indies. Dell was in England on 3 November 1653, when he made a will on the eve of a voyage: he was planning to sail first to Ireland, then to Virginia and finally to New England. In May 1654, in New England, he acknowledged that he had sold to Samuel Symonds two of the Irish youths he had brought over at the order of 'the State of England', for £26. On 19 February 1654/5, Dell bought a shop and land from John Milam*, who had gone to Waterford in Ireland. The inventory of Dell's estate, 6 September 1655, amounted to £1506 14s 7d.

> Darrett Rutman, *Winthrop's Boston: portrait of a puritan town, 1630–1649* (New York: Norton, 1965), 191; *WJ*, 693–4; *NEHGR* 5: 442–3, 8: 77; *Suffolk Deeds* I, 285.

DUMMER, Richard (*c.*1598–1679)

Richard Dummer, a merchant and miller, son of John Dummer of Swaythling near Bishopstoke, Hampshire, emigrated in 1632. Initially, he settled at Roxbury, where he became a church member and built a watermill. He was admitted a freeman on 6 November 1632. In 1635 Dummer moved to Newbury, where the town granted him a farm of 500 acres and liberty to build a mill. He served as a magistrate but was disarmed in 1637 for supporting the antinomian Anne Hutchinson. John Eliot noted that it was Dummer's wife, Mary, who led him astray and died soon after. Dummer was at Portsmouth, Rhode Island, in August 1638. By 1640 he was back in Newbury. He had crossed swords with John Winthrop over antinomianism. Winthrop noted how Dummer sent £100 in 1640 to support his rival as governor, Thomas Dudley.

Dummer went back to England on at least two occasions. He returned home in 1637 and came back to Massachusetts the following year, bringing over his brother Stephen Dummer* and his family. Just before they set sail for New England in 1638, the provisions he and Stephen were laying up for the voyage – beef, bacon, cheese, beer, meal, malt – were impounded by a local constable, after the High Sheriff of Southampton ordered a search for foodstuffs that were to be taken to New England. Dummer was in England again, 1650–1, when he proved the will of Thomas Nelson*: Nelson's widow, Joan*, was Dummer's niece. Dummer administered Nelson's estate in New England. Joan Nelson had returned to England, and stayed there.

Apart from these brief visits, Dummer stayed in Newbury. He served on several occasions as a deputy to the Massachusetts General Court, and held office in town government. He died there, 1679.

D.G. Allen, *In English ways* (Chapel Hill, NC: University of North Carolina Press, 1981), 96, 101, 102, 180, 182; *WJ*, 69, 77n., 101, 144n., 201n., 204n., 215, 326; Bernard Bailyn, *The New England merchants in the seventeenth century* (Cambridge, MA: Harvard University Press, 1955), 53; *GMB* 588–95.

DYER, Mary (d. 1660) and William

Mary Dyer initially settled in Boston, with her husband William. On 13 December 1635, 'Willyam Dyer milliner and Marie his wife' were admitted to the church. William became a freeman of Massachusetts on 3 March 1635/6. During the Antinomian Controversy, both Mary and William had strong sympathies with Anne Hutchinson. When Mary gave birth to a deformed stillborn baby in October 1637, Hutchinson was among the midwives. In a step that fits into a wider tradition of providential narratives, John Winthrop believed the 'monstrous birth' to be a sign of divine judgment against antinomian errors. The Massachusetts authorities disenfranchised William Dyer for his beliefs in November 1637. William and Mary Dyer left Boston in 1638 for Rhode Island, and became pioneers of settlement at Portsmouth, then at Newport.

Mary Dyer went to England in 1651, and William followed soon afterwards. William returned to Rhode Island in 1653. Mary came back in 1657. In England, Mary had become a Quaker. In 1659 she felt called to go from Rhode Island into the Bay Colony. In Boston, she was condemned to death for her Quaker beliefs on 18 October 1659, but reprieved after pleas by her son. She returned to Rhode Island but insisted on travelling to Massachusetts again. She was condemned on 31 May 1660 and hanged the next day.

GM 2: 379–85; David D. Hall, ed., *The Antinomian Controversy, 1636–1638* (Durham, NC: Duke University Press, 1990), 200, 214, 262, 280–1, 393, 394; *WJ*, 241n., 253–5; Carla Gardina Pestana, *Quakers and baptists in colonial Massachusetts* (Cambridge: Cambridge University Press, 1991), 32–4, 37. On monstrous births: Alexandra Walsham, *Providence in early modern England* (Oxford: Oxford University Press, 1999), 194–203, 218–19, 221–2.

ANB, ODNB.

ELMES, Rodolphus (c.1620–1711/2)

Rodolphus Elmes of Southwark emigrated in 1635, as a servant, aged fifteen. He settled at Scitutate, in Plymouth Colony. In 1644, he married Catherine Whitcomb. On 25 August 1653, his mother – Sarah Elmes, a widow of St Saviour's, Southwark – left him a bequest: 'I doe give unto my loving sonne Rodolphus Elmes (now in parts beyond the seas) the sum of £10 if hee shalbe living at the time of my decease.' Sarah Elmes's will was proved on 20 April

1654. Elmes set off for England in the autumn of 1656, and it seems likely part of the purpose was to claim his legacy. He had to borrow money to pay for the journey. On 2 October 1656, he promised to repay John Floyd of Boston £6 'for my passage and moneys lent', in London, no later than 30 April 1657. Elmes returned to Scituate in 1657 and died there on 19 March 1711/2.

C.E. Banks, *Planters of the Commonwealth* (Boston, MA: Houghton Mifflin, 1930), 144; *Suffolk Deeds* II, 294; NA, PROB 11/234/487, will of Sarah Elmes, widow of Saint Saviour in Southwark, Surrey, 20 April 1654; *GM* 2: 424–6, 7: 329.

FEAKE, Robert

Robert Feake of St Nicholas Acons, London, emigrated in 1630. He was a goldsmith in old England and a merchant in New. Feake settled at Watertown. He was one of its wealthiest settlers. The local landmark 'Mount Feake' took its name from him. He became a freeman of Massachusetts on 18 May 1631, and later that year married Elizabeth (Fones) Winthrop, widow of Henry, son of Governor John Winthrop. Feake decided to go to Connecticut, a decision perhaps reinforced by sympathies with the defeated antinomians. He joined in the purchase of Greenwich, 1640, with Daniel Patrick. Elizabeth Feake may have become involved with Patrick, who was murdered in 1644. c.1647 Thomas Lyon (son-in-law to Elizabeth by her first marriage) lived with them, 'My Father being distracted I might bee a helpe to her': Feake was showing signs of mental illness. Elizabeth was by then seeking a divorce, which she obtained from the Dutch authorities, to marry William Hallett. Feake made over half his assets to his wife and Hallett.

Feake left for England abruptly from Boston, soon after 6 October 1647, when he ordered that his estate, some of which was 'mixed' with that of Hallett, should not be touched 'till he saw how God would deale with him in England'. The purpose of his visit is unclear. He left without making any provision for his family, except for asking Lyon and a friend to prevent Elizabeth and Hallett from making away with his estate and taking his children. (However, according to John Winthrop Jr*, Feake had agreed Hallett should manage his estate. Legal difficulties ensued as the Dutch authorities and those of New Haven could not agree on the rights of Elizabeth and Hallett; John Winthrop Jr intervened on their behalf.) On 4 March 1649/50, Feake was pardoned by the House of Commons for an unstated crime, possibly for taking an oath of allegiance to the Dutch, by then regarded by the English as a hostile power.

Feake was back in Watertown by September 1650. He lived as a pauper, kept by the town until his death in 1663.

C.E. Banks, *Planters of the Commonwealth* (Boston, MA: Houghton Mifflin, 1930), 72; *NEHGR* 3: 91; *WP* III, 287; I.M. Calder, *The New Haven Colony* (New Haven, CT: Yale University Press, 1934), 62; *WP* V, 179, 214–16, 238, 298–300, 323–4; 4 *MHSC* 6: 521–2n., Middlesex Probate Recs., Admin. 7437; *GMB* 656–60; Roger Thompson, *Divided we stand: Watertown, Massachusetts, 1630–80* (Amherst, MA: University of Massachusetts Press, 1994), 187–9, see also 7, 42–3, 57, 68, 108, 114.

GARDNER, Peter (c. 1617–1698)

Peter Gardner, a carpenter, emigrated in 1635 on the *Elizabeth*, aged eighteen. Gardner settled at Roxbury, Massachusetts. He married Rebecca Crooke in May 1646. On 12 December 1646 he and Rebecca appointed an attorney to collect a legacy from her father in Hammersmith. Rebecca joined the Roxbury church, but Peter did not. By the late 1640s he was active as a merchant, sending tobacco from Rhode Island to London. Gardner visited London at least twice. In October 1648, Nicholas Rice of Boston made Gardner his attorney to collect bequests in England, in advance of Gardner setting sail. Back in London, Gardner met Robert Smith*, who was keeping the Golden Lion Tavern in Fetter Lane. Gardner gave Smith news of his sister Mary. In 1650, Gardner was in London again, and visited Smith with messages and tokens. Smith suggested his sister Mary should send him over a son for him to adopt as his heir. Gardner died at Roxbury on 5 November 1698.

> GM 3: 12–16; Aspinwall, 68, 160–1, 411, 412; David Cressy, *Coming over: migration and communication between England and New England in the seventeenth century* (Cambridge: Cambridge University Press, 1987), 267–8, citing Mass. Archives, 15A: 11–12.

GIFFORD, John

John Gifford originally came to New England in the 1630s as 'Major [Edward] Gibbons man'. Little is known about his activities at this time. He was probably an apprentice clerk. Gifford went back to England in the early 1640s and worked for his father, who ran the ironworks in the Forest of Dean, Gloucestershire. In 1650, parliament ordered the destruction of the furnaces and forges there, because of their heavy charcoal consumption. This put Gifford out of a job. He was head-hunted by the undertakers of the ironworks at Saugus, near Lynn, and came over to New England again. In the 1650s, Gifford visited England. He threw his considerable energies into raising money and into fighting off litigation about mismanagement. He raised technical expertise at the ironworks but also took the company to financial collapse.

> E.D. Hartley, *Ironworks on the Saugus* (Norman, OK: University of Oklahoma Press, 1957), 139–40, and *passim*; Bernard Bailyn, *The New England merchants in the seventeenth century* (Cambridge, MA: Harvard University Press, 1955), 68–70.

GORTON, Samuel (1593–1677)

Samuel Gorton was born in Gorton, Lancashire, and became a clothier in London. He and his wife Mary emigrated in 1636. They arrived in Boston at a time when the heat of the Antinomian Controversy was fiercest but – although it seems certain Samuel Gorton had antinomian sympathies – the Gortons did not take engage in the dispute. They settled outside the boundaries of Massachusetts, in Plymouth Colony. However, within a short time

Gorton clashed with the authorities there, and in 1638 he was banished for his lay preaching and radical beliefs. He went to Rhode Island, where he clashed first with William Coddington*, then with Roger Williams*. In 1642 Gorton and his followers founded a new settlement at Shawomet (Warwick), Rhode Island. Here, too, controversy followed. When American Indian leaders complained to Massachusetts that Gorton had cheated them, the Bay Colony sent a force to capture the Shawomet settlers and to put them on trial for heresy. Gorton and his followers were sentenced to hard labour, but pressure from England forced the Massachusetts authorities to commute the penalty. Gorton was allowed to leave the colony. He came up with an ingenious strategy to out-manoeuvre the powers-that-be in Boston: he invited Narragansett Indians to submit directly to the authority of the English king, and put themselves (and Gorton) under the king's protection.

In 1644 Gorton sailed for London, to put his case to the earl of Warwick's commission, appointed by parliament to administer the colonies. He set off from New Netherland, avoiding the hostile territory of Boston, in company with his supporters John Greene and Randall Holden. Massachusetts despatched Edward Winslow* in 1646, as an agent to counter Gorton. Back in London, Gorton won what he wanted: he secured a right to Shawomet. On his return to New England in 1648, Gorton re-named the settlement Warwick, in honour of the earl. Gorton presided over Warwick, with his own unique brand of mystical spiritual teaching, until his death in 1677.

Publications See *ODNB*.

Philip F. Gura, *A glimpse of Sion's glory: puritan radicalism in New England, 1620–1660* (Middletown, CT: Wesleyan University Press, 1984), 276–303; Graeme J. Milne, 'New England agents and the English Atlantic, 1641–1666' (PhD dissertation, University of Edinburgh, 1993), 302–4 and *passim*.

ANB, ODNB.

HALL, Samuel (1610–1679/80)

Samuel Hall, a merchant, arrived in New England in 1633, but at first stayed only a year. In November 1633 he set off to explore the Connecticut River. John Winthrop noted the return of Hall and his companions in January 1633/4, 'havinge lost themselues and endured muche miserye'. In October 1634 Hall was fined five shillings for 'drunkenness by him committed ashipboard'. Hall returned to England soon after this, but soon travelled from England to New England again. He is likely to be the Samuel Hall who set sail for New England in May 1635, on the *Elizabeth & Ann*. Hall settled at Ipswich, Massachusetts, where he had difficulty persuading the town to allocate him land. In December 1635 Nathaniel Ward* wrote to John Winthrop explaining that Hall had caused offence by 'the company he brought to towne and his manner of cominge before the town'; there had been private drinking in Hall's house. Ward assured Winthrop he was ready to encourage Hall, but acknowledged that the town had 'of late but somewhat too late . . . bene carefull on whome they bestowe lotts, being awakened therto by the confluence of many ill and doubtfull persons'. Hall joined the Artillery Company in 1638. In 1640 he moved to Salisbury, where in the 1650s he served on juries and as a deputy for the town at the Massachusetts General Court.

Hall made at least two visits to England, 1640–60, and returned to England for good in or just after 1662. In December 1643 he was away in England when the Essex Quarterly Court fined him 25 shillings for beating a young girl. The Massachusetts General Court records show he was in England again in May 1653. Later, he resettled in England. He made his will, as a 'gentleman' of Langford, near Maldon in Essex, on 13 November 1679 (proved 25 January 1679/80). Among his bequests were ten shillings apiece to twenty 'silenced ministers', and £100 to New England for settlers affected by the Boston fire of 1676 and by the Indian Wars. His wife Sarah died at Langford soon afterwards. Her bequests included ten shillings apiece to twenty nonconformist ministers or their widows in Essex, and the same again in the City of London. She left the residue of her estate to buy cloth for the poor of Newbury, Hampton and Amesbury in New England.

> D.G. Allen, *In English ways* (Chapel Hill, NC: University of North Carolina Press, 1981), 277; *GD*; *WJ*, 108–9; *WP* III, 215–16; *Artillery Company*, 62; Waters, 780–2; *GMB* 844–8; *GM* 2: 367, 3: 195.

HAWKINS, Thomas (d. 1648)

Thomas Hawkins, a shipwright of Stepney in Middlesex, was granted land at Charlestown in 1636, but by 1643 had moved to Boston. He was in England with Nehemiah Bourne* in 1639. Hawkins put his shipbuilding skills to use in New England, but also captained ships in trade with Maine, the West Indies, England and the Mediterranean. In 1643, with Edward Gibbons of Boston, he backed Charles La Tour against Charles d'Aulnay, to break d'Aulnay's blockade of the St John River. Hawkins built the ship *Sea Fort*, and survived its shipwreck off the Spanish coast on a journey to England in 1644. In April 1645 his ship was wrecked again on the same spot. On an Atlantic crossing to England in 1648, Winthrop reported, 'God was pleased to change his voyage and send him to heaven.'

> *WJ*, 473, 474, 598–600, 641–2, 762, 765; 4 *MHSC* 7: 297n.; *WP* IV, 153–5; *WP* V, 70, 78, 114, 119, 237, 277, 280; Aspinwall, 86; Roger Thompson, *From deference to defiance: Charlestown, Massachusetts, 1629–1662* (Boston, MA: New England Historic Genealogical Society, 2012), 17, 27, 53, 149, 153, 164–5, 168, 258n.; W.H.M. Wilcox, 'Thomas Hawkins', *NEHGR* 151: 193–216.

HAYDEN, James

James Hayden, a mariner, joined the Charlestown church on 13 September 1635. On 11 February 1636/7 he was granted a houseplot, and on 9 March became a freeman. He was a Charlestown ferryman by 1646. He also plied the Atlantic as a seaman. In 1652, Hayden was resident at St Dunstan in the East, London. By 1653, he was back in Charlestown acting as a ferryman across the Charles River again, and accused of abusing and endangering his passengers. He died at Barbados in 1665.

GM 3: 277–80; Roger Thompson, *From deference to defiance: Charlestown, Massachusetts, 1629–1662* (Boston, MA: New England Historic Genealogical Society, 2012), 18n., 50, 65, 150, 155n., 191, 211n.

HAYNES, John

John Haynes emigrated in 1633 and settled at Cambridge, moving to Hartford in 1637. He was governor of Massachusetts Bay in 1635 and governor or deputy-governor of Connecticut almost continually in the 1640s and 1650s. He was father to Hezekiah Haynes*, John Haynes* and Roger Haynes*.

On 27 October 1646, Haynes made a will: 'called to the undertaking of a voyage into my native country of England and duly weighing according to my measure the difficultes and hardships I am liable and exposed to therein, especially in these declining days of mine when my sun cannot be far from setting'. The precise reasons that took Haynes to England are unclear. He soon returned to New England. After he died in 1654, his will of 1646 was presented and proved.

GMB 893–7. ANB, ODNB.

HIBBINS, William (d. 1654)

William Hibbins, a merchant from Boston, Lincolnshire, emigrated in 1638 and settled at Boston. He became a church member on 28 September 1639 and a freeman of Massachusetts on 13 May 1640. He served as a representative in 1640 and 1641. Hibbins was chosen to go to England as an agent with Hugh Peter* and Thomas Weld*. On 25 July 1641, the Boston church granted him 'letters of Commendation where he should find liberty to enjoy the Ordinances of Christ in England'. (For the work of Hibbins, Peter and Weld as agents, see Hugh Peter.) Unlike Weld and Peter, Hibbins soon returned to New England. In 1642, he 'made a public declaration to the church in Boston, of all the good providences of the Lord towards him in his voyage to and fro'. He was elected an assistant in May 1643 and thereafter until his death in 1654. His wife Ann (who had been excommunicated by the Boston church in 1640) was executed for witchcraft in 1656.

R.P. Stearns, 'The Weld-Peter mission to England', *Colonial Society of Massachusetts, Publications*, 32 (1937), 185–246; *Boston CR*, 26, 34; *NEHGR* 3: 187; *WP* IV, 340–1; *WJ*, 312, 321, 345–6, 353–4, 402, 403, 431; Graeme J. Milne, 'New England agents and the English Atlantic, 1641–1666' (PhD dissertation, University of Edinburgh, 1993), 303 and *passim*.

HOBART, Joshua (d. 1716/7)

Joshua Hobart, the son of Peter Hobart, minister at Hingham, Massachusetts, graduated BA alongside his brother Jeremiah at Harvard in 1650. Both brothers became freemen of Hingham, Massachusetts, on 18 May 1653. In 1655 Joshua Hobart sailed for Barbados, where he married Margaret, the daughter of William Vassall*, on 16 April 1656. Hobart sailed on to London, where he arrived on 5 July. A colonist called 'Hobart' was minister at New Ross, Ireland, c.1656. Hobart was back in New England by 18 July 1657, perhaps only briefly, when as 'Joshua Hubbard', on behalf of his late wife Margaret, he signed a deed of sale for Vassall's estate at Scituate. He seems to have gone away from New England again – his whereabouts are unknown – but returned to Massachusetts in 1669. In 1672 a congregational church at Hingham, Norfolk (where Robert Peck* had been minister), sent a messenger to Boston to find 'an honest and godly minister'. Joshua Hobart's father, Peter, had grown up at Hingham. Joshua Hobart responded to the invitation from Norfolk and in 1674 was ordained as minister to the congregational church. He went back to New England by 1694 and died at Southold, Long Island, in February 1716/7.

BPL, MS. Am. 1506 v.1 no. 6 [printed 4 *MHSC* 8: 4]; St J.D. Seymour, *The puritans in Ireland, 1647–1661* (Oxford: Clarendon Press, 1921), 214.

CC, Sibley.

HOLMES, William

'Lieutenant William Holmes', who settled at Plymouth in 1632, was commissioned to train the settlers of Plymouth and Duxbury in the use of arms. He took part in an expedition to establish a trading post on the Connecticut River in 1633, and led a company against the Pequot Indians in 1637. Holmes was in New England until July 1641, but then makes no appearance in the surviving records for some years: he may have been back in England, fighting in the civil wars. 'Major William Holmes' was in Boston, Massachusetts, by 1649: he made a will in which he bequeathed to his four nieces, should they choose to pursue a claim, the arrears of pay due to him 'for being a soldier and commander in the army and service of the king and parliament'.

GMB 979–81.

HUCKENS, Thomas

Thomas Huckens of Boston joined the Artillery Company in 1637. He was said to have served in the English civil wars under William Rainborowe*.

Artillery Company, 28.

HUDSON, William Jr

William Hudson, son of William Hudson*, became a church member at Boston on 13 June 1640 and a freeman of Massachusetts on 12 October. He was an 'innholder', and a trader with interests in London and Barbados.

Hudson left New England late in 1643, with Nehemiah Bourne*, John Leverett*, Francis Lisle* and Israel Stoughton* to join the parliamentary army. He was an ensign in Leverett's foot company, in Colonel Thomas Rainborowe's regiment. Hudson returned to New England, c. May 1645. His wife Ann was suspected of adultery while he was away. Hudson had committed the care of his family and business to Henry Dawson, his servant and a fellow church member. Winthrop described Dawson as:

> a yonge man of good esteeme for pietye & sincerity [(]but his wife was in England) who in tyme grewe ouer familiar with his masters wife (a yonge woman no member of the Churche) so as she would be with him ofte in his chamber, &c & one night 2: of the servants . . . perceived him to goe vp into their dames chamber . . .

Ann Hudson admitted only immodest behaviour. She and Dawson wore halters at the place of execution and were publicly whipped; the church excommunicated Dawson, 3 August 1645, for 'wanton dallyances'. Later, Ann Hudson joined the Boston church. William Hudson continued to trade from Boston with London and Barbados.

Boston CR, 30, 44–5, 56; *NEHGR* 3: 188; *WJ*, 605, 609–10, 763; Aspinwall *passim*; *GMB* 1036.

INCE, Jonathan (d. 1657)

Jonathan Ince is likely to be the son of Jonathan Ince, who lived at Hartford, and later at Boston. Ince graduated BA from Harvard in 1650, and MA in 1653. For nineteen days in the summer of 1652, at a daily stipend of ten shillings, he worked as artist to an expedition to find the source of the Merrimack River. His last bill at Harvard was in December 1653. He moved to New Haven, and on 12 December 1654 married Mary Miles.

Ince set sail for England, 6 November 1657, on a ship captained by James Garrett. The ship went down, and Ince lost his life. Also lost were John Davis*, Thomas Mayhew* and Nathaniel Pelham*. John Eliot had written a letter for Ince to carry to England, to present to the Corporation for the Propagation of the Gospel in New England. Eliot recommended Ince to the Corporation as a godly scholar, skilled in learning and pronouncing 'the Indian language'. He hoped Ince would assist him in teaching the Indians when he returned to New England.

Harvard Recs. III, 60n; 1 *MHSC* 1: 202; Joseph B. Felt, *The ecclesiastical history of New England*, 2 vols (Boston, MA: Congregational Library Association, 1862), II, 163.

CC, Sibley.

JAY, Walter

Walter Jay of Boston was in Tavistock, Devon, in April 1660. Thomas Larkham* recorded in his diary: 'Given to Walter Jay, of New England, taken by the Ostenders, 1s (besides 5s of the Deacons) and a pair of breeches.' The deacons acted on behalf of the congregational church Larkham had formed in the parish. The parishioners gave money too. Tavistock's vestry minutes, under 'Briefes colected in our parish', 29 April 1660, noted: 'Collected for a Company goinge to new England taken by the Ostenders the sume of 02-06-06.' Jay may have been the mariner Walter Joy, who gave a deposition in Boston before William Hibbins in November 1653.

The diary of Thomas Larkham, 1647–1669, ed. Susan Hardman Moore, Church of England Record Society, 17 (Woodbridge: Boydell and Brewer, 2011), 221; DRO, Tavistock Vestry Minutes, 1660–1740, 428A/PV1, fol. 6; *WP* VI, 344–5.

JOSSELIN, Abraham (c.1615–1670)

Abraham Josselin [Joslin, Joceling] was the son of Thomas Joslin of Barham, Suffolk, and a cousin of Ralph Josselin (*ODNB*), minister of Earls Colne, Essex. Thomas Joslin sailed for New England in 1635 on the *Increase*, with his wife Rebecca and five children. Joslin settled first at Hingham, but subscribed to the town covenant at the new settlement of Lancaster in 1654. Abraham, his eldest son, was not listed as a passenger in 1635, but was mentioned in Thomas Joslin's will, dated 9 May 1660.

Abraham 'Joceling' married Beatrice 'Hamson' (Hampson) in London on 19 November 1642. It is not clear whether Abraham had already been in New England but at some point he settled there: perhaps before 1645; or by 1660, when he had a child baptised in Boston (4 July). He may have been a mariner. Early in March 1644/5, Ralph Josselin recorded a visit from him:

> My cousin Abraham Josselin came to us from New England about by the Canaryes, after a sad long jorney & one tedious fight with a kings pyratt: heard by him of ye welfare of ye plantacon for which god be praised.

On 27 April 1645, Ralph Josselin noted that Abraham was about to return across the Atlantic: 'My Cousin Abraham with mee he is going into New England, the Lord blesse him and prosper him.' Josselin noted another brief visit in February 1657/8: 'my Cosin Ab. Josselin with mee from New-England'. Abraham Josselin went back to New England in March 1658 (with another relative, Grace Josselin, who seems to have come back from New England in 1656). Ralph Josselin sent 'divers things testimonies of my love' to his New England cousins – ten shillings, a book, gloves, a handwritten account of recent national and international news.

Abraham Josselin, and his wife and children, were killed in the Indian massacre at Lancaster, Massachusetts, in 1676.

GM 4: 117–21; *The diary of Ralph Josselin 1616–1683*, ed. Alan Macfarlane (Oxford: Oxford University Press, 1976), 35, 39, 382, 419, 421; Waters, 765; D.G. Allen, *In English ways* (Chapel Hill, NC: University of North Carolina Press, 1981), 254; C.E. Banks, *A history of York, Maine* (Boston, MA: Calkins Press, 1931), 70; *Vital records of Lancaster, Massachusetts, 1643–1850* (online database, *AmericanAncestors.org*. New England Historic Genealogical Society, 2008), 16, 19.

KEAYNE, Sarah

Sarah Keayne was the wife of Benjamin Keayne* and daughter-in-law of the Boston merchant Robert Keayne. She followed Benjamin back to England and acquired a reputation as a radical: 'My she Cosin Keane is growne a great preacher', Stephen Winthrop* reported in March 1645/6. Sarah Keayne returned to New England by November 1646, when the Boston church admonished her for 'Irregular prophesying in mixt Assemblies and for Refusing ordinarilie to heare in the Churches of Christ'. In October 1647 she was excommunicated for ignoring the earlier admonishment, and for 'falling into odious, lewd, and scandalous uncleane behaviour'. By this time Keayne had ended his marriage: the church records described Sarah as 'sometimes the wife of Mr Benjamin Keayne but who Devorsed from him'.

WP V, 70, 143–4, 189n., 351; *Boston CR*, 25, 29, 37, 46, 49.

KENT, Joshua and Mary

Joshua and Mary Kent settled at Dedham, Massachusetts. Joshua was listed as a townsman in 1643, and became a church member on 9 November 1644. The Dedham church records noted that in January 1644/5, Joshua Kent 'went for England with our testimonial but to returne againe . . . he returned 1645'. Although Kent came back to New England, he left again in December 1647. This time the church was less pleased: 'with his wife he returned to England 10m 1647 his reasons not well satisfying his freinds or church here'. After the outbreak of the Second Civil War, Joshua and Mary Kent came back to Dedham in October 1648: 'upon the troubles arising againe in England and wares ther 1648 he returned with his wife againe about the 8m that yeare'. Between these two visits to England, on 6 May 1646, Joshua Kent was admitted a freeman of Massachusetts. Mary Kent joined the church at Dedham on 2 April 1654.

Dedham CR, 28, 33, 37; *NEHGR* 3: 191.

KERMAN, Captain (d. 1644)

John Winthrop recorded how 'Kerman', a shipmaster, left New Haven in December 1642 with a cargo of clapboards to deliver to the Canaries, 'being earnestly commended to the Lord's protection by the church there'. Near the destination, Turkish pirates boarded the boat; fierce hand-to-hand fighting ensued, but the sailors beat off the attackers with only one English life lost. Later, Winthrop recorded how 'Captain Kerman', travelling in the *Sea Fort*, drowned in December 1644 off Spain (also aboard were Giles Firmin*, Thomas Hawkins* and Abraham Pratt*).

> *WJ*, 463–4, 598–9, 759, 762. (Not John Carman of Roxbury, *GMB* 311–13, nor John Kirman of Lynn and Sandwich, *GMB* 1133–5.)

LANE, Job

Job Lane, a carpenter of Dorchester, Massachusetts, was in England in June 1647 when his uncle, Thomas Howell of Marshfield in Massachusetts, named him as an executor. Lane was later of Malden and Billerica, Massachusetts.

> *NEHGR* 3: 194, 4: 282–3, 5:179; see also 11: 102–12, 231–41, 'Lane Family Papers'.

LEADER, Richard

Richard Leader was employed in 1645, by the 'Adventurers in the Iron Works', to succeed John Winthrop Jr* as manager at the Saugus ironworks. Later, a dispute developed, as the ironworks ran into debt and suspicions were aroused about Leader's commercial activities. In 1650 he left the employment of the Adventurers and went to England to raise support for a sawmill in Maine. On his return to Massachusetts he was prosecuted for slandering the colonial authorities, and the church and town of Lynn. Leader admitted his offence, and was fined heavily: £200, and £50 costs. Part of the case against him revolved around hostile comments to fellow-passengers on the Atlantic voyage: the General Court, however, voted to take the view that its jurisdiction did not reach to words 'spoken neere about the midway betweene this and England'. Leader went north and settled in Maine. He arranged with David Selleck of Boston to transport two hundred men and women from Ireland to Virginia and New England, to work as indentured servants. He went to England again to raise capital for salt-making and sugar refining in Barbados. During this visit, in 1653, John Reeve and Lodowick Muggleton claimed to have converted him to Muggletonianism. Leader's Caribbean ventures failed and he returned to Maine in 1661.

> *Mass. Recs.* 3: 227, 257; E.D. Hartley, *Ironworks on the Saugus* (Norman, OK: University of Oklahoma Press, 1957), 117–38.

MAYHEW, Thomas (*c.* 1620–1657)

Thomas Mayhew, son of the minister Thomas Mayhew (*ANB*), emigrated with him from Tisbury, Wiltshire, in 1632. Thomas Mayhew senior settled at Watertown in 1634, and moved to Nantucket in 1647. Mayhew moved to work with his father at Nantucket and became the first minister at Martha's Vineyard.

Mayhew sailed for England in November 1657, on the same ship as John Davis*, Jonathan Ince* and Nathaniel Pelham*. The ship went down and all lives were lost. It is likely that Mayhew was returning on business related to his Indian ministry, and intended to come back to New England.

GMB 1245.

MORSE, John (1607/8–1657)

John Morse was baptised at Redgrave, Suffolk, on 28 February 1607/8, the son of Samuel and Elizabeth Morse. He was a tailor. His father Samuel Morse, a husbandman, had emigrated in 1635 on the *Increase* with his wife and two younger children. John Morse settled in Dedham in 1637 and soon married 'Annis'. He became a church member on 1 March 1640/1, and a freeman of Massachusetts on 13 May 1640. He moved to Boston in 1654. On 29 November 1655, he sold land in Dedham that had come to him from his father, Samuel Morse.

John Morse was in England for the early months of 1656, perhaps on personal business or for trade. On 18 December 1655, he made a will, 'undertakeing a voyage for England, being not without much hazard . . . I doe Carry a Considerable part of my Estate to venture at sea, with my selfe . . . I thinke it my dutie to take care of my wife and Children'. He is likely to be John Morse who returned to New England on the *Speedwell* in May 1656.

Dedham CR, 22; *NEHGR* 1: 132–3; 10: 221; 83: 290; *GM* 5: 172, 173. (Not to be confused with John and Mary Morse* of Boston, who returned to England in 1654.)

MUNNINGS, Mahalaleel (*c.*1632–1659/60)

Mahalaleel Munnings, the son of Edmund Munnings* and brother of Hopestill*, Return and Takeheed*, emigrated with his family at the age of three (listed as 'Michelaliell Monings') and settled at Dorchester in 1635. In New England, he grew up to be a merchant.

Mahalaleel Munnings travelled to England in the early 1650s, perhaps when his parents returned to Essex for good. By 1655, in New England, he had married Hannah Wiswall: their son Mahalaleel, 'born at his grand ffather wiswall house', was baptised at Dorchester on 9 September 1655. Munnings soon set off for England again, but returned to Massachusetts in the summer of 1656: he is listed as a passenger on *Speedwell*, which left Gravesend in May. He was across the Atlantic again in September 1657, when the Dorchester church witnessed his daughter Hannah's baptism, 'her ffather then not come ffrom England'.

Munnings was dismissed to the new church at Boston on 9 October 1659. He drowned in the Boston mill creek, 27 February 1659/60. His wife's grandparents, Thomas and Ann Smith, wrote from London to warn John Wiswall not to be executor for his son-in-law: 'he oweth here yet five or six hundred pounds besides . . . what hee oweth in New England and Barbados I know not'. Mahalaleel Munnings had charged a bill on John Wiswall's brother Adam in London, to pay Henry Ashurst £160 or £170, which Adam Wiswall had refused to honour.

Dorchester CR, 32, 167, 168; *NEHGR* 1: 132; 7: 273–4; 10: 176–7; Alison Games, *Migration and the origins of the English Atlantic world* (Cambridge, MA: Harvard University Press, 1999), 142–3, 203–4, 278n.44 (as 'Michelalial' Munnings). Mahalaleel is a biblical name: Genesis 5:12.

NEWGATE, John (d. 1665)

John Newgate of Southwark, a hatter, felter and haberdasher, was the father of Nathaniel Newgate*. His family came from Horningsheath, Suffolk, near Bury St Edmunds. A John Newgate of Horningsheath left a bequest in 1642 to 'my brother, John Newgate, now living in the parts beyond the seas called New England'.

Newgate emigrated in 1633 with his third wife Ann and several children. They settled at Boston, where Ann must have become a church member soon after, because their daughter Hannah, born at Boston on 1 August 1633, was baptised a few days later. John became a church member on 3 August 1634 – 'John Newgate, hatter' – and a freeman of Massachusetts on 4 March 1634/5.

John Newgate visited England once, perhaps twice, before his death in Boston in 1665. In 1638, he went back to sell land at Horningsheath. On 23 October 1638 he made a will, in anticipation of the voyage. He had returned to New England by 25 July 1639, when Thomas Lechford* recorded Newgate's successful sale of lands in Suffolk. Newgate perhaps went to England again at the end of 1646: he was appointed as an attorney, 12 December, to collect a bequest from Blackfriars, London. On 28 December 1649, John Newgate appointed his son Nathaniel as his attorney, to take possession of a house and lands in Bury St Edmunds, Suffolk.

GMB 1327–32; Darrett Rutman, *Winthrop's Boston: portrait of a puritan town, 1630–1649* (New York: Norton, 1965), 73; Lechford *NB*, 16–19, 131; Aspinwall, 68, 269.

NEWGATE, Nathaniel

Nathaniel Newgate, the son of John Newgate*, came over at the same time as his father. In 1648 Nathaniel was fined £10 for selling guns to Indians. The fine was later reduced to £2, in consideration of 'his youth, & the respect which may be given to his well deserving parents'. On 28 December 1649 Nathaniel was appointed as attorney by his father to take possession of a house and lands in Bury St Edmunds, Suffolk. Newgate probably left for England soon after this.

Newgate, a merchant, may have travelled more than once to England. He was in London, and about to return to Boston, in June 1653: John Hart of London, a merchant late of 'Bylboe', appointed him as his agent to recover debts from Captain Francis Norton, John Allen and Nicholas Davison* of Charlestown. Newgate died in London in September 1668. He made his will there as Nathaniel Newdigate alias Newgate.

GM 4: 72, 6: 354; Aspinwall, 269; *Suffolk Deeds* I, 313, II, 124–7; Waters, 1273–4.

PARDON, William

William Pardon settled at Weymouth, Massachusetts, as a labourer. Letters of attorney granted to him in December 1645 suggest he left for England that month, heading for the West Country. On 5 December, Edward Poole of Weymouth gave Pardon power of attorney to receive bequests for his wife Sarah from Edmund Pinney and Elizabeth Standerwick of Broadway, Somerset. On 15 December, Christopher Collins of Braintree, husband of Jane Greepe, authorised Pardon to collect money due to his wife from Justinian Pearce of Plymouth, merchant: the commission was to be fulfilled in person; Pardon was not granted power of substitution.

Aspinwall, 12, 14.

PIERCE, William (d. 1641)

William Pierce [Peirce], a shipmaster from Ratcliffe, Middlesex, settled at Boston in 1632. He was admitted to the church before 14 October that year, and became a freeman of Massachusetts on 14 May 1634. He served as a selectman in 1634 and was appointed to a committee on the fishing trade in 1635. He was the author of the first pamphlet printed by Stephen Day at Cambridge, Massachusetts, an almanac for 1639.

Pierce traversed the Atlantic many times and kept a base in London: John Winthrop described his wife as 'a godly woman of the church in Boston, dwelling sometimes in London'. Winthrop often mentioned Pierce in his *Journal*, from the first arrival of the Winthrop fleet in 1630 until Pierce's death at the hands of Spanish troops on Providence Island, 13 July 1641.

Pierce may have been related to another Captain Pierce, recommended by John Winthrop Jr* in 1660 to an enquirer who (in the changed climate of the Restoration) was thinking of going to New England:

> there is one Capt. Peirse (he may be found on the Exchange), a master of a ship, who hath lived long in New England and hath relation to it still, though I think upon a marriage hath his habitation in London or neere; he useth every yeare to bring passengers. He is an honest man, and may be usefull to be knowne to such as intend hither.

Publication *An almanack for the year of our Lord 1639. Calculated for New England. By Mr William Pierce, mariner* (Cambridge, MA, 1639).

GMB 1472–8; Darrett Rutman, *Winthrop's Boston: portrait of a puritan town, 1630–1649* (New York: Norton, 1965), 75; *Boston CR*, 13; *WJ*, 32, 352, 356–7 and *passim*; Karen Ordahl Kupperman, *Providence Island, 1630–1641: the other puritan colony* (Cambridge: Cambridge University Press, 1993), 341; 5 *MHSC* 8: 68.

POWELL, Michael (d. 1672/3)

Michael Powell of Woolverstone, Suffolk, emigrated to New England in 1639 and settled at Dedham. He became a church member on 16 April 1641 and a freeman of Massachusetts on 2 June 1641. He was Dedham's schoolmaster. Powell set off in December 1646 to visit England, to judge from various letters of attorney granted to him by fellow colonists: on 5 October, Oliver Cocke of Salisbury appointed Powell to take possession of a house and land in Framlingham, Suffolk; on 10 December, Barbara Weld of Roxbury gave him power of attorney for her business in England, should Thomas Bell* fall sick; on 12 December, Peter and Rebecca Gardiner made Powell their attorney to receive a legacy due to Rebecca from her late father, Roger Crooke of Hammersmith. Powell soon returned to Massachusetts. He moved from Dedham to Boston in 1649.

Dedham CR, 25; *NEHGR* 3: 188; *WJ*, 708; Aspinwall, 50, 67–8.

SAFFIN, John

John Saffin sued Joseph Greene for defamation. Nicholas Morris of 'the County of Northumberland, Gent.' provided a document to support Saffin, dated December 1656. Morris testified that Saffin was never distempered with strong drink and only associated with the 'best sort' – 'I having knowne John Saffin of New England marchant for the space of allmost three yeares he having kept his store at my house.' Saffin won the case.

Middlesex Court Recs., 1656/20/1.

SCOTT, Robert (d. 1653/4)

Robert Scott came to Boston in 1633 and was admitted to the church on 15 December, 'late servant to our brother John Sampford'. He became a freeman of Massachusetts on 7 December 1636. Over the next decade he developed his career and social standing as a haberdasher and merchant. He collaborated with Robert Harding*, and acted as Harding's agent in New England.

Scott may have travelled to England on more than one occasion, but William Aspinwall's* records show something of his activity in the mid-1640s. Scott crossed the Atlantic to England late in December 1644, to judge from letters of attorney he was given at that time. On 16 December, John Rogers of Watertown, clothier, appointed Scott to collect bequests due from his father, Thomas Rogers of Moulsham near Chelmsford, Essex (with power to substitute another attorney). On 20 December, John Compton of Boston, clothier, gave Scott authority to claim and rent out land in England (with power to substitute another attorney). On 23 December, Abraham Page of Boston, tailor, commissioned Scott to collect all legacies, rents and other monies due to him in England (with no power of substitution). It is not clear how long Scott stayed in England. He was back in New England by 18 August 1646, when Aspinwall gave a certificate to attest the measure of '5 pieces of ffrench linen' – '353 English Ells' – received 'from Joshua Woolnow of London by Robert Scott of Boston'. Aspinwall's records contain many other references to Scott's trading activities. In 1649 Benjamin Negus wrote to John Winthrop Jr* on behalf of 'Mr Robart Scott And Partners' about a cargo of cloth Scott was shipping from Boston to Pequot (New London) and the produce Scott expected to receive by return.

GMB 1638–41; *Boston CR*, 17; *NEHGR* 3: 94; Aspinwall, 14, 15, 29 and *passim*; *WP* V, 331.

SLYE, Robert

Robert Slye, a Boston merchant, was in London in July 1651 when he witnessed a letter of attorney from two haberdashers to the colonist John Richards to reclaim a debt in New England. The letter was recorded in New England on 20 May 1652.

Suffolk Deeds I, 203–4.

SMITH, Benjamin

Benjamin Smith, 'late of Boston in New England yeoman' was in England on 24 February 1650/1, when he was given a power of attorney by Henry Willis of Bury St Edmunds, fellmonger, and Martha Hues, Mary Biggs and Ann Langhorne, widows of London. All, including Smith, were relatives of the late Nicholas Willis of Boston, and the letter of attorney concerned claims on his estate. Smith was his nephew.

Smith returned to New England later that year. On 20 November 1651, the letter of attorney from England was accepted by the Suffolk Court. On 11 December, Smith declared he had been given full satisfaction by the overseers of Nicholas Willis's estate, not only for what had been due to him and his family, but also for what had been due to Willis's relatives in England.

Suffolk Deeds I, 158–60.

USHER, Hezekiah (d. 1676)

Hezekiah Usher settled in Cambridge, Massachusetts, by 1639. By 1645 he had moved to Boston. He was the first bookseller and publisher in the English colonies and also an immensely successful Atlantic trader: at his death he left an estate valued at £14,000.

Usher visited England at least twice between 1640 and 1660. He sail for England late in 1649, soon after Josias Stanborough of Southampton, Long Island, gave Usher two letters of attorney, to deal with rents from property in Kent and Oxfordshire (with power to substitute one attorney). In February

1649/50, Henry Dunster wrote that he had not long before sent a letter to John Phillip* in England, 'by Brother Usher by way of Malago'. Usher went to England again in the winter of 1657/8, to procure type and paper for printing the *Great Indian Bible* (1660–3) on behalf of the New England Company. He probably travelled with John* and Elizabeth Harwood (Elizabeth was Usher's sister).

Shepard's confessions, 70, 182; *NEHGR* 3: 96, 23: 410; Aspinwall, 103–4; MHS, MS N-1143, 'Henry Dunster Notebook, 1628–54', fol. 117; Waters, 626n.

WADE, Jonathan (c.1612–1683)

Jonathan Wade probably emigrated from Denver, Norfolk, where he still had land in 1657. He arrived in New England on the *Lyon* in 1632, and settled at Charlestown. 'Jonathan Wade and Susanna his wife' were admitted to the church on 25 May 1633. Jonathan became a freeman of Massachusetts, 14 May 1634. His brother Thomas, a merchant, was in New England briefly in 1635. In 1636, Wade moved to Ipswich and became a successful merchant and tavern keeper. He made agreements for joint trade with other merchants in Ipswich. In later court proceedings, a witness testified that Wade had spoken to him sometime after the Indian war (1637) 'about his affairs in England, that is the trouble he had in obtaining good title to his land there, which he had done'.

Wade's landholdings in England, and his trading activities, took him back to England more than once. He was in London in the late 1650s: on 9 April 1656, he witnessed the sale of Thomas Venner's* house to John Lowle; on 17 June 1657, he made a will, witnessed by the merchants William Peake and Samuel Sedgwick*. His will mentioned land in Norfolk in the parish of Denver, near Downham Market. Wade was back in New England by 1658, but made another visit to England in 1669: he made a will when he was about to set sail. He mentioned rents from his English property and money owed to 'Sir William Peak'.

In 1682, in a petition to the Massachusetts General Court, Wade turned the clock back to 1629: that was when he became 'an adventurer and participant with the patentees and undertakers concerning this Colony of the Massachusetts'. He had put in 'into the common stock £50 and into the joint stock £10 or more for which they promised land here upon our arrival'. More than six decades on, Wade claimed his fair share of the land that had been denied him and demanded his money back with interest.

Wade died in 1683, leaving property in old and New England, and various invalid wills, sparking off legal disputes among his sons.

Charlestown CR, 191; *NEHGR* 3: 92; D.G. Allen, *In English ways* (Chapel Hill, NC: University of North Carolina Press, 1981), 133, 134, 136, 276; *Suffolk Deeds* II, 315a–316; *GD*; *Essex Court Recs.* II, 62–3, IX, 124. *GMB* 1883–8; *GM* 7: 182–3 (Thomas Wade).

WELD, Joseph (c.1599–1646)

Joseph Weld was the brother of Thomas Weld*. Both were sons of Edmund Weld, a linen draper of Sudbury, Suffolk. Joseph Weld emigrated from Sudbury and settled at Roxbury, Massachusetts, in 1635.

Weld made his living as a merchant and innkeeper. He and his wife were church members. He became a freeman on 3 March 1635/6. He joined the Artillery Company in 1637 and served as deputy for Roxbury at the General Court in 1636, 1637, 1638, 1641, 1643 and 1644. In November 1637, the antinomian Anne Hutchinson was kept under house arrest at Weld's home in Roxbury, in the aftermath of her trial, 'committed to Mr Joseph Weld until the court shall dispose of her'.

Weld went to England in 1644. He and Stephen Winthrop* were arrested in London over a legal dispute with Alderman William Berkeley and his brother Isaac, sparked off by a decision against Berkeley in the General Court at Boston. Thomas Weld and Sir Henry Vane Jr* secured their release. Joseph Weld soon went back to New England, but the ramifications of the case dragged on after his death.

Weld died of 'of a cancer in his tongue and jaws' on 7 October 1646. In December, his widow Barbara appointed Thomas Bell* of Roxbury as her attorney, to collect anything owed to her husband in England.

GM 7: 280–8; Mass. Recs. 1: 207, 2: 135; WP V, 194–5; WJ, 550n., 607–8; Roxbury CR, 80, 84, 173; Aspinwall, 66–7.

WILLIAMS, Roger (1603?–1683)

Roger Williams, minister and founder of Rhode Island, was born in London. He attended Pembroke College, Cambridge, and graduated with a BA in 1627. He stayed on at Cambridge for a time but in 1629 took a post as household chaplain to Sir William Masham of High Laver, Essex. He married a maid in the household, Mary Bernard, who was a daughter of the minister Richard Bernard (ODNB) and brother to Masakiell Bernard*.

Roger and Mary Williams emigrated in 1631. Roger Williams's views quickly proved controversial. He was invited to become teacher of the Boston church but declined on the grounds that the congregation had not separated fully from the Church of England. In an effort to evade the straitjacket of Massachusetts' orthodoxy, he moved to Salem, to Plymouth, then back to Salem. The Massachusetts authorities banished him in 1635. Williams left the Bay Colony in 1636 and moved south into Narragansett Indian territory, modern Rhode Island. He named his new settlement 'Providence', in light of 'God's merciful providence unto me in my distress'. This community had Williams's ethos of 'soul liberty' at its heart, and embraced religious toleration. In his pursuit of purity, Williams reached a point where he belonged to no church and would only pray with his wife. His separatist views were anathema to his father-in-law, Richard Bernard, who (after an early experiment with separatism, c.1606) had become a vigorous campaigner against separation and was suspicious of New England practice on this front.

Williams went to England twice, in 1643–4 and in 1651–3. On both occasions, he was sent as an agent. In 1643, he went to London to defend the settlements around Narragansett Bay, including Providence, from territorial claims by Massachusetts. Williams stopped Massachusetts' plans by securing a parliamentary patent for 'Providence Plantation' in 1644. He also spent time publishing tracts against the intolerance of the Massachusetts authorities. In 1651, Williams travelled to London again, this time to counter William Coddington* of Aquidneck. Coddington had secured a new commission from parliament to act as governor: Williams wanted this annulled and the patent of 1644 reaffirmed. Williams returned to New England without fulfilling this mission. However, John Clarke took over the negotiations. Clarke secured a letter from Cromwell, which urged all the settlements around Narragansett Bay to abide by the 1644 patent. In 1663, Clarke returned to New England with a fresh charter from Charles II for Rhode Island and Providence Plantations, which enshrined religious toleration.

Williams's career can be traced in Edwin S. Gaustad, *Roger Williams* (New York and Oxford: Oxford University Press, 2005); E.S. Morgan, *Roger Williams: the church and the state* (New York: W.W. Norton, 1987); *The correspondence of Roger Williams*, ed. Glenn LaFantasie (Hanover, NH: University Press of New England, 1998); *GMB* 2007–10. See also *Pilgrims*, 46–7 (on Richard Bernard's critique of New England); Graeme J. Milne, 'New England agents and the English Atlantic, 1641–1666' (PhD dissertation, University of Edinburgh 1993), 306 and *passim*.

ANB, ODNB.

WINTHROP, John Jr (1605–1676)

John Winthrop Jr, the son of John Winthrop, first came to New England in 1631. He had married Martha Fones at Groton, Suffolk, in February 1630/1. Winthrop settled initially in Boston, but became a founder of Ipswich, Massachusetts, in 1633. He went back to England in 1634 after the death of his wife. He married Elizabeth Reade in London on 6 July 1635 and returned to New England later that year.

Winthrop's interest in science, alchemy, medicine and mystical piety was evident in the 1620s and 1630s. He was also a great entrepreneur. He moved to settle Pequot Plantation (New London) in 1646, where he promoted lead-mining, potash and saltpetre production, salt-works and innovative farming methods. His skills as a physician drew people from all over New England. Winthrop was elected governor of Connecticut in 1657, and was re-elected every year but one until his death.

From 1641 to 1643, he travelled in England and on the Continent to recruit investors and expertise for ironworks at Saugus, Massachusetts. In 1661–3 he made a successful journey to London, and secured a new charter for Connecticut in 1662.

Winthrop's interest in science, medicine, alchemy and mystical piety made him a natural associate of leading scientists like Samuel Hartlib (*ODNB*) and Robert Boyle (*ODNB*). He became one of the original fellows of the Royal Society in 1663.

David Como, *Blown by the spirit: puritanism and the emergence of an antinomian underground in pre-Civil-War England* (Stanford, CA: Stanford University Press, 2004), 415–25; Robert C. Black, *The younger John Winthrop* (New York and London: Columbia University Press, 1966); E.D. Hartley, *Ironworks on the Saugus* (Norman, OK: University of Oklahoma Press, 1957), 44–58 and *passim*.

ANB, ODNB.

Bibliography

Manuscript sources

American archives

AMERICAN ANTIQUARIAN SOCIETY, WORCESTER, MASSACHUSETTS

Misc. MSS Boxes, 'B'. Richard Blinman, 'An Answeare to divers Reverend Elders of New England', c.1657.
Russell Family, Sermons and Sermon Notes. Richard Russell's Sermon Notebook, 1649–51.

BOSTON PUBLIC LIBRARY, BOSTON, MASSACHUSETTS

MS Am. 1502/1. Miscellaneous letters.
MS Am. 1506. Cotton Papers.

CAMBRIDGE, MASSACHUSETTS, CITY CLERK'S OFFICE, CITY HALL

Cambridge Town Records, 1632–1703 (transcript).

CONNECTICUT HISTORICAL SOCIETY, HARTFORD

The Wyllys Papers.

CONNECTICUT STATE LIBRARY, HARTFORD

Milford, First Congregational Church Records, 1639–1837.

GUILFORD, CONNECTICUT, TOWN CLERK'S OFFICE

Guilford Records, Volume A.
Guilford Records, Volume B.

HISTORICAL SOCIETY OF PENNSYLVANIA, PHILADELPHIA

Gratz Sermon Collection, Historical Society of Pennsylvania Manuscript Collection 250B, Box 1. John Pynchon's notes of sermons by George Moxon at Springfield, Massachusetts, 1649.

MASSACHUSETTS ARCHIVES, BOSTON

Massachusetts Archives Collection, 1629–1799
    Volume 10. Ecclesiastical, 1637–1679.
    Volume 15B. Estates, 1636–1671.
    Volume 45. Lands, 1622–1726.
    Volume 58. Literacy, 1645–1774.
    Volume 67. Military, 1643–1675.

Volume 106. Political, 1638–1700.
Volume 240. Hutchinson Papers (Vol. 1, 1625–1650).
Early records of Middlesex County, Massachusetts
    Middlesex County Court Record Book, I, 1649–1663.
    Middlesex County Court Files, 1649–1663.
    Middlesex County Probate Records, First Series, 1648–1876.

MASSACHUSETTS HISTORICAL SOCIETY, BOSTON

Ms. SBd–151. Abraham Browne: volume of reminiscences, 1653–1668.
Ms. N–1143. Henry Dunster Notebook, 1628–1654.
Ms. N–2195. Miscellaneous Manuscripts Collection, 1600–1972.
Ms. N–2196. Miscellaneous Bound Manuscripts Collection, 1629–1908.
Ms. N–2232. Saltonstall Family Papers.

MASSACHUSETTS, MIDDLESEX SOUTH DISTRICT REGISTRY OF DEEDS, CAMBRIDGE

Middlesex Deeds, I, II, III.

MASSACHUSETTS, SOUTHERN ESSEX COUNTY REGISTRY OF DEEDS, SALEM

Essex Deeds.

PHILLIPS LIBRARY, PEABODY ESSEX MUSEUM, SALEM, MASSACHUSETTS

Essex County Quarterly Court Records.
Essex County Quarterly Court File Papers.
Essex County Probate Records (microfilm).

British archives

BODLEIAN LIBRARY, UNIVERSITY OF OXFORD

Rawlinson MS D. 934. Papers relating to proceedings of the Corporation for the Propagation of the Gospel in New England, 1649–1656.
Rawlinson MS D. 1481.346. Samuel Campion's account of nonconformists in the Marches of Wales, 1676.
Rawlinson MSS, Letters, 52, 53. Correspondence and papers of Philip, Lord Wharton.
Tanner MSS 68, 220. Papers relating to the diocese of Norwich.

BRITISH LIBRARY, LONDON

Additional MS 4276.
Egerton MS 2519. Papers of General Samuel Desborough, 1651–1660.
Lansdowne MS 821. Letters to Henry Cromwell.
Loan 9. Diary of Thomas Larkham, 1650–1669.

CATHEDRAL ARCHIVES AND LIBRARY, CANTERBURY

CCA-U37/1. Register, Minute and Account Book of Canterbury Congregational Church, 1645–1715.

CUMBRIA RECORD OFFICE AND LOCAL STUDIES LIBRARY, WHITEHAVEN

MS YDFCCL 3/1. The Register of Cockermouth Congregational Church, 1651–1771.

DEVON RECORD OFFICE, EXETER

482A add 2/PR1. Tavistock Parish Register, 1614–1793.
428A/PV1. Tavistock Vestry Minutes, 1660–1740.
Q/S 1/9. Quarter Sessions Order Book, 1652–61.
QS/B 1652, Easter – Michaelmas. Quarter Sessions, court files.

DR WILLIAMS'S LIBRARY, LONDON

Richard Baxter, Correspondence.
MS 38.59. A.G. Matthews's Notes of Nonconformist Ministers' Wills.

EAST SUSSEX RECORD OFFICE, LEWES

FRE/5421–FRE/5634. Letters from John Allin to Dr Philip Frith and Samuel Jeake of Rye, Sussex, 1663–74.

ESSEX RECORD OFFICE, CHELMSFORD

D/AEA 41. Archdeaconry of Essex Act Book, 1636–1638.
Essex Assize Files, 1650s; Quarter Sessions Rolls and Order Books, 1650s.

LAMBETH PALACE LIBRARY, LONDON

MSS COMM. III/1–7. Registers of Presentations and Approvals of Ministers, 1654–1660.
MSS COMM. V/5, VII/2. Day Books of the Trustees for the Maintenance of Ministers; Augmentation Order Books.
MSS COMM. XIIa, XIIb. Copies of Parochial Surveys, 1647–1657.

LONDON BOROUGH OF TOWER HAMLETS, LOCAL HISTORY LIBRARY AND ARCHIVE

W/SMH/A/1. Records of Stepney Meeting: Church Book, 1644–1894.

THE NATIONAL ARCHIVES, LONDON

Prerogative Court of Canterbury (PCC) wills, in series PROB 11.
[Online at http://www.nationalarchives.gov.uk/records/wills.htm.]
RG 4/3098. Suffolk, Wrentham (Independent), Births and Baptisms, 1650–1785.
RG 4/4414. London, Stepney, Bull Lane (Independent), Births and Baptisms, 1644–1837; Marriages, 1646–1677.
SP16/261, 278, 302, 312, 324, 334, 346, 349, 361. State Papers Domestic: Charles I, 1625–1649.
SP19/95. State Papers Domestic: The Commonwealth [1642–1660]. Order Book of the Committee for the Advance of Money.
SP25/99. State Papers Domestic: The Commonwealth [1642–1660]. Committee for the Advance of Money.

NORFOLK RECORD OFFICE, NORWICH

NCR Case 16d/6. Norwich City Assembly Book of Proceedings, 1642–1668.
FC 19/1. Norwich Old Meeting Congregational Church. Church Book, 1642–1839.
FC 31/1. Great Yarmouth, Middlegate Congregational Church. Church Book, 1643–1855.

SUFFOLK RECORD OFFICE, LOWESTOFT BRANCH

1337/1/1, Wrentham Congregational Church. Church Book, 1649–1971.
168/D1/1, Wrentham Parish Register: births, 1602–1731; marriages, 1603–1714; deaths, 1603–1676.

Selected primary printed sources

[Anon.]. *New Englands first fruits*. London, 1643.
[Anon.]. *A strange metamorphosis in Tavistock, or the Nabal-Naboth improved a Judas*. London, 1658.
Aspinwall, William. *A volume relating to the early history of Boston, containing the Aspinwall Notarial Records from 1644 to 1651*. Boston, MA: Report of the Record Commissioners, 32, Municipal Printing Office, 1903.
Aston, Sir Thomas. *A remonstrance against presbitery*. [London], 1641.
[Baxter, Richard]. N.H. Keeble and Geoffrey F. Nuttall, eds. *A calendar of the correspondence of Richard Baxter* (2 vols). Oxford: Clarendon Press, 1991.
Bell, Susanna. *The legacy of a dying mother to her mourning children, being the experiences of Mrs Susanna Bell*. London, 1673.
[Boston]. Pierce, Richard D., ed. *The records of the First Church in Boston 1630–1868*, I. Boston, MA: Colonial Society of Massachusetts, *Publications*, 39, 1961.
Bradford, William. *Of Plymouth Plantation, 1620–1647*, ed. Samuel E. Morison. New York: Knopf, 1963.
Bradstreet, Anne. *The complete works of Anne Bradstreet*. Edited by Joseph R.McElrath Jr and Allan P. Robb. Boston, MA: Twayne, 1981.
Bush, Sargent, Jr, ed. *The correspondence of John Cotton*. Chapel Hill, NC and London: University of North Carolina Press, 2001.
Calder, Isabel M., ed. *Letters of John Davenport, puritan divine*. New Haven, CT: Yale University Press, 1937.
Calendar of State Papers: colonial series, 1574–1660. London: Longman, Green, Longman & Roberts, 1860.
Calendar of State Papers: colonial series, America and West Indies, 1661–1668. London: Longman, 1880.
Calendar of State Papers: domestic series, of the reign of Charles I (23 vols). London: Longman & Co., 1858–97.
Calendar of State Papers: domestic series, of the Commonwealth (13 vols). London: Longman & Co., 1875–86.
Calendar of State Papers: domestic series, of the reign of Charles II (28 vols). London: Longman, 1860–1939.
[Cambridge]. George Selement and Bruce C. Woolley, eds. *Thomas Shepard's confessions*. Boston, MA: Colonial Society of Massachusetts, *Publications*, 58, 1981.
[Charlestown]. James F. Hunnewell, ed. 'The first record-book of the First Church in Charlestown, Massachusetts', *NEHGR*, 23 (1869), 187–91, 279–83.
Child, Major John. *New-Englands Jonas cast up at London*. London, 1647.
[Cockermouth, Cumbria]. *The Cockermouth congregational church book (1651–c.1765)*, ed. R.B. Wordsworth. Cumberland and Westmorland Antiquarian and Archaeological Society Record Series, XXI, 2012.
[Connecticut]. *A digest of early Connecticut probate records*. Online database: http://www.NewEnglandAncestors.org. Boston, MA: New England Historic Genealogical Society, 2006.
[Connecticut]. J.H. Trumbull, ed. *The public records of the Colony of Connecticut*

prior to the union with New Haven Colony, 1665 (15 vols to 1776). Hartford, CT, 1850–1890.

Connecticut vital records to 1870. Online database, http://www.AmericanAncestors.org, New England Historic Genealogical Society, 2011. From original typescripts, Lucius Barnes Barbour Collection, 1928.

Cotton, John. *Gods promise to his plantation*. London, 1630.

Dissenting Academies Online. [A project of the Dr Williams's Centre for Dissenting Studies, London.] http://www.english.qmul.ac.uk/drwilliams/portal.html.

[Dedham]. D.G. Hill, ed. *The record of baptisms, marriages, and deaths, and admissions to the church and dismissals therefrom, transcribed from the church records in the town of Dedham, Massachusetts*. Dedham, MA, 1888.

[Dorchester]. C.H. Pope, ed. *Records of the First Church at Dorchester . . . 1636–1734*. Boston, MA, 1891.

'Dunster Papers'. Massachusetts Historical Society, *Collections*, 4th series, 2 (1854), 190–8.

Eaton, Samuel and Timothy Taylor. *A defence of sundry positions and scriptures alleged to justify the congregationall-way*. London, 1645.

——. *The defence of sundry positions and Scriptures for the congregational-way justified*. London, 1646.

——. *A just apologie for the church of Duckenfeild in Cheshire*. London, 1647.

Edwards, Thomas. *Gangraena, or a catalogue and discovery of many . . . errours, heresies, blasphemies and pernicious practices* (3 parts in 1 volume). London, 1646.

Emerson, Everett, ed. *Letters from New England*. Amherst, MA: University of Massachusetts Press, 1972.

English Short Title Catalogue. Online at http://estc.bl.uk.

[Essex County]. Essex Deeds. Southern Essex County Registry of Deeds, Salem, Massachusetts. Document images and indices online at http://www.salemdeeds.com.

[Essex County]. *The probate records of Essex County, Massachusetts*, 1, 1635–1664. Salem, MA: Essex Institute, 1916.

[Essex County]. G.F. Dow, ed. *The records and files of the Quarterly Courts of Essex County, Massachusetts* (8 vols). Salem, MA: Essex Institute, 1911–21.

Firmin, Giles. *Separation examined*. London, 1652.

——. *The real Christian*. London, 1670.

——. *Weighty questions discussed*. London, 1692.

G[lanville], F[rancis], D[igory] P[olwhele], W[alter] G[odbear], N[icholas] W[atts], W[illiam] H[ore]. *The Tavistocke Naboth turned Nabal*. London, 1658.

Gookin, Daniel. *To all persons whom these may concern in the several townes and plantations of the United Colonies, in New England*. Cambridge, MA, 1656.

Harvard College records, I. Boston, MA: Colonial Society of Massachusetts, *Publications*, 15, 1925.

Harvard College records, III. Boston, MA: Colonial Society of Massachusetts, *Publications*, 31, 1935.

Harvard College records, IV. Robert W. Lovett, ed. *Documents from the Harvard University archives, 1638–1750*. Boston, MA: Colonial Society of Massachusetts, *Publications*, 49, 1975.

Heywood, Oliver. *The Rev. Oliver Heywood, B.A., 1630–1702; his autobiography, diaries . . .* ed. J.H. Turner (4 vols). Brighouse, Yorkshire: A.B. Bayes, 1882–5.

[——]. *Oliver Heywood's life of John Angier of Denton*, ed. E. Axon. Chetham Society, New Series, 97. Manchester: Chetham Society, 1937.

Hooke, William. *New Englands teares, for old Englands feares*. London, 1641.

——. *New-Englands sence of old-England and Irelands sorrows*. London, 1645.

Hutchinson, Thomas. *The history of Massachusetts from . . . 1628 until 1750* (2 vols). Salem, MA: Thomas Cushing, 1795.

Hutchinson, Thomas. *The Hutchinson Papers. A collection of original papers relative to the history of the Colony of Massachusetts-Bay* (2 vols). Albany, NY: Publications of the Prince Society, 1865.

[Johnson, Edward]. *Johnson's wonder-working Providence, 1628–1651*, ed. J. Franklin Jameson. New York: Barnes and Noble, 1952.

Josselin, Ralph. *The diary of Ralph Josselin 1616–1683*, ed. Alan Macfarlane. Oxford: Oxford University Press, 1976.

Keayne, Robert. *The apologia of Robert Keayne*, ed. Bernard Bailyn. New York: Harper and Row, 1965.

[Knollys, Hanserd]. *The life and death of . . . Mr Hanserd Knollys*. London, 1692.

Larkham, Thomas. *The diary of Thomas Larkham, 1647–1669*, ed. Susan Hardman Moore. Church of England Record Society, 17. Woodbridge, Suffolk: Boydell and Brewer, 2011.

Larkham, Thomas. *The wedding-supper*. London, 1652.

——. *Naboth, in a narrative and complaint of the church of God at Tavistock*. London, 1657.

——. *Judas hanging himselfe*. [London?], 1658.

Lechford, Thomas. *Plain dealing: or, newes from New-England*. London, 1642.

——. *A note-book kept by Thomas Lechford, Esq., lawyer, in Boston, Massachusetts Bay, from June 27, 1638, to July 29, 1641*. Transactions and Collections of the American Antiquarian Society, 7. Cambridge, MA: J. Wilson & Co., 1885.

[Martindale, Adam]. *The life of Adam Martindale*, ed. R. Parkinson. Chetham Society, Old Series, IV. Manchester: Chetham Society, 1845; reprint Manchester: Chetham Society, 2001.

[Massachusetts]. N.B. Shurtleff, ed. *Records of the Governor and Company of the Massachusetts Bay in New England (1626–1686)* (5 vols in 6). Boston, MA, 1853–4. Reprint, New York: AMS Press, 1968.

Massachusetts Historical Society. *Collections of the Massachusetts Historical Society*. Boston, MA: The Society, 1792–.

Mather, Cotton. *Memoirs of the life of the Rev. Increase Mather D.D.* London, 1724.

——. *Magnalia Christi Americana; or, the ecclesiastical history of New England*, ed. T. Robbins (2 vols). Hartford, CT: Silas Andrus & Son, 1853.

Mather, Increase. *A brief relation of the state of New England, from the beginning of that plantation to this present year, 1689*. London, 1689.

——. 'The autobiography of Increase Mather', ed. Michael G. Hall, *Proceedings of the American Antiquarian Society*, 71 (1961), part 2, 280–7.

'Mather Papers'. Massachusetts Historical Society, *Collections*, 4th series, 8 (1868).

Matthews, Marmaduke. *The Messiah magnified by the mouthes of babes in America*. London, 1659.

Meserole, Harrison T., ed. *Seventeenth century American poetry*. New York: Doubleday & Co., 1968.

[Middlesex County]. Middlesex County, MA: Abstracts of Court Records, 1649–1675, http://www.AmericanAncestors.org, New England Historic Genealogical Society, 2003.

[Middlesex County]. Robert H. Rodgers, *Middlesex County records of probate and administration, 1649–76* (3 vols). Boston, MA: New England Historic Genealogical Society, 1999, 2001; Rockland, ME: Picton Press, 2005.

[Middlesex County]. Middlesex County, MA: Index to Probate Records, 1648–1871, http://www.AmericanAncestors.org, New England Historic Genealogical Society, 2003.

[New Haven]. C.J. Hoadly, ed. *Records of the Colony and Plantation of New Haven* (2 vols). Hartford, CT, 1857–8.

[New Haven] F.B. Dexter, ed., *New Haven town records*. Vol. 1, 1649–1662. New Haven, CT, 1917.

Newcome, Henry. *The autobiography of Henry Newcome*, ed. R. Parkinson. Chetham Society Old Series XXVI, XXVII. Manchester, 1852.

Nickolls, J., ed. *Original letters and papers of state addressed to Oliver Cromwell*. London, 1743.

Patient, Thomas. *The doctrine of baptism*. London, 1654.

Perkins, William. *A cloud of faithfull witnesses, leading to the heavenly Canaan, or a commentary on the 11. chapter to the Hebrewes*. London, 1607.

Peter, Hugh. *A dying fathers last legacy to an onely child*. London, 1660.

[Prynne,William]. *Newes from Ipswich*. Ipswich [i.e. London?], 1636.

——. *Independency examined, unmasked, refuted*. London, 1644.

——. *A full reply to certaine briefe observations and anti-queries on Master Prynnes twelve questions about church-government*. London, 1644.

Pynchon, William. *The meritorious price of our redemption*. London, 1650.

Rogers, John. *Ohel or Beth-shemesh: a tabernacle for the sun*. London, 1653.

[Roxbury]. *Roxbury land and church records*. Sixth Report of the Boston Record Commissioners. Boston, MA: Rockwell and Churchill, 1884.

[Rowley]. Blodgette, G.B. and M. Mighill, eds. *The early records of the town of Rowley, Massachusetts*, I, 1639–1672. Rowley, MA, 1894.

Ryther, John. *A plat for mariners*. London, 1672.

[Salem]. Pierce, Richard D., ed. *Records of the First Church in Salem, Massachusetts, 1629–1736*. Salem, MA: Essex Institute, 1974.

[Salem]. *Town records of Salem, Massachusetts: 1634–1659*, ed. W.P. Upham. Salem, MA: Essex Institute, 1869.

The Saltonstall Papers, 1607–1815, ed. R. E. Moody (2 vols). Massachusetts Historical Society, *Collections*, 80, 81. Boston, MA: Massachusetts Historical Society, 1972–4.

Suffolk Deeds, ed. W.B. Trask (12 vols). Boston, MA: Rockwell and Churchill, 1880–1902.

[Thurloe, John]. *A collection of the state papers of John Thurloe*, ed. T. Birch (7 vols). London, 1742.

Walker, John. *An attempt towards recovering an account of the numbers and sufferings of the clergy*. London, 1714.

Ward, Nathaniel. *The simple cobler of aggawam in America*. London, 1647.

Weld, Thomas. *An answer to W[illiam] R[athband] his narration*. London, 1644.

[——]. *A short story of the rise, reign and ruine of the antinomians*. London, 1644.

——. *A brief narration of the practices of the churches in New-England*. London, 1645.

[Weld, Thomas]. 'By a friend to truth, and an enemy to lyes'. *A vindication of Mr Weld. Wherein the case between him and his opposers, is truly stated, and the church-way of Christ soberly asserted*. London, 1658.

Wigglesworth, Michael. *The diary of Michael Wigglesworth 1653–1657: The conscience of a puritan*, ed. E.S. Morgan. Gloucester, MA: Peter Smith, 1970.

Winslow, Edward. *Good newes from New-England*. London, 1624.

——. *New-Englands salamander*. London, 1647.

Winthrop, John. *The Journal of John Winthrop*, ed. Richard S. Dunn, James Savage and Laetitia Yeandle. Cambridge, MA and London: Harvard University Press, 1996.

The Winthrop Papers, 1498–1654, ed. Allyn B. Forbes et al. (6 vols). Boston, MA: Massachusetts Historical Society, 1929–.

Wood, William. *New Englands prospect*. London, 1634.

Woodbridge, Benjamin. *Justification by faith*. London, 1652.
——. *The method of grace in the justification of sinners*. London, 1656.
The Wyllys Papers . . . 1590–1796. Collections of the Connecticut Historical Society, 21. Hartford, CT: Connecticut Historical Society, 1924.
Young, Alexander. *Chronicles of the Pilgrim Fathers of the Colony of Plymouth, from 1602 to 1625*. Boston, MA: C.C. Little & James Brown, 1841.

Selected secondary sources, printed and online

Allen, D.G. *In English ways: the movement of societies and the transferal of English local law and custom to Massachusetts Bay in the seventeenth century*. Chapel Hill, NC: University of North Carolina Press, 1981.
American National Biography (24 vols). Oxford and New York: Oxford University Press, 1999. [ANB Online at http://www.anb.org, 2005–.]
Anderson, R.C., G.F. Sanborn and M.L. Sanborn, eds. *The Great Migration: immigrants to New England, 1634–1635*, 7 vols. Boston, MA: Great Migration Study Project, New England Historic Genealogical Society, 1999–2011. Online at http://www.AmericanAncestors.org.
Anderson, R.C., ed. *The Great Migration begins: immigrants to New England 1620–1633*, 3 vols. Boston, MA: Great Migration Study Project, New England Historic Genealogical Society, 1995. Online at http://www.AmericanAncestors.org.
Anderson, Virginia DeJohn. *New England's generation: the Great Migration and the formation of society and culture in the seventeenth century*. Cambridge: Cambridge University Press, 1991.
Armitage, David and Michael J. Braddick, eds. *The British Atlantic world, 1500–1800*. New York and Basingstoke: Palgrave Macmillan, 2002.
Aylmer, G.E. *The state's servants: the civil servants of the English Republic, 1649–1660*. London: Routledge and Kegan Paul, 1973.
Bailyn, Bernard. *The New England merchants in the seventeenth century*. Cambridge, MA: Harvard University Press, 1955.
——. *Atlantic history: concept and contours*. Cambridge, MA: Harvard University Press, 2005.
Barnard, T.C. *Cromwellian Ireland: English government and reform in Ireland*. Oxford: Oxford University Press, 1975.
Barnes, Thomas G. 'Thomas Lechford and the earliest lawyering in Massachusetts, 1638–1641', in Daniel R. Coquillette, Robert J. Brink and Catherine S. Menard, eds, *Law in colonial Massachusetts*, 3–38. Boston, MA: Colonial Society of Massachusetts, Publications, 62, 1984.
Bozeman, Theodore Dwight. *To live ancient lives: the primitivist dimension in puritanism*. Chapel Hill, NC and London: University of North Carolina Press, 1988.
——. *The precisianist strain: disciplinary religion and antinomian backlash in puritanism to 1638*. Chapel Hill, NC and London: University of North Carolina Press, 2004.
Breen, Louise A. *Transgressing the bounds: subversive enterprises among the puritan elite in Massachusetts, 1630–1692*. Oxford and New York: Oxford University Press, 2001.
Breen, Timothy and Stephen Foster, 'Moving to the New World: the character of early Massachusetts immigration', *William and Mary Quarterly*, 3rd Series, 30 (1973), 189–222.
Bremer, Francis J. *Puritan crisis: New England and the English civil wars, 1630–1670*. New York & London: Garland, 1989.
——, ed. *Puritanism: transatlantic perspectives on a seventeenth-century Anglo-American faith*. Boston, MA: Massachusetts Historical Society, 1993.

——. *Congregational communion: clerical friendship in the Anglo-American puritan community, 1610–1692*. Boston, MA: Northeastern University Press, 1994.

——. *John Winthrop: America's forgotten founding father*. New York and Oxford: Oxford University Press, 2003.

——. *First founders: American puritans and puritanism in an Atlantic world*. Durham, NH: University of New Hampshire Press, 2012.

Brotton, Jerry. *The sale of the late king's goods: Charles I and his art collection*. London: Macmillan, 2006.

Bush, Sargent, Jr. 'Thomas Hooker and the Westminster Assembly', *William and Mary Quarterly*, 3rd series, 29 (1972), 291–300.

Caldwell, Patricia. *The puritan conversion narrative: the beginnings of American expression*. Cambridge: Cambridge University Press, 1983.

Canny, Nicholas and Philip D. Morgan, eds. *The Oxford handbook of the Atlantic world, 1450–1850*. New York and Oxford: Oxford University Press, 2011.

Capp, Bernard S. *The Fifth Monarchy men*. London: Faber, 1972.

Capp, Bernard S. *Cromwell's navy: the fleet and the English Revolution, 1648–1660*. Oxford: Clarendon Press, 1989.

Cell, Gillian T. *English enterprise in Newfoundland 1577–1660*. Toronto: University of Toronto Press, 1969.

Clergy of the Church of England Database. http://www.theclergydatabase.org.uk/index.html

Colonial collegians: biographies of those who attended American colleges before the War for Independence, ed. Conrad Edick Wright. Boston, MA: Massachusetts Historical Society and New England Historic Genealogical Society, 2005. Electronic resource: CD-ROM. Online at http://www.AmericanAncestors.org.

Como, David R. *Blown by the Spirit: puritanism and the emergence of an antinomian underground in pre-Civil-War England*. Stanford, CA: Stanford University Press, 2004.

Cooper, James F., Jr. *Tenacious of their liberties: the congregationalists in colonial Massachusetts*. Oxford and New York: Oxford University Press, 1999.

Cressy, David. *Coming over: migration and communication between England and New England in the seventeenth century*. Cambridge: Cambridge University Press, 1987.

Delbanco, Andrew. *The puritan ordeal*. Cambridge, MA: Harvard University Press, 1989.

Dow, Frances D. *Cromwellian Scotland, 1651–1660*. Edinburgh: Donald, 1979.

Durston, Christopher. *Cromwell's major-generals: godly government during the English Revolution*. Manchester and New York: Manchester University Press, 2001.

Fender, Stephen. *Sea changes: British emigration and American literature*. Cambridge: Cambridge University Press, 1992.

Fernandez, Angela. 'Record-keeping and other trouble-making: Thomas Lechford and law reform in colonial Massachusetts', *Law and History Review*, Summer 2005, http://www.historycooperative.org/journals/lhr/23.2/fernandez.html.

Firth, C.H. and G. Davies, *The regimental history of Cromwell's army* (2 vols). Oxford: Clarendon Press, 1940.

Fischer, David Hackett. *Albion's seed: four British folkways in America*. Oxford: Oxford University Press, 1989.

Fletcher, Anthony. *A county community in peace and war: Sussex 1600–1660*. London: Longman, 1975.

Foster, Stephen. *The long argument: English puritanism and the shaping of New England culture, 1570–1700*. Chapel Hill, NC and London: University of North Carolina Press, 1991.

Games, Alison. *Migration and the origins of the English Atlantic world*. Cambridge, MA and London: Harvard University Press, 2001.

Gentles, Ian. *The New Model Army in England, Ireland and Scotland, 1645–53*. Oxford: Blackwell, 1992.

Gildrie, R.P. *Salem, Massachusetts, 1626–1683: a covenant community*. Charlottesville, VA: University Press of Virginia, 1975.

Gragg, Larry. *Englishmen transplanted: the English colonization of Barbados, 1627–1660*. Oxford and New York: Oxford University Press, 2003.

Greaves, Richard L. and Robert Zaller, eds. *Biographical dictionary of British radicals in the seventeenth century* (3 vols). Brighton: Harvester Press, 1982–4.

Greene, Jack and Philip D. Morgan, eds. *Atlantic history: a critical appraisal*. New York: Oxford University Press, 2009.

Gura, Philip F. *A glimpse of Sion's glory: puritan radicalism in New England, 1620–1660*. Middletown, CT: Wesleyan University Press, 1984.

Halcomb, Joel. 'A social history of congregational religious practice during the Puritan Revolution'. PhD dissertation, University of Cambridge, 2009.

Hall, David D. *The faithful shepherd: a history of the New England ministry in the seventeenth century*. Chapel Hill, NC: University of North Carolina Press, 1972; 2nd edn, Cambridge, MA: Harvard University Press, 2006.

——, ed. *Puritans in the New World: a critical anthology*. Princeton, NJ and Oxford: Princeton University Press, 2004.

——. *Ways of writing: the practice and politics of text-making in seventeenth-century New England*. Philadelphia, PA: University of Pennsylvania Press, 2008.

Handlin, Lilian. 'Dissent in a small community', *New England Quarterly*, 58 (1985), 193–220.

Hardman, Susan. 'Return migration from New England to England, 1640–1660'. PhD dissertation, University of Kent at Canterbury, 1986.

Hardman Moore, Susan. 'Arguing for peace: Giles Firmin on New England and godly unity', in R.N. Swanson, ed., *Unity and diversity in the Church*, 251–61. Studies in Church History, 32. Oxford: Blackwell, 1996.

——. '"Pure folkes" and the parish: Thomas Larkham in Cockermouth and Tavistock', in Diana Wood, ed., *Life and thought in the northern Church c.1100–c.1700*, 489–509. Woodbridge, Suffolk: Boydell Press, 1999.

——. *Pilgrims: New World settlers and the call of home*. New Haven, CT and London: Yale University Press, 2007.

Hartley, E.N. *Ironworks on the Saugus*. Norman, OK: University of Oklahoma Press, 1957.

Hill, Christopher. 'Puritans and "The dark corners of the land"', in his *Change and continuity in seventeenth century England*, 3–47. London: Weidenfeld and Nicolson, 1974.

History of Parliament Online, http://www.historyofparliamentonline.org/.

Howell, Roger. 'Thomas Weld of Gateshead: the return of a New England puritan', *Archaeologia Aeliana*, 4th series, 48 (1970), 303–32.

Hughes, Ann. *Gangraena and the struggle for the English Revolution*. Oxford: Oxford University Press, 2004.

——. '"The public profession of these nations": the national Church in Interregnum England', in Christopher Durston and Judith Maltby, eds, *Religion in revolutionary England*, 93–114. Manchester and New York: Manchester University Press, 2007.

Kishlansky, Mark. *The rise of the New Model Army*. Cambridge: Cambridge University Press, 1979.

Kittredge, G.L. 'Dr Robert Child the Remonstrant', Colonial Society of Massachusetts, *Publications*, 21 (1919), 1–146.

Knight, Janice. *Orthodoxies in Massachusetts: rereading American puritanism.* Cambridge, MA: Harvard University Press, 1994.

Kupperman, Karen Ordahl. *Providence Island, 1630–1641: the other puritan colony.* Cambridge: Cambridge University Press, 1993.

——. *The Atlantic in world history.* New York and Oxford: Oxford University Press, 2012.

Kurlansky, Mark. *Cod: a biography of the fish that changed the world.* London: Vintage, 1999.

Laurence, Anne. *Parliamentary army chaplains, 1642–1651.* Woodbridge, Suffolk: Royal Historical Society, 1990.

Little, Patrick and David L. Smith. *Parliaments and politics during the Cromwellian Protectorate.* Cambridge: Cambridge University Press, 2007.

Liu, Tai. *Puritan London: a study of religion and society in the City parishes.* London and Toronto: Associated University Presses, 1986.

Maclear, J.F. 'New England and the Fifth Monarchy: the quest for the millennium in early American puritanism', *William and Mary Quarterly*, 3rd series, 32 (1975), 223–60.

Matthews, A.G. *Calamy revised.* Oxford: Clarendon Press, 1934. Reprint, Oxford: Clarendon Press, 1988.

Matthews, A.G. *Walker revised.* Oxford: Clarendon Press, 1948. Reprint, Oxford: Clarendon Press, 1988.

Milne, Graeme J. 'New England agents and the English Atlantic, 1641–1666'. PhD dissertation, University of Edinburgh, 1993.

Morison, Samuel Eliot. *The founding of Harvard College.* Cambridge, MA: Harvard University Press, 1935.

——. *Harvard College in the seventeenth century* (2 vols). Cambridge, MA: Harvard University Press, 1936.

Morrill, John. *Cheshire, 1630–1660: county government and society during the English Revolution.* London: Oxford University Press, 1974.

Munk, William, ed. *The roll of the Royal College of Physicians of London*, I, 1518–1700. London: Longman, Green, Longman and Roberts, 1861. Online at http://munksroll.rcplondon.ac.uk/

New England Historical and Genealogical Register. Boston, MA: New England Historic Genealogical Society, 1847–. Online database: http://www.AmericanAncestors.org, New England Historic Genealogical Society, 2001–.

Newman, Simon P. 'Nathaniel Ward, 1580–1652: an Elizabethan puritan in a Jacobean world', *Essex Institute Historical Collections*, 127 (1991), 313–26.

Nuttall, G.F. *The Holy Spirit in puritan faith and experience.* Oxford: Blackwell, 1946. Reprint, Chicago, IL and London: University of Chicago Press, 1992.

——. *Visible saints: the congregational way, 1640–1660.* Oxford: Blackwell, 1957.

Oxford Dictionary of National Biography (61 vols). Oxford: Oxford University Press, 2004–. [Oxford DNB Online at http://www.oxforddnb.com, 2005–.]

Pestana, Carla Gardina. *Quakers and baptists in colonial Massachusetts.* Cambridge: Cambridge University Press, 1991.

——. *The English Atlantic in an age of revolution, 1640–1661.* Cambridge, MA and London: Harvard University Press, 2004.

Pettit, Norman. 'God's Englishman in New England: his enduring ties to the motherland', Massachusetts Historical Society, *Proceedings*, 101 (1989), 56–70.

Powell, Sumner Chilton. *Puritan village: the formation of a New England town.* Middletown, CT: Wesleyan University Press, 1963.

Reynolds, Matthew. *Godly reformers and their opponents in early modern England: religion in Norwich c.1560–1643.* Woodbridge, Suffolk: Boydell Press, 2005.

Riley, Stephen T. 'Abraham Browne's captivity by the Barbary pirates, 1655', in P.C.F. Smith, ed., *Seafaring in colonial Massachusetts*, 31–42. Boston, MA: Colonial Society of Massachusetts, *Publications*, 52, 1980.

Roberts, Oliver A. *History of the ... honourable Artillery Company of Massachusetts, 1637–1688* (4 vols). Boston, MA: A. Mudge and Son, 1895–1901.

Rutman, Darrett. *Winthrop's Boston: a portrait of a puritan town, 1630–1649*. New York: Norton, 1972.

Sachse, William. 'Harvard men in England 1642–1714', Colonial Society of Massachusetts, *Publications*, 35 (1942–6), 120–31.

——. 'The migration of New Englanders to England, 1640–1660', *American Historical Review*, 53 (1947–8), 251–78.

——. *The colonial American in Britain*. Madison, WI: University of Wisconsin Press, 1956.

Seymour, St J.D. *The puritans in Ireland, 1647–1661*. Oxford: Clarendon Press, 1921. Reprint, Oxford: Clarendon Press, 1969.

Shaw, W.A. *A history of the English Church during the Civil Wars and under the Commonwealth, 1640–1660* (2 vols). London: Longman, Green, 1900.

Sibley, J.L. *Biographical sketches of graduates of Harvard University ... 1642–1689* (3 vols). Cambridge, MA: C.W. Sever, 1873–85.

Simmons, R.C. 'Richard Sadler's account of the Massachusetts churches', *New England Quarterly*, 42 (1969), 411–25.

Spurlock, R. Scott. *Cromwell and Scotland: conquest and religion, 1650–1660*. Edinburgh: John Donald Publishers, 2007.

Stearns, R.P. 'The Weld-Peter mission to England', Colonial Society of Massachusetts, *Publications*, 32 (1937), 188–246.

——. *The strenuous puritan: Hugh Peter, 1598–1660*. Urbana, IL: University of Illinois Press, 1954.

Steele, Ian K. *The English Atlantic 1675–1740*. Oxford: Oxford University Press, 1986.

Steiner, B.C. *A history of the plantation of Menunkatuck and of the original town of Guilford, Connecticut*. Baltimore, MD: privately printed, 1897.

Stout, Harry S. 'The morphology of remigration: New England university men and their return to England, 1640–1660', *Journal of American Studies*, 10 (1976), 151–72.

Surman Index Online, http://surman.english.qmul.ac.uk/. Online database of C.H. Surman's biographical card index at Dr Williams's Library, London.

Thompson, Roger. *Mobility and migration: East Anglian founders of New England*. Amherst, MA: University of Massachusetts Press, 1994.

——. *Divided we stand: Watertown, Massachusetts, 1630–1680*. Amherst, MA: University of Massachusetts Press, 2001.

——. *Cambridge cameos: stories of life in seventeenth-century New England*. Boston, MA: New England Historic Genealogical Society, 2005.

——. *From deference to defiance: Charlestown, Massachusetts, 1629–1662*. Boston, MA: New England Historic Genealogical Society, 2012.

Thwing, Annie Haven. 'Inhabitants and estates of the town of Boston, 1630–1800' [electronic resource] and *The crooked and narrow streets of the town of Boston, 1630–1822* (originally published Boston, MA: Marshall Jones Company, 1920). CD ROM. Boston, MA: Massachusetts Historical Society and New England Historic Genealogical Society, 2001.

Tomalin, Claire. *Samuel Pepys: the unequalled self*. London: Penguin Books, 2002.

Tyack, N.C.P. 'Migration from East Anglia to New England before 1660'. PhD dissertation, University of London, 1951.

Underdown, David. *Fire from heaven: life in an English Town in the seventeenth century.* London: Fontana, 1993.
Van Dixhoorn, Chad, ed. *The Minutes and Papers of the Westminster Assembly 1643-1652* (5 vols). Oxford: Oxford University Press, 2012.
Wall, Robert Emmet. *Massachusetts Bay: the crucial decade, 1640-1650.* New Haven, CT: Yale University Press, 1972.
Walsham, Alexandra. *Providence in early modern England.* Oxford: Oxford University Press, 1999.
Waters, Henry F. *Genealogical gleanings in England.* Boston, MA: New England Historic Genealogical Society, 1901.
Webster, Tom. *Godly clergy in early Stuart England: the Caroline puritan movement c.1620-1643.* Cambridge: Cambridge University Press, 1997.
White, B.R. 'Thomas Patient in England and Ireland', *Irish Baptist Historical Society Journal*, 2 (1969-1970), 36-48.
——. *Hanserd Knollys and radical dissent in the 17th century.* London: Friends of Dr Williams's Library, 31st Lecture, 1977.
Winship, Michael P. 'Contesting control of orthodoxy among the godly: William Pynchon reexamined', *William and Mary Quarterly*, 3rd series, 54 (1997), 795-822.
——. 'William Pynchon's *The Jewes synagogue*', *New England Quarterly*, 71 (1998), 290-7.
——. *Making heretics: militant protestantism and free grace in Massachusetts, 1636-1641.* Princeton, NJ and Oxford: Princeton University Press, 2002.
Worthley, Harold Field. *An inventory of the records of the Particular (Congregational) Churches of Massachusetts gathered 1620-1805.* Harvard Theological Studies, 25. Cambridge, MA and London: Harvard University Press, 1970.
Wright, Stephen. *The early English Baptists, 1603-1649.* Woodbridge, Suffolk: Boydell Press, 2006.

Index

Bold figures refer to biographical entries. New England settlements are entered individually, alphabetically, along with modern State names. Places in England are listed under historic counties.

Adams, Ann, of Dedham (MA) **31**, 32
Adams, Ferdinando, shoemaker of Dedham 7, 11, 18n.61, **31–2,** 182, 183
Adams, Thomas, lord mayor of London 265
Alcock, George, of Roxbury **334**
Alexander, William, earl of Stirling 112, 293
Allen, Ann, of Charlestown **32,** 33, 34
Allen, Robert, of Norwich 32, 33, 182
Allen, Thomas, minister 10, **32–5,** 140, 158, 172, 182, 186, 221, 223, 225, 270, 273
Allin, John, minister of Dedham (MA) 35, 251, 254
Allin, John Jr, Harvard graduate, minister, physician **35–6,** 203, 251, 283
ambivalence toward settlers going back to England 8–10, 91
Ambrose, Joshua, Harvard graduate and minister **36**
Ambrose, Nehemiah, Harvard graduate and minister **36–7**
Ambrose, Peter, of Toxteth (Lancashire) 36–7
Ames, Joan, widow of William 37
Ames, John, Harvard student **37**
Ames, William, theologian 20, 37, 243, 251, 337
Ames, William Jr, Harvard graduate and minister of Wrentham (Suffolk) **37–8,** 203, 221, 223, 241, 243, 252, 253, 291
Andrewes, Sir Thomas, regicide and lord mayor of London 203
Andros, Sir Edmund, colonial governor 200, 287
Angier [*née* Aspinwall], Hannah 38
Angier, John, minister of Denton (Lancashire) 38, 39, 40, 99
Angier, John Jr, Harvard graduate and minister **38–9**
Anglo-Dutch Wars xxvi, xxvii, 61, 93, 124, 135, 143, 156, 186, 190, 274, 343
Antigua xxii, 51
Antinomian Controversy (1636–8), antinomians, free grace debate xxiii, 22, 25, 39, 48, 50, 70, 107, 108, 155, 159, 163, 168, 169, 177, 194, 207, 215, 224, 252, 286, 305, 310, 311, 315, 329–30, 348, 349, 350, 357, 358, 359, 360, 361, 376
'Grindletonians' 194
see also orthodoxy and dissent in Massachusetts; religious toleration
Armine, Lady Mary, benefactor 244
army, English, parliamentarian (1640s) and republican (1649–60) xxv, xxvi, xxvii, 53, 59, 84, 89, 93, 98, 145, 148, 149, 166, 169, 178, 306
army in Ireland (1642, 1646–7, 1649–60) xxvi, xxvii, 84, 152, 153, 178, 212, 232, 245, 260, 341, 345
army in Scotland (1651–60) xxvi, 92, 93, 99, 106, 119, 135, 154, 167, 264, 327, 328, 341, 345
colonial soldiers in xxv, 5, 59, 84, 89, 92, 93, 106, 119, 145, 148, 152, 153, 154, 166, 185, 188, 194, 212, 256, 260, 264, 286, 295, 327, 328, 341, 345, 365, 366
colonial surgeons in 108, 188, 255–6, 267, 286
colonists as army chaplains 77, 82–3, 93, 98, 99, 129, 130, 135, 152, 162, 169, 178, 198, 203, 212, 232, 245, 260, 322
Ashmole, Elias, astrologer and antiquary 80
Ashurst, Henry, London merchant 370
Aspinwall, Elizabeth 39, 40
Aspinwall, William, Boston notary and Fifth Monarchist 22, 23n.78, 38, **39–40,** 61, 118, 127, 147, 283, 295, 297–8, 373–4
Aston, Sir Thomas, of Cheshire 98
Astwood, John, of Milford (CT) 5, **41,** 42, 132, 285
Astwood, Sarah, of Boston (MA) 41, **42**
Atlantic crossings
costs 11
life aboard 13–14
passenger lists 2, 18n.62, 22
prevailing winds and Gulf Stream 12
provisions 13, 358
sea-raids from pirates and corsairs 10, 80, 355, 368

INDEX 393

seasonal patterns 13
shipwrecks 10, 49, 88, 108, 124, 239, 255, 295, 321, 363, 369
speed 12
storms 10, 12, 13, 14, 113, 252, 266, 273, 310
Winthrop Fleet (1630) xxii, 20, 150, 239, 257, 278, 299, 346, 347, 372
see also sea-captains, shipmasters, mariners; ships, transatlantic
Austin, Mr, of New Haven **42**
Austin, Francis, of Guilford (CT) **42**, 174
Avery, Elizabeth, prophet 329
Avis, Elizabeth, maidservant **43**

Bachiler, Stephen, minister **44–5**, 160, 261, 272, 355
Baker, John, religious radical **45–6**, 240
Balch, Freeborn, mariner **46**
baptism 57, 70, 89, 102, 168, 184, 202, 231, 234, 253
baptists xxv, 10, 13, 22, 54, 56, 59, 61, 66, 86, 92, 97, 113, 129, 130, 169, 210–11, 226, 231–2, 274, 288, 293, 298, 312, 314, 325, 327–8, 329, 341, 349
see also orthodoxy and dissent in Massachusetts; religious toleration
Barbados xxii, 48, 93, 94, 161, 230, 291, 296, 297, 299, 355, 364, 365, 366, 369, 370
Barbon [Barebone], Praisegod 300
Barnard, Tobias, Harvard graduate 8n.20, **46**, 65, 68, 93, 203, 267
Barnstable (MA) 81, 102, 148–9, 205, 206, 272
Barrington, Lady Joan 138
Barrington, Sir Thomas 277, 278
Bartholomew, Richard, of Salem **47**
Bartlet, William, minister of Bideford (Devon) 58, 201
Baxter, Richard, minister 57, 78, 104, 109, 198, 214, 257, 258, 279, 330, 331
Beadle, John, minister 37
Bedfordshire 68, 273
Bell, Susanna, of Roxbury and London **47–8**, 172
Bell, Thomas, of Roxbury and London 7, **47–8**, 122, 131, 156, 281, 315, 373, 376
Bell, Thomas, of Boston (MA) **48**
Bellamy, John, of New Haven **49**
Bellingham, Richard, governor of Massachusetts 49, 63, 217, 218, 236, 268–9
Bellingham, Samuel, Harvard graduate and doctor **49**, 65, 68, 93, 199, 267
Bendall, Edward, Boston entrepreneur 7, **50–1**, 117
Bendall, Freegrace, Atlantic trader 10, **51**, 188

Bendall, Hoptfor, Atlantic trader **51**
Benn, William, minister of Dorchester (Dorset) 73, 199, 201
Bennett, Robert, army officer and religious radical 149
Berkshire 69, 138, 329, 330, 331
Bermuda 162, 282–3, 291
Bernard, Masakiell, clothier **52**, 148, 376
Bernard, Richard, minister of Batcombe (Somerset) 52, 376
Betscombe, Richard, of Hingham (MA) **52**
Bidgood, Mary, of Ipswich (MA), abandoned by Richard **52–3**
Bidgood, Richard **53**
Birch, Thomas, parliamentarian army officer 98
Birden, John, Harvard graduate and minister **53**, 203, 303
Bisby [Bisbey], William, of London 64
Biscoe, John, minister 53
Biscoe, John, army colonel 53
Biscoe [Briscoe], Nathaniel, of Watertown 10, **53–4**, 288
Biscoe, Richard, of Uxbridge (Middlesex) 53
Bishop, Townsend, of Salem **54–5**
Blackborne, James, customs official 55
Blackborne, Robert, naval official 55
Blackborne [Blackburn], Walter and Elizabeth 11, **55**
Blackwell, Elidad, London minister 35, 289
Blackwood, Christopher, baptist minister 17n.55, **55–6**, 232
Blake, Robert, army officer and naval commander 295
Blinman, Richard, minister **56–8**, 77, 206, 256
Bond, Sampson, minister 250
books
acquiring books for Harvard and schools 57, 98, 246
dangerous for women 142
illegal distribution, 1630s 345
libraries sold to the New England Company 161, 312
literacy in New England 4
manuscripts lost at sea 124, 255
manuscripts taken to London for printing 23, 141
promoting or critiquing New England xxi, xxiii, xxiv, xxv, xxvi, 139, 183, 244, 311, 318, 324, 325, 336, 352
print culture and religious debate 22
printing press, Harvard Yard xxiv, 23, 118, 310, 372
sermons, catechisms, law codes from New England 34, 40, 140, 141, 208

Boston (MA) *passim*
 church 33, 38, 39, 45, 46, 51, 59, 61, 69, 70, 88, 96, 108, 112, 118, 122, 126, 131, 148, 155, 157, 166, 168, 170–1, 182, 185, 186, 187, 188, 194, 196, 199, 206, 227, 230, 240, 241, 261, 293, 313, 315, 320, 327, 329, 334, 347, 350, 351, 364, 366, 368, 376
 Thursday lecture 113, 249
Bosvile, Godfrey 105, 235, 236
Bourne [*née* Earning], Hannah 58, 59, 60, 61, 96, 196
Bourne, Nehemiah, mariner, shipbuilder, naval official 6, 10, **58–62**, 92, 96, 112, 124, 143, 155, 185, 186, 188, 196, 244, 250, 274, 280, 286, 319, 323, 350, 363, 366
Boyes, Matthew, of Rowley (MA) 11, **62–3**, 67, 230
Boyes [Boyse], Joseph, minister 63
Boyle, Robert, natural philosopher 79, 283, 378
Brackenbury, John, mariner 181, 201, **354**
Brackett, Richard, of Boston and Braintree (MA) **334**
Bradford, William, governor of Plymouth Colony 182, 324, 336, 338, 340, 343, 351
Bradshaw, Lord John, lawyer and regicide 111, 153
Bradstreet, Anne, poet xxvi, 63, 64, 307
Bradstreet, Samuel, Harvard graduate and doctor **63–4**
Bradstreet, Simon, governor of Massachusetts 63, 268, 305
Branford (CT) 64, 98, 163
Brecy [Brasie, Bressey], Mr **64–5**
Brecy [Brasie, Bressey], Mrs 64, **65**
Brereley, Roger, of Yorkshire 194
Brereton, Sir William, Cheshire parliamentarian 39, 98, 213
Brewster, Francis, of New Haven **65**
Brewster, Francis, of Wrentham (Suffolk) 37, 38
Brewster, Nathaniel, Harvard graduate and minister 8n.20, **65–7**, 68, 93, 130, 157, 161, 191, 203, 204, 221, 232, 267
Brewster, Robert, of Wrentham (Suffolk) 37, 253
Bridge, William, minister of Great Yarmouth (Norfolk) 38, 65, 66, 221, 233, 302, 325
Bridges, Robert, of Lynn **354–5**
Brigham, Sebastian, of Rowley (MA) 62, **67**, 218
Bright, Francis, minister 17n.55, 346
Brooke, Lord *see* Greville, Robert
Brooks, Thomas, London minister 48, 83, 221

Brown, Hugh, fisherman and mariner **67–8**
Brown, John and Samuel **335**
Browne, Abraham, Boston mariner **355**
Brownrigg, Ralph, bishop of Exeter 167
Bruise, 'Goodman', of Boxford (Suffolk) **335**
Buckinghamshire
 Aston Clinton 285
 Great Hampden 184
 Leckhampstead 142
 Marsworth 141
 Wooburn 263
 Wraysbury 258, 279
Buckmaster, Laurence, Boston mariner **68**
Bulkeley, John, Harvard graduate and minister 8n.20, 65, **68–9**, 93, 202, 203, 267, 269, 271
Bulkeley, Peter minister 68
Bullock, Edward, husbandman, of Dorchester (MA) **69**
Burden, Ann, of Boston (MA), Quaker 22, **69–70**, 116
Burden, George, of Boston, shoemaker and tanner 11, **70**, 114, 116, 210
Burdett, George, informer, army chaplain, conformist 17n.55, **70–2**, 160, 168
Burr, Jonathan, minister 254
Burroughes, Jeremiah, minister 76, 233
Bury, William, of Boston (MA) **72**
Busby, John, of Boston (MA) **72–3**
Butler Henry, Harvard graduate and minister **73**

Caffinch, John, of New Haven 7, **74**, 255, 316
Calcard, Edward **355–6**
Cambridge (MA) xxii, xxiii, xxiv, 21, 23, 24, 37, 58, 63, 76, 82, 84, 85, 86, 89, 118, 122, 128, 132, 141, 154, 157, 160, 189, 198, 202, 203, 207, 219, 222, 223, 228, 229, 235, 236, 237, 238, 251, 252, 253, 254, 255, 265, 277, 278, 281, 284, 287, 289, 304, 337, 338, 341, 364, 372, 374
Cambridge Platform (1648) xxvi, 325
Cambridge, University of 32, 38, 55, 70, 79, 82, 89, 91, 97, 105, 107, 109, 116, 128, 132, 136, 139, 150, 157, 160, 167, 168, 170, 177, 194, 213, 220, 229, 232, 239, 242, 250, 261, 266, 268, 272, 284, 304, 308, 310, 314, 320, 337, 342, 376
Cambridgeshire 341
 Abbotsley 41
 Elsworth 91
 Eltisley 90, 337
Canary Islands 12, 367
Cape Ann (MA) xxi, xxii, 57, 256, 261
Carleton, Edward, of Rowley (MA) 11, 62, 67, **74–5**, 218

Caribbean xxii, xxiii, xxvii, 5, 12, 15, 41, 50, 94, 122, 151, 154, 182, 243, 245, 274, 325, 358, 364, 369
　Cromwell's 'Western Design' xxvii, 122, 274
　see also Providence Island
Carter, Joseph, of Newbury (MA) **75–6**
Chaplin, Clement, of Hartford **76**
Charles I xxii–xxvi, 2, 5, 8, 106, 109, 130, 152, 153, 245, 331, 345
　art collection sold *see* Winslow, Edward
Charles II and the Restoration of the monarchy (1660) xxvi, xxviii, 1, 2, 5, 6, 91, 93, 135, 140, 186, 276, 330, 350, 377
Charlestown (MA) xxii, 10, 32, 33, 34, 39, 45, 58, 59, 60, 86, 124, 126, 134, 147, 148, 157, 158, 159, 161, 162, 174, 187, 189, 207, 220, 227, 255, 260, 273–4, 322, 337, 354, 357, 363, 364, 371, 375
Chauncy, Charles, president of Harvard 77, 78, 229
Chauncy, Ichabod, physician 77, 78, 271
Chauncy, Isaac, minister 77, **78**
Chesapeake 15
Cheshire 12, 39, 98, 99, 162, 213, 214
　Astbury 213
　Barrow 98
　Bredbury 100
　Chester 40, 56, 66, 96, 98, 99, 130
　Didsbury 268
　Dukinfield 98, 99
　Great Budworth 97, 337
　Knutsford 98
　West Kirby 97, 99
Chickering, Henry, yeoman 11, **356**
Child, Dr Robert, metallurgist, physician, agriculturalist 75, **79–80**, 106, 113, 234, 239, 266, 268, 283, 299, 322, 332
children
　fund to transport poor children to New England 59, 92, 244
　left behind in New England 152, 195–6, 269, 278, 295, 328
　sent for from England 81
Chillenden, Edmund, baptist 329
Church of England
　bishops *see* Brownrigg, Ralph; Cosin, John; Harsnett, Samuel; Laud, William; Lloyd, George; Rutter, Samuel; Skinner, Robert; Williams, John; Wren, Matthew
　Court of High Commission xxiv, 31, 33, 70, 98, 152, 168, 177, 206, 233, 234, 272, 316
　dioceses xxiii, 19
　　Chichester 284

　　Ely 262
　　Exeter 12
　　Lincoln 141, 320
　　Norwich 31, 72
　　Salisbury 337
　　York 272
　religious policies of the 1630s and emigration to New England 19–20
Church in revolutionary England
　colonists and gathered churches, laity 23, 46, 101, 132, 134, 155, 189, 196–7, 232, 285, 292, 302, 313, 329
　colonists and gathered churches, ministers 33, 37, 66, 98, 129, 130, 169, 172, 175, 178–80, 194, 199, 201, 214, 221, 253, 312, 318
　colonists as parish ministers ('public preachers') 33, 35, 36, 39, 50, 66, 68, 73, 76, 78, 104, 109, 110, 126, 129, 132, 134, 136, 137, 138, 145, 149, 161, 169, 171–2, 175, 178, 184, 193, 199, 201, 208, 210, 213, 221, 223, 234, 249–50, 252, 261–2, 262–3, 266, 271, 273, 276, 281, 289, 307, 308, 309, 312, 315, 322, 329, 331
　colonists' certificates to support admission to parish livings 35, 37, 48, 50, 60, 69, 73, 78, 104, 110, 136, 138, 145, 149, 160, 193, 197, 201, 203, 212, 213, 219, 221, 223, 245, 262, 263, 281, 289, 304, 306, 308, 309, 315
　Commission for the Propagation of the Gospel in the Four Northern Counties 281
　'Ejectors', lay county commissioners for removing unsuitable ministers xxvii, 68, 99, 109, 138, 139, 172, 195, 214, 223, 266, 271, 309, 322, 329, 331
　'Triers', or Commissioners for the Approbation of Public Preachers xxvii, 180, 208, 210, 245
　Voluntary Associations of the 1650s
　　Cumberland 282
　　Devon 201
　　Essex 109
　　Worcestershire 109, 214
　see also congregationalists; ministers; presbyterians
churches in New England *see* New England Way
'city on a hill' 26
Civil Wars, English xxiv, xxv, xxvi
　impact on migration 5, 47, 249
　see also army
Clarke, John, of Newport (RI) 325, 357, 377
Clarkson, Laurence, religious radical 231, 260

Clements, John, of Haverhill (MA) and Ireland **80**, 356
Clements, Robert 80, **356**
climate in New England 3, 4, 9, 63
cloth, clothes, clothiers 4, 11, 48, 52, 53, 62, 63, 185, 225, 227, 228, 255, 274, 288, 294, 295, 320, 354, 361, 363, 373, 374
Cockram, William, of Hingham (MA) **80–1**
Coddington, William, merchant and official of Rhode Island 123, 159, **357**, 362, 377
Cogan, Abigail 81
Cogan, Henry, of Barnstable (MA) **81–2**
Cogswell, John, of Ipswich (MA) 82
Cogswell, John Jr, of Ipswich **82**, 340
Cobbett, Thomas, minister 226
Cokayn, George, minister 242
Collins, John, Harvard graduate and minister 48, **82–3**, 132, 136, 156, 202, 287, 320
colonial agents in England xxiv, xxvi, 4, 17n.55, 32, 41, 83, 84, 92, 120, 124, 144, 151, 183, 186, 199, 236, 237, 243–4, 269, 270, 287, 299, 309, 310, 311, 319, 324, 325, 327, 336, 354, 357, 362, 364, 377
communion or Lord's Supper xxi, 19, 20, 31, 33, 70, 97, 168, 170, 224, 227, 252
Concord (MA) 68, 314
congregationalists, congregationalism
  in England xxv, 10, 23, 33, 34, 37, 38, 58, 65, 66, 73, 77, 78, 83, 86, 98, 99, 101, 109, 110, 129, 130, 131, 132, 136, 140, 147, 159, 172, 175, 176, 178–80, 189, 193, 194, 195, 196–7, 199, 201, 202, 203, 208, 213, 214, 221, 223, 245, 252, 253, 271, 272, 282, 285, 291, 292, 298, 302, 308, 312, 313, 314, 318, 335, 347, 365, 367
  in New England *see* New England Way
Cooke, George, colonist and military governor in Ireland 6, **84–5**, 242, 247, 269, 278
Cooke, Joseph, of Cambridge (MA) 84, **85**, 277, 341
Corbet, Clement, chancellor to bishop of Norwich 31, 33, 233, 234, 251
Corbet, John, in Ireland **85–6**, 201, 298
Corlet, Elijah, schoolmaster 86
Cornwell, Francis, baptist 56
Corporation for the Propagation of the Gospel in New England *see* New England Company
Cornwall
  Fowey 242, 249
  Launceston 149, 250
  Mylor 249, 250
  St Buryan 149
Corporation for the Propagation of the Gospel in New England *see* New England Company
Cosin, John, bishop of Durham 126
Cotton, John, minister of Boston (MA) xxiii, xxv, 10, 33, 34, 40, 45, 76, 113, 124, 126, 127, 150, 166, 182, 183, 184, 185, 194, 199, 220, 221, 236, 249, 252, 254, 259, 266, 268, 269, 271, 299, 304, 313, 315, 316, 329, 330, 347, 348, 351, 357
County Durham
  Boldon 309
  Gateshead 21, 312
  Ryton 309
  Whickham 154
covenants
  church 9–10, 20, 37, 39, 99, 126, 149, 179, 180, 224, 244, 252, 291, 317, 352
  civil 9, 74, 90, 135, 163, 316
  release from 9–10
Covert, Richard, London merchant 181
Coytmore, Thomas, sea-captain 260
Cradock, Matthew, London merchant and colonial investor 150, 346, 357
Cradock, Walter, Welsh congregationalist 213
Crane, Robert 271, **335**
Cranford, James, London minister 193
Cromwell, Henry, Lord Deputy of Ireland xxvii, 66, 84, 90, 129, 130, 161, 203–4, 232, 309
Cromwell, Oliver, Lord Protector xxvi–xxviii, 2, 5, 7, 26, 34, 41, 46, 66, 90, 91, 93, 122, 129, 130, 137–8, 139, 161, 171, 185, 245, 246, 274, 292, 298, 300, 312, 325, 341, 342, 377
Cumberland 175, 179, 281
  Carlisle 93, 281–2
  Cockermouth 175, 179, 281, 282
Cushman, Robert, grocer and colonial agent 334, **336**
Cutter, William, of Cambridge (MA) 11, 21, **86–7**, 118, 126, 154, 210, 264, 300

Dalton, Timothy, minister 44, 152
Danson, Thomas, minister 199
Darley, Henry, politician 105, 114
Davenport, John, minister xxiii, 9, 14, 41, 46, 57, 61, 65, 89, 92, 97, 98, 102, 121, 124, 138, 139, 140, 143, 163, 187, 192, 193, 210, 218, 219, 243, 252, 254, 265, 270, 275, 289, 310, 316, 327
Davis, Barnabas, tallow chandler **336–7**
Davis, John, joiner **88**, 295
Davis John, Harvard graduate 64, **88**, 239, 366, 369

Davis, John, minister of Dover (Kent) 196, 201
Davison, Nicholas, of Charlestown **357–8**, 371
Dawson, Henry, Boston labourer 366
Day, Wentworth, colonist, soldier and Fifth Monarchist **88–9**, 301
debate about the legitimacy of emigration to New England 19
debt, debtors 42, 50, 82, 151, 212, 226, 271, 292, 294, 295, 297, 338, 340, 369
Dedham (MA) xxiii, 7, 11, 31, 33, 35, 107, 170, 196, 222, 233, 235, 240, 251, 252, 291, 356, 368, 370, 373
Delaware xxiv, 174, 192, 274, 275
Dell, George, shipmaster **358**
Denton, Richard, minister **89–90**
Derbyshire 124
Desborough [*née* Whitfield], Dorothy 90–1
Desborough [Disbrowe], Isaac 41, **337**
Desborough, John *see* Disbrowe, John
Desborough [Disbrowe], Samuel, of Guilford (CT) 5n.10, 6, 8, 41, **90–1**, 92, 106, 135, 163, 164, 269, 316, 319, 337
Devon
  Axmouth 138, 139
  Bampton 116
  Barnstaple 102, 112, 198, 201, 206, 354
  Bideford 177, 201, 338
  Calverleigh 145
  Colyton 339
  Crediton 176, 177, 212
  Exeter 47, 148, 176, 179, 180, 187, 201, 203
  Great Torrington 198
  Harberton 201
  Heavitree 123, 193
  Holbeton 118
  Northam 175, 177, 211
  Northleigh 148
  Pinhoe 116
  Plymouth 55, 58, 112, 116, 149, 178, 179, 187, 190, 195, 201, 230, 355, 372
  Plympton St Mary 102
  Tavistock 175–80, 181, 212, 354, 356, 367
  Teignmouth 356
  Tiverton 145
  Westleigh 58
  Winkleigh 341
Disbrowe [Desborough], John, parliamentarian army officer and politician 90, 187, 337
dissenters leave New England for England 10, 22
  see also Antinomian Controversy; baptists; Quakers; orthodoxy and dissent in Massachusetts; religious toleration
Dorchester (MA) xxii, 3, 58, 59, 69, 73, 81, 96, 102, 104, 117, 137, 144, 145, 148, 187, 189, 190, 197, 199, 200, 202, 213, 215, 216, 220, 254, 264, 278, 286, 287, 291, 295, 303, 308, 339, 369, 370
Dorchester Company of Adventurers xxi, xxii, 12, 150
Dorset
  Beaminster 137, 144
  Bridport 52, 73, 81
  Dorchester 73, 81, 150, 199, 201, 278
  Fordington 150, 201
  Gillingham 262
  Lyme Regis 177
  Netherbury 137
  Owermoigne 203
  Symondsbury 52, 73, 303
  Weymouth 52, 117, 137, 148, 150, 199
doubts about the wisdom of settling in New England 3, 143, 150
Dover [Northam] (NH) 71, 168, 169, 177, 211, 340, 355–6
Downing, Emmanuel, lawyer and colonial entrepreneur 59, 75, **91–3**, 94, 112, 190, 235, 240, 244, 267, 274, 327
Downing, Sir George, Harvard graduate, diplomat, financial reformer 6, 8n.20, 65, 68, 91, 92, **93–4**, 202, 203, 236, 267, 328
Downing, Joshua **94**
Downing, Lucy 83, **91–3**, 94, 119, 221, 267
Duckenfield [Duckenfeild], Robert, army officer 56, 98
Duckett, Charles, army officer 167
Dudley, Thomas, governor of Massachusetts 69, 166, 182, 184, 237, 271, 331, 346, 347, 358
Dummer, Richard 44, 94, 217, 218, 348, **358–9**
Dummer, Stephen and Alice, of Newbury (MA) 22, **94–5**, 217, 261–2, 276, 358
Dunkirk 77, 122
Dunster, Henry, president of Harvard 21, 68, 84, 86, 118, 119, 126, 191, 193, 198, 207, 210–11, 237, 253, 265, 269, 277, 278, 287, 356, 375
Durant, John, minister of Canterbury (Kent) 201
Duxbury (MA) 174, 281, 294, 365
Dyer, Mary, Quaker xxviii, **359**
Dyer, William, antinomian 123, **359**

Earning, Katherine, widow 58, 60, **96**
East Anglia 6, 9, 12, 47, 70, 160, 196, 234, 252, 351
Eaton, Alexander, Wapping apothecary 228, 229
Eaton [formerly Yale], Ann, baptist 10, **96–7**, 142, 143, 332, 333
Eaton, Hannah **97**, 142, 332

Eaton, Nathaniel, disgraced head of Harvard 17n.55, 54, 58, 251, 265, 277, 321, **337–8**
Eaton, Samuel, minister 17n.55, 56, 96, **97–101**, 129, 130, 161, 214, 298, 337
Eaton, Theophilus, governor of New Haven Colony and husband of Ann xxviii, 92, 96–7, 98, 102, 121, 124, 134, 142, 143, 144, 187, 192, 265, 284, 332
Eaton, Theophilus Jr **97**, 142, 332
Edwards, Elizabeth, of Salem and Great Yarmouth 23, **101**
Edwards, Nathaniel **101**
Edwards, Thomas, shoemaker 11, **101**, 280
Edwards, Thomas, author of *Gangraena* 22, 57, 93, 98, 109, 169, 178, 196–7, 231, 241, 247, 311, 312, 357
Eeles, John, of Dorchester (MA) **102**
Eliot, John, minister 41, 48, 122, 161, 220, 245, 254, 271, 306, 310, 318, 326, 366
Elmes, Rodolphus, of Scituate **359–60**
emigration to New England *see* migration
Endecott, John, governor of Massachusetts xxii, 151, 152, 186, 191, 226, 243, 263
Essex 109, 193, 252, 341
  Bishop's Stortford 193
  Boreham 126, 188
  Bures 128, 235, 237, 238
  Chelmsford 141, 271, 373
  Coggeshall 77, 133, 271, 272, 286, 335, 342
  Colchester 84, 108, 109, 170, 171, 271, 308
  Copford Hall 133, 341
  Debden 350
  Dedham 107, 170, 222, 233, 235, 240
  Dengie *see* Tillingham
  Earls Colne 235, 271, 367
  Fordham 68, 160
  Gravesend 131, 152, 201, 203, 277, 370
  Great Yeldham 84, 85
  Henham 193
  High Laver 52, 193, 376
  Kelvedon 271
  Langford near Maldon 271, 363
  Lawford 240
  Little Baddow 141, 299
  Nazeing 41, 126
  Ovington 110
  Pebmarsh 84
  Prittlewell 299
  Radwinter 215
  Rayleigh 242, 243
  Ridgewell 109
  Shalford 109
  Shenfield 307
  South Hanningfield 104, 245
  Springfield 257
  Stanway 85, 133
  Stondon Massey 304, 307
  Tendring 146
  Terling 13, 309, 310, 312, 357
  Tillingham 215, 216
  Wanstead 136
  Wickford 243, 263–4
Evance, John, of New Haven 91, **102**
Evance [later Hatsell], Susanna, of New Haven 65, **102**
Exeter (NH) 45, 194, 220, 261, 315, 355
'extraordinary cause' for leaving England and duty to return if times change 20
emigration as 'exile' 19, 71, 72, 128, 144, 177, 182, 208, 234
Eyre, William, minister in Salisbury (Wiltshire) 77, 329, 331
Eyton, Sampson, Harvard student **102–3**

Fairfield, Daniel, convicted of child abuse **104**, 152
Fairfield (CT) 190, 249
Farnworth, Joseph, Harvard student and minister **104–5**, 245
fast days in New England for England xxiv, 139
Feake, Robert, goldsmith and merchant **360**
Fenwick, Dorothy and Elizabeth **107**
Fenwick, George, of Saybrook (CT) and governor of Edinburgh and Leith 10, 86, 90, **105–7**, 118, 203, 236, 249, 264, 269, 316, 317
Fenwick, Mary 105, **107**
Fiennes, Nathaniel, politician and army officer 285
Fiennes, William, first Viscount Saye and Sele xxiii, 105, 150, 269, 316, 336, 347
Fifth Monarchists 6, 40, 66, 89, 130, 169, 232, 289, 300, 341, 349
Firmin, Giles, minister 7, 14n.46, 21–2, **107–10**, 246, 255, 271, 305, 369
Firmin, Susan, Giles Jr and Nathaniel 107–10
fish, fishermen, fishmongers xxi, 9, 11, 12, 13, 55, 67, 112, 116, 148, 150, 177, 185, 261, 298, 335, 346, 357, 372
Flavell, John, minister 201
Fleetwood, Lord Charles 66, 160, 210, 232, 245, 341
Fletcher, Edward and Mary, of Boston (MA) **110–11**
Fletcher, William, minister 111
Floyd [Lloyd] Richard, member of New England Company **111**, 237, 350
Fogg, Ralph, of Salem 55, **111–12**, 300
Foote, Joshua, London merchant 70, 72
Forbes, James, minister in Gloucester (Gloucestershire) 110, 111, 199

Forrett, James, colonial agent **112**
Foster, Samuel, mathematician 147
Fowle, Margaret 112, 113
Fowle, Thomas, Boston merchant and Remonstrant 55, 59, 75, 79, 92, 106, **112–14**, 127, 185, 239, 249, 266, 274, 299, 325, 332, 345
Fox, George, Quaker 195
Franklin, William, blacksmith **114**, 210
Frith, Philip, of Rye (Sussex) 35, 284
Fugill, Thomas, disgraced surveyor 7, **114–15**, 133, 219
furs, fur trade 9, 13, 47, 112, 116, 127, 174, 257, 344

Gardiner, Sir Christopher 150, **338–9**, 346, 347
Gardner, Peter, merchant 280, **361**
Garnesey, Elizabeth, of York (ME) **116**
Gibbons, Edward, Boston merchant 60, 113, 116, 127, 361, 363
Gibbons, Margaret, widow of Edward **116**
Gibson, Mary **116–17**
Gibson, Richard, minister 17n.55, **116–17**
Gifford, Abigail, widow 334, **339**
Gifford, John, ironworker **361**
Gilbert, Thomas, of Taunton (MA) 50, **117**, 189, 221
Gill, Arthur, ship carpenter **117–18**
Gill, Thomas **118**
Gillett, Jonathan **339**
Gloucester (MA) 57, 256, 279
Gloucestershire 110, 198
    Bagendon 110–11
    Badgeworth 217
    Forest of Dean 361
    Gloucester 111, 136, 199
    Tetbury 336
    Tewkesbury 336
    Todenham 293
Glover, John, Harvard graduate and physician 86, **118–19**, 201
Glover, Jose [Joseph], minister 118–19
Glover, Roger, died at the siege of Edinburgh Castle (1650) 118, **119**
Goad, Thomas, apprentice **339**
Godfrey, Edward, of York (ME) 46, **120**, 149
Godfrey, Oliver, of York (ME) **120**
Goffe, William, regicide and major-general xxviii, 122, 138, 140, 270, 318, 319
Goodwin, John, London minister 285
Goodwin, Thomas, English congregationalist 10, 129, 132, 136, 147, 155, 193, 203, 245, 285
Goodyear, Mrs, died at sea 121, 174
Goodyear, Stephen, of New Haven **120–1**, 124, 174, 192, 219, 284

Gookin, Daniel, merchant 64, **121–2**
Gookin, Sir Vincent 121
Gookin, Vincent 121
Gorges, Sir Ferdinando, promoter of colonization xxi, xxiii, 120, 123, 140, 150, 160, 338, 339–40, 344, 346
Gorges, Robert 123, **339–40**
Gorges, Thomas 71, **123**
Gorges, William 123, **340**
Gorton, Samuel, of Shawomet 68, 84, 106, 236, 324, 325, 326, 357, **361–2**
Gould, Jeremiah, of Rhode Island **123**
Graves, Thomas, shipbuilder and rear-admiral 59, 60, **124**, 135
'Great Migration' *see* migration
Greenhill, William, minister at Stepney (Middlesex) 96, 129, 131, 134, 156, 172, 203, 221, 233, 236, 292, 322, 325
Greenwich (CT) 360
Gregson, Thomas, of New Haven 121, **124–5**, 174, 192, 255
Greville, Robert, second Baron Brooke xxiii, 150, 316, 336, 347
Griffiths, George, London minister 129, 130
Guernsey (Channel Islands) 198–9
Guilford (CT) 8, 11, 41, 42, 74, 90, 91, 135, 163, 164, 317–18, 319, 350

Hadden [Hawden, Hawdon], George, Harvard graduate 86, **126**
Haines, Samuel, servant 82, **340**
Half-Way Covenant *see* New England Way
Hall, Samuel, merchant **362–3**
Hampshire
    Basingstoke 138
    Bishopstoke 94, 95, 262, 276, 277, 358
    Burghclere 330
    Highclere 330
    Hook 139
    Kings Worthy 138
    Knights Enham 78
    Newton Stacey 44
    North Baddesley 276, 277
    Portsmouth 198, 223, 322, 323, 344
    Romsey 53, 217, 277
    Stoneham 44, 217
    Titchfield 223
    Upper Clatford 139
    Wherwell 44
    Winchester 261, 318, 319
Hampton (NH) 44, 45, 272, 355, 363
Harding, Robert, Atlantic trader 112, 113, **126–7**, 184, 185, 188, 266, 325, 373
Harding, Robert, in Ireland **127–8**
Harlakenden, Elizabeth and Mary **128**, 238
Harlakenden, Roger 84, 85, 128, 235, 236
Harrison, John Jr, law student **340–1**

Harrison, Thomas, minister 50, 66, 98, 115, **128–31**, 161, 201, 202, 203, 204, 213, 232, 298, 325

Harrison, Thomas, parliamentarian army officer and regicide 89, 260

Harsnett, Samuel, bishop of Norwich 232, 233

Hartford (CT) xxiii, 24, 64, 76, 88, 133, 141, 143, 189, 279, 284, 303, 341, 352, 364, 366

Hartlib, Samuel, educational reformer and writer 80, 378

Haverhill (MA) 75, 80, 108, 305, 306, 356

Harvard, John, minister 32, 33

Harvard College
  early difficulties 54, 251, 265, 277, 337–8
  graduates and students go to England xxiv, xxvi, 1, 6, 7, 8, 17, 18, 35, 36, 37, 38, 46, 49, 53, 63, 64, 65, 68, 73, 77, 78, 82, 88, 93, 102–3, 104, 126, 132, 133, 136, 137, 138, 146, 157, 191, 192, 193, 197–8, 200–1, 202, 203, 205, 210, 211, 213, 222, 229, 239, 245, 252, 262, 265, 267, 281, 283, 284, 287, 289, 303, 304, 306, 309, 316, 320, 323, 326, 327, 329, 365, 366
  presidents *see* Chauncy, Charles; Dunster, Henry; Hoar, Leonard; Mather, Increase; Oakes, Urian; Rogers, John

Harwood [*née* Usher], Elizabeth 131–2, 375

Harwood, John, merchant tailor **131–2**, 219, 375

Hatherley, Timothy, felt-maker and merchant **341**

Hatley, Philip, of Milford (CT) 41, **132**, 156, 285

Hatsell, Henry, naval official and politician 102

Hawkins, Thomas, shipwright and sea-captain 58, 127, 255, 280, **363**, 369

Hay, William, MP 35

Hayden, James, mariner **363–4**

Haynes, Hezekiah, deputy major-general 6, 91, 132, **341–2**, 364

Haynes, John, governor of Connecticut 85, 132, 143, 190, 236, 341, **364**

Haynes, John Jr, Harvard graduate and minister 85, **132–3**, 341, 364

Haynes, Roger, Harvard student and soldier 132, **133**, 341, 364

Hefford [Heifer, Heyford], Samuel, of Ipswich (MA) **133**

Hempstead, Long Island (NY) 89

Herefordshire 56, 142

Hertfordshire 12, 41, 132
  Little Hadham 41
  St Albans 296, 297
  Ware 77

Hewson, John, army officer and regicide 129

Heywood, Oliver, minister 89, 100, 138, 194

Hibbins, William, colonial agent 18n.61, 92, 148, 241, 243–4, 311, **364**, 367

Higginson, Charles **133**

Higginson, Elizabeth 219, 255

Higginson, Francis, minister 133, 134, 135

Higginson, Francis Jr, minister **134**, 263

Higginson, John, minister 134, 317, 318, 319

Higginson, Samuel, naval officer **134–5**

Higginson, Theophilus, of New Haven 254, 255, 318

Higginson, Timothy, naval officer **135**

Hingham (MA) 11, 52, 80, 81, 148, 196, 215, 234, 280, 365, 367

Hoadley, John, of Guilford (CT) 91, **135–6**, 316, 317

Hoar, Leonard, president of Harvard 83, **136**, 172, 211, 223

Hobart, Joshua, Harvard graduate and minister 299, **365**

Hobart, Peter, minister 81, 148, 215, 234, 365

Holland, Cornelius, politician and regicide 160

Holland, Jeremiah, Harvard graduate and minister **137**, 203

Hollard, Angel, shoemaker 11, 137

Hollingworth, Richard, Lancashire minister 98–9

Holmes, William **365**

Hooke, Ebenezer **137**

Hooke [*née* Whalley], Jane **137–8**

Hooke, John, minister **138**, 219

Hooke, Walter, chaplain **138–9**

Hooke, William, minister xxiv, 12n.34, 33, 46, 57, 104, 136, 137, 138, **139–40**, 172, 193, 198, 219, 270, 289, 322

Hooke, William, merchant **140–1**

Hooker, John, son of Thomas **141–2**

Hooker, Thomas, minister xxiii, 76, 141, 252, 255, 304, 310, 311, 316, 334

Hopkins [*née* Yale], Ann 96, **142**, 143, 332, 333

Hopkins, Edward, of Hartford 6, 61, 91, 106, **142–4**, 155, 186, 192, 281, 319, 323, 332, 333, 350

Horsford [Hosford], William, of Windsor (CT) **144–5**

hostility towards settlers who left 8–10

Houghton, Robert, of Southwark 185, 244, 273, 274

Howe, John, minister 198, 201

Hubbard, Benjamin, of Charlestown **147**, 158

Hubbard, 'Fra:' *see* Hubbard, Nathaniel

Hubbard, Nathaniel **146–7**, 201

Hubbard, William, Harvard graduate, minister, historian 8n.20, 63, 65, 68, 93, 146, 267, 317, 335

INDEX

Huckens, Thomas **365**
Hudson, William, Boston baker **148**, 366
Hudson, William Jr, innkeeper 47, 59, 72, 148, 185, 188, 286, **366**
Hughes, George, of Plymouth (Devon), minister 149, 178, 179, 201
Hull (MA) 206, 207
Hull, John, merchant and mintmaster 49, 51, 285, 287
Hull, Joseph, minister 10, 12n.34, 52, **148–9**, 245
Humfrey, John, colonist and parliamentarian army officer xxiv, 6, 10, 104, **150–3**, 154, 226, 235, 243, 245, 251, 260, 269, 300, 310
Humfrey, John Jr, parliamentarian army officer **154**
Humfrey, Joseph **154**
Hutchin, George, wheelwright **154**
Hutchinson, Anne, of Boston, antinomian xxiii, xxiv, 50, 88, 108, 126, 155, 163, 183, 194, 224, 230, 305, 310, 315, 350, 357, 358, 359, 376
  grandchildren baptized at Stepney 156
Hutchinson, Edward, colonist and brother-in-law of Anne **155**, 194
Hutchinson, Richard, brother-in-law of Anne, London merchant 55, 111, 143, 155–6, 192, 193
Hutchinson, Richard, of Boston and London, son of Anne 22, 111, 132, 143, **155–6**, 192, 285

Ince, Jonathan, Harvard graduate 64, 88, 239, **366**, 369
Independents, Independency, in England xxv, 57, 68, 83, 98, 109, 129, 130, 131, 146, 162, 178, 209, 232, 241, 242, 245, 247, 252, 306, 325, 357
  see also congregationalists
inheritance
  conditional on living in New England 72, 167, 353
  return to England triggered by 9, 36, 188, 212, 260, 308
invitations to leave New England xxvi, 7, 8, 10, 33, 63, 85, 92, 128, 171, 191, 206, 208, 234, 245, 247, 249, 298, 317, 354
Ipswich (MA) xxiii, 20, 44, 53, 62, 63, 82, 85, 108, 119, 129, 146, 198, 200, 217, 230, 261, 263, 268, 269, 276, 280, 294, 296, 297, 298, 304, 305, 335, 340, 342, 348, 362, 375, 377
Ireland
  Carrickfergus, Co. Antrim 205, 296, 298
  Castledermot, Co. Kildare 80

  Drogheda, Co. Louth 161
  Dublin 56, 66, 70, 91, 97, 99, 127, 129, 130, 162, 191, 198, 202, 203, 204, 211, 232, 255, 289, 298
  Kilkenny 56, 232
  Limerick, Co. Limerick 71, 162, 292
  Lisburn, Co. Antrim 80
  New Ross, Co. Wexford 365
  Roscrea, Co. Tipperary 281
  Rosegarland Castle, Co. Wexford 212
  Waterford, Co. Waterford 210, 211, 232, 358
  Wexford, Co. Wexford 56, 84
  see also army in Ireland; invitations to leave New England
ironworks
  New Haven xxvii, 121
  Saugus xxv, xxvi, 79, 92, 152, 244, 274, 354, 355, 361, 369, 377
Isles of Shoals 116, 120, 149, 343

James, Abraham, Harvard student and minister **157**, 203
James, Thomas, minister 121, 147, **157–9**, 171, 263, 308
Jay, Walter, mariner **367**
Jeake, Samuel, of Rye (Sussex) 35
Jeffreys, Robert, settler and financial administrator **159–60**
Jenner, Thomas, minister 65, 66, 99, 129, 130, **160–2**, 204, 213
Jennings, Richard, minister 170, **342–3**
Jennison, William, of Watertown **162–3**
Jessey [Jacie], Henry, minister 111, 169, 218, 335
Jollie, Thomas, minister 194
Jones, John, minister 249
Jones, Lord Philip, governor of Swansea 208, 209
Jones, Thomas, of Guilford (CT) 91, **163**
Jordan, Thomas, of Guilford (CT) 11, 91, **164**, 316, 319
Josselin, Abraham, colonist **367–8**
Josselin, Grace, colonist 367
Josselin, Ralph, of Earls Colne (Essex) 68, 237, 271, 342, 367–8
Josselyn, John, travel writer 345
Jupe, Benjamin, of Boston **164–5**, 166, 212

Keayne, Benjamin, London merchant 164, **166–7**, 368
Keayne, Robert, Boston merchant 164, 166–7, 212, 278, 295, 344, 368
Keayne [*née* Dudley], Sarah, radical preacher 166, **368**
Kem, Samuel, minister 238

401

Kent 12, 56, 79, 135, 198, 245
  Ashford 73, 281, 282
  Canterbury 121, 197, 201, 213, 262, 282, 336
  Chatham 148
  Cranbrook 56, 282, 288, 316
  Dover 196, 197, 201, 221, 282
  Greenwich 178
  Horsmonden 262–3
  Lenham 164
  Maidstone 94, 271, 282
  Northfleet 79
  Rolvenden 135
  Sandwich 199, 201, 203, 281, 282
  Seale 120
  Stockbury 55
  Tenterden 7, 74
  West Farleigh 271
  Wilmington 120
Kent, Joshua and Mary, of Dedham (MA) **368**
Kerman, shipmaster **368–9**
Kiffin, William, baptist 213, 232
Kirby, Francis, London merchant 75–6
Knight, William, minister **167–8**
Knollys, Hanserd, baptist minister 13, 17n.55, 22, 71, **168–70**, 177–8, 232, 293, 349, 355
Knowles, John, minister 34, 48, 121, 136, 140, 158, **170–3**, 270, 298, 321, 322, 342
Knowles, John, antitrinitarian 99

Lahorne, Rowland, cordwainer **174**
Lamberton, George, merchant 42, 49, 65, 121, 124, **174**, 192, 321
Lancaster (MA) 220, 349, 367
Lancashire 12, 99, 198, 214
  Birch 98
  Bolton le Moors 89
  Burtonwood 204
  Childwall 36
  Denton 38, 40, 99, 100
  Gorton 99, 361
  Manchester 38, 39, 99, 276
  Much Woolton 200, 202
  Prescot 213
  Prestwich 39
  Ringley 39
  Toxteth 36, 37
  Walton 36
Lane, Job, of Dorchester (MA) 123, 131, **369**
Larkham, George, minister in Cumberland **175**, 211, 281, 282,
Larkham, Jane **175–6**, 181, 211
Larkham, Patience 175, **176–7**, 181, 211
Larkham, Patience, daughter of Thomas see Miller, Joseph and Patience

Larkham, Thomas, minister at Tavistock (Devon) 7, 12n.34, 17n.55, 117, 169, 175, 176, **177–81**, 201, 211, 212, 354, 355, 356, 367
Larkham, Thomas Jr **181**, 211
Latham, William, *Mayflower* emigrant **182**
Laud, William, archbishop of Canterbury xxi, xxii, xxiii, xxiv, xxv, 71, 77, 141, 243, 245, 246, 304, 310, 311, 316
Laudian policies in the 1630s xxiii, 7, 19, 20, 182, 243, 304, 350
Lechford, Thomas, of Boston, lawyer and critic of New England 11, 18n.61, 22, 31, 32, 57, 139, 160, 169, 170, 171, **182–3**, 184, 190, 234, 243, 251, 261, 273, 286, 336, 371
Leader, Richard, ironworker 79, 92, **369**
Leete, William, of Guilford (CT) 8, 41, 91, 135, 163, 164, 317
Leicestershire
  Ab Kettleby 262
  Pickwell 309
  Wanlip 309, 312
Lely, Sir Peter, artist 185
Lenthall, Robert, minister 10, 17n.55, 22, 126, **183–4**
letters of attorney for business in England 23, 47, 50, 52, 60, 65, 96, 102, 105, 113, 114, 117, 127, 148, 154, 185, 188, 196, 228, 295, 297, 361, 371, 372, 373
Leverett, John, governor of Massachusetts 59, 61, 83, 120, 127, 144, 172, **184–6**, 188, 274, 275, 286, 325, 366
Leverett [née Sedgwick], Sarah 185, **186**
Ley, Sir James, third earl of Marlborough 343
Lincolnshire 13, 39, 48, 75, 156, 169, 170, 235, 237, 263
  Aby 315, 322
  Alford 155, 194
  Belleau 168, 315, 332, 350
  Bilsby 314
  Boston xxiii, 76, 184, 235, 357, 364
  Butterwick 320
  Horbling 63
  Humberston 168
  Leverton 320
  Lincoln 286, 322
  Louth 168
  Saleby 314
  Scartho 168, 169
  Skirbeck 157, 320
  Sutterton 230
  Swaby 315, 332
  Swineshead, Smeeth Hall 237
Ling, Benjamin, of New Haven **187**, 192
Lippincott, Richard and Abigail, of Boston, Quakers 22, **187–8**

Lippincott, Remember, Restore, Freedom, Increase and Preserve 188
Lisle, Francis, barber-surgeon 51, 55, 59, 185, **188**, 286, 366
Lloyd, George, bishop of Chester 96
Lloyd, Richard *see* Floyd, Richard
Llwyd, Morgan, minister 256
London, City of
  Bunhill Fields, burial ground 61, 83, 140, 202
  Fire of London (1666) 48
  Great Plague (1665) 35, 48, 119, 172, 232, 283
  parishes
    All Hallows Barking 48, 173, 300
    All Hallows Lombard Street 132, 285
    All Hallows Staining 45
    All Hallows the Great 172
    St Andrew Undershaft 35, 289
    St Antholin 83, 223
    St Augustine's Watling Street 128
    St Benet Gracechurch 201, 203, 223
    St Botolph without Aldgate 117, 164
    St Dunstan in the East 129, 132, 155, 221, 285, 364
    St Giles Cripplegate 83, 194, 242, 312, 335
    St Helen's Bishopsgate 76
    St James Piccadilly 304
    St Katharine by the Tower 69, 172, 334
    St Katherine Coleman 323
    St Leonard Eastcheap 102, 221
    St Leonard Shoreditch 261
    St Magnus the Martyr 219
    St Margaret Moses 262, 291
    St Margaret's Fish Street 221
    St Martin-in-the-Fields 97
    St Martin Ironmonger Lane 262
    St Martin Ludgate 138
    St Martin Orgar 289
    St Mary Aldermanbury 102, 289
    St Mary Axe 188
    St Mary le Bow 128
    St Michael's Crooked Lane 55
    St Nicholas Acons 289, 360
    St Olave's Hart Street 144
    St Sepulchre Holborn 182, 243
    St Stephen's Coleman Street 97, 102, 119, 142, 144, 192, 193, 218, 219, 265, 275, 285, 332
    St Thomas the Apostle 283
  prisons
    Fleet 142, 143
    Ludgate 120
    Newgate 46, 169
  Savoy Chapel, Hospital, Palace 138, 140
    see also Savoy Conference
  streets
    Bell Lane, Spitalfields 83
    Birchin Lane 167, 212
    Cannon Street 172
    Cheapside 55, 111
    Coleman Street
      Bell Alley 231
      Swan Alley 300
    Downing Street 6, 94
    Duke's Place, Aldgate 83
    Eastcheap 172
    Fenchurch Street 202
    Fetter Lane 280, 361
    Fish Street 123
    Foster Lane 112, 283
    Gracechurch Street 72
    Leadenhall Street 219
    Lime Street, Paved Alley 83, 202
    Mark Lane 45, 78
    Pudding Lane 131–2
    Red Cross Street 242
    Seething Lane 48, 144, 301, 323
    Spittleyard, Bishopsgate 140
    West Harding Street 140
  The [Royal] Exchange 79, 131, 322, 327, 372
  Tower of London and Tower Hill xxiv, 6, 7, 231, 242, 248, 282, 300, 301, 311, 323, 334, 341, 345
London merchants *see* Andrewes, Sir Thomas; Ashurst, Henry; Bell, Thomas; Bellamy, John; Bisby, William; Brewster, Francis; Cogswell, John; Covert, Richard; Craddock, Matthew; Davison, Nicholas; Eaton, Theophilus; Evance, John Foote; Joshua; Gregson, Thomas; Harwood, John; Hopkins, Edward Houghton, Robert; Hutchinson, Richard; Kirby, Francis; Lynd, Simon; Malbon, Richard; Newman, Robert; Peake, William; Pennoyer, William; Pocock, John; Rowe, Owen; Sedgwick, Robert; Tomson, Robert; Woodcock, William; Yale, David; Yale, Thomas
Longe, Joseph, returned to England to collect a legacy 117, **188–9**
Lord, Robert and Rebecca **189**, 292
Lothropp, John, minister 56, 148, 205, 272
Lowle, Mary, orphan **190**
Lowry, Thomas, minister 272, 309
Ludlow, Edmund, regicide 190
Ludlow, Roger, colonial governor and jurist 6, 66, 76, **190–1**, 255
Lynd, Simon, London merchant 50

Lynn (MA) 44, 85, 145, 146, 150, 152, 154, 166, 171, 172, 207, 226, 231, 265, 266, 293, 295, 320, 321, 337, 352, 355, 361, 369
Lyon, Richard, sent to Harvard as tutor to William Mildmay **191**, 211

Machin, John, Cheshire minister 213–4
Mainwaring, Roger, bishop of St David's 206
Malbon, Richard, merchant 121, 124, 143, **192–3**, 219
Malbon, Samuel, Harvard student and minister 192, **193–4**, 201, 219
Malden (MA) 63, 137, 174, 185, 191, 207–8, 215, 279, 369
major-generals, Cromwellian xxvii, 90, 138, 187, 318, 319, 341
Manchester, earl of *see* Montagu, Edward
Marblehead (MA) 279
Marsden, Gamaliel, minister 195, 204
Marshall, Christopher, minister 10, 175, **194–5**, 271
Marshall [*née* Hutchinson], Sarah 194, 195
Marshall, Stephen, minister of Finchingfield (Essex) 109
Marshall, Thomas, of Rye (Sussex) 35
Martha's Vineyard 318, 369
Martin, Francis, merchant 60, **195–6**
Martin, Isaac, of Hingham (MA) **196**
Maryland xxiii
Mascall, Robert **196–7**, 282
Massachusetts Artillery Company 39, 47, 50, 51, 55, 84, 85, 88, 110, 126, 146, 166, 167, 185, 188, 210, 228, 230, 236, 260, 267, 274, 277, 286, 293, 295, 300, 313, 322, 327, 331, 354, 363, 365, 376
Mather, Increase, Harvard graduate, minister and president of Harvard 1, 3, 5, 49, 57, 77, 138, **197–200**, 201, 202, 204, 308, 313, 314, 316
Mather, Nathaniel, minister 49, 83, 85–6, 118, 146, 156, 193, 197, 199, **200–2**, 203, 222, 281, 282, 289, 298, 354
Mather, Richard, minister xxv, 3, 52, 73, 158, 197, 198, 220, 254, 259
Mather, Samuel, minister 7, 8, 35, 46, 53, 65, 66, 68, 99, 102, 129, 130, 137, 157, 162, 193, 197, 198, 201, **202–4**, 232, 267, 222, 232, 267, 281, 289, 303, 329
Matthews, Katherine 205, 206, 208, 209
Matthews, Lemuel, student at Oxford and minister **205**, 206, 209
Matthews, Manasseh, Harvard student and minister **205**, 206, 209
Matthews, Marmaduke, minister 10, 149, 185, 191, 205, **206–9**, 210
Matthews, Mordecai, Harvard graduate and minister 205, 206, **209–10**

Maverick, John, minister 12n.34
Maverick, Samuel, Remonstrant 75, 79, 113, 120, 192, 239, 299, 322
Mayhew, Thomas, minister 127, 161, 318, 369
Mayhew, Thomas Jr, minister 64, 88, 239, 366, **369–70**
Members of Parliament 35, 37, 53, 90, 93, 105, 106, 123, 130, 143, 160, 213, 237, 323, 328, 341
Metcalfe, Michael, of Norwich (Norfolk) and Dedham (MA) 33
Middlesex
  Bethnal Green 89, 131
  Hackney 45
  Isleworth 171, 223, 321, 322
  Stepney 46, 67, 70, 96, 99, 131, 133, 134, 135, 156, 172, 189, 221, 227, 232, 236, 261, 273, 292, 299, 322, 329, 357, 363
  Twickenham 171, 322
  Uxbridge 53
  Wapping 46, 58, 61, 69, 104, 172, 228, 229, 260, 322
migration
  back from New England 4–5
    character 5–8
    extent 1, 16–18
    friction over departures 8
    motives 9–12
  'Great Migration' of the 1630s 2, 3–4
    background of emigrants 3–4
    motives 18–22
  to New England in the 1660s 5
Milam [Mileham, Millard, Mylam], John, of Boston (MA) 11, 86, 114, 127, **210–11**, 300, 358
Mildmay, Sir Henry, parliamentarian and regicide 136, 191, 211
Mildmay, William, Harvard graduate 136, 191, **211**
Miles, John, baptist 226
Milford (CT) 5, 41, 85, 132, 184, 285
Miller, John, minister 171, 210
Miller, Joseph and Patience 175, 176, 181, **211–12**
ministers
  as migrants to and from New England 16–17, 19–22
  ex-colonists conform at or after the Restoration 36, 39, 71, 126, 132–3, 134, 138, 141, 167, 205, 210, 262, 263, 284, 289, 310, 320, 330, 338
  ex-colonists ejected or resign at the Restoration 34, 35, 36, 38, 57, 66, 68, 73, 78, 104, 109, 111, 130, 136, 140, 145, 149, 159, 169, 172, 175, 180, 193, 195, 199, 201, 204, 209, 214, 215, 221, 223, 253, 262, 271, 282, 308, 309, 322, 330, 331

see also Church in revolutionary England
Minter, Desire, *Mayflower* emigrant **343**
Mitchell, Jonathan, Harvard graduate and minister 35, 68, 137, 157, 193, 198, 203, 222, 223, 267, 281, 287, 303, 329
Montagu, Edward, earl of Manchester and parliamentarian 169, 188
Morse, John, Boston salt-maker 11, 164, 165, **212–13**, 262, 274, 291, 370
Morse, John, Dedham tailor 213, **370**
Morse [*née* Jupe], Mary, of Boston (MA) 164, 165, 166, **212–13**, 370
Morton, Thomas, lawyer xxi, 92, 150, 324, 338, **343–4**, 346, 347
Moulson, Lady Ann, benefactor 244
Moxon, George, minister 145, **213–14**, 258, 279
Moxon, George Jr, minister **214–15**
Munnings, Edmund and Mary, of Dorchester (MA) **215–16**, 370
Munnings, Hopestill 215, **216**, 370
Munnings, Mahalaleel 14, 215, 216, 295, **370–1**
Munnings, Return 3, 197, 215–16, 370
Munnings, Takeheed 215, **216**, 370
Murcot, John, minister 99

navy, Cromwellian xxvi, 5, 61, 124, 134, 135, 143, 144, 155–6, 185–6, 323
  naval chaplains 201, 213, 214, 221
  naval commissioners 6, 61, 118, 143, 155, 186, 319, 323, 350
Nayler, James, Quaker 195
Neale, Walter, fur trader **344**
Nelson [Dummer], Joan 94, **217**, 358
Nelson, Thomas, of Rowley (MA) 74, **217–8**, 358
Netherlands 19, 37, 169, 243, 245, 347
  Amsterdam 193, 310
  Franeker 337
  Leiden 49, 77, 79, 134, 267, 294, 324, 336, 350
  Rotterdam 33, 37, 61, 81, 141, 202, 243, 251, 263
  The Hague 93
  see also Anglo-Dutch war; New Netherland
New England Company xxi, xxvi, 33, 48, 57, 111, 150, 161, 237, 245, 250, 312, 318, 325, 326, 335, 349, 366, 375
New England Way xxv, xxvi, 15, 20, 21–2, 26, 33, 79, 89, 109, 160, 244, 266–7, 271, 311, 313, 352
  Half-Way Covenant 57, 308
New Haven (CT) xxvii, 2, 7, 9, 39, 42, 49, 57, 64, 65, 74, 88, 97, 98, 102, 112, 114, 115, 120, 121, 124, 125, 133, 134, 135, 138, 139, 140, 142, 143, 144, 158, 171, 174, 187, 192, 193, 218, 219, 254, 255, 265, 275, 284, 289, 295, 316, 319, 320, 321, 332, 333, 337, 360, 366, 368
New Haven Colony xxiv, xxv, xxviii, 1, 10, 41, 89, 97, 121, 124, 187, 192, 219, 316, 319, 350
New Jersey 35, 187
New London (CT) *see* Pequot Plantation
New Model Army *see* army
New Netherland xxii, xxvii, 5, 41, 89, 91, 146, 164, 186, 190, 192, 246, 274, 275, 292, 324, 360, 362
Newbury (MA) xxiii, 22, 44, 45, 72, 76, 94, 190, 240, 262, 276, 277, 294, 331, 348, 358, 359, 363
Newcome, Henry, minister 99, 214, 268
Newfoundland 12, 13, 17, 57, 60, 177, 199
Newgate, John, Boston hatter **371**
Newgate, Nathaniel, Boston merchant **371**
Newman, Robert, of New Haven 114, 121, 193, **218–9**, 255, 284
Newman, Samuel, minister 160, 194
Newport (RI) 126, 159, 184, 289, 357, 359
news, newsbooks, newsletters xxi, xxiii, 5, 17, 21, 25, 47, 57, 58, 65, 79, 115, 128, 237, 250, 251, 328, 340, 354, 367
Norcrosse, Jeremiah and Adrean **219–20**
Norcrosse [*née* Gilbert], Mary **220–1**
Norcrosse, Nathaniel, minister 10, 117, 170, **220–1**
Norfolk 233, 341, 357
  Alby 66, 161
  Barrow Apton 196
  Blofield 193
  Denver 375
  Egmere 221
  Great Yarmouth 23, 38, 44, 65, 66, 70, 71, 72, 81, 101, 149, 193, 221, 225, 252, 291, 292, 294, 301, 302, 313
  Harleston 313, 314
  Hingham 11, 232–3, 234, 280, 365
  Horstead with Staninghall and Coltishall 161
  Irstead 65
  Little Walsingham 219, 221
  Pulham Market, Pulham [St] Mary 313
  Neatishead 65
  Norwich 7, 10, 32–4, 72, 182, 194, 221, 223, 224, 225, 232–3, 251, 252, 273, 313, 345
  Shropham 280
  Thetford 76
  Waterden 221
Northamptonshire 127, 137, 189, 260, 277, 297
Northumberland 106, 373
  Berwick-upon-Tweed 106

Northumberland (cont.)
  Brinkburn 105
  Heddon 160
  Hexham 312
  Newcastle-upon-Tyne 21, 69, 70, 86, 87, 93, 106, 126, 264, 310, 349
  Stannington 126
Norton, John, minister 198, 217, 220, 258, 268, 305
Nottinghamshire
  Cotgrave 50
  Kirkton and Screveton 137
  Worksop 52
Noyes, James, minister 330, 331
Nye, Philip, minister 10, 129, 147, 203, 316, 325

Oakes, Urian, president of Harvard 136, 201, 203, **222–3**, 287
Okey, John, army officer and regicide 93, 154
Oliver, Mary, of Salem 7, 22, 33, **223–5**, 227
Oliver, Thomas, of Salem 33, 223, 224, **225–6**
orthodoxy and dissent in Massachusetts 10, 22, 25, 26, 184, 185, 237, 246, 305, 328, 350, 376
  see also Antinomian Controversy; baptists; Quakers; religious toleration
Ottley, Adam, of Lynn **226**
Owen, John, English congregationalist 10, 68, 83, 129, 131, 136, 193, 203, 219, 245, 271, 308, 325
Oxford, University of 36, 44, 56, 103, 118, 138, 139, 141, 148, 175, 183, 190, 192, 193, 203, 206, 249, 267, 287, 289, 304, 312, 316, 321, 329, 330

Padua, University of 79, 267, 338
Page, Margaret, of Salem **227**
Palgrave, Anne, of Charlestown and Stepney (Middlesex) **227**, 232
Pardon, William, labourer **372**
Parish, Thomas, of Cambridge (MA) **227–9**
Parish, Thomas, Harvard graduate 228, **229**
Parker, Nicholas, of Boston (MA) **229–30**
Parker, Thomas, minister 294, 329, 330, 331
Parrat, Francis, of Rowley **230**
Parsons, William, of Boston **230**
Patient, Thomas, baptist preacher 22, 66, 204, **231–2**
Paulin, Sebastian, apprentice **344–5**
Peake, William, London merchant 375
Pearse [Pierce], John, mariner 227, **232**
Peck, Joseph 11, 234
Peck, Robert, minister 11, 17n55, 21, **232–5**, 251, 365
Pelham [formerly Harlakenden], Elizabeth **235**

Pelham, Frances, Hannah, Jemima, John, Katherine, Mary 128, 235, **238–9**
Pelham, Herbert, of Cambridge (MA) and Bures (Essex) 84, 105, 111, 128, 140, 150, 172, **235–8**, 239, 251, 269, 270, 271, 325, 326, 350
Pelham, Nathaniel, Harvard graduate 64, 128, **238–9**
Pelham, Penelope 128, 235, 237, **238**, 325–6
Pelham, William 128, **239**
Pell, John, mathematician and minister 66
Pell, Thomas, of New Haven 65
Pemerton [Pemberton], John, Boston weaver **239–40**
Penn, Sir William, naval officer 274
Penn, William, Quaker and founder of Pennsylvania 162
Pennoyer, William, London merchant 250
Penton, Edward, distributes illegal tract **345**
Pepys, Samuel, diarist 144, 323
Pequot Plantation [New London] 57, 129, 206, 249, 327, 349, 374, 377
Pequot War (1637) xxiii, 145–6, 190, 275, 286, 345, 365
Perkins, William, theologian 20
Pestell, William, naval captain 301
Pester, William, of Salem **240**
Peter [Peters], Deliverance **241–2**, 243, 246
Peter [Peters], Elizabeth **242**
Peter [Peters], Hugh, minister xxv, 4, 6, 17n.55, 18n.61, 32, 37, 46, 60, 84, 92, 93, 104, 105, 109, 130, 149, 150, 151, 152, 153, 154, 182, 183, 203, 226, 241, **242–9**, 250, 251, 260, 263, 277, 278, 306, 309, 310, 311, 328, 364
Peter [Peters], Thomas, minister 60, 106, 107, 127, 206, 242, **249–50**, 325
Petto, Samuel, Suffolk minister 314
Phillip [née Ames], Elizabeth 251, 252, 253
Phillip [Phillips], John, minister of Wrentham (Suffolk) 7, 10, 11, 17n.55, 21, 35, 37–8, 152, 221, 234, **250–4**, 278, 291, 321, 356, 375
Phillips, George, minister 171, 251, 288
Phips, Sir William, colonial governor 200
Pierce, Mark, schoolteacher 124, 219, **254–5**
Pierce, William, sea-captain 151, 196, 267, 268, **372**
Pierson, Abraham, minister 194
Piscataqua xxi, xxiv, 80, 116, 120, 168, 177, 344
Player, John, of Canterbury (Kent), minister 197
Plymouth and Plymouth Colony xxi, xxii, xxv, 1, 2, 57, 77, 81, 111, 113, 117, 139, 148, 149, 174, 205, 206, 294, 299, 324, 334, 336, 338, 341, 343, 344, 345, 351, 359, 361, 365, 376

Pocock, John, London merchant 112
Polewhele, Theophilus, minister 201
'popery', fear of 19
  see also religious purity, quest for
population of New England 17
  distinctive character of 3–4
Portsmouth (NH) xxi, 45, 149, 340
Portsmouth (RI) 39, 155, 159, 358, 359
Potter, Vincent, regicide 46, 112, **345–6**
Powell, Michael **373**
Powell, Vavasor, minister 89, 256, 347
Powning, Henry, colonial merchant 301
Pratt, Abraham, Bay Colony surgeon, and Joanna 14n.46, 108, **255–6**, 369
presbyterians, presbyterianism xxiv, xxv, xxvi, 22, 73, 78, 79, 86, 89, 98, 99, 104, 109, 130, 159, 175, 197, 200, 213, 252, 257, 261, 263, 266, 301, 306, 307, 308, 309, 311, 312, 318, 329, 330, 331, 341, 357
  see also Edwards, Thomas, author of Gangraena
Prichard, Hugh, of Roxbury **256**
print culture see books
Providence
  harnessed a wide variety of motives for migration 19, 20
  judgments from 9–10
Providence Island xxii, xxiii, xxiv, 3, 70, 114, 151, 182, 300, 372
Prudden, Peter, minister 41, 132, 285
Prynne, William, pamphleteer and lawyer xxiii, 11, 31, 182, 183, 345
Pynchon [formerly Samford], Frances 257, 258, 278
Pynchon, John, of Springfield 213, 258
Pynchon, William, Springfield entrepreneur and fur trader 10, 213, 214, 236, **257–9**, 278–9

Quick, John, minister 84
Quakers xxvii, xxviii, 22, 69–70, 86, 99, 134, 162, 187, 195, 208, 271, 279, 312, 314, 329, 341, 347, 357, 359
  see also orthodoxy and dissent in Massachusetts; religious toleration

Rainborowe, Thomas, parliamentarian army officer 59, 84, 185, 260, 286, 327, 366
Rainborowe [Rainsborough] William, parliamentarian army officer 58, 59, 89, 152, 185, 245, **260–1**, 327, 365
Rákóczy, George, Prince of Transylvania 182
Ramsey, Thomas, Catholic agent 312
Ranew, Nathaniel, minister 109
Rashley, Jonathan, minister 261, 262
Rashley, Nathaniel, minister 262

Rashley, Thomas, minister 22, **261–2**, 276, 331
Ratcliffe, Philip, servant 338, **346**, 347
Rathband, William, minister 158, 311
Rawson, Edward, Harvard graduate and minister 213, **262–3**
Reade, Thomas, governor of Stirling 6, 106, **263–4**, 327
Reading (MA) 266
Reed, William and Mabel of Woburn (MA) 87, **264–5**
Rehoboth (MA) 11, 196
religious purity, quest for 20, 21, 160, 179, 208, 253, 269, 314, 318, 349, 352, 376
religious toleration xxv, xxvii, 10, 11, 61, 129, 185, 237, 246, 253, 305, 307, 328, 347, 350, 376, 377
Remonstrant Controversy xxv, 75, 79, 106, 113, 185, 239, 249, 266, 268, 299, 322, 324, 325, 332
return migration to England see migration
Revell, John, London fishmonger **346**
Rich, Sir Nathaniel, colonial investor and politician 304
Rich, Nathaniel, army colonel 160, 167
Rich, Robert, second earl of Warwick xxii, 50, 126, 336
  Warwick commission for colonial government 84, 106, 236, 247, 269, 325, 362
Richmond Island (ME) 116, 195
Robinson, Luke, MP 160
Rogers, Daniel, minister of Wethersfield (Essex) 109
Rogers, Ezekiel, minister of Rowley (MA) 62, 63, 114, 202, 217, 218, 268, 304, 305
Rogers, John, minister of Dedham (Essex) 107, 170, 233, 235
Rogers, John, of Ipswich (MA), preacher, physician, Harvard president 85–6, 146, 200–1, 222, 281, 298
Rogers, John, Fifth Monarchist 130, 232, 289
Rogers, Nathaniel, minister of Ipswich (MA) 62, 63, 268, 305, 342
Rolls, Samuel, minister 223
Rowe, Nathaniel, Harvard student 8, **265**, 321
Rowe, Owen, London merchant and regicide 8, 265
Rowley (MA) xxiv, 11, 49, 62, 63, 67, 74, 75, 114, 171, 202, 217, 218, 230, 276
Roxbury (MA) xxii, 7, 41, 42, 47–8, 55, 62, 76, 104, 122, 160, 172, 207, 220, 229–30, 243, 245, 250, 255, 256, 257, 264, 271, 279, 280, 288, 294, 299, 310, 318, 334, 358, 361, 373, 376
Rutter, Samuel, bishop of Sodor and Man 39

Saco (ME) 44, 116, 160, 161
Sadler, John, Master of Magdalene College, Cambridge 32
Sadler, Richard, minister 22, 127, 185, **266–7**, 321, 325
Saffin, John, merchant **373**
Salem (MA) xxii, 23, 37, 47, 54, 61, 63, 67, 71, 91, 92, 93, 101, 104, 107, 111, 112, 134, 150, 151, 154, 171, 213, 220, 224, 225, 227, 231, 240, 241, 242, 243, 245, 247, 251, 261, 263, 264, 279, 287, 291, 300, 302, 318, 320, 323, 335, 344, 346, 358, 376
Salisbury (MA) 141, 315, 363, 373
Saltonstall, Henry, Harvard graduate and physician 8n.20, 65, 68, 93, 203, **267**, 347
Saltonstall [née Gurdon], Muriel 237, **268**, 269
Saltonstall, Sir Richard 105, 150, 235, 267, 268, 269, 336, **347**
Saltonstall, Richard 68, 84, 90, 106, 140, 172, 217, 218, 236, 237, 247, 256, **268–70**, 305, 347
   sought release from his vow to stay in New England 269
Saltonstall, Rosamund 267
Saltonstall, Samuel 267
Sampson, William, minister 73
Sams, John, minister 68, 77, **271–2**, 335
Sanborn [Samborne], Stephen, of Hampton 44, 45, **272**
Saugus (MA) *see* ironworks
Savile, John, first baron Savile 194
Savile, Thomas, first earl of Sussex 195
Savoy Conference (1658) 140, 282
Savoy Conference (1661) 330
Saxton, Peter, minister 14, 17n.55, 18n.61, **272–3**
Saybrook (CT) xxiii, xxv, 105, 106, 107, 114, 187, 249, 275, 303, 316
schools, schoolmasters xxv, 48, 54, 57, 73, 86, 88, 121, 130, 139, 144, 152, 157, 158, 169, 171, 176, 177, 184, 205, 220, 223, 250, 252, 265, 271, 308, 321–2, 323, 329, 331, 337, 373
Scituate (MA) 56, 77, 78, 81, 113, 148, 264, 272, 273, 299, 341, 360, 365
Scobell, Henry 66, 149, 262, 318
Scotland xxiv, xxv, xxvi, xxviii, 5, 6, 58, 79, 82–3, 90–1, 92, 93, 99, 106, 112, 118, 119, 135, 146, 154, 163, 167, 201, 203, 257, 269, 327, 328, 345
   Aberdeen 118, 328
   Dunbar, battle of (1650) xxvi, 341
   Edinburgh xxiv, xxvi, 83, 90, 92, 93, 106, 119, 135, 327

   Leith 90, 106, 135, 163, 203
   Scottish MPs *see* Members of Parliament
   Scottish universities 90, 106
   Stirling castle 264, 327
Scott, Robert 127, **373–4**
Scrope, Adrian, army officer and regicide 172
sea-captains, shipmasters, mariners 6, 10, 14, 25, 42, 50, 52, 59–61, 67, 68, 80–1, 94, 96, 102, 121, 124, 133, 134, 135, 145, 151, 162, 189, 201, 230, 232, 260, 268, 273, 279, 292, 300, 329, 354, 355, 358, 363, 364, 367, 368–9, 372
   see also Atlantic crossings
Sedgwick, Joanna 32, 34, **273**, 274, 275
Sedgwick, Robert, of Charlestown xxvii, 59, 92, 112, 154, 185–6, 212, 244, 273, **273–5**
Sedgwick, Samuel **275**, 375
Sedgwick, Sarah *see* Leverett, Sarah
Sedgwick, William, army chaplain 273
Seely, Robert, of New Haven **275–6**
Sewall, Henry Jr and Jane, of Newbury (MA) 22, 94, 261, **276–7**
Sewall, Samuel, diarist 49, 94, 202, 230, 261, 270, 277
Sharpe, Thomas, leatherseller 334, **347–8**
Shepard, Hannah 278
Shepard, Samuel, of Cambridge (MA) 58, 84, **277–8**
Shepard, Thomas, minister of Cambridge (MA) 37, 114, 160, 202, 203, 242, 246, 254, 264, 277, 311, 337
Sherman, John, minister 220
ships, naval 61, 135
ships, transatlantic
   Abigail 70, 215
   Adventure, built at Charlestown 323
   Angel Gabriel 82, 340
   Anne 294
   Arbella 346
   Blessing 299, 336
   Confidence 58
   Defence 84, 85, 264, 277
   Elizabeth 314, 361
   Elizabeth & Ann 76, 159, 189, 345, 362
   Elizabeth Dorcas 276
   Fellowship, built at New Haven 174, 192, 295, 321
   Griffin 155, 339
   Hector 343
   Hercules 281
   Hopewell 41, 117, 211, 337, 352
   Increase 88, 228, 367, 370
   Jewel 346
   John Adventurer 292
   Lions Whelp 255
   Lyon 268, 299, 346, 347, 375
   Mary Anne 81, 225

Mary & Jane 357
Mary Rose, wrecked in Boston harbour 50
Marygould 137, 148, 196
Mayflower xxi, 182, 274, 324, 336, 343, 351
Merchant 59
Paragon 72
Planter 296, 297
Plough 44
Rebecca 339
Sea Fort, built at Boston 14, 108, 255, 363, 369
Sparrow 58, 75
Speedwell 336, 357, 370
Supply 79, 113, 266
Susan & Ellen 268
Trial, first ship built at Boston 59
Unicorn 185
William & Francis 44
see also Atlantic crossings
Shrimpton, Edward, London merchant 89
Shrimpton, Henry, Boston merchant 89
Shropshire
   Bishops Castle 338
   Eaton Constantine 215
   Ludlow 266
   Walcot 56
   Whixall 266
Shute, Samuel, local politician 215
Sibbes, Richard, theologian 254
Simpson, John, Fifth Monarchist 89
Simpson, Sidrach, minister 129, 325
Skinner, Ralph, bishop of Oxford 141
Slye, Robert, Boston merchant **374**
Smith, Benjamin, of Boston **374**
Smith, Erasmus, merchant and educational benefactor 130
Smith, Henry and Ann, of Springfield (MA) 213, 258, **278–9**
Smith, James Jr **279**
Smith, Nathaniel, of Malden (MA) 101, **279–80**
Smith, Richard, of Shropham (Norfolk) and Ipswich (MA) **280**
Smith, Robert, London wine cooper **280**, 361
Smith, Samuel, London minister 201, 203, 223
Smith, Zephaniah, tanner and minister **281**
Somerset 56, 73, 117, 148, 172, 339, 340
   Batcombe 52, 123, 148, 196
   Bristol 57, 58, 69, 77, 112, 117, 125, 127, 140, 141, 172, 190, 232, 279, 285, 346
   Broadway 148, 372
   Crewkerne 148
   Portbury 190
   Taunton 81, 82, 123, 295
   Yeovil 73
Spain xxvii, 12, 14, 42, 80, 108, 250, 255, 267, 356, 369

Spencer, John, of Ipswich (MA) 335, **348**
Springfield (MA) 145, 213, 257–8, 279
Stalham, John, of Terling (Essex), minister 68, 82, 271
Stamford (CT) 89
Stansby, Robert, of Westhorpe (Suffolk) 44, 71, 160, 305
Starr, Comfort, minister 193, 197, 201, **281–2**
Stirk [Starkey], George, Harvard graduate and physician 35, 79, **282–4**
Stollyon, Abraham, of New Haven 121, 219, **284**
Stone, John, Harvard graduate **284–5**
Stone, Samuel, minister 203, 271, 284
Stonehill, Henry, of Milford 41, 132, 156, **285**
Storer, Richard, of Boston and Braintree **285**
Stoughton, Israel, merchant and army officer 59, 167, 185, 188, 190, **286–7**, 322, 366
Stoughton, John, minister 286
Stoughton, William, Harvard graduate, minister, colonial magistrate 267, 286, **287**, 289
Stowe, John, of Roxbury (MA) and Cranbrook (Kent) **288**
Stowers, John, of Watertown (MA) and Parham (Suffolk) **288–9**
Stratford (CT) 190, 276, 292
Stucley, Lewis, of Exeter (Devon), minister 145, 201
Sudbury (MA) 236, 237, 239
Suffolk 24, 31, 44, 71, 196, 341
   Assington 166, 235, 237, 268
   Barham 367
   Boxford 335
   Bury St Edmunds 47, 76, 371, 374
   Coddenham 308
   Combs 342–3
   Framlingham 291, 373
   Frostenden 37
   Groton 327, 328, 335, 377
   Grundisburgh 342
   Hadleigh 76
   Haverhill 214, 304, 310
   Hemingstone 132–3
   Ipswich 7, 31, 72, 91, 107, 167, 182, 234, 308, 342
   Kersey 50
   Nayland 227, 228, 229
   Needham Market 158, 159, 308
   Parham 288–9
   Redgrave 370
   Semer 76
   South Cove 37
   Southwold 38, 80–1
   Sudbury 107, 196, 202, 310, 334, 351, 376
   Walberswick 65
   West Creeting 159, 308

Suffolk (*cont.*)
  Westhorpe 160, 305
  Woolverstone 373
  Wrentham 11, 35, 37, 38, 221, 250–4, 291, 356
Surrey 135, 245
  Barnes 184
  Kingston-upon-Thames 348
  Ockley 316
  Southwark 76, 131, 185, 212, 244, 255, 273, 274, 338, 341, 359, 371
  Sutton 118
Sussex 32, 135, 235, 245, 284
  Lewes 282
  Rumboldswyke 287
  Rye 35–6, 55, 56
  Warminghurst 106
Swinfield, Raphael, of Dublin **289**
Swinnock, Joseph, Harvard student and minister **289–90**
Sydenham, William, army officer and Dorset politician 201
Sykes, William, clothier in the East Riding of Yorkshire 62
Symmes, Zechariah, minister 33, 157, 220, 259

Tare, Jane and Richard, of Boston **291**
Taunton (MA) 117, 139, 166
Taylor, Jeremy, bishop of Down, Connor and Dromore 205
Taylor, Timothy, Cheshire minister 98–9, 100, 161, 296, 298
Thomason, George, book collector 258, 307
Thompson, Edmund and Martha, of Salem **291**
Thompson, William, minister 121, 158, 171, 259
Thornton, Thomas, minister **291–2**
Thurston, Richard and Martha 189, **292**
Tillam, Thomas, poet and religious radical 22, 312, 334, **348–9**
Tillinghast, John, Fifth Monarchist 66
timber, transatlantic trade in 9, 13, 47, 61, 357
Tinker, John 58, **349**
Tomlins, Edward, carpenter and religious radical **293**
Tomson, Robert, merchant and naval officer 6, 111, 140, 143, 144, 155, 317, 323, **349–50**
Topping, Richard and Alice, of Boston **293**
Topsfield (MA) 167
Tracy, Stephen, cloth-worker **294**
transatlantic trade 7, 11, 12, 47, 48, 50, 51, 58, 62, 72, 86, 112, 116, 121, 127, 131, 139, 162, 181, 185, 210, 257, 260, 274, 297, 327, 344, 354, 357, 363, 366, 372, 374

see also cloth, fish, furs, timber
Traske, John, antinomian 215
Travers, Henry, of Newbury (MA) **294**
Trotman, John and Katherine, of Boston (MA) **294–5**
Trowbridge, Thomas, of New Haven **295**
Tullie, Timothy, of Carlisle, minister 281, 282
Turner, Nathaniel, of New Haven 174, **295–6**
Tuttle, Hannah **296**, 297
Tuttle, Joanna **296–7**
Tuttle, John, of Ipswich (MA) 86, 171, 201, 296–7, **297–8**
Twisse, William, minister 329

Usher, Hezekiah, bookseller and merchant of Boston (MA) 99, 131, 355, **374–5**

Vane, Sir Henry Jr, politician and author 6, 10, 22, 39, 46, 61, 105, 106, 151, 155, 248, 258, 311, 315, 343, **350–1**, 376
Vassall, Samuel, merchant and politician 299
Vassall, William, merchant 79, 113, 127, 185, 266, **299–300**, 325, 346, 365
Venables, Robert, parliamentarian army officer 274
Venner, Alice 300, 301
Venner, Thomas, cooper and Fifth Monarchist 6, 11, 40, 46, 56, 86, 89, 112, 169, 202, 210, **300–1**, 312, 375
Vere, Lady Mary, patron of ministers in England 65
Vermace [Vermais, Vermase, Fermayes, 'ffermais', 'ffirmace'], Mark, of Salem **301–2**
Vines, Richard, of Saco (ME) 160–1
Virginia xxi, 17n.55, 121, 128, 129, 158, 162, 171, 190, 235, 258, 300, 338, 343, 358, 369

Wade, Joan, deserted her husband **303**
Wade, Jonathan 275, 301, **375**
Wales xxvii, 206, 208, 210, 256, 266, 270
  Carmarthenshire 208
  Commission for the Propagation of the Gospel in Wales 208
  Denbighshire 56, 256, 332
  Glamorgan
    Llancarfan 208, 210
    Llangyfelach 206, 208
    Penmaen 206
    Reynoldston 210
    Swansea 205, 208–9, 210
  Monmouthshire
    Chepstow 56, 57
    Llanmartin 57
    Llanvaches 56

Wales, Elkanah, minister in the West Riding of Yorkshire 62, 63
Walton, William, minister 12n.34
Walver, Abraham, Harvard graduate and minister 53, 203, **303**
Ward, James, Harvard graduate 203, **304**, 306, 309
Ward, John, minister, of Haverhill (MA) 62, 108, 305
Ward, John, minister of Norwich 304
Ward, Nathaniel, minister 20, 108, 109, 160, 245, 268, **304–7**, 309, 362
Ward, Samuel, minister of Ipswich (Suffolk) 31, 304
Ward, Seth, bishop of Exeter 338
Warham, John, minister 12n.34, 257
Warwick, earl of see Rich, Robert
Warwickshire 94, 345
 Coventry 276, 277
 Fenny Compton 321, 352, 353
 Warwick 276
Waterhouse, Ann 308
Waterhouse, Thomas, minister 159, **308–9**
Watertown (MA) xxii, 10, 54, 72, 162, 171, 219, 220, 228, 239, 260, 267, 275, 288–9, 347, 360, 369, 373
Weld, Barbara 47, 373, 376
Weld, Edmund, Harvard graduate and minister **309**
Weld, John, Harvard student and minister 262, 304, **309–10**
Weld, Joseph, of Roxbury 47, 55, 256, 262, 271, 304, 309, 310, 328, 376
Weld, Judith 241
Weld, Thomas, minister xxv, 4, 7, 13, 17n.55, 18n.61, 21, 32, 47, 59, 92, 161, 183, 241, 243–5, 252, 254, 262, 271, 278, 304, 309, **310–13**, 315, 349, 364, 376
Wells (ME) 46, 315
West Country 9, 12, 82, 150, 166, 201, 203, 250, 286, 355, 372
 see also Cornwall, Devon, Dorset, Somerset
Westgate, John, of Boston **313–14**
Westminster Assembly of Divines xxv, 196, 244, 252, 254, 305
Westmorland, Kirkby Stephen 134
Wethersfield (CT) xxiii, 64, 76, 89, 275, 353
Weymouth (MA) xxi, 52, 123, 137, 148, 159, 160, 161, 183–4, 196, 340, 372
Whalley, Edward, regicide and major-general xxviii, 50, 122, 138, 140, 270
Wharton, Lord Philip 134, 158–9, 200, 263
Wheat, Joshua **314**
Wheelwright, John, minister 39, 48, 70, 147, 155, 156, 168, 194, 220, 261, **314–15**, 332, 348, 350, 355, 357
White, John, of Dorchester (Dorset) 150

White, Nathaniel, Harvard graduate and minister **316**
Whitfield, Dorothy 316, 318, 319
Whitfield, Henry, minister xxvi, 74, 90, 105, 135, 163, 164, **316–19**
 Henry Whitfield House, Guilford (CT) 317
Whitfield, Mary 319
Whitfield, Nathaniel, customs official 11, 91, 140, 164, **319–20**, 350
Whiting, John, Harvard graduate and minister **320**
Whiting, Samuel, minister 226, 298
Wilkes, Thomas, haberdasher **320**
Wilkes, William and Joan **320–1**
Williams, John, bishop of Lincoln 168
Williams [*née* Bernard], Mary 376
Williams, Roger, of Providence (RI) xxiii, xxv, 52, 84, 147, 158, 241, 243, 269, 325, 357, 362, **376–7**
Willis, Thomas, schoolmaster 171, 172, 265, **321**
Willis, Thomas Jr, minister 171, **321–2**
Willoughby, Francis, naval commissioner and colonial magistrate 6, 61, 79, 118, 143, 144, 155, 227, 244, 275, 319, **322–4**, 350, 357
Willoughby, William, naval commissioner 244, 322–3
Wilson, John, minister of Boston (MA) 45, 57, 88, 160, 166, 182, 220, 254, 259, 262, 315, 330, 347, **351**
Wiltshire 52, 78, 82, 190, 262, 331, 337, 340, 348, 369
 Barford St Martin 261, 329, 331
 Compton Bassett 77
 Maiden Bradley 73
 Market Lavington 73
 Salisbury 262, 329, 330, 337
 Stanton Fitzwarren 329, 330
 Woodborough 77, 78
Windsor (CT) 102, 144–5, 190, 257, 281, 286, 292, 330, 339, 349
Winslow, Edward, *Mayflower* emigrant and governor of Plymouth Colony xxi, xxvi, 6, 50, 56, 57, 79, 111, 113, 127, 129, 144, 153, 159, 161, 185, 236, 237, 245, 249, 250, 274, 299, 306, 318, **324–6**, 336, 350, 351, 362
 sells Charles I's art collection 6, 153, 325
Winslow, Gilbert **351**
Winslow, Josiah, Harvard student 237, 238, 239, 325, **326**
Winslow, Penelope *see* Penelope Pelham
Winslow, Susanna 324–6
Winthrop, Adam 84, 92, 129
Winthrop, Fitz John, governor of Massachusetts 92, 122, 264, **327**

Winthrop, John, governor of Massachusetts xxii, xxvi, 3, 8, 9–10, 13, 14, 17, 18n.62, 21, 26, 31, 42, 44, 45, 50, 54, 57, 58, 59, 60, 71, 74–5, 79, 84, 91, 93, 96, 105, 106, 107, 108, 109, 113, 115, 116, 120, 124, 128–9, 142, 147, 148, 149, 150, 151, 152, 157, 158, 159, 160, 163, 166, 169, 171, 177, 178, 183, 184, 188, 190, 192, 194, 195, 206, 213, 220, 223–4, 226, 236–7, 239, 240, 241, 242, 243, 246, 247, 249, 250, 251, 255, 257, 260, 261, 265, 268, 283, 284, 286, 293, 299, 304, 305, 310, 311, 315, 322–3, 327, 328, 338, 339, 340, 343, 344, 349, 350, 358, 359, 360, 362, 363, 366, 368–9, 372

Winthrop, John Jr, colonial governor 12, 18n.61, 59, 61, 65, 76, 79, 92, 105, 107, 120, 122, 129, 131, 134, 137, 139, 140, 147, 150, 152, 187, 190, 206, 212, 219, 221, 235, 241, 242, 243, 244, 245, 247, 249, 250, 263, 268, 274, 283, 285, 305, 319, 327, 335, 339, 340, 342, 346, 350, 360, 369, 372, 374, **377–8**

Winthrop [née Rainborowe], Judith 260, 327, 328

Winthrop, Martha 185, 260

Winthrop, Samuel 81

Winthrop, Stephen, parliamentarian army officer 6, 92, 166, 167, 250, 260, **327–8**, 349, 368, 376

witch trials 213, 228, 287, 364

Witheredge [Witheridge], Edward, merchant and naval captain **329**

Woburn (MA) 264–5

Wood, William xvii, xxiii, **352**

Woodbridge, Benjamin, Harvard graduate and minister 8n.20, 22, 65, 68, 93, 203, 261, 267, **329–30**, 331

Woodbridge, John, minister 22, 261, 329, **330–1**

Woodbridge, Mercy 331

Woodcock, William, London merchant and colonial investor 336

Woodmancey, John, colonial merchant 301

Worcestershire 109, 127, 214, 266, 324, 351
  Worcester, battle of (1651) xxvi, 325

Wren, Matthew, bishop of Norwich xxiii, xxiv, 7, 21, 31, 32, 72, 182, 233, 234, 251

Wright, Laurence, Cromwell's physician 193, 328

Wyllys, George, of Hartford, governor of Connecticut 8, 21, 126, 143, 341

Wyllys, George Jr, broke his promise to make New England his home 8, 21, 143, 341, **352–3**

Wyllys, Mary, of Hartford 64

Wyllys, Samuel, Harvard graduate and colonial magistrate 133, 342

Yale, David, merchant 11, 47, 48, 75, 79, 96, 112, 113, 127, 142, 143, 156, 192, 239, 299, 315, **332**, 333

Yale, Elihu 97, 332

Yale, Thomas 96, 142, 332, **333**

Yale, Ursula 332

Yarmouth (MA) 44, 149, 205, 206, 210, 292

York (ME) 46, 71, 116, 120, 140, 149, 221, 344

Yorkshire
  City of York 63, 74, 98, 272
  East Riding
    Bridlington 263
    Cottingham 217
    Holme-on-Spalding-Moor 67
    Hornsea 74
    Hull 62, 128
    Rowley 114, 217
  North Riding
    Edstone 63
    Newton-on-Ouse 272
    Welburn 63
  West Riding
    Edlington 272
    Grindleton 194
    Halifax 89
    Healaugh 134
    Leeds 62, 63, 272, 273
    Silkstone 70
    Topcliffe 175, 195
    Wakefield 194, 213
    Woodkirk [West Ardsley] 194, 195
    Wragby 267, 268

CPSIA information can be obtained
at www.ICGtesting.com
Printed in the USA
BVOW06s0717230317
478732BV00011B/12/P